KT-408-636

# NORTHERN FRANCE
## AND THE PARIS REGION

© Philip Coblentz/Brand X Pictures

**Chief Editor**               Cynthia Clayton Ochterbeck

## THE GREEN GUIDE NORTHERN FRANCE AND THE PARIS REGION

| | |
|---|---|
| **Editor** | Gaven R. Watkins |
| **Contributing Writer** | Terry Marsh |
| **Production Coordinator** | Natasha G. George |
| **Cartography** | Alain Baldet, Michèle Cana, Peter Wrenn |
| **Photo Editor** | Lydia Strong |
| **Proofreader** | Jonathan P. Gilbert |
| **Layout & Design** | Heinrich Grieb and Alison Rayner |
| **Cover Design** | Laurent Muller and Ute Weber |

**Contact Us:**

The Green Guide
Michelin Maps and Guides
One Parkway South
Greenville, SC 29615
USA
☎1-800-423-0485
www.michelintravel.com
michelin.guides@us.michelin.com

Michelin Maps and Guides
Hannay House
39 Clarendon Road
Watford, Herts WD17 1JA
UK
☎01923 205240
www.ViaMichelin.com
travelpubsales@uk.michelin.com

**Special Sales:**

For information regarding bulk sales,
customized editions and premium sales,
please contact our Customer Service
Departments:
USA     1-800-432-6277
UK       01923 205240
Canada 1-800-361-8236

**Note to the Reader**
While every effort is made to ensure that all information printed in this guide is
correct and up-to-date, Michelin Apa Publications Ltd. accepts no liability for
any direct, indirect or consequential losses howsoever caused so far as such
can be excluded by law.

# One Team ...
# A Commitment to Quality

There's just one reason our team is dedicated to producing quality travel publications—you, our reader.

Throughout our guides we offer **practical information**, **touring tips** and **suggestions** for finding the best places for a break.

**Michelin driving tours** help you hit the highlights and quickly absorb the best of the region. Our descriptive **walking tours** make you your own guide, armed with directions, maps and expert information.

We scout out the attractions, classify them with **star ratings**, and describe in detail what you will find when you visit them.

**Michelin maps** featured throughout the guide offer vibrant, detailed and easy-to-follow outlines of everything from close-up museum plans to international maps.

Places to stay and eat are always a big part of travel, so we research **hotels and restaurants** that we think convey the essence of the destination and arrange them by geographic area and price. We walk you through the best shopping districts and point you towards the host of entertainment and recreation possibilities on offer.

We **test**, **retest**, **check and recheck** to make sure that our guidebooks are truly just that: a personalized guide to help you make the most of your visit. And if you still want a speaking guide, we list local tour guides who will lead you on all the boat, bus, guided, historical, culinary, and other tours you shouldn't miss.

In short, we remove the guesswork involved with travel. After all, we want you to enjoy exploring with Michelin as much as we do.

**The Michelin Green Guide Team**

# PLANNING YOUR TRIP

**MICHELIN DRIVING TOURS**     **12**

**WHEN AND WHERE TO GO**     **14**
Themed Tours................... 14
Seasons......................... 16

**KNOW BEFORE YOU GO**     **17**
Useful Websites ................. 17
Tourist Offices................... 17
International Visitors ........... 19
Accessibility.................... 21

**GETTING THERE**     **21**
By Plane ....................... 21
By Ship ........................ 21
By Train........................ 22
By Coach/Bus ................... 22

**GETTING AROUND**     **22**
Public Transportation........... 22
Driving in France ............... 23

**WHERE TO STAY AND EAT**     **25**
Where to Stay .................. 25
Where to Eat ................... 28

**WHAT TO SEE AND DO**     **30**
Outdoor Fun ................... 30
Spas .......................... 34
Activities for Children........... 34

**CALENDAR OF EVENTS**     **36**

**SHOPPING**     **41**

**SIGHTSEEING**     **42**

**BOOKS AND FILMS**     **47**

**USEFUL WORDS & PHRASES**     **49**

**BASIC INFORMATION**     **52**

# INTRODUCTION TO NORTHERN FRANCE

**NATURE**     **58**
Picardy ......................... 59
Nord-Pas-de-Calais.............. 60
Artois.......................... 60
Flanders ....................... 61
Île-de-France................... 62
Forests......................... 63
Gardens in the Île-de-France ..... 66

**HISTORY**     **68**
Timeline ....................... 68

**ART AND CULTURE**     **72**
Architectural Drawings ......... 72
Living like Kings ................ 79
Interior Decoration ............. 80
Religious and Civil Architecture .. 82
Monasteries in Île-de-France..... 86
Rural Housing in the North...... 89
Military Architecture............ 90
Faience and Porcelain in
   Île-de-France.................. 91
Stained Glass................... 92
Landscape Painting............. 94
Northern Folklore and Traditions . 97

**THE REGION TODAY**     **100**
Economy....................... 100
Food and Drink................. 102

**SYMBOLS**

   **Tourist Information**
   **Hours of Operation**
   **Periods of Closure**
   **A Bit of Advice**
   **Details to Consider**
   **Entry Fees**
   **Especially for Children**
   **Tours**
   **Wheelchair Accessible**

# CONTENTS

## DISCOVERING NORTHERN FRANCE

Abbeville . . . . . . . . . . . . . . . . . . . . . . . 106
Albert . . . . . . . . . . . . . . . . . . . . . . . . . 107
Amiens . . . . . . . . . . . . . . . . . . . . . . . . 109
Arras . . . . . . . . . . . . . . . . . . . . . . . . . 120
Parc Astérix . . . . . . . . . . . . . . . . . . . . 128
Auvers-sur-Oise . . . . . . . . . . . . . . . . . 130
Avesnes-sur-Helpe . . . . . . . . . . . . . . . 132
Bailleul . . . . . . . . . . . . . . . . . . . . . . . . 137
Barbizon . . . . . . . . . . . . . . . . . . . . . . . 140
Bavay . . . . . . . . . . . . . . . . . . . . . . . . . 142
Beauvais . . . . . . . . . . . . . . . . . . . . . . . 143
Bergues . . . . . . . . . . . . . . . . . . . . . . . . 149
Boulogne-sur-Mer . . . . . . . . . . . . . . . . 151
Musée de l'Air et
    de l'Espace du Bourget . . . . . . . . . . 160
Château de Breteuil . . . . . . . . . . . . . . 161
Calais . . . . . . . . . . . . . . . . . . . . . . . . . 164
Cambrai . . . . . . . . . . . . . . . . . . . . . . . 168
Cassel . . . . . . . . . . . . . . . . . . . . . . . . . 172
Abbaye de Chaalis . . . . . . . . . . . . . . . 174
Château de Chantilly . . . . . . . . . . . . . 177
Chartres . . . . . . . . . . . . . . . . . . . . . . . 185
Le Chemin des Dames . . . . . . . . . . . . . 195
Compiègne . . . . . . . . . . . . . . . . . . . . . 196
Corbie . . . . . . . . . . . . . . . . . . . . . . . . . 208
La Côte d'Opale . . . . . . . . . . . . . . . . . 211
Coucy-Le-Château-Auffrique . . . . . . . . 214
Crécy-en-Ponthieu . . . . . . . . . . . . . . . 216
Château de Dampierre . . . . . . . . . . . . . 218
Disneyland Resort Paris . . . . . . . . . . . . 220
Douai . . . . . . . . . . . . . . . . . . . . . . . . . 227
Dunkerque . . . . . . . . . . . . . . . . . . . . . 232
Château d'Écouen . . . . . . . . . . . . . . . . 236
Château de Ferrières . . . . . . . . . . . . . . 238
Fontainebleau . . . . . . . . . . . . . . . . . . . 240
Forêt de Fontainebleau . . . . . . . . . . . . 251
Guînes . . . . . . . . . . . . . . . . . . . . . . . . . 257
Coupole d'Helfaut-Wizernes . . . . . . . . . 258
L'Isle-Adam . . . . . . . . . . . . . . . . . . . . . 259
Abbaye de Jouarre . . . . . . . . . . . . . . . 261
Jouy-en-Josas . . . . . . . . . . . . . . . . . . . 263
Laon . . . . . . . . . . . . . . . . . . . . . . . . . . 265
Lille . . . . . . . . . . . . . . . . . . . . . . . . . . . 270
Maintenon . . . . . . . . . . . . . . . . . . . . . 285
Maisons-Laffitte . . . . . . . . . . . . . . . . . 287
Marly-le-Roi . . . . . . . . . . . . . . . . . . . . 289
Parc ornithologique du Marquenterre . 293
Meaux . . . . . . . . . . . . . . . . . . . . . . . . 295

Meudon . . . . . . . . . . . . . . . . . . . . . . . 298
Milly-la-Forêt . . . . . . . . . . . . . . . . . . . 300
Montfort-l'Amaury . . . . . . . . . . . . . . . 302
Montmorency . . . . . . . . . . . . . . . . . . . 305
Montreuil . . . . . . . . . . . . . . . . . . . . . . 308
Moret-sur-Loing . . . . . . . . . . . . . . . . . 310
Morienval . . . . . . . . . . . . . . . . . . . . . . 313
Grottes-Refuges de Naours . . . . . . . . . 314
Colline de Notre-dame-de-Lorette . . . . 315
Noyon . . . . . . . . . . . . . . . . . . . . . . . . 316
Château d'Olhain . . . . . . . . . . . . . . . . 318
Vallée de l'Ourcq . . . . . . . . . . . . . . . . . 319
Paris . . . . . . . . . . . . . . . . . . . . . . . . . . 323
Péronne . . . . . . . . . . . . . . . . . . . . . . . 334
Château de Pierrefonds . . . . . . . . . . . . 336
Poissy . . . . . . . . . . . . . . . . . . . . . . . . . 339
Abbaye de Port-Royal-des-Champs . . . 342
Provins . . . . . . . . . . . . . . . . . . . . . . . . 344
Le Quesnoy . . . . . . . . . . . . . . . . . . . . . 348
Rambouillet . . . . . . . . . . . . . . . . . . . . . 349
Forêt de Rambouillet . . . . . . . . . . . . . . 352
Château-Fort de Rambures . . . . . . . . . . 354
La Roche-Guyon . . . . . . . . . . . . . . . . . 355
Abbaye de Royaumont . . . . . . . . . . . . . 358
Rueil-Malmaison . . . . . . . . . . . . . . . . . 360
St-Amand-les-Eaux . . . . . . . . . . . . . . . 362
St-Cloud . . . . . . . . . . . . . . . . . . . . . . . 364
St-Denis . . . . . . . . . . . . . . . . . . . . . . . 367
St-Germain-en-Laye . . . . . . . . . . . . . . . 372
Forêt de St-Gobain . . . . . . . . . . . . . . . 377
St-Leu-d'Esserent . . . . . . . . . . . . . . . . 379
St-Omer . . . . . . . . . . . . . . . . . . . . . . . 380
St-Quentin . . . . . . . . . . . . . . . . . . . . . 385
St-Riquier . . . . . . . . . . . . . . . . . . . . . . 387
St-Valery-sur-Somme . . . . . . . . . . . . . . 389
Sceaux . . . . . . . . . . . . . . . . . . . . . . . . 391
Senlis . . . . . . . . . . . . . . . . . . . . . . . . . 393
Sèvres . . . . . . . . . . . . . . . . . . . . . . . . . 399
Soissons . . . . . . . . . . . . . . . . . . . . . . . 400
La Baie de Somme . . . . . . . . . . . . . . . . 403
Vallée de la Somme . . . . . . . . . . . . . . . 405
La Thiérache . . . . . . . . . . . . . . . . . . . . 408
Château et Parc de Thoiry . . . . . . . . . . 412
Le Touquet-Paris-Plage . . . . . . . . . . . . 414
Valenciennes . . . . . . . . . . . . . . . . . . . . 419
Abbaye et Jardins de Valloires . . . . . . . 421
Château de Vaux-le-Vicomte . . . . . . . . 423
Château de Versailles . . . . . . . . . . . . . . 427
Parc du château de Versailles . . . . . . . . 445
Ville de Versailles . . . . . . . . . . . . . . . . . 454
Villeneuve-d'Ascq . . . . . . . . . . . . . . . . 459
Villers-Cotterêts . . . . . . . . . . . . . . . . . 462

Index . . . . . . . . . . . . . . . . . . . . . . . . . 464
Maps and Plans . . . . . . . . . . . . . . . . . 476
Legend . . . . . . . . . . . . . . . . . . . . . . . . 478

# HOW TO USE THIS GUIDE

## Orientation

To help you grasp the "lay of the land" quickly and easily, so you'll feel confident and comfortable finding your way around the region, we offer the following tools in this guide:

- ⌾ Detailed table of contents for an overview of what you'll find in the guide, and how the guide is organized.
- ⌾ Map of Northern France and the Paris Region at the front of the guide, with the Principal Sights highlighted for easy reference.
- ⌾ Detailed maps for major cities and villages, including driving tour maps and larger-scale maps for walking tours.
- ⌾ Map of eight Regional Driving Tours, each one numbered and color coded.
- ⌾ Principal Sights organized alphabetically for quick reference.

## Practicalities

At the front of the guide, you'll see a section called "Planning Your Trip" that contains information about planning your trip, the best time to go, different ways of getting to the region and getting around, and basic facts and tips for making the most of your visit. You'll find driving and themed tours, and suggestions for outdoor fun. There's also a calendar of popular annual events. Information on shopping, sightseeing, kids' activities and sports and recreational opportunities is included as well.

## WHERE TO STAY

We've made a selection of hotels and arranged them within the cities by price category to fit all budgets (⌾ *see the Legend on the cover flap for an explanation of the price categories*). For the most part, we've selected accommodations based on their unique regional quality, their Northern France feel, as it were. So, unless the individual hotel embodies local ambience, it's rare that we include chain properties, which typically have their own imprint. If you want a more comprehensive selection of accommodations, see the red-cover **Michelin Guide France**.

## WHERE TO EAT

We thought you'd like to know the popular eating spots in Northern France and the Paris Region. So we selected restaurants that capture the Northern France experience—those that have a unique regional flavor and local atmosphere. We're not rating the quality of the food per se. As we did with the hotels, we selected restaurants for many towns and villages, categorized by price to appeal to all wallets (⌾ *see the Legend on the cover flap for an explanation of the price categories*). If you want a more comprehensive selection of dining recommendations, see the red-cover **Michelin Guide France**.

## Attractions

Principal Sights are arranged alphabetically. Within each Principal Sight, attractions for each town, village, or geographical area are divided into local Sights or Walking Tours, nearby Excursions to sights outside the town, or detailed Driving Tours—suggested itineraries for seeing several attractions around a major town. Contact information, admission charges and hours of operation are given for the majority of attractions. Unless otherwise noted, admission prices shown are for a single adult only. Discounts for children, seniors, students, teachers, etc. may be available; be sure to ask. If no admission charge is shown, entrance to the attraction is free.

If you're pressed for time, we recommend you visit the three- and two-star sights first: the stars are your guide.

## STAR RATINGS

Michelin has used stars as a rating tool for more than 100 years:

| ★★★ | Highly recommended |
| ★★ | Recommended |
| ★ | Interesting |

## SYMBOLS IN THE TEXT

Besides the stars, other symbols in the text indicate sights that are closed to the public ⚊; on-site eating facilities ✕; also see 👀; breakfast included in the nightly rate 🖙; on-site parking 🅿; spa facilities Spa; camping facilities △; swimming pool 🏊; and beaches ⚓.

See the box appearing on the Contents page and the Legend on the cover flap for other symbols used in the text.

See the Maps explanation below for symbols appearing on the maps.

Throughout the guide you will find peach-coloured text boxes or sidebars containing anecdotal or background information. Green-coloured boxes contain information to help you save time or money.

## Maps

All maps in this guide are oriented north, unless otherwise indicated by a directional arrow. The term "Local Map" refers to a map within the chapter or Tourism Region. See the map Legend at the back of the guide for an explanation of other map symbols. A complete list of the maps found in the guide appears at the back of this book.

Addresses, phone numbers, opening hours and prices published in this guide are accurate at press time. We welcome corrections and suggestions that may assist us in preparing the next edition. Please send your comments to:

Michelin Maps and Guides
Hannay House
39 Clarendon Road
Watford, Herts WD17 1JA
UK
travelpubsales@uk.michelin.com
www.michelin.co.uk

Michelin Maps and Guides
Editorial Department
P.O. Box 19001
Greenville, SC 29602-9001
USA
michelin.guides@us.michelin.com
www.michelintravel.com

*Landsailing*

S. Sauvignier/ MICHELN

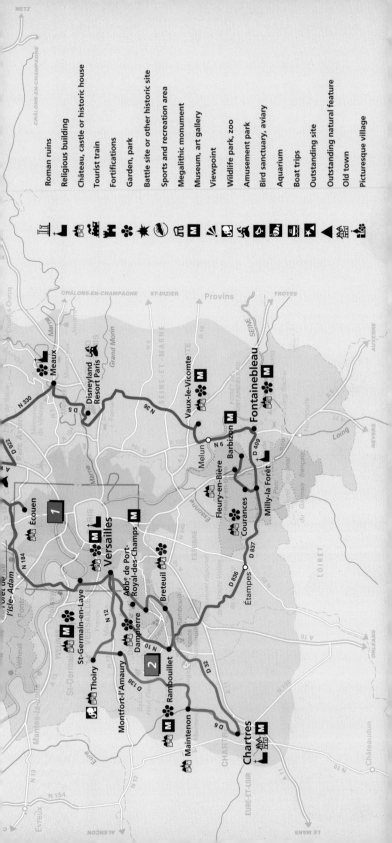

Roman ruins

Religious building

Château, castle or historic house

Tourist train

Fortifications

Garden, park

Battle site or other historic site

Sports and recreation area

Megalithic monument

Museum, art gallery

Viewpoint

Wildlife park, zoo

Amusement park

Bird sanctuary, aviary

Aquarium

Boat trips

Outstanding site

Outstanding natural feature

Old town

Picturesque village

Meaux

Disneyland Resort Paris

Vaux-le-Vicomte

Fontainebleau

Melun

Barbizon

Milly-la-Forêt

Fleury-en-Bière

Courances

Ecouen

Versailles

Abbé de Port-Royal-des-Champs

Breteuil

Étampes

St-Germain-en-Laye

Thoiry

Dampierre

Montfort-l'Amaury

Rambouillet

Maintenon

Chartres

# MICHELIN DRIVING TOURS

## 1 Royal Palaces of Île de France

*420km/261mi starting from St-Germain-en-Laye*
This large circuit, centred on Paris, embraces the most impressive royal residences in France. Just on the outskirts of Paris, the Château of St-Germain-en-Laye is especially interesting for the prehistoric art collection. Écouen is home to the national museum of the Renaissance. Vaux-le-Vicomte displays wonderful symmetry and landscape design, while visitors are moved by the sad fate of the man who built it. Fontainebleau, on the edge of the large forest of the same name, evokes the imperial grandeur of Napoleon and echoes of his downfall, and Versailles, of course, is legendary for its splendour and its role in history.

## 2 From Versailles to Chartres through Rambouillet Forest

*168km/105mi starting from Versailles*
The forest of Rambouillet was once the favoured hunting ground of kings and, later, presidents of France. Many parts are open to the public and the establishment of the Haute Vallée de la Chevreuse Regional Nature Park has preserved typical local villages and churches. Breteuil and Dampierre are in beautiful natural settings, ideal places to spend some time outdoors. On the way to Chartres, the forests give way to a vast plain across which the cathedral spires, seen for some distance, pinpoint the city. It is not difficult to imagine how pilgrims must have felt as they neared this awesome building. After admiring the renowned stained-glass windows and the inlaid labyrinth, or maybe enjoying a tour with the cathedral guide, it is worth exploring the Old Town along the banks of the River Eure, with its beautiful half-timbered houses and narrow streets.

## 3 Castles and Cathedrals

*510km/317mi starting from Amiens*
This tour meanders through the countryside of Picardy into Oise, a landscape that is easy on the eye, with huge expanses (and some very small ones, too, at the edge of villages) of barley and wheat, dotted with wildflowers. After Beauvais, you enter the distinctive landscape of the Bray, where groves and meadows alternate. The village of Gerberoy is one of 'The Most Beautiful Villages of France', a place of lovely half-timbered houses. And as you contemplate the many marvellous Gothic churches, don't forget to stop and enjoy the regional cuisine of Picardy, which includes many vegetable-based dishes such as hearty soups, and the tasty *ficelle Picarde*, a form of stuffed pancake.

## 4 The valleys of Picardy

*350km/218mi starting from Amiens*
This is a good tour to make when all the family is along for the ride, as there is something for everyone. Follow the meandering route of the River Somme from Amiens, and maybe make a stop to visit the Samara Prehistoric Park or Naours, where an amazing network of underground passageways is big enough to shelter 3,000 people. When you reach the coast, the Parc Ornithologique du Marquenterre offers 3,000 hectares of pine forests, sand and mud flats that are an irresistible invitation for thousands of migratory birds. Nearby, if you're not too squeamish, is the Escargotière du Marquenterre, where edible snails are bred and sold. Leave time for water

play, or time for a snooze on the warm sand at Berck-sur-Mer or Le Touquet-Paris-Plage. The delightful gardens at Valloires are likely to be less crowded than the beach, and offer a lovely and restful interlude.

## 5 The Artois region

*300km/186mi starting from Arras*
This mining region has always shown a strong festive spirit and if you happen to visit at carnival time, you may even see jolly giants roaming the streets of Douai, and be carried away by the festivities. You may stop at any time to enjoy a moment in a traditional brasserie or listen to the chiming of a carillon, one of the many village bell towers found throughout northern France. In the Fine Arts Museum in Valenciennes, you can admire works by Bosch and Rubens. On your way to Lille and French Flanders, you may wish to take advantage of the natural benefits of the spring water at Saint-Amand. Then on to Béthune and its Grand Place, and south to the medieval castle of Olhain in the heart of the mining area.

## 6 The Opal Coast

*250km/155mi starting from Boulogne.*
Catch the fresh sea breezes as you drive along the cliff-top roads or stop to clamber in the dunes and play on the beaches of the Côte d'Opale. Many travellers enjoy a tour of the busy harbours at Boulogne and Calais; there are also traditional craftsmen at work in the region: a stop-over in Desvres, for example, is a chance to see unique ceramics being made. Inland from Boulogne the countryside is a patchwork of fields, trees and hedgerows; the Audomarois wetlands are a protected area where you may visit the Regional Nature Park's exhibition areas or enjoy nature discovery walks. If you are feeling hot and tired, why not take a boat ride on the 'water-gangs', canals running between the fields, and home to many species of waterfowl. Seafood lovers will find everything they crave here, and the fresh local produce is a lovely complement to other regional specialities.

## 7 Belfries in Flanders

*250km/155mi starting from Lille*
Leave the friendly city of Lille behind and head out to the hills and dales of Flanders. This little region has a style of its own, as you will soon see by observing the architecture of the fortified villages, the belfries, churches and mills, and inside the charming little eateries and watering holes known locally as *estaminets*. Local brewers contribute to the fun when traditional festivities are held. This corner of France is a favourite with those who love good beer!

## 8 The Avesnois countryside

*350km/218mi starting from St-Quentin*
Heading east from St-Quentin, the road follows the Oise Valley dotted with fortified churches. This is where Maroilles, a strong-tasting cheese, is produced. The drive then takes you through the region known locally as l'Avesnois, named after the main town, Avesnes-sur-Helpe, and close to the Belgian border. In fact, there are two rivers named Helpe, the Majeure and the Mineure, which flow through the Regional Nature Park. Since the Middle Ages, the landscape has been marked by small villages set around the mills and forges that sprung up beside powerful abbeys. There are plenty of opportunities to stop along this part of the itinerary and enjoy the amenities of the park. On your way south from Bavay and its Gallo-Roman remains, stop in Cateau-Cambrésis to admire works by Matisse. Between Cambrai and St-Quentin, the Riqueval tunnel runs through the plateau separating the Somme and Escaut rivers.

# WHEN AND WHERE TO GO

## Themed Tours

### HISTORY TOURS

These are itineraries based, for the most part, on architectural heritage presented in its historical context. There are several historical routes in the area covered in this guide:

- **Route du Camp du Drap d'Or**: the "Cloth of Gold" route from Calais to Arras. Information from the Association Route du Camp du Drap d'or, 20 rue Clemenceau, 62340 Guînes, ☎ 03 21 35 24 90.
- **Route des Archers**: evoking the battle of Agincourt, when the French knights were defeated by the English archers during the Hundred Years War. Contact the Agincourt tourist office, ☎ 03 21 47 27 53.
- **Route des Valois**: the Valois dynasty in the heart of the forests of Retz and Compiègne. Contact M. de Montesquiou, abbaye de Longpont, 02600 Longpont, ☎ 03 23 96 01 53.
- **Route du Lys de France et de la Rose de Picardie**: "Lily of France and Rose of Picardy" route from St-Denis to Boulogne-sur-Mer, via Écouen, Royaumont, l'Isle-Adam, Gerberoy, Poix-en-Picardie, St-Riquier, Rue and Montreuil. Apply to the Château de Troissereux, 60112 Troissereux, ☎ 03 44 79 00 00.
- **Route du Roy Soleil**: châteaux occupied by the Sun King Louis XIV. These and other special itineraries are the subjects of brochures that can be found in most local tourist offices.

### CULTURAL HERITAGE

- **Route des villes fortifiées** – This itinerary was set up by an association for the promotion of the **walled towns** of the Nord-Pas-de-Calais region. It includes 13 of the area's main citadels: Arras, Avesnes-sur-Helpe, Bergues, Boulogne-sur-Mer, Calais, Cambrai, Condé-sur-l'Escaut, Gravelines, Lille, Maubeuge, Montreuil-sur-Mer, Le Quesnoy and St-Omer. The itinerary is 500km/310mi in length, but is subdivided into shorter sections that provide many possibilities for excursions and tours. Each of the towns has a *Route des villes fortifiées* signpost at its entrance, accompanied by a logo. A map and brochure telling the history of each town are available from the local tourist offices and from the **Comité Régional de Tourisme du Nord-Pas-de-Calais** (🕭 *Local tourist offices*).
- **Route des Abbayes en Yvelines** is a tourist itinerary that passes via the Cistercian abbey of Les Vaux-de-Cernay and the abbey of Port-Royal-des-Champs, associated with the history of Jansenism.
- **Chemins des Retables** – Several tours enable visitors to discover the rich interior of churches in the Flanders region. Contact the Association des Retables de Flandre, BP 6535, 59386 Dunkerque Cedex, ☎ 03 28 68 69 78.
- **Route des Maisons d'Ecrivains** opens the door to residences of famous authors in the Île-de-France, including Chateaubriand, Zola and Dumas. Information centre: 13 avenue d'Eylau, 75116 Paris, ☎ 01 47 27 45 51.
- **Route des Jardins et châteaux** – around Paris: parks and châteaux in Île-de-France, including Breteuil, Sceaux, Courances, Fontainebleau, and St-Cloud.
- **Route des Impressionnistes en Val d'Oise** – Impressionist painters in the Val d'Oise region, Auvers-sur-Oise, Pontoise, L'Isle-Adam, Vétheuil, La Roche-Guyon, Argenteuil… in the footsteps of Manet, Daubigny, Pissarro, Renoir

and Van Gogh. Information,
☎01 30 29 51 00.

- **Balades au pays des Impression-nistes** – Nine municipalities situated along the River Seine form what is known as Impressionist country, including Carrières-sur-Seine, Bougival, Louveciennes, Marly-le Roi, le Port-Marly, Le Pecq-sur-Seine and Noisy-le-Roi. A leaflet is available from the tourist offices in these towns.

## TRADITIONS

**Windmills** – Once a common sight in the region, surviving examples of windmills have been taken under the wing of a local association which has begun to restore and develop them. The **Centre Régional de Moulinologie**, Musée des Moulins, 59650 Villeneuve-d'Ascq, ☎ 03 20 05 49 34, can provide brochures, maps and books on the subject. Most of the windmills cited in this guide are open to visitors.
On the plains of the Beauce and Brie, a few sails still catch the wind from time to time, and you can buy freshly ground flour there. Listed below are a few operating windmills where visitors are welcome, at least for a look around the outside of the mill.
In the Beauce *(located off the A 10 "Allainville" exit or, from Orléans, the "Allaines-Chartres" exit)*:

- **Ouarville**: Open 2.30-6pm, Sundays from Easter to 1 November. ☎ 02 37 22 13 87.
- **Levesville-la-Chenard**: Sunday afternoons, June to the end of August, or by appointment. ☎ 02 37 22 13 10.
- **Sannois**: on Mont Trouillet *(near Enghien-les-Bains)*, open Sundays 1.30-6.30pm. Contact the Sannois town hall *(mairie)* ☎ 01 39 98 20 00.

The following windmills are described in the Sights section of this guide.

- Moulin de St-Maxent (ᑭ see ABBEVILLE).
- Moulin Den Leeuw at Pitgam (ᑭ see BERGUES).
- Moulins de CASSEL, Steenmeulen (at Terdeghem), Drievemeulen,

Noordmeulen near Steenvoorde, Moulin Deschodt at Wormhout (ᑭ see CASSEL).

- Noord-Meulen (ᑭ see HOND-SCHOOTE).
- Oudankmeulen at Boeschepe (ᑭ see BAILLEUL).
- VILLENEUVE D'ASCQ (windmill and museum).

The association's annual windmill festival is held around the region in June.

**Carillons** – Chiming bells are part of everyday life in many towns in northern France and particularly in Flanders. A carillon consists of several bells hung in a bell-tower or belfry. The bells ring out different refrains to indicate the hour, the quarter and the half hour. The word comes from a medieval term "quadrillon", a peal of four bells ringing in harmony. In the Middle Ages, clocks were mechanical; they included small bells that the bell-ringer struck using a mallet or hammer. After a gradual increase in the number of bells, the mallet was replaced by a keyboard. The automatic system with cylinders, used in some places, is progressively being replaced by an electrical system that is easier to maintain.
The main carillons in the Nord-Pas-de-Calais area are as follows:

- **Tourcoing** – Eglise St-Christophe: 61 bells
- **Douai** – Town hall: 62 bells
- **Bergues** – Belfry: 50 bells
- **Avesnes-sur-Helpe** – Collégiale St-Nicolas: 48 bells
- **Capelle-la-Grande** – Belfry: 49 bells
- **Dunkerque** – Tour St-Eloi: 48 bells
- **Le Quesnoy** – Town hall: 48 bells
- **St-Amand-les-Eaux** – Tower on the abbey church: 48 bells
- **Seclin** – Collégiale St-Piat: 42 bells
- **Orchies** – Church: 48 bells

Carillon concerts are held regularly in certain towns *(for information, contact the tourist office)*.

## LOCAL CRAFTS AND INDUSTRY

Below are a few suggestions for visits; it is usually necessary to make an appointment.

**Usine élévatoire de Tribardou** –Route de Charmentray, 77450 Tribardou, ☎ 01 60 09 95 00. Guided tours year-round, on request, 1€. This factory, situated a few miles from Meaux, uses an impressive waterwheel to pump water from the River Marne and supply the Ourcq canal; an interesting insight into 19C technical methods.

**Météo-France** – Centre départemental des Yvelines, 3 rue Teisserenc-de-Bort, 78190 Trappes, ☎ 01 30 66 47 80. This regional weather station is open to the public on Thursdays only.

**Verrerie d'art de Soisy-sur-École** – Le Moulin de Noues, BP 2, 91840 Soisy-sur-École, ☎ 01 64 98 00 03. Visit of the glassworks, exhibition centre and salesroom.

**Coca Cola Entreprise** – 1-3 rue J.J.-Rousseau, ZAC Les Radars, 91350 Grigny, ☎ 01 69 02 20 00; daily except weekends 10am-5pm.

# Seasons

## CLIMATE

While the beaches of the Opal Coast are spectacular, stretching out for 1km/0.5mi at low tide, the relatively cool weather and the chilly waters of the Channel are generally more appealing for shell-seekers, horseback riders, landsailers and kite-flyers than for swimmers. In the winter months, the coast is often buffeted by strong winds. Statistically, June is the sunniest month on the coast, August the warmest. The highest period of rainfall is in November, and the lowest in April (for a total of 170 days per year). Peak summer temperatures usually hover around 25°C/77°F.

Inland, the winters are chilly, and darkness comes early in the northern latitudes. As spring turns to summer, the days become long and warm, and by June the sun lingers until after 10pm. Spring and autumn provide a chance to explore the valleys of the Aa, Canche, Authie and Somme, and the different regional nature parks.

Spring in Île-de-France offers a glorious contrast between the vivid yellow of rapeseed fields against the green background of the copses and forests, while autumn in the oak and beech woods of Compiègne, Rambouillet, Sénart or St-Germain is accompanied by the warm colours of changing leaves.

## WEATHER FORECAST

**National forecast:** ☎ 32 50
**Local forecast:** ☎ 0 892 68 02 XX, where XX is the number of the département (e.g. for the Nord – ☎ 0 892 68 02 59).
This information is also available on www.meteofrance.com.

## WHAT TO PACK

As little as possible! Cleaning and laundry services are available everywhere. Most personal items can be replaced at reasonable cost. Try to pack everything into one suitcase and a small bag. Porter help is in limited or non-existent in rural France, and new purchases simply add to the original weight. If you think it may be necessary, take an extra bag for packing new purchases, shopping at the open-air market, carrying a picnic etc. Be sure luggage is clearly labelled and old travel tags removed. Do not pack medication in checked luggage; keep it with you.

# KNOW BEFORE YOU GO

## Useful Websites

**www.ambafrance-uk.org**
The French Embassy's website provides basic information (geography, demo-graphics, history), a news digest and business-related information. It offers special pages for children, and pages devoted to culture, language study and travel.

**www.visiteurope.com**
The European Travel Commission provides useful information on travelling to and around 27 European countries, and includes links to some commercial booking services.

**www.franceguide.com**
The French Government Tourist Office site is packed with practical information and tips for those travelling to France. The home page has a number of links to more specific guidance, for American or Canadian travellers for example, or to the FGTO's London pages.

**www.FranceKeys.com**
This site has plenty of practical information for visiting France. It covers all the regions, with links to tourist offices and related sites. Very useful for planning the details of your tour in France!

**www.franceway.com** is an on-line magazine which focuses on culture and heritage. For each region, there are also suggestions for activities and practical information on where to stay and how to get there.

**www.paris.org**
Paris Pages is a collection of everthing useful for visiting Paris. It is lively and well illustrated. Categories include museums, cafés, hotels, restaurants, current events and exhibits, stores and shops, public transportation and a discussion group.

**www.pas-de-calais.com** is the regional tourist office site, with a complete English version. On it, you will find maps, useful addresses, scheduled events, and information for booking *gîtes*, other furnished accommodation, and bed and breakfast establishments. There is a space for e-mailing your specific questions for reply.

**www.picardietourisme.com** / **www.picardy.org** are two sites dedicated to promoting Picardy, and provide masses of information not only on basics like accommodation and where to eat, but on history, culture and recreation.

## Tourist Offices

### FRENCH TOURIST OFFICES ABROAD

For information, brochures, maps and assistance in planning a trip to France, travellers should apply to the official French tourist office in their own country:

**AUSTRALIA – NEW ZEALAND**
 **Sydney** – BNP Building, 12 Castlereagh Street, Sydney, New South Wales 2000. ☎ (02) 9 231 52 44, Fax: (02) 9 221 86 82.

**CANADA**
 **Toronto** – 30 St Patrick's Street, Suite 700, Toronto, ONT M5T 3A3. ☎ (416) 979 7587.
 **Montreal** – 1981 McGill College Avenue, Suite 490, Montreal PQ H3A 2W9. ☎ (514) 288-4264, Fax: (514) 845 48 68.

**EIRE**
 **Dublin** – 10 Suffolk St, Dublin 2. ☎ (1) 679 0813, Fax: (1) 679 0814.

**UNITED KINGDOM**
 **London** – 178 Piccadilly, London W1J 9AL. ☎ (09068) 244 123, Fax: (020) 793 6594.

**UNITED STATES**
 **East Coast: New York** – 444 Madison Avenue, NY 10022. ☎ 212-838-7800, Fax: (212) 838 7855.
 **Midwest: Chicago** – 676 North Michigan Avenue, Suite 3360, Chicago, IL 60611. ☎ (312) 751 7800, Fax: (312) 337 6339.

*Senlis*

**West Coast: Los Angeles** –
9454 Wilshire Boulevard, Suite 715,
Beverly Hills, CA 90212. ☎(310)
271 6665, Fax: (310) 276 2835.

## TOURIST OFFICES IN FRANCE

Visitors may also contact local tourist
offices for more information, including
brochures and maps. The addresses
and telephone numbers of tourist
offices are listed after the symbol ▯
within the towns and places in the
Sights section of this guide. Below,
the addresses are given for local
tourist offices of the *départements*
and *régions* covered in this guide.

### REGIONAL TOURIST OFFICES

**Île-de-France** – Comité Régional
du Tourisme, 11 r. du Faubourg-
Poissonnière – 75009 Paris.
☎01 73 00 77 00.

**Nord-Pas-de-Calais** – Comité
Régional du Tourisme, 6 place
Mendès-France, 59028 Lille.
☎ 03 20 14 57 57.
www.crt-nordpasdecalais.fr

**Picardie** – Comité Régional du
Tourisme, 3 rue Vincent Auriol, 80011
Amiens 1. ☎ 03 22 22 33 63.
www.picardietourisme.com

### DEPARTMENTAL TOURIST OFFICES

#### PICARDY

**Aisne** – 24-28 avenue Charles-de-
Gaulle, 02007 Laon. ☎ 03 23 27 76
76. www.evasion-aisne.com

**Oise** – 19 rue Pierre-Jacoby,
BP 80822, 60008 Beauvais.
☎03 44 45 82 12.
www.oisetourisme.com

**Somme** – 21 rue Ernest-Cauvin,
80000 Amiens. ☎03 22 71 22 71.
www.somme-tourisme.com

#### NORD-PAS-DE-CALAIS

**Nord** – 6 rue Gauthier-de-
Châtillon, BP 1232, 59013 Lille.
☎03 20 57 59 59. www.cdt-nord.fr

**Pas-de-Calais** – route La
Trésorerie, BP 79, 62126 Wimille.
☎03 21 10 34 60. www.pas-de-
calais.com

#### ÎLE DE FRANCE

**Essonne** – 19 rue Mazières,
91000 Evry. ☎01 64 97 35 13.
www.tourisme-essonne.com

**Eure-et-Loir** – 10 rue du Docteur
Maunoury, BP 67, 28002 Chartres.
☎ 02 37 84 01 00.
www.tourisme28.com

**Hauts-de-Seine** – 8 place de la
Défense, Courbevoie, 92974 Paris-
la-Défense. ☎01 46 93 92 92.
www.tourisme-hautsdeseine.com

**Seine-et-Marne** – 11 rue Royale,
77300 Fontainebleau. ☎ 01 60 39
60 39.  www.tourisme77.net

**Seine-St-Denis** – 140 avenue
Jean-Lolive, 93695 Pantin. ☎ 01 49
15 98 98. www.tourisme93.com

**Val de Marne** – 38 quai Victor-
Hugo, 94500 Champigny-sur-
Marne. ☎ 01 55 09 16 20.

www.tourisme-valdemarne.com
**Val-d'Oise** – Château de la Motte,
95270 Luzarches.☎ 01 30 29 51
00. www.val-doise-tourisme.com
**Yvelines** – 2 place André-Mignot,
78012 Versailles. ☎ 01 39 07 71 22.
www.tourisme.yvelines.fr

**TOURIST INFORMATION CENTRES**
The **Espace du tourisme d'Île-de-
France**, Carrousel du Louvre, 99 rue de
Rivoli, 75001 Paris, ☎ 08 26 16 66 66,
is a handy tourist information bureau
open daily, 10am-7pm.
The **Espace du tourisme d'Île-de-
France et Seine-et-Marne**, place des
Passagers du Vent, 77700 Chessy-Marne-
la-Vallée, ☎ 01 60 43 33 33, is a tourist
information kiosk close to the RER
station at Disneyland/Disney Village.

The **Espace accueil tourisme CDT
Seine-St-Denis**, Stade de France,
porte H, 93216 St-Denis-La-Plaine,
☎ 01 49 46 08 11, is an information
centre located in the new stadium
inaugurated in 1998.

The complete collection of Michelin
**maps and guides** is on sale in the
Espace Michelin, 32 avenue de l'Opéra,
75002 Paris, ☎ 01 42 68 05 20.

ॐ See the *Admission times and
charges* for the addresses and
telephone numbers of local tourist
offices (*Syndicats d'Initiative*). These
offices provide information on craft
courses and itineraries with special
themes – wine tours, history tours,
artistic tours. Nineteen towns and
areas, labelled **Villes et Pays d'Art
et d'Histoire** by the Ministry of
Culture, are mentioned in this guide
(Amiens, Arras, Beauvais, Boulogne-
sur-Mer, Cambrai, Compiègne,
Douai, Laon, Lille, Meaux, Noyon,
Pontoise, Provins, St-Denis,
St Germain-en-Laye, St-Omer,
St Quentin, Senlis and Soissons).
They are particularly active in
promoting their architectural and
cultural heritage and offer guided
tours by highly qualified guides as
well as activities for 6- to 12-year-
old children. More infor-mation is
available from local tourist offices
a nd from **www.vpah.culture.fr**
(french language version only).

# International Visitors

| Embassies and Consulates | | | |
|---|---|---|---|
| Australia | Embassy | 4 rue Jean-Rey, 75015 Paris | ☎ 01 40 59 33 00 – Fax: 01 40 59 33 10. |
| Canada | Embassy | 35 avenue Montaigne, 75008 Paris | ☎ 01 44 43 29 00 – Fax: 01 44 43 29 99. |
| Eire | Embassy | 4 rue Rude, 75016 Paris | ☎ 01 44 17 67 00 – Fax: 01 44 17 67 60. |
| New Zealand | Embassy | 7 ter rue Léonard-de-Vinci, 75016 Paris | ☎ 01 45 01 43 43 – Fax: 01 45 01 43 44. |
| South Africa | Embassy | 59 Quai d'Orsay, 75007 Paris | ☎ 01 53 59 23 23 – Fax: 01 53 59 23 33 |
| UK | Embassy | 35 rue du Faubourg St-Honoré, 75008 Paris | ☎ 01 44 51 31 00 – Fax: 01 44 51 31 27. |
| | Consulate | 16 rue d'Anjou, 75008 Paris | ☎ 01 44 51 31 01 (visas). |
| USA | Embassy | 2 avenue Gabriel, 75008 Paris | ☎ 01 43 12 22 22 – Fax: 01 42 66 97 83. |
| | Consulate | 2 rue St-Florentin, 75001 Paris | ☎ 01 42 96 14 88. |

## ENTRY REQUIREMENTS

**Passport** – Nationals of countries within the European Union entering France need only a national identity card; in the case of the UK, until such time as there may be national identity cards, this means your passport. Nationals of other countries must be in possession of a valid national **passport**. In case of loss or theft, report to your embassy or consulate and the local police.

**Visa** – No **entry visa** is required for Canadian, US or Australian citizens travelling as tourists and staying less than 90 days, except for students planning to study in France. If you think you may need a visa, apply to your local French Consulate.

**US citizens** should obtain the booklet *Safe Trip Abroad*, which provides useful information on visa requirements, customs regulations, medical care etc for international travellers. Published by the Government Printing Office, it can be ordered by phone – ☎ (202) 512-1800 – or consulted online (www.access.gpo.gov). General passport information is available by phone toll-free from the Federal Information Center (item 5 on the automated menu), ☎ 800-688-9889. US passport application forms can be downloaded from http://travel.state.gov.

## CUSTOMS REGULATIONS

Apply to the Customs Office (UK) for a leaflet on customs regulations and the full range of duty-free allowances; available from HM Customs and Excise, Thomas Paine House, Angel Square, Torrens Street, London EC1V 1TA, ☎ 08450 109 000. The US Customs Service offers a publication *Know Before You Go* for US citizens: for the office nearest you, consult the phone book, Federal Government, US Treasury (www.customs.ustreas.gov).

There are no customs formalities for holidaymakers bringing their caravans into France for a stay of less than six months. No customs document is necessary for pleasure boats and outboard motors for a stay of less than six months, but the registration certificate should be kept on board. Americans can take home, tax-free, up to US$ 400 worth of goods (limited quantities of alcohol and tobacco products); Canadians up to CND$ 300; Australians up to AUS$ 400 and New Zealanders up to NZ$ 700.

Residents from a member state of the European Union are not restricted with regard to purchasing duty-paid goods for private use or personal consumption.

| Duty-Free Allowances | |
| --- | --- |
| Spirits (whisky, gin, vodka etc) | 10 litres |
| Fortified wines (vermouth, port etc) | 20 litres |
| Wine (not more than 60 sparkling) | 90 litres |
| Beer | 110 litres |
| Cigarettes | 800 |
| Cigarillos | 400 |
| Cigars | 200 |
| Smoking tobacco | 1 kg |

## HEALTH

First aid, medical advice and chemists' night service rotas are available from chemists (*pharmacie*) identified by a green cross sign. All prescription drugs should be clearly labelled; it is recommended that you carry a copy of the prescription.

It is advisable to take out comprehensive travel insurance which also covers medical expenses as medical treatment in French hospitals or clinics is not free. **Nationals of non-EU countries** should check with their insurance companies about policy limitations. Reimbursement can then be negotiated with the insurance company according to the policy held.

**British and Irish citizens** should apply to the Department of Health and Social Security **before travelling** for a EuropeanHealth Insurance Card, which entitles the holder to urgent treatment for accident or unexpected illness in EU countries – see www.nhs.uk. A refund of part of the costs of treatment can be obtained on application in person or by post to the local Social Security Offices (*Caisse Primaire d'Assurance Maladie*).

**Americans** concerned about travel and health can contact the International Association for Medical Assistance to Travelers, which can also provide details of English-speaking doctors in different parts of France: ☎ (716) 754-4883.

**The American Hospital of Paris** is open 24hr for emergencies as well as consultations, with English-speaking staff, at 63 boulevard Victor-Hugo, 92200 Neuilly-sur-Seine, ☎ 01 46 41 25 25. Accredited by major insurance companies.

**The British Hospital** is just outside Paris in Levallois-Perret, 3 rue Barbès, ☎ 01 46 39 22 22.

## Accessibility

The sights described in this guide that are easily accessible to people of reduced mobility are indicated in the 'Admission times and charges' section by the ♿ symbol.

On TGV and Corail trains operated by the national railway (SNCF), there are special wheelchair slots in 1st class carriages available to holders of 2nd class tickets. On Eurostar and Thalys, special rates are available for accompanying adults. All airports are equipped to receive physically disabled passengers.

Web-surfers can find information for slow walkers, mature travellers and others with special needs at www.access-able.com.

For information on museum access for the disabled contact Les Musées de France, Service Accueil des Publics Spécifiques, 6 rue des Pyramides, 75041 Paris Cedex 1, ☎ 01 40 15 80 72.

**The Michelin Guide France** and the **Michelin Camping Caravaning France** indicate hotels and campsites with facilities suitable for physically handicapped people.

# GETTING THERE

## By Plane

Various international and other independent airlines operate services to Paris (Charles-de-Gaulle/Roissy located 27km/14mi north of Paris, Orly located 16km/10mi south, and Beauvais-Tillé). There are also direct flights from London to Lille-Lesquin Airport, located 15min from the centre of Lille in northern France. Contact airlines and travel agents for information on package-tour flights with rail or coach link-ups or fly-drive schemes.

## By Ship

**From the UK or Ireland:**
There are numerous **cross-Channel services** (passenger and car ferries, hovercraft) from the United Kingdom and Ireland, and also the rail Shuttle through the Channel Tunnel (**Le Shuttle-Eurotunnel**, ☎ 0990 353-535, www.eurotunnel.com). For details apply to travel agencies or to:

- **P&O Ferries** Channel House, Channel View Road, Dover, Kent. CT17 9JT, ☎ 08705 980 333, www.poferries.com
- **Norfolk Line** Norfolk House Eastern Docks, Dover, Kent. CT16 1JA, ☎ 0870 870 10 20 www.norfolkline-ferries.co.uk
- **Brittany Ferries** Millbay Docks; Plymouth, Devon PL1 3EW. ☎ 0990 360 360, www.brittany-ferries.com
- **Portsmouth Commercial Port (and ferry information)** George Byng Way, Portsmouth, Hampshire PO2 8SP. ☎ 01705 297 391, Fax 01705 861 165,

www.portsmouth-port.co.uk
🚢 **Irish Ferries** 50 West Norland Street, Dublin 2. ☎ (353) 16-610-511, www.irishferries.com
🚢 **Seafrance** Eastern Docks, Dover, Kent CT16 1JA. ☎ 01304 212696, Fax 01304 240033, www.seafrance.fr

## By Train

All rail services throughout France can be arranged through Rail Europe in the UK. ☎ 08708 304 862; www.raileurope.co.uk).
**Eurostar** runs from **London** (Waterloo) to **Paris** (Gare du Nord) in under 3hr (up to 20 times daily), or **Lille** (Europe) in 2hr (up to 10 times daily). There is a once daily service (every day of the year) running directly from the UK to **Marne La Vallee Disneyland**, taking 3hr.
Bookings and information ☎ 08705 186 186 (£5 booking fee applies) in the UK; www.eurostar.com.
Rail Europe can also book Eurostar travel on ☎ 08708 303 862 or www.raileurope.co.uk.
**Eurailpass, Flexipass** and **Saverpass** are travel passes which may be purchased in the US. Contact your travel agent or **Rail Europe,** 178 Piccadilly, London W1V OBA, ☎ 0990 848 848. Information on schedules can be obtained on www.raileurope.com, www.sncf.fr. There are numerous **discounts** available when you purchase your tickets in France, from 25-50% below the regular rate. These include discounts for using senior cards and youth cards (cards that must be purchased, and showing your name and a photograph), and lower rates for 2-9 people travelling together (no card required, advance purchase necessary). There are a limited number of discount seats available during peak travel times, and the best discounts are available for travel during off-peak periods.
Tickets for rail travel in France must be validated (*composter*) by using the (usually) orange automatic date-stamping machines at the platform entrance (failure to do so may result in a fine).
The French railway company, SNCF, operates a telephone information, reservation and prepayment service in English from 7am to 10pm (French time). In France call ☎ 08 36 35 35 39 (when calling from outside France, drop the initial 0).

## By Coach / Bus

**Eurolines (UK),** 4 Cardiff Road, Luton, Bedfordshire, LU1 1PP. ☎ 08705 143219, Fax 01582 400694.
**Eurolines (Paris),** 22 rue Malmaison, 93177 Bagnolet. ☎ 01 49 72 57 80, Fax 01 49 72 57 99.
**www.eurolines.com** is the international website with information about travelling all over Europe by coach (bus).

# GETTING AROUND

## Public Transportation

The **Paris Visite** pass allows unlimited travel on the entire RATP network in the Paris and Île-de-France area and includes the metro, RER, bus, tram and suburban trains, depending on the geographical zone (1-3 for the inner zone and 1-5, 6, 7 or 8 for the outer suburbs of Île-de-France). Valid for 1, 2, 3 or 5 consecutive days, it can be purchased in main metro and all RER stations, or abroad. Information: ☎ 08 36 68 77 14, www.ratp.fr.
Other passes are also available on the RATP network, including the *carte orange hebdomadaire* for travel from daily in zones 1-8, or the **Mobilis** card, issued with a voucher, and valid for one day.
**Metro** lines are identified by a number. Some of them extend into the suburbs:

St-Denis or Asnières on line 13, Créteil on line 8.

For **RER** lines A, B, C, D, E, which extend into the outer suburbs, cost depends on the distance travelled.

Six Parisian railway stations (Austerlitz, Est, Lyon, Montparnasse, Nord, St-Lazare) provide suburban train links to the towns of the Île-de-France region. Stations are open from 6am to 9pm. The cost of travelling on the *transilien SNCF* (Île-de-France regional network) varies according to length of journey, ☎ 01 53 90 20 20 (6am-10pm).

There is a very frequent service to Lille by TGV (1hr) from the Gare du Nord. Arras is under an hour away from the capital, again by TGV. Travel to Amiens takes 1-2hr, depending on the number of stops made, while Beauvais takes a little over 1hr; information/reservations: ☎ 08 36 35 35 35, www.sncf.fr.

# Driving in France

The area covered in this guide is easily reached by main motorways and national routes. **Michelin map 726** indicates the main itineraries as well as alternate routes for avoiding heavy traffic during busy holiday periods, and gives estimated travel times. **Michelin map 723** is a detailed atlas of French motorways, indicating tolls, rest areas and services along the route; it includes a table for calculating distances and times. The latest Michelin route-planning service is available on **www.ViaMichelin. com**. Travellers can calculate a precise route using such options as shortest route, route avoiding toll roads or a Michelin-recommended route and gain access to tourist information (hotels, restau-rants, attractions). The service is available on a pay-per-route basis or by subscription.

The roads are very busy during the holiday period (particularly weekends in July and August) and, to avoid traffic congestion, it is advisable to follow the recommended secondary routes (signposted as *Bison Futé – itinéraires bis)*. The motorway network includes rest areas (*aires de repos*) and petrol stations (*stations-service*), usually with restaurant and shopping complexes attached, about every 40km/25mi, so that long-distance drivers have no excuse not to stop for a rest every now and then.

## DOCUMENTS

Travellers from other European Union countries and North America can drive in France with a valid national or home-state **driving licence**. Always carry your passport and UK driving licence with you when motoring abroad. Remember, you may be asked to produce these at any time in addition to your motor insurance and vehicle registration documents. An **international driving licence** is useful because the information on it appears in nine languages (keep in mind that traffic officers are empowered to fine motorists). An international licence is available in the UK from the AA or the RAC, or in the US from the National Automobile Club, 1151 East Hillsdale Blvd., Foster City, CA 94404, ☎ 650-294-7000 or, www.national-autoclub.com; or contact your local branch of the American Automobile Association. For the vehicle, it is necessary to have the registration papers (logbook) and a nationality plate of the approved size.

Certain motoring organisations (AA, RAC, AAA) offer accident **insurance** and breakdown service schemes for members. Check with your current insurance company in regard to coverage while abroad. If you plan to hire a car using your credit card, check with the company, which may provide liability insurance automatically (and thus save you having to pay the cost for optimum coverage).

## HIGHWAY CODE

The minimum driving age is 18. Traffic drives on the right. All passengers must wear **seat belts**. Children under the age of 10 must ride in the back seat. Headlights must be switched on in poor visibility and at night; use sidelights only when the vehicle is stationary.

Do not drive using only sidelights. In the case of a **breakdown**, a red warning triangle or hazard warning lights are obligatory. The possibility exists that in the next few years it may become compulsory also to wear high visibility vests in the event of breakdown. In the absence of stop signs at inter-sections, cars must **yield to the right**. Traffic on main roads outside built-up areas (priority indicated by a yellow diamond sign) and on roundabouts has right of way. There are many **roundabouts** especially on the edge of towns; you must slow down when you approach one and yield to the cars in the circle. Vehicles must stop when the lights turn red at road junctions and may filter to the right only when indicated by an amber arrow.

The regulations on **drinking and driving** (limited to 0.50g/l) and **speeding** are strictly enforced – usually by an on-the-spot fine and/or confiscation of the vehicle.

## Speed Limits

Although liable to modification, these are as follows:

- toll motorways (*autoroutes*) 130kph/80mph (110kph/68mph when raining);
- dual carriageways and motorways without tolls 110kph/68mph (100kph/62mph when raining);
- other roads 90kph/56mph (80kph/50mph when raining) and in towns 50kph/31mph;
- outside lane on motorways during daylight, on level ground and with good visibility – minimum speed limit of 80kph/50mph.

## Parking Regulations

In town there are zones where parking is either restricted or subject to a fee; tickets should be obtained from the ticket machines (*horodateurs* – small change necessary) and displayed inside the windscreen on the driver's side; failure to display may result in a fine, or your vehicle being towed away and impounded. Other parking areas in town may require you to take a ticket when passing through a barrier. To exit, you must pay the parking fee (usually there is a machine located by the exit – *sortie*) and insert the paid-up card in another machine which will lift the exit gate.

## Tolls

In France, most motorway sections are subject to a toll (*péage*). You can pay in cash or with a credit card (Visa, Mastercard).

## CAR RENTAL

There are car rental agencies at airports, railway stations and in all large towns throughout France. European cars have manual transmission; automatic cars are available in larger cities only if an advance reservation is made. Drivers must be over 21; between ages 21-25, drivers are required to pay an extra daily fee; some companies allow drivers under 23 only if the reservation has been made through a travel agent. It is relatively expensive to hire a car in France; it is worth checking, when you buy your air ticket, to check whether it is possible to take advantage of **fly-drive offers**. There are many on-line services that will look for the best prices on car rental around the globe. **Nova** can be contacted at www.rentacar-worldwide. com or ☎ 0800 018 6682 (free phone UK) or ☎ 44 28 4272 8189 (calling from outside the UK). All of the firms listed opposite have Internet sites for reservations and information.

| Rental Cars – Central Reservation in France | |
|---|---|
| **Avis:** | ☎ 08 20 05 05 05 |
| **Europcar:** | ☎ 08 25 82 54 57 |
| **Budget France:** | ☎ 08 25 00 35 64 |
| **Hertz France:** | ☎ 01 47 03 49 12 |
| **SIXT-Eurorent:** | ☎ 08 20 00 74 98 |
| **National-CITER:** | ☎ 01 45 22 77 91 |
| **Baron's Limousines:** | ☎ 01 45 30 21 21 |

## MOTORHOME RENTAL

**Worldwide Motorhome Rentals** offers fully equipped campervans for rent. You can view them on the

company's website.
☏ 888- 519-8969 *US toll-free*
☏ 530-389-8316 *outside the US*
Fax 530-389-8316.
www.mhrww.com

🚐 **Overseas Motorhome Tours Inc**.
organises escorted tours
and individual rental of
recreational vehicles:
☏ 800-322-2127 *US*
☏ 1-310-543-2590 *outside the US*
www.omtinc.com.

## FUEL

French service stations dispense:
🚙 *sans plomb 98* (super unleaded 98)
🚙 *sans plomb 95* (super unleaded 95)
🚙 *diesel/gazole including high grade diesel* (diesel)
🚙 *GPL* (LPG).
Petrol is less expensive in France than in the UK, but higher than in the US. Prices are listed along the motorways. It is cheaper to fill up after leaving the motorway; check the large hyper-markets on the outskirts of town.

# WHERE TO STAY AND EAT

*Hotel and Restaurant listings fall within the description of each region. 🪙 For coin ranges, see the Legend on the cover flap.*

## Where to Stay

The map opposite illustrates a selection of holiday destinations that are especially recommended for their accommoda-tion and leisure facilities, and their pleasant setting. It shows **overnight stops**, fairly large towns that should be visited and that have good accom-modation facilities, as well as traditional destinations for a **short break**, which combine accommodation, charm and a peaceful setting. As far as Paris and Lille are concerned, the influence they exert in the region and the wealth of monuments, museums and other sights to which they are home make them the ideal setting for a **weekend break.**

## FINDING A HOTEL

**The Green Guide** is pleased to offer a new feature: lists of selected hotels and restaurants for this region. The **Address Books** throughout the Sights section provide descriptions and price ranges of typical places to stay and eat with local flair. The Legend at the back of this guide explains the symbols and abbreviations used in these sections. We have reported the prices and conditions as we observed them, but of course changes in management and other factors may mean that you will find some discrepancies. Please feel free to keep us informed of any major differences you encounter.
Use the **Map of places to stay** *(opposite)* to identify recommended places for overnight stops. For an even greater selection, use the **Michelin Guide France,** with its famously reliable star-rating system and hundreds of establishments all over France.
Book ahead to ensure that you get the accommodation you want, not only in tourist season but year-round, as many towns fill up during trade fairs, arts festivals etc. Some places require an advance deposit or a reconfirmation. Reconfirming is especially important if you plan to arrive after 6pm.
For further assistance, **Loisirs Accueil** is a booking service that has offices in some French *départements* – for further information, contact the tourist offices listed above or the Fédération nationale des services de réservation Loisirs-Accueil, 280 boulevard St-Germain, 75007 Paris, ☏ 01 44 11 10 44; www.resinfrance.com.
A guide to good-value, family-run hotels, **Logis et Auberges de France**, is available from the French Tourist Office, as are lists of other kinds of accommodation such as hotel-châteaux, bed-and-breakfasts etc.

**Relais et châteaux** provides information on booking in luxury hotels with character: 15 rue Galvani, 75017 Paris, ☎ 01 45 72 90 00; likewise **Chateaux and Hotels de France**, ☎ 01 72 72 92 02, www.chateauxhotels.com.

**Economy Chain Hotels** – If you need a place to stop en route, these can be useful, as they are inexpensive (30-45 € for a double room) and generally located near the main road. While breakfast is available, there may not be a restaurant; rooms are small, with a television and bathroom. Central reservation numbers:

- **Akena** ☎ 01 69 84 85 17
- **B&B** ☎ 0892 782 929
- **Mister Bed** ☎ 01 46 14 38 00. www.misterbed.fr
- **Villages Hôtel** ☎ 03 80 60 92 70

The hotel companies below offer slightly more expensive lodgings, (from 58 €) and offer a few more amenities and services.

- **Campanile** ☎ 01 64 62 46 46
- **Kyriad** ☎ 0825 003 003

Many chains have on-line reservations:

- **Etap** 0 892 688 900. www.etaphotel.com
- **Ibis** 0 825 882 222. www.ibishotel.com

## Renting a cottage, Bed and Breakfast

The **Maison des Gîtes de France** is an information service on self-catering accommodation in the Northern France region (and the rest of France). *Gîtes* usually take the form of a cottage or apartment decorated in the local style where visitors can make themselves at home, or bed and breakfast accommodation (*chambres d'hôtes*) which consists of a room and breakfast at a reasonable price.

Contact the Gîtes de France office in Paris: 59 rue St-Lazare, 75439 Paris Cedex 09, ☎ 01 49 70 75 75, or their representative in the UK, **Brittany Ferries** (*address above*). The Internet site, **www.gites-de-france.fr**, has a good English version. From the site, you can order catalogues for different regions illustrated with photographs of the properties, as well as specialised catalogues (bed and breakfasts, farm

stays etc). You can also contact the local tourist offices which may have lists of available properties and local bed and breakfast establishments.

The **Fédération nationale Clévacances**, 54 boulevard de l'Embouchure, BP 2166, 31022 Toulouse Cedex 09, ☎ 05 61 13 55 66, www.clevacances.com, offers a wide choice of accommodation (rooms, flats, chalets and villas) throughout France.

The **Fédération des Stations vertes de vacances et Villages de neige** (6 rue Ranfer-de-Bretenières, BP 71698, 21016 Dijon Cedex, ☎ 03 80 54 10 50; www.stationsvertes.com) is an association which promotes almost 600 rural localities throughout France, selected for their natural appeal as well as for the quality of their environment, their accommodation and the leisure activities available.

### Farm Holidays

Three guides, *Guide des fermes-auberges, Bienvenue à la ferme* and *Vacances et week-ends à la ferme*, list the addresses of farms providing guest facilities which have been vetted for quality and for meeting official standards. For more information, apply to local tourist offices (*addresses above*).

## HOSTELS, CAMPING

To obtain an International Youth Hostel Federation card (there is no age requirement, and there is a senior card available too) you should contact the IYHF in your own country for information and membership applications (UK ☎ 01727 855215; US ☎ 202 783 6161; Canada ☎ 613-273 7884; Australia ☎ 61-2-9565-1669). There is a new booking service on the Internet (www.hihostels.com), which you may use to reserve rooms as much as six months in advance.

The main youth hostel association (*auberges de jeunesse*) in France is the **Ligue Française pour les Auberges de la Jeunesse**, 67 rue Vergniaud, 75013 Paris, ☎ 01 44 16 78 78; www.auberges-de-jeunesse.com. There are numerous officially graded **camp sites** with varying standards of

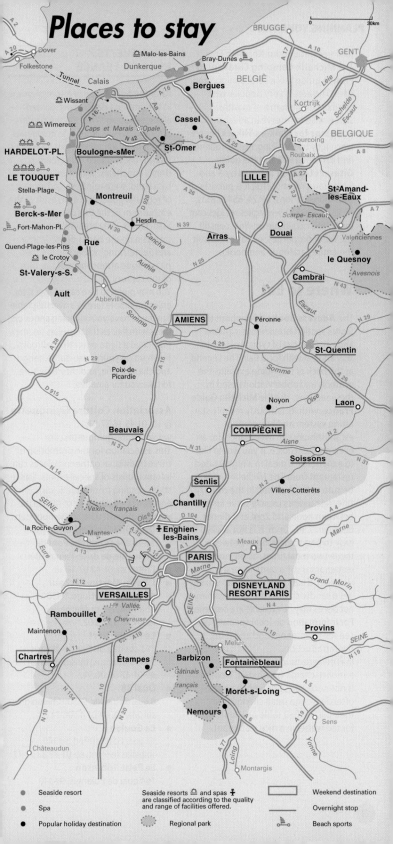

facilities throughout Northern France. The **Michelin Camping Caravaning France** guide lists a selection of camp sites. The area is very popular with campers in the summer months, so it is wise to reserve in advance.

**Lodgings for Walkers/Hikers** People who enjoy bike walking, hiking, touring, and canoeing will find the guide **Gîtes d'étapes et refuges** by A and S Mouraret most useful. It is published by Rando-Éditions, BP 24, 65421 Ibos, ☎ 05 62 90 09 90. www.gites-refuges.com (order the catalogue on-line, consult the list of properties, or pay to consult the entire catalogue and book).

# Where to Eat

The **Address Books** throughout the Sights section provide descriptions and price ranges of typical places to stay and eat with local flair. The Legend at the back of this guide explains the symbols and abbreviations used in these sections. Use the **Michelin Guide France**, with its famously reliable star-rating system and hundreds of establishments all over France, for an even greater choice. If you would like to experience a meal in a highly rated restaurant from The Michelin Guide, be sure to book ahead! In the country-side, restaurants usually serve lunch between noon and 2pm and dinner between 7.30-10pm. It is not always easy to find something in between those two meal times, as the non-stop restaurant is still a rarity in rural France. However, a hungry traveller can usually get a sandwich in a café, and ordinary hot dishes may be available in a *brasserie*. For information on local specialities, see the chapter on food and drink in the Introduction.

In French restaurants and cafés, a service charge is included. Tipping is not necessary, but French people often leave the small change from their bill on their table or about 5% for the waiter in a nice restaurant.

## "GUINGUETTES" IN ÎLE-DE-FRANCE

After the golden age of Impressionism in the late 19C, dance halls located along canals and rivers in the country-side around Paris, known as *guinguettes*, gradually disappeared from Île-de-France. These dance halls, serving drinks and meals, with music provided by a band, were reintroduced as part of regional policy and as a result of the enthusiasm of the Culture Guinguette association. They are now springing up again on the banks of the Marne and Seine, bringing back to life the picturesque atmosphere of the turn of the century.

You may prefer to be a casual spectator, enjoying simple fare at a riverside table. But if you have your dancing shoes on, dress with flair as the regu-lars do (men may need a tie to enter the ballroom). Brush up on your passo doble, tango and cha-cha-cha, and they'll be sure to take you for a native.

### Association Culture Guinguette

🛈 ☎ 01 45 16 37 51; www.culture-guinguette.com This association for the promotion of these traditional gathering places can inform tourists of special events. Dance styles ranging from athletic rock to energetic polka by way of the classic waltz are practised in the member clubs:

- **Domaine Ste-Catherine** 22-24 allée Centrale, Pont de Créteil, île de Brise-Pain, 94000 Créteil ☎ 01 42 07 19 18.
- **L'Île du Martin-Pêcheur** 41 quai Victor-Hugo, 94500 Champigny-sur-Marne ☎ 01 49 83 03 02.
- **Le Moulin Vert** 103 chemin du Contre-Halage, 94500 Champigny-sur-Marne ☎ 01 47 06 00 91.
- **Quai 38** 8 quai du Viaduc, 94500 Champigny-sur-Marne, ☎ 01 47 06 24 69.
- **La Goulue** 17 quai Gabriel-Péri, 94340 Joinville-le-Pont, ☎ 01 48 83 21 77.
- **Le Petit Robinson** 164 quai de Polangis, 94340

Joinville-le-Pont, ☎ 01 48 89 04 39.

- **Chez Gégène**
  162 quai de Polangis, 94340
  Joinville-le-Pont, ☎ 01 48 83 29 43;
  www.chez-gegene.fr
- **La Grenouillère**
  68 avenue du 11-Novembre,
  St-Maur-des-Fossés, 94210 La
  Varenne-St-Hilaire, ☎ 01 48 89 23 32.
- **Le Canotier**
  2 rue du Bac, 77410, Précy-
  sur-Marne, ☎ 01 60 01 62 12.
- **L'Auberge Charmante**
  20 quai de la Rive-Charmante,
  93160 Noisy-le-Grand,
  ☎ 01 45 92 94 31.

## FERMES-AUBERGES

These farm inns may or may not offer
accommodation. They serve farm
produce and local speciality dishes. They
are open at weekends but advanced
booking is required. Contact the Association des fermiers aubergistes de
France, **Ferm'Auberge**, Les Perriaux,
89350 Champignelles, ☎ 03 85 45 13 22.

## BRASSERIES IN NORTHERN FRANCE

The best place to discover the friend-
liness of people in the north of France
is in one of the many **brasseries** (the
name derives from the French for
"brewery"; hot and cold dishes are
usually available all day long) often

located on the main square. This is also
the best place to taste inexpensive
traditional dishes like *moules et frites*,
or a brown-sugar tart, washed down
with a glass of beer. The ambience is
lively well into the night.

## ESTAMINETS

Food and drink are also served in cafés
known locally as *estaminets* (originally,
a café where smoking was permitted).
The warm, unpretentious atmosphere
is typical of the region, as is the good
beer served there.

- **De Vierpot**
  125 Complexe Joseph-Decanter,
  59299 Boeschepe (ᗷ *see BAILLEUL*).
- **Het Blauwershof**
  9 rue d'Eecke, 59270 Godewaersvelde (ᗷ *see CASSEL*).
- **'T Kasteelhof**
  8 rue St-Nicolas, 59670 Cassel
  (ᗷ *see CASSEL*).
- **L'Estaminet flamand**
  6 rue des Fusilliers-Marins, 59140
  Dunkerque (ᗷ *see DUNKERQUE*).

## GASTRONOMY IN NORTHERN FRANCE

### The Coast
Boulogne is France's leading fresh
fish port. In addition to the gourmet
restaurants serving fish soup, turbot
with cream sauce, *sole meunière*,
or a fish platter known as *la gainée*

*Outdoor café in Lille*

consisting of three different types of fish with a shrimp sauce, there are also fishmongers' stalls selling cod, herring and fresh eels.

## Picardy

Soup has pride of place in this region and one of the best-known is the *soupe des hortillons*, made with fresh vegetables. Water fowl is used in many different ways, for example duck or snipe pâté. The *ficelle picarde* is a ham pancake rolled up and filled with mushrooms then smothered in béchamel sauce and baked in the oven until the top is crisp and golden. Leek quiche also forms part of a simple but delicious meal.

### Gourmet guide

The Picardy region boasts places that appeal to the gourmet tourist interested in discovering local specialities. Among the spots that have been awarded the *Site remarquable du goût* (for "remarkable taste sensations") distinction are Houille, Loos and Wanbrechies, on the outskirts of Lille, known for *genièvre* (a juniper-flavoured eau-de-vie similar to gin); the port of Boulogne famous for its fish; the market gardens of the Marais Audomarois in St-Omer; and the *Hortillonnages* marshland in Amiens, for fruit and vegetables (traditional floating market on the 3rd Sunday in June, canal festival in September). You can obtain detailed information on local gastronomy by contacting:

- **Comité de Promotion Nord-Pas-de-Calais** 5 avenue Roger-Salengro, BP 39, 62051, St-Laurent-Blangy Cedex, ☎ 03 21 60 57 86; www.comitedepromotion-npdc.com
- **Comité de Promotion Picardie** 19 bis rue A.-Dumas, 80026 Amiens Cedex 3.

# WHAT TO SEE AND DO

## Outdoor Fun

### SWIMMING

Bathing conditions are indicated by flags on beaches which are monitored by lifeguards (no flags means no lifeguards): green indicates it is safe to bathe and lifeguards are on duty; yellow warns that conditions are not that good, but lifeguards are still in attendance; red means bathing is forbidden as conditions are too dangerous. Quality control tests take place regularly from June onward. Well-equipped beaches offer facilities such as swimming pools, water-skiing, diving, jet skiing, landsailing, kite-flying, rowing etc. Information is available from local tourist offices.

### SAILING AND WINDSURFING

The Paris region boasts around 15 lakes and half a dozen locations on the River Seine and River Marne where sailing is available. There are a number of sports and recreation parks (*bases de loisirs*), where windsurfing and dinghy or catamaran sailing are possible, occasionally combined with other activities such as tennis, swimming, horse riding, golf or water-skiing. Among others, these centres include St-Quentin-en-Yvelines, D 912, 78190 Trappes, ☎ 01 30 62 20 12; Moisson-Mousseaux, 78840 Moisson, ☎ 01 34 79 33 34; Jablines/Annet, 77450 Jablines, ☎ 01 60 26 04 31 and Cergy-Neuville, rue des Étangs, 95001 Cergy-Neuville, ☎ 01 30 30 21 55. There are sailing schools all along the coast of northern France from Bray-Dunes to Auly-Onival. Some of the inland lakes are also ideal for these sports, for example the Val-Joly recreation area in the Avesnois region (♿ *see map under L'AVESNOIS*), the Etangs de la Sensée and Escaut, and the Lac de Monampteuil near Soissons. For information, contact the:

- **Fédération française de voile**, 55 avenue Kléber, 75784 Paris Cedex 16, ☎ 01 45 53 68 00; www.ffvoile.org

⚓ **France station Voile – Nautisme et Tourisme**, 17 rue Boissière, 75116 Paris, ☎ 01 44 05 96 55; www.france-nautisme.com.

## CANOEING AND KAYAKING

**Canoes**, propelled by a single-bladed paddle, are ideal for family day trips from a base or down a river. **Kayaks**, propelled by a double-bladed paddle, are more suitable for exploring lakes and the lower part of rivers. **Sea-kayaks** are narrower and longer and beginners are advised to start out in the company of an experienced guide.

## FRESHWATER FISHING

The area around Paris offers many lakes and rivers for anglers of all levels, moreover northern France is crossed by many rivers, waterways and lakes; a paradise for anglers, especially along the Somme, Course, Lys, Aisne, Oise, Aa rivers and in the Seven-valleys region (Canche, Authie, Ternoise etc).
The map-brochure with commentary entitled *Pêche en France* can be obtained from the Conseil Supérieur de la Pêche, 134 avenue de Malakoff, 75016 Paris, (☎ 01 45 02 20 20) or from the *Fédération de Pêche* (angling union) in each département.
Obligatory fishing permits (*cartes de pêche*) are often for sale on site in cafés or sports shops located near popular spots. Between 1 June and 30 September, it is possible, in certain places, to obtain a special holiday fishing permit (*permis de pêche "vacances"*), valid for a fortnight. Day permits are available for fishing in some of the region's lakes.

## SEA FISHING

Day or half-day fishing trips are organised along the coast of northern France. The equipment is supplied by the organisers. Information can be obtained from:
**Fédération Française des Pêcheurs en Mer**, Résidence Alliance, centre Jorlis, 64600 Anglet, ☎ 05 59 31 00 73.

## WALKING

There is an extensive network of well-marked footpaths in France which make rambling (*la randonnée pédestre*) a breeze. Several **Grande Randonnée (GR)** trails, recognisable by the red and white horizontal marks on trees, rocks and in town on walls, signposts etc, go through the region. Along with the GR, there are also the **Petite Randonnée (PR)** paths, which are usually blazed with blue (2hr walk), yellow (2hr 15min-3hr 45min) or green (4-6hr) marks. Of course, with appropriate maps, you can combine walks to suit your desires. To use these trails, obtain the *topo-guide* for the area published by the

*Simple pleasures*

Y. Tierny/MICHELIN

**Fédération Française de la Randonnée Pédestre.** Their information centre is at 14 rue Riquet, 75019 Paris, ☎ 01 44 89 93 93, www.ffrp.asso.fr. Some English-language editions are available. Another source of maps and guides for excursions on foot is the **Institut National Géographique (IGN),** which has a boutique in Paris at 107 rue de la Boétie (off the Champs-Elysées); to order from abroad, visit the website (www.ign.fr) for addresses of wholesalers in your country. Among their publications, France 1M903 is a map showing all of the GR and PR in France (4.90€); the "Série Bleue" and "Top 25" maps, at a scale of 1:25 000 (1cm = 250m), show all paths, whether waymarked or not, as well as refuges, camp sites, beaches etc.

The **Conseil général du Nord** publishes, jointly with the **Association Départementale de la Randonnée**, itineraries covering various distances, with maps and information. Contact the **Comité Départe-mental de Tourisme du Nord** (*address under Local tourist offices above*).

An association publishes a guide (*Guide des Sentiers de Promenade dans le Massif Forestier de Fontainebleau*) on the famous forest south-east of Paris – a popular spot for ramblers, climbers, mushroom hunters and cyclists on day trips – and provides guided tours that are open to all. For a programme, please send an international reply coupon to **Association des Amis de la Forêt de Fontainebleau**, 26 rue de la Cloche, BP 14, 77301 Fontainebleau Cedex, or call ☎ 01 64 23 46 45 (answering machine); www.aaff.org. To join up with fellow ramblers, try the **Randonneurs d'Ile-de-France club**, 92 rue du Moulin-Vert, 75014 Paris, ☎ 01 45 42 24 72, www.rifrando.asso.fr, which organises walks in the region (*small membership fee*).

## CYCLING

The network of country roads is ideal for cycling. Lists of cycle hire shops are available from local tourist offices. Bikes are carried free of charge on many regional trains and on the Paris-Amiens-Boulogne line. Cycle tours are easy to organise as there are cycle hire firms near or in train stations close to the main forests.

The **Fédération française de Cyclotourisme**, 8 rue Jean-Marie-Jégo, 75013 Paris, ☎ 01 44 16 88 88, supplies itineraries covering most of France, outlining mileage, the level of difficulty of routes and sights to see. Mountain biking (*VTT*), or off-road cycling, has become very popular in France. There are many tracks laid out in the region, suitable for both new and experienced riders.

The **Office National des Forêts** edits publications for mountain-bike enthusiasts – Guides VTT Evasion (numbers 1 to 8). They include itineraries covering between 15km/9mi and 30km/18mi. www.onf.fr, click on *La Boutique*.

The **Fédération Française de Cyclisme** – 5 rue de Rome, 93561 Rosny-sous-Bois Cedex, ☎ 01 49 35 69 24 also publishes a guide with over 27 000mi of marked mountain-biking tracks, available on their website: www.ffc.fr.

## RIDING

The Nord-Pas-de-Calais and Île-de-France regions have hundreds of miles of bridle paths running through forests or along the coast.

The **Comité National de Tourisme équestre**, 9 boulevard Mac-Donald, 75019 Paris, ☎ 01 53 26 15 50, publishes an annual review called *Cheval Nature, l'officiel du tourisme équestre en France*. It lists all the possibilities for riding by region and département.

Addresses of riding stables and information on bridle paths are available from:

- **Association Régionale de Tourisme équestre Nord-Pas-de-Calais,** Le Paddock, 62223 St-Laurent-de-Blangy, ☎ 03 21 55 40 81.
- **Association Régionale de Tourisme équestre Picardie**, 8 rue Fournier-Sarlovèze, B.P.

20636, 60203 Compiègne Cedex,
☎ 03 44 40 19 54 (Mon and
Tue afternoons).

 **Association Régionale de
Tourisme équestre d'Île-de-
France (ARTEIF),** 1 rue Barbès,
95260 Beaumont-sur-Oise,
☎ 01 34 70 05 34. The brochure
*Chevauchée en Île-de-France* lists
the main centres in the region and
their activities.

## HORSE FARM

It is possible to visit the Haras national
de Bréviaires, a few miles north of
Rambouillet. Guided tours (*1hr 30min*)
on Saturdays at 3pm. Closed August.
5€. ☎ 01 34 57 85 38.

## GOLF

Golfers can enjoy their favourite sport
and take part in competitions in the
region. Courses abound in the Nord-
Pas-de-Calais region, in pleasantly
rustic settings taking players up hill
and over dale, on the edge of forests,
or overlooking the sea. Contact the
Comité Régional de Tourisme (*address
under Local tourist offices above*) to
obtain the brochure entitled *Golfs
Nord-Pas-de-Calais*. Picardy has golf
courses in Fort-Mahon, Quend-Plage,
Grand-Laviers, Nampont-Saint-Martin,
Salouel (3km/2mi from Amiens) and
Querrieu (7km/4mi from Amiens).

**Ligue de golf de Picardie**, Rond-
point du Grand Cerf, Lys-Chantilly,
60260 Lamorlaye, ☎ 03 44 21 26 28.
**Fédération française de golf**,
68 rue Anatole-France, 92309 Levallois-
Perret Cedex, ☎ 01 41 49 77 00;
www.ffgolf.org.

## LANDSAILING

Landsailing uses a strange combination
of a three-wheeled go-kart and a sail-
boat. Powered solely by the wind, they
may exceed 100kph/62mph on the vast
stretches of fine, hard sand along the
coasts of northern France. In addition
to landsailers, there are also speedsail
boards which resemble windsurfing
boards on wheels.
For information, contact the
**Fédération Française de Char à voile**,
19 rue des Sables, 62600 Berck-sur-Mer,
☎ 03 21 89 99 10; www.ffcv.org.

## KITE FLYING

This is another popular activity in
northern France, particularly on the
beaches. To obtain a good kite and learn
how to fly it, it is advisable to join a club
or an association (addres-ses are available
from local tourist offices). For general
information, contact the **Fédération
française de vol libre** (hang-gliding,
paragliding and kite-flying), 4 rue de
Suisse, 06000 Nice, ☎ 04 97 03 82 82;
www.ffvl.fr.

*Landsailing*

S. Sauvignier/ MICHELIN

## ROCK CLIMBING

The Île-de-France area offers climbers numerous possibilities for all levels at a number of natural sites; the most renowned and best equipped for bouldering are to be found in and around **Fontainebleau Forest**. The highest rocks are at Larchant and the Dame Jouanne. The Massif des Trois-Pignons offers remarkable scenery and many different levels of difficulty. Bouldering may look easy, but requires good technique and adherence to safety procedures, and is best practised with club or professional climbers.
**Fédération Française de la Montagne et de l'Escalade**, 8 quai de la Marne, 75019 Paris, ☎ 01 40 18 75 50.
**Club alpin Île-de-France**, 24 rue Laumière, 75019 Paris, ☎ 01 53 72 88 00.
**Centre européen d'escalade**, 3 rue des Alouettes, Senia 219, 94320 Thiais, ☎ 01 46 86 38 44.
**Mur Mur**, 55 rue Cartier-Bresson, 93500 Pantin, ☎ 01 48 46 11 00 or boulevard Garibaldi, 92130 Issy-les-Moulineaux, ☎ 01 58 88 00 22.
Good indoor installations.

## GO-KARTING

There are several tracks in the Paris region, including:
**RKB Racing Kart Buffo**, RN 19, BP3, 77390 Les Étards (35km/22mi from Paris), ☎ 01 64 07 61 66; www.rkb.fr; kart rental available from age 7 upwards.
**Aérodrome de Pontoise-Cormeilles**, 95650 Boissy-l'Aillerie, ☎ 01 30 73 28 00; www.rkc.fr; three tracks including one for kids; open 9am-7.30pm.

## SKIING

In the north, Noeux-les-Mines has been converted into a ski resort without snow! Even so, the artificial runs are quite enjoyable.
**Loisinord**, rue Léon-Blum, 62290 Noeux-les-Mines, ☎ 03 21 26 84 84; two runs: a main one and one for learning; skiing instructor from the French skiing school available. Open year-round.

# Spas

## SPECIALISED CENTRES

**Enghien-les-Bains** has the only spa centre in Île-de-France. It specialises in throat ailments, skin diseases and rheumatism, but there are also programmes purely for relaxation lasting from 1 to 6 days. **Les Thermes**, 87 rue du Général-de-Gaulle, 95880, ☎ 01 39 34 12 00.
In the northern part of the region, **St-Amand-les-Eaux** specialises in respiratory complaints and rheumatism.
**Les Thermes**, 1303 route Fontaine-Bouillon, ☎ 03 27 48 25 00.
Information is available from:
**Union Nationale des Établissements Thermaux**, 1 rue Cels, 75014 Paris, ☎ 01 53 91 05 75; www.france-thermale.org.
**Chaîne thermale du Soleil/Maison du Thermalisme**, 32 avenue de l'Opéra, 75002 Paris, ☎ 01 44 71 37 00; www.sante-eau.com.

## SEA-WATER THERAPY

**Le Touquet** is a well-known seaside resort with a sea-water therapy (*thalassothérapie*) centre offering a wide range of treatments (health, fitness, post-natal, dietetics, personalised programmes etc).
**Institut Thalassa**, sea front, ☎ 03 21 09 86 00; **Centre Thalgo**, Park Plaza hotel, 4 boulevard de la Canche, ☎ 03 21 06 88 84; **Aqualud**, boulevard de la Mer, ☎ 03 21 05 90 96; www.aqualud.com.
Information is available from:
**Fédération Mer et Santé, 8 rue d'Isly**, 75008 Paris, ☎ 01 44 70 07 57; www.mer-et-sante.asso.fr.
**Maison de la thalassothérapie**, 5 rue Denis-Poisson, 75017 Paris, ☎ 08 25 07 97 07.

# Activities for Children

The region abounds in parks, and various attractive sites and features as well as leisure activities which will appeal to children; in the Sights

# Horse Racing

The Paris region has the largest number of race tracks anywhere in France, hosting all types of horse races. **France Galop** specialises in improving breeds of horses in France and manages the flat racing tracks in the Paris area: 46 place Abel-Gance, 92655 Boulogne Cedex, ☎ 01 49 10 20 30; www.france-galop.com.

| Track | Trotting | Flat course | Steeplechase | Main races |
|---|---|---|---|---|
| Chantilly | – | ● | – | Prix du Jockey-Club (June) |
| | | | | Prix de Diane-Hermès (June) |
| Enghien | ● | – | ● | Prix de l'Atlantique (April) |
| | | | | Prix d'Europe (July) |
| | | | | Grand Steeple-Chase (October) |
| Longchamp | – | ● | – | Grand Prix de Paris (June) |
| | | | | Arc de Triomphe (October) |
| Maisons-Laffitte | – | ● | Cross-country | Prix Robert Papin (July) |
| St-Cloud | – | ● | – | Grand Prix de St-Cloud (July) |
| | | | | Critérium de St-Cloud (October) |

The region also includes the Parisian race tracks of Auteuil (steeplechases) and Vincennes (trotting races).

section, the reader's attention is drawn to these features by the symbol [Kids].
Below is a selection of some of the numerous theme parks and recreational areas in the regions covered in this guide.

## Northern France
**Aqualud**, 62520 Le Touquet, ☎ 03 21 05 90 96 (  see le TOUQUET).
**Olhain**, Parc départemental de Nature et de Loisirs (  see Château d'OLHAIN).
**Prés du Hem**, 7 avenue Marc-Sangnier, 59280 Armentières, 15km/9mi NW of Lille, ☎ 03 20 44 04 60 (  see LILLE).
**Val Joly**, Parc départemental, 59132 Eppe-Sauvage, ☎ 03 27 61 83 76 (  see see AVESNES-SUR-HELPE).
**Loisinord**, 62290 Nœux-les-Mines, ☎ 03 21 26 89 89; water sports and downhill skiing on an artificial slope.

## Île-de-France
**Parc Astérix**, 60128 Plailly, ☎ 08 92 68 30 10; www.parcasterix.fr (  see Parc ASTÉRIX).
**Disneyland Resort Paris**, 77777 Marne-la-Vallée, ☎ 01 60 30 60 30; advance booking, schedules and prices at www.disneylandparis.com (  see DISNEYLAND RESORT PARIS).
**Mer de Sable**, 60950 Ermenonville, ☎ 03 44 54 18 48 (  see Abbaye de CHAALIS).
**France Miniature**, 78990 Elancourt, ☎ 01 30 16 16 30 (  see FRANCE MINIATURE).
**Thoiry**, 78770 Thoiry, ☎ 01 34 87 52 25 (  see THOIRY).

## Puppets
The north is an area traditionally known for its puppets (marionnettes) and a few theatres continue to give shows, to the great delight of children and adults alike:
**Théâtre Le Grand Bleu**, 36 avenue Max-Dormoy, Lille, ☎ 03 20 09 88 44.
**Théâtre Louis Richard**, 26 rue du Château, Roubaix, ☎ 03 20 73 10 10.
**Théâtre du Broutteux**, 11 bis place Ch.-Roussel, Tourcoing, ☎ 03 20 27 55 24.
**Musée des Marionnettes du monde**, Buire-le-Sec, ☎ 03 21 81 80 34.
**Théâtre "Chès Cabotans d'Amiens"**, rue E.-David, Amiens, ☎ 03 22 22 30 90.

# CALENDAR OF EVENTS

## Festivals and Fairs

### FEBRUARY-MARCH

**Chambly** "Bois-Hourdy" folk festival.
☎ 0139 37 44 00.
**Maubeuge** – Jazz Manège:
international festival of jazz.
☎ 03 27 65 65 4.
www.lemanege.com

### END OF MARCH

**Amiens** International jazz
festival. ☎ 03 22 97 79 79.
www.amiensjazzfestival.com

### MARCH-APRIL

**Seine-Saint-Denis** Banlieues Bleues
jazz festival. ☎ 01 49 22 10 10.
www.banlieuesbleues.fr.

### SATURDAY APRIL TO DECEMBER

**Chartres** "Les samedis musicaux de
Chartres" (classical music, jazz,
folk music). Information at the
Office de tourisme, place de la
Cathédrale. ☎ 02 37 27 18 52.

### APRIL

**Abbeville et baie de Somme**
Bird Film Festival (screenings,
exhibits, nature walks, lectures).
☎ 03 22 24 02 02.
www.festival-oiseau.asso.fr
**Valenciennes** Action and Adventure
film festival. ☎ 03 27 29 55 40.
www.festival-valenciennes.com

### PALM SUNDAY WEEKEND (FRIDAY TO MONDAY)

**Coulommiers** Cheese and wine fair.
☎ 01 64 03 88 09.

### LAST SUNDAY IN APRIL

**Fortified towns in the
Nord-Pas-de-Calais** Regional
fortified towns festival.
☎ 03 28 82 05 43.

### MAY

**Boulogne-sur-Mer** Music & Ramparts.
☎ 03 21 10 88 10.
**Marly-le-Roi** Fête du parc.
☎ 01 30 61 61 35.

### 2ND SUNDAY IN MAY

**Rambouillet** Lily-of-the-Valley festival.
☎ 01 34 83 21 21.

### WHITSUN WEEKEND

**St-Quentin** "Fêtes du Bouffon".

### END OF MAY

**Lille** "Montgolfiades" balloon festival.
☎ 03 20 05 40 62.
**Laon** Euromédiévales (banquet,
displays, medieval markets).
☎ 03 23 22 30 34.
**Tourcoing** Medieval market,
European Knights Tournament.
☎ 03 20 28 13 20.

### MAY-JUNE

**Auvers-sur-Oise** International Music
Festival. ☎ 01 30 36 77 77.

### 1ST WEEKEND IN JUNE

**Bièvres** Photo fair. ☎ 01 43 22 11 72.

### MID JUNE (ODD-NUMBERED YEARS)

**Aérodrome du Bourget**
International Air and Space Show.
☎ 01 53 23 33 33).

### 3RD WEEKEND IN JUNE

**Lille** Fêtes de Lille:
various events around the city.
**Provins** Medieval festival.
☎ 01 64 67 02 60.

## 3RD SUNDAY IN JUNE

**Gerberoy** "Fête des roses".
**Windmills around the region**
National Windmill Day.
Information: ARAM.
☎ 03 20 05 49 34.

## 23 JUNE

**Long** "Feux de la Saint-Jean"
mid-summer festival.
☎ 03 21 31 80 21.

## JUNE-JULY

**Saint-Denis** Festival of classical music.
☎ 01 48 13 06 07.

## LATE JUNE-MID AUGUST

**St-Germain-en-Laye** "Fête des
Loges" fun fair. ☎ 01 30 87 21 70.

## SATURDAY OR SUNDAY
## JUNE-SEPTEMBER

**Royaumont** Concerts at the abbey.
☎ 01 34 68 05 50.
www.royaumont.com

## JULY

**Côte d'Opale** Music Festival.
☎ 03 21 30 40 33.
**St-Riquier** Classical music festival.
☎ 03 22 28 82 82
**Desvres** Fête de la faïence
(earthenware festival).

## 1ST SUNDAY IN JULY

**Noyon** Red fruit market.

## AROUND 14 JULY

**Bray-Dunes** World Folklore Festival.
☎ 03 28 26 61 09.

## JULY-AUGUST

**Hardelot** Classical Music Festival.
☎ 03 21 83 51 02.

*Big Thunder Railroad at Disneyland Paris*

## 4TH SUNDAY IN JULY

**Buire-le-Sec** Crafts and Trades Fair.

## END JULY

**St-Omer** Procession of floats on the canal.

## TUESDAY, THURSDAY
## AND SATURDAY AT 9.15PM
## IN LATE JULY AND AUGUST

**Chartres** "Soirées Estivales"
(summer nights festival).
☎ 02 37 18 26 26.

## JULY-SEPTEMBER

**Sceaux** "Festival de l'Orangerie".
☎ 01 46 60 07 79.

## ONE WEEK IN MID AUGUST

**Wimereux** Wimereux during the
Belle Époque.

## FIRST FORTNIGHT IN AUGUST

**Le Touquet** International music festival.
☎ 03 21 06 72 00.

## AUTUMN

**Versailles** Baroque music concert series.
☎ 01 39 20 78 10.

## SEPTEMBER-OCTOBER

**Throughout Île-de-France** Festival:
concerts. ☎ 01 58 71 01 01.

## Les nieulles

The name of these little biscuits (pronounced nee-uls) comes from the Spanish niola, which means "crumb". In 1510, a banquet was held in the reception rooms of the Hôtel de Ville, presided by the Count of Luxembourg, Lord of Armentières. When the guests had finished feasting, the Count stepped out on the balcony. A crowd of children gathered below, holding their hands out for alms. The Count flung the crumbs from the cake at them, as if they were so many hungry birds.

**In Picardie** "Festival des cathédrales".
☎ 03 22 22 44 94.

### 1ST SUNDAY IN SEPTEMBER

**Arleux** Garlic Fair.
**Melun** Antiques Fair and Brie
  cheese market.

### 1ST WEEKEND IN SEPTEMBER

**Lille** "Grande braderie" flea market
  and sale.

### 2ND SUNDAY IN SEPTEMBER

**Armentières** "Fête des Nieulles".

### LAST WEEKEND IN SEPTEMBER (ODD-NUMBERED YEARS)

**Senlis** "Rendez-vous de Septembre":
  car-free city, music festival in the
  streets on odd-numbered years,
  last weekend in the month.
  ☎ 03 44 53 06 40.

### LATE SEPTEMBER-EARLY OCTOBER

**Chatou** "Grande foire nationale
  aux jambons" (ham fair).
  ☎ 01 47 70 88 78.

### 1ST WEEKEND IN OCTOBER

**Steenvoorde** Hops festival.

### 1ST SUNDAY IN OCTOBER

**Suresnes** "Fête des Vendanges":
  street theatre festival.
  ☎ 01 41 18 18 76.

### OCTOBER

**Barbizon** Painting awards.
  ☎ 01 60 66 40 24.
**Lille** Festival de Lille.
  ☎ 03 20 52 47 23.

*Flying high at Berk-Plage*

Y. Thierry/MICHELIN

### 3RD SUNDAY IN OCTOBER

**Sains-du-Nord** Cider festival.

### MID OCTOBER-MID NOVEMBER

**Tourcoing** Jazz Festival.
☎ 03 20 28 96 99.

### NOVEMBER

**St-Jean-de-Beauregard** Fairs:
"Fruits and vegetables from
the past and present".
☎ 01 60 12 00 01.

### 2ND WEEKEND IN DECEMBER

**Licques** Turkey festival.

### 24 DECEMBER

**Boulogne-sur-Mer** "Fête des
Guénels" (a guénel resembles
a jack-o'-lantern, carved out
of a beet!).

## Pageants,
## "Son et Lumière,"
## Fountains

### APRIL-OCTOBER

**Provins** Falconry show.
☎ 01 64 20 26 26.

*Provins – Jousting tournament*

### 2ND AND LAST SATURDAY OF THE MONTH (3-6PM)

**Vaux-le-Vicomte** Fountains in the
garden. ☎ 01 64 14 41 90.

### SUNDAY (11AM-NOON AND 3.30-5PM)

**Versailles** Fountains and music in the
palace garden. ☎ 01 39 24 88 88.

### MAY-SEPTEMBER

### 3RD SUNDAY OF THE MONTH

**Parc de Marly-le-Roi** Grand fountain.
☎ 01 30 61 61 35.

*Garlic Festival*

*Landsailing competition*

## MAY-MID OCTOBER

### SATURDAY BETWEEN 8.00PM AND MIDNIGHT

**Vaux-le-Vicomte** Candlelight tour of château and gardens.
☎ 01 64 14 41 90.
www.vaux-le-vicomte.com

### SUNDAY IN JUNE-JULY

**St-Cloud** Fountains. ☎ 01 41 12 02 90.

### MID-JUNE-AUGUST

**Provins** Jousting tournament in the moat. ☎ 01 64 60 26 26.

### MID-JUNE-MID JULY, LATE AUGUST AND FIRST THREE WEEKS IN SEPTEMBER

### FRIDAY AND SATURDAY

**Meaux** "Son et lumière".
☎ 01 64 33 02 26.

### 3RD WEEKEND IN JUNE

**Chantilly** "Nuits de Feu" international fireworks competition, on even-numbered years.
☎ 03 44 45 18 18.

### CERTAIN SATURDAYS JULY-SEPTEMBER

**Versailles** "Grandes Fêtes de Nuit au bassin de Neptune", fireworks, fountains and music in the palace garden.
☎ 01 30 83 78 88.

### SEPTEMBER

**Moret-sur-Loing** "Son et lumière" ("Reflections of History").
☎ 01 60 70 41 66.

## Sporting Events

### FEBRUARY

**Le Touquet** "Enduro des sables": motorbike endurance race.
**Liévin** International athletics meeting (mid-month).

### END MARCH-END NOVEMBER

**Fontainebleau** La Solle racetrack open. ☎ 01 60 74 99 99. Sunday (11am-noon and 3.30-5pm).

# SHOPPING

Most of the larger shops are open Mondays to Saturdays from 9am to 6.30 or 7.30pm. Smaller, individual shops may close during the lunch hour. Food shops (grocers, wine merchants and bakeries) are generally open from 7am to 6.30 or 7.30pm; some open on Sunday mornings. Many food shops close between noon and 2pm and on Mondays. Bakery and pastry shops sometimes close on Wednesdays. Hypermarkets usually stay open non-stop until 9pm or later.

People travelling to the USA cannot import plant products or fresh food, including fruit, cheeses and nuts. It is acceptable to carry tinned products or preserves.

## Recovering the Value Added Tax

In France a sales tax (VAT or Value Added Tax ranging from 5.5% to 19.6%) is added to almost all retail goods – it can be worth your while to recover it. VAT refunds are available to visitors from outside the EU only if purchases exceed US $200 per store, but repeat visits to a store can be combined. The system works in large stores which cater to tourists, and in luxury stores and other shops advertising "Duty Free." Show your passport, and the store will complete a form that is to be stamped (at the airport) by a European customs agents. The sum due can be collected at the airport or by mailing the forms from home.

## Local Specialities

### FOOD AND DRINK

The famous **Brie** cheese comes from Meaux, east of Paris, but also from Coulommiers and Melun further south. Meaux also produces a gourmet **mustard** made according to a traditional recipe. Northern France's cheeses include the mild **Mont-des-Cats** and the stronger-flavoured **Maroilles**, first produced by monks in the 10C, and often used in regional dishes. **Beer** is Northern France's traditional drink and there are many varieties to be enjoyed along the "route des Brasseurs" (the brewers' trail). Liqueurs from Île-de-France include the **Noyau de Poissy**, made from brandy flavoured with apricot stones, and the famous **Grand Marnier** produced in Neauphle-le-Château, west of Versailles (the distillery is located opposite the church; tour by appointment, ☎ 01 30 07 80 85).

### HANDICRAFT

There is a wide choice of beautiful objects to take home including: **porcelain** manufactured in Sèvres (one of the Paris suburbs) and in Arras, **earthenware** from Desvres, **pottery** from Sars-Poteries, **glassware** and **crystal** from Arques, **lace** from Calais, **puppets** from Amiens.

*Brie de Meaux*

S. Sauvignier/ MICHELIN

# SIGHTSEEING

## Tourist trains

**Le p'tit train de la Haute-Somme** – South of Albert, 3km/2mi from Bray-sur-Somme, there is a narrow-gauge railway running from Froissy to Dompierre via the Cappy Tunnel (300m/325yd). The round trip covers a distance of 14km/9mi and takes about 1hr 30min. A visit to the railway museum rounds off the trip ( see *Admission times and charges: Vallée de la SOMME, Froissy*).

**Le Chemin de Fer de la Baie de Somme** – A train of old carriages with platforms runs through fields and salt marshes from Noyelles to Le Crotoy, St-Valéry-sur-Mer and Cayeux-sur-Mer ( see *Admission times and charges: Baie de SOMME*).

**Chemin de Fer Touristique du Vermandois** – From St-Quentin to Origny-Ste-Benoîte (44km/27mi round trip) via Ribemont. A steam train or an old-fashioned rail motor car crosses and then runs alongside the Canal de la Sambre in Oise.
For information and bookings, contact Laure Peillon, C.F.T.V., BP 152, 02104 St-Quentin Cedex, ☎ 03 23 07 88 38.

**Chemin de Fer Touristique de la vallée de l'Aa** – The journey runs for 15km/9mi from Arques to Lumbres along the old branch of the St-Omer to Boulogne-sur-Mer line. It enables a visit to be made to the Fontinettes barge lift and stops at the Coupole d'Helfaut-Wizernes Second World War rocket-launching pad. Information can be obtained from Mr Chambelland at Bayenghem-lès-Seninghem, ☎ 03 21 12 19 19.

**Tramway Touristique de la vallée de la Deûle** – Trips by tram along a metre-gauge track over 3km/1.8mi between Marquette and Wambrechies in the suburbs of Lille. For information, contact AMITRAM, 1521 rue de Bourbourg, 59670 Bavinchove, ☎ 03 28 42 44 58. www.amitram.asso.fr.

## Bird's-eye views

### TOURIST FLIGHTS

A 35min plane flight is one of the highlights of a weekend break (2 days and nights) in the Oise *département*: contact Loisirs Accueil at the **Comité Départementale du tourisme de l'Oise**, ☎ 03 44 45 82 12.
Other tourist flights are organised by the following:

*Baie de Somme – All aboard!*

**Flying Production**, Lille-Marcq airport, 59910 Bondues, ☎ 03 20 89 91 52; www.flying-production.com. Plane or helicopter flights over Monts des Flandres, Caps Gris-Nez and Blanc-Nez, Le Touquet, Wissant.

**Aéroclub de St-Omer**, Plateau des Bruyères, BP 7, 62967 Longuenesse, ☎ 03 21 38 25 42; flights over the Helfaut-Wizernes rocket-launching-pad area and the Marais audomarois.

**ULM flights** are available from Dreux or Viabon daily from April to October, depending on weather conditions; contact **Loisirs Accueil Eure-et-Loir**, 10 rue du Dr-Maunoury, BP 67, 28002 Chartres Cedex, ☎ 02 37 84 01 00. www.tourisme28.com; also from Abbeville: contact **Ludair**, Abbeville airport, 80132 Buigny-St-Maclou, ☎ 03 22 24 36 59 or 06 03 28 66 96; flights over the Baie de Somme.

### HOT-AIR BALLOONING

Take off from Moret-sur-Loing with professional bilingual pilots on a tour of the landscapes which inspired the Impressionists or of the hunting grounds of the French kings: from April to October, mornings and evenings, depending on the weather: **France Montgolfières**, 24 rue de Paris, 77240 Champs-sur-Marne, ☎ 01 47 00 66 44 (www.franceballoons.com). This company is certified by the civil aviation authority. Flights also available in other areas of France. Also available from La Roche-Guyon with **Airshow**, 6 rue du Faubourg-Poissonnière, ☎ 01 53 24 95 47 and from Hazebrouck with **Club Montgolfière Passion**, 253 rue d'Aire, 59190 Hazebrouck, ☎ 03 28 41 65 59.

### Tethered Balloon Rides

Tethered rides are organised outside the Parc préhistorique de Samara, near Amiens: **Samara**, 80310 La Chaussée-Tirancourt, ☎ 03 22 51 82 83.

## For Travel into Britain

A quick trip over the Channel to Kent or even London is possible if you have time to spare (passport required): **From Calais** – 75min by ferry to Dover. Seafrance offers day trips to Canterbury, by bus from Calais to Dover and train from Dover to Canterbury. ☎ 0 825 044 045.

The **Eurotunnel** is situated at Coquelles *(3km/2mi from the coast)*. For those travelling by car, the **Shuttle** links Calais with Folkestone, 24hr 7 days a week. The journey lasts 35min, 28 of which are spent in the tunnel. ☎ 09 90 35 35 35.

**From Paris or Lille** – For those travelling by train, Eurostar takes 3hr for the journey from Paris-Gare du Nord to London-Waterloo, or 2hr from

### Tourist Passes

The **Paris Museum Pass** allows free direct entry to the permanent collections of 60 museums and monuments **in and around Paris**. Valid for 1 day (25 €), 3 consecutive days (44 €) or 5 consecutive days (62€), it can be purchased in participating museums and monuments, at major metro stations, the tourist information bureau at the Carrousel du Louvre, and at the National Tourist Bureau in the Champs Elysées. Information: ☎ 01 44 61 96 60. Connect to www.intermusees.com for participating museums and hyperlinks.

The **Passeport Intersites**, obtainable free of charge, allows access at reduced rates to a number of monuments in the **Val-d'Oise** *département*, including the Château de la Roche-Guyon, Château d'Auvers, Château d'Ecouen and Royau-mont Abbey. ☎08 01 01 95 95.

The **Passeport pour Auvers-sur-Oise** works on the same principle – the first sight at a full price, then subsequent visits to other sights in the town are at a reduced rate. The passport includes the Auberge Ravoux, Musée Daubigny, Château d'Auvers, Maison-atelier de Daubigny and the Musée de l'Absinthe.

Lille-Europe (♿*see above, Getting there by rail*).
To obtain tourist information in Paris, contact the **Office du tourisme de la Grande Bretagne**, BP 154-08, 75363 Paris Cedex 08, ☎ 01 58 36 50 50 (Mon-Fri 10am-5pm); www.visitbritain.com/fr.

# Cruising the Waterways

The rivers and canals once plied by well-laden barges constitute over 1 000mi of navigable waterways providing holidaymakers with an opportunity to enjoy a cruise or hire their own boat; both excellent ways of visiting the region.
The **Comité Régional de Tourisme d'Île-de-France** has joined with the Paris Port Authority and Voies Navigables de France to publish a brochure on boating opportunities in Île-de-France, *Prenez le large en Île-de-France*. They can also provide the *Tourisme fluvial – Guide pratique*, which gives addresses of rental agencies and marina facilities. Likewise, the **Comité Regional de Tourisme du Nord-Pas-de-Calais** (*address under Local tourist offices above*) publishes a brochure on the area's inland waterway network.

*River cruise on the Seine, Paris*

©Photodisk, Inc.

## CRUISES AND BOAT RENTALS:

🛥 **Marne Loisirs** –
Chemin des 2 rivières –
77 260 La Ferté sous Jouarre,
☎ 03 85 53 76 70;
www.marne-loisirs.fr.
Live-aboard boat rentals (no permit required) for 2 to 12 people.

🛥 **Continental Waterways** –
This operator has a fleet of luxury hotel-barges, offering all-inclusive 6-night cruises. One of them, the "Anacoluthe", cruises on the River Seine and River Yonne between Bougival and Joigny and includes a Paris cruise by night. In the US ☎ (800) 676-6613, Fax (212) 688-5456 (www.continentalwaterways.com).

🛥 **Nogent-sur-Marne Marina** –
Quai du Port, 94130 Nogent-sur-Marne, ☎ 01 48 71 41 65.
Peddle boats and small motor boats for rent.

🛥 **Arques Plaisance** –
Base nautique, rue d'Alsace,
62510 Arques, ☎ 03 21 98 35 97.
River launches for hire for a day, a weekend or a week; river permit or pilot on board.

🛥 **Locaboat Plaisance** –
Small barges for hire on the River Somme (departure from Cappy); reservations: Port au Bois, BP 150, 89303 Joigny Cedex ☎ 03 86 91 72 72; www.locaboat.com

🛥 **Somme Plaisance** –
27 rue Georges-Clemenceau, 80110 Moreuil, ☎ 03 22 09 75 50.
Boat rental (4-10 people), departure from Corbie.

Maps of waterways are available from:
🛥 **Éditions Grafocarte-Navicarte**, 125 rue Jean-Jacques-Rousseau, BP 40, 92132 Issy-les-Moulineaux Cedex, ☎ 01 41 09 19 00.
🛥 **Éditions du Plaisancier**, 43 porte du Grand-Lyon, 01700 Neyron, ☎ 04 72 01 58 68.

*A brisk walk along the Côte d'Opale*

## BOAT TRIPS

In the Audomarois region
(👁 *see ST-OMER*).

Around the market garden
district of Amiens (👁 *see AMIENS: Hortillonnages*).

**Paris Canal** –
Bassin de La Villette,
19-21 quai de la Loire, 75019 Paris,
☎ 01 42 40 96 97. On the canals of
Paris and along the meanders of the
Marne (Paris-Chennevières-Paris).

**Un canal, deux canaux** –
BP 69, 77440 Lizy-sur-Ourcq,
☎ 01 60 01 13 65.

**Tourisme Accueil Val-d'Oise** –
Château de la Motte, rue François-
de-Ganay, 95270 Luzarches,
☎ 01 30 29 51 00. Boat trips, lunch
or dinner cruises from La Roche-
Guyon, Auvers and Pontoise.

# Nature Parks and Reserves

**Regional nature parks** have brought
a breath of fresh air to the landscapes
of the Île-de-France region and
northern France. They are promoted
as protected areas, not only in regard
to the natural environment but also
for traditional lifestyles, crafts and
trades. Information can be obtained
from the *Maison du Parc* associated
with each one.

South of Paris, the Château de
Dampierre, the Château de Breteuil
and the Abbaye de Port-Royal-des-
Champs (*see description in the Sights
section*) are within the **Parc naturel
régional de la Haute Vallée de
Chevreuse**, created in 1985 (Maison du
Parc, Château de la Madeleine, BP 73,
78460 Chevreuse, ☎ 01 30 52 09 09).
Woods and farmlands alternate on the
plateau along with lush valleys. The
park offers over 200km/125mi of
blazed hiking trails.

*Houseboat on the Somme Canal*

The **Parc naturel régional du Vexin français**, created in 1995 just north of Paris (Maison du Parc, Château de Théméricourt), offers 500km/310mi of marked footpaths as well as cycling tracks and bridle paths.

In the northern area covered in this guide, discover dunes, forests, bays and wetlands by following itineraries on foot, horseback or bike in the region's nature parks which include the **Parc naturel régional de l'Avesnois** (Maison du Parc, Grange Dîmière, 4 cour de l'Abbaye, 59550 Maroilles, ☎ 03 27 77 90 20); the **Parc naturel regional des Caps et Marais d'Opale** (Maison du Parc, le Grand Vannage, 62510 Arques, ☎ 03 21 87 90 90); the **Parc naturel regional Scarpe-Escaut** (Maison du Parc, Le Luron, 357 rue Notre-Dame-d'Amour, 59230 St-Amand-les-Eaux, ☎ 03 27 19 19 70).

## CONSERVATION AREAS

To protect coastal areas, the **Conservatoire du Littoral** (Corderie Royale, rue Jean-Baptiste Audebert, 17300 Rochefort ☎ 05 46 84 72 50) was set up in 1975 to safeguard and maintain ecological balance. There are now 339 protected sites, including the dunes at Garennes-de-Lornel in Pas-de-Calais, the first to be covered by preservation measures.

Various other organisations and centres aim to safeguard ecological systems:

- **Centre Permanent d'Initiatives pour l'Environnement Vallée de Somme**, 32 route d'Amiens, 80480 Dury, ☎ 03 22 33 24 27 *(guided walks, guided tours of the Samara marshland)*.
- **Conservatoire des Sites Naturels de Picardie**, 1 place Ginkgo, Village Oasis, 80044 Amiens Cedex 1, ☎ 03 22 89 63 96.
- **Conservatoire des Sites Naturels du Nord-Pas-de-Calais**, 4 allée Saint-Éloi, ZA La Becquerelle, 59118 Wambrechies, ☎ 03 28 04 53 45.
- **Centre Ornithologique Île-de-France** (CORIF), ☎ 01 48 51 92 00; birdwatching in the Paris region.
- **Ferme pédagogique de Versailles**, Parc du château, near the Hameau de la Reine, Wed and Sat 1.30-4.30pm, 5€, ☎ 01 40 67 10 04.

## WILDLIFE RESERVES

These areas are protected by virtue of the rare or remarkable flora and fauna found there, exceptional geological characteristics, or their role as a way station for migratory species. Some reserves are vast while others are quite modest. Waymarked footpaths allow visitors to observe the natural habitat.

- **le Marais d'Isle**, Aisne (✆ *see St-Quentin*); Maison de la Nature, ☎ 03 23 05 06 50; a footpath enables visitors to walk round the marsh, a sanctuary for migratory birds.
- **la Baie de Somme** (the largest reserve in the region). Information at the Parc Ornithologique du Marquenterre, ☎ 08 36 68 80 21.

# BOOKS AND FILMS

## The Monarchy

### Memoirs Duc De Saint-Simon: 1710-1715 (Lost Treasures)
*Lucy Norton, Editor, (Prion Books, 2000).*
The Duc de Saint-Simon was at the very centre of Louis XIV's court at Versailles, and later played an important role in the regency of the Duc d'Orléans. He stood out amid the intrigue and scheming as a truly pious and honest man. The editor has chosen to concentrate on the entries describing the people at court, and the Duc's keen eye misses no detail. Marcel Proust had high regard for this masterpiece, which he credited with inspiring his own *Remembrance of Things Past*.

### Vatel
*2000, Starring Gérard Depardieu, Uma Thurman; Director: Roland Joffé; Miramax Home Entertainment VHS, DVD.*
This lush period piece tells the story of a doomed Head Steward in love with a Lady in Waiting. The tale of Vatel, *maître d'hôtel* to the Grand Condé at the château of Chantilly, is both true and tragic. It was made famous by Mme de Sévigné. During a dinner party that the Condé gave in honour of Louis XIV at Chantilly, the fish was delayed (perhaps by jealous intriguers). Vatel felt himself to be dishonoured and killed himself with his own sword. The outdoor scenes were shot at Vaux-le-Vicomte, Le Nôtre's favourite garden. The over-the-top festivities, Baroque showgirls and the decadence of the aristocracy are displayed with little left to the imagination; the costumes and wigs are stunning.

### Marie Antoinette: The Journey
*Antonia Fraser, (Anchor Books, 2002). Also available in large-print and audio editions.*
Author of many best-selling histories and biographies, Fraser has mostly written about events in her native England, but here puts her pen to the life of the ill-fated queen. The Queen was much-maligned by rumour in her own time, and many stories of her alleged outrages have persevered, but this book shows how difficult her position was and provides a thoughtful consideration of a woman whose story never fails to fascinate.

### Versailles: A Novel
*Kathryn Davis, (Houghton Mifflin Co, 2002).*
The viewpoint of this historical novel belongs to Queen Marie Antoinette, who arrived in France at age 14 to marry Louis, a distracted young man destined to become the 16th French monarch of that name, and who was to take his wife to the guillotine with him. The style is light, even humorous, but the history is sometimes imperfect. The great palace acts like a character in the novel, first reflecting the glory and power of the kingdom and gradually revealed as an artificial paradise and an ineffective shield from fate. Far from home and never really loved by the people of France, Marie turns her attention to Versailles itself. The story carries her from room to room and through the famous gardens where the life of court played out its final days.

## The World Wars

### Suite Française
*Irène Némirovsky (Vintage Books, 2007).*
In 1941, Irène Némirovsky sat down to write a book that would convey the magnitude of what she was living through by evoking the domestic lives and personal trials of the ordinary citizens of France. Némirovsky's deaith in Auschwitz in 1942 prevented her from seeing the day, 65 years later, that the existing two sections of her planned novel sequence, Suite Française, would be rediscovered and hailed as a masterpiece.

Set in the year France fell to Germany, the book falls into two parts. The first depicts a group of Parisians as they flee the Nazi invasion; the second follows the inhabitants of a small rural community under occupation.

### A Storm in Flanders: The Ypres Salient, 1914-1918: Tragedy and Triumph on the Western Front
*Winston Groom, (Grove Press, 2003).*
The author of *Forrest Gump* is far from whimsical as he describes "the most notorious and dreaded place in all of the First World War, probably of any war in history": the Ypres salient, where "more than a million soldiers were shot, bayon-eted, bludgeoned, bombed, grenaded, gassed, incinerated by flamethrowers, drowned in shell craters, smothered by caved-in trenches, obliterated by underground mines, or, more often than not, blown to pieces by artillery shells." The fields of Flanders were churned into hell on Earth during the pivotal, four-year engagement of the First World War that forever changed our views of warfare. Groom draws on the journals of men and women who were there to depict the terrifying new tactics and technologies employed at Ypres, the ineffable horror of trench warfare and also the heroism and humanity that somehow survived. The town of Ypres (or Ieper) is in Belgium, about 32km/20mi NW of Lille.

### Battle of the Somme
*Gerald Gliddon (Sutton Publishing, 2000).*
Gerald Gliddon is an author and bookseller specialising in the history of the First World War. His book is well researched and covers all of the battles of the Somme, 1916. There are useful descriptions of the many Commonwealth War Graves in the region, and a full list of all military units. The chronology, first-hand reports and extensive bibliography make it well worth reading for serious students of history.

### Good-Bye to All That: An Autobiography by Robert Graves
*(Anchor, 1958. The new edition has been edited and annotated with an introduction by Graves' nephew and biographer).*
First published in 1929 when the author was 34, this book serves as a memoir for the whole generation of Englishmen who suffered in the First World War. A poet, historical novelist, and critic, Graves' autobiography is his bitterest work. He lashes out at his class, the petty cruelties of England's elite schools, his military superiors, the horrors of trench warfare. The underlying theme is the extinction of the elite society of the Edwardian upper classes. The rough scenes of atrocities, suicides, murders and heroic rescues follow one another and build up to an emotional charge that defines Graves' experience. He makes little mention of his poetry or the other famous authors he knew; his marriage and the birth of his children are discussed in an unemotional tone. This aspect of the book, which was written shortly after the war, shows how the battlefield left the survivors numb and "shell-shocked" long after they had returned home.

## General Interest

### More More France Please
*Helens Frith Powell (Gibson Square, 2007).*
What do you do when a semi-feral dog bites off the nose of a guest at your first French dinner? Where do you go if you don't want to see any compatriots? What do you do when your well dries up? In this book, the author writes about the real life sotires of herself and fellow Brits in France, revealing some surprising details about what goes on behind the façades of life in France.

### The Snow Goose
*Paul Gallico, (Random House, 1988).*
*For readers age ten and up.*
This wonderful tale has been in print since 1941, and the 50th anniversary edition has new colour illustrations. A reclusive hunchback and a timid country girl meet and together care for a wounded snow goose. It is sentimental, but full of the magic of love. When

Fritha watches the recovered snow goose soar away, she sees "the soul of Rhayader taking farewell of her before departing forever."

## Germinal

*Emile Zola, translated by Leonard W. Tancock (Viking Press; Reprint edition November 1954). Also available as an audio cassette, and VHS (a Claude Berry film, 1996, starring Gérard Dépardieu). Misery at its most miserable. This novel is a realistic depiction of the living* conditions of the miners of northern France in the 1860s. The 13th book in the author's Rougon-Macquart cycle, it is also a complex novel of ideas and an engrossing account of the drama of everyday life. The hero is a newcomer who tries to force improvements by organising resistance to the mine owners. The consequences of the strike are terrible. By the time Zola died, in 1902, the book had become so emblematic that the crowd at his State funeral chanted "Germinal! Germinal!"

# USEFUL WORDS & PHRASES

## Architectural Terms

👆 *See the ABC of Architecture in the Introduction*

## Sights

| | |
|---|---|
| **abbaye** | abbey |
| **arc-boutant** | flying buttress |
| **beffroi** | belfry |
| **chapelle** | chapel |
| **cimetière** | cemetery |
| **cloître** | cloisters |
| **cour** | courtyard |
| **couvent** | convent |
| **écluse** | lock (canal) |
| **église** | church |
| **gothique** | Gothic |
| **halle** | covered market |
| **jardin** | garden |
| **mairie** | town hall |
| **maison** | house |
| **marché** | market |
| **monastère** | monastery |
| **moulin** | windmill |
| **musée** | museum |
| **place** | square |
| **pont** | bridge |
| **port** | port/harbour |
| **quai** | quay |
| **remparts** | ramparts |
| **romain** | Roman |
| **roman** | Romanesque |
| **tour** | tower |

## Natural Sites

| | |
|---|---|
| **barrage** | dam |
| **belvédère** | viewpoint |
| **cascade** | waterfall |
| **corniche** | ledge |
| **côte** | coast, hillside |
| **étang** | pond/mere |
| **falaise** | cliff |
| **forêt** | forest |
| **grotte** | cave |
| **lac** | lake |
| **marais** | marsh |
| **plage** | beach |
| **rivière** | river |
| **ruisseau** | stream |
| **signal** | beacon |
| **source** | spring |
| **vallée** | valley |

## On the Road

| | |
|---|---|
| **car park** | parking |
| **diesel** | diesel/gazole |
| **driving licence** | permis de conduire |
| **east** | Est |
| **garage (for repairs)** | garage |
| **left** | gauche |
| **LPG** | GPL |
| **motorway/highway** | autoroute |
| **north** | Nord |
| **parking meter** | horodateur |
| **petrol/gas** | essence |
| **petrol/gas station** | station essence |
| **right** | droite |
| **roundabout** | rond-point or giratoire |

| | |
|---|---|
| **south** | Sud |
| **toll** | péage |
| **traffic lights** | feux |
| **tyre** | pneu |
| **unleaded** | sans plomb |
| **west** | Ouest |
| **wheel clamp** | sabot |
| **zebra crossing** | passage clouté |

## Time

| | |
|---|---|
| **today** | aujourd'hui |
| **tomorrow** | demain |
| **yesterday** | hier |
| **winter** | hiver |
| **spring** | printemps |
| **summer** | été |
| **autumn/fall** | automne |
| **week** | semaine |
| **Monday** | lundi |
| **Tuesday** | mardi |
| **Wednesday** | mercredi |
| **Thursday** | jeudi |
| **Friday** | vendredi |
| **Saturday** | samedi |
| **Sunday** | dimanche |

## Numbers

| | |
|---|---|
| **0** | zéro |
| **1** | un |
| **2** | deux |
| **3** | trois |
| **4** | quatre |
| **5** | cinq |
| **6** | six |
| **7** | sept |
| **8** | huit |
| **9** | neuf |
| **10** | dix |
| **11** | onze |
| **12** | douze |
| **13** | treize |
| **14** | quatorze |
| **15** | quinze |
| **16** | seize |
| **17** | dix-sept |
| **18** | dix-huit |
| **19** | dix-neuf |
| **20** | vingt |
| **30** | trente |
| **40** | quarante |
| **50** | cinquante |
| **60** | soixante |
| **70** | soixante-dix |
| **80** | quatre-vingts |
| **90** | quatre-vingt-dix |
| **100** | cent |
| **1 000** | mille |

## Shopping

| | |
|---|---|
| **antiseptic** | antiseptique |
| **bank** | banque |
| **bakery** | boulangerie |
| **big** | grand |
| **butcher shop** | boucherie |
| **chemist's/drugstore** | pharmacie |
| **closed** | fermé |
| **cough mixture** | sirop pour la toux |
| **entrance** | entrée |
| **exit** | sortie |
| **fishmonger's** | poissonnerie |
| **grocer's** | épicerie |
| **newsagent, bookshop** | librairie |
| **open** | ouvert |
| **painkiller** | analgésique |
| **plaster (adhesive)** | pansement adhésif |
| **post office** | poste |
| **pound (half kilo)** | livre |
| **push** | pousser |
| **pull** | tirer |
| **shop** | magasin |
| **small** | petit |
| **stamps** | timbres |

## Food and Drink

| | |
|---|---|
| **beef** | bœuf |
| **beer** | bière |
| **butter** | beurre |
| **bread** | pain |
| **breakfast** | petit-déjeuner |
| **cheese** | fromage |
| **chicken** | poulet |
| **dessert** | dessert |
| **dinner** | dîner |
| **duck/young duck** | canard/caneton |
| **eel** | anguille |
| **fish** | poisson |
| **fork** | fourchette |
| **fruit** | fruits |
| **glass** | verre |
| **ham** | jambon |
| **house wine** | vin de maison |
| **ice cream** | glace |
| **ice cubes** | glaçons |

| | |
|---|---|
| **jug of water** | carafe d'eau |
| **jug of wine** | pichet de vin |
| **knife** | couteau |
| **lamb** | agneau |
| **lunch** | déjeuner |
| **lettuce salad** | salade |
| **meat** | viande |
| **mineral water** | eau minérale |
| **mixed salad** | salade composée |
| **mussels** | moules |
| **orange juice** | jus d'orange |
| **oysters** | huîtres |
| **plate** | assiette |
| **pork** | porc |
| **red wine** | vin rouge |
| **salt** | sel |
| **sparkling water** | eau gazeuse |
| **spoon** | cuillère |
| **still water** | eau plate/non-gazeuse |
| **sugar** | sucre |
| **tap water** | eau du robinet |
| **turkey** | dinde |
| **vegetables** | légumes |
| **white wine** | vin blanc |
| **yoghurt** | yaourt |

## Personal Documents and Travel

| | |
|---|---|
| **airport** | aéroport |
| **credit card** | carte de crédit |
| **customs** | douane |
| **passport** | passeport |
| **platform** | voie |
| **railway station** | gare |
| **shuttle** | navette |
| **the Shuttle** | le Shuttle |
| **suitcase** | valise |
| **train/plane ticket** | billet de train/d'avion |
| **wallet** | portefeuille |

## Clothing

| | |
|---|---|
| **coat** | manteau |
| **jumper** | pull |
| **raincoat** | imperméable |
| **shirt** | chemise |
| **shoes** | chaussures |
| **socks** | chaussettes |
| **stockings** | bas |
| **suit** | costume/tailleur |
| **tights** | collant |
| **trousers** | pantalon |

## Useful Phrases

| | |
|---|---|
| **goodbye** | au revoir |
| **hello/good morning** | bonjour |
| **excuse me** | excusez-moi/pardon |
| **thank you** | merci |
| **yes/no** | oui/non |
| **please** | s'il vous plaît |
| **Do you speak English?** | Parlez-vous anglais? |
| **I don't understand** | Je ne comprends pas |
| **Talk slowly** | Parlez lentement |
| **Where's...?** | Où est...? |
| **When does the ... leave?** | A quelle heure part...? |
| **When does the ... arrive?** | A quelle heure arrive...? |
| **When does the museum open?** | A quelle heure ouvre le musée? |
| **When is breakfast served?** | A quelle heure sert-on le petit-déjeuner? |
| **What does it cost?** | Combien cela coûte? |
| **Where is the nearest petrol/gas station?** | Où se trouve la station essence la plus proche? |
| **Where are the toilets?** | Où sont les toilettes? |
| **Do you accept credit cards?** | Acceptez-vous les cartes de crédit? |
| **Can I have a receipt, please?** | Puis-j'avoir un reçu, s'il vous plaît? |

# BASIC INFORMATION

## Communications

### PUBLIC TELEPHONES

Most public phones in France use prepaid phone cards (*télécartes*), rather than coins. Some telephone booths accept credit cards (Visa, Mastercard/Eurocard). *Télécartes* (50 or 120 units) can be bought in post offices, branches of France Télécom, *bureaux de tabac* (cafés that sell cigarettes) and newsagents and can be used to make calls in France and abroad. Calls can be received at phone boxes where the blue bell sign is shown; the phone will not ring, so keep your eye on the little message screen.

### Emergency numbers

| | |
|---|---|
| Police: | 17 |
| **SAMU (Paramedics):** | 15 |
| **Fire (Pompiers):** | 18 |

### NATIONAL CALLS

French telephone numbers have 10digits. Paris and Paris region numbers begin with 01; 02 in northwest France; 03 in northeast France; 04 in south-east France and Corsica; 05 in south-west France.

### INTERNATIONAL CALLS

To call France from abroad, dial the country code (33) + 9-digit number (omit the initial 0). When calling abroad from France dial 00, then dial

### To use your personal calling card

| | |
|---|---|
| AT&T | ☎ 0-800 99 00 11 |
| Sprint | ☎ 0-800 99 00 87 |
| MCI | ☎ 0-800 99 00 19 |
| Canada Direct | ☎ 0-800 99 00 16 |

### International Dialling Codes
*(00 + code)*

| | | | |
|---|---|---|---|
| Australia | ☎ 61 | New Zealand | ☎ 64 |
| Canada | ☎ 1 | United Kingdom | ☎ 44 |
| Eire | ☎ 353 | United States | ☎ 1 |

the country code followed by the area code and number of your correspondent.
**International Information**, US/Canada: 00 33 12 11
**International operator**: 00 33 12 + country code
**Local directory assistance**: 12 Toll-free numbers in France begin with 0 800.

### MOBILE PHONES

In France these have numbers which begin with 06. Two-watt (lighter, shorter reach) and eight-watt models are on the market, using the Orange (France Télécom) or SFR networks. *Mobicartes* are prepaid phone cards that fit into mobile units. Mobile phone rentals (delivery or airport pickup provided):
**A.L.T. Rent A Phone**
☎ 01 48 00 06 06E-mail altloc@jve.fr
**Rent a Cell Express**
☎ 01 53 93 78 00, Fax 01 53 93 78 09
**Ellinas Phone Rental**
☎ 01 47 20 70 00

## Electricity

The electric current is 220 volts. Circular two-pin plugs are the rule. Adapters and converters (for hairdryers, for example) should be bought before you leave home; they are on sale in most airports. If you have a rechargeable device (video camera, portable computer, battery charger), read the instructions carefully or contact the manufacturer or shop. Sometimes these items only require a plug adapter; in other cases you must use a voltage con-verter as well or risk ruining your appliance.

## Public Holidays

Public services, museums and other monuments may be closed or may vary their hours of admission on the following **public holidays**:
National museums and art galleries are generally closed on Tuesdays; municipal museums are generally closed on Mondays. In addition to the usual school holidays at Christmas and in the spring and summer, there are long mid-term breaks (10 days to a fortnight) in February and early November.

| 1 January | New Year's Day (*Jour de l'An*) |
|-----------|-------------------------------|
| | Easter Day and Easter Monday (*Pâques*) |
| 1 May | May Day (*Fête du Travail*) |
| 8 May | VE Day (*Fête de la Libération*) |
| Thurs 40 days after Easter | Ascension Day (*Ascension*) |
| 7th Sun-Mon after Easter | Whit Sunday and Monday (*Pentecôte*) |
| 14 July | France's National Day (*Fête de la Bastille*) |
| 15 August | Assumption (*Assomption*) |
| 1 November | All Saint's Day (*Toussaint*) |
| 11 November | Armistice Day (*Fête de la Victoire*) |
| 25 December | Christmas Day (*Noël*) |

## Post / Mail

Post offices open Mondays to Fridays, 8am to 7pm, Saturdays, 8am to noon. Smaller branch post offices often close at lunchtime between noon and 2pm and in the afternoon at 4pm.

Postage via air mail to:
- ✉ UK: letter (20g) 0.55 €
- ✉ North America: letter (20g) 0.90 €
- ✉ Australia and NZ: letter (20g) 0.90 €

Stamps are also available from newsagents and tobacconists.
Stamp collectors should ask for *timbres de collection* in any post office.
General Delivery (*Poste Restante*) mail should be addressed as follows: Name, Poste Restante, Poste Centrale, post code of the *département* followed by town name, France. **The Michelin Guide France** gives local post codes.

## Money

### NOTES AND COINS

Since 17 February 2002, the **euro** has been the only currency accepted as a means of payment in France. It is divided into 100 cents or centimes. Old notes in French francs can only be exchanged at the Banque de France (2012 is the last date for this exchange).

### BANKS

Although business hours vary from branch to branch, banks are usually open from 9am to noon and 2pm to 5pm and are closed either on Mondays or Saturdays. Banks close early on the day before a bank holiday. A passport is necessary as identification when cashing travellers cheques in banks. Commission charges vary and hotels usually charge more than banks for cashing cheques.
You can obtain use **ATM machines** in France to get cash directly from your bank account (with a debit card) or to use your credit card to get a cash advance. Be sure to remember your PIN number; you will need it to use cash dispensers and to pay with your card in shops, restaurants, etc. Visa is the most widely accepted credit card, followed by Mastercard; other cards, credit and debit (Diners Club, Plus, Cirrus, etc) are also accepted in some cash machines. American Express is

more often accepted in premium establishments. Most places post signs indicating which card they accept; if you don't see such a sign and want to pay with a card, ask before ordering or making a selection.

**Before you leave home, check with the bank that issued your card for emergency replacement procedures, and ask them to note that your credit card is likely to be used abroad for a while.** Carry your card number and emergency phone numbers separate from your wallet and handbag; leave a copy of this information with someone you can easily reach. If your card is lost or stolen while you are in France, call one of the following 24-hour hotlines:

| | |
|---|---|
| **American Express** ☎ 01 47 77 70 00 | |
| **Visa** ☎ 08 36 69 08 80 | |
| **MasterCard/Eurocard** ☎ 01 45 67 84 84 | |
| **Diners Club** ☎ 01 49 06 17 50t | |

These numbers are also listed at most ATM machines.

You must report any loss or theft of credit cards or travellers cheques to the local police who will issue you with a certificate (useful proof to show the issuing company).

## PRICES AND TIPS

Since a service charge is automatically included in the prices of meals and accommodation in France, it is not necessary to tip in restaurants and hotels. However, if the service in a restaurant is especially good or if you have enjoyed a fine meal, an extra tip (this is the *pourboire*, rather than the *service*) will be appreciated. Usually a few euros will suffice. Some restaurants may ask you to add a percentage tip to your bill before paying by credit card. This is always optional. Restaurants usually charge for meals in two ways: a menu that is a fixed-price menu with 2 or 3 courses, sometimes a small pitcher of wine, all for a stated price, or à la carte, the more expensive way, with each course ordered separately.

Cafés have very different prices, depending on where they are located. The price of a drink or a coffee is cheaper if you stand at the counter (comptoir) than if you sit down (salle) and sometimes it is even more expensive if you sit outdoors (terrasse).

## DISCOUNTS

Significant discounts are available for senior citizens, students, young people under the age of 25, teachers, and groups for public transportation, museums and monuments and for some leisure activities such as the cinema (at certain times of day). Bring student or senior cards with you, and bring along some extra passport-size photos for discount travel cards.

The **International Student Travel Confederation** (www.isic.org), global administrator of the International Student and Teacher Identity Cards, is an association of student travel organisations around the world. ISTC members collectively negotiate benefits with airlines, governments, and providers of other goods and services for the student and teacher community, both in their own country and around the world. The non-profit association sells international ID cards for students, under-25-year-olds and teachers (who may get discounts on museum entrances, for example). The ISTC is also active in a network of international education and work exchange programmes.

The corporate headquarters address is Herengracht 479, 1017 BS Amsterdam, The Netherlands ☎ 31 20 421 28 00; Fax 31 20 421 28 10.

# Time

France is 1hr ahead of Greenwich Mean Time (GMT). France goes on daylight-saving time from the last Sunday in March to the last Sunday in October. In France "am" and "pm" are not used but the 24-hour clock is widely applied.

# CONVERSION TABLES

## Weights and Measures

| 🇪🇺 | 🇺🇸 | 🇬🇧 | |
|---|---|---|---|
| **1 kilogram (kg)**<br>6.35 kilograms<br>0.45 kilograms | **2.2 pounds (lb)**<br>14 pounds<br>16 ounces (oz) | **2.2 pounds**<br>1 stone (st)<br>16 ounces | *To convert kilograms to pounds, multiply by 2.2* |
| **1 metric ton (tn)** | **1.1 tons** | **1.1 tons** | |
| **1 litre (l)**<br>3.79 litres<br>4.55 litres | **2.11 pints (pt)**<br>1 gallon (gal)<br>1.20 gallon | **1.76 pints**<br>0.83 gallon<br>1 gallon | *To convert litres to gallons, multiply by 0.26 (US) or 0.22 (UK)* |
| **1 hectare (ha)**<br>**1 sq. kilometre (km²)** | **2.47 acres**<br>0.38 sq. miles<br>(sq.mi.) | **2.47 acres**<br>0.38 sq. miles | *To convert hectares to acres, multiply by 2.4* |
| **1 centimetre (cm)**<br>**1 metre (m)** | **0.39 inches (in)**<br>3.28 feet (ft) or 39.37 inches<br>or 1.09 yards (yd) | **0.39 inches** | *To convert metres to feet, multiply by 3.28; for kilometres to miles, multiply by 0.6* |
| **1 kilometre (km)** | **0.62 miles (mi)** | **0.62 miles** | |

## Clothing

| Women | 🇪🇺 | 🇺🇸 | 🇬🇧 |
|---|---|---|---|
| | 35 | 4 | 2½ |
| | 36 | 5 | 3½ |
| | 37 | 6 | 4½ |
| Shoes | 38 | 7 | 5½ |
| | 39 | 8 | 6½ |
| | 40 | 9 | 7½ |
| | 41 | 10 | 8½ |
| | 36 | 6 | 8 |
| | 38 | 8 | 10 |
| Dresses | 40 | 10 | 12 |
| & suits | 42 | 12 | 14 |
| | 44 | 14 | 16 |
| | 46 | 16 | 18 |
| | 36 | 06 | 30 |
| | 38 | 08 | 32 |
| Blouses & | 40 | 10 | 34 |
| sweaters | 42 | 12 | 36 |
| | 44 | 14 | 38 |
| | 46 | 16 | 40 |

| Men | 🇪🇺 | 🇺🇸 | 🇬🇧 |
|---|---|---|---|
| | 40 | 7½ | 7 |
| | 41 | 8½ | 8 |
| | 42 | 9½ | 9 |
| Shoes | 43 | 10½ | 10 |
| | 44 | 11½ | 11 |
| | 45 | 12½ | 12 |
| | 46 | 13½ | 13 |
| | 46 | 36 | 36 |
| | 48 | 38 | 38 |
| Suits | 50 | 40 | 40 |
| | 52 | 42 | 42 |
| | 54 | 44 | 44 |
| | 56 | 46 | 48 |
| | 37 | 14½ | 14½ |
| | 38 | 15 | 15 |
| Shirts | 39 | 15½ | 15½ |
| | 40 | 15¾ | 15¾ |
| | 41 | 16 | 16 |
| | 42 | 16½ | 16½ |

Sizes often vary depending on the designer. These equivalents are given for guidance only.

## Speed

| KPH | 10 | 30 | 50 | 70 | 80 | 90 | 100 | 110 | 120 | 130 |
|---|---|---|---|---|---|---|---|---|---|---|
| MPH | 6 | 19 | 31 | 43 | 50 | 56 | 62 | 68 | 75 | 81 |

## Temperature

| Celsius (°C) | 0° | 5° | 10° | 15° | 20° | 25° | 30° | 40° | 60° | 80° | 100° |
|---|---|---|---|---|---|---|---|---|---|---|---|
| Fahrenheit (°F) | 32° | 41° | 50° | 59° | 68° | 77° | 86° | 104° | 140° | 176° | 212° |

*To convert Celsius into Fahrenheit, multiply °C by 9, divide by 5, and add 32.*
*To convert Fahrenheit into Celsius, subtract 32 from °F, multiply by 5, and divide by 9.*
NB: Conversion factors on this page are approximate.

*Lille – Grand Place*

S. Sauvignier/ MICHELIN

# INTRODUCTION TO NORTHERN FRANCE

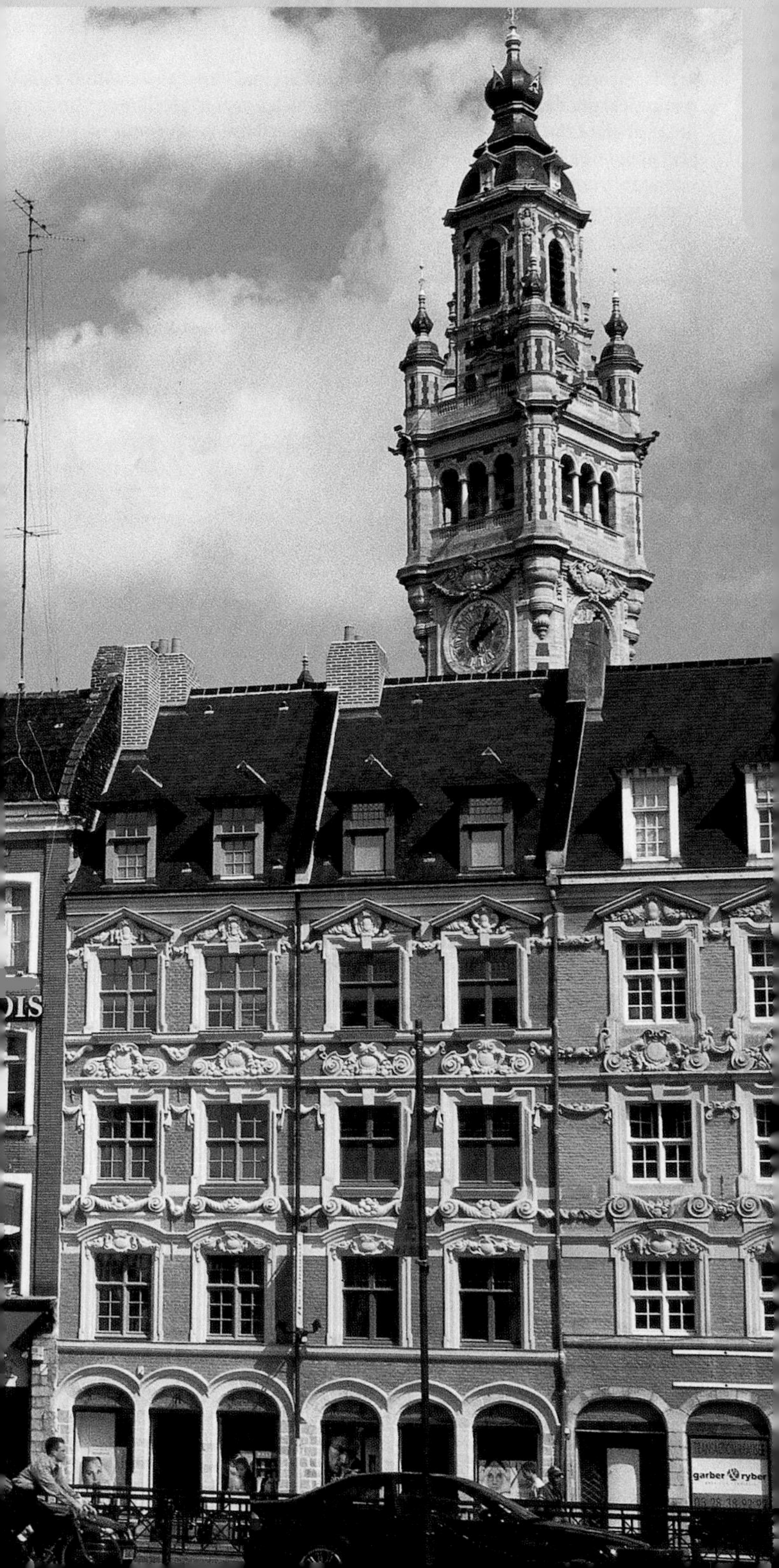

# NATURE

Artois, Picardy and Île-de-France (the region around Paris) all lie within a vast geological area known as the Paris Basin, which borders on Flanders and the great plain of Northern Europe. The landscapes of the Basin comprise forests, lush alluvial valleys with slow-flowing rivers, and limestone plateaux providing rich arable land. The climate is mild in summer and temperate in winter, with damp springs and autumns.

# Picardy

This region, to the north of Île-de-France, is composed of three separate *départements*: **Somme, Aisne and Oise.**

## SOMME

**Somme** really is a land of contrasts from the towering chalk cliffs of Mers-les-Bains and Ault to the leafy valleys of the Thiérache. It is a region with the best reserves of game-filled ancient forest in northern Europe, its biggest tidal estuary, and the largest expanse of sand dunes. Wide skies, secretive marshlands, cosy villages nestling among rolling farmland and orchards, or the open country of the Haute Somme characterise the area.

## AISNE

To the east, **Aisne** is identified by large farms, often complemented by a sugar refinery or a distillery. St-Quentin, the administrative and industrial centre of the *département*, is the principal town. The voluptuous landscape of Aisne is lush with cereals and the *bocage* of dairy cattle, rolling green hills and fields of gold that ripple away to the horizon. Among the folds, tiny communities, mostly of less than 100 souls, gather around a series of Middle Age fortified churches, built as a quick and temporary defence against the passage of plundering neighbours.

## OISE

To the south, marking the transition to the Île-de-France, the Valois region of **Oise** has a mantle of forests and miles of wheat fields invariably bright in spring with poppies and other wildflowers. The Oise may be close to Paris, but it doesn't live in its shadow. In the **Vimeu** region, the chalk has decomposed into flinty clay, and the cold, damp ground has created a mixed landscape of farmland crisscrossed by hedges and trees, cider-apple orchards and small, scattered villages. Near Beauvais the chalky, silt-covered plateau suddenly reveals a verdant hollow: the **Pays de Bray,** a wooded area interspersed with meadows where stock-farming is the main activity.

## RIVERS AND VALLEYS

The verdant wide-mouthed valleys are bisected by the Somme, Authie and Canche rivers. These waters flow so slowly they have difficulty in making their way, losing themselves in ponds and marshes full of fish and waterfowl. The floors of the valleys are a mix of old peat bogs, rows of poplars, arable and stock-farming fields and in a few places, on the outskirts of towns like Amiens, floating vegetable gardens (*hortillonnages*) surrounded by canals.

Towns and cities have developed along the valleys: Montreuil on the Canche; Doullens on the Authie; Péronne, Amiens and Abbeville on the Somme.

The capital of Picardy is **Amiens**, a great industrial centre with factories producing tyres, electronics, video games, domestic appliances, car parts and chemical products. In Oise the main town is **Beauvais**, and in Aisne it's **Laon**.

## MARITIME LANDSCAPE

To the south, near Ault, the Picardy plateau meets the sea, ending in a sharp cliff of white chalk banded with flint.

The bay, not surprisingly, is a huge and dangerous place to be, though it does seem to be suffering from coastal erosion. In 1878, it comprised 86 sq km; in 1993 that was down to 73 sq km, and today is about 70 sq km – one estimate puts it at 40sq km. The tide goes out as much as 14 kilometres, the second largest ebb in France, leaving behind tricky sandbanks, muddy channels and large expanses of sea grass; when it comes back in it does so rather more quickly than it went out.

North of the Somme Bay a maritime plain called the **Marquenterre** area has been created by debris torn from the Normandy coast and carried northward by the currents, gradually forming an offshore bar. Only the Somme, Authie and Canche rivers have carved a passage to the sea; there are therefore few large ports but several seaside resorts,

*The Opal Coast at the Site des deux Caps*

the largest of them, Le Touquet, seated beside the dunes.

The coastal plain lies between the dunes and the old coastal bar, which is marked by a noticeable cliff. The drained and dried plain is now used for fields of wheat and oats, and for raising salt-pasture lambs on the grassy shores known as *mollières*.

In the past St-Valery-sur-Somme, Le Crotoy and Étaples were important ports; today they harbour only fishing boats and yachts.

# Nord-Pas-de-Calais

The northernmost region of France, Nord-Pas-de-Calais comprises two dé-partements: **Nord**, and **Pas-de-Calais**. Locally, but now generally throughout France, the region takes in the former provinces of Artois and Flanders, though the borders are not easy to define.

# Artois

The former province of Artois lies on an extension of the Picardy plateaux, a rise of land running northwest to southeast. It ends in an escarpment of about 100m (Vimy Ridge, Notre-Dame de Lorette Hill) which divides the Paris Basin from the Anglo-Belgian Basin. The great plain of Flanders begins at the foot of this escarpment.

The well-watered hills of Artois are however bare to the south-east, in the **Ternois** region where there are out-crops of chalk; to the north-west, the chalky top layer of soil has decomposed into flinty clay resulting in lush, damp countryside which includes Hesdin Forest and mixed agricultural and meadow land.

## BOULONNAIS

The **Boulonnais** region forms an enclave in the chalk layer, revealing outcrops of harder, older rocks. The landscape here is very different from neigh-bouring areas. In the north, the Upper Boulonnais forms a chalky pla-teau which in places reaches over 200m/650ft in altitude. In the area where the land forms a hollow, the Lower Boulonnais, the wooded coun-tryside is dotted with whitewashed farms. The clay has created meadows that are used for rearing the dappled-grey "Boulonnais draughthorses" and for other stock-breeding. The soil also supports the Desvres and Boulogne forests, while the Hardelot Forest grows in sandier soil.

Boulogne, France's foremost fishing port, stands at the mouth of the River Liane. To the north, the edge of the calcareous plateau forms the cliffs of the Opal Coast (👁 *see La CÔTE D'OPALE*).

## HAINAUT AND CAMBRÉSIS

**Hainaut** (capital: Valenciennes) and **Cambrésis** (capital: Cambrai) are extensions of the chalky plateaux of Artois and Picardy. They are also cov-ered with a thick layer of silt that is ideal for growing sugar beets and wheat, with excellent per-acre harvests. The plateaux are divided by wide river val-leys such as those of the Scarpe, Sam-bre, Selle and Escaut (Scheldt). Mead-ows of fodder crops and pasture give them the look of farming country. The forests of St-Amand and Mormal appear where there is flinty clay, the result of decomposition of the chalk.

*Montreuil-sur-Mer — Rue du Clape-en-Bas*

## THIÉRACHE AND AVESNOIS

These two relatively hilly regions form the tail of the Ardennes uplands, covered at the western end by marl and chalk mixed with marl. The **Thiérache** is a damp region, part forest and part pasture. When carefully drained the cold, non-porous ground provides pasture for cows. The dairies produce butter, cheese and condensed milk. The **Avesnois** is crossed by the River Helpe Majeure and River Helpe Mineure, tributaries of the River Sambre. This region resembles the Thiérache, but is marked by summits rising to over 250m/820ft in places. It is also an area of pastureland famous for its dairy cows and cheeses, especially Maroilles.

## Flanders

The Flemish plain, which continues into Belgium, is bounded to the south by the hills of Artois and to the east by the plateaux of Hainault and Cambrésis.

## COASTAL FLANDERS

The wet and windy *Blooteland* (bare land protected by dunes separating the area from the sea) has been gradually reclaimed from the sea since the Middle Ages. The engineers, including the famous **Coebergher**, who came mostly from the Low Countries, drained the land gradually using great dams, canals and pumps, thus creating the marshes (*Moëres*). Today it is a low-lying region where the grey clay yields crops of sugar-beets, cereals, flax and chicory, and the nearby pastures are grazed by sheep, pigs, horses and cattle. The flat countryside, scattered with great isolated farms built around square courtyards, is dominated by belfries, bell-towers, windmills and, on the coast, the factory chimneys and harbour cranes of Dunkirk and Calais.

## INLAND FLANDERS

Known as *Houtland* (wooded land) in contrast to the bare coastal area, the "Flemish lowlands" consist of lush countryside divided by rows of poplars, willows or elms. The censes, white-walled Flemish farms with red roofs, stand out against this green background.

A series of summits extends into Belgium, comprising the **Monts des Flandres** range. In addition to providing beautiful meadows where cows, horses and pigs thrive, the rich soil is also used for growing various crops such as cereals, fruit and vegetables in gardens among the St-Omer canals, and plants for industrial processing (hops near Bailleul, flax in the Lys Valley, chicory, sugar beets). However, two small areas between Lille and Douai are different: the bare plateaux of the **Mélantois** and the **Pévèle** regions. The coal fields (*see Econ-*

*omy*) stretching from Béthune to Valenciennes have given rise to a "black country" marked by slag-heaps, brick mining towns and mine-shaft frames.

Between the Lys Valley and the River Escaut (Scheldt) lies the industrial conurbation of Lille-Roubaix-Tourcoing-Armentières. Once a major textile centre (**&** *see LILLE*), it is currently undergoing extensive urban renewal.

# Île-de-France

## PAYS DE FRANCE

This arable plateau extending between St-Denis, Luzarches and the Dammartin-en-Goële ridge was in the heart of royal territory. The layer of marl covering the subsoil has made the area extremely fertile, and the huge fields are planted with wheat and beet.

## PARISIS

**Parisis** lies between the River Oise and River Seine and the Pays de France. The area was once occupied by the Gauls, who gave it its name and christened the French capital. Parisis is an alluvial plain with few rivers that slopes toward the Seine. It is dominated by limestone hillocks covered in sand or grit.

Beyond the industrial suburbs of Paris, market gardens and orchards spread along the limestone slopes of the plain, while the sandy stretches are forested.

## SENLISIS

Geographers and historians have often grouped this region with Valois, but in fact it was part of the Crown territory, the central core of Île-de-France. Senlisis, which is bordered by the Oise, the Dammartin-en-Goële ridge and the Valois itself, is one of the most picturesque regions near the capital. Arable land is found on the silty soils, while the sandy areas have favoured the development of forestry.

## VALOIS

**Valois** is surrounded by Senlisis and the Oise, Automne and Ourcq rivers. It acquired strategic importance as early as Roman times and has remained one of the most important regions in French history. First a county, then a duchy, Valois was twice given to one of the king's brothers. On two occasions the descendants of this royal line, known as the Princes de Valois, acceded to the throne.

## MULTIEN

**Multien** is an area of rolling landscapes and ploughed fields bounded by the River Marne, the Valois and the Goële ridge. It was the scene of fierce combat in September 1914.

## FRENCH VEXIN

Three rivers border this limestone platform: the **Oise**, the **Epte** and the **Seine**. West of the River Epte is the Normandy Vexin. The loess covering is an extremely fertile topsoil which favours cereal cultivation, especially wheat, and vegetable crops. Cattle rearing is concentrated in the valleys planted with poplar trees. The Buttes de Rosne, a series of outliers stretching from Monneville to Vallangoujard, are wooded. They include the strip of land running north of the Seine.

## MANTOIS

**Mantois** is an enormous plateau situated between the River Eure and River Oise. It consists of forests to the east and arable land to the west. The small towns dotting its many valleys are well worth a visit.

## HUREPOIX

Bounded by Mantois, Beauce, Fontainebleau Forest and the Seine, the **Hurepoix** region has suffered from recent urbanisation. However, by avoiding major roads and referring to map no 106, you will enjoy exploring its varied landscapes.

## GÂTINAIS

The **Gâtinais** is defined by the River Seine and the Hurepoix, Beauce and Champagne regions. The French Gâtinais, a clay plateau, lies east of the River Loing while the Orléanais Gâtinais (to the west) is an area of sand and sandstone. This second area is covered by Fontainebleau Forest, popular because of its splendid groves and sandstone boulders. The lush valley of the Loing, which attracted a number of well-known artists to the area (Corot, Millet), is dotted with charming small towns.

## FRENCH BRIE

**French Brie** is located between the River Seine and River Grand Morin and has Champagne Brie as its northern border. Historically, the former belonged to the king of France, while the latter was the property of the Comte de Champagne. The area is watered by four meandering rivers – Seine, Marne, Petit Morin and Grand Morin – and has many large farms specialising in large-scale wheat, sugar-beet and vegetable cultivation. French Brie contains sites as varied as the Chateau de Vaux-le-Vicomte and Disneyland Paris.

# Forests

Île-de-France has some magnificent forests, including Rambouillet, Compiègne and Fontainebleau, which feature among the finest in the country. The forests form a "green ring" around Paris that is a delight for weekend hikers, bikers and horseback riders, among others.
Woods and forests have a timeless appeal: lush greenery in springtime, shaded groves in summer, the deep russet tones of autumn or the crisp frosts of winter. Forests also provide a multitude of fauna and flora to study, or flowers, fruit, nuts and mushrooms to harvest in season. Many also have charming picnic areas. Those who take time to understand the life cycle of a forest also understand its infinite variety.

## STATE AND PRIVATE FORESTS

Three types of forest exist in France: state, private and local. The most interesting for walkers are the state forests, as they have an extensive network of roads, paths and lanes, and their magnificent groves form a picturesque setting. The aim of the forest rangers is to preserve the natural habitat. The most beautiful French forests used to feature protected forest zones known as "artistic reserves" in which unusually striking trees were left untouched by the axe, even when they died. This practice was given up in favour of "biological reserves". Forests on private estates are not open to the public, apart from the roads that run through them.

## TREES

Like all living things, trees breathe, reproduce and need nourishment. Mineral nutrients are drawn from the earth by the roots and distributed to all parts of the tree via the sap running through the trunk and leaves.
Different trees require different kinds of soil. Chestnut trees, for instance, cannot survive on limestone soils, whereas oaks will flourish on a variety of soils.
Trees, like other plants, breathe through their leaves and reproduce through their flowers. Flowers will bear fruit if they are fertilised by pollen of their own species. Very few trees have hermaphrodite flowers – presenting both male and female characteristics – like roses, acacias etc. Consequently the pollen is usually carried from the male flower to the female flower by insects, or sometimes by the wind. Trees may also reproduce by their shoots; thus, when a youngish tree trunk is razed to the ground, a number of stool shoots will emerge from the stump. Conifers do not produce offshoots.
The trees of Île-de-France fall into two categories: deciduous and coniferous.
**Deciduous** – These trees shed their leaves every autumn and grow them again in the spring. Beeches, oaks, hornbeams, birches and chestnut trees belong to this category.

**Coniferous** – In place of leaves, coniferous species have needles which they shed regularly throughout the year. The needles are renewed every four to five years. Their sap contains resin – they are also known as resinous trees – and the fruit is generally cone-shaped. Pines, cypresses, cedars and fir trees are all conifers, as is the larch, which loses its needles every year.

## TREES OF THE ÎLE-DE-FRANCE FORESTS

Most species of deciduous trees can be found around Paris. The most common are listed below.

**Oak** – One of the most esteemed forest trees, the oak's hard but beautiful wood is used both for carpentry and ornamental woodwork. In former times oak bark was much sought after by local tanners. Some of the oaks tower 40m/132ft high with trunks over 1m/3ft in diameter. Trees can be felled up to the age of 250 years.

**Beech** – Although it resembles the oak in its habit, beech is slightly more elegant. The wood is mainly used for everyday furniture and railway sleepers but it is also popular as fuel. The trunk is cylindrical, the bark smooth and shiny; young shoots have a crooked, gnarled appearance. Beeches grow as tall as oaks but are not commercially viable beyond 120 years.

**Hornbeam** – A remarkably tough species, the hornbeam resembles the beech; it also lives to the same age, but is shorter and its bark features numerous grooves.

**Chestnut** – This tree can grow to great heights and can live for several hundred years, but is generally felled much younger as very old chestnut trees become hollow and prone to disease. Its wood was traditionally used by the cooperage industry for making staves, posts and stakes; nowadays it is used for the production of chipboard. Chestnut trees will grow only on siliceous soil.

**Birch** – Even when it reaches 25m/82ft in height the birch retains a graceful, slim trunk of white bark – which peels off in fine layers – and shimmering leaves. Damp, sandy soil is an excellent terrain for all varieties of birch. Although it is excellent firewood, it is mainly used in making wood pulp for the paper industry.

**Scots Pine** – This species, the most commonly found conifer in Île-de-France, is ideal for reafforestation, particularly in sandy terrain. Since the mid-19C it has been planted in plots of land where there is meagre or non-existent vegetation. Scots pines have short needles (4-6cm/1.5-2.5in) which grow in

*A Chestnut Tree in Bloom*

pairs, smallish cones (3-5cm/1-2in) and reddish-ochre bark.

Foresters often plant Scots pines alongside exotic or Mediterranean (maritime pine) resinous species. A great favourite is the Corsican pine, a tall, handsome tree with a perfectly straight trunk. It can grow to 50m/165ft, but old trees develop large grey patches on their bark.

## THE SCIENCE OF FORESTRY

If a forest is not tended, it will invariably deteriorate. In order to develop fully and reach their proper size, trees must be given breathing space and be placed in an environment which meets their specific requirements. The first step in a reafforestation campaign is to plant fir trees, which have few needs and produce wood in a very short time. Their roots retain the earth, otherwise washed away by surface water, and the needles build up thick layers on the ground. Next, hornbeams, birches and beeches are planted to increase the fertility of the soil, and finally oaks. Many of the beech groves are left as this species is considered to be commercially profitable.

**Rotations** – The prime concern of foresters is always to have trees ready for felling. Consequently, when trees are felled foresters ensure they are immediately replaced with seedlings. For example, a forest may be divided into 10 units, and every five years the unit with the oldest trees is cleared and then replanted. Thus, within 50 years the forest is entirely renewed while remaining commercially viable, a technique known as rotation.

Forest managers try to avoid exposing a large sector of the forest, as leafy plants such as hazel and mulberry trees can set in and choke the young shoots. Two, three or four groups within each sector are formed according to the trees' approximate age, and a programme of successive felling is planned. This ensures that only limited areas are deforested at any one time.

Whatever the rotation for a given forest, its appearance is bound to change depending on the thickness of the vegetation and the forestry techniques applied.

*Birch Tree*

There are three types of plantation in Île-de-France:

**Groves** – After the land has been sown, the weaker shoots are choked by the stronger ones in a process of natural selection. The trees, planted fairly close to one another, spread vertically. After some time the land is cleared around the finer species to encourage them to develop, and eventually these are the only ones that remain. This grove, where the widely spaced trees are all the same age, is called a *futaie pleine*; the rotation is rather long, 50 or even 80 years for very tall trees. *Futaie jardinée* is another type of grove, in which the trees are planted and cut at different times, so that the sector features a variety of "age groups"; older trees are always felled first.

A fully matured grove is a truly impressive sight, with its powerful trunks and its rich canopy of foliage producing subtle effects of light and shade.

**Copses** – The trees are younger. Rotation ranges from 5 to 30 years, depending on whether pit props, logs for heating or firewood is wanted. A copse is a sector of forest where a group of mature trees have been cut down. The shoots growing around the stump develop into a multitude of young bushy, leafy trees.

**Copses with Standards** – If, when cutting a copse, the finest trees are left standing, these will dominate the new shoots. If they survive a series of fellings, they will grow to be extremely strong. The utilisation of copses with standards produces both fuel wood (from the copses) and timber for industrial purposes (from the older species).

## FAUNA AND FLORA

Forests contain not only trees but also countless varieties of plants and animals. Hunts are still organised in certain forests.

Nature lovers will find forests fascinating as the rich, damp soil is remarkably fertile, sustaining moss, lichen, mushrooms, grasses, flowers, shrubs and ferns.

**Flowers** – April is the season of laburnum, hyacinths and daffodils. May brings hawthorn, lily-of-the-valley, columbine and the delightful catkins of the hazel tree. In June there is broom, heather, campanula, scabious and wild pinks. During the autumn, russet and gold leaves are as attractive as the forest flowers.

**Fruit** – Wild strawberries and succulent raspberries ripen during July and August, while blackberries can be harvested in August and September together with the new crop of hazelnuts. October is the time for sloes and sweet chestnuts.

**Mushrooms** – Some varieties of mushrooms – Russula virescens, chanterelle comestible and mousseron – are always edible. Other species are difficult to identify and may be dangerous. If in doubt, mushroom pickers should consult a professional mycologist or a local chemist (*pharmacien*) who is trained to identify mushrooms.

# Gardens in the Île-de-France

Three successive trends defined the official canons of ornamental gardening in Île-de-France, the home of many royal residences.

## 16C

During the 16C gardens were not considered as an essential part of an estate, but merely in the same category as outbuildings. They were generally of geometric shape and resembled a chessboard, where each of the squares contained carefully trimmed spindle and box forming arabesques and other elaborate patterns. These motifs were called *broderies*. Gardens were enclosed within a sort of cloister made of stone or greenery, from which visitors could enjoy a good view of the garden. Paths featuring fragments of marble, pottery and brick cut through the grounds. Though water did not play any significant part in the general appearance of the gardens, there were basins and fountains encircled by balustrades or tall plants. They were there to be observed in their own right and for people to admire the ornamental statues and water displays.

Most of them have now disappeared, at least in Île-de-France. There is, however, an outstanding example in Villandry in the Loire Valley ( see The Green Guide, Châteaux of the Loire).

*Château de Vaux-le-Vicomte and its fountain*

A. Cassaigne/ MICHELIN

# 17C-EARLY 18C: THE FORMAL GARDEN

Although **André le Nôtre** cannot be credited with "inventing" the **formal French garden**, he was the one person who raised this art form to absolute perfection. Its purpose was twofold: to enhance the beauty of the château it surrounded and to provide a superb view from within. The garden's main features were fountains, trees, statues, terraces and a sweeping perspective.

The château was fronted by a "Turkish carpet" of parterres with flowers and evergreen shrubs forming arabesques and intricate patterns. These were symmetrically flanked by basins with fountains, usually adorned with statues. Fountains were also placed on the terrace bearing the château and the upper lawns, which was the starting-point of the central perspective along a canal or a green carpet of lawn (*tapis vert*) lined with elegant groves of tall trees.

The groups of trees planted along the perspective were designed to be perfectly symmetrical. They were crossed by a network of paths, with clearings at the intersections offering splendid vistas extending into the far distance. Hedges lined the paths, concealing the massive tree trunks and providing a backdrop for marble statues. As hedges were fragile and expensive to maintain, however, most were later removed or greatly reduced in height from their original 6-8m/20-26ft. Each grove of trees featured a "curiosity": perhaps a fountain with elaborate waterworks, a colonnade or a group of sculpted figures.

The enormous variety of designs and styles used for the parterres and surrounding trees, bushes and hedges ensured that these formal gardens were never monotonous. They were conceived as an intellectual pursuit, giving pleasure through their stately proportions and perspectives, the skilful design and the sheer beauty of each detail.

# LATE 18C-19C: THE LANDSCAPE GARDEN

In the 18C, manipulating the landscape into rigid geometric patterns was no longer fashionable. The tendency instead was to imitate nature. The landscape garden – also called the Anglo-Chinese garden – consisted of lush, rolling grounds dotted with great trees and rocks, pleasantly refreshed by streams and tiny cascades. A rustic bridge might cross a river flowing into a pond or lake covered with water-lilies and surround-ed by willow trees, and a mill or dairy might add the final touch to this Arcadian scene. The 18C fascination for philosophy, characteristic of the Age of Enlightenment, was also reflected in contemporary gardening, which saw the introduction of symbolic or exotic monuments or *"fabriques"* (a technical term originally referring to architectural works depicted in paintings).

Antique temples and medieval ruins were particular favourites, while tombs and mausoleums became popular just before the Revolution. Chinese and Turkish sculptures were also fashionable. An unfinished temple, for instance, would remind visitors of the limits of science, while an oriental pagoda standing beside a crumbling tower symbolised the fragility of human achievements.

Sentimentality, romance and melodrama were popular features of many art forms. Such trends also affected landscape gardens, giving rise to a number of new sights including the secret lovers' grotto, the bench of the tired mother, the grave of the rejected suitor etc.

Most of these estates were ravaged during the Revolution, and few of their fragile monuments survived. Efforts are now being made to restore what was left. The most outstanding example of an 18C folly in the region is the Cassan Pagoda at L'Isle-Adam.

Particularly fine gardens may still be found at Versailles, Vaux-le-Vicomte, Chantilly, Courances, St.-Cloud, Sceaux, Champs, Fontainebleau, Rambouillet and Ferrières.

# HISTORY

## Timeline

### CELTS AND ROMANS

**Circa 300 BC** The north of Gaul occupied by a Celto-Germanic tribe, the Belgae.

**153 –** First Roman soldiers enter Gaul.

**57 –** Belgian Gaul conquered by Caesar. Bavay, Boulogne and Amiens become important Roman centres.

**AD 1C-3C** Roman peace. Northern France becomes part of the province of Second Belgium (capital at Reims).

**406 –** German tribes invade Gaul.

### MEROVINGIANS AND CAROLINGIANS

**486 –** Territory from the Somme to the Loire rivers occupied by Clovis following the defeat of the Roman army at Soissons: his kingdom was called Francia in Latin.

**534-36 –** Franks conquer Burgundy and acquire Provence.

**6C and 7C** Creation of bishoprics and founding of many abbeys.

**751 –** Pepin crowned first Carolingian king of the Franks.

**800 –** Charlemagne crowned Holy Roman Emperor.

**9C and 10C** Norman and Hungarian invasions. Withdrawal of the abbeys into the towns.

**911 –** The Duchy of Normandy created after the Treaty of St Clair-sur-Epte, ending the Normans' ambitions in Île-de-France.

**987 –** Hugh Capet, duke and suzerain of the land extending from the Somme to the Loire rivers, crowned the first King of France, in Senlis.

### THE MIDDLE AGES

**11C and 12C** Period of prosperity. Development of the cloth-making industry in Flanders, Artois and Picardy. Towns obtain charters and build belfries.

**1066 –** William, duke of Normandy, conquers England.

**1095 –** Pope Urban II preaches the first crusade at Clermont.

**1154 –** Henry II becomes king of England and establishes the Angevin Empire of Britain and western and southern France.

**1214 –** Battle of Bouvines: victory for Philippe Auguste over the Count of Flanders and his allies King John of England, the Holy Roman Emperor Otto IV and the counts of Boulogne and Hainault.

**1272 –** Ponthieu under the authority of the kings of England.

**1314 –** Flanders annexed by Philip the Fair.

**1337 –** Beginning of the Hundred Years War (1337-1453). The death of Philip the Fair and his three sons ("the accursed kings") results in a problem of succession: Philip the Fair's nephew, Philip de Valois, preferred by the French barons over his grandson, Edward III, King of England. The following century marked by battles between the French and the English who lay claim to the French Crown, as well as between the Armagnacs, supporters of the family of Orléans, and the Burgundians, supporters of the dukes of Burgundy.

**1346 –** Battle of Crécy: victory for Edward III of England.

**1347 –** Calais surrendered to the English with the famous episode of the Burghers of Calais.

**1348 –** The Black Death

**1369 –** Marriage of Philip the Bold, Duke of Burgundy, with Marguerite, daughter of the Count of Flanders: Flanders under Burgundian authority.

**1415 –** Battle of Agincourt: victory for Henry V of England.

**1420 –** The Treaty of Troyes signed by Isabeau of Bavaria, wife of the mad king Charles VI, depriving the Dauphin of his rights of succession and designating her son-in-law, Henry V of England, heir to the French throne.

**1422 –** Death of Charles VI. France divided between the English, the Burgundians and the Armagnacs. Charles VII, the legitimate heir, resident in Bourges.

**1430 –** Joan of Arc taken prisoner at Compiègne, and burned at the stake in 1431, in Rouen.

**1435 –** Reconciliation of France and Burgundy in the Treaty of Arras.

**1441 –** English supremacy over Île-de-France ends with the liberation of Pontoise.

**1477 –** Invasion of Picardy, Artois, Boulonnais and Hainault by Louis XI following the death of Charles the Bold; only Picardy subsequently held. Marriage of Marie of Burgundy, daughter of Charles the Bold, to Maximilian of Austria: Flanders brought under Hapsburg control.

Battle of Bouvines, Horace Vernat

RMN

## FROM THE BOURBONS TO THE REVOLUTION

**16C –** Through the House of Hapsburg, Flanders included in the empire of Charles V of Spain.

**1520 –** Meeting between Henry VIII of England and François I at the Field of the Cloth of Gold, Guînes.

**1529 –** Peace of Dames signed at Cambrai: claims to Artois and Flanders renounced by François I.

**1557 –** St-Quentin taken by the Spanish.

**1558 –** Calais taken from the English by the Duke of Guise.

**1562 –** Beginning of the Wars of Religion (1562-1598).

**1585 –** Philip II of Spain allied with the Catholic League (Treaty of Joinville).

**1593 –** Henry of Navarre converts to Catholicism after capturing most of Île-de-France; crowned King Henri IV of France.

**1598 –** Edict of Nantes grants religious tolerance to the Huguenots.

**1659 –** Following the Treaty of the Pyrenees, marriage agreed between Louis XIV and Maria-Theresa of Spain; Artois brought under French sovereignty.

**1661 –** The construction of a huge palace at Versailles commissioned by Louis XIV.

**1663 –** Marriage of Louis XIV with Maria-Theresa, who according to local custom was to inherit all of the Brabant region from her mother. When the inheritance passes to another heir, Louis XIV declares the war of "Devolution" on the Spanish Low Countries.

**1668 –** Walloon Flanders given to Louis XIV by the Treaty of Aix-la-Chapelle.

**1678 –** Louis XIV allowed to annex the other northern towns by the Treaty of Nimegen.

**1713 –** The borders of northern France established definitively (Treaty of Utrecht).

**1789 –** French Revolution. Declaration of the Rights of Man, Storming of the Bastille and formation of the National Assembly.

## FROM THE FIRST TO THE SECOND EMPIRE

**1802 –** Treaty of Amiens: peace with Britain.

**1803 –** Napoleon's army mustered at the Boulogne Camp for a possible invasion of England.

**1804 –** Napoleon crowns himself Emperor of France.

**1814 –** France invaded. Unconditional abdication by Napoleon at Fontainebleau. Louis XVIII, returned from exile in England, is enthroned in 1815.

**1840 –** Attempted uprising against King Louis-Philippe organised by Louis-Napoleon in Boulogne.

**1848 –** Louis-Napoleon elected President of the Republic; crowned Emperor (Napoleon III) in 1852.

**1870-71** Franco-Prussian War. End of the Second Empire signalled by the defeat at Sedan: the Third Republic proclaimed. Paris besieged by Prussians:

Alsace and part of Lorraine given up under the Treaty of Frankfurt.

## 20TH CENTURY

**1914 –** Outbreak of the First World War. France attacked by German armies through neutral Belgium; four years of bloody trench warfare follow.

**1915 to 1918** Battles throughout northern France and Flanders: in Artois (Neuville-St-Vaast, Vimy), in Picardy (Somme Valley, Chemin des Dames in the Aisne Valley, St Quentin) and in Île-de-France (Ourcq Valley, Battle of the Marne).

**1918 –** 11 November: armistice signed in Compiègne Forest.

**1919 –** End of the war with the Treaty of Versailles.

**1939 –** Outbreak of the Second World War. In June 1940 France overrun by the German army; occupation of much of the country. The "French State", established at Vichy, collaborates closely with the Germans. The north of France cut off from the rest of the country by a boundary. France's honour saved by General de Gaulle's Free French forces and by the courage of the men and women of the Resistance.

By 1942 all France occupied; the French fleet scuttled at Toulon. Allied landing in Normandy in June 1944, and in the south of France in August: Paris liberated. The "Dunkirk pocket" retaken by the Allies. The German surrender signed at Reims on 7 May 1945.

**1976 –** Creation of the "Île-de-France" administrative region.

**1987 –** Start of building works for the Channel Tunnel linking France and England.

**1994 –** 6 May: official opening of the Channel Tunnel.

**1996 –** Inauguration of Evry Cathedral.

**1998 –** Inauguration of the Stade de France in St-Denis for the World Cup, won by the French team.

## 21ST CENTURY

**2004 –** Lille is designated a European Capital of Culture, a distinction that gives cities a chance to showcase its cultural life and development.

**2007 –** Nicolas Sarkozy is elected President of France: the 6th President of French Fifth Republic, the 23rd President of the French Republic and Co-Prince of Andorra. One of his first 'social' acts was to admit singer Barbra Streisand the Office of Légion d'Honneur.

**2007 –** Paris is one of ten venues in France to host the 2007 Rugby World Cup.

# ART AND CULTURE

## Architectural Drawings

### Religious architecture

**MANTES-LA-JOLIE – Ground plan of Notre-Dame (12C-14C)**

Basilical plan without transept: the sacristy was added in the 13C, the radiating chapels and the Chapelle de Navarre in the 14C.

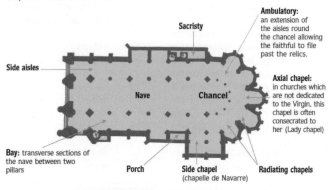

**Ambulatory:** an extension of the aisles round the chancel allowing the faithful to file past the relics.

**Sacristy**

**Side aisles**

**Nave**

**Chancel**

**Axial chapel:** in churches which are not dedicated to the Virgin, this chapel is often consecrated to her (Lady chapel)

**Bay:** transverse sections of the nave between two pillars

**Porch**

**Side chapel** (chapelle de Navarre)

**Radiating chapels**

**CHARTRES – Notre-Dame Cathedral**

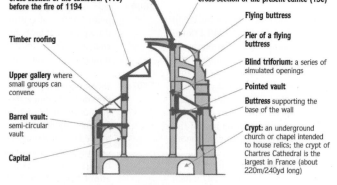

**Cross-section of the cathedral (11C) before the fire of 1194**

**Cross-section of the present edifice (13C)**

**Timber roofing**

**Flying buttress**

**Pier of a flying buttress**

**Blind triforium:** a series of simulated openings

**Upper gallery** where small groups can convene

**Pointed vault**

**Buttress** supporting the base of the wall

**Barrel vault:** semi-circular vault

**Crypt:** an underground church or chapel intended to house relics; the crypt of Chartres Cathedral is the largest in France (about 220m/240yd long)

**Capital**

**RAMPILLON – Main doorway of the church (13C)**

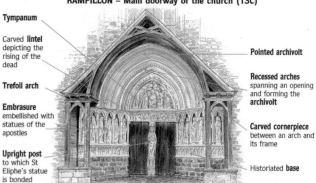

**Tympanum**

Carved **lintel** depicting the rising of the dead

**Trefoil arch**

**Embrasure** embellished with statues of the apostles

**Upright post** to which St Eliphe's statue is bonded

**Pointed archivolt**

**Recessed arches** spanning an opening and forming the **archivolt**

**Carved cornerpiece** between an arch and its frame

**Historiated base**

R. Corbel/MICHELIN

## AMIENS – West front of the cathedral (13C)

The vast cathedral is the edifice which best reflects the blossoming of Rayonnant Gothic architecture.

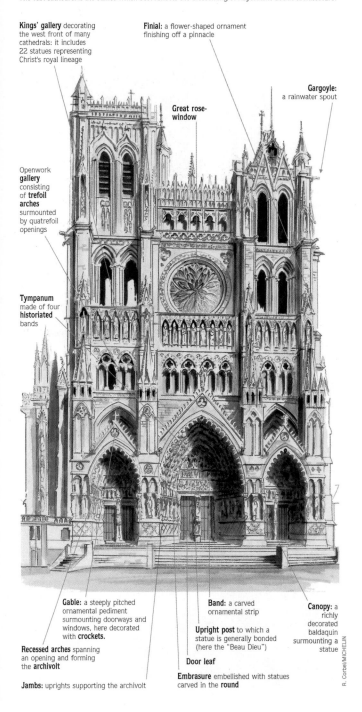

**Kings' gallery** decorating the west front of many cathedrals: it includes 22 statues representing Christ's royal lineage

**Finial:** a flower-shaped ornament finishing off a pinnacle

**Gargoyle:** a rainwater spout

**Great rose-window**

Openwork **gallery** consisting of **trefoil arches** surmounted by quatrefoil openings

**Tympanum** made of four **historiated** bands

**Gable:** a steeply pitched ornamental pediment surmounting doorways and windows, here decorated with **crockets.**

**Recessed arches** spanning an opening and forming the **archivolt**

**Jambs:** uprights supporting the archivolt

**Band:** a carved ornamental strip

**Upright post** to which a statue is generally bonded (here the "Beau Dieu")

**Door leaf**

**Embrasure** embellished with statues carved in the **round**

**Canopy:** a richly decorated baldaquin surmounting a statue

R. Corbel/MICHELIN

## BEAUVAIS – East end of the cathedral (13C)

In spite of the missing spire (which collapsed in 1573) and nave (never built owing to lack of funds), the cathedral has a magnificent chancel representing the apogee of Gothic building techniques with vaulting soaring to a height of 48m/157ft.

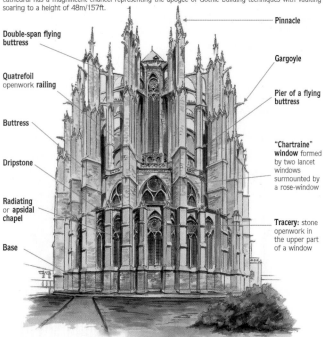

Pinnacle

Double-span flying buttress

Gargoyle

Quatrefoil openwork **railing**

Pier of a flying buttress

Buttress

"Chartraine" **window** formed by two lancet windows surmounted by a rose-window

Dripstone

Radiating or **apsidal** chapel

Tracery: stone openwork in the upper part of a window

Base

## SENLIS – Notre-Dame Cathedral (12C-13C)

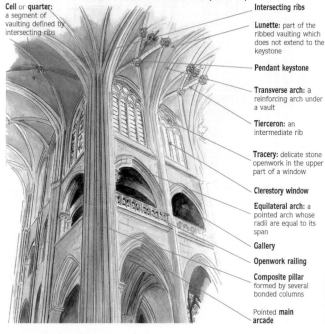

**Cell** or **quarter:** a segment of vaulting defined by intersecting ribs

Intersecting ribs

**Lunette:** part of the ribbed vaulting which does not extend to the keystone

Pendant keystone

**Transverse arch:** a reinforcing arch under a vault

**Tierceron:** an intermediate rib

**Tracery:** delicate stone openwork in the upper part of a window

Clerestory window

**Equilateral arch:** a pointed arch whose radii are equal to its span

Gallery

Openwork railing

**Composite pillar** formed by several bonded columns

Pointed **main arcade**

R. Corbel/MICHELIN

## AIRE-SUR-LA-LYS – Organ of the collegiate church (1653)

This richly carved organ comes from the former Cistercian abbey of Clairmarais near Aire-sur-la-Lys.

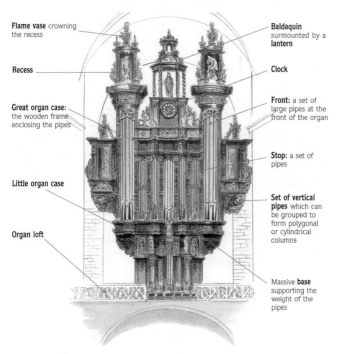

**Flame vase** crowning the recess

**Recess**

**Great organ case:** the wooden frame enclosing the pipes

**Little organ case**

**Organ loft**

**Baldaquin** surmounted by a **lantern**

**Clock**

**Front:** a set of large pipes at the front of the organ

**Stop:** a set of pipes

**Set of vertical pipes** which can be grouped to form polygonal or cylindrical columns

Massive **base** supporting the weight of the pipes

## QUAËDYPRE – High altar and altarpiece of the church (late 17C)

In the 17C and 18C, altarpieces were architectural compositions towering above the altar and intended to channel the congregation's religious fervour.

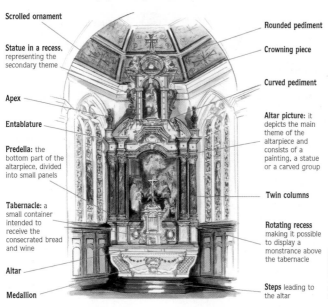

**Scrolled ornament**

**Statue in a recess,** representing the secondary theme

**Apex**

**Entablature**

**Predella:** the bottom part of the altarpiece, divided into small panels

**Tabernacle:** a small container intended to receive the consecrated bread and wine

**Altar**

**Medallion**

**Rounded pediment**

**Crowning piece**

**Curved pediment**

**Altar picture:** it depicts the main theme of the altarpiece and consists of a painting, a statue or a carved group

**Twin columns**

**Rotating recess** making it possible to display a monstrance above the tabernacle

**Steps** leading to the altar

R. Corbel/MICHELIN

## Civil architecture

### Château de COURANCES (16C-17C)

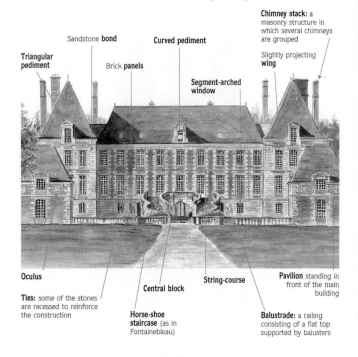

Chimney stack: a masonry structure in which several chimneys are grouped

Sandstone **bond**

Curved pediment

**Triangular pediment**

Slightly projecting **wing**

Brick **panels**

**Segment-arched window**

Oculus

**Ties:** some of the stones are recessed to reinforce the construction

Central block

Horse-shoe staircase (as in Fontainebleau)

String-course

Balustrade: a railing consisting of a flat top supported by balusters

Pavilion standing in front of the main building

### Château de CHANTILLY stables – Dome (1721-1740)

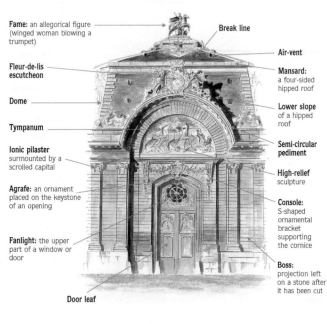

Fame: an allegorical figure (winged woman blowing a trumpet)

Break line

Air-vent

**Fleur-de-lis escutcheon**

**Mansard:** a four-sided hipped roof

**Dome**

**Lower slope** of a hipped roof

**Tympanum**

**Ionic pilaster** surmounted by a scrolled capital

**Semi-circular pediment**

**High-relief** sculpture

**Agrafe:** an ornament placed on the keystone of an opening

**Console:** S-shaped ornamental bracket supporting the cornice

**Fanlight:** the upper part of a window or door

**Boss:** projection left on a stone after it has been cut

Door leaf

R. Corbel/MICHELIN

## RUE – Belfry (15C)

Symbolising the power of the city, the belfry was used as a watchtower as well as the aldermen's meeting place.

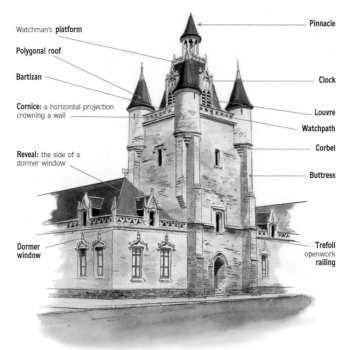

Watchman's **platform**

Polygonal roof

Bartizan

**Cornice:** a horizontal projection crowning a wall

**Reveal:** the side of a dormer window

Dormer window

Pinnacle

Clock

Louvre

Watchpath

Corbel

Buttress

Trefoil openwork **railing**

## ARRAS – Façades overlooking the Grand'Place (15C-17C)

Left is the Hôtel des Trois Luppars (1467), the oldest house lining the square, right is a house dating from 1684.

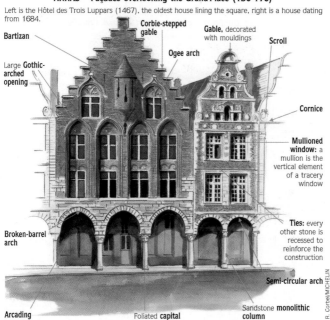

Bartizan

Corbie-stepped gable

Ogee arch

**Gable,** decorated with mouldings

Scroll

Large **Gothic-arched opening**

Cornice

**Mullioned window:** a mullion is the vertical element of a tracery window

Broken-barrel arch

**Ties:** every other stone is recessed to reinforce the construction

Semi-circular arch

Arcading

Foliated **capital**

Sandstone **monolithic column**

R. Corbel/MICHELIN

### CHATOU – 19C pavilion

This type of pavilion, built of course-grained limestone, is characteristic of suburban domestic architecture.

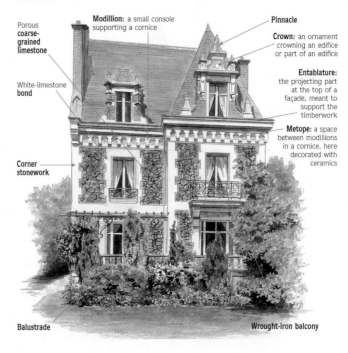

Porous **coarse-grained limestone**

**Modillion:** a small console supporting a cornice

**Pinnacle**

**Crown:** an ornament crowning an edifice or part of an edifice

**Entablature:** the projecting part at the top of a façade, meant to support the timberwork

White-limestone **bond**

**Metope:** a space between modillions in a cornice, here decorated with ceramics

**Corner stonework**

**Balustrade**

**Wrought-iron balcony**

## Military architecture
### LE QUESNOY – Fortifications (12C and 17C-19C)

These well-preserved fortifications, remodelled by Vauban from 1667 onwards, are set in green surroundings.

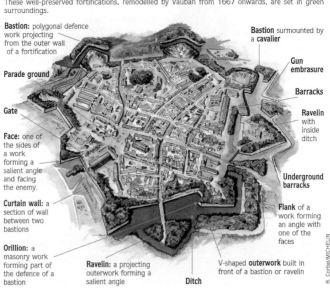

**Bastion:** polygonal defence work projecting from the outer wall of a fortification

**Bastion** surmounted by a **cavalier**

**Gun embrasure**

**Parade ground**

**Barracks**

**Gate**

**Ravelin** with inside ditch

**Face:** one of the sides of a work forming a salient angle and facing the enemy.

**Underground barracks**

**Curtain wall:** a section of wall between two bastions

**Flank** of a work forming an angle with one of the faces

**Orillion:** a masonry work forming part of the defence of a bastion

**Ravelin:** a projecting outerwork forming a salient angle

V-shaped **outerwork** built in front of a bastion or ravelin

**Ditch**

R. Corbel/MICHELIN

# Living Like Kings

After the 15C, medieval castles were converted from fortresses into residential châteaux. Windows were enlarged, doors and openings were richly adorned. Towers, once strategic elements of the defensive structure, became decorative features, along with crenellated battlements and moats. By the second half of the 16C, such characteristics had become superfluous. Façades were embellished with statues and rows of superimposed columns. Roofs were high and presented a single slope.

The Château d'Écouen is a fine example of the French Renaissance style, as is the Richelieu Pavillon of the Louvre (1546-1654), in Paris. The style, which succeeded Gothic as the style dominant in Europe after the mid-16C, first developed in Italy. The name describes the "rebirth" of interest in Roman and Greek art and learning. By the early 17C, the Classical style of architecture had emerged, as expressed in the magnificence of royal palaces.

## FRANÇOIS I (REIGNED 1515-47)

The early phase of the French Renaissance culminated in the François I style (⌖ see FONTAINEBLEAU). The decorative aspects mingle Gothic embellishments with elements inspired by Italian art, and the design features round arches and symmetrical composition. Many of the elegant buildings erected by the monarch bear his distinctive emblem: a crowned salamander.

## HENRI IV (R. 1589-1610) – LOUIS XIII (R. 1610-43)

Louis XIII was strongly influenced by the Henri IV style (Place des Vosges, Paris), which marked the beginnings of the Classical period of French architecture. The principal characteristics of this style, which prevailed during the first half of the 17C, are the exact symmetry of the main building and the use of brick panels set into white stonework. Carved ornamentation is limited and sober. Most often, the design is a central block flanked by two end pavilions (⌖ see Château de COURANCES). Louis XIII built the first palace in Versailles in this style, in brick, stone and slate.

## LOUIS XIV (R. 1643-1715)

Under the skilful hand of François Mansart, civil architecture gave up its straightforward character and acquired a less domestic, nobler appearance. The early period shows columns and pilasters that stand the height of a single floor of the château. Triangular and arched pediments top doorways and windows. Numerous chimneys sprout from the high roofs (⌖ see Château de MAISONS-LAFITTE).

Châteaux built during the second period are characterised by a high ground floor, a very high first floor and a relatively low second floor. A balustrade conceals the roof. The horizontal lines of the building are broken by rows of sturdy columns and tall windows. Ornamental sculpture is limited to the rooftop and the summit of the front pavilions, and inspired by classical models. Versailles represents the culmination of the high Classical period.

## LOUIS XV (R. 1715-74)

After 1700, the Louis XIV style and its harsh angles were mellowed by soft, rounded contours. Under Louis XV, oval spaces and curved surfaces were favoured. Windows and pediments display intricate ornamentation, while the rest of the façade remains austere, without columns; the roof is formed by two sloping planes (⌖ see the stables at CHANTILLY). Over time, Classical yielded more and more to Rococo (also known as Baroque classicism in France), which is distinguished by profuse, often semi-abstract ornamentation, and lightness of colour and weight.

## LOUIS XVI (R. 1774-92)

The influence of the elegant Louis XV style is still apparent in works of this period, but over-abundant curves are replaced by right angles. Columns make a conspicuous comeback, placed on unadorned façades. This phase is known

## Interior Decoration

*Fontainebleau – Galerie François I, fresco by Primaticcio*
**Renaissance: First Fontainebleau School** – Ornate decoration in a free interpretation of the Italian masters. The frescoes framed by stuccowork are above the wainscoting. Coffered ceilings and rafters.

*Gros-Bois – Dining Room*
**Louis XIII style** – The decorative features are more restrained. Above the wainscoting are huge tapestries or frescoes. The ceiling rafters are visible but in most instances the coffering has disappeared.

*Versailles – Salon de Vénus*
**Louis XIV style** – The decoration is luxurious in the materials used but understated in design. Marble panels decorate the walls. The ceiling is divided into painted compartments separated by gilded stuccowork.

*Champs – Mme de Pompadour's bedchamber*

**Louis XV style** – Right angles have been banished. Curves, scrolls and arabesques soften straight lines. Light-coloured wainscoting has replaced the marble panels. Mouldings with plant and floral motifs, volutes, cartouches and shells.

*Versailles – Louis XVI's gaming room*

**Louis XVI style** – The decoration is still elegant and light in colour, but straight lines have come back into fashion. The severity of the rectangular panels is relieved by reeds and ribbons or garlands.

*Compiègne – Napoleon's bedchamber*

**Empire style** – Antique green or crimson-red hangings have replaced the wainscoting. Straight lines and semicircular arches predominate. Heavy mouldings and motifs stand out against the dark woodwork.

as "Classicist", for many of the decorative motifs are inspired by Antiquity, a trend that introduced the so-called Pompeian and the Empire styles that followed (👉 see VERSAILLES: Petit Trianon). The French Revolution brought an abrupt end to building in this style.

# Religious and Civil Architecture

Île-de-France and the regions north of Paris offer a rich variety of architectural styles: Gallo-Roman at Bavay; Romanesque at Morienval, Rhuis and Chartres; Gothic architecture throughout Île-de-France where it was born, and the later Flamboyant Gothic mainly in Picardy; Renaissance influence at Amiens and Cassel; Classical architecture in and around Paris; and Baroque in Flanders. Many of the earliest buildings of note were constructed for religious purposes, and the development of architectural styles is best understood through them. A church consisted basically of a chancel reserved for members of the clergy, where the high altar and the reliquaries were located, and of a nave for the congregation. This simple layout characterised the early churches, built on a basilical plan. During the Romanesque period the plan of the church developed into the shape of a cross. The vestibule (narthex) at the entrance received those who had not been baptised, and the nave was enlarged with aisles. In places of pilgrimage, an ambulatory and side aisles were added to the chancel to facilitate processions. Architects followed this layout as it was convenient for celebrating Mass and easy to build.

## ROMANESQUE (11C-12C)

Architects in Romanesque times knew how to build huge, lofty churches, but as the heavy stone vaulting often caused the walls to settle or cave in they made the windows as small as possible and added aisles surmounted by galleries to support the sombre nave.

One of the main types of roofing in Romanesque churches is groined vaulting, in which two identical barrels meet at right angles. The barrel in line with the nave is supported by the transverse arch, while the one set at a right angle is supported by the main arch or by a recess in the wall. Rhuis and Morienval churches and the Royal Doorway of Chartres Cathedral are splendid examples of Romanesque art.

## GOTHIC (12C-15C)

The transition from Romanesque to Gothic architecture – which originated in Île-de-France – was a slow, natural process that developed in response to the demand for wider, higher and lighter churches. Gothic art, typified by quadripartite vaulting and the use of pointed arches, evolved from sombre 12C Romanesque sanctuaries into light 13C churches and the extravagantly ornate buildings of the 15C. It is rare to find a church with entirely unified features reflecting a given period in history. Building a church was a costly and lengthy operation subject to changes in public taste and building methods as the work progressed. Toward the late 13C famous personalities and guilds were granted the privilege of having a chapel built in their honour in one of the side aisles. In exchange they were expected to make a generous contribution toward the building or its maintenance.

**Architects** – The names of the architects of great religious edifices are known to us only from the Gothic period onwards, through texts or through inscriptions carved around the "labyrinths" outlined on cathedral floors. That is how Robert de Luzarches was revealed as responsible for the plans of Amiens Cathedral.

The most outstanding master builder in the north of France, however, was undoubtedly **Villard de Honnecourt**, born near Cambrai. The towers of Laon Cathedral, Vaucelles Abbey (*south of Cambrai*), and the chancels at St-Quentin and Cambrai (*no longer extant*) have all been attributed to him.

**West fronts** – Most main façades were set facing west. Nave and aisles had their own doorway flanked by buttresses that were bare in the 12C and 13C, ornate in the 15C. The tympanum featured ornamentation, and in the 14C its gable was elaborately carved. 13C rose windows were fairly small; in the 14C they were enlarged across the west front to provide light for the nave. As windows grew larger, façades became more delicate. A gallery was built at the base of the towers to break the rigid vertical perspective created by the buttresses and bell-towers; in the 15C this was reduced to a balustrade and the gables further embellished.

Ideally, west fronts were to be richly decorated with stone carvings, but in many cases they were the last part to be completed. Architects were often obliged to forego ornamentation, and even towers, owing to insufficient funds. In other cases, even the transepts were given remarkable façades (*see Chartres*).

**Spires** – After lightening the façades of Gothic churches, architects turned to the spires. By the Flamboyant period the open-work masonry was markedly ornate. In the 19C many bell-towers in the region were given a spire by followers of Viollet-le-Duc.

**Flying buttresses** – In Early Gothic churches the pillars in the nave were supported by masonry concealed in the galleries. During the 12C these walls were reduced to arches (⚓ *see below*) supported by sturdy piers. Soon afterwards the galleries themselves were replaced with a row of flying buttresses outside. A number of high openings could therefore be incorporated into the church interior, producing a far more luminous nave.

From then on, tall churches can be schematically described as stone frames consisting of columns supporting diagonal arches and resting on two or three levels of flying buttresses. The buttresses were in turn supported by a series of tall pillars bearing pinnacles.

**Diagonal arches** – Toward the end of the 11C groined vaulting was extremely common; but, as it was difficult to build and liable to crack, a group of architects from England, Milan and Île-de-France decided to reinforce the groins.

They found that by building the diagonal arches first and by consolidating them with a small amount of rubble, vaulting that was both sturdy and light was achieved.

By supporting this vaulting on a series of arches, so that the weight of the masonry would have to be borne at the springing, the architects could dispense with the walls in between the arches and replace them with stained-glass windows; this in turn greatly enhanced the luminosity of the interiors.

This significant development heralded the age of quadripartite vaulting.

**Vaulting** – Quadripartite vaulting, in which the thrust is supported by four main arches, is easy to install in a square-shaped bay. In the 12C bays were enlarged and it was no longer possible

| **Transitional** (12C) | **Early Gothic** (early 13C) | **High Gothic** (late 13C-early 14C) | **Flamboyant** (15C and 16C) |

to build them square, as the pillars propping up the walls would have been too far apart. The problem was initially resolved by covering the bays two by two, thus forming a square again. An extra transverse arch was then added and made to rest on slim pillars alternating with stout piers.

This type of vaulting – upheld by three diagonal arches – is known as sexpartite vaulting because of the number of its divisions.

When more sophisticated diagonal arches were made to support the vaulting above rectangular bays, the intermediary resting points were eventually discarded.

After the 15C, Flamboyant architects put in additional, decorative ribbing of complex design that formed liernes and tiercerons, and subsequently stars and intricate networks. The main supporting arches were flanked by ornamental arches of no practical use. The keystones – usually pendant – grew thinner and longer.

**Elevations** ( *see illustrations*) – Gothic elevations reflect the continual search for higher and lighter buildings.

**Transitional Gothic (A)** – The term Transitional Gothic covers the birth and early stages of Gothic architecture, from about 1125 to 1190. The first use of diagonal vaulting in France appeared over the ambulatory in the Romanesque abbey church at Morienval.

Though some Romanesque details – such as semicircular arches – can still be observed in early Gothic buildings, there were several significant changes. The new interiors presented four-storey elevations consisting of high clerestory windows at the top lighting the nave directly, a triforium (a narrow, arcaded passageway below the clerestory), a gallery – instrumental in supporting the walls as high up as possible – and arcading at ground level. There were often openings behind the gallery but never behind the triforium.

The pillars of the main arches initially consisted of a thick column; this was later replaced by twinned columns supporting the arches and the colonnettes above. Laon Cathedral is a good example of Early Gothic architecture. Semi-circular transept endings like the famous south arm at Soissons Cathedral were also a feature.

**Early Gothic (B)** – This great period (c1180-1250), when Gothic architecture was in its ascendancy, produced some of France's finest masterpieces, among them Chartres Cathedral ( *see illustration*). Characteristics include: arches and windows pointed and shaped like a lancet; clerestory windows surmounted by a round opening; the gallery replaced by external flying buttresses. The numerous colonnettes originating from the vaulting rested on the shaft that bore the weight of all the main arches. This pier was generally a large round column flanked by four colonnettes.

**High Gothic (C)** – This was the golden age of the great cathedrals in France, lasting from about 1250 and the reign of St Louis to around 1375 when the Hundred Years War blocked the progress made by medieval architects.

At this time High Gothic, known as "Rayonnant" in French, reached its peak: the three-storey elevation (large arcades, triforium – the wall at the back now pierced with stained glass – and tall clerestory windows) lightened the nave and formed one huge single stained-glass window in the chancels of churches with no ambulatory; the wall area was reduced to a minimum and the springers supporting the vaulting were doubled by another series of arches. In many cases the colonnettes started from the ground, at the point where they surround the pillar of the main arches. Two slight mouldings – level with the main arches and the springers – were the only features to break the vertiginous ascent. Beauvais Cathedral is the most outstanding example of High Gothic ( *see illustration*).

**Flamboyant Gothic (D)** – This last stage in Gothic architecture, which could develop no further, succumbed to ornamental excess, aided by the fine, easily worked Picardy stone.

The style owes its name to the flame shapes in the tracery of the bays and rose windows, and to the exuberant carved and sculpted decoration which tended to obscure the structural lines of the buildings: doorways were crowned with open-work gables, balustrades were surmounted by pinnacles, vaulting featured complex designs with purely decorative arches (called liernes and tiercerons) converging on ornately worked keystones. The triforium disappeared, replaced by larger clerestory windows. Arches came to rest on columns or were continued by ribbing level with the pillars. The latter were no longer flanked by colonnettes. In some churches, the ribs formed a spiral around the column.

**Flemish civil architecture** – From the late 13C the particular nature of Flemish Gothic architecture manifested itself in the civic buildings, belfries and town halls erected by the cities that had obtained charters.

**Belfries** – Symbol of the town's power, the belfry was either an isolated building (Bergues, Béthune) or part of the town hall (Douai, Arras, Calais). It was built like a keep with watchtowers and machicolations. The rooms above the foundations – which housed the prison – had various functions, such as guardroom. At the top, the bell-room enclosed the **chimes**. Originally these consisted of only four bells. Today they often number at least 30 bells which play every hour, half-hour and quarter-hour. The bell-room is surrounded by watchtowers from which the sentry looked out for enemies and fires. At the very top is a weather vane symbolising the city: thus the lion of Flanders stands at Arras, Bergues and Douai.

**Town halls** – Town halls are often imposing with striking, richly embellished façades: niches, statues, gables and pinnacles might adorn the exterior.

Inside, the large council chamber or function room had walls decorated with frescoes illustrating the history of the town.

The most beautiful town halls (Douai, Arras, St-Quentin, Hondschoote, Compiègne) were built in the 15C and 16C. Many suffered damage and modification over the centuries and some were completely rebuilt in their original style, as at Arras.

## RENAISSANCE (16C)

Renaissance architecture, under the influence of Italian culture, favoured a return to classical themes: columns with capitals imitating the Ionic and Corinthian orders; façades decorated with niches, statues and roundels; pilasters flanking the windows. Quadripartite vaulting was replaced by coffered ceilings and barrel vaulting. Architects introduced basket-handled arches and semicircular or rectangular openings. Inverted brackets replaced flying buttresses. West fronts, and sometimes the north and south façades too, kept their heavy ornamentation. Spires were replaced by small domes and lantern towers.

Isolated examples of Renaissance art –

*Moret-sur-Loing – Maison de François I*

B. Kaufmann/ MICHELIN

*Abbaye de Royaumont*

R. Kaufmann / MICHELIN

not widely adopted in the north of France – are the Maison du Sagittaire in Amiens and the Hôtel de la Noble Cour in Cassel.

## BAROQUE AND CLASSICAL (17C-18C)

**Architecture** – Through the 17C and 18C, architecture presented two different faces. One was Baroque, dominated by irregular contours, an abundance of exuberant shapes, generous carving and much ornamentation. The other was Classical, a model of stateliness and restraint, adhering strictly to the rules of Antiquity with rows of Greek columns (Doric, Ionic and Corinthian), pedimented doorways, imposing domes and scrolled architraves. The Baroque style flourished in Flanders, Hainault and Artois which fell under Spanish influence, while the Classical style found favour in Picardy and Île-de-France.

The Baroque Chapelle du Grand Séminaire in Cambrai is one of many religious buildings erected in the 17C following the influence of the Counter Reformation and its main engineers, the Jesuits. Civil buildings include the House of Gilles de la Boé in Lille and the Mont-de-Piété in Bergues. The Mint in Lille, with its bosses and richly carved ornamentation, exemplifies **Flemish Baroque**.

The Petit Trianon at Versailles is a famous example of Classical architecture.

In Arras, Baroque and Classical elements were combined for the town's splendid main squares framed by houses with arcades and volutes. Combined elements can also be seen at the abbeys in Valloires and Prémontré and at the Château de Long.

**Sculpture** – The finely grained and easily worked chalky stone found in Picardy was used for much decorative work. By the 13C the "picture carvers" in Amiens and Arras were already displaying the specific Picardy traits discernible throughout later centuries: lively, finely detailed figures going about their everyday life. The calendar at Amiens is a good example of this engaging art.

In the late 15C and early 16C the Picardy wood carvers (*huchiers*) became renowned through their work on the stalls in Amiens Cathedral; the door panels in St Wulfram's in Abbeville; and the finely worked frames of the "Puy-Notre-Dame" paintings.

Baroque art favoured abundant decorative sculpture. Buildings were covered with a profusion of ornamental fruit, flowers, cornucopias, putti, niches, statues, vases etc.

# Monasteries in Île-de-France

A considerable number of priory, convent and abbey ruins are to be found in Île-de-France, and numerous districts and street names recall the many religious communities that have not survived.

**Abbeys in the history of Île-de-France** – Abbeys would not exist if people didn't feel a strong calling to take up ecclesiastical duties. At the same time, there would be no abbeys if the clergy had not been given any land. After the 5C, when the victorious Franks divided up the Gallo-Roman territory, it would have been impossible for any religious community to survive without the help of donations. There were many aspiring monks in France up to the 18C, and the different communities were almost entirely dependent on the generosity of benefactors. As the suzerain of Île-de-France was none other than the supreme ruler of France, the king, this region was graced with an abundance of local monasteries.

In the early days of Christianity, during the late 4C, Île-de-France was covered with forests; but the land was also fertile and the area attracted monks who wanted to live in peace and escape the terrible famine ravaging the country. Soon afterwards the Merovingian monarchs, who had been strongly backed by the clergy, encouraged the creation of religious foundations, to which they made considerable contributions. The wealthy Carolingians continued to endow these abbeys, and the practice was kept up by the Capetians and their vassals for over 800 years (Chaalis and Royaumont).

French kings favoured monasteries because the monks used to reclaim uncultivated land and because the monasteries were constantly praying for their patrons. Religious faith was strong from the 10C to the 17C, and kings made donations to abbeys for a variety of reasons: to thank God for a victory, to seek expiation for an offence committed against the Church, to express their own personal belief or to offer a dowry to dowager queens or royal princesses about to take the veil.

**Religious Orders** – The term abbey does not apply to just any Christian community whose members lead a frugal, secluded life. In fact it designates a group of men or women, placed under the authority of an abbot or an abbess, who live according to a rule approved by the Pope. The monks' day is usually divided into chores related to community life, and spiritual and liturgical duties, which are the main purpose of the association.

All abbeys have an abbot or abbess, who generally enjoys the same rank as a bishop. He or she is elected by fellow companions and incarnates the spiritual and temporal leader of the abbey. After the 16C, the Pope gave the king of France the right to appoint abbots and abbesses. These prelates were called commendatory abbots and usually lived in the king's entourage.

Sometimes, to administer new domains or to fulfil the wish of a patron who wanted to receive monks on his land, the abbots would build a priory. This small community was supervised by a prior who was answerable to the abbey. The Cistercians set up many granges, farming colonies run by lay brothers.

**Monastic Rules** – The Benedictine Order – created by St Benedict in the 6C – was undoubtedly the order which flourished the most in France. Its members founded over 1 000 abbeys throughout the country. The Benedictine rule was subsequently reformed, leading to the creation of two additional orders.

The first originated in the late 10C from Cluny in Burgundy, but unfortunately all the Cluniac houses died out during the Revolution. The second – the Cistercian Order – was, and still is, extremely powerful. It was St Bernard of Cîteaux, also a native of Burgundy, who founded the order in the 11C. A firm believer in asceticism, he introduced a number of new rules: elaborate ceremonies and the decoration of churches were condemned; monks could no longer be paid tithes, nor receive or acquire land; strict rules were laid down on diet, rest was limited to seven hours and monks had to sleep in their clothes in a common dormitory.

They shared their time between liturgical worship ( 6-7 hours a day). manual labour, study and contemplation. In the 17C, Abbot de Rancé added further austerities to the Cistercian rule (silence, diet). This new rule was named after La Trappe, the monastery near Perseigne

Halluin

St-Vaast-en-Cambrésis

Maintenay

Villeneuve-d'Ascq

Wormhout

where it originated. It is presently enforced in abbeys of strict observance.

The other two main orders that founded abbeys in France were the Augustinian friars and the Premonstratensian canons, both dating from the 12C.

Other communities include the Carmelite Order, the Order of St Francis (Franciscans and Capuchins), the Order of Preachers and the Society of Jesus (Jesuits). They do not follow monastic rules, nor do they found abbeys. Their activities (missionary work, caring for the sick) bring them into contact with the lay world. They live in convents or houses under the authority of the prior, the Mother Superior etc.

A collegiate church is occupied by a community of canons accountable to their bishop.

**Monastic buildings** – The cloisters are the centre of an abbey; the four galleries allow the nuns or the monks to take their walks under cover. One of the cloister walls adjoins the abbey church, while another gives onto the chapterhouse where monks meet to discuss community problems under the chairmanship of the abbot. The third gallery opens onto the refectory and the fourth onto the calefactory, the only room with heating where the monks study or do manual labour.

The dormitory is generally placed above the chapter-house. It communicates with the church by means of a direct staircase so that the monks could more readily attend early morning and night Mass.

**Lay brothers** – These are believers who cannot or choose not to take holy orders and therefore have a different status. They spend most of their time in the fields and the workshops, and have their own dormitory and refectory. They may not enter the chapter-house or the chancel of the church. Since the Vatican II Council (1962-65) lay brothers have become more and more involved in the life of the community.

Visitors are not allowed to enter the "enclosure" and are lodged in the guesthouse. The poor are housed in the almshouse.

Monasteries also include an infirmary, a noviciate, sometimes a school, and the buildings needed to run the abbey: barns, cellars, winepress, stables and cowsheds.

## Rural Housing in the North

**The Coast, Inland Flanders and Artois** – Whether in Picardy, Artois or Flanders, the same type of houses can be found along the coast: long and low to form a defence against the west winds which often bring rain. They are capped by high-pitched roofs covered with Flemish S-shaped tiles called *pannes*. Their whitewashed walls are cheered by brightly coloured doors and shutters; the bases of the buildings are tarred against the damp.

Behind this apparent uniformity lie very different construction techniques.

In Picardy the walls consist of daubing on wood laths; in certain areas the surface is left plain, as in Ponthieu, but it is more usually whitewashed, giving a spruce look in summer to the flower-bedecked villages along the River Canche and River Authie.

In Flanders the usual building material is more generally brick, sandy coloured in maritime areas and ranging from red to purplish or brown farther inland. The great Lille and Artois regional farms, known as "**censes**", are built around a courtyard with access through a carriage gateway often surmounted by a dovecote.

Some large, partly stone-built farms in the Boulonnais hills are actually old seigniorial homes with a turret or fortifications, giving the impression of a manor house.

**Hainaut, Avesnois, Thiérache and Soissonnais** – In the Hainaut and Avesnois regions houses are massively built, usually consisting of one-storey brick buildings with facings and foundations in regional blue stone. Their slate roofs are reminiscent of the nearby Ardennes region.

Construction in the Thiérache region, the land of clay and wood, consists of daubing and brick with slate roofs. There are many old dovecotes in the region, either over carriage gates or free-standing in courtyards. Villages in close proximity to one another huddle around their fortified churches (👉 *see La THIÉRACHE*).

The houses in the Soissonnais region are similar to those of Île-de-France. Beautiful white freestone is used for walls and crow-stepped gables, contrasting with flat, red roof tiles which take on a patina with the years.

**Windmills** – In the early 19C there were nearly 3 000 windmills in northern France. Today no more than a few dozen still exist, registered, protected and restored by the Association Régionale des Amis des Moulins du Nord-Pas-de-Calais (ARAM).

**Post mills** – Built of wood, these mills are the most common in Flanders. The main body of the structure and the sails turn around a vertical post. On the exterior – the side opposite the sails – a beam known as the "tail" is linked to a wheel which is turned to position the entire mill according to the wind direction. Some fourteen of this type remain in northern France, including those at Boeschepe, Cassel, Hondschoote, Steenvoorde, Villeneuve d'Ascq and St-Maxent.

On a **tower mill** (or smock mill when made of wood) only the roof, to which the sails are attached, turns. This type of mill is more massive and is usually built of brick or stone; the Steenmeulen at Terdeghem near Steenvoorde is the only one still in working order, but there are other fine specimens at Templeuve and Watten (Nord) as well as Achicourt, Beuvry, Guemps (Pas-de-Calais), and Louvencourt (Somme).

**Water mills** – Water mills can also be seen throughout the region, particularly in the Avesnois, Ternois, Thiérache and Valenciennes areas. The shape and size of the wheel, which is the essential part of the mill, depends on the rate of flow of the river and on the specific features of the site. Some of these mills are open to the public: Felleries, Sars-Poteries, Marly (Nord), Esquerdes, Maintenay, Wimille and Wissant (Pas-de-Calais).

# Military Architecture

Of the defensive systems in the north of France, relatively few date from the Middle Ages: the town walls of Boulogne and Laon, and the castles at Coucy, Rambures, Picquigny, Lucheux, Septmonts and Pierrefonds. In contrast, numerous 17C star fortifications along the northeastern border have been preserved, some in their entirety, as at Bergues and Le Quesnoy, others only partially: Avesnes, Maubeuge, Cambrai, Douai, St-Omer and Péronne.

**Before Vauban** – It was under the last of the Valois kings that the military engineers, who had studied Italian examples, adopted a system of curtain walls defended at the corners by bastions. Bastions in the shape of an ace of spades with projections were introduced to protect the men defending the curtain wall. This feature can be seen at Le Quesnoy. Bastions and curtain walls, usually with stone bonding, were crowned with platforms bearing cannon. Raised towers allowed the moats or ditches and surrounding area to be watched. In the 17C Henri IV employed an engineer, **Jean Errard** (1554-1610) nicknamed the Father of French Fortification, who specialised in castrametation. In the north Errard fortified Ham and Montreuil and built the citadels at Calais, Laon, Doullens and Amiens which still stand today. In 1600 he published an authoritative *Treatise on Fortification* which served until Vauban's time.

**The Age of Vauban** – Inspired by his predecessors, **Sébastien le Prestre de Vauban** (1633-1707) established a system of his own characterised by bastions with half-moons surrounded by deep moats. Making the most of the natural obstacles and using local materials (brick in the north), he also tried to give an aesthetic quality to his works by adorning them with carved monumental stone gateways as at Bergues, Lille and Maubeuge.

On the coast and along the border of Flanders and Hainaut, Vauban established a long line of double defences, known as the "**pré carré**". These two close lines of fortresses and citadels were designed to prevent the enemy's passage, and to ensure mutual back-up in case of attack.

The first line consists of 15 sites from Dunkirk and Bergues to Maubeuge, Philippeville and Dinant. The second runs a little way behind and includes 13 towns extending from Gravelines and St-Omer to Avesnes, Marienbourg, Rocroi and Mézières. Some of these strongpoints were Vauban's own creations such as the citadel at Lille, which he himself called the "Queen of Citadels"; others existed already and were remodelled.

For over a century this group of fortifications succeeded in defending the north of France, until the invasions of 1814 and 1815.

During the French campaign in 1940 Le Quesnoy, Lille, Bergues, Dunkirk, Gravelines and Calais all formed solid strongholds protecting the retreat of the Franco-British armies.

**Atlantic Wall** – The concrete bunkers of the Atlantic Wall that stretch along the coastline were erected by the **Todt Organisation**, which from 1940 used prisoners of war for the task. The Nord-Pas-de-Calais region was considered a war zone against England, and in 1944 about 10000 constructions were counted on the French coast. In the deep forests of Eperlecques and Clairmarais enormous concrete installations were built for launching the V1 and V2 rockets on London. The Eperlecques Bunker (&#9758; *see St-Omer*), today designated a historic monument, is one of the most impressive examples of this type of monumental concrete architecture, along with the fort at Mimoyecques (&#9758; *see Guînes*).

# Faience and Porcelain in Île-de-France

## FAIENCE

This term is commonly applied to all ceramics made of porous clay and glazed with waterproof enamel. The enamel was initially transparent but, in the 9C, it became opaque thanks to the discovery in the Middle East of tin glaze. The Arabic influence throughout the Mediterranean Basin led to the development of faience in Moorish Spain and Italy from the 15C onwards. The Spanish island of Majorca gave its name to "Majolica ware", the term describing Italian Renaissance ceramics. The name "faience" may derive from Faenza, the Italian town renowned for its majolica. Faience developed in France in the 16C and 17C with leading pottery centres such as Nevers and Rouen. The latter influenced the early producers of faience in Île-de-France such as Pierre Chicaneau who settled in St-Cloud in 1674. In the 18C, as porcelain became more popular, the number of potteries increased in the region and the first pieces of porcelain were produced. The famous ceramist Jacques Chapelle set up the works in **Sceaux** in 1748 and circumvented the Vincennes-Sèvres monopoly on faience by creating "Japanese-style faience". The Rococo style, vivid colours, and original decorations, many of them in relief, brought success to Sceaux until the end of the 18C. This period was marked by the discovery in England of "fine faience" or white lead-glazed earthenware. Its reasonable cost and elegance, along with the exceptionally liberal conditions laid down in the Treaty of Vergennes (1786), ensured its popularity and its massively imported into France. This know-how was gradually taken over in Île-de-France by the works in **Montereau**, **Creil** and **Choisy-le-Roi**. However, the end of the 19C confirmed the preference for porcelain, and faience went into a decline.

## PORCELAIN

Porcelain was discovered in China in the 12C. It is a thin, white ceramic ware that is slightly translucent. Body and glaze are fired together. In the 16C, the popularity of porcelain from the Far East led to numerous experiments in Europe to try and achieve a product that would rival it. The high level of imports by the French East India Company is indicative of European interest in this mysterious technique. Craftsmen did not know the exact nature of the paste used by the Chinese and they progressed by trial and error, using processes similar to the ones used for faience. A very fine marl used on its own was vitrified by the introduction of a sort of glass called frit. The resulting ceramic was "soft-paste" porcelain that could be scratched by steel.

In the early 18C, the basic ingredient of porcelain, white china clay, was discovered in Saxony. The secrets of the production process were jealously kept in Meissen, near Dresden. In France, it was not until 1769 that the output from a white china clay quarry near St-Yriex in the Limousin area enabled craftsmen to produce "hard-paste" porcelain. Sèvres produced porcelain exclusively from the beginning of the 19C onwards. This new product, in which body and glaze were fired together at a very high temperature (1 400°C/2 500°F), was very strong but more difficult to decorate.

Only five colours are suitable for high-temperature firing – blue, green, yellow, purplish brown and reddish orange. The introduction of low-firing techniques revolutionised the production of faience and porcelain. The enamel was fired in succession at low temperatures, enabling the use of a wide range of fresh, vivid colours.

The porcelain works in **St-Cloud** (1697-1766) were the first to master the techniques required to produce "soft-paste" porcelain. It was famous for its "white" ware and applied gilding that differed greatly from the technique used by Sèvres. Numerous porcelain works opened in quick succession in the 18C, with the backing of princes or the royal family. The works in **Chantilly** (1725-1800), for example, were set up by Cirquaire Cirou with the support of Louis-Henri de Bourbon, Prince de Condé. In **Mennecy**, it was the Duke de Villeroy who provided the necessary patronage in the face of ever-increasing privileges granted to some of the works. The one with the highest level of support was in **Vincennes**. Madame de Pompadour and Louis XV both took a keen interest in the company that set up works in **Sèvres** in 1756. The earliest designs were "natural" flowers and the works gradually specialised in the production of dinner services, statuettes and even veritable pictures in porcelain. Because of the processes used, the decoration and enamel combined perfectly, giving an incomparable blending. In its early days, the Sèvres porcelain works enjoyed exclusive rights to the use of gold on all its products. Even now, unless there is some technical reason against it, all its products must include some gold. "Biscuit-ware", another speciality of these works, is the term used to describe a production method in which the body of the paste is left unglazed so that the gracefulness of the statuettes is not altered.

## Stained Glass

Since the early Middle Ages, church windows have been adorned with coloured glass. Unfortunately, none of these very early works have survived.

During the Gothic period, master glassmakers played an important role in the completion and ornamentation of churches. Thanks to them, both the clergy and the congregation could appreciate the shimmering light that came streaming through the roundels. Stained glass is not purely decorative, however. To the Church it is an invaluable teaching aid, permanently communicating catechism, sacred history and the lives of the saints.

### THE ART OF MAKING STAINED GLASS

Stained-glass windows consist of juxtaposed pieces of coloured glass held together by strips of lead. The window is divided into panels to ensure perfect solidity. When the various coloured pieces have been selected and cut to shape, the glassmaker completes the shading and details of the figures with touches of **grisaille**, a brownish pigment containing silica that is painted on and blends with the glass in the melt. The glass panels are then reassembled and fixed in place in the window. Patches of lichen may develop on stained-glass windows; it starts to attack the lead after 100 years and has been known to break through the glass after 300 to 400 years. However, it is man rather than erosion who is to blame for the disappearance of numerous early stained-glass windows: in the 18C many were dismantled and replaced by plain glass, which afforded a better view of the aisles.

## The development of stained glass

Technical developments in glass-making were prompted by artistic trends but also by the search for greater economy and the wish to produce lighter tones.

**12C** – Stained-glass windows were small, with fairly heavy borders. The ornamentation around the main figures was extremely limited.

**13C** – To ensure perfect cohesion between the panels and the leading, the iron armatures were fastened to the walls.

The clerestory windows presented tall, isolated figures. The lower windows, which could be observed more closely, had medallions depicting scenes from the lives of the saints. This genre is known as historiated stained glass. Panels included architectural features and embellishments. Borders were heavy and the scenes show a marked attempt at realism. Historiated roundels were set in a grisaille framework enhanced by brightly painted rose-windows. The daily lives of craftsmen were evoked in lively anecdotal scenes. The lower windows were generally divided into panels composing geometric motifs (stars, diamonds, clover-leaves).

**14C** – The loss of wealth led to a considerable increase in window space. For reasons of economy, more and more **grisaille** was produced, its starkness softened by delicate shading and graceful foliage motifs. Angels and rosy cherubs adorned the barer parts of the windows. Borders became smaller and lettering made an appearance. In the second half of the 14C glassmakers discovered that silver staining could be used to accentuate a variety of bright colours: yellow on a white background, light green on blue, amber on red etc.

**15C** – The leading was no longer produced using a plane, but instead stretched on a wire-drawing bench: the lead strips were thinner, therefore more flexible and able to hold together larger and thinner panes of glass than previously. Glassmakers worked with a lighter type of glass, and the colours used in the decoration were less vivid. In some churches, two thirds of the window was taken up by grisaille. These panels featured Gothic canopies with high gables and openwork pinnacles. The craftsmanship was of a remarkable quality, and master glassmakers began to sign their own work, introducing original themes.

**16C** – Stained glass drew inspiration from the works of the great painters and contemporary engravings. Glassmakers had become masters at cutting glass from large sheets – using a diamond and no longer a red-hot iron – and they also excelled at painting with enamels. Stained-glass windows developed into large, transparent paintings in which minute attention was given to detail, perspective and design. In some buildings religious themes were replaced by classical scenes taken from Antiquity.

**17C and 18C** – The use of coloured glass decreased. Stained glass was painted and decorated with enamels.

*12C–13C stained glass, Cathédrale de Chartres*

S. Sauvignier/ MICHELIN

*Moret bridge by Alfred Sisley (1893)*

## Landscape Painting

Although many painters were employed in the internal decoration of châteaux and abbeys around Paris, it was not until the 19C that painters began to show an interest in the surrounding landscapes.

Until the 18C, French masters had used landscapes merely as a background to their work, either as a decorative element or to enhance the atmosphere through composition and colour. It was so poorly regarded that often a major artist painting a portrait or other subject would leave the background landscape to be painted by a studio assistant. The two most celebrated French landscape painters were the 17C classicists Nicolas Poussin and Claude Lorrain. Poussin gave his views the heroic qualities of his subject and Lorrain painted scenes of a lost, idyllic Antiquity.

### CAMILLE COROT (1796-1875)

Corot was the pioneer of contemporary landscape painting in France. He lived in Barbizon from 1830 to 1835 and worked outdoors in Fontainebleau Forest and all over Île-de-France, studying the contrasts and soft hues of light in the undergrowth, along shaded paths and on the edge of the plain. He later took up painting lakes in a search for more delicate variations; the ponds at Ville-d'Avray (south of St-Cloud), with their subtle reflections, were his favourites.

### PAINTERS OF THE OISE

The group was founded in 1845 by two of Corot's followers, Charles-François Daubigny and Jules Dupré. Daubigny (1817-78) liked to paint the rippling waters of the River Oise and the greenery and blossoms of the orchards and groves. He led a peaceful life: his work paid well and received universal acclaim. He could often be found working on the Île de Vaux near Auvers, or in a small rowing boat he had converted into a studio. Jules Dupré (1811-89), a close friend of Théodore Rousseau, used darker colours and belonged to the Barbizon School. He seldom left his house in L'Isle-Adam.

In 1865 the lithographer and satirical cartoonist Honoré Daumier (1808-79) moved from the capital to Valmondois in Île-de-France, when he met with serious financial difficulties.

In 1866 **Camille Pissarro** (1830-1903) initially settled in Pontoise for two years. Uninterested in the nearby streams and rivers, he concentrated on meadows, grassy slopes, country villages and street scenes featuring peasant women, which he portrayed in a deliberately poetic manner. His gift for expressing light, his qualities as a teacher and his kindness made him the father figure of the Impressionist movement.

## THE BARBIZON SCHOOL

Its representatives drew inspiration from the landscapes of Fontainebleau Forest and the nearby Bière plain. The founder of the movement was **Théodore Rousseau** (1812-67) who settled in a modest country cottage in 1847 and stayed there until his death. Diaz and Charles Jacque were among his close friends. They remained cheerful and humorous despite the lack of success of their paintings and their consequent penury. It was only towards the end of the Second Empire that their talent was acknowledged. Troyon (1810-65) specialised in rural scenes representing cattle. Barye, the highly respected animal sculptor, also took up landscape painting because of his love of nature. The charms and hardships of country life were portrayed particularly well in the work of **Jean-François Millet** (1814-75), who lived in Barbizon from 1849 until his death.

The artists of this school generally favoured the dark colours of tree bark and undergrowth, and their preferred subjects included dusk, soft lighting and stormy skies. These sombre tones were criticised by their detractors, who claimed they painted with "prune juice".

Around 1865 a new group of artists fell under the spell of these magical woodlands and Pierre-Auguste Renoir, Alfred Sisley and Claude Monet settled in Chailly. Though they did not associate themselves with the Barbizon community, they did accept advice from their elders. Diaz encouraged the young Renoir to work with lighter tones. Here too the seeds of Impressionism were being sown.

## IMPRESSIONISM

The second-generation artists wanted their work to capture the essence of light itself and to reflect the vibrant quality of colour. The term "Impressionist" was actually coined by a sarcastic journalist in 1874, but was adopted by the group as they felt it conveyed the double revolution they had brought about in the field of painting.

**The Impressionist Revolution** – The Impressionist movement revolutionised artistic conventions on two counts: it paid little attention to form and it invented a new technique. Until then, the representation of reality was fundamentally important, and no artist would have dared to neglect the lines and shapes of his subject, whether a portrait, still-life painting or landscape. Painters showed little concern for light and its effects, considered a minor component, and priority was given to subject matter. For the Impressionists, light and the analysis of its effects became the principal subject; all the rest – contours, scenes, people – was simply an excuse to paint light.

Religious and historical works, as well as family portraits and everyday scenes, were no longer interesting in themselves. The Impressionists' favourite subjects were those that played with light: water, snow, fabrics, flesh, flowers, leaves, or fruit.

They wished to capture the infinite depths of the skies, the shimmering of light on water, a dress or a human face. When depicting the undergrowth, they wanted to show how the russet tones glitter in sunlight, how bright colours sparkle.

Such fleeting and indefinite concepts were no longer attainable using traditional techniques. As priority was given to the vibration of light around the edges of objects, the process that applied paint along contours was banished. Traditionally, the layers of paint were applied slowly and acquired their definite colour after the oil had solidified. They were then coated with varnish to produce a transparent effect and to give depth to the colours. Naturally this technique was far too lengthy to capture the ephemeral quality of light. As a consequence, the Impressionists developed a technique more suited to their purpose that involved very little oil and dispensed with varnish. Their art consisted in applying quick, small dabs of colour. The exact shade was conveyed by the juxtaposition of touches of pure colour, the final effect being assessed by the eye of the viewer.

The Impressionists were harshly criticised, even insulted at times, and it was only after a 20-year struggle that their work was fully acknowledged. Île-de-France – with its rivers, lakes, gardens, orchards, showers of rain, mists, elegant ladies and regattas – provided them with countless sources of inspiration.

## THE PAINTERS

The Impressionist School was founded in Honfleur where **Claude Monet** (1840-1926), a painter from Le Havre, was encouraged by the seascape specialist Eugène Boudin to paint landscapes. **Boudin** (1824-98), a friend of Corot's, was also a precursor of Impressionism: his paintings are full of air and light. Following his example, Monet and later the Dutch artist Jongkind worked on the luminosity of the landscapes around the Seine estuary. They were joined by Bazille and **Sisley**, whom they had befriended in Gleyre's studio, and began to paint around Fontainebleau Forest too, though they remained separate from the Barbizon School. Pissarro, Cézanne and Guillaumin, who met at the Swiss Academy, were called "The Famous Three" (*Le Groupe des Trois*).

The painters were strongly supported by **Édouard Manet** (1832-83), one of their elders who was upsetting artistic conventions and scandalising the public with his bold colours and compositions. It was Manet who encouraged the Impressionists to pursue their efforts at painting light. In 1863, following clashes between the artists and the official salons that refused to show these new works, a now-famous independent exhibition of the rejected works (Salon des Refusés) was set up on the orders of Napoleon III. It gave birth to, and led to the naming of, the Impressionist movement.

In 1871 small groups of amateur painters, pupils and friends, including **Paul Cézanne**, joined Pissarro at Pontoise and Docteur Gachet in Auvers. Another group based in Argenteuil and Louveciennes included **Renoir**, Monet, Sisley and Edgar Degas, who had originally studied under Ingres. Monet's innovative technique put him at the head of the movement and inspired both Manet and later Berthe Morisot.

In the 1880s, Renoir moved to Chatou just west of Paris, where he frequented the Maison Tomaise, a restaurant first opened in 1815 and now restored. After 1880 the group broke up, but its members remained faithful to painting with light colours. Sisley moved to Moret, drawn to the River Loing, while Monet settled in Giverny on the banks of the Epte ( see *The Green Guide Normandy*). For practical reasons, Pissarro left the Oise Valley to live in Eragny, near Gisors. **Georges Seurat** (1859-91) remained in Paris but concentrated on the landscapes around the capital and along the Channel coast. His technique amounted to breaking down the subject matter into small dabs of colour, each consisting of a series of dots (*points*). Maximilien Luce (1858-1941) also experimented with this method – known as Pointillism or Divisionism – in the vicinity of Mantes. Cézanne later returned to Aix-en-Provence where, through the use of colour, tone and accentuated outlines, he developed stylised masses that laid the foundations for the Cubist movement.

Renoir travelled to Algeria and Venice, which inspired him to paint some of his finest works. Degas and Toulouse-Lautrec (1846-1901) lived in Paris. They were fascinated by circuses and theatres where swirling dancers and performers were bathed in complex illuminations created by artificial lighting.

## THE DAWN OF THE 20C

The followers of the **Nabis** and **Fauve** movements, which preceded Cubism and the new art forms born in the wake of the First World War, also set up their easels – and sometimes even their studios – in the picturesque outskirts of Paris. On his return from a stay in Pont-Aven, where Paul Gauguin had shown him the magic of composing in flat, bold colours, Paul Sérusier converted his friends from the Académie Julian to the same style and formed the Nabis movement (a Hebrew word meaning prophet). **Maurice Denis** (1870-1943) became the leader of the group, which included Bonnard, Roussel, Vuillard, Maillol, Vallotton and others.

The early Fauves (meaning "wild beasts")

included extremely diverse artists – Matisse, Dufy, Braque, Derain, Vlaminck, Rouault, Marquet. Their paintings of bright, even violent colour created an uproar when they were first shown. The painters, never a coherent group, were influenced by the paintings of **Van Gogh,** who had died in 1890 leaving a collection of brilliant canvases composed of strong, vigorous brushstrokes of pure colour.

The coasts and countryside of the north of France and the region around Paris continue to attract many artists.

# Northern Folklore and Traditions

*For dates of festivals and other events see the Calendar of Events in the Practical information section.*

The people of Picardy and the north of France belong to the "Picardy nation" that used to spread from Beauvais to Lille and from Calais to Laon, extending as far as Tournai and Mons. The common language of this "nation" formed a bond between its inhabitants, who are known for being hard workers with a taste for good food and lively merrymaking. Even now, the slightest excuse is found to celebrate or get together in an *estaminet* (the Walloon word for a café) for a beer or two. Natives of Flanders, Artois, Lille and Picardy all have this same fondness for gatherings which is reflected in their many group activities: carnivals, celebrations, patron saint's days, village fairs and associations (each village has its own band).

## THE DUCASSE OR KERMESSE

The words *ducasse* (from *dédicace*, meaning a Catholic holiday) and *kermesse* ("church fair" in Flemish) now both designate a town or village patron saint's day. This holiday has preserved aspects of its religious origins (Mass and procession) but today also includes stalls, competitions, traditional games, jumble sales etc.

## CARNIVALS

Carnival time is an occasion to dress up in costume and watch parades of floats and giant figures. It traditionally takes place on Shrove Tuesday (*Mardi Gras*) – as in Dunkirk, where it lasts for three days – but in reality carnival parades take place throughout the year in the North.

## FAMOUS GIANTS

Giants originate from various myths, legends and stories, and include:
- **legendary founders**, such as Lydéric and Phinaert in Lille;
- **famous warriors** like the Reuzes from Dunkirk and Cassel, said to originate from Scandinavia;
- **historic figures**, such as Jeanne Maillotte in Lille, the inn-keeper who fought off the "Howlers"; the beautiful Roze in Ardres, who saved the town from dragonnades; the Elector of Bergues, portraying Lamartine; Roland in Hazebrouck, one of Baudouin of Flanders' Crusaders, who distinguished himself at the taking of Constantinople;
- **famous couples**, like Martin and Martine, the two "Jack o' the Clocks" of Cambrai; Colas and Jacqueline, the gardeners of Arras; Arlequin and Colombine in Bruay; Manon and Des Grieux in Hesdin;
- **popular figures**, like Gédéon, the bell-ringer of Bourbourg, who saved the belfry chimes from being stolen; the pedlar Tisje Tasje of Hazebrouck, symbol of the Flemish spirit, with his wife Toria and his daughter Babe Tisje; Pierrot Bimberlot in Le Quesnoy; and Ko Pierre, a drum major, in Aniche;
- **legendary heroes**: Gargantua in Bailleul; Gambrinus, the king of beer, in Armentières; Yan den Houtkapper, the woodcutter who made a pair of wooden boots for Charlemagne, in Steenvoorde; Gayant of Douai, said to have delivered the town from brigands;
- **representatives of trades**, like the vegetable gardener Baptistin in St-Omer; the miner Cafougnette in

Yan den Houtkapper
*Steenvoorde*

Martin and Martine
*Cambrai*

Gayant and his wife
*Douai*

The Sailor's wife
*Grand-Fort Philippe*

Mother Reuze
*Cassel*

R. Corbel/ MICHELIN

Denain; and the fisherman Batisse in Boulogne;

● or simply a **child**, like the famous Binbin in Valenciennes.

Giants are often accompanied by their families – as they do marry and are given large families – and are surrounded by skirted horses, devils, bodyguards and wheels of fortune. Sometimes they have their own hymn, such as the Reuzelieds in Dunkirk and Cassel.

**Materials** – Traditionally the giants' bodies are made from a willow frame on which a painted papier mâché head is placed. Once dressed in their costumes, the giants are then carried by one or more people who make them dance in the procession. The tallest is Gayant in Douai, who is 8.40m/28ft tall. As giants are often now made of heavier materials (steel tubing, cane, plastic), they are frequently pulled along in carts or on wheels rather than carried.

## TOWN CHIMES

Chimes in town belfries, which regularly sound out their melodic tunes, lend a rhythm to life in northern French towns. Since the Middle Ages, when four bells were tapped by hand with a hammer, there have been many additions: a mechanism, a manual keyboard, pedals, all of which have made it possible to increase the number of bells (62 in Douai) and to increase the variety of their sounds.

Carillon concerts are held in Douai, St-Amand-les-Eaux and Maubeuge (east of Valenciennes).

## TRADITIONAL GAMES AND SPORTS

Traditional entertainments remain popular: marionettes, ball games, real tennis, ninepins, darts, lacrosse (an ancestor of golf), archery (which is also a traditional sport of the Valois area), cock-fighting, pigeon-breeding etc. A popular bar game is the *billard Nicolas*, where players squeeze a bulb to blow a marble across a round playing area.

**Archery** – In the Middle Ages archers were already the pride of the counts of Flanders, who would have the archers accompany them on all their expeditions. As soon as individual towns were founded the archers formed associations or guilds. They appeared at all public ceremonies, dressed in brightly coloured costumes, brandishing the great standard of their association.

Today archery is practised in several ways. A method particular to the North is vertical or "perch" shooting, which consists in firing arrows upward to hit dummy birds attached to gratings suspended from a pole. At the top of this pole, about 30m/98ft off the ground, is the hardest target of all, the "**poppinjay**" (*papegaï*). Archers must hit this bird with a long, ball-tipped arrow and the winner is proclaimed "King of the Perch". In winter the sport is practised indoors: arrows are shot horizontally at a slightly tilted grating. Still grouped in brotherhoods, the archers gather every year to honour their patron, St Sebastian.

**Crossbow** – The art of the crossbow, which also dates from the Middle Ages, has its own circle of enthusiasts organised in brotherhoods. Their gatherings, colourful events featuring these curious weapons from another time, are often given evocative names such as the King's Crossbow Shoot.

**Javelin** – This feathered arrow measuring 50-60cm/20-24in is thrown into a tightly tied bundle of straw which serves as a target. It is the same principle as for the game of darts, which is played in many cafés.

**The Game of "Billons"** – A *billon* is a tapering wooden club about 1m/3ft long, weighing about 2-3kg/4-7lb. Two teams throw their *billons* in turn towards a post 9m/30ft away. The aim is to land the narrower end of the club nearest to the post and this may be achieved by dislodging the *billons* of the opposing team.

**Bouchon** – Teams face each other in cafés, and knock down the cork and wood "targets" with their metal paddles. The best players participate in competitions at local festivals.

**Pigeon-Breeding** – Pigeon fanciers (*coulonneux*) raise their birds to fly back to the nest as quickly as possible. For pigeon-racing competitions, which are very popular, the birds are carried in special baskets to a distance of up to 500km/310mi and must then return to their dovecote at record speed. A pigeon can fly over 100km/60mi per hour on average.

**Singing Finch Competitions** – Finches have also become part of the folklore in the north of France, where they participate in trilling contests. Some can trill as many as 800 times an hour.

# THE REGION TODAY

## Economy

### NORD-PAS-DE-CALAIS

The Nord-Pas-de-Calais area has had a high population density since the Middle Ages due to its landscapes, geographical location, temperate climate and agricultural resources. It has always been a major trading area, whose towns acquired wealth from textiles and trade very early on in their history and enjoyed a great deal of autonomy, symbolised by their belfries.

The region also has a coastal belt that includes Boulogne, France's leading fishing port. The Pas-de-Calais, the busiest maritime area in the world, constitutes the French side of the Straits of Dover, the narrowest stretch of water between the continent and Great Britain and the main trade route to Northern Europe.

The industrial infrastructure in the Nord-Pas-de-Calais region is still the second largest in France. Although industrial employment is decreasing overall, the area's small and medium-size enterprises are implementing modernisation strategies aimed at expansion, especially in the export market. In doing so, they are taking full advantage of the proximity of vast European markets and the ease of access afforded by the Nord-Europe high-speed train, the Channel Tunnel and the dense network of roads. This situation has attracted a great deal of foreign investment (it is the leading region in France for international investors, including Coca-Cola, MacCain, IBM, Rank Xerox, 3M etc).

## METALLURGY

The discovery and extraction of coal in the 19C attracted heavy industries (mining, iron and steelmaking) to the area. Mining ceased in 1990, leaving deep scars. Reconversion is currently underway.

The iron and steel industry has been through many crises over the past few decades. Formerly, the main criteria leading to the opening of a works was proximity to raw materials. Since the 1960s, economies have acquired a global dimension which, in addition to a reduction in transport costs, has led to the importing of raw materials with higher mineral contents. The foundries and steelworks then moved toward ports, and numerous traditional industrial sites closed down. Meanwhile, Dunkirk acquired one of the most efficient steelworks in Europe and Gravelines was selected as the site for an ultra-modern aluminium works (Pechiney).

French rail equipment (especially the VAL, the driverless subway first built in Lille in 1983 and now exported worldwide) is produced mainly in the Valenciennes and Douai areas. The automobile industry has plants in Douai (Renault), Maubeuge (MCA, a Renault subsidiary), Douvrain (Française des Mécaniques) and Hourdain (Peugeot-Fiat).

The chemicals industry (9 000 jobs) has developed in the field of organic chemistry using tar and other coal byproducts.

## TEXTILES AND GLASSWARE

The textile and clothing industries, which had been traditional employers since the Middle Ages, have been seriously affected by international competition (especially from Third World countries where wages are low). This has led to a need for huge increases in productivity in a market subject to the uncertainties of fashion. The enormous efforts made to achieve technical and commercial modernisation and train workers are unable to stem the constant flow of lay-offs. Despite these difficulties, the Nord-Pas-de-Calais area still supplies the entire national production of linen (Lys Valley), 95% of worsteds, 22% of woollen fabrics, 38% of thread and 20% of cottons, not to mention the famous Calais and Caudry lace.

The glassware and crystal industries include the PPG works in Boussois, Sicover in Aniche and, best-known of all, the Arques glass and crystal works which has achieved an outstanding increase in turnover and now exports to 160 countries.

## FOOD-PROCESSING

The food-processing industry is now the region's leading sector. Regional produce supplies flour mills and biscuit factories in the Lille area, starch works, breweries etc. Chicory refineries enjoy a worldwide reputation. Beets have engendered a whole industrial sector with crushing mills, sugar and other refineries, and distilleries. All of these buildings have given the plain its own particular landscape near Cambrai and Thumeries. Canning factories produce 30% of the total national production of tinned vegetables and ready prepared meals and 50% of fish (Boulogne).

## NEW SECTORS

The region's geographical situation is ideal for the expansion of several different services (accounting for 62% of total jobs) including logistics, distribution, tourism, business services etc. Mail order is also an important sector of employment. With a steadily increasing work force of 18 000, it provides regional companies with a wide range of business opportunities. Of the 10 largest French companies in this sector, five operate from this area. The top two are La Redoute and Trois Suisses.

## COAL FIELDS

Coal extraction in the coal fields of the Nord-Pas-de-Calais area dates from the 18C. The deposit in this region lies at the western end of a large coal depression which extends into Belgium (Borinage at Mons, Charleroi coal fields) and Germany (Ruhr coal fields).

After 270 years of extraction, all the mines have now closed.

### Closure of the mines

The pits employed up to 220 000 people in 1947, but a decline in the yield from these mines started to appear in the late 1950s. In 1959, when productivity still reached 29 million tonnes, a plan of progressive shutdown was implemented which led to the closure of the last pit on 21 December 1990.

### Industrial Recycling

A range of different industries developed around the working of the mines: production of oval coal briquettes, foundry and special coke; the manufacture of facing bricks; the sale of mine gas; the production of electricity in power stations which run largely on fuel products gathered from the slag heaps; the use of shale, also from slag heaps, for road foundations and as ballast for railway lines. Over 300 either flat or conical slag heaps remain today, about 70 of which are still commercially exploitable. With the prospect of imminent closure, the mining companies formed subsidiaries to take over from them; these make up the industrial group Filianor.

## PICARDY

Despite being a rural area, Picardy nonetheless sustains lively industrial activities. Traditionally the region's industry was textiles, but this has largely been replaced by metal-based industries (agricultural and car equipment, mopeds etc). Chemical products include glass (St-Gobain) and rubber (tyres in Amiens) in particular.

Linked to agriculture, the sugar refineries, food-manufacturing plants and especially the canning factories – based in the Santerre area at Estrée, Rosières and Péronne – all play an important part in the region.

## ÎLE-DE-FRANCE

**A high population density** – Although Île-de-France covers only 2.2% of the surface area of France, over 18% of the French population resides in the province. This huge concentration of over 10 million inhabitants has gradually focused around the natural junctions of the Seine, Marne and Oise river basins. These large, slow rivers separate vast plateaux bearing rich countryside including the Brie and Beauce regions, and the large forests of Fontainebleau, Halatte, Rambouillet, Marly and St-Germain.

Today the development of the Paris region tends to respect these natural tracts and instead focuses urban and economic growth around the new towns: Cergy-Pontoise, Évry, St-Quentin-en-Yvelines, Marne-la-Vallée and Melun-Sénart.

**The foremost industrial region in France** – The Paris region employs over 15% of the national labour force. Alongside the various industries (metallurgy, mechanical engineering, electrical and electronics manufacturing, chemicals, clothing and fashion), highly specialised and ultra-modern businesses have also developed.

The Paris and Île-de-France region is the foremost business market in France.

# Food and Drink

## THE CUISINE OF PICARDY

Soups are the great local specialities, in particular those made from tripe, pumpkin (*potiron*) or frogs (*grenouille*), as well as the famous vegetable soup (*soupe des hortillons*) and the stuffed pancakes in a creamy mushroom sauce (*ficelle Picarde*). The people of Picardy and Artois love their vegetables: beans from Soissons, Laon artichokes, St Valery carrots, peas from the Vermandois and leeks which are used in a delicious pie, the *tarte aux poireaux*.

Starters include duck pâté in a pastry

case (*pâté de canard en croûte*) – prepared in Amiens since the 17C – snipe pâté (*pâté de bécassines*) from Abbeville and Montreuil, eel pâté (*pâté d'anguilles*) from Péronne.

Duck, snipe and plover, eel, carp and pike from the River Somme are often on the menu. Seafood (shrimps known as *sauterelles*, cockles called *hemons*) is common, as well as sole, turbot, fresh herring and cod, often cooked with cream.

## FLEMISH CUISINE

Flemish cooking, washed down with beer and often followed by a glass of gin or a *bistouille* (coffee with a dash of alcohol), contains several typical dishes:

- ✂ rabbit with prunes or raisins and pigeon with cherries;
- ✂ home-made potted meat made from veal, pork fat, rabbit and sometimes chicken (*potjevleesch*);
- ✂ mixed stew of veal, mutton, pork offals, pork fat and vegetables (*hochepot*);
- ✂ braised beef in a beer sauce flavoured with onions and spices (*carbonade*);
- ✂ eel sautéed in butter and stewed in a wine sauce with herbs (*anguille au vert*);
- ✂ small smoked herrings, a speciality of Dunkirk (*craquelots*).

Among the other specialities of the north of France are chitterling sausages (*andouillettes*) from Arras and Cambrai, trout from the River Canche and River Course, and cauliflowers from St-Omer.

## CHEESES OF THE NORTH

Local cheeses, except for the one from **Mont des Cats**, are strong. Most come from the Thiérache and Avesnois regions rich in pastureland. The best is **Maroilles**, created in the 10C by monks from Màroilles Abbey: it has a soft centre with a crust soaked in beer, similar to cheese from Munster. The other cheeses in the region are derived from it: **Vieux Lille**, also called Maroilles Gris (grey Maroilles); **Dauphin** (Maroilles with herbs and spices); **Cœur d'Avesnes** or Rollot; and the delicious **Boulette** d'Avesnes (Maroilles with spices, rolled in paprika). **Flamiche au Maroilles**, a creamy, highly flavoured quiche, is one of the most famous dishes from the northern region of France.

## BRIE

The Brie region in Île-de-France is famous for its soft cow's milk cheeses with surface mould. There are two types, Brie and double or triple-cream cheeses (**Lucullus, Grand Vatel, Gratte-Paille** etc) often made from the fat left over from the production of Brie, a legendary cheese that already enjoyed a reputation for excellence in the 13C. Brie was as popular with the commoners of Paris as with royalty, and it was the outright winner of a competition organised during the Congress of Vienna in 1815 bringing together all the best cheeses from throughout Europe. There are certain characteristics common to all Brie cheeses. They are made from partially skimmed raw cow's milk, the rind is white with reddish marks, the cheese is soft in texture and pale yellow in colour, the fat content is approximately 45%, and the maturing period does not exceed seven weeks. Setting these features aside, several varieties of Brie have developed and they differ depending on the area of production. The best-known are Brie de Meaux and Brie de Melun.

## CAKES

The local pancakes (*crêpes*), waffles and sweet breads (*tartines and brioches*) can make entire meals in themselves; the brioches with bulging middles are called *coquilles*.

Tarts, such as the delicious *tartes au sucre* sprinkled with brown sugar, are often served for dessert. Sweets are accompanied by the light, chicory coffee which people from the region drink at any time of the day.

## BEER

Gambrinus, the king of beer, is greatly revered in the north of France, as is St Arnould, the patron saint of brewers.

Beer (*la bière*) was already known in Antiquity. In Gaul it was called *cervoise*. During the Middle Ages brewing beer was a privilege of the monasteries. It spread enormously in Flanders under John the Fearless, Duke of Burgundy and Count of Flanders, who developed the use of hops.

### The Brewing Process

Beer is obtained by the mashing and fermentation of a mixture of water and malt, flavoured with hops. Barley grains are soaked in water (malting) until they germinate. The malted barley, dried and roasted in a kiln, becomes **malt**. This is powdered and then mixed with pure water and hops and cooked, according to each manufacturer's secret procedure. This operation, called brewing, transforms the starch in the malt into sugar and makes it possible to obtain the **wort**. With the addition of a raising agent, the wort begins to ferment.

Beer brewing was formerly undertaken simply by a brewer, with his boy handling a sort of pointed shovel (*fourquet*), but is now a large and sophisticated industry.

Much French beer and lager (paler, "aged" beer containing more bubbles and often less alcohol) is produced in the Pas-de-Calais region, which is rich in water, barley and hops. The hops grown in Flanders have a particularly strong flavour. The largest breweries are in the areas around Lille-Roubaix and Armentières, and the Scarpe and Escaut (Scheldt) river valleys. Today, there are only 17 left, although many small breweries are now operating locally.

Different beers have their own characteristics: the slightly bitter lager (*bière blonde*) of the north; the relatively sweet and fruity dark beer (*bière brune*) or the richly flavoured, amber-red beer (*bière rousse*).

## GIN

Gin is still produced in Houlle, Wambrechies and Loos. Another drink produced in Loos is an aperitif called *chuchemourette*, consisting of *crème de cassis* and gin.

*The Hall of Mirrors, Château Versailles*

RMN

# ABBEVILLE

POPULATION 24 567

MICHELIN LOCAL MAP 301: E-7

Abbeville (pronounced Abb'ville) is the capital of the Ponthieu region and stands on the edge of the River Somme, about 20km/12mi from the sea. In the 19C artists flocked to its medieval streets overlooked by the towers of the Collégiale St-Vulfran; since the Second World War, the city has taken on a more modern aspect.

**Information:** Office du tourisme d'Abbeville, 1 pl. Amiral-Courbet, 81000. ☎03 22 24 27 92. www.ot-abbeville.fr.

## A Bit of History

### Medieval Conflicts

The town derives its name from the Latin *Abbatis Villa* meaning Abbot's Villa, and originally developed around the country house of the abbot of St-Riquier. From the 13C to the 15C, Abbeville became the property of the English, the Burgundians and the French, depending on the outcome of the struggles for possession of the Somme Valley. Abbeville finally became French under Louis XI in the 15C.

## Sights *2hr*

### Collégiale St-Vulfran

St Wulfram's Collegiate Church, which looks like a cathedral, was begun in 1488; the west front was built first, but construction of the nave was interrupted in 1539 owing to lack of money, and it was not until the 17C that the chancel was finished in neo-Gothic style.

**Central Doorway** – The door has preserved its Renaissance panels, given by

Jehan Mourette, the head of a brotherhood of poets (Confrérie du Puy Notre-Dame d'Abbeville). In the centre, the figures of the Evangelists are framed by St Peter (*left*) and St Paul (*right*). Scenes from the life of the Virgin Mary can be seen above a frieze of horsemen.

**Interior** – Note the abstract stained-glass windows in the chancel which were designed by William Epstein.

### Musée Boucher-de-Perthes★

24, rue Gontier Patin, 80100 Abbeville. ⏱*Open daily except Tue, 2-6pm.* ⏱*Closed 1 Jan, 1 May, 14 Jul, 1 Nov, 25 Dec.* ☎ *03 22 24 08 49.* ⊚*1€.*

Facing the square, which is graced by the statue of the local sailor, Admiral Courbet (1827-85), stand the museum buildings: a 13C belfry, a small 15C edifice (formerly the Mint) and a new building to the rear. The museum houses medieval sculpture, ceramics and tapestries, paintings from the 16C to the 18C and 17C furniture from Picardy. Note, in particular, a work by Camille Claudel and a superb silver Virgin and Child (1568) as well as the Boucher de Perthes prehistoric collections and a mammoth tooth discovered on Ault beach.

### Église du St-Sépulcre

⏱*May to Sep. Daily except Mon and Tue 2-6pm, 1-5pm.* ☎ *03 22 24 10 41.*

Originally built in the 15C, and reconstruct-ed in the 19C in the Flamboyant Gothic style. Little remains of the 15C building. The contemporary **stained-glass windows★★** by Alfred Manessier represent *The Passion* and the *Resurrection of Christ.*

*S. Sauvignier/ MICHELIN*

*Collégiale St. Vulfran*

# Excursions

## Château de Bagatelle★

*133 rte de Paris.* Closed 1 Jan, 1 May, *14 Jul, 1 Nov, 25 Dec.* ☎ *03 22 24 02 69.* *www.chateaudebagatelle.com.*
Abraham Van Robais had Bagatelle built c1740 as his villa in the country, where he could relax and receive his business clients. It originally consisted of only the ground floor to which was added, 15 years later, an attic storey with bull's-eye windows to provide living accommodation; the mansard roof dates from about 1790. In spite of subsequent additions this is a charming residence, characterised by a harmony and unity of style.
**Interior** – Guided tours: mid-Jul to end Aug (45min). Open daily except Tue 2-6pm. 8€. Reception rooms: Rococo decoration, 18C furniture, delicately painted panelling. A graceful double staircase with a wrought-iron balustrade was ingeniously adapted to fit the hall, to give access to the low-ceilinged first-floor rooms.
**Grounds** – mid-Jul to end Aug, daily except Tue 2-6pm; Sep to mid-Oct and mid-May to mid-Jul, daily except Tue, Sat and Sun, 2-4.30pm. 4€. The formal French garden is adorned with statues and the botanical park contains a large and varied collection of plants, including some rare species.

## Monts de Caubert

*5km/3mi west of Abbeville.* At the first sharp bend before a road junction, turn left onto the narrow road running along the crest of the rise. Some 1.5km/1mi farther on is a wayside cross from which there is a good **view** over the Somme Valley, Abbeville and the plains of Ponthieu beyond.

## The Vimeu Region

The Vimeu region of Picardy, between the River Somme and River Bresle gets its name from a tributary of the latter. It seems like an isolated plateau, grooved by green valleys with hedged meadows full of apple trees. This farming country also contains many châteaux and villages hidden among the trees. Making locks and wrought-ironwork have been traditional occupations of the area since the 17C.

## Musée des Industries du Vimeu

*Place Gilson, 80130 Friville-Escarbotin.* *20km/12.4mi west of Abbeville.* Open Mar to Oct, Sun, Tue, Wed, 2.30-4.30pm. 3.50€. ☎ *03 22 26 42 37.* The museum traces the history of small-scale metalwork: locksmithery, taps and fittings, ironmongery, ship chandlery etc. The ground floor displays 19C machines (pedal-worked drill) and reconstructed workshops. Among the collections of locks, bars and bolts, note the display of 135 padlocks, the smallest of which is made from a gold coin.

# ALBERT

POPULATION 10 065
MICHELIN LOCAL MAP 301: I-8

The town, which was originally called Ancre for the river which flows through it, was the seat of a marquess; the title was acquired in 1610 by Marie de Medici's favourite, Concino Concini. Following his tragic death in 1617, which heralded the queen mother's disgrace, Louis XIII offered Ancre to Charles d'Albert, Duc de Luynes, who gave it his name. Albert was almost totally destroyed during the Battle of the Somme in 1916 and the Battle of Picardy in 1918 (*see* Introduction: History). Today it is a well-planned, modern town boasting 250 Art Deco façades. Méaulte, a large suburb to the south, is the home of aircraft factories founded by Potez but now run by Aérospatiale.

**Information:** Office du tourisme d'Albert, 9 r. Gambetta, 80300 ☎ 03 22 75 16 42. www.ville-albert.fr.

*Château de Bagatelle*

## Sights

### Musée des Abris 'Somme 1916'

*Open Jun-Sep: 9.30am-6pm: Feb-May and early Oct to mid-Dec: 9am-noon, 2-6pm. Closed 1 Jan and 25 Dec. 4€ 03 22 75 16 17. www.musee-somme-1916.org.*

An underground air-raid shelter (1939) houses a moving exhibition of wartime memorabilia and conditions illustrating the daily life of soldiers during the First World War.

## Battlefields

*Round trip of 34km/21mi – 1hr.*

A circuit east and north of Albert commemorates the British and South African soldiers under Douglas Haig who fell during the Allied attack in the summer of 1916 (Battle of the Somme). For detailed information about the battle, visit the Historial de la Grande Guerre in Péronne (see PÉRONNE).

### Mémorial de Thiepval

*Open all year: May-Oct 10am-6pm. Rest of year 9am-5pm. 03 22 75 16 42.*

The Germans turned the village into an underground fortress which was besieged by the British during the summer of 1916. The brick-built triumphal arch overlooking the Ancre Valley bears the names of 73 367 British soldiers. Thiepval is the largest and one of the most emotive memorials to the missing from any war in which British soldiers have died.

### Parc-mémorial de Beaumont-Hamel★

*Guided tours in French and English.* This wind-swept plateau was the site of a battle fought by the Newfoundland Division in July 1916 on the opening day of the Battle of the Somme. The monument, topped by a Newfoundland Caribou, includes a viewing platform: **view** of the battlefield.

### Mémorial de Pozières

The village, barring the way to Thiepval hill, was taken by Australian and Canadian forces. The names of 14 690 men who went missing in action are engraved on the Australian memorial. In commemoration, after the war the Australians named a village in Queensland, Pozières.

### Mémorial de Longueval

*Open Apr to mid-Oct, 10am-5.45pm; mid-Oct to Mar, 10am-3.45pm. Closed Mon and public holidays from mid-Nov to end Jan. 03 22 85 02 17.*

In July 1916, the Germans dropped shells containing tear gas on the South African positions. It cost the Allies 90 000 lives during five days of fierce fighting to regain what was subsequently named "Devil's Wood." The memorial and the museum, housed in a small-scale replica of Capetown Castle, commemorate the many South African soldiers who lost their lives during both World Wars.

### Rancourt

Three war cemeteries (French, British and German) are located here. The memorial to French soldiers killed during the Battle of the Somme bears 8 566 names.

# AMIENS★★

**POPULATION 136 000**
**MICHELIN LOCAL MAP 301: G-8**

Amiens, the capital of Picardy, is an important communications centre and the setting for a beautiful cathedral. Devastated during the two World Wars, it is now essentially a modern town, sheltering the precious remains of its past in picturesque areas. The delicious gastronomic specialities include chocolate wafers, macaroons, pancakes filled with ham and mushrooms with a white sauce *(ficelles picardes)* and the famous duck pâtés in pastry *(pâtés de canard en croûte)*.

▪ **Information:** Office de tourisme d'Amiens – 6 bis r. Dusevel, 80000 – ☎ 03 22 71 60 50 – www.amiens.com/tourisme.

▸ **Orient Yourself:** The majority of the city's attractions sit on the south bank of the Somme River, some clustered around the cathedral, others a little farther west and southwest. Consider taking a 2hr art and history tour for an overview of the city *(see Address Book)*. Good shopping areas are rue du Hocquet and place du Don. Cross the River Somme to explore the narrow streets of Quartier St-Leu.

▪ **Parking:** There are several parking areas near the cathedral and on the perimeter roads enclosing the cathedral district.

▪ **Don't Miss:** The cathedral, of course, but also the marvellous Picardy Museum. If you love gardens, make a point of visiting the Hortillonnages.

▪ **Organizing Your Time:** Allow at least 1hr-2hr to see the cathedral. The walking tour at a leisurely pace requires 1hr, as does the Picardy Museum.

▪ **Especially for Kids:** There's the Marionnette Theatre featuring puppet shows for children *( see Address Book)*. Also an aquarium and insectarium near the Hortillonnages will delight kids of all ages.

▪ **Also See:** Corbie, le parc Samara, and la cité souterraine de Naours.

## A Bit of History

In Gallo-Roman times Amiens was the capital of a Belgian tribe, the Ambiani; in the 4C the town was converted to Christianity by Firmin and his companions. In 1218 the Romanesque church on the site was destroyed by fire. Bishop Evrard de Fouilloy and the people of Amiens immediately decided to build a replacement, something exceptional, worthy of sheltering the "head of John the Baptist," the precious relic, albeit a fragment, brought back in 1206 from the fourth crusade by Wallon de Sarton, canon of Picquigny.

### Steely Assaults

The valleys of the River Somme and River Aisne were major obstacles to invaders from the north, and being the bridgehead, Amiens suffered many attacks. In 1918, during the Battle of Picardy, the town was attacked by Ludendorff and bombarded with 12 000 shells. It was set ablaze in 1940 during the Battle of the Somme. In 1944 its prison was the target of a dangerous aerial attack aimed at helping the im-prisoned Resistance members to escape (Operation Jericho).

### Local Heroes

Amiens was the birthplace of several writers including **Choderlos de Laclos** (1741-1803), famous for *Les Liaisons Dangereuses*, Paul Bourget (1852-1925) and **Roland Dorgelès** (1885-1973), author of *Les Croix de Bois*, as well as the physician **Édouard Branly** (1844-1940) who invented the coherer, a device for detecting radio waves. **Jules Verne** (1828-1905) lived in Amiens from 1871 until his death.

## Address Book

*⌚For coin ranges, see the Legend on the cover flap.*

### TOURS

Guided tours *(90min-2hr)* highlighting the art and history of Amiens offered mid-Jun to mid-Sep. daily except Sun at 2.30pm; rest of the year Sat. at 2.30pm. 5.50 €. Contact the Tourism Office *(above)*.

### WHERE TO STAY

⌂ **Hôtel Alsace-Lorraine** – *18 rue de la Morlière* – ☎ *03 22 91 35 71* – *www. alsace-lorraine.fr.st* – *14 rms* – ⌂ *7€*. You won't regret having chosen this comfortable little hotel hidden behind an imposing carriage entrance just a five-minute walk from the train station. The rooms, brightened with colourful fabrics, give onto the charming inner courtyard, guaranteeing a good night's sleep.

⌂⌂ **Hôtel Carlton** – *42 rue de Noyon* – ☎ *03 22 97 72 22* – *www.lecarlton.fr* – *23 rms:* ⌂ *8.50€* – *restaurant* ⌂⌂. Go beyond the 19C facade of this attractive building and discover the modern, agreeably plush interior. Every room features waxed furniture and murals. Their restaurant, Le Bistrot, is more simply decorated; grilled meat is the mainstay here.

⌂⌂ **Mme Lemaitre (Bed and Breakfast)** – *26 r. Principale, 80480 Creuse* – *14km/8.5mi SW of Amiens* – ☎ *03 22 38 91 50* – *closed winter* – ⌷ – *6 rms*. A gorgeous late-18C residence nestled in a spacious garden featuring ancient trees. White walls and furniture with a regional slant characterize the comfortable bedrooms. Downstairs, there's a snug sitting room warmed by a handsome period fireplace.

⌂⌂ **Le Petit Chateau (Bed and Breakfast)** – *2 rue Grimaux, 80480 Dury – 6km/3.6mi S of Amiens via N 1 dir. Beauvais* – ☎ *03 22 95 29 52* – *http:// perso.orange.fr/am.saguez* – ⌷ – *4 rms*. Offering all the advantages of the countryside, yet only 10 minutes from downtown Amiens, a massive 19C residence whose comfortable guest rooms are housed in an outbuilding. Collecting old automobiles is the owner's hobby, and he will be delighted to show you his treasures.

### WHERE TO EAT

⌂⌂ **Le Bouchon** – *10, rue Alexandre Fatton* – ☎ *03 22 91 14 32* – *www.lebouchon.fr* – *closed Sun evening, Sep to Jun*. A Parisian-style bistro near the railway station specialising in typically Lyonnais dishes and traditional cuisine of the region; a relaxed, "no fuss" atmosphere.

⌂ **Ale factory (Les Artisans Brasseurs)** *18 port d'Amont, quartier St Leu* – ☎ *03 22 72 69 85* – *closed mid-Jul to mid-Aug, Sat lunch and Sun*. A brick building set on the banks of the Somme. Alsatian specialities (flammeküches and sauer-krauts) are served, in addition to more traditional dishes, all to be washed down with one of the beers brewed on the site. The décor is a blend of wood and metal.

⌂ **Le T'chiot Zinc** – *18 rue de Noyon* – ☎ *03 22 91 43 79* – *closed Mon lunch and Sun*. Housed in a former bakery built in 1643, this highly charming eatery has a typical bistro decor with alcoves and photos of Old Amiens. The menu proposes solid, traditional cuisine, featuring suckling pig and the mouthwatering caqhuse: pork cooked with onions, white wine and crème fraîche.

⌂⌂ **Les Marissons** – *Pont de la Dodane* – ☎ *03 22 92 96 66* – *les-marissons.fr* – *Sat lunch, Sun and Wed lunch*. Search no further! The place to be in the Saint-Leu quarter is right here, in this old maritime workshop transformed into a restaurant. The flowery mini-garden becomes a terrace in summer, while in winter diners sit under the sloping wooden frame in a pleasant decor of handsome beams and round tables.

⌂ **L'Os à Mœlle** – *12 r. Flatters* – ☎ *03 22 92 75 46* – *closed 2 to 21 Jan, Sun evening, Mon and Tue*. In this small restaurant in the centre of the village, be prepared to sample bone marrow! Behind its modest façade and with a décor in the style of a bistrot *spécialités du terroir* are served.

⌂ **Le Petit Poucet** – *52 rue des Trois-Cail-loux* – ☎ *03 22 91 42 32 daily except Mon, 8am-7.30pm (Sun, 7pm)*. This attractive pink-faced establishment is very popular with the people of Amiens who come here for a slice of quiche, a ficelle picarde (baked crepes, stuffed and rolled), or a mixed salad for lunch, a delectable chocolate for tea, or a box of divine pastries to enjoy at home.

## SHOWTIME AND ART

**"Amiens, the cathedral in living colour"** – The artist Skertzò uses light effects to highlight the polychromatic entranceways of the Amiens cathedral's western facade. The presentation is simply fantastic! It is held from mid-June to September at dusk, and from mid-December to early January at 8pm. Commentary in French and then English.

**Comédie de Picardie** – *62 rue des Jacobins – ☎ 03 22 22 20 20 – www. comdepic.com – Mon-Fri 1pm-7pm, Sat 1pm-6pm. Closed Aug, public holidays, Sun except performance days. 11 to 46€.* This venerable old manor, entirely restored, houses a very pretty 400-seat theatre. The region's creative and dramatic hub, it produces 15 different shows for a total of 250 performances per season.

**La Lune des Pirates** – *17 quai Bélu – ☎ 03 22 97 88 01 – www.lalune.net. Closed mid-Jul to end Aug (tickets at Fnac).* Formerly a very popular café, the Pirates' Moon has become a showcase for contemporary music. It also holds exhibitions and cultural happenings.

**Théâtre de Marionnettes** – *Chés Cabotans d'Amiens –* [🚸] *31 rue Édouard-David, quartier St-Leu – ☎ 03 22 22 30 90 – www.ches-cabotans-damiens.com. Exhibitions: Apr-Aug from Tue to Sun 10am-noon, 2pm-6pm except Sun morning; mid-Oct to Mar from Tue to Sun 2pm-6pm. Performances: mid-Jul-mid-Aug from Tue to Sun: 6pm; 15 Oct to end Mar: Sun (except public holidays and Christmas week) 3pm; additional shows during school holiday weekdays at 2.30pm – 10 € (children: 5 €).* An actor performs, a marionette becomes alive. The puppets all have their own history and language (French or Picard) plus remarkably ex-pressive faces that can be admired in the ground-floor exhibition. This fascinating show for all audiences takes place in a veritable miniature theatre with a beautifully designed set.

**Laurent-Devime** – *34 r. du Chêne – 80260 St-Gratien – ☎03 22 40 16 71.* This storyteller offers entertainment in a variety of forms: Picard evenings, storytelling walks in the country or city, marionettes and shows inspired by *kamishibaï*, Japanese image-based theatre. Traditional Picardy games workshop.

## SHOPPING

**Atelier de Jean-Pierre Facquier** – *67 rue du Don – ☎ 03 22 92 49 52 or 03 22 39 21 74 – Tue-Fri 2pm-6.30pm, Sat 10am-noon, 2pm-6pm – closed 1 week in summer.* Transforming them into traditional and invented wooden figurines, Monsieur Facquier carves life into pieces of wood before your eyes. Madame Facquier sews their clothes using fabric chosen with care. Each unique character is a genuine work of art.

**Caveau St-Loupien – La Galerie Gourmande** – *19 rue de la République-Galerie des Jacobins – ☎ 03 22 72 40 40 – www.caveau-saint-loupien.com – Mon 2.30pm-7.30pm, Tue-Sat 10.30am-7.30pm, public holidays (mornings).* A specialist in regional gastronomy: here you will find a vast selection of local mustards, wine jellies, red fruit preserves, terrines and regional dishes in addition to just about every sort of beer and ale brewed in Picardy, locally produced lemonades and syrups (rose, violet, lavender...), Picard aperitifs and, naturally, genuine Amiens macaroons.

**Jean Trogneux** – *☎ 03 22 71 17 17 – www.trogneux.fr. daily except Sun, 9.30am-12.15pm, 1.45-7pm – closed 25 Dec and 1 Jan.* The city's speciality since the 16C, the Amiens macaroon, with its blend of almonds and honey, is ever popular. The Trogneux family, confectioners and chocolatiers for five generations, sell more than two million of them every year! The shop also carries a nice selection of local products.

**Marché sur l'eau** – The local market gardeners, who grow their produce in canal-bordered, floating wetlands (*hortillonnages*), come to market Saturday mornings, Place Parmentier. Once a year, on 3rd Sunday in June, market is held as in years gone by. The gardeners, wearing traditional attire, come via flatbottomed boats and unload their produce onto the docks.

# Cathédrale Notre-Dame★★★

*Open Jul–Aug 11am, 2.30–5.15pm; Apr–Jun & Sep, 3pm & 4.30pm (Sat, Sun and public holidays 2.30–5.15pm; rest of year, 5.45pm. Closed Mar, 1 Jan, 1 May, 4th Sun of Sep, 25 Dec. 3€ (child, free).*

Amiens Cathedral is the largest Gothic building in France (145m/475ft long with vaults 42.5m/139ft high).

The plans of the church were entrusted to **Robert de Luzarches** who was succeeded by Thomas de Cormont and then his son Renaud. The cathedral was begun in 1220 and the speed with which it was built explains the remarkable unity of style, though the towers remained uncrowned until the beginning of the 15C. The cathedral was later restored by Viollet-le-Duc. It miraculously escaped damage in 1940.

## Exterior

The west front (*see illustration in the Introduction*) of Amiens Cathedral has a horizontal emphasis, consisting of several bands: the three doorways; the two galleries including the **Kings' Gallery** with its enormous figures; the great Flamboyant rose-window (renewed in the 16C) framed by twinned open bays; and the small **bell-ringers' gallery** topped by light arcading between the towers. Elegant sculptures – some damaged by pollution – further enhance the ensemble. The **central doorway** is framed by the Wise and Foolish Virgins who, together with the Apostles and the Prophets on the piers, escort from a respectable distance the famous **Beau Dieu**, a noble and serene Christ standing on lavender and basil. He is the focal point of this enormous carved Bible. The tympanum portrays the Last Judgment presided over by a more archaic and severe God.

The **left doorway** is dedicated to **St Firmin** the evangelist of Amiens and to the Picardy region. The quatrefoils on the base enclose representations of a **Calendar** symbolised by the signs of the Zodiac and the Labours of the Months. The **right doorway** is dedicated to the **Mother of God**.

▶ *Walk along impasse Voron.*

On the north side, note the statue of Charles V (**4**) on the 14th buttress supporting the tower.

Go round the cathedral to the right, passing a giant St Christopher (**1**), an Annunciation (**2**), and, between the 3rd and 4th chapels, a pair of woad merchants with their sack (**3**).

▶ *Follow rue Cormont to place St-Michel.*

From here there is a fine view of the **east end** with its pierced flying buttresses, and the soaring lead-covered chestnut **spire** (112.70m/370ft high).

S. Sauvignier/ MICHELIN

*"Beau Dieu" – central doorway of the cathedral*

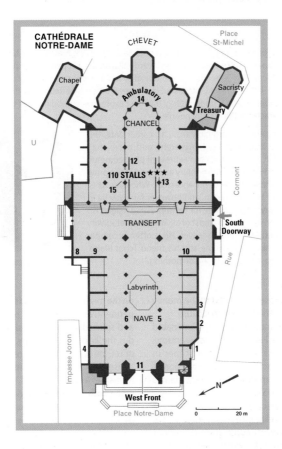

CATHÉDRALE NOTRE-DAME

CHEVET

Place St-Michel

Chapel

Ambulatory
14

Sacristy

Treasury

CHANCEL

U

12

110 STALLS ★★★

15

13

TRANSEPT

South Doorway

Cormont

8  9

10

Rue

Labyrinth

Impasse Joron

3

6  NAVE  5

2

4

1

11

N

West Front

Place Notre-Dame

0        20 m

▶ *Retrace your steps and enter the cathedral through the south doorway.*

The **south doorway**, known as the Golden Virgin Doorway because of the statue which used to adorn the pier, is dedicated to St Honoré who was bishop of Amiens. Visitors can mount the 307 steps to the top of the **North tower** (via the South tower and Rose gallery), for a close up view of the spires and statuary atop the cathedral, and a wide-angle view of the city below.

### Interior

🕐 *Apr-Sep 6.30am-6.30pm; Oct-Mar, 6.30am-5.30pm.* ☎ *03 22 71 60 50.*
The sheer size and the amount of light inside the cathedral are striking. The **nave** is the highest in France, reaching 42.50m/139ft. Its elevation consists of large and exceptionally high arcades surmounted by a band of finely detailed

foliage, a blind triforium and a clerestory; 13C recumbent **bronze effigies**★ of the cathedral's founding bishops lie in the third bay: Evrard de Fouilloy (5) and Geoffroy d'Eu (6); the latter faces towards St-Saulve Chapel which contains a figure of Christ in a long gold robe.
On the flagging, renewed in the 19C, the meandering lines of the labyrinth have been restored. In the past the faithful would follow the lines on their knees, as a Way of the Cross. At the centre, the names of those responsible for the cathedral are inscribed: Robert de Luzarches and Thomas and Renaud de Cormont (the original stone is in the Picardy Museum).
The **north transept** is adorned with a 14C rose-window with star-shaped central tracery. The font (8), to the left of the door, dates from 1180 and was originally used to wash the dead. On the west wall a painted sculpture in four

## Puppets

Famous for its string puppets dating back to about 1785, Amiens now boasts its own puppet theatre. Known in the Picardy dialect as *cabotans*, the puppets are about 50cm/19in in height, carved out of wood and operated from above. The king of St-Leu (a district that existed in medieval times) is **Lafleur**. He is the leader of the *cabotans* and is undoubtedly the most expressive embodiment of the spirit and character of the Picardy people.

Since the 19C, but arguably from an earlier date, this mythical, truculent, bold, irreverent, and brave character with a fiery temper has expressed plain common sense and described the nobility and pride of the province in the language of his ancestors. Wherever he is, wherever he comes from, and however far away he is, he is always recognisable for his impressive height, his characteristic gait, and most of all, his 18C valet's livery of beautiful red Amiens velvet. He is often accompanied by his wife Sandrine and his friend Tchot Blaise. His motto is "Drink, eat and do nothing."

*Lafleur and Sandrine*

Office Culturel, Amienstv

parts represents Christ and the money lenders in the Temple **(9)** (1520).

The south transept, which is illuminated through a Flamboyant rose-window, bears on its west wall four scenes in relief **(10)** portraying the conversion of the magician Hermogene by St James the Great (1511).

The perspective back down the nave reveals its elegance and the boldness of the organ loft supporting the **great organ (11)** (1442) with its delicate golden arabesques, crowned by the majestic rose-window at the west end.

The chancel is enclosed within a beautiful 18C choir screen, wrought by Jean Veyren. The 110 Flamboyant **stalls★★★ (12)** were created between 1508 and 1519 by the master cabinet-makers Arnould Boulin, Antoine Avernier and Alexandre Huet. They are arranged in two rows and surmounted by wooden tracery, and are presided over by two master-stalls destined for the king and the dean of the chapter. Over 4 000 figures

on the misericords, stall ends, canopies, pendentives and brackets realistically and spiritedly evoke Genesis and Exodus, the life of the Virgin Mary, and scenes of 16C life in Amiens. One worker carved himself holding his mallet and inscribed his name: Jehan Turpin.

In the **ambulatory** on the right, on the choir screen above two recumbent effigies, eight remarkable carved and coloured stone groups (1488) under delicate Gothic canopies evoke the life of **St Firmin (13)**, his martyrdom and his exhumation by St Saul three centuries later. The highly expressive figures are wearing 15C dress: the nobles in sumptuous attire, the humble poorly dressed and the executioner in curious breeches. Behind the main altar, facing the central chapel containing a 19C gilded statue of the Virgin Mary, are the tomb of Cardinal de la Grange (1402) and the much larger tomb of Canon Guislan Lucas, famous for its **Weeping Angel (14)** carved by Nicolas Blasset .(1628). In

## Confrérie du Puy Notre-Dame

This literary and religious society devoted to the glorification of the Virgin Mary was founded in Amiens in 1389. The master of the brotherhood was elected on an annual basis and used to recite his "royal hymn" from a podium or *puy*. The refrain or *palinode* was unusual in that it was a play on words based on the name of the donor who from 1450 onwards was required to offer to the cathedral a votive painting referring to the theme of the *palinode*.

the apsidal chapels vestiges of the 13C stained-glass windows remain.

The choir screen north of the chancel bears scenes from the **life of St John** (15) (1531) *(read from right to left)*.

# Walking Tour

▶ *Start near the cathedral, and cross the river via the Dodane bridge.*

## Quartier St-Leu★

Several arms of the Somme flow through this district, which has undergone widescale renovation in an effort to preserve its special charm. Craft and antique shops, cafés and restaurants now occupy the spaces where tanners, millers, weavers and dyers once worked. A flea market takes place in place Parmentier on the second Sunday of every month.

From the bridge known as **Pont de la Dodane**, there is a fine **view** of the cathedral. A stroll through the streets (rue Bélu, rue des Majots, rue Motte, rue d'Engoulvent) lined with small colourful half-timbered houses gives a feel of the area's discreet charm.

Église St-Leu, a 15C hall-church with three aisles, has a 16C Flamboyant Gothic bell-tower.

Kids The **Théâtre des Marionnettes** is nearby (☞ *see Address Book*).

▶ *Return to place Notre-Dame and walk along the south side of the cathedral which is best viewed from the pedestrian street leading to place Aguesseau.*

On the corner of the law courts, a low-relief sculpture by J Samson (1830) depicts the story of St Martin's Cloak.

## Maison du Sagittaire et Logis du Roi

The King's Lodging (1565), featuring a pointed-arch door decorated with a Virgin with a Rose, is the seat of the **Rosati** of Picardy, a society with the motto "Tradition, Art and Literature." The adjacent building is the **Sagittarius House** (1593) with its Renaissance front, which owes its name to the sign of

the Zodiac embellishing its two arches.

## Old Theatre

The Louis XVI façade was the work of Rousseau in 1780; the building now houses a bank. Three large windows are framed by elegant low-relief sculptures depicting garlands, medallions, muses and lyres.

## Bailliage

The restored front is all that remains of the bailiff's residence built under François I in 1541, presenting mullioned windows, Flamboyant gables and Renaissance medallions. On the right, note the "fool" wearing a hood with bells.

## Bell-tower

The enormous bell-tower in place au Fil consists of a square 15C base and an 18C belfry surmounted by a dome. Looking down rue Chapeau-des-Violettes, you will see the **Église St-Germain**, built in Flamboyant Gothic style in the 15C; its tower leans slightly.

On your way back to the cathedral, stop by the statue of Marie without a shirt, a half-naked little nymph symbolising spring, carved by Albert Roze in the pompous style in fashion at the turn of the last century.

## Hortillonnages★

*Maison des Hortillonnages, 54, bd Beauvillé. Apr-Oct guided boat tours (1hr) (in French), daily from 2pm. 5.30€. ☎ 03 22 92 12 18.*

These small vegetable gardens known as **aires** have been worked since the Middle Ages by market gardeners or *hortillons* (from the Latin *hortus* meaning garden) who supplied the local population with fruit and vegetables. The gardens stretch over an area of 300ha/740 acres amid a network of canals or **rieux** fed by the many arms of the River Somme and River Arve. At present, fruit trees and flowers are tending to replace vegetables and the gardeners' huts are becoming weekend holiday homes.

The "**market-on-the-water**" to which the market gardeners come to sell their produce is held every year on the third Sunday in June.

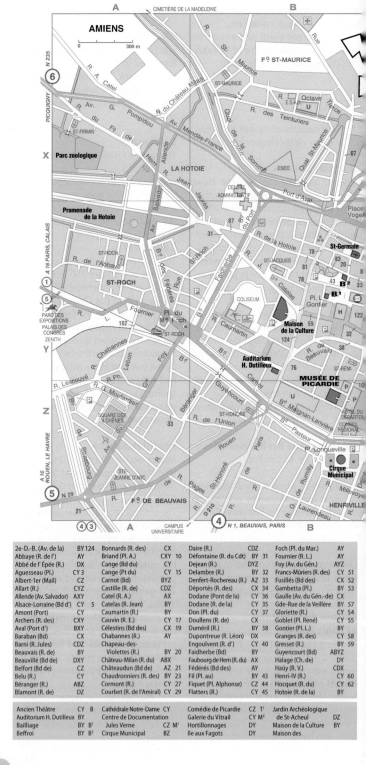

AMIENS

| | | | | | | |
|---|---|---|---|---|---|---|
| 2e-D.-B. (Av. de la) | BY 124 | Bonnards (R. des) | CX | Daire (R.) | CDZ | Foch (Pl. du Mar.) | AY |
| Abbaye (R. de l') | AY | Briand (Pl. A.) | CXY 10 | Défontaine (R. du Cdt) | BY 31 | Fournier (R. L.) | AY |
| Abbé de l' Épée (R.) | DX | Cange (Bd du) | CY | Dejean (R.) | DYZ | Foy (Av. du Gén.) | AYZ |
| Aguesseau (Pl.) | CY 3 | Cange (Pt du) | CY 15 | Delambre (R.) | BY 32 | Francs-Mûriers (R. des) | CY 51 |
| Albert-1er (Mail) | CZ | Carnot (Bd) | BYZ | Denfert-Rochereau (R.) | AZ 33 | Fusillés (Bd des) | CX 52 |
| Allart (R.) | CYZ | Castille (R. de) | CDZ | Déportés (R. des) | CX 34 | Gambetta (Pl.) | BY 53 |
| Allende (Av. Salvador) | AXY | Catelas (R. Jean) | BY | Dodane (Pont de la) | CY 36 | Gaulle (Av. du Gén.-de) | CX |
| Alsace-Lorraine (Bd d') | CY 5 | Catel (R. A.) | AX | Dodane (R. de la) | CY 35 | Gde-Rue de la Veillère | BY 57 |
| Amont (Port) | CY | Caumartin (R.) | BY | Don (Pl. du) | CY 37 | Gloriette (R.) | CY 54 |
| Archers (R. des) | CXY | Cauvin (R. E.) | CY 17 | Doullens (R. de) | CX | Goblet (Pl. René) | CY 55 |
| Aval (Port d') | BXY | Célestins (Bd des) | CX 19 | Duméril (R.) | BY 38 | Gontier (Pl. L.) | BY |
| Baraban (Bd) | CX | Chabannes (R.) | AY | Dupontreue (R. Léon) | DX | Granges (R. des) | CY 58 |
| Barni (R. Jules) | CDZ | Chapeau-des-Violettes (R.) | BY 20 | Engoulvent (R. d') | CY 40 | Gresset (R.) | BY 59 |
| Beauvais (R. de) | BY | Château-Milan (R. du) | ABX | Faidherbe (Bd) | BY | Guyencourt (Bd) | ABYZ |
| Beauville (Bd de) | DXY | Châteaudun (Bd de) | AZ 21 | Faubourg de Hem (R. du) | AX | Halage (Ch. de) | DY |
| Belfort (Bd de) | CZ | Chaudronniers (R. des) | BY 23 | Fédérés (Bd des) | CY | Haüy (R. V.) | CDX |
| Belu (R.) | CY | Cormont (R.) | CY 27 | Fil (Pl. au) | BY 43 | Henri-IV (R.) | CY 60 |
| Béranger (R.) | ABZ | Courbet (R. de l'Amiral) | CY 29 | Fiquet (Pl. Alphonse) | CZ 44 | Hocquet (R. du) | CY 62 |
| Blamont (R. de) | DZ | | | Flatters (R.) | CY 45 | Hotoie (R. de la) | BY |

| | | | | | | |
|---|---|---|---|---|---|---|
| Ancien Théâtre | CY B | Cathédrale Notre-Dame | CY | Comédie de Picardie | CZ T¹ | Jardin Archéologique | |
| Auditorium H. Dutilleux | BY | Centre de Documentation | | Galerie du Vitrail | CY M² | de St-Acheul | DZ |
| Bailliage | BY B¹ | Jules Verne | CZ M¹ | Hortillonnages | DY | Maison de la Culture | BY |
| Beffroi | BY B² | Cirque Municipal | BZ | Ile aux Fagots | DY | Maison des | |

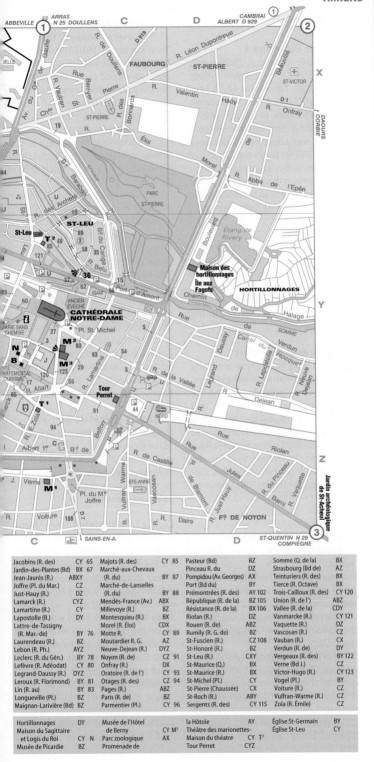

| | | | | | | |
|---|---|---|---|---|---|---|
| Jacobins (R. des) | CY 65 | Majots (R. des) | CY 85 | Pasteur (Bd) | BZ | Somme (Q. de la) | BX |
| Jardin-des-Plantes (Bd) | BX 67 | Marché-aux-Chevaux | | Pinceau R. du | DZ | Strasbourg (Bd de) | AZ |
| Jean-Jaurès (R.) | ABXY | (R. du) | BY 87 | Pompidou (Av. Georges) | AX | Teinturiers (R. des) | BX |
| Joffre (Pl. du Mar.) | CZ | Marché-de-Lanselles | | Port (Bd du) | BY | Tierce (R. Octave) | BX |
| Just-Hauy (R.) | DZ | (R. du) | BY 88 | Prémontrées (R. des) | AY 102 | Trois-Cailloux (R. des) | CY 120 |
| Lamarck (R.) | CYZ | Mendès-France (Av.) | ABX | République (R. de la) | BZ 105 | Union (R. de l') | ABZ |
| Lamartine (R.) | CY | Millevoye (R.) | BZ | Résistance (R. de la) | BX 106 | Vallée (R. de la) | CDY |
| Lapostolle (R.) | DY | Montesquieu (R.) | BX | Riolan (R.) | DZ | Vanmarcke (R.) | CY 121 |
| Lattre-de-Tassigny | | Morel (R. Éloi) | CDX | Rouen (R. de) | ABZ | Vaquette (R.) | DZ |
| (R. Mar.-de) | BY 76 | Motte R. | CY 89 | Rumilly (R. G. de) | BZ | Vascosan (R.) | CZ |
| Laurendeau (R.) | BZ | Moutardier R. G. | AZ | St-Fuscien (R.) | CZ 108 | Vauban (R.) | CX |
| Lebon (R. Ph.) | AYZ | Neuve-Dejean (R.) | DYZ | St-Honoré (R.) | BZ | Verdun (R. de) | DY |
| Leclerc (R. du Gén.) | BY 78 | Noyon (R. de) | CZ 91 | St-Leu (R.) | CXY | Vergeaux (R. des) | BY 122 |
| Lefèvre (R. Adéodat) | CY 80 | Onfray (R.) | DX | St-Maurice (Q.) | BX | Verne (Bd J.) | CZ |
| Legrand-Daussy (R.) | DYZ | Oratoire (R. de l') | CY 93 | St-Maurice (R.) | BX | Victor-Hugo (R.) | CY 123 |
| Leroux (R. Florimond) | BY 81 | Otages (R. des) | CZ 94 | St-Michel (Pl.) | CY | Vogel (Pl.) | BY |
| Lin (R. au) | BY 83 | Pages (R.) | ABZ | St-Pierre (Chaussée) | CX | Voiture (R.) | CZ |
| Longueville (Pl.) | BZ | Paris (R. de) | BZ | St-Roch (R.) | ABY | Vulfran-Warme (R.) | CZ |
| Maignan-Larivière (Bd) | BZ | Parmentier (Pl.) | CY 96 | Sergents (R. des) | CY 115 | Zola (R. Émile) | CZ |

| | | | | | | |
|---|---|---|---|---|---|---|
| Hortillonnages | DY | Musée de l'Hôtel | | la Hôtoie | AY | Église St-Germain | BY |
| Maison du Sagittaire | | de Berny | CY M³ | Théâtre des marionettes- | | Église St-Leu | CY |
| et Logis du Roi | CY N | Parc zoologique | AX | Maison du théâtre | CY T² | | |
| Musée de Picardie | BZ | Promenade de | | Tour Perret | CYZ | | |

# Additional Sights

## Musée de Picardie★★

*48 rue de la République.* ♿ *Open daily (except Mon) 10am-12.30pm, 2-6pm. Closed 1 Jan, 1 and 8 May, 14 Jul, 1 and 11 Nov and 25 Dec. 4.50 € – No charge, 1st Sun each month.* ☎ *03 22 97 14 00.*

The building housing the Picardy Museum was constructed between 1855 and 1867 for the Picardy Society of Antiquaries and is an imposing example of Napoleon III architecture. In the rotunda, the American artist Sol LeWitt created a mural using Indian ink wash.

### Archaeology

This department is housed in the basement. In addition to the Egyptian antiquities (serpentine statuette of Imenhotep) and Ancient Greek exhibits (head of Kuros) the collection includes items uncovered during digs in the region.

### Sculpture and objets d'art

On the ground floor. There are many objects representing **medieval art**. The sculptures formerly adorned the cathedral or various churches and abbeys in the region that have been destroyed over the years. In addition to the works by local sculptors Albert Roze (*Head of an Old Woman from Picardy*) and Nicolas Blasset (*Ecce Homo*), sculpture is represented by 19C Romantic and Realist works.

### Painting

The Grand Salon contains huge historical paintings (18C-19C) by Van Loo and Vernet.

Enormous murals by Puvis de Chavannes adorn the main stairway and first-floor rooms. The Notre-Dame du Puy gallery and part of the following room house the works of art of the Confrérie du Puy Notre-Dame d'Amiens.

Some of these paintings on wood have retained their sumptuous frames, fashioned by those who carved the cathedral stalls. François I is recognisable in the panel with a Renaissance canopy (1518) entitled *Au juste poids, véritable balance* ("For just weight, true scales"); Henri IV appears under the Gothic canopy bearing the poem entitled *Terre d'où prit la vérité naissance* ("Land where Truth was born") (1601). The remarkable *Virgin with Palm Tree* (1520) in its high openwork wood frame shows the Virgin Mary surrounded by saints and the donors and their families, with Amiens Cathedral in the background.

The Nieuwerkerke gallery presents 17C paintings from the Spanish School (Ribera and El Greco), the Dutch School (Frans Hals) and the French School (Simon Vouet).

Subsequent rooms exhibit 18C French painting including works by Oudry, Chardin, Fragonard and Quentin de La Tour, as well as the nine *Chasses en pays étrangers* (Hunts in Foreign Lands) by Parrocel, Pater, Boucher, Lancret, Van Loo and De Troy for Louis XV's small apartments at Versailles. Italian masters (Guardi, Tiepolo) express the charm of Venetian painting.

The Charles-Dufour gallery is dedicated to 19C French landscape painters and in particular to the Barbizon School (Millet, Isabey, Corot, Rousseau). Modern art is represented by Balthus, Masson, Fautrier, Dubuffet, Picasso and Picabia.

## Musée de l'hôtel de Berny★

*Musée d'Art local et d'Histoire régionale – 36 rue Victor Hugo – ⚠ Closed for restoration until 2012.* ☎ *03 22 97 14 00.*

The **Hôtel de Berny** was built in 1633 to accommodate the meetings of the treasurers of France.

## Centre International Jules-Verne

*2 rue Charles Dubois* ♿ *Open Apr-Sep, daily, 10am-12.30pm, 2-6.30pm. Mar, 2 6.30pm (Sat, Sun 11am-6.30pm). Rest of year, 10am-12.30pm, 2-6pm (Sat, Sun, 2-6pm). Closed 1 Jan, 1 May, 25 Dec. 5€.* ☎ *03 22 45 45 75.*

**Jules Verne** (1828-1905) was born in Nantes but spent much of his life in Amiens where he wrote *Around the World in Eighty Days, Michel Strogoff*. He played an active part in local life and was a town councillor. His home, the so-called "House with a Tower" provides a vast amount of information about the writer and his works (more than 20 000 documents). It also contains a reconstruction of his study, a number of personal

*Quartier St-Leu*

effects, a model of the *Nautilus*, and his portrait in the form of a hologram.

## Hôtel Bouctot-Vagniez

*36 rue des Otages.* ◷*Open Mon–Fri 9am-noon, 2-5pm.* ◷*Closed public holidays. No charge.* ☎ *03 22 82 80 80.*
This "bourgeois" mansion, built in 1912 in neo-Gothic style to rival the aristocratic mansions surrounding the cathedral, symbolised the success of a family of textile merchants.

## Jardin archéologique de St-Acheul

*10, rue Raymond Gourdain.* ♿ ◷*Open Jul-Aug and mid-Apr to end Apr, 10am-noon, 2-7pm (weekends and public holidays, 2-7pm); Jan to mid-Apr, May-Jun and Sep to Christmas, 9am-12.30pm, 2 5.30pm (weekends and public holidays, 2-5.30pm).* ◷*Closed over Christmas period.* ◆ *No charge, but guided tour by appointment 6€.* ☎ *03 22 47 82 57.*
St-Acheul, one of the suburbs of Amiens, has, since 1872, given its name to a Palaeolithic period, the Acheulian. Numerous bifacial tools were discovered on this site. The garden of St Acheul extends across a former gravel quarry in a pleasant rural setting which has not altered the character of the original site. A footbridge leads to an observation

tower (19m/62ft) which offers a panoramic view of the site, the Somme Valley and Amiens. Cross sections and diagrams show the successive stages which led to the formation of the valley.
A long alleyway dotted with panels, known as the **fil du temps** (Time line), lists the most important dates in Man's evolution: it takes you on a journey back in time and space to 450 000 BC and leads to the entrance of the garden where a **geological cross section** shows the successive layers of sediment accumulated since that time. Descriptive panels, a viewing table and a key of the cross section explain the history of the area.

## Parc zoologique d'Amiens

*139 r. du Fbg-de-Hem.* 🧒 ◷*Open Apr-Sep, 10am-6pm (Sun and public holidays, 10am-7pm); Oct-Mar, Wed, Sat, Sun, public and school holidays, 2-5pm.* ◷*Closed 1 Jan, 24-25 and 31 Dec.* ✆*4 € (child, 3€) (Free, 14 Jul).* ☎*03 22 69 61 12.*
Bordering the Promenade de la Hotoie (18C) and its lake, the zoo was recently redesigned within a pleasant landscaped park crisscrossed by several arms of the River Selle: home to swans, pelicans and cranes. The zoo is committed to the protection of endangered species and not one of its 450 inmates was captured in its natural environment.

# ARRAS★★

POPULATION 1024 206
MICHELIN LOCAL MAP 301: J-6

Arras, the capital of the Artois region, hides its little-known artistic beauties, the 18C Grand-Place and place des Héros, behind a serious, reserved appearance. The city, a religious, military and administrative centre, is surrounded by boulevards that replaced the old Vauban-like fortifications. Chitterling sausages (*andouillettes*) and chocolate hearts are the local gastronomic specialities.

- **Information:** Hôtel de ville, pl. des Héros, 62000 Arras, ☎ *03 21 51 26 95*. www.ot-arras.fr.
- ▶ **Orient Yourself:** The centre of the town is marked by three large squares, the Grande Place, the Place des Héros, and the Petite Place. These are surrounded by many buildings restored to their pre-war World War One conditions, notably the Gothic town hall and the 19th-century cathedral.
- **Parking:** There are (paid) parking areas in and around the centre of Arras. Try the one near the tourist information office.
- **Don't Miss:** La Grande Place and the place des Héros.
- **Organizing Your Time:** Start with a walk around the centre of town. which will give you a feel for the place. Allow about 1 hr.
- **Especially for Kids:** Cité Nature is a popular attraction
- **Also See:** the hill on which stands Notre-Dame-de-Lorette; the Canadian War Memorial at Vimy.

## A Bit of History

**Influence in the Middle Ages** – The Roman town of Nemetacum, capital of the Atrebates, was founded on the slopes of Baudimont hill, which is still known today as La Cité. In the Middle Ages the town developed from a grain market around the Benedictine abbey of St Vaast into a centre of woollen cloth manufacture, and later became a cradle of art, patronised by bankers and rich Arras burghers.

In terms of literature, the town is famous for its troubadours (*trouvères*) such as **Gautier d'Arras, Jean Bodel**, author of *Le Jeu de saint Nicolas*, and above all the 13C **Adam de la Halle** who brought dramatic art to Arras with his play **Le Jeu de la Feuillée**.

Grand'Place

R. Kaufmann/ MICHELIN

## Address Book

*For coin ranges, see the Legend on the cover flap.*

### TOURISM INFORMATION

Hôtel de ville, pl. des Héros, 62000 Arras, ☎ *03 21 51 26 95*. www.ot-arras.fr

### WHERE TO STAY

**Le Clos Grincourt (Bed and Breakfast)** – *18 rue du Château, 62161 Duisans – 9km/5.4mi W of Arras via N 39 then D 56 – ☎ 03 21 48 68 33 – reservations required Nov-Mar. 3 rms.* A tree-lined lane leads to a lovely bourgeois house that went into construction under Louis XIV, but was not completed until the days of Napoleon III. The rooms are like little apartments; all have views over the flower-filled garden. Hospitable, attentive reception.

**Château de Saulty (Bed and Breakfast)** – *82 rue de la Gare, 62158 Saulty – 19km/11.5mi SW of Arras dir. Doullens via N 25 – ☎ 03 21 48 24 76 – closed Jan – 5 rms.* This château, built in 1835, looks very fine in its 45ha/112 acre park at the village edge. After a cosy night spent in one of the smart, spacious guest rooms, your breakfast starring home-made jams and juice may inspire a stroll through the fruit orchard.

**Hôtel Diamant** – *5 pl. des Héros – ☎ 03 21 71 23 23 – www.arras-hotel-diamant.com. – 12 rms – 8 €.* This hotel enjoys a choice location on the Place des Héros at the foot of the belfry. The reception is very pleasant and the rather small rooms are impeccably maintained.

**Hotel Le Manoir de Gavrelle** – *35 rte Nationale, 62580 Gavrelle – 11km/6.6mi NE of Arras via N 50 dir. Douai – ☎ 03 21 58 68 58 – www.lemanoir62.net – closed 3 wks in Aug, 2nd half of Dec and Sun evening – 19 rms – 6 € – restaurant.* One of the pleasures of staying in this bourgeois manor set in a park is that the windows open onto a picturesque view of the verdant countryside. Simple, clean rooms housed in the former stables. The restaurant serves traditional French cuisine.

### WHERE TO EAT

**La Taverne de l'Écu** – *18-20 rue Wacquez-Glasson – ☎ 03 21 51 42 05 – closed Sun evening.* Traditional brasserie fare and local specialities to satisfy appetites of all sizes! Located in a pedestrianised street, this tavern has been decorated with flair. Try the *écuflette*, a house recipe based on the *flammenküche*, a creamy Alsatian pizza-like delicacy.

**La Table du Troubadour** – *43 bd Carnot – ☎ 03 21 71 34 50 – closed Sun.* The owner wants her restaurant to be unique – and it is! She has created a treasure trove of copper kettles, photos by Doisneau, old enamel stoves, a record player, dollies, a pram, and so on. The food is made from market-fresh ingredients and the dishes are worthy of a whisk-wielding French grandmother.

**Les Grandes Arcades** – *8-12 Grand'Place – ☎ 03 21 23 30 89.* Two formulas are available at this restaurant situated on the splendid Grand'Place: a brasserie menu and a proper restaurant menu. Don't forget to have a look at the magnificent 15C vaulted cellar below. A few renovated, personalized bedrooms are available.

### TAKE A BREAK

**Pâtisserie Yannick-Delestrez** – *50 pl. des Héros – ☎ 03 21 71 53 20. Tue-Sun, 8am-7.30pm – closed 1st week in Feb and end Aug.* For the past 100 years, this pastry shop has been delighting gourmet palates with its *Cœur d'Arras* (a gingerbread confection), *Petits Rats d'Arras*, waffles and other toothsome house recipes. In addition to sweetmeats and pastries, the tearoom serves salads and hot quiches.

### ON THE TOWN

**Irish Pub** – *7 pl. des Héros – ☎ 03 21 71 46 08 – noon-1am; Sat, 3.30pm-2am; Sun, 3.30pm-1am; public holidays from 3pm.* The name tells the game: wooden tables, a waxed parquet, a good choice of beer and music with a Celtic accent transport patrons to the Emerald Isle. When the weather warms up, you may enjoy your mug of the frothy on the terrace. Theme evenings.

## SHOWTIME

**Théâtre d'Arras** – 7 pl. du Théâtre – ☎ 03 21 71 66 16. Tue-Sat, 2pm-7.15pm – closed Jul-Aug. This pretty théâtre à l'italienne seating 400 is listed as a historic building. The varied programming features music and drama. Events drawing larger crowds are held in the casino.

## SPORT

**Stade d'eau vive (fresh water stadium) – Base nautique Robert-Pecqueur** – R. Laurent-Gers, 62223 St-Laurent-Blangy – 2km/1.2mi NE of Arras – ☎ 03 21 73 74 93 – Mon-Fri, 8am-noon, 2pm-5pm; Sat-Sun by reservation –closed end Dec to mid-Jan. 10€ to 18 €. Originally designed for the 2004 Olympic Games, this 300m/985ft long, 12m/40ft wide artificial torrent was excavated between the Scarpe lock and one of its overflow branches. Kayaks, rafts and canoes may be rented here at very reasonable prices.

## SHOPPING

**Andouillette d'Arras** – Available in all the local delicatessens, Arras andouillette is prepared from calf's stomach seasoned with parsley, shallots, herbs, spices and juniper. It is eaten with a smidgen of mustard and a dab of crème fraîche.

**Caudron** – 11-15 pl. de la Vacquerie – ☎ 03 21 71 14 23 – Mon 2pm-7pm, Tue-Sat 9am-noon, 2.30pm-7pm. Although this craftsman works with imported porcelain (the Arras factory closed in 1790), his blazing hot kiln allows the colour to spread elegantly over the porcelain surface, thereby reproducing the legendary Arras blue. The shop sells very handsome pieces inspired by traditional patterns such as the flowery barbeau and the tree of life.

**Markets** – Traditional markets held at the Place des Héros on Wednesday, and the Grand'Place on Saturday mornings.

From 1384 the manufacture of high-warp tapestries, under the patronage of the dukes of Burgundy, brought Arras widespread fame – and the word arras passed into English to indicate a tapestry wall-hanging. After the Renaissance, this activity decreased as Beauvais and Antwerp took over.

**Youth of "The Incorruptible"** – **Maximilien de Robespierre**, whose father was an Artois Council barrister, was born in Arras in 1758. Orphaned at an early age, the young man became the protégé of the bishop and received a scholarship to attend the Louis-le-Grand School in Paris. Robespierre became a barrister on his return to Arras and was not only accepted by the Arras Academy but also affiliated with the **Rosati** (an anagram of "Artois") poetic society. During this period the pale young man, later the spirited leader of the Revolution, courted young ladies for whom he wrote verse.

In Arras, Robespierre knew **Joseph Lebon** (1765-95), a member of the Oratorian order who was mayor of the town during the Reign of Terror. During this time the former priest presided over the destruction of many churches and regularly sent aristocrats and rich farmers to the guillotine set up in place du Théâtre. Lebon himself was later to perish under the blade in Amiens.

**Arras and the Battles of Artois** – During the First World War, the front was until 1917 constantly near Arras which suffered heavy shelling as a result. The most violent conflicts took place in the strategically important hills north of the town. After the Battle of the Marne the retreating Germans fought to hold on to them, their backs to the rich coal basin, clinging to Vimy Ridge and the slopes of Notre-Dame-de-Lorette Hill. In the autumn of 1914 they emerged to attack Arras, but were stopped after battles at Ablain-St-Nazaire, Carency and La Targette.

In May and June 1915 **General Foch**, in command of the French forces in the north, attempted to pierce the German ranks; his troops took Neuville St-Vaast and Notre-Dame-de-Lorette. The attack failed at Vimy however, which was won only in 1917, by the Canadians.

# Walking Tour: Main Squares

## Grand'Place and place des Héros★★★

The two main squares in Arras, the theatrical Grand'Place and place des Héros, joined by the short rue de la Taillerie, are extremely impressive. They existed as early as the 11C, but have seen many transformations through the centuries. Today's magnificent façades are fine examples of 17C and 18C Flemish architecture. The local council of the period was careful to control the town's development, permitting citizens to construct only "in stone or brick, with no projecting architectural elements." The façades – formerly embellished with carved shop signs, of which a few remain – rest on monolith-columned arcades which protected market stallholders and customers alike from inclement weather. As evening comes the squares take on a different charm when the gables, discreetly floodlit, stand out against the night sky.

The smaller and livelier of the two squares, **place des Héros**, is surrounded by shops and overlooked by the belfry.

▶ *Stand facing the town hall and take rue D.-Delansorne, which starts in the left-hand corner of place des Héros and leads to rue Paul-Doumer.*

On the corner of rue Doumer stands the **Palais de Justice** (Law Courts), the former seat of the Artois government (1701), embellished with Corinthian pilasters and its side entrance (1724) decorated with Regency shells.

▶ *From rue Doumer, follow the second or third side street on the left.*

## Place du Théâtre

During the Revolution, the guillotine stood in this lively square. The **theatre** dates from 1784 (its façade has been restored). It was built where the fish market stood; it faces the **Ostel des Poissonniers** (1710), a narrow Baroque house carved with sea gods and mermaids. In rue des Jongleurs, note the majestic 18C Hôtel de Guines; no 9 rue

Robespierre was the former residence of the famous revolutionary.
**Maison Robespierre** – Robespierre lived (1787-89) in this house. It has been turned into a **Musée du Compagnonnage** (crafts guild), which displays masterpieces by some of the best craftsmen in France (*Compagnons du Tour de France*).

▶ *Walk across the square and take rue St-Aubert on your right; place du Wetz-d'Amain is a little farther on the left.*

## Place du Wetz-d'Amain

The square is graced by a pretty Renaissance house, to which a Classical stone porch was added later. It served as refuge to the monks of Mont St-Éloi.

▶ *Turn back, follow rue du Gén.-Barbot which crosses rue St-Aubert; turn left on rue A.-Briand; Église Notre-Dame-des-Ardents is on your left. One of the streets on the right leads to place V.-Hugo and the lower town.*

## Église Notre-Dame-des-Ardents

Fragments of the Holy Taper, a miraculous candle entrusted by the Virgin Mary to two minstrels to cure ergotic poisoning in the 12C, are safeguarded. The silver reliquary is to the left of the high altar, in a latticed recess (*lighting below, to the right*).

▶ *Follow one of the streets on the right to reach place Victor-Hugo and the lower town.*

## Basse-ville

This district lies between the town and the citadel. It is arranged around the lovely, octagonal **place Victor-Hugo**, built in 1756, where the cattle market used to be held. Follow rue des Promenades towards the **Jardins du Gouverneur** and **Jardin des Allées**: a **stele** erected in honour of the Rosati depicts a marquess and a 20C man watching a procession of muses.

The **Citadel** (🕑 mid-Jun to mid-Sep, Sun, 3.30pm, guided visits (2h). 🎟 4.60€. ☎ 03 21 51 26 95) stands just across boulevard du Général-de-Gaulle; the octagonal stronghold designed by Vauban

| | | |
|---|---|---|
| 29-Juillet R. du | BY | 54 |
| 33 Pl. du | BY | 55 |
| 4-Crosses R. des | BZ | |
| Adam R. Paul | AY | 2 |
| Agaches R. des | BY | 3 |
| Albert-Ier-de-Belgique R. | BY | 4 |
| Amiens R. d' | AYZ | |
| Ancien-Rivage Pl. de l' | BY | 5 |
| Archicourt R. | BZ | |
| Augustine R. des | BCY | |
| Barbot R. du Gén. | BY | 6 |
| Baudimont R. | AY | |
| Baudimont Rd-Pt | AY | 7 |
| Besnier Bd G. | AY | |
| Blanc R. Louis | BY | |
| Bodel R. J. | CY | |
| Branly R. E. | CZ | |
| Breton R. E. | CZ | |
| Briand R. A. | BZ | |
| Carabiniers-d'Artois R. des | AY | 8 |
| Cardinal R. du | CZ | 9 |
| Carnot Bd | BCZ | |
| Churchill Av. W. | AY | |
| Crespel Bd | AZ | |
| Crinchon R. du | BCY | |
| Croix-de-Grès R. de la | AY | |
| Degeorges R. F. | BZ | |
| Delasorne R. D. | BZ | 10 |
| Douai R. de | CZ | |
| Doumer R. P. | BY | 12 |
| Dutilleux R. C. | CZ | |
| Ernestale R. | BZ | 13 |
| Faidherbe Bd | CYZ | |
| Ferry R. J. | AY | 15 |
| Foch R. Maréchal | CZ | 16 |
| Fours R. des | ABZ | |
| Fusillés Av. des | AZ | |
| Gambetta R. | BCZ | |
| Gaulle Bd du Gén.-de | AZ | |
| Gouvernance R. de la | BY | 18 |
| Guy Mollet Pl. | CY | 19 |
| Hagerue Carrefour | BZ | |
| Halette R. A. | AY | |
| Héros Pl. des | BCYZ | |
| Jeanne-d'Arc R. | BZ | |
| Kennedy Av. J. | AZ | 24 |
| Leclerc Av. du Maréchal | BCZ | |
| Legay R. | CY | |
| Legrelle R. E. | BCZ | 25 |
| Leroy R. V. | CY | |
| Liberté Bd de la | ABY | |
| Madeleine Pl. de la | BY | 28 |
| Marché-au-Filé R. du | BY | 30 |
| Marseille Pl. de | BZ | 31 |
| Méaulens R. | BY | |
| Mémorial-des-Fusillés Av. du | AZ | |
| Michelet R. | BY | |
| Michonneau Av. P. | CY | |
| Notre-Dame-de-Lorette Villa | BY | |
| Paix R. de la | AY | |
| Pasteur R. | CZ | |
| Pont-de-Cité Pl. du | ABY | |
| Préfecture Pl.de la | AY | |
| Président-Allende Bd | AYZ | |
| Quatre-Crosses R. des | BZ | |
| Rivage Q. du | BY | |
| Robespierre R. | BZ | 34 |
| Ronville R. | CZ | 35 |
| Rosati R. des | CY | |
| St-Aubert R. | BY | |
| St-Michel R. | CYZ | |
| St-Quentin R. de | CZ | |
| Ste-Claire R. | AZ | 37 |
| Ste-Croix R. | CY | 39 |

| | | |
|---|---|---|
| Salengro R. | BY | |
| Schuman Bd R. | BCY | |
| Strasbourg Bd de | CZ | 42 |
| Taillerie R. de la | CY | 43 |
| Tchécoslovaquie Pl. de | BY | |
| Teinturiers R. des | BY | 45 |
| Théâtre Pl. et R. | BZ | 47 |
| Turenne R. de | BY | |
| Vauban Bd | BZ | |
| Verdun Cours de | AZ | 49 |
| Victor-Hugo Pl. | AZ | 51 |
| Wacquez-Glasson R. | CZ | 52 |
| Wetz-d'Amain Pl. du | BY | 53 |

| | | |
|---|---|---|
| Ancienne Abbaye St-Vaast | BY | |
| Cathédrale | BY | |
| Citadelle | AZ | |
| Hôtel de Guines | BY | F |
| Hôtel de ville et Beffroi | BY | H |
| Jardins du Gouverneur et des Allées | AZ | |
| Maison Robespierre | BY | E |
| Mur des Fusillés | AZ | |
| Mémorial Britannique | AZ | |
| Palais de Justice | BZ | J |
| Théâtre | BZ | T |
| Église Notre-Dame-des-Ardents | BZ | |

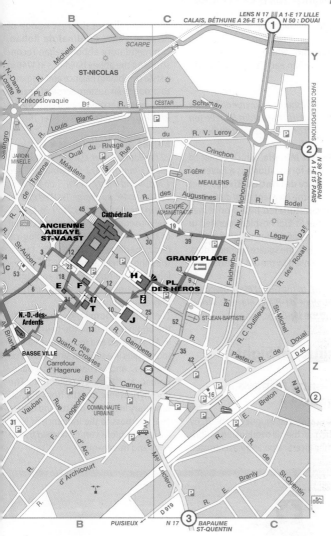

was built between 1668 and 1672 . It is composed of five bastions. A model of the fortifications is displayed in the entrance hall. The tour includes the arsenal and the Baroque Chapelle St-Louis.

Avenue du Mémorial des Fusillés leads to the **Mur des Fusillés** where 217 members of the Resistance movement were executed during the Second World War. The memorial was inaugurated in 1949.

▶ *Return to place V.-Hugo and walk to the Cité district via rue Victor-Hugo. Then take the cours de Verdun on the right; cross place du 33e and continue along rue de Châteaudun leading to rue d'Amiens.*

## Cité

**Place de la Préfecture** was the heart of medieval Arras. Today the *préfecture* (county council) occupies the former bishop's palace, finished in 1780. Opposite, the Église St-Nicolas-en-Cité (1839) stands on the site of Notre-Dame-de-la-Cité Cathedral, which was destroyed between 1798 and 1804. It houses a triptych depicting the *Climb to Calvary*, painted in 1577 by P Claessens of Bruges. Follow rue Baudimont on the right for 135m/150yd to reach **place du Pont-**

de-Cité. The name recalls the bridge on the River Crinchon (now flowing underground), which linked the Cité to the town when each had its own fortifications.

▶ *From the square, follow rue de Turenne which skirts the Jardin Minelle (on the left) and leads to quai du Rivage.*

The **Jardin Minelle**, which replaced the town's fortifications, is a haven of peace. **Place de l'Ancien-Rivage** is set back from the pleasant *quai du Rivage*. The square-turreted house on it was the former St-Éloi hospice, founded in 1635 by one of the town's goldsmiths. Until the 19C, the square formed a dock that was linked to the old harbour.

▶ *Return to the Grand'Place along rue du Mont-de-Piété, place G.-Mollet and rue Ste-Croix.*

## Additional Sights

## Ancienne Abbaye St-Vaast★★

The old abbey was founded in the 7C by St Aubert on the hill overlooking a tributary of the River Scarpe, and was entrusted

with the relics of the first bishop of Arras, St Vaast. **Cardinal de Rohan**, commendatory abbot, began reconstructing the abbey buildings in 1746 in a style combining balance and elegance to produce an austere sense of beauty; they were deconsecrated during the Revolution, then restored after 1918.

### Musée des Beaux-Arts★

*22 rue Paul Doumer. ◐Open daily except Tue 9.30am–noon, 2–5.30pm. ◐Closed 1 Jan, 1 and 8 May, 14 Jul, 1 and 11 Nov, 25 Dec. ◧4€ no charge 1st Wed and 1st Sun in the month. ☎ 03 21 71 26 43.*

The museum offers a splendid account of the town's history: archaeological finds, medieval sculpture, 15C tapestries, the cathedral treasury, 17C porcelain and paintings (French and Dutch schools, large religious works) and pre-Impressionist paintings.

The **Italian Room** (**1**) decorated with the original lion from the belfry (1554) in Arras is used as a reception area. The tour begins in a series of small rooms on the left (**2** and **3**) containing the Gallo-Roman archaeology collection. The porphyry statue of Attis from a 2C-3C sanctuary in honour of Attis and Cybele bears witness to the influence of Near Eastern religions carried abroad by the army and merchants.

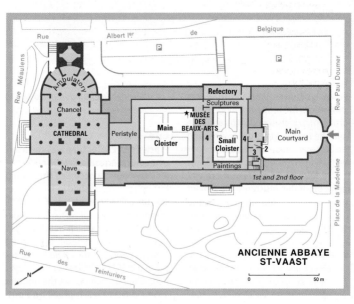

ANCIENNE ABBAYE
ST-VAAST

The **galleries around the small cloister** (4), known as the Cour du Puits, contain some fine medieval sculptures and paintings: Virgin and Child by Pépin de Huy, tapestries made in Arras (legend of St Vaast); note in particular the 13C **Anges de Saudémont**★ with their delicately rendered curly hair, almond-shaped eyes and faint smile. The 16C is illustrated by triptychs by **Bellegambe** (Adoration of the Christ Child) and an Entombment by Vermeyen.

**Refectory** – A tapestry bearing the arms of Cardinal de Rohan hangs above the great marble fireplace.

**Grand cloître** – The spacious main cloister, which used to lead through a peristyle into the minster, contains capitals carved with garlands and rosettes. The **staircase** is decorated with a fine series of paintings by Giovanni Baglioni (1571-1644).

The **first floor** is given over to paintings from the 16C to 18C by the French School (Vignon, Nicolas de Largillière, Boullongne, Vien, Bouliar, Doncre) and the Dutch School (Brueghel the Younger, Adriaen Van Utrecht, Barent Fabritius, a student of Rembrandt, and Rubens). 17C and 18C sculpture.

The **Salle des Mays de Notre-Dame** owes its name to the works that were given to Notre-Dame Church in Paris every springtime between 1603 and 1707 by the guild of gold- and silver-smiths. It contains huge works by La Hyre, Sébastien Bourdon, Louis de Boullongne, Philippe de Champaigne, Joseph Barrocel and Jouvenet.

On the **2nd floor**, the rooms on the front of the building contain the ceramics collections from the 16C to the 19C: Italian and glazed earthenware, and Arras and Tournai porcelain decorated with light, delicate motifs (note the "**Buffon bird dinner service**" commissioned by the Duc d'Orléans in 1787).

Around the small cloister are works by various schools of early-19C French landscape artists including Corot and Dutilleux. One spacious room is given over to large 19C works (**Delacroix, Chassériau**). Next to this room is the Salle Louise-Weiss containing 19C small paintings by Monticelli, Ribot and Ravier.

14C funerary mask – Musée des Beaux-Arts

*Musée des Beaux-Arts*

## Cathédrale

*Open Jun-Sep, Sat 3pm and by request at the tourist office. May-Oct, Sun 10.30am-12.30pm, 2.30-6pm; rest of year, daily except Sun and public holidays, 2.30-6pm. ☎ 03 21 51 26 95. Entrance in rue des Teinturiers.*

The old abbey church of St Vaast was built according to plans prepared by Contant d'Ivry in the 18C. It was finished in 1833 and elevated to a cathedral, to replace Notre-Dame-de-la-Cité.

The Classical façade is graced by a monumental flight of steps; the luminous interior presents an Antique splendour. A line of lofty columns bearing Corinthian capitals flanks the nave, transept and chancel. Enormous 19C statues of saints, from the Pantheon in Paris, adorn the side aisles.

The right transept is decorated with large frescoes.

## Hôtel de Ville and Belfry

*Combined tickets giving admission to the Hotel de Ville, the Belfry and the Souterrains are available from the Office de Tourisme 7.20€ (child, 4.20€). ☎ 03 21 51 26 95. www.ot-arras.fr.* **Hotel de Ville** – *Guided visits (30min) Open Jul-Aug: Wed and Sun 3pm. 2€.*

### Belfry★

*Open May-Sep, 9am-6.30pm (Sun, 10am-1pm, 2.30-6.30pm); Oct-Apr, 9am-noon, 2-6pm (Sun, 10am-12.30pm, 2.30-6.30pm; Mon, 10am-noon, 2-6pm) 2.60€ (child, 1.70€).*

The town hall was destroyed in 1914 and rebuilt in the Flamboyant style. The beautiful front, with its uneven arches, stands on the western side of place des Héros, and the graceful 75m/246ft belfry, with its 40-bell peal, rises over the more severe-looking Renaissance wings. Downstairs, an audio-visual presentation on the history of Arras is an excellent introduction to the town.

**Circuit des souterrains**

☞ *Guided tours 45min-tour: daily 10am-noon, 2-6pm (Sun and public holidays, 10am-12.30pm, 2.30-6.30pm.* ⏱ *Closed 1 Jan and 25 Dec.* ☞ *4.50€.*
The 10C galleries, cut into the limestone bank on which the town stands, served as a refuge in wartime (during WWI the British set up a field hospital here) and above all as an enormous wine cellar; the caves (boves) are at the ideal temperature for storing wine.

# PARC ASTÉRIX★★

MICHELIN LOCAL MAP 312: G-6 OR MAP 106 FOLD 9
30KM/18.6MI NORTH OF PARIS

**Astérix the Gaul, hero of the famous cartoon strip by Goscinny and Uderzo known throughout the world and translated into several languages, provides the theme for this 50ha/123 acre fun park; it is a fantasy world for all ages that offers a journey into the past. The park opened in 1989. The Gauls, and in particular Astérix's friends, the mighty Obelix who follows him everywhere, Panoramix (Getafix) who prepares magic potions, Assurancetourix (Cacofonix) the bard and Abraracourcix (Vitalstatistix) the chief of the tribe are the heroes, but beware the Romans are never very far away!**

▸ **Orient Yourself:** Access from Paris: *By car: A 1 motorway, exit "Parc Astérix". By train: RER line B to Roissy-Charles-de-Gaulle, then by shuttle bus to the park.*

## Visit

*Allow a whole day.* 🧒 ⏱ *Opening days vary from year to year: ask for information or visit the web site. Likewise, times vary according to the time of year, but are usually 10am-6pm or 9.30am-7pm (Jul-Aug).* ⏱ *Closed from early Nov to end*

*Mar.* ☞ *35€(child, 25€; under 3 years, free).* 🅿 *Parking 6€ per day.* ☏ *08 92 68 30 10. www.parcasterix.fr. An admission ticket to the Parc Astérix gives access to all of the shows and attractions for the entire day (except for games of skill and video games).*

The park presents reconstructed "historical" sections, various attractions, shows and audio-visual displays and offers a choice of snacks and meals.

### WHERE TO STAY

⊖⊖🛏 **Hôtel des Trois Hiboux**
*– Parc Astérix, 60128 Plailly –*
☏ *03 44 62 68 00 – hoteldestroishiboux@ parcasterix.com – closed mid-Oct to mid-Mar –* 🅿 *–96 rms –* �

 *12.50€ – restaurant* ⊖⊖*. According to legend, each of the three forests surrounding the amusement park used to be the territory of one owl (hibou). Perhaps you'll fall asleep to the lullaby of their songs in one of the cosy bedrooms of this hotel where they are said to convene. Sweet dreams!*

### Via Antiqua

Situated at the entrance to the park, this "street" is lined with houses symbolising, in their architecture, Astérix's various journeys across Europe (Germany, Helvetica, Hispania etc).

### Gaule antique

The very heart of this area is the Gallic Village d'Astérix, consisting of huts where visitors can meet Obelix with his menhirs, Panoramix and Assurance-

*Styx River Ride*

tourix the bard in his hut perched in the treetops. Here and there are fights, festivities or hunting scenes. The **Balade d'Astérix** reveals a few strange scenes and a tour of the **Forêt des Druides** attracts young and not-so-young visitors alike. Nearby, the atmosphere is much damper at the **Grand Splatch★**. The most popular site is a Stone Age village built on piles. An ingenious delivery system called **Menhir Express★★** takes anybody who dares on a trip through a network of canals bristling with surprises! You will love the ride known as the **Trace du Hourr★★★** aboard a small train racing along a bobsleigh track at 60kph/37mph.

## Grèce antique

The entrance to this part of the park is marked by the colonnade from the Temple of Zeus. The **Vol d'Icare** (Icarus' flight) takes visitors out of Daedalus' labyrinth, but you still have to defeat the terrible **Hydre de Lerne**.

## Empire romain

In the arena are terrible fights between gladiators and some amazing circus acts performed by the **Stars de l'Empire**. If you wish to know what is afoot in the Gallic village, join the **Espions de César★** (Caesar's spies) who have devised a very efficient surveillance system (5m/16ft above ground level). And why not brave Hell itself on the **Descente du Styx★**.

## Moyen Âge

A long journey in time takes place along **Avenue de Paris★★**. Ten centuries of history are illustrated here, each period represented by people in costume, typical shops and the avenue's own special atmosphere. The Middle Ages live again with street entertainers, glassmakers and potters living and working in dark, mysterious streets.

## Temps modernes

Going on holiday has not always been plain sailing as you can see from the numerous adventures to be encountered along the **Nationale 7** main road to the south of France. However, it may not be necessary to leave for the country as the **Oxygénarium★★** has been specially designed to offer city dwellers the combined benefits of water and fresh mountain air: guaranteed thrills! More excitement is round the corner with **Goudurix★★**, a gigantic roller coaster taking visitors through a succession of vertiginous drops, swooping round corners, and going into spins and loops, all at breathtaking speed.

This trip through time ends in 1930, in **Main basse sur la Joconde★★**, a splendid enactment of a historical detective story during which a gang of thieves attempts to steal the *Mona Lisa*.

# AUVERS-SUR-OISE★★

POPULATION 6 820

MICHELIN LOCAL MAP 305: E-6 OR MAP 106 FOLD 6

This village stretches over 7km/4.5mi from the River Oise to the escarpment edging the Vexin plateau. The old path, now a series of narrow streets winding their way from Valhermeil to Cordeville, still carries the memory of the artists who brought it fame. Here and there, panels indicate the scenes portrayed by Impressionist painters. It is the district around the church, however, which constitutes the favourite "place of pilgrimage" for art lovers.

Doctor **Paul Gachet** (1828-1909) moved to Auvers in 1872. An enthusiastic painter and engraver, with an unquenchable thirst for novelty, he was the centre of attraction for a new generation of painters known as the "Impressionists," who came to stay and paint locally.

🛈 **Information:** Manoir des Colombières, r. de la Sansonne, 95430 Auvers-sur-Oise, ☎ 01 30 36 10 06.

▸ **Orient Yourself:** Auvers-sur-Oise lies just 20 miles northwest of Paris, along the A 115. SNCF depart from Gare du Nord or Gare St-Lazare, changing at Pontoise.

👁 **Don't Miss:** Use the map available at the tourist office to locate the various sites with ease.

🕐 **Organizing Your Time:** Spend a full day here to have a look at the home of Dr Gachet and the Maison du Pendu immortalised by Cézanne. The surrounding area brims with scenic beauty, thanks to the vast fields of corn that so inspired the artists and where Van Gogh ended his life on 29 July 1890. Throughout the town, 19 panels display copies of works painted in Auvers by Pissarro, Daubigny, Van Gogh, Cézanne, Corot and others.

**Kids Especially for Kids:** The 17C Château d'Auvers.

## In Van Gogh's Footsteps

During his stay in Auvers, Van Gogh was extremely active. The restful countryside where he hoped to find peace after his internment in Provence encouraged his quest for freedom and his frantic need to work, with the result that he completed more than 70 paintings in a very short time.

### Auberge Ravoux★

*Place de la Mairie –* 🕐*Open 10am-6pm (except Mon and Tue).* 🕐*Closed mid-Nov to mid-Mar.* 💶*5 €.* ☎ *01 30 36 60 60.*
Known as the **Maison de Van Gogh**, this is actually the inn where Van Gogh stayed for two months before his tragic death. Feeling terribly guilty towards his brother Theo, on whom he was entirely dependent, Van Gogh shot himself in the chest while he was out in a field; he died two days later in the room he occupied in the Auberge Ravoux. He was 37 years old. The inn has been carefully restored and has retained its interior decoration and its sphere of activity (*local cuisine and wines*). Outside are panels describing the artist's eventful life. The small garret he occupied has remained unchanged and, despite the absence of furniture, gives an insight into the ascetic conditions under which he lived (*tours restricted to five visitors at a time because of the lack of space*). The tour ends with a moving audio-visual presentation illustrating Van Gogh's stay in Auvers.

▸ *Follow rue des Colombières past the museum and studio of Charles-François Daubigny (👁 see Additional Sights).*

A path to the right leads to a cemetery set among the corn fields that Van Gogh loved to paint.

### Vincent and Theo Van Gogh's Graves

*Rue Émile-Bernard.* The famous Dutch

painter's tomb stands against the left-hand wall. His brother Theo, who gave him moral support all his life and who died soon after him, rests by his side.

## Additional Sights

### Musée de l'Absinthe

*44 rue Alphonse Callé.* ⏰*Open Jun to mid-Sep daily except Mon and Tue 1.30-6pm. Mid-Sep to end May (closed mid-Dec to end Feb) Sat-Sun and public holidays 11am-6pm.* 🎫*5€.* ☎*01 30 36 83 26.*

The famous green liqueur reached the peak of its popularity in the cafés of the 19C. It was often described as the **"green muse"** and was closely linked to the life of the artists of the day who spent a great deal of time in cafés. The documents, posters and objects displayed in the museum bring back to life the history of a drink which had a profound social influence until it was banned in 1915.

### Musée Daubigny

*Rue de la Sansonne –* ⏰ *Open Apr-Oct, 2-6pm. Nov-Mar, 2-5pm (weekends, 5.30pm).* ⏰*Closed Mon and Tue.* 🎫*4€.* ☎ *01 30 36 80 20.*

Housed in the Manoir des Colombières, this museum displays a collection of 19C paintings, water colours, drawings and engravings illustrating the birth of Impressionism: works by Daubigny and Goeneutte, an engraver and painter who portrayed elegant Parisian women. There are also contemporary works of art.

### Maison-Atelier de Daubigny★

*61 rue Daubigny –* ⏰ *Open Easter to 1 Nov Thu-Sun and public holidays 2 6.30pm.* 🎫*5€.* ☎ *01 34 48 03 03.*

**Charles-François Daubigny** (1817-78), a landscape painter, settled in Auvers on the advice of his friend Camille Corot. He had a studio-house built in 1861 and asked his family and friends to take part in the interior decoration. Charles, his son Karl and his daughter Cécile as well as Corot and Daumier left their marks of artistic inspiration on the walls and doors. Daubigny loved to paint on the River Oise, aboard a small specially designed boat. Later on, Monet followed his example. In 1890, Van Gogh painted Daubigny's

garden; in his last letter to his brother Theo, he gives details about the colours he chose for the painting and asks his advice.

### Château d'Auvers

*50 rue de Léry –* ♿ *Audio tours (1hr30min, last admission 1hr30min before closing).* ⏰*Open daily (except Mon) Apr-Sep 10.30am-6.00pm (weekends 6.30pm). Oct-Mar 10.30am-4.30pm (weekends 5.30pm).* ⏰*Closed 25 Dec and first 3 weeks in Jan.* 🎫*10€ (children 6€).* ☎*01 34 48 48 40. www.chateau-auvers.fr.*

**Kids** This 17C château, which has been restored and laid out with extensive use of audio-visual presentations, offers visitors a chance to enjoy a **Journey Back to the Days of the Impressionists**★ and gain some insight into the wonderful adventure that was Art in the 19C. Using reconstructions of interiors and the projection of some 600 works, it brings to life the Paris of the time, a city undergoing immense change thanks to the work of Baron Haussmann, and a city where the wealthy middle classes led a bustling, frivolous life with little appreciation of the new style of painting.

Although some of the artists fed on the capital's atmosphere for their works (Degas, Toulouse-Lautrec), most of them preferred to travel on the brand-new railway from Paris to the seaside in search of new sources of inspiration. They found it in the open-air bars (*guinguettes*) in Asnières and Chatou, along the banks of the Seine and the Oise (Argenteuil, Vétheuil, Auvers-sur-Oise etc.), in the lush countryside of the Paris basin (haystacks by Monet and Thornley), in the sea, the harbours (Le Havre), the cliffs (Étretat) and the beaches.

---

**WHERE TO EAT**

🍽️ **Auberge Ravoux** – *Opposite the town hall –* ☎ *01 30 36 60 60 – www.ariv.asso.fr/ravoux.htm – closed 10 Nov to 10 Mar, Sun evening and Mon – reservations required – 28/35 €.* This old artists' café, with its late 19C decor, was Van Gogh's last home. Very pleasant, history-rich atmosphere, a pretty serving counter and large tables of solid wood. Traditional cuisine and wine from small vintners.

# AVESNES-SUR-HELPE

POPULATION 5 003

MICHELIN LOCAL MAP 302: L-7

This quiet town, which stands, has preserved some of its Vauban-like fortifications. It is the ideal starting point for drives through the Avesnois region with its patchwork of hedged-in meadows and slate-roofed hamlets. From here you can also explore the hiking trails of the Parc naturel régional de l'Avesnois (ⓒ see Maroilles below).

In the 17C, a Protestant from Avesnes, Jessé de Forest, left his home town to go and live in America. He settled on Long Island, where the district of Forest Hills was later named after him.

🛈 **Information:** 41 pl. du Gén.-Leclerc, 59440 Avesnes-Sur-Helpe, ☏ 03 27 56 57 20. www.avesnes-sur-helpe.com

▶ **Orient Yourself:** On the south bank of the River Helpe-Majeure close to the Belgian border, and closer to Brussels (68 miles) than to Paris (158 miles)

🅿 **Parking:** On street parking (limited).

🕭 **Don't Miss:** Taste the local cheeses, Maroilles and Dauphin.

## Walking Tour

### Grand'Place

The town's narrow main square is surrounded by old houses with high slate roofs.

### Hôtel de Ville

A double staircase with wrought-iron balustrades fronts the 18C Classical town hall in blue Tournai stone.

▶ *Walk round the church and follow rue d'Albret.*

### Square de la Madeleine

Located on top of one of the bastions, this provides a bird's-eye view of the Helpe Valley.

## Excursions

### Cartignies

*6km/3.7mi southwest along D 424.*
The village boasts some 40 **blue-stone oratories.**

### Pont-de-Sains

*10km/6.2mi southeast along D 951.*
Picturesque setting. The castle once belonged to Talleyrand, then to his niece, the Duchess of Dino.

### Maroilles

*12km/7.5mi west along D 962.*
This place is famous for its cheeses, Maroilles and Dauphin, which used to be the speciality of the former Benedictine abbey (a few 17C buildings can still be seen). There's also a lovely watermill. The **Maison du Parc Naturel Régional de l'Avesnois** (*Grange dîmière, 4 cour de l'Abbaye, 59550 Maroilles;* ☏ *03 27 77 51 60. www.parc-naturel-avesnois.fr;* 🕑 *open daily (except weekends and public holidays) 9am-noon, 2-5pm; May-Sep daily (except Sat) 3-7pm)* provides useful information about hiking tours in the area, the countryside with its hedged-in fields and the local cultural heritage.

## Driving Tour

### Avesnois Region★★ *Round-trip*

This region, which lies south of Maubeuge and extends along the Belgian border, is known for its undulating countryside of orchards, woodlands and pastures, through which meander the River Helpe-Majeure and River Helpe-Mineure, and for its pretty villages of brick, slate and stone. Of the many small bandstands, built on village squares by the foundries of the Sambre Valley, only about 20 have survived. The finest are in Beugnies, Floursies, Marbraix, Solre-le-Château, Avesnes, Cartignies, Dourlers and Trélon.

The vast forests and the cluster of lakes around Liessies and Trélon are traces of a period when the great abbeys – Maroilles, Liessies and St-Michel – dominated the region, constructing mills and forges on every river.

Many small industries developed in the 18C and 19C: glassmaking at Sars-Poteries, Trélon and Anor, wood turning at Felleries, spinning at Fourmies, marble quarrying at Cousoire etc. Today the museums at Sars-Poteries, Felleries, Trélon and Fourmies recall the time when the region was highly populated and active.

▸ *Leave Avesnes by D 133 (east) towards Liessies.*

## Ramousies

The 16C **church** contains two beautiful Renaissance altarpieces from Antwerp workshops that once belonged to Liessies Abbey. One depicts the life of St Sulpice; the other represents the Passion. The 13C crucifix is from the oldest calvary in northern France.

▸ *Continue along D 80 to Felleries.*

## Felleries

Since the 17C the town's inhabitants have specialised in bois-joli: turned wood and cooperage. These workshops developed at the same time as the textile industry, the former making bobbins and spindles for the latter.

**The Moulin des Bois-Jolis Museum**
(& ☉*Open Apr-Oct: 2-6pm, Sat-Sun and public holidays 2.30-6.30pm.* ⊚*3.50€.* ☎ *03 27 59 03 46*), housed in a 16C watermill, brings together a wide variety of treen (wooden) items made in Felleries: butter moulds, salt boxes, spindles, tops etc.

## Sars-Poteries

Since the 15C the earth around Sars has been used by potters, and many small pottery workshops exist locally while the larger factories specialising in pipes, ducts etc have all closed. In the 19C, two glassworks were set up specialising in dinner services and bottles. In 1900, they employed a work force of 800 but by 1938 the economic slump forced them to close.

## Musée-Atelier du Verre★

*1 rue du Général de Gaulle –* ☉*Open daily except Tue 10am-12.30pm, 1.30-*

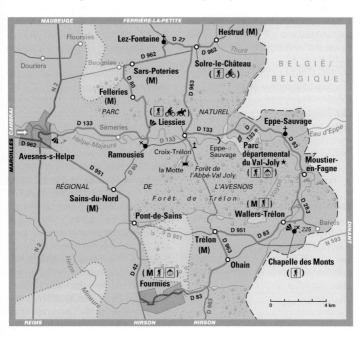

6pm. ○Closed 1 Jan, 1 May, 25 Dec.
∞3€. ☎ 03 27 61 61 44.
Housed in the former home of the glassworks manager, this museum boasts an
unusual collection of popular glassware
made by the workers for their own use.
The pieces were nicknamed *bousillés*
(meaning "made after working hours")
and they enabled the workers to make
full use of their talent, artistry and
imagination.

There are highly ornate engraved lamps,
large dishes, "revenge inkwells" (so named
because the glass workers did not know
how to write, but they had the most beautiful inkwells), and strange "Passion
bottles" containing representations of
the instruments of Christ's Passion (these
bottles were taken on pilgrimages to
Notre-Dame de Liesse). As a result of local
digs, the museum has built up a collection of grey-sandstone objects with glazed
cobalt-blue decoration (17C and 18C).

In association with the glass workshop,
the museum welcomes international
artists and, by doing so, extends its
contemporary glass collection.

The menhir, known as the **Pierre de
Dessus-Bise**, stands on place du Vieux
Marché. According to tradition, sterile
women who sit on it become able to
bear children.

The **watermill** north of the village was
built in 1780 and still contains its great
wheel and workings.

▶ *Take D 962 east, then turn left
3km/1.9mi farther on.*

### Lez-Fontaine
In the 15C **church** the wooden vaults
are decorated with paintings dating
from 1531.

▶ *Follow D 27 to Solre-le-Château.*

### Solre-le-Château
The seigniorial château no longer exists
but there are still many 17C and 18C
houses. The sober Renaissance **town
hall** (late 16C) has an austere bell-tower.
A covered market was held on the ground
floor; note the Gothic writing on the
keystones.

▶ *Walk through the archway leading
to place Verte.*

The lovely 16C Gothic **church** is made
of local blue stone. The powerful **belfry**
was part of the fortifications; its base
forms a most unusual porch, open on
three sides. The mauve spire (1612) is
crowned by a large bulb with openings
where the watchman stood. Inside the
church there is a double transept, wooden
barrel-vaulting with carved tie-beams
in the nave and diagonal vaulting in the
chancel. The church also contains an
18C organ, 16C stained glass and Renaissance woodwork. The square is surrounded by fine 17C and 18C houses (*if
the church is closed, ask at the town hall
next door*).

▶ *Take D 962 towards Grandrieu.*

### Hestrud
The **Musée de la Douane et des
Frontières** (*Customs museum*, ○ *open
daily (except Tue) 10am-7pm (Mon, 10am-
noon);* ○ *closed mid-Dec to mid-Jan;*
∞2€; ☎03 27 59 28 48) housed in the
former customs building, illustrates the
history of the borders of the Avesnois
region since 1659: smuggled goods,
customs officers' uniforms.

▶ *Return to Soire and follow D 963
to Liessies.*

### Liessies
The village originated with an 8C Benedictine abbey which had exclusive use
of the surrounding woods. The abbey
prospered and by the 17C the abbots
were powerful lords, but the Revolution
led to the break up of the 13C abbey
church and the monastic buildings.
The **Église St-Jean-et-Ste-Hiltrude**
stands near the site of the old abbey. The
**abbey park**, situated near the church,
is open to the public. Several trails
enable visitors to discover the local fauna
and flora as well as former monastic
buildings. ☞ *Tours of the park* ○*Daily
(except Sun afternoons Jan-Feb and from
mid-jul to end Aug) 9am-noon, 2-7pm,
Sun 9.30am-1pm, 3-7pm.* ☎ *03 27 61 81 66.*
The village is the starting point of an
excursion to the 18C **Château de la Motte**,

## Address Book

*For coin ranges, see Legend on the cover flap.*

### WHERE TO STAY

**Les Prés de la Fagne (Bed and Breakfast)** – *2 r. Principale, 59132 Baives – (1km/0.6mi E of Wallers-Trelon) – ☎ 03 27 57 02 69 – www.lespresdelafagne.fr.st – closed Jan-Feb – ⚄ – 4 rms – meals ⚌.* A new gem in an antique setting. This tastefully restored 17C barn successfully blends different eras – some guest rooms even have a bathtub at the foot of the bed! Horse rides available for seasoned riders.

**La Villa Mariani (Bed and Breakfast)** – *5 Grand'Place, 59740 Solre-le-Château – ☎ 03 27 61 65 30 – 3 rms.* Savour the tranquillity of a wooded garden and the charm of old walls after having set your luggage down in one of the rooms of this 19C house on the village square. Contemporary art exhibitions are regularly held on the premises.

### WHERE TO EAT

**Marquais** – *R. du Gén.-de-Gaulle – ☎ 03 27 61 62 72, www.hoteldumarquais.com – ⊞ – 11 rms – ⚌ 6.00€.* The family ambience that reigns in this lovely inn will warm your visit to the north. Period pieces and painted brick give the bedrooms a certain panache and the breakfast table set in the hall adds to the ambient charm. Leisure time may be divided between a brisk bout of tennis, a relaxing read in the garden and a visit to the Verre workshop-museum.

**Auberge de Châtelet** – *Les Haies-à-Charmes, 59440 Dourlers – ☎ 03 27 61 06 70 – closed mid- to end-Aug, Sun and public holiday evenings.* Charmingly rustic interior with exposed beams, panelling and tiled floor is an ideal place to stop for lunch if you've been out walking. Try the *boulette d'Avesnes* a variety of the famed *maroilles* cheese .

**L'Estaminet** – *83 Grand-Rue, 59550 Maroilles – ☎ 03 27 77 78 80 – closed Sun evening.* The unassuming facade gives no hint of this establishment's popularity, and yet it is always packed. Chalk its reputation up to the particularly warm decor and reception, and the plentiful, savoury cuisine centering on maroilles, a flavourful local cheese.

### POTTERY TOUR

**Poterie Maine** – *Rte Nationale – ☎ 03 27 61 68 11 – Mon-Fri 10am-noon, 2pm-6.30pm, Sat, Sun and public holidays 3pm-7pm.* Workshops may be visited by appointment. Pottery produced here since 1862.

---

built of red brick, and to **l'Abbé-Val Joly Forest**.

The 18C **Calvaire de la Croix-Trélon** stands to the east of the intersection of the Trélon road (D 963) and the Château de la Motte access road.

▸ *From Liessies follow D 133 along the Helpe Valley.*

The road becomes more winding, and the slopes are increasingly covered with thick woods.

### Parc Départemental du Val-Joly★

The construction of the dam at Eppe-Sauvage on the Helpe-Majeure created a magnificent reservoir surrounded by the wooded banks of the River Helpe and its tributary, the Voyon. The park has many leisure facilities including swimming, tennis, sailing, fishing, riding, hiking and mountain biking, archery, and boating or pedalo. There is also an aquarium (22 tanks). The park includes a camp site with bungalows for hire as well as shopping and catering facilities.

### Eppe-Sauvage

This village, close to the Belgian border, nestles in a pretty location in the hollow of a basin formed where the River Helpe and River Eau d'Eppe meet. In the **Église St-Ursmar**, with its 16C chancel and transept, there are two remarkable 16C painted wood triptychs.

After Eppe-Sauvage, the valley opens out and becomes less wooded; marshes,

## Blue-stone Oratories

Blue-stone oratories have been built in the Avesnois and Thiérache regions since 1550; they are located in various places, mostly on the roadside, but also in fields, along ancient footpaths and even in woods or set in walls. These characteristic constructions consist of a narrow shaft surmounted by a fine recess, closed off by wire mesh as in Le Favril or Dimont, and a larger crowning piece. Each recess was intended to hold one or several polychrome statues carved by the clog makers of Mormal Forest. The oratories were erected for various reasons: in thanksgiving for a cure (as in Bérelles), to ask for a favour, to assert a certain social status, to abide by a family tradition. The Avesnois region is said to possess more than 700 blue-stone oratories including some 40 of them in the village of Cartignies alone.

called *fagnes*, are frequent along its floor. A beautiful manor farm may be seen.

### Moustier-en-Fagne

This small village derives its name from a 16C priory, or *moustier*. Olivetan Benedictines, who devote themselves to painting icons, live in the monks' quarters. They are near the **church** dedicated to St Dodon, the hermit invoked for back ailments, who was originally from this village. A handsome **manor house** with crow-stepped gables, built in 1520, is visible (left) on entering Moustier-en-Fagne.

▶ *Continue south and, 2km/1mi beyond Moustier, fork left onto D 283, then turn right.*

The top of a knoll (225m/738ft high) affords a clear **view** of **Trélon Forest**.

### Wallers-Trélon

Built entirely in blue stone, this beautiful village owes its unique appearance to the numerous quarries nearby. Nature trails allow visitors to discover the unusual flora of the **Monts de Baive**, which flourishes owing to the chalky soil.

To learn more about the blue stone in all its forms, take a tour of the exhibition in the **Maison de la fagne** (○*open Jul-Aug 2-6pm (weekends and public holidays 2.30-6.30pm); Apr-Jun and Sep-Oct weekends and public holidays, 2.30-6.30pm.* ⊕*2.50€.* ☎ *03 27 60 66 11).*

▶ *Take D 83 south; turn right onto D 951 to Trélon.*

### Trélon

Formerly known for its glass industry, Trélon is today the location of the **Atelier-musée du verre** (*rue Clavon;* ♿ ○*open Apr-Oct, 9am-noon, 2-6pm; Sat, Sun and public holidays, 2.30-6.30pm.* ⊕*5€.* ☎ *03 27 59 71 02),* a branch of the Fourmies-Trélon Folk Museum. In the heart of the old hall of the 19C glassworks, which still contains two kilns from 1850 and 1920 together with their equipment, glass workers demonstrate the blowing and shaping of glass.

▶ *Follow D 963 then D 83 to Fourmies.*

### Sains-du-Nord

The **Maison du Bocage** (*rue J.B. Lebas –* ○*open Apr-Oct 2-6pm (Sat, Sun and public holidays 2.30-6.30pm).* ⊕*3.50€.* ☎ *03 27 59 82 24),* a branch of the Fourmies-Trélon Folk Museum, has been established in a 19C farm. Exhibitions present life and work in the woodlands and pastures of the Avesnois (stock farming, cheese-making etc).

# BAILLEUL
### POPULATION 14 146
### MICHELIN LOCAL MAP 302: E-3

Situated in the hilly area known as Monts de Flandre, the town of Bailleul was damaged in 1918 during the last German onslaught in this region. It was rebuilt in authentic Flemish style. The Shrove Tuesday Carnival, headed by the giant Gargantua, offers Doctor Picolissimo the opportunity of throwing tripe to the crowd. The drive through the Monts de Flandre, described below, shows that Flanders is not as flat as some people say. A strange event takes place in July every year, the Fête des Épouvantails (the Festival of Scarecrows): at the end of the procession, the scarecrows are burnt and the popular ball can begin.

- **Information:** 3 Grand'Place, 59270 Bailleul, ☎ 03 28 43 81 00.
- **Orient Yourself:** Almost on the border with Belgium, and 150 miles north of Paris via the A 1.
- **Don't Miss:** A tour of the belfry with its superb view.
- **Organizing Your Time:** Spend half a day here, and then maybe stay over for a relaxing lunch.
- **Also See:** Lille.

## Sights

### Grand-Place
In spite of having been destroyed eight times, Bailleul and its Grand-Place have always regained their typically Flemish atmosphere. Before settling down in a local tavern with a glass of "3 Monts" beer, have a closer look at the town hall and its belfry in neo-Flemish style. The brick façade decorated with corner stones features a proclamation balcony.

### Rue du Musée
The street is lined with fine houses, in particular no 3, the town's cultural centre with its Marguerite-Yourcenar hall.

### Beffroi
*Guided tours Jul to mid-Sep Tue, Sun and public holidays 11am, Wed and Fri at 4pm, Sat at 3pm. Apr to June and Sep Sat at 3pm, Sun at 11am (June to Sep, 2nd and 4th Fri, 7pm). 2.50€. ☎03 28 43 81 00.*
The belfry towering over the town hall housed the cloth market in medieval times. There is a 13C Gothic room at ground level and from the watch-path at the top, the vast **panorama**★ includes the plain and Monts de Flandre to the north and the slag heaps of the mining area to the south. When the weather is clear, the city of Lille is visible. The peal of bells chimes well-known Flemish tunes.

### Musée Benoît-Depuydt
*24 rue du musée. ⏱Open daily (except Tue) 2-5.30pm. ⏱Closed 1 May, 25 Dec-1 Jan. 3.30€, no charge 1st Sunday in the month. ☎ 03 28 49 12 70.*
Founded in 1859, this elegant museum displays glazed earthenware from Delft and Northern France, porcelain from China and Japan, 16C to 18C furniture and carved wood as well as paintings from the Flemish, French and Dutch schools. Note in particular a breast-feeding Virgin Mary by Gérard David and an Adoration of the Magi by Pieter

### Lace-making today
In the 17C, lace-making was already a local tradition, but it reached its height during the 19C, when there were as many as 800 lace-makers in the area. The first school was founded in 1664. Lace-making declined from 1900 onwards, because of the introduction of machines. Today the tradition lives on. The International Lace-making Weekend takes place every third year (third weekend in July, scheduled for 2007) with the participation of lace-makers worldwide.

## Address Book

*For coin ranges, see the Legend on the cover flap.*

### WHERE TO STAY

**Auberge du Vert Mont** – *1318 r. du Mont-Noir, 59299 Bœschepe – ☎ 03 28 49 41 26. Closed Mon lunch and Tue lunch off-season – 7 rms – ⚏ 6.50€ – restaurant.* This red brick inn perches upon the village heights. Smart bedrooms overlook the valley. Pleasant country-style dining room decorated with wooden clogs, barrels and wheels. Kids' games and a small animal park.

### WHERE TO EAT

**Estaminet 'De Vierpot'** – *125 complexe Joseph-Decanter, 59299 Bœschepe – 12km/7.2mi N of Bailleul via D10 – ☎ 03 28 49 46 37. Closed Mon, Apr to Jun and Sep; Jul to Aug; Mon and Tue, Oct to Mar.* This inviting tavern at the foot of a restored mill is a model of northern hospitality. Typical decor dating from the 1900s, with an old stove and wooden benches. The menus offer *planches flamandes*, quiches, crepes, and a choice of more than 50 beers.

### A COLD BREW

**Ferme-brasserie Beck** – *Eckelstraete – ☎03 28 49 03 90 – Sat from 7pm, Sun from 5pm. Closed Dec-Feb.* Guided tours of the farm-brewery and tasting sessions.

---

Brueghel. In addition, a large tapestry from Flanders (18C) and 19C portraits hang in the museum.

### Maison de la Dentelle

*6 Rue du Collège – ♿ ⏰Open daily (except Sun and public holidays) 1.30-5pm. ⏰Closed 25 Dec-1 Jan. ⚏2.50€. ☎ 03 28 41 25 72.*
The school occupies a Flemish-style house; the pediment is decorated with a lace-maker and her spinning wheel. Every year some 100 students learn the technique of bobbin lace-making.

### Conservatoire Botanique National de Bailleul

*Hameau de Haendries – ⏰Open Apr to mid-Oct daily (except weekends) 9am-noon, 1.30-5pm. June to end-Sep, guided visits possible on Fri or Sat afternoons, make inquiries. ⏰Closed mid-Oct to end Mar and public holidays. ⚏3€. (Guided tours, 5€) No charge in June. ☎03 28 49 93 07.*
Housed on the 30ha/74-acre estate of a restored Flemish farm, this national botanical conservatory specialises in vegetation from Northern France. The medicinal garden contains some 700 plants and the botanical gardens are dedicated to the preservation of more than 600 endangered species. The GR

128 footpath, which crosses the Monts de Flandre, goes through the estate. Picnic tables, a viewing table and nature trails are available for visitors.

## Driving Tour

### Northern heights
*Allow half a day.*
This itinerary will take you through the Flemish countryside into Belgium. On the way, you will see hills, mills, typical local taverns and taste "special" beer and soft cheese.

▶ *Follow D 23 then turn left on D 223.*

On your right (on the Belgian side) is **Mont Kemmel** crowned by a hotel. On the same side but closer is **Mont Rouge** (Rodeberg).

▶ *Turn left again on D 318.*

### Mont Noir
Straddling the border between France and Belgium, Mont Noir (Black Hill), so called owing to its dark wooded slopes, is part of the Monts de Flandres range (altitude 170m/558ft). A path leads to the artificial grotto (1875) dedicated to Notre-Dame de la Salette.

## Saint-Jans-Cappel

This village lies at the foot of Mont Noir, immortalised in *Archives du Nord (How Many Years)*, the autobiographical work of writer and French Academy member **Marguerite Yourcenar** (1903-87) who spent her childhood years here.

From the **Parc Marguerite-Yourcenar**★, the view extends towards Ypres, Mont Rouge and Mont des Cats, surmounted by its monastery. The sea and Artois hills are visible in clear weather.

Within the Parc, the **Villa Mont-Noir**★, dating from the 1920s, is a cultural and literary centre which welcomes resident European writers.

*Le sentier des jacinthes*, a marked trail (2hr 30min) running along the slopes of Mont Noir, is dotted with the writer's quotations.

The **Musée Marguerite-Yourcenar** displays documents, photographs, a video presentation of her life and works as well as works by local artists who illustrate the beauty of the region. *Guided visits (45min) Open Apr-Sep Sun 3.30-5.30pm, and at other times by arrangement. 2€. ☎ 03 28 42 20 20.*

▶ *Follow D 10 north to Berthen and turn left.*

## Mont des Cats

Also known as Catsberg (altitude 158m/ 514ft), this hill is part of the Monts de Flandres range. It lies in pleasant undulating countryside where fields of hops, poplar trees, and red roofs form the "humanised landscape" defined by geographer Brunhes. Gourmets know this area for its wonderful cheeses which are similar to Port-Salut. On top of the hill are the neo-Gothic buildings of a Trappist monastery – **Abbaye Notre-Dame-du-Mont** – founded in 1826 and restored since that time.

## Centre d'accueil C. Grimminck

*Open daily (except Tue) 10am-noon, 2.30-6pm, Sun 12.15-1pm and 2.30-6pm, Mon 2.30-6pm. Closed 1st week in Jan, Good Friday and 25 Dec. ☎ 03 28 43 83 70.* The centre consists of an exhibition hall, a shop selling products from the monastery and a room where the monks' daily life is the subject of an audio-visual presentation.

▶ *Turn back and follow D 10 to Boeschepe.*

## Boeschepe

The village of Boeschepe at the foot of Mont des Cats has a restored windmill, the **Ondankmeulen** (the mill of ungratefulness). *Guided tours (30min) Jul-Aug 3-6pm. Apr-Jun and Sep, Sun 3-6pm. 1.50€. ☎ 03 28 42 50 70*, next to a delightful bar *(estaminet)*, which sells some 50 different kinds of beer.

▶ *Follow D 139 past the Belgian border and continue to Poperingue.*

## Poperinge

The inhabitants are known as **Keikoppen**, "Tough Heads". On the Grand'Place, a stone weighing 1 650kg/3 638lb testifies to this reputation. The Cathédrale St-Bertinus, a Flemish hall-church, is a fine example of the transition from the Romanesque style to the Gothic style.

▶ *Leave Poperinge via N 308 towards Dunkerque and turn left to Watou, also in Belgium.*

## Watou

This village is ideal for anyone wishing to sample the authentic atmosphere of an *estaminet* (a bar), where the locals drink beer while playing various games.

▶ *Return to Bailleul along D 10.*

# BARBIZON★★

POPULATION 1 499

MICHELIN LOCAL MAP 312: E-5 OR MAP 106 FOLD 45

10KM/6MI NORTH-WEST OF FONTAINEBLEAU – LOCAL MAP SEE FORÊT DE FONTAINEBLEAU

Lying on the edge of the Fontainebleau Forest, the village of Barbizon, which was part of Chailly until 1903, was a popular spot with landscape painters (*see Introduction: Landscape Painting*) and still carries memories of the artists who made it famous. The Bas-Bréau coppices nearby are reminders of a time when, according to the Goncourt brothers, "every tree was like an artist's model surrounded by a circle of paint-boxes."

**Information:** 55 Grande-Rue, 77630 Barbizon, ☎01 60 66 41 87.

## A Bit of History

### The Barbizon School
Breaking the rules of studio work and official art, the Barbizon artists were landscape painters who perfected the technique of working directly from nature after two great masters: **Théodore Rousseau** (1812-67) and **Jean-François Millet** (1814-75). The local people were happy to welcome these nature-loving artists who rose at dawn and whose genius and mischievous nature enlivened local weddings and banquets. Next came the writers, seduced by the beauty of the forest and the congenial atmosphere of this small, international community: George Sand, Henri Murger, the Goncourt brothers, Taine etc. Thereafter, Barbizon remained a fashionable spot.

Millet, a patriarch with nine children, died after a life of hard work, his eyes forever riveted on the landscapes of the Bière plain. Like Rousseau, he was buried at **Chailly Cemetery** (*2km/1.2mi north along D 64; plan of graveyard at entrance*).

## Sights

### La Grande Rue

This long high street (Grande Rue) lined with hotels, restaurants and villas. Many of these buildings bear commemorative plaques of the artists who stayed there.

### Auberge du Père Ganne★
*92 grande rue.* ⏰*Open daily (except Tue) 10am-12.30pm, 2-5.30pm.* ⬤*5€.* ☎*01 60 66 22 27.*

*"The Gleaners" by Millet (Musée d'Orsay, Paris)*

## Address Book

*For coin ranges, see the Legend on the cover flap.*

### WHERE TO STAY

**La Ferme des Vosves (Bed and Breakfast)** – *155 r. de Boissise, 77190 Village de Vosves – 10km/6mi N of Barbizon –* ☎ *01 64 39 22 28. Closed at New Year. 2 rms. www.fermedevosves.com.* Take your time and enjoy the pretty gardens of this old farm nestled in the heart of a village overlooking the Seine. The bedrooms are simply furnished, and the quietness, the hospitable welcome and modest prices make this an excellent place to stay.

### WHERE TO EAT

**Le Relais de Barbizon** – *2 av. du Gén-de-Gaulle –* ☎ *01 60 66 40 28. Closed mid Aug, mid to end Dec, Tue evening and Wed.* A modest little inn at the village entrance. Enjoyable dining room with a section set aside for family gatherings. Cuisine made from fresh ingredients; a variety of fixed-price menus.

**L'Angelus** – *31 Grande-Rue –* ☎ *01 60 66 40 30. Closed mid-Jan to mid-Feb; Mon-Tue.* This rustic inn

takes its name from one of the works of Millet, painted at Barbizon. You're sure to appreciate the relaxing atmosphere and traditional cuisine.

### ON THE TOWN

**Bizon's Club** – *1 r. Grande rue –* ☎ *01 60 66 40 01, www.bizonsclub.fr – Fri-Sun 11pm 'til dawn.* The Forest of Fontainebleau's foremost discotheque manages to be hip, selective and convivial... the perfect balance! The younger crowd congregates on the big dance floor with techno music; more mature patrons prefer the small club downstairs with music from the 1980s.

### SHOPPING

**Verrerie d'Art** – *Le Moulin des Noues, 91840 Soisy-sur-École – 13km/8.5mi NW of Barbizon –* ☎ *01 64 98 00 03, www.verrerie-art-soisy.fr. Closed 1 May and 20 July – 20 Aug: Tue-Sat 10am-12:30pm, 2-6pm; Sun 2.30-6pm.* Set in a pretty park with a river, this glassmaker's atelier has opened its doors so that you can learn how glass is blown and handcrafted. A short film, an exhibition and a boutique round out the visit.

This was a popular meeting-place for artists, many of whom had rooms here. The inn is now the **Musée Municipal de l'École de Barbizon**. A lively educational audio-visual display describes "Ganne's painters" who revolutionised art and brought life and laughter to the inn by their tricks. On the ground floor, three recently restored rooms are representative of their habit of decorating all the wood panelling in the inn as a means of paying for their keep. They decorated cupboards, doors, the sideboard, the fireplace, in fact any flat surface, all of them ideal as supports for the talents of the artists. On the first floor the museum has numerous paintings indicating the influence of Barbizon on Impressionists through the "Back to Nature" theme: works by Camille Corot, Charles Jacque, Jules Dupré, Ferdinand Chaigneau, Georges Gassies and Eugène Lavieille.

**Maison de Rousseau** *(55 Grande-Rue).* The home of Théodore Rousseau is behind the war memorial

**Maison-atelier de Jean-François Millet**
*27 Grande-Rue . ⓘOpen 9.30am-12.30pm, 2-5.30pm. ⓘClosed 1 Jan and 25 Dec.* ☎*01 60 66 21 55.*
Millet's home and studio for 25 years contains etchings of some of Millet's most famous paintings: *The Angelus*, *The Gleaners* and others. In the dining room, there are drawings and engravings by Millet. The living room is reserved for exhibitions of contemporary works.

**Monument de Rousseau et Millet**
A bronze medal embedded in the rock is the work of Henri Chapu. Behind this monument, a plaque set into another rock commemorates the centenary of the setting up of the first artistic reserve in 1853 at the instigation of Rousseau.

# BAVAY★

POPULATION 3 581
MICHELIN LOCAL MAP 302: K-6

Bavay was originally the capital of the old Belgian tribe the Nervii; today it is a small town with low houses, known for its confectionery called "Chiques de Bavay". At the time of Caesar Augustus, Bagacum was an important town in Roman Belgium. It was a judicial and administrative centre, the seat of a curia, a military post and a supply centre situated at the junction of seven roads that led to Utrecht, Boulogne, Cambrai, Soissons, Reims, Trier and Cologne, this last being the busiest. The routes, still recognisable in the present road network, were furrowed by carts which formed ruts, traces of which can be found in the forum.

**Information:** Maison du Patrimoine, r. Saint-Maur, 59570 Bavay, ☎ 03 27 39 81 65. www.mairie-bavay.fr.

## A Bit of History

### Grand' Place
The brickwork of the 17C belfry contrasts with the 18C town hall, built of granite, next to it. A fluted column in the square supports a statue of Brunhilda, Queen of Austrasia, who took a great interest in road networks.

### Remains of the Roman City
In 1942 Canon Bièvelet began searching on a site cleared by bombing in 1940. Excavations revealed the remains of a large group of monumental buildings: a civil basilica, a forum, a portico above a horseshoe-shaped underground gallery (*cryptoporticus*) and a room over a deep cellar stand along an east-west axis. A few houses have also been found south of the walls built after the invasions of the second half of the 3C.

## Visit

**Musée Archéologique** (*2 rue de Gommeries –* ⊙*open daily (except Tue) Apr-Sep 9am-6pm; Oct-Mar 9am-noon, 2-5pm, Sat-Sun and public holidays*

ROMAN REMAINS
0    10 m

VALENCIENNES
R. des Clouteries
(D 932)
R. des Remparts
LE CATEAU-CAMBRÉSIS
MAUBEUGE
Cryptoporticus
FORUM
Excavations
Musée Archéologique
Basilica
Rue de la Réunion
Rue de Gommeries
AVESNES

**A SWEET SHOP**

**La Romaine** – *30 pl. Charles-de-Gaulle* – ☎*03 27 63 10 06 – Daily (except Mon) 7am-7pm. Closed 15 Jul-15 Aug.* This establishment guards the secret of the renowned 'Chiques de Bavay' – sweets flavoured with apple, cherry or coffee. They were purportedly invented by the wives of soldiers under Napoléon I who often chewed tobacco in order to spit out the lead they had ingested while ripping open gunpowder bags with their teeth. Their wives came up with these recipes to give them an alternative to the tobacco-chewing habit.

**A BREWERY**

**Brasserie au Baron** – *place des Rocs, Gussignies* – ☎ *03 27 66 88 61.* Visits of the microbrewery.

*10.30am-noon, 2-6pm.* ⏰ *closed 1 Jan, 1 May, 1 and 11 Nov, 25 Dec-1 Jan.* ⊚*3€, no charge 1st and 3rd Sunday in the month.* ☎ *03 27 63 13 95).* Housed in a large modern building, the archaeological museum exhibits various objects found during excavations. An audiovisual show presents daily life, trade,

religious life and craft activities at the time of Bagacum. The numerous pots, dishes and vases with busts of divinities on them are a reminder that Bavay was an important pottery production centre. Delightful bronze figurines are among the treasures from a bronzefounder's hoard.

# BEAUVAIS★★

POPULATION 59 003

MICHELIN LOCAL MAP 305: D-4

This attractive city, which is the capital of the Oise region and the hometown of talented people such as the fashion designer Givenchy and the plane manufacturer Marcel Dassault, has retained its striking cathedral, an architectural masterpiece almost defying the laws of gravity.

▸ **Information:** Office du tourisme de Beauvais, 1 r. Beauregard, 60000 ☎ 03 44 15 30 30. www.beauvaistourisme.fr.

## A Bit of History

### Bishops and Burghers

Beauvais, the capital of the Belgian tribe the Bellovaci, became a Gallo-Roman city enclosed within walls during the 3C. From the 11C the city had as its lord a bishop, who was often in conflict with the town's wealthy merchants and jealous of their franchises. One of the bishops, Pierre Cauchon, has a dubious claim to fame: while the town wanted to surrender to Charles VII, Cauchon rallied to the English. Chased out of Beauvais in 1429 by the burghers, he took refuge in Rouen where, on 30 May 1431, he sent Joan of Arc to the stake.

### Jeanne Hachette

On 27 June 1472 Beauvais was besieged by Charles the Bold, Duke of Burgundy, who was marching on Paris with 80 000 men. The town had no troops so men and women ran to the ramparts and watched in horror as ladders were laid against the fortifications. Jeanne Laîné, the daughter of a humble craftsman, saw an assailant appear at the top of the wall, a standard in hand. She threw herself on him, tore away his banner and struck him with a hatchet, sending him flying into the moat below. This

example fired the courage of the others; the resistance gained momentum, giving time for reinforcements to arrive. Charles lifted the siege on 22 July. Each year, at the end of June, Beauvais honours Jeanne "Hachette".

### Tapestries

In 1664, Louis XIV founded the **Manufacture Royale de Tapisserie**. The artisans worked on horizontal looms producing low-warp tapestries in wool and silk which are noted for being extremely fine; they were usually used as upholstery. The Manufacture Royale changed its name to Manufacture Nationale in 1804. The workshops, which were evacuated to Aubusson in 1939, were unable to return to Beauvais after the buildings were destroyed in 1940. The looms were relocated to the Gobelins Works in Paris and remained there until Beauvais could welcome them back in 1989.

### Ceramics and stained glass

Pottery making has been going on in the area since Gallo-Roman times. Glazed earthenware and stoneware, manufactured locally since the 15C, have made the Beauvais region one of the great ceramic centres of France.

## Address Book

*For coin ranges, see Legend on the cover flap.*

### WHERE TO STAY

**Hôtel du Cygne** – *24 r. Carnot, Beauvais* – ☎ 03 44 48 68 40 – *21 rms* – ⊡ 8 €. A conveniently located hotel in the heart of old Beauvais. The rooms are simple and well-kept; those looking onto the back are quieter. The breakfast room is of spruce.

**La Ferme du Colombier (Bed and Breakfast)** – *14 r. du Four-Jean-Legros – 60650 Savignies –10km/6mi NW of Beauvais N31 dir. Rouen, then D 1 –* ☎ 03 44 82 18 49 – *– reservations required – 4 rms – Meals .* A holiday on the farmstead! Your (loquacious) neighbours here will be the sheep raised on site. The comfortable, spacious bedrooms, housed in an annex, come with kitchen privileges. Enquire about the rambling tours organized by your hosts.

**Chambre d'Hôte M. et Mme Bruandet** – *13 Hameau de Bellefontaine, Hannaches – 5km/3mi southwest of Gerberoy* – ☎ 03 44 82 46 63 – *http:// bellefontaine.free.fr. Closed Jan – – 3 rms – meal*. Resolutely modern style furniture adorns the rooms and the sculptures in the square courtyard. The imaginative and talented designs were conceived by the owner himself, who is a sculptor by profession. Enquire about local hiking tours.

### WHERE TO EAT

**Hostellerie du Vieux Logis** – *25 rue du Logis-du-Roy, Gerberoy* – ☎ 03 44 82 71 66 – *closed Tue and Sun evenings and Wed; Nov to Feb, closed Mon to Fri evenings*. This half-timbered house blends in nicely with the picturesque village of Gerberoy. The dining hall features wooden frame-work and an impressive brick fireplace. We recommend the "sweet menu" and the "medieval barbecue". Terrace for the summer months, where tea is served in the afternoon.

**Les Canards de la Landelle** – *1 r. des Sablons, 60850 Lalandelle –* ☎ 03 44 81 63 39. Open for lunch daily from 14 Jul to end Aug, Sat evenings from Sep to Jun and Sun lunch all year. Typical of the Bray country, this 18C barn is now an inn starring duck in its multiple forms: the chef whips up magret, civet, confit, cassoulet. In winter, diners enjoy sitting next to the fireplace; in summer patrons congregate on the terrace beneath an ancient walnut tree.

**La Baie d'Halong** – *32 r. de Clermont* – ☎ 03 44 45 39 83. In this restaurant on the edge of town, Ta Kim-Huong offers Vietnamese cuisine, including recipes inherited from his grandmother. You can try a fondue, aromatic soups, or try five-spice chicken.

### SHOWTIME

**Théâtre du Beauvaisis** – *Pl. Georges-Brassens* – ☎ 03 44 06 08 20. *Ticket office open Tue-Fri 1pm-7pm, Sat 4pm-7pm. Closed Mon and public holidays, and Sun except performance days.* Classical and modern theatre, dance, circus, one-man shows, music, comedy, exhibitions.

### SPORT AND LEISURE

**Plan d'eau du Canada** (*Municipal watersports centre*) – *R. de la Mie-au-Roy, Beauvais* – ☎ 03 44 45 33 93. *Mid-Mar to mid-May: 8am-8.30pm; mid-May to mid-Sep: 8am-10pm; mid-Sep to mid-Oct: 8am-8.30pm; mid-Oct to mid-Mar: 8am-6.30pm.* This 30ha/75acre artificial lake is quite popular with the local population. The water-sports complex next to the beach offers rentals of sailing dinghies, canoes, kayaks, pedal-boats, sailboards and more.

**Parc Saint-Paul** – Kids – *47, Rue de l'Avelon, 60650 Saint Paul – 8km/4.8mi W of Beauvais* – ☎ 03 44 82 20 16, *www.parcsaintpaul.com. Apr-Sep 10am-6pm – 12.50€ (children 10.50€).* A amusement park situated on 15ha/37acres of land and water.

### SHOPPING

**Les Canards de la Landelle** – *1 r. des Sablons, 60850 Lalandelle –* ☎ 03 44 81 63 39. Foie gras from the Bray region.

Around 1850, pottery workshops were replaced by ceramic and tile factories which in turn attracted fine pottery workshops in their vicinity. Beauvais' 16C stained glass is also famous, particularly that by the Leprince family.

### Place Jeanne-Hachette

There is a fine statue of the local heroine opposite the town hall with its beautifully restored 18C façade.

### Ruins

On the corner, you will see traces of the Collégiale St-Barthélémy and, opposite, behind the Galerie Nationale de la Tapisserie, the ruins of Gallo-Roman town walls.

### Ancien Palais Épiscopal

The former bishop's palace is a fine architectural ensemble restored in 2000. The 14C fortified doorway is flanked by two large towers with pepper-pot roofs. It was built by Bishop Simon de Clermont de Nesle with 8 000 livres of fines that the town had to pay after a riot in 1306 during which the bishopric was pillaged. At the far end of the courtyard stands the main body of the palace; set ablaze in 1472 by the Burgundians, it was rebuilt around 1500 and retains an elegant Renaissance façade. The buildings house the Musée Départemental de l'Oise.

## Sights

## Cathédrale St-Pierre★★★

The history of the cathedral has been tumultuous. Its unique appearance is due to the great technical drama of its construction and the desperate efforts of the bishops and chapters to raise the necessary funds: an exhausting struggle which was prolonged over four centuries, but finally abandoned before the enormous project was completed. During the Carolingian period (751-987) a small cathedral, Notre-Dame, was erected; known as the **Basse-Œuvre**, now only three of the nave's bays remain complete, adjoining the newer building. In 949 another cathedral was begun, but it was destroyed by two fires. Subsequently, in 1225, the bishop and chapter decided to erect the biggest church of its day, a New Work

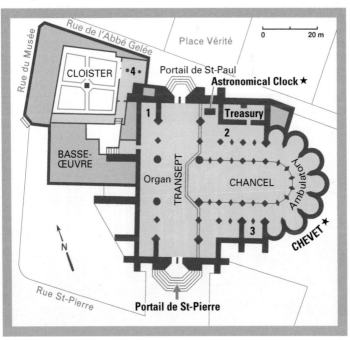

*Beauvais, Église St-Etienne –*
*Detail from the Tree of Jesse*

(**Nouvel-Œuvre**) dedicated to St Peter. While building a grandiose cathedral might seem a reasonable ambition in the Gothic period, in this case aspiration overcame sense. When the construction of the chancel was started in 1238, the clergy and the master builders wanted to better past architects and set a standard even future architects would find difficult to meet: the height to the vault's keystone was to be slightly above 48m/158ft, making the roof (68m/223ft high) about the height of the towers of Notre-Dame in Paris.

It took 25 years to achieve this feat but for once the medieval architects had overestimated their ability. The pillars were too widely spaced and the buttresses on the piers too weak. In 1284 the chancel collapsed: 40 more years of work and an enormous amount of money went into saving it. The three large arches of the chancel's right bays were reinforced by the addition of intermediary piers, the flying buttresses multiplied, the abutments strengthened.

No sooner had this task been finished than the Hundred Years War prevented any continuation. The cathedral still consisted of only a chancel and its dependent parts.

In 1500 the bishop decided to resume work and entrusted the construction of the transept to Martin Chambiges, assisted by Jean Vast; funds were mainly obtained through the sale of exemptions and in 1550, the transept was finally completed.

Unfortunately, instead of building the nave next, it was decided to erect an openwork tower over the transept crossing, surmounted by a spire. The cross at the top of the spire was positioned in 1569, at a height of 153m/502ft (Strasbourg's is 142m/466ft). But as there was no nave to counterbalance the thrusts, the piers gave way on Ascension Day in 1573, just as the procession had left the church.

After that, despite tremendous efforts and sacrifices, the clergy and people of Beauvais were able to restore only the

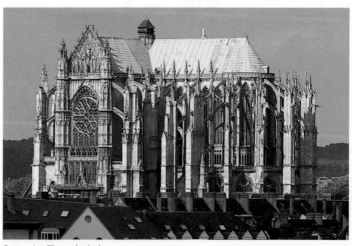

*Beauvais – The cathedral*

chancel and the transept: the unfinished cathedral would never again have a spire, and would never have a nave.

## Chevet★

*See illustration in the Introduction.*
The chancel dates from the 13C. Like the Flamboyant transept arms, it is shored up by flying buttresses with high piers which rise up to the roof. The transept arms were to have been very long and framed by towers.

**South transept façade** – The façade is richly decorated and bears two high turrets flanking the **Portail de St-Pierre** (St Peter's Doorway), the embrasures, tympanum and arching of which are adorned with niches beneath openwork canopies. The doorway is surmounted by a large rose-window with delicate tracery.

**Interior★★★** – The dizzying height of the vaults (almost 48m/157ft high) is immediately apparent. The generous transept is almost 58m/190ft long, and the chancel is extremely elegant. There is an open triforium and the clerestory is 18m/59ft high. Seven chapels open off the ambulatory.

The following, which are of particular interest, are marked on the cathedral map: the "Roncherolles" **stained glass** dating from 1522 (1); the 14C clock (2); the 16C altarpiece (3) and the chapter house (4).

**Stained-glass windows★★** – The transept features most of the 16C compositions. The south rose-window features the Eternal Father in the central medallion. Underneath, 10 Prophets and 10 Apostles or Doctors stand in two rows.

**Astronomical Clock★** – *'Sound and Light' (Son et Lumière) show (30min).* Jul-Aug, 10.40am, 11.40am, 12.40pm, 2.40pm, 3.40pm and 4.40pm; May-Jun and Sep-Oct, 10.40am, 11.40am, 2.40pm, 3.40pm and 4.40pm, weekends 5.40pm; Nov-Apr, 11.40am, 2.40pm and 3.40pm . Closed 1 Jan. 4€. ☎ 03 44 48 11 60. This monumental clock was made by the engineer Louis-Auguste Vérité from 1865 to 1868. It comprises 90 000 parts and has been reassembled several times. The lower part resembles a fortress with numerous windows. In the glazed openings 52 dials show the length of the days and nights, the seasons etc.

To the right of the astronomical clock is an old 14C clock with chimes that play psalms corresponding to the different periods of the year.

**Basse-Œuvre** – Traces remain of the old 10C cathedral built from salvaged Gallo-Roman quarry stones known as *pastoureaux*. It served as the parish church until the 1789 Revolution.

## Église St-Étienne★

The nave and the transept of the church dedicated to St Stephen are Romanesque. Their restraint, softened by the "Beauvais-style" bracketed cornices, contrasts with the architectural richness of the chancel, rebuilt a little after 1500 in a refined Flamboyant style. The chancel, which is higher than the nave, is encircled by chapels. The tower flanking the west front served as the town belfry. The left aisle gives on to a Romanesque doorway with a finely carved tympanum and arching. **Stained-glass windows★★** – The chancel's Renaissance stained-glass windows, by Engrand, are most beautiful; among them is the extraordinary **Tree of Jesse★★★** with its stunning design, colours and translucency.

## Musée Départemental de l'Oise★

*Open daily (except Tue) 10am-noon, 2–6pm (Jul-Sep 10am-6pm). Closed 1 Jan, Easter, 1 May, Whitsun and 25 Dec. 2€, no charge 1st Sunday in the month.* ☎ 03 44 11 43 83, www.cg60.fr.
The collections are displayed on four levels. The **towers at the entrance** to the museum contain the medieval collections: woodcarvings from churches and abbeys, sculpted fragments from some of Beauvais' timber-framed houses and frescoes.

The **upper floors** house the fine arts collections (mainly paintings) from the 16C to the 20C: 16C French School, 17C and 18C Italian and French Schools, and French landscape artists of the 19C including **Corot** (*The Fountain of the French Academy in Rome* and *The Old St-Michel Bridge, Paris*) and **Huet**. There's also an unusual **Bust of the Virgin Mary** by Ingres (1860), while Art Nouveau furniture and Beauvais tapestry work provide an insight into France at the turn of the last century and during the Roaring Twenties.

### Galerie nationale de la Tapisserie

*(22, rue Saint-Pierre. open Apr-Sep daily (except Mon) 9.30am-12.30pm, 2-6pm (last admission 30min before closing); Oct-Mar daily (except Mon) 10am-12.30pm, 2-5pm. closed 1 Jan, 1 May, 25 Dec. ☎ 03 44 15 39 10).* Housed in a low-roofed building beyond the cathedral's east end, the gallery stages exhibitions giving an overview of French tapestry from the 15C to present day.

### Manufacture nationale de la tapisserie

*24, rue Henri Brispot. Guided tours (1hr) Tue-Thu, 2-4.30pm. 3.20€. ☎ 03 44 05 14 28.*
The national tapestry works have, since 1989, been housed in the former slaughterhouses. Today the factory contains about a dozen looms. The entire production is reserved for the State.

## Driving Tours

## Le Pays de Bray

*58km/36mi – allow 2hr*
Carved liked a buttonhole into the chalk of the Paris basin, the landscape of the Bray is one of wide panoramas, of farmland planted with apple orchards, and gently curving valleys. It is also renowned as the place where Swiss-born Charles Gervais 'invented' the soft cheese known as Petit Suisse.

▶ *Leave Beauvais along avenue J.-Mermoz. Turn left towards Gisors (D981). 5km/3mi beyond Auneuil, turn right (D129). Cross the Vauroux, to Lalandelle, and then follow signs for « Table d'orientation » from which there is a fine view over the countryside of Bray. Turn right onto the D22 at the start of the descent.*

At the first turning to the right, you can see a hollow where the strata of the underlying chalk is clearly visible.

▶ *Retrace your route to the crossroads and continue along the D574.*

You pass through the village of Coudray-St-Germer, then descend **(view**★ of Gournay).

### St-Germer-de-Fly

St Germer founded an abbey here in the 7C. The great **church**★ was built between 1150 and 1175. *Guided visits possible; contact tourist office for information ☎ 03 44 82 62 74.*

▶ *Take the D109 towards Cuigy-en-Bray and Espaubourg, and the narrow road along the foot of the steep slopes of the Bray. At St-Aubin-en-Bray turn left. Cross the RN to Fontainettes.*

### Les Fontainettes

Garden pottery manufacture and sandstone piping. This very undulating and wooded region, is the cradle of Beauvais ceramics and pottery.

### Lachapelle-aux-Pots

**Le musée de la Poterie** demonstrates the speciality of the village: exhibition of work by local potters Delaherche and Klingsor. *Open Apr-Oct daily (except Mon), 2-6pm, Sat-Sun and public holidays, 2.30-6.30pm. Closed 1 Jan, 24-25 and 31 Dec, and the Mon of public holidays. 2€. ☎ 03 44 04 50 71 or 03 44 04 50 72.*

### Savignies

This charming village, a stronghold of pottery was surplanted in the 19C by Lachapelle. But you can still find traces of this industry such as chimneys and walls, and a few artists who maintain the tradition.

# BERGUES ★★

POPULATION 4 306

MICHELIN LOCAL MAP 302: C-2

Bergues is a wealthy Flemish town leading a peaceful life within ramparts which overlook a region famous for its pastures, butter and cheese, but growing rich on the wool trade. The yellow-ochre tones of the buildings are reflected in the waters of the moat and canals which partly surround the town. Despite wartime damage, Bergues has retained its old character with winding streets, large squares and the silent quays along the edge of the River Colme.

**Information:** *Pl. de la République, 59380 Bergues, ☎ 03 28 68 71 06. www.bergues.fr.*

## A Bit of History

**The Walled Town** The walls, pierced by four gateways and surrounded by a deep moat, date partly from the Middle Ages (Bierne Gate, Beckerstor, curtain wall east of Cassel Gate) and partly from the 17C. These fortifications were used by the French troops during the defence of Dunkirk, forcing the Germans to use Stukas and flame-throwers to breach them.

## Sights

### Belfry

Open 10am-noon, 2-6pm; Sat, Sun and public holidays, 10am-1pm and 3-6pm. closed Sun (Nov to Feb), 1 Jan, 1 May 1 and 11 Nov and 25 Dec. 2€. ☎ 03 28 68 71 06.

Erected during the 14C, remodelled in the 16C and dynamited by the Germans in 1944, the belfry (54m/ 177ft high) was rebuilt by Paul Gélis who sought to pre-

## Address Book

### WHERE TO STAY

**Au Tonnelier** – 4 rue du Mont de Piété, Bergues. ☎ 03 28 68 70 05, www.autonnelier.com. Closed mid-Aug to early Sep, 22 Dec to 5 Jan, Mon, Tue, Fri lunch and Sun evening –12 rms – 7.50€ – restaurant. Located near the church, this village house sports flower-filled windowboxes in summer. Come in through the old café and take a seat in the cheerful dining room. Simply furnished rooms.

### WHERE TO EAT

**Taverne le Bruegel** – 1 r. du Marché-aux-Fromages, Bergues. ☎ 03 28 68 19 19 – closed 20-30 Dec. The oldest house in Bergues, dating back to 1597, this is a typical, congenial tavern where carbonnade and other Flemish specialities are served in an engaging decor featuring brick walls and wooden furniture.

**Le Cornet d'Or** – 26 r. de l'Espagnole. ☎ 03 28 68 66 27. Closed Sun evening and Mon except public holidays. Don't be put

off by this restaurant's rather austere façade – the traditional cuisine with a nicely modern touch has a solid reputation in these parts. The dining room, sporting exposed beams and floral bouquets, is plush and cosy.

### SHOWTIME

**La Nuit du Miroir aux Alouettes, Anno 1585** – Beffroi, Place de la Republique. ☎ 03 28 68 71 06. 11€ (children: 6 €). An interactive historical event in the walled town. Weekend evenings: end April and early October. Tickets and reservations at the Office du Tourisme.

### LEISURE

**Brasserie Thiriez** – 22 r. de Wormhout, 59470 Esquelbecq. ☎ 03 28 62 88 44. Brewery visits (1hr) by appointment. Tastings Mon-Sat, 10am-7pm; Sun and public holidays by appointment. Closed 1-20 Jan.

**Tourist Tram** – 3pm, 3.45pm, 4.30pm and 5.15pm. 30min: Departs from belfry. 3.80 €.

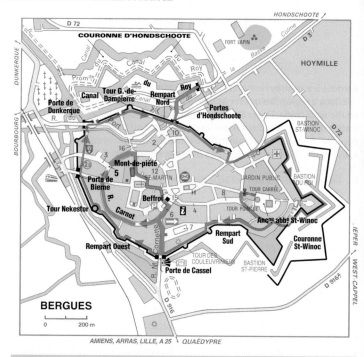

| | | | | | | |
|---|---|---|---|---|---|---|
| Anglaise R. | 2 | Lamartine R. | 6 | Nationale R. | 12 |
| Arsenal R. de l' | 3 | Marché-aux-Bestiaux Pl. | 7 | République Pl. de la | 15 |
| Collège R. du | 4 | Marché-aux-Chevaux R. | 8 | St-Jean R. | 16 |
| Faidherbe R. | 5 | Marché-aux-Poissons Pl. et R. | 10 | | |

serve the main structure of the former edifice while simplifying the exterior decoration. It is made of yellow bricks known as "sand bricks" and is surmounted by the lion of Flanders; the **carillon** comprises 50 bells (*contact tourist office for information on recitals*).

*Belfry*

**Porte de Cassel** This gateway was built in the 17C with a **drawbridge**; its triangular pediment features a carved sun, Louis XIV's emblem. From the outside, there is a view to the right over the **medieval curtain wall** toward the towers of St-Winoc.

**Rempart Ouest** The western rampart was erected in 1635. Beyond the **Poudrière du Moulin** stands the **Tour Nekestor**, dating from the time of the dukes of Burgundy. The wall continues towards the **Porte de Bierne** (16C) with its drawbridge, offering views of the **ruins of a medieval tower** and some **ancient locks**.

**Rempart Nord** The northern rampart links the **Porte de Dunkerque**, which overlooks the beginning of the inner canal, the **Tour Guy-de-Dampierre** (1286), named after the 22nd Count of Flanders and the first **Porte d'Hondschoote**.

**Couronne d'Hondschoote** On the north side of the walls, Vauban used the branches of the River Colme to build an extensive system of bastions and ravelins completely surrounded by large moats filled with carp, pike-perch and tench which serve as a bird sanctuary; viewed from above, this defensive system forms a sort of crown, hence its name.

**Couronne and abbaye de St-Winoc** The Couronne de St-Winoc was designed to protect the abbey of the same name. It comprises three mighty **bastions** (1672-92): the St-Winoc bastion, the King's bastion and the St-Pierre bastion. The **abbey** is accessible from the Couronne across avenue du Général-de-Gaulle. Only ruins remain of this famous Benedictine establishment. Most of the buildings were destroyed during the Revolution; all that survives is the 18C marble front door, the Tour Pointue (rebuilt in 1815) which marks the site of the abbey's façade and the 12C-13C square tower of the transept crossing, supported by reinforced buttresses.

**Rempart Sud** Follow the southern rampart past three small 13C round towers followed by the Faux-Monnayeurs and Couleuvriniers towers to return to the Porte de Cassel.

**Rues Carnot and Faidherbe** These streets are lined with lovely 18C buildings including several mansions such as the **Hôtel de Hau de Staplande**, along rue Carnot.

**Mont-de-piété** This elegant building with a Baroque gable is constructed of brick and white stone, and includes an ingenious combination of decorative elements: pilasters, niches, cartouches, pediments. It was designed by **Wenceslas Coebergher** (1561-1634), an extraordinary character who was a painter, architect, economist and engineer; in the Flanders region he occupied himself with the draining of the Moëres, the marshes near Hondschoote, and introduced the first pawnshops (*monts-de-piété*). This pawnshop was inaugurated in 1633 and continued in business until 1848. The town museum has been housed inside since 1953.

**Musée municipal** (*daily (except Tue), 10am-noon, 2-5pm. closed Jan. 3.50€. ☎ 03 28 68 13 30*). The most outstanding of all the paintings in the municipal museum is undoubtedly the *Hurdy-Gurdy Player*, a vast canvas by **Georges de la Tour** (1593-1652) exhibited on the first floor. There are also works by several 16C-17C Flemish artists including a sketch by Rubens, and portraits by Van Dyck, Cossiers and Simon de Vox. The natural history section on the second floor includes a particularly extensive collection of birds and butterflies.

# BOULOGNE-SUR-MER★★

POPULATION 92 704
MICHELIN LOCAL MAP 301: C-3

Boulogne, once a Roman city, is situated where the Liane Valley opens up after running between steep hills. The town has a rough but appealing look and busy streets. Today it is the largest European centre of the fish trade and home of an international fish-processing complex. Boulogne's illustrious citizens include the literary historian **St Beuve**, (1804-69), the engineer **Frédéric Sauvage** (1786-1857), the inventor of the propeller used in steam navigation, and the Egyptologist **Auguste Mariette**.

▪ **Information:** 24 quai Gambetta, BP 187, 62203 Boulogne-Sur-Mer. ☎ 03 21 10 88 10. www.tourisme-boulognesurmer.com.

▸ **Orient Yourself:** Accessible from the A 16. Amid the newer shopping streets of the ville basse are some of the best food shops in the whole region.

⊛ **Don't Miss:** Nausicaä; the ville haute.

◔ **Organizing Your Time:** Nausicaä will consume around two hours (best visited in the afternoon). Allow a half day to tour the town.

▨ **Especially for Kids:** Nausicaä and its aquariums; the beach at Portel.

⌀ **Also See:** Hardelot; the coast, and Desvres.

# A Bit of History

Boulogne is linked to Bonaparte who from 1803 to 1805 kept his troops mustered at the **Boulogne Camp** in readiness to invade England. On 26 August 1805, Napoleon I, crowned a year earlier, finally abandoned his project in order to set his Grande Armée against the Austrians.

In August 1840 the future Napoleon III tried to raise the town against Louis-Philippe, but the attempt floundered and he was imprisoned in Ham Fort.

**The Father of Egyptology** – The young man from Boulogne, who was working at the Louvre Museum in Paris, left for Cairo in 1850, entrusted with the task of finding Coptic manuscripts. Instead he discovered Memphis, the ancient capital of the Pharaohs. During the following 30 years, **Auguste Mariette** (1821-81) travelled throughout Egypt and was responsible for numerous excavation projects. He also founded the Boulaq Museum, which later became Cairo's Egyptian Museum, and set up the department of Egyptian Antiquities. In 1879 he was promoted to the rank of pasha by the Egyptian authorities.

# Sights

## Nausicaä★★★

*Centre National de la Mer, Boul Ste Beuve.*
**Kids** &. ⓒ*Open Jul-Dec, 9.30am-7.30pm; rest of year, 9.30am-6.30pm.* ⓒ*Closed 3 weeks in Jan (open 2pm on 1 Jan). 25 Dec.* ⓢ*16.50€ (child, 10.80€).* ☎ *03 21 30 99 99. www.nausicaa.fr. Tickets bought within 2h of closure can be used until noon the next day.*

Designed by architect Jacques Rougerie, who specialises in buildings with a maritime theme, and Christian Le Conte, a specialist in museography, **Nausicaä** is the largest sea-life centre in Europe. It aims to provide information about fauna in warm and cold ocean environments and to manage marine resources and the trades linked to them.

The building is dappled with bluish light and filled with aquatic music. There are 36 aquariums with more than 10 000 marine animals from the world's seas.

**Journey through the World's Seas** – The circular aquarium contains jellyfish. After being told about the reproduction cycle of species from tropical seas and the Mediterranean, you go on to discover some magnificent specimens and observe their habits.

Next comes the **Espace Diamant des Thons**, a strange aquarium shaped like a reverse pyramid and containing a shoal of *sérioles* (of the tuna family).

**Man and the Sea** – A long circular corridor illustrates the relationship between man and the sea going back thousands of years. A **celestial dome** forms the setting of the area devoted to resources from the sea and to the dangers which threaten the coastline.

**Tropical Lagoon Village** – You then arrive on the beach of 'Paradise' island surrounded by the greenish-blue waters of a **lagoon**. From the pontoon, you can observe the lagoon full of colourful fish on one side, and the open sea with characteristic shoals of fish on the other.

**Underwater Observatory** – The underwater observatory reveals Californian sea-lions diving and swimming through the waves. The **aerial observatory** shows the same sea-lions stretched out on the rocks in a typical Californian setting of cliffs and log cabins.

An escalator leads to the **hands-on basin**, full of cod, pollack and turbot, where children can stroke thorn-back rays.

The tour takes you to a reduced-scale fish farm where new fish-farming techniques are described. The adjacent area is devoted to various fishing techniques and a film shows night work aboard a trawler in the North Sea.

The visit ends with the spectacular **Anneau des sélaciens**, a panoramic circular tank filled with sharks.

Off the foyer are a cinema (130 seats), a multimedia library, souvenir shops, a restaurant, bar and cafeteria.

## La Ville Basse

The **outer harbour** is protected by two jetties, one, Digue Carnot, is 3 250m/ over 2mi long. The **inner harbour** con-

# Address Book

*For coin ranges, see the Legend on the cover flap.*

## WHERE TO STAY

**Le Clos d'Esch (Bed and Breakfast)** – *126 r. de l'Église, 62360 Echinghen – 4km/2.4mi E of Boulogne. Take D 940 dir. St-Léonard, then D 234 dir. Echingen.* ☎ *03 21 91 14 34. jp-boussemaere@ wanadoo.fr. Closed 23 Dec to end Jan – 4 rms.* If you prefer the tranquillity of the country to the bustle of the city, this is definitely the place for you. At the centre of a small village, this renovated farm is a pleasing halt in a pastoral setting. The upstairs rooms are wonderful!

**Hôtel de la Ferme du Vert** – *62720 Wierre-Effroy – 10km/6mi NE of Boulogne via N 42 and D 234.* ☎ *03 21 87 67 00, www.fermeduvert.com. Closed 15 Dec to 20 Jan – 16 rms – 9€ – restaurant.* Rest and relaxation are inevitable when you stay in this old farm built in the 19C. Although all are different, the rooms share one common denominator: the simple, elegant interior design. The restaurant and cheese shop will delight connoisseurs.

**Hôtel Faidherbe** – *12 r. Faidherbe, 62200 Boulogne-sur-Mer.* ☎ *03 21 31 60 93. Closed Christmas and New Year – 34 rms – 7.50€.* This comfortable and cosy hotel is conveniently located halfway between the centre of town and the port. The white-painted rooms all have wicker furnishings, colourful linens and well-equipped bathrooms.

**Hôtel Métropole** – *51 r. Thiers.* ☎ *03 21 31 54 30, www.hotel-metropole-boulogne.com. Closed 19 Dec to 5 Jan – 25 rms – 9€.* A practical hotel offering modern or rustic bedrooms, all air-conditioned, comfortable and well soundproofed. Dapper breakfast room opening onto a garden.

## WHERE TO EAT

**Le Doyen** – *11 r. du Doyen –* ☎ *03 21 30 13 08. Closed 15 days in Jan and Sun except public holidays.* This is the kind of understated establishment that we love to unearth. The very small

interior is nattily decorated in pastel hues, the welcome is warm indeed, and seafood is the mainstay of the delectable cuisine.

**Restaurant de Nausicaä** – *Bd Ste-Bevue –* ☎ *03 21 33 24 24. Closed Mon evenings – noon-2pm and 7-9.30pm.* This split-level establishment set up inside the Centre National de la Mer commands panoramic views of the beach and harbour entrance.

**La Raterie** – *1744 hameau de la Maloterie, 62720 Wierre-Effroy – 12km/7.2mi NE of Boulogne-sur-Mer via D 238.* ☎ *03 21 92 80 90. www.ferm-auberge-laraterie.com. Closed Sun evening and Mon.* This pretty 18C farm is the perfect introduction to the charm of the local countryside. The inn, furnished with period pieces, a fireplace and a splendid enamelled stove, serves appetizing regional recipes. Vast bedrooms overlook the garden.

## SHOPPING

**Ferme du Puits du Sart** – *62132 Hermelinghen.* ☎ *03 21 85 00 79.* Producer of duck foie gras. Visits and sampling of different products.

**Licques Volailles** – *777, rue de l'Abbé Pruvost, 62850 Licques.* ☎ *03 21 35 05 42.* Licques poultry, a breed that was created by local monks, is renowned throughout France. Worth tracking down.

## ON THE TOWN

**Cabaret Sam** – *24 r. Alexander-Fleming –* ☎ *03 21 87 32 69 ; no reservations; doors open at 8pm. Closed Aug and Jan.* The owners' idea was to make culture accessible to all and they've done an excellent job of it. Absolutely packed on performance evenings, the little 200-seat venue has a very eclectic programme that gives undiscovered stars a chance to shine.

## SPORTS AND LEISURE

**Char à voile Club de la Côte d'Opale** – *272 bd Ste-Beuve –* ☎ *03 21 83 25 48 – www.cvcco.com – daily 8.30am-noon, 2-5.30pm.* Sand yacht and speed sail rentals for 7 years and up.

## Plankton

This generic name refers to organisms that cannot withstand maritime currents. They vary in size from the microscopic phytoplankton (plant plankton), to zooplankton no bigger than the head of a pin, to some kinds of jellyfish, which when extended by their filaments can be dozens of metres long. Plankton is of vital importance. It forms the basis of all marine life, producing organic matter from mineral salts and the energy afforded by sources of light. It generates much of the planet's oxygen.

sists of a tidal dock reserved for ferries, small trawlers and yachts and the Napoleon and Loubet docks for the big fishing boats.

**Quai Gambetta**, overlooked by tall buildings, is busiest when the trawlers unload their catch, some of which is sold on the spot.

**Beach** – Kids Already quite well known in the 18C, the fine, white-sand beach became very fashionable from the mid-19C onwards. Because of its facilities for children and summer leisure activities, the town has been awarded the "Station Kid" label. Sailing, landsailing and speedsail are also available.

**Église St-Nicolas** – The church, standing in place Dalton where the market is held (*Wednesdays and Saturdays*), is the oldest in Boulogne despite its Classical façade. It was built from 1220 to 1250, and underwent many alterations in the 16C (apse, transept, chancel vaults, chapels) and in the 18C when the nave was rebuilt. The 17C high altar features spiral columns and a fine painting of *The Flagellation* by Lehmann, a pupil of Ingres.

## La Ville Haute★★ *3hr*

The upper town, enclosed by ramparts, stands on the site of the old Roman *castrum* or fortified town. It is overlooked by the enormous dome of Notre-Dame basilica and is popular with tourists in summer, offering pleasant strolls along the ramparts or through the streets and past the historic buildings of the walled town.

**Ramparts** – The fortifications were built in the early 13C on the foundations of the Gallo-Roman walls and were strengthened in the 16C to 17C. The ramparts form a rectangle reinforced by the **castle** to the east, and accessed by four gates – Gayole, Dunes, Calais and **Degrés** which is pedestrian only – flanked by two towers. The parapet walkway is accessible from each gateway and offers lovely **views**★ of the town and the port.

At the western corner the **tour Gayette**, a former jail, was the site of the take-off for the balloon flight in 1785 by **Pilâtre de Rozier** and Romain who were attempting to cross the Channel; they crashed near Wimille, just north of Boulogne.

A pyramid-shaped monument surmounted by a statue stands in the garden between Boulevard Auguste-Mariette and the ramparts: it is dedicated to **Mariette** the Egyptologist, whom the statue shows in Egyptian costume.

▶ *Walk through the western Porte des Dunes to place de la Résistance and place Godefroy-de-Bouillon.*

## Fish Trade Centre

Industrial trawlers unload their catch around midnight; coastal-fishing boats come back in the early hours of the morning. The catch is offered for sale and refrigerated during the fish auction (*la criée*) which starts between 6 and 7am. The batches are then sent round to factories for processing. This is completed by 11am and the parcels end up at the harbour station (112 unloading bays, 24 refrigerated-transport companies) to be dispatched to various destinations: Paris/Rungis, Strasbourg, Lyon, Marseille, Bordeaux… and abroad, where they arrive the same day or the next morning at the latest.

*Boulogne-sur-Mer – The fishing port*

**Library** – This is located in the old Annonciades Convent. The 17C buildings and the cloisters house study and exhibition rooms, while the main reading room occupies the 18C chapel with its superb coffered ceiling, visible through the windows from the square.

**Belfry** ✏✏ *Tours daily (except Sun and public holidays)* ◷*Open 8am-6pm (Sat, 8am-noon).* ◷*Closed Sun and public holidays. Free admission.* ☎ *03 21 80 13 12.* The 13C Gothic belfry (*access through the Hôtel de Ville*), has a 12C base (the former keep from the castle of the counts of Boulogne) and an 18C octagonal section at the top. It houses Gallo-Roman statues and regional antique furniture as well as a beautiful stained-glass window portraying Godefroy de Bouillon.The top of the belfry (183 steps) offers an extensive **view**⋆ of Boulogne and its surroundings.

▸ *Place de la Résistance leads into place Godefroy-de-Bouillon located at the junction of the four main streets.*

The square owes its name to the leader of the first crusade, who was a member of the House of Boulogne.

**Hôtel de Ville** – The 18C façade of red brick with stone dressings, contrasts sharply with the primitive Gothic belfry.

**Hôtel Desandrouin** – To the right as you come out of the town hall stands this Louis XVI mansion where Napoleon stayed several times from 1803 to 1811.

▸ *Follow rue de Puits-d'Amour alongside Hôtel Desandrouin and turn right.*

**Rue Guyale** – The merchants' guildhall used to stand on this street, which has been restored and reveals the back of the Annonciades Convent and the rough-stone façades of the old houses.

▸ *From place Godefroy-de-Bouillon take rue de Lille.*

At no 58 is the oldest **house** in Boulogne (12C). The Basilique Notre-Dame stands on the left. Rue du Château on the right leads to the former residence of the counts of Boulogne.

**Basilique Notre-Dame**

*Access via the south transept in rue de Lille.*

The basilica was built from 1827 to 1866 on the site of the old cathedral (destroyed after the Revolution) and has preserved the Romanesque crypt. Inside, a powerful Corinthian colonnade supports the building. The superb, soaring **dome**⋆ with its circle of large statues rises behind the chancel; beyond it, in the central chapel, stands the wooden statuette of Our Lady of Boulogne (Notre-Dame de Boulogne), crowned with

*Boulogne-sur-Mer – Château-musée*

Y. Tierny/ MICHELIN

precious stones. **Crypt** – ⊙*Open daily (except Mon) 2-5pm.* ⊙*Closed 1 Jan, 25 Dec.* ⊛*2€ (child, 1€).* ☎ *03 21 30 22 70.* Under the basilica, a labyrinth of underground passages links 14 chambers. One of them houses the **Treasury**★ which contains religious statues and objects (chalices, reliquaries) from various churches in the region, and the relic of the Holy Blood offered by Philip the Fair to Our Lady of Boulogne.

Continue through several rooms to the **crypt of the painted pillars** dating from the 11C, discovered during the construction of the new basilica.

▶ *Take rue du Château opposite.*

### Château-musée★

*Rue de Bernet.* ⊙*Open daily (except Tue) 10am-12.30pm, 2-5pm, Sun and public holidays 10am-12.30pm, 2.30-5.30pm.* ⊙*Closed 1 Jan, 1 May, 25 Dec. 1€ (under 18, free). Free first Sun in month.* ☎ *03 21 10 02 20.www.ville-boulogne-sur-mer.fr.* Formerly the residence of the counts of Boulogne, this polygonal building was the first in western Europe to abandon the traditional keep. Flanked by round towers, it protected the most vulnerable part of the ramparts facing the plateau. The castle is separated from the ramparts by a moat, which was spanned by a drawbridge.

The archaeology of the Mediterranean is represented by an Egyptian section (sarcophagi and numerous funerary objects, the gift of Mariette the Egyptologist) and also by a beautiful group of **Greek vases**★★ dating from 5-6C BC,

among them a black-figure jug portraying the suicide of Ajax.

Beyond this are rooms containing ceramics and earthenware from the main French and foreign manufacturers, and remarkable pieces of porcelain.

Among the ethnographic collections, the **Eskimo and Aleutian masks**★★ brought back from a voyage to North America by the anthropologist Pinart, and the objects from the South Sea Islands including a Maori battle canoe from New Zealand, are particularly interesting.

The enormous guard-room displays collections from the Middle Ages and the Renaissance: copper and brassware, wood and stone sculptures, Gothic furniture and woodwork, an exceptional glazed earthenware finial, paintings, and coins.

## Additional Sights

### Maison de la Beurière★

⊙*Open daily (except Mon): Mid-Jun to mid-Sep, 10am-12.30pm, 3-6.30pm; mid-Sep to mid-June, 10am-noon, 2-4.30pm.* ⊙*Closed 25 Dec, 1 Jan and 1 May.* ⊛*2€.* ☎ *03 21 30 14 52.*

In the ancient seafaring quarter, at the time known as "la Beurière", but today as St-Pierre, 4 000 people used to live, a third of the entire Boulonnais population. From this time there remains just one narrow, stepped street and five or six houses. The others were destroyed during the Second World War. Here, in one of the last dwellings, dated 1870, a small museum illustrates the life of a seafaring family around 1900.

## Excursions

### Colonne de la Grande Armée★

⊙*Closed mid Jun to end Sep: Wed-Sun, 10.30am-12.30pm, 2.30-6.30pm; rest of year: 10am-noon, 2-4pm.* ⊙*Closed 1 Jan, 1 May, 1 and 11 Nov, 25 Dec.* ⊛*Free.* ☎ *03 21 80 43 69. 3km/2mi north by N 1 and turn left on a small road.*

Designed by the architect **Eloi Labarre** (1764-1833) to commemorate the Boulogne Camp, the column was started in

## Address Book

### WHERE TO STAY IN HARDELOT

🍴🍴 **Hôtel du Parc** – *111 av. Francois-1er.* ☎ *03 21 33 22 11* – 🅿 – *81 rms* – ⌑ *11€* – *restaurant* 🍴🍴🍴. Set amid the trees, this modern hotel is a haven of peace. The rooms, furnished in painted wood and discreet fabrics, are spacious; most open onto nature. Pools, tennis courts and fitness facilities for the sports-minded.

### WHERE TO EAT IN HARDELOT

🍴🍴 **Brasserie l'Océan** – *100 bd Mer, 62152 Hardelot-Plage.* ☎ *03 21 83 17 98.* The sea greeting the shore: ever a sight for sore eyes! In good weather, enjoy the terrace, gently stroked by ocean breezes. Simple, uncomplicated fare featuring (what else?) seafood.

---

1804 but only finished under Louis-Philippe. The column is of marble from nearby Marquise, rises 54m/177ft high and is 4m/13ft in diameter. On its base, a bronze low-relief sculpture portrays Field Marshal Soult offering the plans of the column to the Emperor. A staircase (*263 steps*) leads to the square platform (190m/623ft above sea level) from where the **panorama**★★ extends over the lush countryside of the Boulogne region and, on a clear day, across the Channel as far as the white cliffs of Dover.

### Monument de la légion d'honneur

*2km/1.25mi north by D 940 and a path to the right.*

This obelisk marks the site of the throne on which Napoleon I sat on 16 August 1804 for the second distribution of the Legion of Honour decorations (the first took place on 14 July 1804 at the Invalides in Paris).

### Viewpoint of St-Étienne-au-Mont★

*5km/3mi along D 52 then right up a steep hill (13% grade).*

From the cemetery adjacent to the isolated hilltop church (altitude 124m/407ft), there is a fine **view**★ of the Liane Valley; Boulogne, over which towers the dome of Notre-Dame basilica, can be seen downstream.

### Le Portel

*5km/3mi southwest.*

**Kids** The town has been awarded the "Station Kid" label for the facilities its sandy **beach** dotted with rocks offers children. The resort faces a small isle on which stands **fort de l'Heurt**, built by Napoleon in 1804. A statue of Our Lady of Boulogne watches over the Epi jetty.

| | |
|---|---|
| Basilique Notre-Dame | V |
| Beffroi | X |
| Bibliothèque | X |
| Château-musée | V |
| Gare maritime | Y |
| Hôtel Desandrouin | X K 1 |
| Hôtel de ville | VX H |
| Maison ancienne | V K 2 |
| Maison de la Beurière | Y K 4 |
| Monument à Mariette | V K 3 |
| Musée San Martin | X |
| Musée d'Histoire naturelle | X M |
| Nausicaä | Y |
| Palais de justice | V J |
| Plage | Y |
| Port | Y |
| Porte des Degrés | X |
| Tour Gayette | X R |
| Église St-Nicolas | Z |

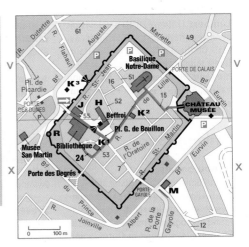

*Typical landscape of the Boulonnais region*

### Hardelot-Plage ♨♨
*15km/9mi south by D 940 and D 113E.*
This elegant seaside sporting resort and "Station Kid" features a magnificent, gently sloping beach of fine sand. Leisure facilities include paths for walking, riding and cycling; golf; sailing; kite-flying; and a country club with tennis courts and a swimming pool.

The **château** north of the village, by the Lac des Miroirs, retains some of its 13C fortifications. In the 19C it was bought by an Englishman who had the château rebuilt in the style of Windsor Castle with crenellations and turrets. The castle now belongs to the municipality.

### Forêt de Boulogne
*10km/6mi east by D 341.*
The road climbs the slopes of **Mont Lambert** (189m/620ft); a television aerial rises from the top. The forest covers 2 000ha/4 940 acres and contains forest roads, bridle paths, parking facilities and picnic areas. The lush Liane Valley borders the forest to the south and east.

## Driving Tour

### Le Boulonnais
*75km/46mi round-trip– about 3hr.*
The Boulonnais is a region of lush countryside. Its complex relief is due to differing geological formations: marble in Marquise, sandstone in Outreau and chalk in Desvres and Neufchâtel, where it lies under a layer of clay. In some places outcrops rise over 200m/656ft in altitude.

The plateau between Guînes and the River Aa is intermittently bare or dotted with copses; here and there great farms surrounded by thickets and pastures grow cereals and sugar beet.

The Wimereux, Liane, Hem and Slack valleys are deep and narrow, providing fertile ground for orchards (cider apples) and meadows. A local breed of cow is found here, in addition to the Northern Blue and the Flemish Red cows; sheep are put out to pasture with Boulonnais draughthorses, powerful grey animals capable of pulling as much as a ton in weight.

The Boulonnais forms part of the nature park known as the **Parc Naturel Régional des Caps et Marais d'Opale** which includes the Boulonnais and Audomarois parks.

▶ *Leave Boulogne eastward along N 42; 3km/2mi on, beyond the roundabout, turn onto D 232.*

This picturesque road, edged with beeches and old elms, descends sharply into the freshness of the **Wimereux Valley** which is carpeted with meadows and scattered with copses.

### Souverain-Moulin
The château and its outbuildings look very attractive in their leafy setting.

| | | | | | | | |
|---|---|---|---|---|---|---|---|
| Alsace R. d' | Z | Farjon R. F. | Z | Pipots R. des | Z | | |
| Aumont R. d' | X 7 | Flahaut R. | V | Porte-Gayole R. de la | Z | | |
| Beaucerf Bd | Z 8 | Folkestone R. de | Y | Porte-Neuve R. | VY 49 | | |
| Bomarsund R. de | Y | Gambetta Quai | Y | Pressy R. de | V 51 | | |
| Boucher-de-Perthes R. | ZX 12 | Gaulle Av. Ch.-de | Y | Prince-Albert Bd du | Z | | |
| Bouillon Pl. G.-de | X | Grande-Rue | Y | Providence R. de la | V 52 | | |
| Branly R. E. | Z | Guyale R. | X 24 | Puits-d'Amour R. | Z 53 | | |
| Bras-d'Or R. du | Z 13 | Hédouin R. | Z | Résistance Pl. | VY 55 | | |
| Camp-de-Droite R. du | Y | Joinville R. | X | St-Jean R. | V | | |
| Cazin R. | Z | Lampe R. de la | Z 32 | St-Louis R. | Y 56 | | |
| Chanzy Bd | Y | Lattre-de-Tassigny Av. de | Y 33 | Ste-Beuve Bd | Y 59 | | |
| Château R. du | V 15 | Lille R. de | XVY 37 | Sauvage Pl. F. | Z | | |
| Clocheville Bd de | Y | Marguet Pont | Z 38 | Thiers R. A. | YZ 60 | | |
| Cloître R. du | V 16 | Mariette Bd A. | Y | Tour-d'Ordre R. de la | Y | | |
| Comte Bd A. | Z | Mitterrand Bd F. | Z 40 | Tour-Notre-Dame R. | VY 61 | | |
| Daunou Bd | Z | Nationale R. | Z | Victoires R. des | Y 63 | | |
| Diderot Bd | Z | Navarin Pl. | Y | Victor-Hugo R. | YZ | | |
| Dutertre R. | VY 20 | Oratoire R. de l' | X | Vivier R. du | Y | | |
| Entente-Cordiale Pont de l' | Z 23 | Paix R. de la | Y | Voltaire Bd | Z | | |
| Euvin Bd | YZ | Perrochel R. de | Z 48 | | | | |
| Faidherbe R. | Y | Picardie Pl. de | V | | | | |

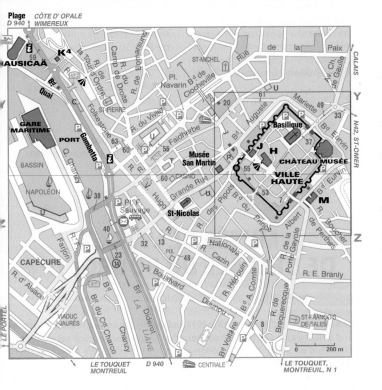

> Take D 233 (east) to Belle, then turn left onto D 238 and right onto D 251. Turn right again onto D 127.

**The Maison du Parc National Régional des Caps et Marais d'Opale** is situated in the **manoir du Huisbois** (*Open daily except Sat, Sun and public holidays, 9am-noon, 2-6pm. Closed 1 and 8 May, 25 Dec. ☎ 03 21 87 90 90*) a beautiful 17C house of local grey stone. The informa-

tion centre provides documentation, a library, a video centre and exhibitions all relating to the Boulonnais.

> From N 42 to Saint-Omer, turn left on D 224 to Licques.

## Licques

Licques is famous for its turkeys introduced in the area in the 17C by the monks of the local abbey.

▶ *From Licques, follow D 191 west through Sanghem and Hermelingen.*

Beyond Le Ventu the road begins to climb, overlooking the entire region. There are beautiful **views**★ over the verdant, undulating Boulonnais countryside.

▶ *At Hardinghen, take D 127 south-west and D 127E to Réty.*

## Rety

The small Flamboyant **church** (late 15C; 12C tower) has decorative stonework which creates a chequered effect. Inside, note the chancel's carved keystone in the centre of a stone crown. The cemetery has been turned into an attractive garden. *To visit enquire at the Mairie, (⟲9.30-11.30am, 2.5pm).* ☎ 03 21 92 89 75.

▶ *Turn left beyond Rety onto D 232. After crossing D 127E, turn right to Hydrequent.*

## Hydrequent

The **Maison du Marbre et de la Géologie** (⟲open Apr-Aug daily (except Mon) 2-6pm. ⟲closed public holidays. ⟲4€. ☎ 03 21 83 19 10. www.parc-opale.com) is a centre concentrating on the formation of marble and coal in the Boulonnais. The marble, which is actually limestone formed during the Carboniferous Era or Jurassic period, is rich in fossils. Some 26 different types of marble exist. The **Marquise quarry** yields a type of "marble" which has been used for many buildings, among them Canterbury Cathedral in England; granules of the rock were used more recently for the vaults of the Channel Tunnel.

▶ *Return to D 232.*

Almost immediately, a pretty **mill** beside the River Slack comes into view (left).

▶ *In Wierre-Effroy take D 234 to Conte-ville-lès-Boulogne, then take D 233 along the banks of the River Wimereux.*

## Wimille

The graves of the aeronauts Pilâtre de Rozier and Romain are in the old cemetery.

▶ *Return to Boulogne.*

# MUSÉE DE L'AIR ET DE L'ESPACE DU BOURGET★★

LE BOURGET AIR AND SPACE MUSEUM

MICHELIN LOCAL MAP 305: F-7, MAP 101 FOLDS 7, 17 OR 106 FOLD 20

Le Bourget airfield was created in 1914 and rapidly became an important airport and military air base. It was from here that Nungesser and Coli set off in their *White Bird* on 8 May 1927 in a doomed attempt to reach the American coast. Thirteen days later, in the early hours of 22 May, Lindbergh successfully landed his *Spirit of St Louis* in Paris, after achieving the first ever non-stop solo flight across the Atlantic. Costes and Bellonte were the first to accomplish this feat in the opposite direction when *Question Mark* landed on 1 September 1930.

## Visit

Kids ⟲ ⟲Open daily (except Mon) 10am-6pm (Oct-Mar until 5pm). ⟲7€ (children: 5€). ☎ 01 49 92 70 62. www.mae.org. The museum has been laid out in the former terminal building at Le Bourget and it boasts some extraordinary col-lections retelling the history of the con-quest of the skies.

The adventure began with **hot air balloons**★ after the experiment carried out by Pilâtre de Rozier and Arlandes in 1783 and a model of their balloon can be seen in the museum, to recall the event. This first success resulted in the rapid

*Musée de l'Air et de l"espace – Concorde*

expansion of ballooning. Later, balloons were to prove very useful in military operations or as a means of transport during the Franco-Prussian war of 1870.

**Grande Galerie★★** – This gallery traces the early years of aviation and has the largest collection in the world dealing with this period. Some of the aircraft were inspired by bionics, among them Clément Ader's strange *Éole*, which was designed after observation of a bat. Among the earliest aircraft, note Farman's *Voisin* (first round trip, 1km/0.6mi, in Issy-les-Moulineaux, 1907), the elegant and popular *Levasseur Antoinette* (1908), the *Blériot-XI* which succeeded in flying across the Channel etc. With the outbreak of the First World War, aviation underwent rapid progress. Aircraft structures and power were increased and the skies became the setting for the first aerial battles.

▶ *Proceed in chronological order via the Hall de l'Espace to the Hall de l'Aviation légère et sportive.*

**Hall de l'Aviation légère et sportive** – This hall contains the famous *Potez-53* (which achieved average speeds of 322kph/200mph over a distance of 2 000km/1 243mi in 1933), the very powerful *Caudron 714R* (900hp), and the *Breguet XIX* "Nungesser-Coli" in which Costes and Le Brix made the first successful crossing of the South Atlantic in 1927.

**Hall des Prototypes français★** – This hall covers the French Air Force since 1945 and contains some amazing prototypes with thermopropulsion such as the *Leduc-016*.

**Hall du Concorde★★** – Fearsome fighters of the Second World War are represented here such as the *Spitfire MK-16* used by the Free French Airforce or the enormous *P-47 Thunderbolt* (a 2 000hp fighter bomber). However, the star is the prototype of *Concorde 001*, the only supersonic aircraft.

▶ *Retrace your steps via the Hall des Prototypes.*

**Hall de l'Espace★** – The conquest of space is represented by launchers and space capsules (the famous **Sputnik** was the Earth's first artificial satellite); in 1965, France became the third power to conquer space after the United States and the USSR through its *Diamant* launcher replaced later by the famous *Ariane* launcher.

# CHÂTEAU DE BRETEUIL★★

MICHELIN LOCAL MAP 311: I-3, MAP 101 FOLD 32 OR 106 FOLD 29

**Known for many years as Bévilliers or Buvilliers, Breteuil is one of the most charming châteaux in the Île-de-France region. It offers fascinating insight into the illustrious Le Tonnelier de Breteuil family, who have been living in the castle since 1712. The estate has several attractive features: its architecture, fine furniture, souvenirs of a family of famous diplomats, a pleasant park and, as a special treat for children, well-known fairy-tale characters.**

# Visit

*Guided tours (45min) from 2.30-5.30pm, Sun, public holidays. Grounds open at 10am. ⊘11.90€ (under 18, 8.90€) ☎ 01 30 52 05 02. www.breteuil.fr.*

The château is built in the Louis XIII style in brick and stone. It consists of a main building flanked by two low wings.

On the first floor, the family memorabilia takes on an interesting dimension thanks to the waxwork figures which bring back to life a few historical events. Louis XVI is shown with Louis-Auguste de Breteuil and Marie-Antoinette, signing the arrest warrant for the Cardinal de Rohan who was implicated in the mysterious affair of the Queen's necklace. In the smoking room, the figures represent Henri de Breteuil, Gambetta and the future Edward VII laying down in 1881 the basis of the Entente cordiale. The château's most outstanding exhibit remains the **Teschen table**★★★, a table inlaid with stones, gems and petrified wood. The play of light across its surface shows it off to its full advantage.

This superb piece of craftsmanship was given to Louis-Auguste de Breteuil (1730-1807) by Empress Maria Teresa of Austria. He had been the successful mediator during discussions leading to the Treaty of Teschen (1779) which put an end to a serious regional conflict between the Empire and Prussia.

### The Park★★

Kids Lying on the edge of a plateau overlooking the upper Chevreuse Valley, the 75ha/185 acre park, where deer roam freely, provides some beautiful views and diverse landscapes. Near the château are the **formal French gardens** created by the Duchênes (father and son) in accordance with Le Nôtre's principles. They include a lake, a 16C dovecote, statues and topiaried yews and boxwood. The **Princes' Garden** is vividly and variously coloured with flowering cherries, roses and some outstanding peonies. A box **maze** occupies one of the terraces of the orangery. Two ponds lower down form an ideal setting for a romantic stroll.

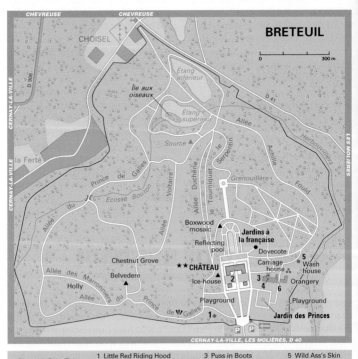

| Perrault's Fairy Tales | 1 Little Red Riding Hood | 3 Puss in Boots | 5 Wild Ass's Skin |
|---|---|---|---|
| | 2 Sleeping Beauty | 4 Tom Thumb | 6 Bluebeard |

**For the best little places, follow the leader.**

Looking for the latest news on today's best hotels and restaurants? Pick up the Michelin Guide and look for the Bib Gourmand and Bib Hotel symbols. With 45,000 addresses in Europe, in every category and price range, the perfect place to dine or stay is never far away.

A better way forward

# CALAIS

POPULATION 104 852

MICHELIN LOCAL MAP 301: E-2

Calais is the leading passenger port in France and the second in the world with a traffic totalling 20 million passengers a year. The town gave its name to the Pas-de-Calais, the strait known on the north side of the Channel as the Straits of Dover. The history of the town has been considerably influenced by its proximity to the English coast, only 38km/23.5mi away. The white cliffs of Dover are often clearly visible from the promenade and the vast sandy beach west of the entrance to Calais harbour. Calais is the ideal starting point for excursions along the Opal Coast to Le Touquet.

**Information:** 12 bd Clemenceau, 62100 Calais, ☎ 03 21 96 62 40. www.ot-calais.fr.

## A Bit of History

### The Channel Tunnel
The "Chunnel" is the realisation of more than two centuries of dreams and unfinished projects.

### From utopia to reality
Over the past 250 years there have been 27 proposals, the oldest of which was made in 1750 by M Desmarets, who wanted to rejoin Britain to the mainland by a bridge, a tunnel or a causeway. From 1834 onwards, Aimé Thomé de Gamond, who is known as the "Father of the Tunnel", put forward several different propositions, all of them technically viable.

### First attempts
In 1880, 1 840m/over 1mi of galleries were dug out on the site called the

*Tunnel digging machine in Coquelles*

Y. Thierry/ MICHELIN

"Puits des Anciens". 2 000m/ 1.25mi were tunnelled out on the English side before the work was stopped. A fresh approach was tried in 1922. The technical progress of the 1960s gave the project a boost but a 400m/433yd gallery was abandoned once again.

### Birth of Eurotunnel
During a Franco-British summit conference in September 1981, the idea of building a fixed link was again mooted by British Prime Minister Margaret Thatcher and French President François Mitterrand. In October 1985, after an international competition, four projects were shortlisted and it was the Eurotunnel project which was finally selected, on 20 January 1986. A Franco-British treaty was signed on 12 February 1986 in Canterbury Cathedral with a view to the construction of the tunnel. The first link between France and England was established on 1 December 1990. The official opening of the tunnel and of the Shuttle service took place on 6 May 1994.

### Facts and figures
Most of the tunnel lies at a depth of 40m/130ft below the seabed, in a layer of blue chalk. Enormous tunnel-digging machines bored their way through the rock at a rate of 800 to 1 000m/867 to 1 083yd a month.

The **trans-Channel link** consists, in fact, of two railway tunnels 7.60m/25ft in diameter connected every 375m/406yd to a central service gallery 4.80m/ 16ft in diameter built for the purposes of ventilation, security, and system maintenance. The tunnels contain a single track and the trains run in one direction only, taking passengers and freight. The tunnels have a total length of 50km/31mi of which 40km/24mi are beneath the Channel.

## The Burghers of Calais

After his success at Crécy **Edward III** of England needed to create a power-base in France. He began the siege of Calais on 3 September 1346, but eight months later had still not been able to breach the valiant defence led by the town governor, Jean de Vienne; in fact, it was famine that forced the inhabitants to capitulate in the end.

Six burghers, led by **Eustache de Saint-Pierre**, prepared to sacrifice themselves in order that the other citizens of Calais would be spared the sword. In thin robes, "barefoot, bareheaded, halters about their necks and the keys to the town in their hands," they presented themselves before the king to be delivered to the exectioner. They were saved by the intercession of Queen Philippa of Hainault.

Calais was in the hands of the English for over two centuries and was liberated only in 1558, by the Duke of Guise. This was a mortal blow to **Mary Tudor**, Queen of England, who said: "If my heart were laid open, the word "Calais" would be engraved on it."

## Calais Lace

Together with Caudry-en-Cambrésis, Calais is the main centre of machine-made lace, employing about 2 000 workers using over 350 looms. Englishmen from Nottingham introduced the industry at the beginning of the 19C; quality was improved around 1830 when the first Jacquard looms were introduced.

Three quarters of the lace made in Calais is exported; 80% of it is used for lingerie, 20% for dresses (wedding gowns, cocktail and evening dresses, off-the-peg and designer clothing). Traditional lace made with the Leavers machine is entitled to a quality label created in 1991, representing a peacock.

# Sights

## Monument des Bourgeois de Calais★★

This famous work by **Rodin**, *The Burghers of Calais*, is located between the Hôtel de Ville and Parc St-Pierre. It dates from 1895 and exemplifies the sculptor's brilliance: the bronze group is simultaneously full of vitality and pathos. Each of the six life-size figures should be admired separately: their veins and muscles exaggerated, their forms tense and haughty. They express the heroic nobility of the men obliged to humiliate themselves before the king of England.

*The Burghers of Calais by Rodin*

Y. Thierry/ MICHELIN

## Address Book

*For coin ranges, see the Legend on the cover flap.*

### WHERE TO STAY

**Hôtel Victoria** – *8 r. du Cdt-Bonningue. ☎ 03 21 34 38 32. www.hotel-victoria-calais.activehotels.com – 14 rms– ☲ 5.50€.* Well situated opposite the lighthouse and a short three-minute walk from the Transmanche station, this small hotel is nothing fancy, but it is impeccably maintained.

**Le Manoir du Meldick (Bed and Breakfast)** – *2528 av. du Gén.-de-Gaulle, Le Fort Vert, 62730 Marck – 6km/3.6mi E of Calais via D 940 and D 119. ☎ 03 21 85 74 34, www.manoir-du-meldick.com – ⊟ – 5 rms.* Just a few minutes from the Calais port, yet far from its crowds, Meldick Manor is sure to please. Rooms are spacious and comfortable.

### WHERE TO EAT

**La Boudinière** – *2691 rte de Waldam, 62215 Oye-Plage – 14km/8.5mi E of Calais via D 119. ☎ 03 21 85 93 14, www.laboudiniere.com. Closed 15 days in Feb, 15 days in Sep and Wed from Oct to Jun.* Lost in the Calais countryside, this little restaurant serves traditional cuisine of excellent quality. The meat served here is top-rate – the owner-chef chooses and cuts the steaks himself. Friendly reception and quiet dining room.

**La Sole Meunière** – *1 bd de la Résistance. ☎ 03 21 34 43 01. www.solemeuniere.com. Closed Sun evening and Mon.* The house speciality is sole, cooked five different ways by the 'sole-ful' chef. Opt for a table by the bay windows for a view of the port. Also offered are other seafood dishes, local cheeses, desserts and fine wines.

**Au Côte d'Argent** – *1 digue G.-Berthe – ☎ 03 21 34 68 07. Closed mid-Feb, mid-Aug to early Sep, 24 Dec-early Jan, Wed eve Sep-Apr, Sun eve and Mon.* Dine in a setting that looks and feels like a boat, as you watch the ferries coming and going.

**Le Channel** – *3 bd de la résistance – ☎ 03 21 34 42 30. Closed late-Jul-early Aug, 23 Dec to 18 Jan, Sun eve and Mon.* A last chance to sample French cuisine before heading for England ! Try the French interpretations of le 'steak pie' or 'jelly'.

## Hôtel de ville

The beautiful and graceful town hall is built of brick and stone in the 15C Flemish style yet dates only from the turn of the last century. The **belfry** (75m/246ft) can be seen for miles in all directions; the sound of its bell is very appealing. Inside, a **stained-glass window** recalling the departure of the English diffuses the sunlight over the grand staircase.

## Place d'Armes

Before the devastation of the war, this was the heart of medieval Calais. Only the 13C **watchtower** has survived. The belfry and the town hall beside it are popular subjects for artists.

To the left is the Bassin Ouest; to the right is the Bassin du Paradis and the rear harbour used as a marina.

## The Lighthouse (Le phare)

*Guided visits (30min) Jun-Sep: 2-6.30pm, Sat-Sun and public holidays 10am-noon, 2-6.30pm; rest of year: Wed 2-5.30pm, Sat-Sun 10am-noon, 25.30pm. Jan and 1 May. 4€ (children: 2€). ☎ 03 21 34 33 34. www.pharedecalais.com.* The lighthouse (53m/174ft tall; 271 steps) was built in 1848 to replace the watchtower beacon. From the top there is a surprisingly wide and splendid panoramic **view**★★ over Calais, the harbour, the basins, the town's stadium, place d'Armes and the unexpectedly large Church of Our Lady.

## Musée des Beaux-Arts et de la Dentelle★

*Open daily (except Tue and public holidays) 10am-noon, 2-5.30pm, Sat 10am-noon, 2-6.30pm, Sun 2-6.30pm. ☎ 03 21 46 48 40.* The fine arts and lace museum gives an insight into changes in sculpture over the 19C and 20C and styles of painting between the 17C and 20C.

**19C and 20C sculpture** is centred on the works of Rodin and the studies he made for *The Burghers of Calais*. The concept of modern sculpture is made quite clear through the works of Rodin's predecessors, including Carrière-Belleuse, Carpeaux, Barye, and of some of his students, Bourdelle and Maillol.

**Paintings from the 17C to the 20C** by

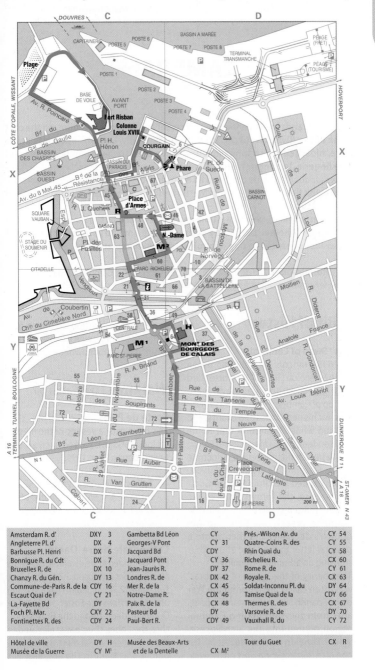

| | | | | | | |
|---|---|---|---|---|---|---|
| Amsterdam R. d' | DXY | 3 | Gambetta Bd Léon | CY | Prés.-Wilson Av. du | CY 54 |
| Angleterre Pl. d' | DX | 4 | Georges-V Pont | CY 31 | Quatre-Coins R. des | CY 55 |
| Barbusse Pl. Henri | DX | 6 | Jacquard Bd | CDY | Rhin Quai du | CY 58 |
| Bonnigue R. du Cdt | DX | 7 | Jacquard Pont | CY 36 | Richelieu R. | CX 60 |
| Bruxelles R. de | DX | 10 | Jean-Jaurès R. | DY 37 | Rome R. de | CY 61 |
| Chanzy R. du Gén. | DY | 13 | Londres R. de | DX 42 | Royale R. | CX 63 |
| Commune-de-Paris R. de la | CDY | 16 | Mer R. de la | CX 45 | Soldat-Inconnu Pl. du | DY 64 |
| Escaut Quai de l' | CY | 21 | Notre-Dame R. | CDX 46 | Tamise Quai de la | CDY 66 |
| La-Fayette Bd | DY | | Paix R. de la | CX 48 | Thermes R. des | CX 67 |
| Foch Pl. Mar. | CXY | 22 | Pasteur Bd | DY | Varsovie R. de | DY 70 |
| Fontinettes R. des | CDY | 24 | Paul-Bert R. | CDY 49 | Vauxhall R. du | CY 72 |

| | | | |
|---|---|---|---|
| Hôtel de ville | DY H | Musée des Beaux-Arts | |
| Musée de la Guerre | CY M¹ | et de la Dentelle | CX M² |
| | | Tour du Guet | CX R |

the Flemish and North-European schools. There are also works by modern and contemporary artists such as Jean Dubuffet (*Landscape around Calais*), Félix Del Marle (*Construction-Colour*), Picasso (*The Old Man, Woman's Face*), Fautrier, Lipchitz, Arp…

The **lace section**, in a former tulle-making factory, deals with machine-made and hand-made lace. The history of lace is illustrated by production techniques, haute-couture dresses, and pieces of lace and lingerie from the 17C to the present day (the museum owns more than 400 000 samples of machine-made lace).

# CAMBRAI ★
### POPULATION 33 738
### MICHELIN LOCAL MAP 302: H-6

Cambrai stands in the centre of a rich cereal and sugar beet region, on the east bank of the River Escaut (or Scheldt). Traditionally, Cambric linen was made here, bleached in the sunny meadows then used to make handkerchiefs and fine lingerie. In gourmet terms, Cambrai is known for its small chitterling sausages (*andouillettes*), its tripe and its mint-flavoured sweets (*bêtises de Cambrai*). The town's heroes are the giants Martin and Martine who are said to have killed the local tyrant.

The town is built of white limestone and is overlooked by the three towers of the belfry, the cathedral and St Gery's Church. Once a military stronghold, Cambrai today looks peaceful, a ring of boulevards having replaced the ramparts.

> **Information:** Office de tourisme, 48 r. de Noyon, 59400 Cambrai. ☎ 03 27 78 36 15. www.cambraiofficedetourisme.com.

## A Bit of History

### The "Swan of Cambrai"
In 1695 François de Salignac de La Mothe-Fénelon (1651-1715), a great lord and famous writer, was made archbishop of Cambrai. **Fénelon** was venerated for his gentleness and charity, and learned while in Cambrai that Rome had condemned his *Maximes des Saints*; this work defended quietism, a doctrine made fashionable by Mme Guyon, which exalted the "Pure Love of God." In response, the former tutor of the Duke of Burgundy first climbed into the pulpit to preach obedience to the Church's decisions and then wrote a pastoral letter to the same effect, thus showing an admirable humility.

The charity of the "Swan of Cambrai" was often called upon during the War of the Spanish Succession; starving peasants from the surrounding Cambrai region poured into the archdiocese, where Fénelon welcomed them. On one occasion a cow was lost on the way.

At once the archbishop set out on foot to find the animal, which he was able to return it to its poor owner.

## Walking Tour *allow 2hr*

### Porte de Paris
This town gate, a vestige of the medieval fortifications, is flanked by two round towers dating from 1390.

> ▶ *Follow avenue de la Victoire towards the town hall, visible at the end of the street. Place du St-Sépulcre appears shortly on the left.*

### Cathédrale Notre-Dame
◔ ↝ *Guided tours available Oct-May: Mon-Thu & Sat, 8am-noon, 2-7pm; Fri, 2-7pm; Sun, 9am-12.30pm, 3-6pm ◑Closed Sun afternoons from Oct-Easter.*
Originally dedicated to the Holy Sepulchre, the abbey church was elevated to the rank of cathedral after the Revolution. It was built in the 18C and has

## Bêtises de Cambrai

These oblong mint-flavoured sweets with a yellow stripe on the side are, according to legend, the result of the fortunate mistake of a 19C confectioner's apprentice. His mother complained that he had once again blundered and made a mistake (*bêtise*), hence the name given to the mint humbugs which were nevertheless appreciated for their digestive and refreshing qualities. Another old legend tells how men who went to an important market held on the 24th day of every month would behave irresponsibly and waste their money on sweets made in front of them!

been altered several times since; the tower dates from 1876. The rounded chapels terminating the transept arms are decorated with large *trompe-l'œil grisailles*, painted in 1760 by the Antwerp artist Martin Geeraerts. Fénelon's tomb, sculpted by David d'Angers in 1826, is in the apsidal chapel.

### Maison Espagnole

(*Tourist office*) This wooden house, its gables sheathed in slate, dates from the late 16C. You can see the medieval cellars and, on the first floor, the oak carvings which once adorned the façade. Note the 17C and 18C private mansions along rue du Grand-Séminaire, rue de l'Epée and rue de Vaucelette. One of these, carefully restored, houses the fine arts museum. As you walk across place Jean-Moulin, note the rounded east end of the chapel of the former St-Julien hospital.

### Église St-Géry

🕐*Open Mon-Sat, 10am-noon, 3-6pm; Sun, 8.15am-noon, 5.30-7.30pm.* ☎ *03 27 78 36 15.*
Overlooked by a tower (76m/249ft tall), the old church of St Aubert's Abbey rises on the site once occupied by a temple believed to have been dedicated to Jupiter Capitolinus. Construction of this austere Classical building lasted from 1698 to 1745. The ambitious plans called for a chancel with an ambulatory and radiating chapels, preceded by a monumental canopy resting on four colossal Baroque columns.
The beautiful **rood screen** (1632) is a good example of the Baroque style with its contrasting red and black marble and its carved decoration creating an impression of movement or even agitation. The monumental pulpit, installed in 1850, was the work of Cam-

brai craftsmen. The north transept houses Rubens' enormous painting, **The Entombment**★★. The 14C **statue** in the south transept was discovered in 1982 during excavations in the crypt and represents a bishop.

▶ *Cross place du 9-Octobre to reach place Aristide-Briand.*

### Place Aristide-Briand

The square was entirely rebuilt after the First World War and is dominated by the majestic lines of the **hôtel de ville** which was rebuilt at the end of the 19C, but set ablaze during the First World War. Its reconstruction in the 1920s, together with that of the square itself, respected the old façade and its Louis XVI peristyle; this was largely due to the commitment of the Parisian architect, Antoine. The hall is surmounted by a columned bell-tower, flanked by the town's two jack-o'-the-clocks, Martin and Martine. According to legend these

L. Lecat/Musée des Beaux-Arts

*Fragment of 14C Annunciation*

two individuals, who appear in parades as giants, were 14C blacksmiths who dealt with the lord ravaging the region by felling him with hammer blows. The bronze figures (2m/6.5ft tall), dressed as turbaned Moors, date from 1512; they strike the town bell with their hammers to sound the hour.

The southwest corner of the square marks the beginning of a long avenue, Mail St-Martin, offering a good view of the 15C-18C **belfry** (70m/230ft tall), which is all that remains of St Martin's Church.

### Porte Notre-Dame

This part of the Baroque 17C fortifications was built at the beginning of the 17C; it owes its name to the statue of the Virgin Mary that adorns the outer face. The gate is unusual for its diamond-shaped stones and its grooved

columns. The sun representing Louis XIV was added to the pediment after the town was captured from the Spanish by the French.

## Additional Sights

### Musée des Beaux-Arts

  ❍*Open daily (except Mon and Tue) 10am-noon, 2-6pm.* ❍*Closed 1 Jan, 1 & 8 May, 15 Aug and 25 Dec.* ◎*3€. No charge 1st Sat-Sun in the month.* ☎ *03 27 82 27 90. www.villedecambrai.com.*

The town museum is housed in a mansion built for the Comte de Francqueville c1720. It has been restored and substantially extended, with the addition of two new buildings.

The **archaeology** department occupies the vaulted 18C cellars. Three themes recall the Gallo-Roman period: ceram-

---

## Address Book

*⚭For coin ranges, see the Legend on the cover flap.*

### WHERE TO STAY

⊝ **Delcambre (Bed and Breakfast)** – *Ferme de Bonavis, 59266 Banteux – 11km/6.6mi S of Cambrai via N 44.* ☎ *03 27 78 55 08, www.bonavis.fr –* ⚭ *– 3 rms.* This former coaching inn with a pleasantly roomy interior was converted to a farm (still working) after World War II; guest rooms, with their high ceilings and parquet floors, are sober and quiet.

### WHERE TO EAT

⊝⊝ **La Taverne de Lutèce** – *68 av. de la Victoire.* ☎ *03 27 78 54 34. Closed Sat and Mon lunch, and Sun.* Come to this simple, rustic tavern and satisfy your appetite with a choice of traditional dishes and a few Picard and Flemish specialities. Convivial, upbeat atmosphere.

⊝⊝ **Le Bouchon** – *31 r. des Rôtisseurs.* ☎ *03 27 78 44 55. Closed 3 weeks in Aug, Mon, Tue and Wed evenings and Sun.* Hidden behind a red brick facade is an affordable eaterie serving ample portions. Eat elbow to elbow in this

relaxed environment. Bistro-style cooking and a 'ch'ti' menu for sampling regional specialities.

⊝**'Chez Dan' Brasserie Boulonnaise** – *18 r. des Liniers.* ☎ *03 27 81 39 77.* Traditional northern hospitality and the warm ambience keep customers coming back to this brasserie with a maritime décor. Simple, reasonably priced cuisine.

### SHOPPING

**Confiserie Afchain** – *ZI de Cantinpré.* ☎ *03 27 81 25 49 – www.betises-de-cambrai.tm.fr. Mon-Fri 9am-noon, 2pm 5pm. Closed 3 wks in Aug, 2 wks at Christ-mas.* The firm Afchain, founded in 1830, is the self-proclaimed originator of the Bêtises de Cambrai bonbons ("Foolishnesses"). A small museum tells the story of this unusual invention. A free guided tour of the confectionary shows the stages of Bêtise making. Advance booking required.

**Confiserie Despinoy** – *Rte Nationale.* ☎ *03 27 83 57 57 – Mon-Fri, 9am-3.30pm – closed Aug and Christmas week.* Another confectionary specialised in Bêtises de Cambrai. Free visits but call ahead.

---

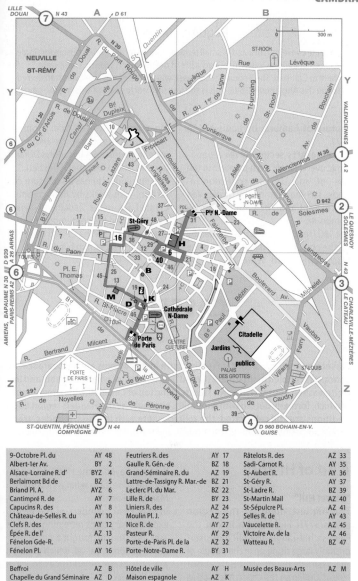

| | | | | | | |
|---|---|---|---|---|---|---|
| 9-Octobre Pl. du | AY 48 | Feutriers R. des | AY 17 | Râtelots R. des | AZ 33 |
| Albert-1er Av. | BY 2 | Gaulle R. Gén.-de | BZ 18 | Sadi-Carnot R. | AY 35 |
| Alsace-Lorraine R. d' | BYZ 4 | Grand-Séminaire R. du | AZ 19 | St-Aubert R. | AY 36 |
| Berlaimont Bd de | BZ 5 | Lattre-de-Tassigny R. Mar.-de | BZ 21 | St-Géry R. | AY 37 |
| Briand Pl. A. | AYZ 6 | Leclerc Pl. du Mar. | BZ 22 | St-Ladre R. | BZ 39 |
| Cantimpré R. de | AY 7 | Lille R. de | BY 23 | St-Martin Mail | AZ 40 |
| Capucins R. des | AY 8 | Liniers R. des | AZ 24 | St-Sépulcre Pl. | AZ 41 |
| Château-de-Selles R. du | AZ 10 | Moulin Pl. J. | AZ 25 | Selles R. de | AY 43 |
| Clefs R. des | AZ 12 | Nice R. de | AY 27 | Vaucelette R. | AZ 45 |
| Épée R. de l' | AZ 13 | Pasteur R. | AY 29 | Victoire Av. de la | AZ 46 |
| Fénelon Gde-R. | AY 15 | Porte-de-Paris Pl. de la | AZ 32 | Watteau R. | BZ 47 |
| Fénelon Pl. | AY 16 | Porte-Notre-Dame R. | BY 31 | | |

| | | | | | |
|---|---|---|---|---|---|
| Beffroi | AZ B | Hôtel de ville | AY H | Musée des Beaux-Arts | AZ M |
| Chapelle du Grand Séminaire | AZ D | Maison espagnole | AZ K | | |

ics, housing and funerals. Exhibits from the Merovingian period include funerary artefacts from sites near Cambrai, Les Rues-des-Vignes (pairs of gilded silver fibulae) and Busigny, all of which were explored in 1986. The section devoted to osteo-archaeology gives a clearer insight into man during the Dark Ages (age of the deceased, traces of disease or illness etc).

The many sculptures come from religious buildings that have been demolished. The set from the Abbaye St-Géry in Les Monts-des-Boeufs (12C) consists of three statue-columns representing the seasons, a capital and small tympana, one of which illustrates the legend of Pyramus and Thisbe. There is a fine 16C **rood screen**★ originally in the chapel of St-Julien Hospital. **Alabaster statues** come from the former cathedral church. A painting by **Van der Meulen** is a graphic description of the

## Beguine convents

Beguine convents consisted of small terraced houses forming an enclosure for single women or widows wishing to lead a life of devotion and charity. There were 11 of them in Cambrai. The Béguinage St-Vaast, which dates from 1354, was transferred to rue des Anglaises in 1545. This is the last such enclosure still existing in France.

capture of Cambrai by Louis XIV in 1677.

The **Fine Arts** section gives a panoramic overview of Dutch painting in the late 16C and 17C. The collection includes still-life paintings by Nicolas Van Veerendael and *The Card Players* by Rombouts.

The 18C French School is represented by Berthelemy (*Esther Fainting*), de Lajoue (*Astronomy*), and Wille (*The Dying Moments of a Beloved Wife*). From the 19C and 20C are portraits, religious subjects and landscapes by Carolus Durand, Boudin, Utrillo, Marquet, Friesz etc.

The museum also has a sculpture collection, with works by Rodin, Camille Claudel, Bourdelle, Zadkine (*Il penseroso*, 1951) and the contemporary artist Georges Jeanclos (he carved the doorway for St-Ayoul Church in Provins).

# CASSEL★

POPULATION 2 290
MICHELIN LOCAL MAP 302: C-3

Cassel is a small town that is Flemish both in its customs and appearance: an enormous cobbled main square (Grand' Place), narrow, winding streets and low whitewashed houses. The town stands at the top of Cassel Hill, the green slopes of which, formerly dotted with windmills, overlook the flat Flanders region. Local traditions are still celebrated: the religious fête with its mass, parades, traditional competitions; archery; the carnival; and the procession of the Reuze giants.

## A Bit of History

### "Cassel Hill"

The highest point of the region (176m/577ft high) and a link in the Flemish hill-range, the hill looks surprisingly large rising up in the middle of the Flemish plain; although about 30km/18mi from the coast, it is used as a landmark by sailors. Its peak is made up of a very hard ferruginous layer.

To the east, **Mont des Récollets** (159m/521ft high) owes its name to a convent of Recollect nuns that stood here from 1615 to 1870.

### Two World Wars

From October 1914 to April 1915 General **Marshall Foch** had his headquarters at Cassel. From here he followed the progress of the battle of Flanders, which was raging on the banks of the Yser. He stayed at the Hôtel de Schoebecque at no 32 in what is now rue du Maréchal-Foch.

In May 1940 members of the British expeditionary corps retreating towards Yser and Dunkirk fought a fierce rearguard action at Cassel, which enabled the bulk of the allied forces to leave from Dunkirk.

## Sights 1hr

### Public Gardens

The gardens at the top of the hill occupy the site of a medieval castle which once incorporated a collegiate church, the crypt of which remains. An equestrian statue of General Foch stands in the middle of the garden.

A tour of the terrace offers an excellent **panorama**★★ (*viewing platforms*) over the picturesque jumble of Cassel's old rooftops, and beyond to the hills of Flanders and the plain, as far as the North Sea and the belfry of Bruges. A local saying maintains that "from Cassel you can see five kingdoms: France, Belgium, Holland, England and, above the clouds, the Kingdom of Heaven".

## Casteel-Meulen

*Guided visits (40min) Apr-Sep 10am-12.30pm, 2-6.30pm. Rest of year Sun, 10am-12.30pm, 2-6.30pm. Closed 1 Jan, 25 Dec. 2.80€. Arrange visits through the Office de tourisme, ☎ 03 28 40 52 55. www.ot-cassel.fr.*

This 18C wooden **windmill** from Arneke was re-erected here to replace the castle's original windmill which burnt down in 1911. It produces flour (there is a bakery on the premises) and also linseed oil. Celebrations take place on 14 July.

## Grand' Place

The main square, irregularly shaped and cobbled, extends along the hillside near the church. It still has an attractive group of 16C, 17C and 18C houses on its

V. Thierry/MICHELIN

*Wormhour – Moulin Deschodt*

south side, among them the Hôtel de la Noble Cour.

## Hôtel de la Noble Cour

A high roof dotted with blind dormer windows crowns the façade, which is entirely of stone – unusual in the North – pierced by large windows with alternately triangular and curvilinear pedi-

---

## Address Book

*For coin ranges, see the Legend on the cover flap.*

### WHERE TO EAT

**La Taverne Flamande** – 34 Grand'Place. ☎ 03 28 42 42 59. Closed Feb school holidays, end Aug, end Oct, Tue evening and Wed – reserv. recommended. After paying your respects to Reuze Papa, the gigantic hero, come try the Flemish specialities served in this tavern on the Grand'Place. Before settling down on the summer terrace surveying the valley, have a look at the splendid counter inside.

**'T Kasteelhof** – 8 r. St-Nicolas. ☎ 03 28 40 59 29. Closed 1 Jan, 3 wks in Jan, 1st wk Jul, 2 wks in Oct, Mon-Wed, 25 Dec – reserv. recommended weekends. Said to be the highest tavern in French Flanders! Come try the regional specialities and purchase local products in the adjoining shop. Saturday night and Sunday lunch Flemish tales are told to patrons as they dine.

**Het Blauwershof** – 9 r. d'Eecke, 59270 Godewaersvelde -12km/7.2mi E of Cassel via D 948 and D 18. ☎ 03 28 49 45 11. Closed Jan, 15 days in summer and Mon. A genuine Flemish tavern whose name means 'Cheaters' Inn.' The decor in the three rooms is a typical hotchpotch, including an old stove, a mechanical piano, a crossbow and the effigy of Gambrinus, King of Beer.

**Au Roi du Potje Vleesch** – 31 r. du Mont-des-Cats, 59270 Godewaersvelde – 12km/7.2mi E of Cassel via D 948 and D 18. ☎ 03 28 42 52 56. Closed Jan and Mon – reserv. weekends. You must go through the delicatessen to find this tavern housed in a former slaughterhouse. The rustic Flemish decor sets the stage for a meal of regional cuisine, the famous potjevleesch (a meat stew) and Henri le Douanier beer, named after the village giant. Before leaving, remember to fill up your shopping basket.

ments; the elegant Renaissance doorway, flanked by grey marble columns, is decorated with Fames in the spandrels and with Sirens and foliate scrolls on the frieze (🕐 *temporarily closed for renovation*). Pending its reopening, the museum stages temporary exhibitions.

### Collégiale Notre-Dame

Foch often came here to pray and meditate in this Gothic Flemish church with three gables, three aisles, three apses and square tower over the transept crossing.

## Excursions

### Steenvoorde

*8km/5mi east by D 948.*

This typical small Flemish town with painted houses under red-tiled roofs was once famous for its sheets; today it is the home of one of the largest dairies in the area.

The town celebrates the legend of its giant, Yan den Houtkapper, a woodcutter who made a pair of everlasting boots for Charlemagne; in return he was given a suit of armour, which he still wears for the processions in which he is the hero.

**Windmills** – Three well-preserved windmills can be seen near the town. Two of them are wooden post mills: the **Drievemeulen** (*on D 948 west; Jul and Aug:* 🚶 *90min guided tours through tourist office.* ⊛*2€ (child, 1€)* ☎ *03 28 42 97 98*), dating from 1776, is a typical oil mill; the **Noordmeulen** (*same hours as for Drievenmeulen*), dating from 1576 with 18C working parts, is a wheat mill. The third, the **Steenmeulen** at Terdeghem (*on D 947 south*), is a truncated brick mill, still in working order (1864). 🚶 *Apr-Sep, guided tours (90min), daily (except Fri and last Sun of month) 9am-noon, 2-6pm.* ⊛*4€.* ☎ *03 28 48 16 10. www.steenmeulen.com.*

### Wormhout

*10km/6mi north via D 218 and D 916.*

**Moulin Deschodt** – 🚶 *Guided visits (1h) 1st and 3rd Sun of Jun, 2nd Sun of Jul, 1st and 2nd Sun of Aug. 3-6pm.* ⊛*2€.* ☎*03 28 62 81 23.* This wooden post mill is the last of 11 windmills which stood in the town in 1780.

**Musée Jeanne-Devos** – 🕐*Open daily except Wed, 2-5pm, 1st two Sundays in the month 3-6pm.* 🕐*Closed 25 Dec, 1 Jan and public holidays.* ⊛*2€.* ☎ *03 28 62 81 23.* This charming Flemish house, flanked by a dovecote and set within lovely gardens at the end of a cul-de-sac, is the old Wormhout presbytery (18C). It was inhabited by Jeanne Devos who collected, until her death in 1989, a multitude of objects from daily life. A photographer by profession, she left thousands of photographs portraying the ordinary and extraordinary lives of the villagers nearby.

# ABBAYE DE CHAALIS★★

MICHELIN LOCAL MAP 305: H-6 OR MAP 106 FOLD 9

The estate lies on the edge of Ermenonville Forest, near the Mer de Sable theme park (👉 *see Excursions*) and, during the 19C, it evoked the gentle, romantic charm suggested by religious contemplation. Later, and up to 1912, Chaalis inspired its last owners to collect works of art and to entertain some of the most notable personalities of their time.

## A Bit of History

### A Prosperous Abbey

Chaalis was a Cistercian abbey (👉*see Introduction: Monasteries in Île-de-France*), built on the site of a former priory in 1136 by Louis the Fat. The monks led a pious and modest country life, husbanding the land, cultivating vines, keeping bees and fishing in the lakes.

M.O.Bernard/ MICHELIN

*Abbaye de Chaalis*

### Decline

During the 16C the abbey was held *in commendam* and the abbots were appointed by the king. The first was Cardinal Ippolito d'Este, son of Alfonso d'Este and Lucrezia Borgia, a distant cousin of François I. Known as Cardinal of Ferrara, this enthusiastic art lover had his private chapel decorated with murals and commissioned fine gardens.

In the 18C the ninth abbot, one of the Great Condé's grandsons, attempted a costly operation to restore the abbey to plans by Jean Aubert, the architect who designed the Great Stables at Chantilly. It was a disaster; after only one side of the building had been completed (1739, currently the Château-Museum) work stopped owing to lack of funds. This financial crisis prompted Louis XVI to close down the abbey in 1785. During the upheaval of the French Revolution, Chaalis was badly pillaged and the greater part of the building destroyed.

### Restoration

The estate frequently changed hands. Romantic painters and poets appreciated the melancholy charm of the old walls and their lush, verdant setting. In 1850 the highly distinguished Mme De Vatry bought the abbey ruins; she converted the 18C building into a château, had the park refurbished and entertained lavishly.

## Visit *1hr*

### Church ruins★

Consecrated in 1219, Chaalis Abbey was the first Cistercian church built in the Gothic style. Of the original buildings there remain a staircase turret, the northern transept arm surrounded by radiating chapels – an unusual feature – part of the chancel and the altar.

### Chapelle de l'abbé★

Built around 1250, the chapel is a fine example of Gothic splendour from the time of the Sainte-Chapelle in Paris. On the right, a bronze bust portraying Mme Jacquemart-André marks the site of her grave. Beyond the chapel a strange 16C crenellated wall with asymmetrical merlons sets the boundaries of the rose

Ph. Gajic/ MICHELIN

*St. Lawrence, by Giotto*

## Patrons of the arts

Of humble origin, Nélie Jacquemart (1841-1912) stayed for long periods, during her childhood, at Madame Vatry's who considered her almost as her daughter. She became acquainted with members of the aristocracy and the upper middle-class who were very useful to her in the pursuit of her career as a fashionable portrait painter, having studied with Léon Cogniet. In 1872, Édouard André, the heir to one of the largest fortunes in banking, commissioned a portrait from her, which still hangs in the private apartments of his Parisian mansion, and they met for the first time on this occasion. In 1881 they got married and their union was a happy one. Having no children, the couple devoted their efforts to collecting beautiful things, mainly from Italy, in the sumptuous mansion on boulevard Haussmann. Nélie André completed this collection after the death of her husband. In 1902, she realised one of her dreams: going to India; however she gave up the idea of a world tour when she learned that the Chaalis estate was for sale. She acquired it and devoted the last years of her life to it.

garden. Above the heavy archway, the coat of arms of Cardinal Louis d'Este, nephew of Cardinal of Ferrara, is displayed. From north of the château there is a fine perspective of the park with its flowerbeds and dazzling lake, restored in the 19C.

### Château-Musée★★

⏱*Open daily, Mar-mid-Nov, 11am-6pm; rest of year, Sun 11am-5pm. Visit to the park, daily, 10am-7pm.* ⏱*Closed 25 Dec.* ⏱*6.50€ (museum, park and rose garden), 3€ (park and rose garden)* ☎ *03 44 54 04 02. www.chaalis.fr.*

The personality and taste of Mme André are revealed as soon as you enter the **Salle des Moines** which houses Italian 15C Gothic furniture, small paintings, two panels from an altarpiece painted by Jean de Bellegambe, many religious statues (14C-16C French) and above all the famous **panels painted by Giotto★★**, depicting St John the Evangelist and St Lawrence.

## Excursions

### Ermenonville

*3km/1mi south on N 330.*
In May 1778 **Jean-Jacques Rousseau** was invited to stay at the Château d'Ermenonville (*private*) by the Marquis de Girardin, who had acquired the estate in 1763, and it is here that Rousseau rekindled his passion for nature; he walked, daydreamed in the park and taught music to his host's children.
The **Parc Jean-Jacques Rousseau**★ (⏱*times vary; call for current information;* ⏱*closed end of Dec;* ⏱*2€;* ☎*03 44 54 96 67*) was transformed by the marquess from sandy, swampy land into a superb landscaped garden in the French style with shaded paths, graceful vistas, elegant rockeries and follies.

### Mer de Sable★

*0.5km/0.25mi south on N 330.* ♿ ⏱*Open mid-May-Sep: 10am or 10.30am-7pm or 7.30pm (depending on the day)* ⏱*Closed Mon-Fri in Sep; Fri in Jun* ⏱*18.50€ (children 3-11: 15€).* ☎ *08 25 25 20 60. www. merdesable.fr.*

The sand deposits date from the Tertiary Era, at the end of the Ice Age this region was probably one vast sandy moor covered with wild heather.

Kids The landscape has been developed into a themed park evoking China, the Wild West or Morocco through characteristic scenery. The small train tour of the desert and the shows are complemented by various thrilling attractions (white-water rides, head-first slides etc) and more peaceful games. A glass-blower demonstrates his skill and sells his productions on the site.

# CHÂTEAU DE CHANTILLY★★★

**MICHELIN LOCAL MAP 305: F-5 OR MAP 106 FOLD 8**

The name Chantilly brings to mind a château, a forest, a racecourse and the world of horse racing in general. Because of its remarkable setting, its park and the treasures in its museum, the Château de Chantilly is considered one of the major sights in France. Chantilly is also rapidly becoming an important cultural centre, thanks to the activities of the Centre des Fontaines, with its library boasting 600 000 titles (philosophy, art, religion etc).

**Information:** Office de tourisme de Chantilly, 60 av. du Mar. Joffre, 60631 Chantilly. ☎ 03 44 67 37 37. www.chantilly-tourisme.com.

## A Bit of History

**From Cantilius to the Montmorency** – Over the past 2 000 years, five castles have occupied this part of the Nonette Valley. Above the ponds and marshes of the area rose a rocky island where **Cantilius**, a native of Roman Gaul, built the first fortified dwelling. His name and achievement gave birth to Chantilly. In the Middle Ages the building became a fortress belonging to the Bouteiller de France, named after the hereditary duties he carried out at the court of the Capetians; originally in charge of the royal cellars, the Bouteiller was one of the king's close advisers.

In 1386 the land was bought by the chancellor, Mr d'Orgemont, who had the castle rebuilt. The feudal foundations bore the three subsequent constructions. In 1450 the last descendant of the Orgemont married one of the Barons of Montmorency and Chantilly became the property of this illustrious family. It remained in their possession for 200 years.

**Constable Anne, Duc de Montmorency** – Anne de Montmorency was a devoted servant to a succession of six French kings from Louis XII to Charles IX. This formidable character gained a reputation as warrior, statesman, diplomat and patron of the arts. For 40 years, apart from a few brief periods, he remained the leading noble of the land, second to the king. Childhood friend and companion-in-arms to François I, close adviser to Henri II, he even had some influence over Catherine de' Medici, who looked favourably upon the man who had advised her on cures for her infertility.

*Château de Chantilly*

D. Pazery/ MICHELIN

Constable Anne owned 600 fiefs, over 130 castles and estates, four mansions in Paris and numerous posts and offices. He was immensely wealthy. When he went to court he was escorted by 300 guards on horseback. Through his five sons and the husbands of his seven daughters, he controlled most of the country's highest positions and had connections with Henri II, as well as with all the other most distinguished French families.

In 1528 the feudal castle of the Orgemont was demolished and the architect Pierre Chambiges replaced it with a palace built in the French Renaissance style. On a nearby island Jean Bullant erected the charming château which still stands today; the Petit Château. It was separated from the Grand Château by a moat – now filled in – which was spanned by two superimposed bridges. An aviary was set up in the tiny garden on the island. Constable Anne ordered great loads of earth and built the terrace which bears his statue.

**The last love of Henri IV** – Henri IV often stayed at Chantilly, with his companion-in-arms Henri I de Montmorency, the son of Constable Anne. At the age of 54 the king fell in love with his host's ravishing daughter Charlotte, aged only 15. He arranged for her to marry Henri II de Bourbon-Condé, a shy and gauche young man, whom the king hoped would prove an accommodating husband. The day after the wedding, however, Condé left the capital with his wife. Henri IV ordered them to return to Paris. The young couple fled to Brussels, where they stayed under the protection of the king of Spain. Henri IV raged, implored, threatened and even went as far as to ask the Pope to intervene. Only when he was murdered by Ravaillac did the two fugitives return to France.

**Henri de Montmorency** – Encouraged by Louis XIII's brother, the scheming Gaston d'Orléans, Henri II de Montmorency plotted against Richelieu. He was defeated at Castelnaudary near Toulouse and made a prisoner after receiving 18 wounds, including five by bullets. By way of an apology, he bequeathed to Cardinal Richelieu the two *Slave* sta ues by Michelangelo, now in the Louvre; those at Chantilly and Écouen are replicas.

**The Great Condé** – Charlotte de Montmorency and her husband the Prince of Condé – the couple persecuted by Henri IV – inherited Chantilly in 1643 and the château remained family property until 1830. Descendants of Charles de Bourbon, like Henri IV, the Princes of Condé were of royal blood and the heir apparent to the title was called the Duke of Enghien.

The Great Condé was the son of Charlotte and Henri II. He applied himself to renovating the Château de Chantilly with the same energy and efficiency he had shown in military operations. In 1662 he commissioned Le Nôtre to redesign the park and the forest. The fountains at Chantilly were considered the most elegant in France and Louis XIV made a point of outclassing them at Versailles. The work lasted 20 years and the result was a splendid achievement, part of which still stands today.

**The Last of the Condés** – The Prince of Condé died at Fontainebleau in 1686, to the king's great dismay. During the religious ceremony preceding the burial, Bossuet delivered a funeral oration which became famous.

The great-grandson of the Great Condé, Louis-Henri de Bourbon, alias "Monsieur le Duc", was an artist with a taste for splendour, who gave Chantilly a new lease on life. He asked Jean Aubert to build the Grandes Écuries, a masterpiece of the 18C, and set up a porcelain factory which closed down in 1870.

The Château d'Enghien was built on the estate by Louis-Joseph de Condé in

*Henri IV*

1769. His grandson the Duke of Enghien, who had just been born, was its first occupant. The father of the newly born baby was 16, his grandfather 36. The young prince died tragically in 1804; he was seized by the French police in the margravate of Baden and shot outside the fortress of Vincennes on the orders of Bonaparte.

During the French Revolution the main building was razed to the ground, though the smaller château was spared. Louis-Joseph was 78 when he returned from exile. His son accompanied him back to Chantilly and the two of them were dismayed: their beloved château was in ruins and the park in a shambles. They decided to renovate the estate. They bought back the plots of their former land, restored the Petit Château, redesigned and refurbished the grounds. The prince died in 1818, but the duke continued the work. He was an enthusiastic hunter and at the age of 70 he still hunted daily. Thanks to his efforts, Chantilly became the lively, fashionable place it had been in the years preceding the Revolution. As in former times, the receptions and hunting parties attracted crowds of elegant visitors. The renovation and restoration work was a source of income for the local population.

The duke was worried by the Revolution of 1830, which raised his cousin Louis-Philippe to the throne, and considered returning to England. A few days later, he was found hanging from a window at his castle in St-Leu. He was the last descendant of the Condé.

**The Duke of Aumale** – The Duke of Bourbon had left Chantilly to his great-nephew and godson the Duke of Aumale, the fourth son of Louis-Philippe. This prince gained recognition in Africa when he captured Abd el-Kader and his numerous relations. The Revolution of 1848 forced him to go into exile and he returned only in 1870; in 1873 he presided over the court martial which sentenced Marshal Bazaine. From 1875 to 1881 the duke commissioned Daumet to build the Grand Château in the Renaissance style. This castle, the fifth, still stands today. Back in exile between 1883 and 1889, he died

in 1897 and the Institute of France inherited his estate at Chantilly, together with the superb collections that constitute the Condé Museum.

## Visit

### The Château★★★

*guided visits (30min):* ⏱*Open daily (except Tue) Mar-Oct 10am-6pm. Nov-Feb 10.30am-12.45pm, 2-5pm (weekends and public holidays, 10.30am-5pm) (last admission 45min before closing).* ✆*8€ (4-12, 3.50€; 13-17, 7€).* ☎ *03 44 62 62 62. www.chateaudechantilly.com.*

From Chapelle-en-Serval, crossing Chantilly Forest, the château suddenly rises into view from the carrefour des Lions; it appears to be floating on the water in a superb setting of rocks, ponds, lawns and stately trees.

From Paris, take N 16; do not drive through the town but turn right after the lower road and into the shady Route de l'Aigle which skirts the racecourse.

The road from Senlis through Vineuil offers a good view of the château and its park; leaving Vineuil, turn left at each junction.

Try to picture the Château de Chantilly at the time of the Condé when the two main buildings were still divided by an arm of water: the 16C Petit Château (or barbican) and the Grand Château, for which Daumet used the foundations of the former stronghold.

Cross the constable's terrace, which bears the equestrian statue of Anne de Montmorency, and enter the main courtyard through the main gateway (Grille d'Honneur), flanked by the two copies of Michelangelo's *Slaves*.

The Duke of Aumale did not intend to establish a **museum**★★ for educational purposes; he merely wanted to build up a fine art collection. He therefore hung the works in chronological order of purchase though favourite ones were sometimes placed in a separate room. The curators have respected his layout.

According to the terms of the duke's legacy, the Institute must agree "to make no changes to the interior and exterior architecture of the château."

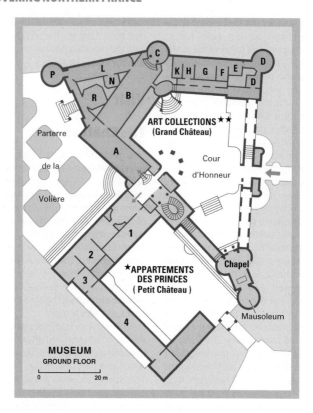

**MUSEUM**
GROUND FLOOR

0          20 m

ART COLLECTIONS ★★
(Grand Château)

Parterre

de la

Volière

Cour
d'Honneur

★APPARTEMENTS
DES PRINCES
( Petit Château )

Chapel

Mausoleum

Moreover, it is not allowed to lend any of the exhibits.

*The reception hall is the starting point for guided tours of the chapel and the various apartments as well as for unaccompanied tours of the collections. if a group has already formed, it is best to* *join it . It is advisable to interrupt a visit to the collections if the custodians announce a guided tour of the apartments.*

*Cabinet des Livres*

D. Pazery/ MICHELIN

## Appartements des Princes★

Situated in the **Petit Château**, this suite, occupied by the Great Condé and his descendants, was embellished with Regency and Rococo **wainscoting★★**, especially in the 18C thanks to the Duke of Bourbon. It was not occupied by the Duke of Aumale who had taken up residence on the ground floor.

The antechamber and part of the library, the work of the Duke of Aumale, are located on the site of the old moat.

**Cabinet des Livres★** (Library) (1)

This contains a splendid collection of manuscripts, including **The Rich Hours of the Duke of Berry** (*Les Très Riches Heures du duc de Berry*) with 15C illuminations by the Limbourg brothers. This extremely fragile document is not permanently exhibited but visitors may see a facsimile by Faksimile Verlag of Luzern.

## Address Book

♿*For coin ranges, see Legend on the cover flap.*

### WHERE TO STAY

⊜⊜ **Pavillon St-Hubert** – *In Toutevoie, on the banks of the Oise – 60270 Gouvieux – 3.5km/2mi W of Chantilly via D 909.* ☎03 44 57 07 04. 🅿 – 18 rms – 🍽 8€ – *restaurant* ⊜⊜. A former hunting lodge and its lovely garden by the Oise offering small rooms reminiscent of the inns of yore. The dining room, furnished in the Louis XIII style, is adorned with hunting trophies. Terrace in the shade of sycamore trees, with the Oise River in the background.

⊜⊜🍽 **Château de la Tour** – *60270 Gouvieux – 3.5km/2mi W of Chantilly via D 909.* ☎ 03 44 62 38 38. *Closed Christmas period.* 🅿 – 41 rms – *restaurant* ⊜⊜🍽. This early 20C domain, formerly belonging to a famous banker, overlooks a spacious park that can be contemplated from the terrace. There are modern and old-fashioned bedrooms available for the asking; elegant dining rooms with a Louis XIII flair.

### WHERE TO EAT

⊜⊜ **La Capitainerie "Les Cuisines de Vatel"** – *in the château – 60500 Chantilly.* ☎ 03 44 57 15 89. www.restaurantfp-chantilly.com. *Closed Tue and evenings – reserv. advisable.* One would be hard put to find a more prestigious setting for a restaurant than this one, located under the ancestral arches of kitchens once governed by the illustrious chef Vatel. The inviting decor features copper ware, porcelain, old ovens, the original brick fireplace and leather chairs. The menu changes with the seasons.

⊜⊜🍽 **Auberge le Vertugadin** – *44 r. du Connétable, 60500 Chantilly.* ☎ 03 44 57 03 19. *Closed Sun evening.* Follow the road to the Château de Chantilly to find this 19C manor with green window frames and shutters. There are two dining rooms to choose from, countrified or gentrified, plus a gravel terrace. The fixed-price and à la carte menus evolve with the seasons.

⊜⊜🍽 **La Belle Bio** – *22 r. du Connétable, 60500 Chantilly – 0.5km/0.3mi from the Château.* ☎ 03 44 57 02 25. *Closed Sun evening and Mon.* No, you're not entering a grocer's shop, but rather a '100% organic' restaurant. The colourful decor is charming, and the menu is chock full of tasty, imaginative dishes (fish, meat, vegetables). Highly recommended.

### RIDE ON THE CANAL

**L'hydrophile** – *Château de Chantilly, 60500 Chantilly.* ☎ 03 44 57 35 35 – *early Mar to late Oct: daily 10am-7pm, weather permitting; closed Nov-Feb.* The hydrophile takes you on a half-hour electric boat ride on the grand canal and in the moats of the château, amidst native aquatic fauna.

---

Another interesting reproduction is the psalter of Queen Ingeburge of Denmark. Among the ornamental motifs feature the monogram of the Duke of Aumale (H O for Henri d'Orléans) and the Condé coat of arms (France's "broken" coat of arms with a diagonal line symbolising the younger branch of the family).

**Chambre de Monsieur le Prince (2)**

This title referred to the reigning Condé Prince, in this instance the Duke of Bourbon (1692-1740), who installed a wainscot at the far end of the room, into which were embedded panels painted by C Huet in 1735. The famous Louis XVI commode was designed by Riesener and made by Hervieu.

**Salon des Singes (3)**

A collection of monkey scenes (*singeries*) dating from the early 18C is a masterpiece by an anonymous draughtsman; note the fire screen depicting the monkeys' reading lesson.

**Galerie de Monsieur le Prince (4)**

The Great Condé had ordered his own battle gallery, which he never saw completed (1692). The sequence was interrupted from 1652 to 1659 during his years of rebellion. A painting conceived by the hero's son portrays him stopping a Fame from publishing a list of his

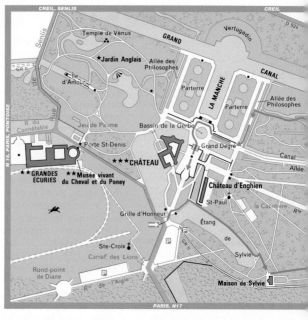

treacherous deeds and asking another Fame to issue a formal apology.

## Chapelle

An **altar**★ attributed to Jean Goujon and some 16C wainscoting and stained-glass windows from the chapel at Écouen were brought here by the Duke of Aumale. The apse contains the **mausoleum** of Henri II de Condé (*see above*) (bronze statues by J Sarrazin taken from the Jesuit Church of St-Paul-St-Louis in Paris) and the stone urn which received the hearts of the Condé princes. Up to the Revolution, the Condé necropolis was at Vallery in Burgundy, where another sepulchral monument celebrating Henri II still stands.

## The Collections★★ (Grand Château)

▶ Cross the Galerie des Cerfs **(A)** with its hunting theme; note the 17C Gobelins tapestries.

**Galerie de Peinture** (**B**) – The variety of paintings here reflects the eclectic tastes of the Duke of Aumale. Military events are illustrated on huge canvases (*Battle on the Railway Line* by Neuville, Meissonnier's *The Cuirassiers of 1805*).

Orientalism is well represented with Gros' work, *The Plague Victims* of Jaffa, H Vernet's *Arab Sheikhs holding Council*, and *The Falcon Hunt* by Fromentin. Note, too, the famous portrait of *Gabrielle d'Estrées in her Bath* (16C French school), the portraits of Cardinals Richelieu and Mazarin by Philippe de Champaigne, and *The Massacre of the Holy Innocents* by Poussin.

**Rotonde** (**C**) – The *Loreto Madonna* by **Raphael, Piero di Cosimo's** por-trait of the ravishing Simonetta Vespucci, who is believed to have been Botticelli's model for his *Birth of Venus*, and Chapu's kneeling statue of Joan of Arc listening to voices are exhibited here.

**Salle de la Smalah et Rotonde de la Minerve** (**D**) – Family portraits of the Orléans (17C, 18C and 19C) and of Louis-Philippe's relations in particular: Bonnat's picture of the Duke of Aumale at the age of 68.

**Cabinet de Giotto** (**E**) – A room devoted to Italian Primitives: *Angels Dancing in the Sun* (Italian School, 15C).

**Salle Isabelle** (**F**) – Numerous 19C paintings including *Moroccan Guards* by Delacroix, *Horse Leaving the Stables* by Géricault, and *Françoise de Rimini* by Ingres.

**Salle d'Orléans** (**G**) – The glass cabi-

nets contain **soft-paste Chantilly porcelain** manufactured in the workshops founded in 1725 by the Duke de Bourbon (armorial service bearing the Condé coat of arms or the Duke of Orléans' monogram).

**Salle Caroline** (**H**) – 18C painting has pride of place here, with portraits by Largillière and Greuze, *Young Woman Playing with Children* by Van Loo, *The Worried Lover* and *The Serenade Player* by Watteau, or *Snowstorm* by Everdingen.

**Cabinet des Clouet** (**K**) – A precious collection of small and extremely rare **paintings**★★ executed by the **Clouets**, Corneille de Lyon etc portraying François I, Marguerite de Navarre (stroking a little dog) and Henri II as a child etc.

**Galerie de Psyché** (**L**) – The 44 **stained-glass windows** (16C) that tell the story of the loves of Psyche and Cupid came from Constable Anne's other family home, Château d'Écouen.

**Santuario**★★★ (**N**) – This houses the museum's most precious exhibits: Raphael's *Orléans Madonna*, *The Three Ages of Womanhood*, also known as *The Three Graces*, by the same artist; *Esther and Ahasuerus*, the panel of a wedding chest painted by Filippino Lippi and 40 miniature works by Jean Fouquet, cut out of Estienne Chevalier's book of hours, a splendid example of French 15C art.

**Cabinet des Gemmes** (**P**) – This contains jewels of stunning beauty. The Pink Diamond, alias the Great Condé (a copy of which is permanently on show), was stolen in 1926 and subsequently found in an apple where the thieves had hidden it. The room also boasts an outstanding collection of enamels and miniatures.

**Tribune** (**R**) – Above the cornice of this polygonal room are painted panels representing episodes from the life of the Duke of Aumale and the house of Orléans. The paintings include *Autumn* by **Botticelli**, *Love Disarmed* and *Pastoral Pleasures* by **Watteau**, a portrait of Molière by **Mignard**, and on the "Ecouen Wall", three superb works by **Ingres**: a self-portrait, *Madame Devaucay* and *Venus*.

**Petits Appartements**★ Access by the stairway off the reception hall. The Duke of Aumale had these private apartments designed and decorated by painter Eugène Lami specially for his marriage in 1844.

## Park★★

&#9855; &#128337;*Open Apr-Oct: 10am-6pm; Nov-Mar: 10.30am-5pm.* 4€ (4-12, 2.50€; 13-17, 3.50€). ☎ 03 44 62 62 62.

**Jardin anglais** –The landscaped English-style garden was laid out on the surviving relics of Le Nôtre's park in 1820. Its charm derives from the pleasant groves (plane trees, swamp cypresses, weeping willows) rather than from the symbolic monuments: remains of a Temple of Venus and of Love (Île d'Amour).

**Chapelle St-Jean** – The chapel was erected on the estate by Constable Anne in 1538, with six other chapels, in memory of the seven churches of Rome he had visited in order to gain the indulgences granted to those who undertook this pilgrimage. He obtained from the Pope the same privileges for the chapels at Chantilly. Two other chapels still stand on the estate: St Paul's, located behind the Château d'Enghien and Ste-Croix, on the lawns of the racecourse.

▶ *Take allée Blanche along the banks of the Canal des Morfondus.*

**La Chute** – These tiered waterfalls mark the start of the Grand Canal.

▶ *Return along allée Blanche; cross the Canal des Morfondus at the footbridge.*

**Le Hameau** – Dating from 1775, this was built before the more famous Trianon at Versailles. Under the influence of Jean-Jacques Rousseau, French princes used to seek new horizons by creating miniature villages.

The mill and a few half-timbered buildings used to accommodate a kitchen, a dining room and a billiard room. The barn provided a drawing room that was restored by the Duke of Aumale. All the big parties included supper in this charming spot in the park.

▶ *Skirt the brook by the small village.*

**Parterres** – The parterres are framed by two avenues of young lime trees, called "The Philosophers' Path" because the great writers who visited Chantilly used to pace up and down the shaded avenue, exchanging their views and ideas. The circular Vertugadin lawns lie along the line of La Manche, flanked by delightful stretches of water. Between La Manche and the round basin (Bassin de la Gerbe) stands Coysevox's statue of the Great Condé, framed by the effigies of La Bruyère and Bossuet (statues of Molière and Le Nôtre, seated, may be seen in the near distance). A monumental stairway (Grand Degré) leads from the parterres up to the terrace; on either side of these imposing steps are grottoes, their carved decoration representing rivers.

**Le Potager des Princes** – *17 r. de la Faisanderie.* ⏰*Open daily (except Tue), 2-7pm.* 🚷*7.50€.* ☎ *03 44 57 40 40. www.potagerdesprinces.com.*

Originally designed by André Le Nôtre and Jean-Baptiste de la Quintinie, this garden includes an area reserved for farmyard animals, an orchard, a rose garden and a vegetable garden where medicinal and culinary herbs grow next to traditional vegetables.

**Grandes écuries★★ (Stables)**

Jean Aubert's masterpiece constitutes the most stunning piece of 18C architecture in Chantilly. The St-Denis Gate-

way – built astride the road leading to town – marks the site of an uncompleted pavilion. The most attractive façade of the stables overlooks the racecourse.

## Musée Vivant du Cheval et du Poney★★

♿⏰*Open Apr-Oct and Jul-Oct: 10.30am-6.30pm; May-Jun: 10.30am-6pm; Nov-Mar: daily except Tue, 2-5.30pm (Sat-Sun and public holidays, 10.30am-6.30pm).* 🚷*8.50€.* ☎ *03 44 57 40 40. www.musee-vivant-du-cheval.fr.*

This museum is brought to life by the 28 saddle and draught animals – 18 horses and 10 ponies – bred in France or in the Iberian Peninsula which occupy the stalls and boxes built in the days of the Duke of Aumale.

# Forêt de Chantilly

The vast wooded area has been reshaped by hunting enthusiasts over 500 years. The network of paths through the forest is suitable for country walks, and the light soil favours riding activities; training sessions take place at carrefour du Petit Couvert every morning. The forests of Coye, Orry and Pontarmé are reserved for walkers.

## Château de la Reine Blanche

In 1825 this old mill was restored in the troubadour style by the last of the Condés, the Duke of Bourbon, who used it as a hunting pavilion. It stands on the site of a legendary château believed to have been built by Queen Blanche of Navarre, wife of Philippe VI of Valois, after her husband's death around 1350. Part of the lodge is now occupied by a pancake house. An avenue of age-old beeches completes this delightful **site**★.

## Étangs de Commelles

These were used as fishponds by the monks from Chaalis Abbey. The road provides access to the car parks and to the causeways that crisscross the water, which makes it possible to explore the area around the ponds on foot.

# CHARTRES★★★

POPULATION 40 361

MICHELIN LOCAL MAP 311: E-5 OR MAP 106 FOLDS 37 AND 38

Chartres is the capital of Beauce, France's famous corn belt, but for tourists the town is known mainly for the Cathedral of Our Lady, a magnificent edifice, now a UNESCO World Heritage Site, which reigns supreme over a picturesque setting of monuments and old streets.

- **Information:** Pl. de la Cathédrale, 28000 Chartres. ☎ 02 37 18 26 26. www.chartres-tourisme.com.

- ▶ **Orient Yourself:** Chartres lies off the A 11. The town is situated on a knoll on the left bank of the River Eure, in the heart of the Beauce. The cathedral dominates the Old Town, known as the Quartier St-André. The central district holds the shopping

- **Parking:** There is a large underground car park at Le Bouef Couronne, and street parking (paid) along the boulevard de la Résistance and the boulevard Maurice Violette.

- **Don't Miss:** For a bird's-eye view of the cathedral, stand behind the Monument aux Aviateurs Militaires, a memorial to the French Air Force high above the east bank of the river. The **view**★ is impressive. A few typical gable ends are visible in the old town and the roofs of two churches, St-Aignan and St-Pierre.

- **Organizing Your Time:** Allow 90min to 2hr to visit the cathedral and at least 4hr to visit the Additional Sights (the tour of the agricultural museum, which is west of town, requires a minimum 2hr alone).

- **Also See:** The windmills of the Beauce Plain.

## A Bit of History

### A Town with a Destiny

Since ancient times Chartres has always had a strong influence over religious matters. It is believed that a Gallo-Roman well on the Chartres plateau was the object of a pagan cult and that in the 4C this was transformed into a Christian cult by the first evangelists. Adventius, the first known bishop of Chartres, lived during the middle of the 4C. A document from the 7C mentions a bishop Béthaire kneeling in front of

*Chartres Cathedral*

B. Kauffmann/ MICHELIN

Notre-Dame, which points to the existence of a Marian cult.

In 876 the chemise said to belong to the Virgin Mary was given to the cathedral by Charles the Bald, confirming that Chartres was already a place of pilgrimage. Up to the 14C the town of Chartres continued to flourish.

### The Pilgrimage

Chartres Cathedral was consecrated to the Assumption of the Virgin Mary in 1260; in the Middle Ages it attracted many pilgrims.

In 1912 and 1913 the writer and poet **Charles Péguy** (1873-1914) made the pilgrimage to Chartres. The strong influence it had on his work inspired a small group of enthusiasts after the First World War to follow suit and led, in 1935, to the establishment of the "Students' Pilgrimage" (*during Whitsun*).

### An exceptional man

In the **Église St-Jean-Baptiste** in the Rechèvres district to the north of the town lies the body of the abbot **Franz Stock**, whose tomb is still a place of pilgrimage.

This German priest, chaplain to the prisons of Paris from 1940 to 1944, refused to retreat with the Wehrmacht and was taken prisoner. At the Morancez prison camp near Chartres he founded a seminary for prisoners of war and was the Superior there for two years. He died in February 1948 at the age of 43.

# Visit

# Cathedral★★★

*Allow 1hr 30min.* The 4 000 carved figures and the 5 000 characters portrayed by the stained-glass windows demanded a lifelong commitment from the specialists who studied them.

### A Swift Construction

The building rests upon the Romanesque cathedral erected by Bishop Fulbert in the 11C and 12C: there remain the crypt, the towers and the foundations of the west front, including the Royal Doorway, and fragments of the Notre-Dame-de-la-Belle-Verrière stained-glass window. The remaining sections of the cathedral were built in the wake of the Great Fire of 1194; princes and dignitaries contributed generously to the work, while the poor offered their labour.

These efforts made it possible to complete the cathedral in 25 years, and to add on the north and south porches 20 years later, with the result that the architecture and decoration of Notre-Dame form a harmonious composition almost unparalleled in the history of Gothic art. By some miracle, the Wars of Religion, the French Revolution and the two World Wars spared the famous basilica, which Rodin referred to as "the Acropolis of France" on account of its aesthetic and spiritual value. Only the cathedral's "forest" – the superb roof timbers – were destroyed by flames in 1836, and subsequently replaced by a metal framework.

Beneath the cathedral close, where it is planned to build an international medieval centre, archaeological excavations covering an area of some 1 200m2/12 912sq ft are currently in progress. The remains of two 13C houses have been uncovered.

## Exterior

### West front

The two tall spires and the Royals Doorway form one of the most perfect compositions encountered in French religious art. The New Bell-Tower on the left was built first; the lower part dates back to 1134. Its present name dates from the 16C, when Jehan de Beauce erected a stone spire (115m /377ft high) to replace the wooden steeple which had burned down in 1506. The Old Bell-Tower (c 1145-64), rising 106m/384ft, is a masterpiece of Romanesque art, forming a stark contrast to the ornate Gothic construction. The Royal Doorway and the three large windows above date from the 12C. Everything above this ensemble was built at a later date: the rose-window (13C), the 14C gable and the king's gallery featuring the kings of Judah, the ancestors of the Virgin Mary. On the gable, the Virgin Mary is depicted presenting her son to the Beauce area.

The **Royal Doorway**★★★ (Portail Royal), a splendid example of Late Romanesque architecture (1145-70), represents the life and triumph of the Saviour. The Christ in Majesty on the central tympanum and the statue-columns are famous throughout the world. The elongated features of the biblical kings and queens, prophets, priests and patriarchs study the visitors from the embrasures. While the faces are animated, the bodies remain rigid, in deliberate contrast to the figures adorning the arches and the capitals. The statues were primarily designed to be columns, not human beings.

### North porch and doorway

Leave the west front on your left and walk round the cathedral, stepping back to get a clear view of its lines. The nave is extremely high and unusually wide. The problem of how to support it was brilliantly resolved with the construction of three-tiered flying buttresses; the lower two arcs were joined together by colonnettes. The elegant Pavillon de l'Horloge near the New Bell-Tower is the work of Jehan de Beauce (1520).

The ornamentation of the north porch is similar to that of the doorway, executed at an earlier date. Treated more freely than those on the Royal Doorway, the characters are elegant and extremely lively, illustrating a new, more realistic approach to religious art. The statue of St Modesta, a local martyr who is pictured gazing up at the New Bell-Tower, is extremely graceful.

Once again, the decoration of the three doors refers to the Old Testament. The right door pays tribute to the biblical heroes who exercised the virtues recommended in the teachings of Christ. The central panel shows the Virgin Mary and the Prophets who foretold the coming of the Messiah. The door on the left presents the Annunciation, Visitation and Nativity, together with the Vices and Virtues.

In the bishop's garden, the raised terrace commands a view of the town below lying on the banks of the lower River Eure. Before reaching the garden gate, look left and note the archway straddling a narrow street. It used to open into the Notre-Dame cloisters.

### East end

The complexity of the double-course flying buttresses – reinforced here with an intermediate pier as they cross over the chapels – and the succession of radiating chapels, chancel and arms of the transept are stunning. The 14C St Piat Chapel, originally separate, was joined to Notre-Dame by a stately staircase.

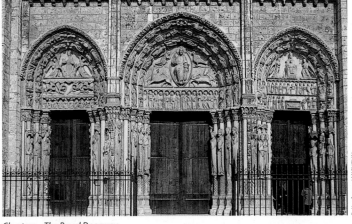

*Chartres – The Royal Doorway*

B. Kaufmann/ MICHELIN

### South porch and doorway

Here, the upper stonework is concealed by a constellation of colonnettes. The perspective of these planes, stretching from the arches of the porch to the gables, confers to this arm of the transept a sense of unity that is lacking in the north transept.

The theme is the Church of Christ and the Last Judgment. In the Middle Ages, these scenes would usually be reserved for the west portal, but in this case the Royal Doorway already featured ornamentation. Consequently, the scenes portraying the Coming of a New World, prepared by the martyrs, were destined for the left-door embrasures, while those of the Confessors (witnesses of Christ who have not yet been made martyrs) adorn the right door.

Christ reigns supreme on the central tympanum. He is also present on the pier, framed by the double row of the 12 Apostles with their lean, ascetic faces, draped in long, gently folded robes.

Among the martyrs, note the statues standing in the foreground: St George and St Theodore, both admirable 13C representations of knights in armour. These figures are quite separate from the columns – the feet are flat and no longer slanted – and are there for purely decorative purposes.

The most delightful feature of the sculpted porch is the display of medallions, grouped in sets of six and placed on the recessed arches of the three doorways: the lives of the martyrs, the Vices and Virtues etc.

Returning to the west front, note the Old Bell-Tower and its ironical statue of a donkey playing the fiddle, symbolising man's desire to share in celestial music. At the corner of the building, stop to admire the tall figure of the sundial Angel.

### Access to the Bell-Tower★

*Open Mar-Sep 9am-12.30pm, 2-6pm (Sun, 2-6pm). Oct-Apr, 9am-12.30pm, 2-5pm, (Sun 2-5pm) – last ascent 30min before closure. Closed 1 Jan, 1 May and Mon, Whitsun (afternoons), 25 Dec. 6.50€. 02 37 21 22 07. www.monum.fr.*

The tour (*195 steps*) leads round the north side and up to the lower platform of the New Bell-Tower. Seen from a height of 70m/230ft, the buttresses, flying buttresses, statues, gargoyles and Old Bell-Tower are most impressive. It is still possible to recognise the former Notre-Dame cloisters thanks to the old pointed roof. Enclosed by a wall right up to the 19C, this area was frequented by clerics, especially canons.

## Interior

The nave (16m/52ft) is wider than any other in France (Notre-Dame in Paris 40ft; Notre-Dame in Amiens 46ft), though it has single aisles. The vaulting reaches a height of 37m/121ft and the interior is 130m/427ft long. This nave is 13C, built in the style known as early or lancet Gothic. There is no gallery; instead, there is a blind triforium (*see illustration in the Introduction: Religious Architecture*). In a place of pilgrimage of this importance, the chancel and the transept had to accommodate large-scale ceremonies; they were therefore wider than the nave. In Chartres, the chancel, its double ambulatory and the transept form an ensemble 64m/210ft wide between the north and south doorways.

Note the gentle slope of the floor, rising slightly towards the chancel; this made it easier to wash down the church when the pilgrims had stayed overnight.

The striking state of semi-darkness in the nave creates an element of mystery which was not intentional: it is due to the gradual dimming of the stained glass over the centuries.

### Stained-glass windows★★★

The 12C and 13C stained-glass windows of Notre-Dame constitute, together with those of Bourges, the largest collection in France. The Virgin and Child and the Annunciation and Visitation scenes in the clerestory at the far end of the chancel produce a striking impression.

### West front

These three 12C windows used to throw light on Fulbert's Romanesque cathedral and the dark, low nave that stood behind, which explains why they are so long.

The scenes (*bottom to top*) illustrate the fulfilment of the prophecies: (*right*) the Tree of Jesse, (*centre*) the childhood and life of Our Lord (Incarnation cycle) and (*left*) Passion and Resurrection (Redemption cycle).

You can feast your eyes on the famous 12C "Chartres blue", with its clear, deep tones enhanced by reddish tinges, especially radiant in the rays of the setting sun. For many years, people believed that this particular shade of blue was a long-lost trade secret. Modern laboratories have now established that the sodium compounds and silica in the glass made it more resistant to dirt and corrosion than the panes made with other materials and in other times. The large 13C rose-window on the west front depicts the Last Judgment.

### Transept

This ensemble consists of two 13C rose-windows, to which were added a number of lancet windows featuring tall figures. The themes are the same as those on the corresponding carved doorway: Old Testament (north), the End of the World (south).

The north rose (*rose de France*) was a present from Blanche of Castille, mother of St Louis and Regent of France, and portrays a Virgin and Child. It is characterised by the fleur-de-lis motif on the shield under the central lancet and by the alternating Castile towers and fleurs-de-lis pictured on the small corner lancets. The larger lancets depict St Anne holding the infant Virgin Mary, framed by four kings or high priests: Melchizedek and David stand on the left, Solomon and Aaron on the right.

The centre roundel of the south rose shows the risen Christ, surrounded by the Old Men of the Apocalypse, forming two rings of 12 medallions. The yellow and blue chequered quatrefoils represent the coat of arms of the benefactors, the Comte de Dreux Pierre Mauclerc and his wife, who are also featured at the bottom of the lancets.

The lancets on either side of the Virgin and Child depict four striking figures – the Great Prophets Isaiah, Jeremiah, Ezekiel and Daniel – with the four Evangelists seated on their shoulders.

The morality of the scene is simple: although they are weak and lacking dignity, the Evangelists can see farther than the giants of the Old Testament thanks to the Holy Spirit.

### Notre-Dame-de-la-Belle-Verrière★ (1)

*See Illustration in the Introduction.* This is a very famous stained-glass window. The Virgin and Child, a fragment of the window spared by the fire of 1194, has been mounted in 13C stained glass. The range of blues is quite superb.

**Other stained-glass windows** – The aisles of the nave and the chapels around the ambulatory are lit by a number of celebrated stained-glass windows from the 13C verging on the sombre side. On the east side, the arms of the transept have received two works of recent making, in perfect harmony with the early fenestration: St Fulbert's window (*south transept*) (2), donated by the American Association of Architects (from the François Lorin workshop, 1954), and the window of Peace (*north transept*) (3), a present from a group of German admirers (1971).

The Vendôme Chapel (4) features a particularly radiant 15C stained-glass window. It illustrates the development of this art, which eventually led to the lighter panes of the 17C and 18C.

Chartres Cathedral – Central window of the west front: Detail of the Redemption cycle

H. Champollion/ MICHELIN

## Parclose ★★

The screen was started by Jehan de Beauce in 1514 and finished in the 18C. This fine work consists of 41 sculpted compositions depicting the lives of Christ and the Virgin Mary. These Renaissance medallions, evoking biblical history, local history and mythology, contrast sharply with the Gothic statues of the doorways.

## Chancel

The marble facing, the Assumption group above the high altar and the low-relief carvings separating the columns were added in the 18C.

## Organ (5)

The case dates from the 16C.

## Vierge du Pilier (6)

This wooden statue (c 1510) stood against the rood screen, now sadly disappeared. The richly clothed Virgin is the object of a procession celebrated annually.

## Treasury

*Closed to the public.*
Chapelle St-Piat has been built to house the cathedral treasury. It is linked to the east end of the cathedral by a Renaissance staircase. Inside are some superb items of church plate.

## Chapelle des Martyrs

This chapel has been refurbished and now contains the **Virgin Mary's Veil**, laid out in a beautiful glass-fronted reliquary. Pilgrims used to pray to this veil, calling it a tunic or "Holy Chemise."

## Crypt★

*Guided tours (30min) Apr-Oct daily (except Sun and public holidays) at 11am, 2.15pm, 3.30pm and 4.30pm (end Jun to mid-Sep: additional tour at 5.15pm). Nov-Mar daily (except Sun and public holidays) at 11am and 4.15pm. Closed 1 Jan, 21 Jun, 25 Dec. 2.30€. 02 37 21 56 33.*
The entrance is outside the cathedral, on the south side (*see plan above*). This is France's longest crypt (220m/722ft long). It dates largely from the 11C and features Romanesque groined vaulting. It is a curious shape; the two long galleries joined by the ambulatory pass under the chancel and the aisles and give onto seven chapels. The central area, which has been filled in, remains

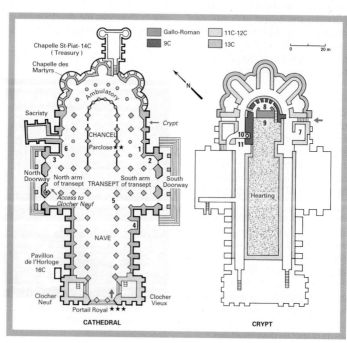

CATHEDRAL

CRYPT

## Address Book

🍴 *For coin ranges, see the Legend on the cover flap.*

### WHERE TO STAY

🛏 **La Ferme du Château (Bed and Breakfast)** – *in Levesville, 28300 Bailleau-l'Évêque – 8km/5mi NW of Chartres via N 154 and D 134.* ☎ 02 37 22 97 02. *3 rms: meals* 🍴🍴. This elegant Beauce farm offers pretty, comfortable rooms that have been decorated with a light hand. Neighbouring a small château, the farm is very quiet and its kind, hospitable owners are very discreet – a quality we appreciate!

🛏🛏🖥🛏 **Hôtel Le Grand Monarque** – *22 pl. des Épars.* ☎ 02 37 18 15 15. *www.bw-grand-monarque.com – 50 rms – 🍴 12 € – restaurant* 🛏🛏🖥🛏. A 16C coaching inn at the heart of the city. The comfortable rooms have a personal touch; some are embellished with cheerfully flowered patterns and canopies while others are more sober. Snug dining room with ornamental wood carvings and works of art.

### WHERE TO EAT

🍴 **Le Pichet** – *19 r. du Cheval-Blanc.* ☎ 02 37 21 08 35 – *www.info28.com/lepider. Closed Tue evening and Wed.* Just down the street from the cathedral, a very friendly little bistro that suits our tastes. Inside, there is a pleasant jumble of bric-a-brac: wooden chairs, a collection of coffeepots, pitchers, old street signs and other good stuff. The food is traditional French cuisine.

🍴🍴 **Le Café Serpente** – *2 r. du Cloître Notre-Dame.* ☎ 02 37 21 68 81. *www.le-cafe-serpente.com. Closed evenings of 24 and 31 Dec – reserv. requested in winter.* A bicycle on the ceiling, posters on the walls and enamelled plaques in the stairwell comprise the decor of this thoroughly genial old café opposite the cathedral. On your plates: appetizing salads, brasserie fare and authentic cuisine at all hours.

🍴🍴 **Le Tripot** – *11 pl. Jean-Moulin.* ☎ 02 37 36 60 11. *Closed last 2 weeks of Aug, Sun-Mon.* This house built in 1553 used to accommodate a real tennis court called 'Le Tripot'. Well-preserved rustic interior and contemporary cuisine.

### SHOPPING

**Galerie de Chartres** – *7 r. Collin-d'Harleville.* ☎ 02 37 88 28 28, *www.interencheres.com – showings: Mon and Fri, 9am-noon, 2-6pm.* This establishment organises auctions for an international clientele every weekend in the 16C Eglise Sainte-Foy (ceramics, weapons, stamps, silverware, cameras, radios etc.). Specialises in the sale of collectable dolls and toys.

**Marché aux légumes et volailles** – *Pl. Billard.* Each Saturday morning, the covered Vegetable and Poultry Market displays colourful stands featuring authentic Beauce produce. This carrousel of sights, tastes and fragrances is one of the most popular markets in the area.

**Atelier Loire** – *16 r. d'Ouarville, 28300 Lèves – Just north of Chartres on the way to Dreux, 2km/1.2mi from the cathedral –* ☎02 37 21 20 71 – *www.galerie-du-vitrail.com – guided tours, Fri 2.30pm; closed Aug and public holidays.* A century-old, stately residence set amidst a park and adorned with stained-glass creations is the home of this atelier founded in 1946 by Gabriel Loire, and continued today by his grandchildren. The art and technique of making stained glass are carefully explained, beginning with artists' models (as designed by Adami, Miro or Fernand Léger, for example) and ending with the finished product created by master glass crafters.

### ON THE TOWN

**Brûlerie les Rois Mages** – *6 r. des Changes.* ☎ 02 37 36 30 52 – *Tue-Sat 9.15am-12.15pm, 1.30-7.15pm.* Enter this "retro" coffee-roasting shop and choose among the wide variety of coffees roasted on site and the dozens of teas to enjoy in the brûlerie or take home.

**La Chocolaterie** – *14 pl. Marceau.* ☎ 02 37 21 86 92 – *Tue-Sat, 8am-7.30pm; Sun-Mon 10am-7.30pm.* A highly useful address for stocking up on gourmet treats to take home as souvenirs, such as macaroons or Mentchikoffs, a local chocolate speciality. The very cosy tearoom offers sofas and a fireplace; there's a pleasant terrace in summer.

unexplored. Of the seven radiating chapels, only three are Romanesque. The other four were added by the master architect of the Gothic cathedral to serve as foundations for the chancel and the apse of the future building.

### St Martin's Chapel (7)

Located by the south gallery, this chapel houses the originals of the statues on the Royal Doorway: the sundial Angel etc.

▶ *A staircase, starting from the ambulatory, leads down to a lower crypt.*

### Crypt St-Lubin (8)

This crypt served as the foundations of the 9C church. A thick, circular column with a visible base backs onto a Gallo-Roman wall (**9**), its bond easily recognisable by the alternating bricks and mortar. The crypt was a safe place that protected the cathedral treasures in times of social unrest or natural disaster. Thus, the chemise of the Virgin Mary survived the Great Fire of 1194.

### Puits des Saints-Forts (10)

The lower part of this 33m/108ft deep shaft has a square section characteristic of Gallo-Roman wells. The coping is contemporary. The name dates back to 858; it is believed that several Christian martyrs from Chartres were murdered during a Norman attack, and their bodies thrown down the well.

### Chapelle Notre-Dame-de-Sous-Terre (11)

A sacred retreat where pilgrims indulge in fervent praying. Since the 17C the chapel, together with the north gallery of the crypt, has played the part of a miniature church. It originally consisted of a small alcove where the faithful came to venerate the Virgin Mary. The interior of the chapel and its decoration were refurbished in 1976. On this occasion, the 19C statue of the Virgin Mary was replaced by a more hieratic figure, based on the Romanesque model, enhanced by a Gobelins tapestry.

| | |
|---|---|
| Ballay R. Noël | A 5 |
| Bourg R. du | A 10 |
| Brèche R. de la | A 12 |
| Cardinal-Pie R. du | A 14 |
| Changes R. des | A |
| Cheval-Blanc R. du | A 19 |
| Cois R. aux | A 22 |
| Cygne Pl. du | A |
| Guillaume R. Porte | A 41 |
| Herbes Pl. aux | A 43 |
| Marceau Pl. | A |
| Marceau R. | A |
| Petite Cordonnerie R. de la | A 57 |
| Pied-Plat Tertre du | A 58 |
| Poissonnerie Pl. de la | A 60 |
| Soleil-d'Or R. du | A |
| Teinturiers Q. des | A 72 |

| | |
|---|---|
| Escalier " de la Reine Berthe " | A B |
| Grenier de Loens Centre International du Vitrail | A E |
| Maison à pans de bois | A F |
| Musée des Beaux-Arts | A M² |
| Passerelle | A S |

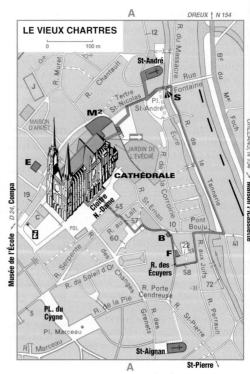

LE VIEUX CHARTRES

# Additional Sights

## Old Town★ (Quartier St-André and Banks of the Eure)

*Follow the route indicated on the plan below.* This pleasant walk leads past the picturesque hilly site, the banks of the River Eure, an ancient district recently restored and the cathedral which is visible from every street corner. In the summer season, a small **tourist train** tours the old town.

## Église St-André

🕑*Temporarily closed for restoration.*
☏ 02 37 21 03 69.

This Romanesque church (*deconsecrated*) was the place of worship of one of the most active and densely populated districts in town. Most of the trades were closely related to the river: millers, dyers, curriers, cobblers, tanners, drapers, fullers, tawers, serge makers etc. The church was enlarged in the 13C, and in the 16C and 17C it received a chancel and an axial chapel resting on arches that straddled the River Eure and rue du Massacre. Unfortunately, both these structures disappeared in 1827 leaving a much less picturesque church.

*Cross the Eure by a metal footbridge.* There is a good **view**★ of the old humpback bridges. At the foot of the shortened nave of St Andrew's lie the remains of the arch that once supported the chancel. *Wander upstream.* The washhouses and races of former mills have been prettily restored. Rue aux Juifs leads through an ancient district that has recently been renovated, featuring cobbled streets bordered by gable-ended houses and old-fashioned street lamps.

**Rue des Écuyers** – This is one of the most successful restoration schemes of the old town. At nos 17 and 19 the houses have 17C doorways with rusticated surrounds, surmounted by a bull's-eye window. Stroll along the street to rue aux Cois. The corner building is a delightful half-timbered villa, with an overhang in the shape of a prow. Opposite stands Queen Bertha's stair turret, a 16C structure, also half-timbered.

# Central District

## Place du Cygne

The street has been widened into a little square planted with trees and shrubs (*flower market on Tuesdays, Thursdays and Saturdays*) and is at present an oasis of calm in this lively shopping district in the town centre.

At the end of rue du Cygne, on place Marceau, a monument celebrates the memory of the young local general who died at Altenkirchen (1796) at the age of 27. His ashes have been shared among Chartres (funeral urn under the statue on place des Épars), the Panthéon and the Dome Church of the Invalides in Paris.

## Église St-Pierre★

This 12C and 13C Gothic church used to belong to the Benedictine abbey of St-Père-en-Vallée. The belfry-porch dates from pre-Romanesque times. The **Gothic stained-glass windows**★ can be traced back to the late 13C and early 14C, before the widespread introduction of yellow staining.

The oldest stained glass is that in the south bays of the chancel, portraying tall, hieratic figures from the Old Testament.

## Monument de Jean Moulin

**Jean Moulin** was *préfet* (chief administrator) of Chartres during the German invasion; on 8 June 1940, despite having been tortured, he resisted the enemy and refused to sign a document claiming that the French troops had committed a series of atrocities. As he was afraid of being unable to withstand further torture, he attempted to commit suicide.

Moulin was dismissed by the Vichy government in November 1940 and, from then on, he planned and coordinated underground resistance, working in close collaboration with General de Gaulle.

Arrested in Lyon on 21 June 1943, he did not survive the harsh treatment he received from the Gestapo.

## Grenier de Loëns

From the 12C onward, this half-timbered barn with treble gables in the courtyard of the old chapter house was used to store the wine and cereals offered to the clergy as a tithe. Renovated to house the **Centre international du Vitrail** (&. ◷ *open 9.30am-12.30pm, 1.30-6pm, Sat-Sun and public holidays 10am-12.30pm, 2.30-6pm. ◷ closed 1 Jan, 25 Dec.* ⌖4€. ☎ *02 37 21 65 72. www.centre-vitrail.org*) which organises stained-glass exhibitions, the building now features a large hall with beautifully restored roof timbering and a magnificent 12C cellar with three aisles.

## Musée des Beaux-Arts

◷*Open daily (except Tue): May-Oct, 10am-noon, 2-6pm (Sun and public holidays 2-6pm). Nov-Apr, 10am-noon, 2-5pm (Sun and public holidays, 2-6pm). ◷Closed 1 Jan, 1 and 8 May, 1 and 11 Nov, 25 Dec.* ⌖2.70€ – *ticket combined with the Maison Picassiette: 5.80€).* ☎ *02 37 36 41 39. www.ville-chartres.fr.*

The museum is housed in the old bishop's palace and occupies the first terrace of the bishopric's gardens. The large, handsome edifice which was built over four centuries consists of a 15C section arranged around an interior courtyard, a 17C and 18C façade, and an early-18C wing overlooking the garden. The old sacristy, close to the chapel, houses 12 unusually large **enamels**★ representing the Apostles, by Léonard Limousin.

The museum's new rooms house the permanent modern art collections as well as temporary exhibitions. There are several works by Vlaminck (*The House in Auvers, Red Bouquet with Anemones*) and J Guérin (*Flower Woman with the Poplar*). The South Sea Island collection and works by master glass painter Navarre are also on show.

## Le COMPA: Conservatoire du Machinisme et des Pratiques Agricoles

*West of the town by D 24.* &. ❧ *Tours (90min): ◷Open daily (except Mon) 9am-12.30pm, 1.30-6pm (weekends and public holidays 10am-12.30pm, 1.30-7pm). ◷Closed 1 Jan, 1 May, 1 Nov, 25 Dec.* ⌖3.80€. ☎*02 37 84 15 00. www.lecompa.com.*

The museum is located in a strikingly converted, semicircular former railway shed. The spacious, modern-looking building, encircled by neat lawns offering a good view of Chartres and the cathedral, contains splendid, gleaming old machines and tools of copper, wrought iron or wood.

**Tools and machines** – At the museum's core stands an assortment of machines grouped according to function: seeders, binder-harvesters, combine-harvesters.

**Land, men and methods** – A comparison of two farming concerns in different regions of France, in 1860 and today, provides a better understanding of rural life. Ploughs from around the world illustrate the diversity in methods used by workers on the land.

**Galerie des inventeurs et des inventions** – The 80m/262ft-long gallery introduces the figures responsible for major agricultural developments over the centuries.

The ideas and innovations of Pliny the Elder, Olivier de Serres, Henri de Vilmorin and, more recently, Ferguson and the national agricultural research centre (INRA) are explained through information panels and fascinating interactive displays.

**Salle des tracteurs** – The tour ends with an exhibition of tractors, the oldest dating from 1816, the most recent from 1954.

## Musée de l'École

&. ◷*Open daily (except Sat-Sun) 10am-noon, 2-6pm (last admission 4.30pm).*

*Ph. Galic/ MICHELIN*

*Sawyer Massey tractor (1910)*

Closed public holidays. 3.50€.
02 37 30 07 69.
A classroom, belonging to the old teachers' training college, houses teaching aids and furniture evoking the schools of yesteryear: abacuses, magic lanterns using paraffin, books advocating humanist ethics, a collective money-bank with a separate compartment for each pupil etc.

**Maison Picassiette**
*22 rue du Repos.* Open daily (except Tue): Apr and Nov 10am-noon, 2-5pm (Sun and public holidays 2-5pm). May-Oct 10am-noon, 2-6pm (Sun and public holidays, 2-6pm). Closed 1 and 8 May, and 1 and 11 Nov. 4.30€ (ticket combined with the musée des Beaux-Arts). 02 37 34 10 78. www.ville-chartres.fr.
Built and decorated by Raymond Isidore (1900-64), this house offers an amazing medley of naive art. Numerous monuments and religious scenes are suggested by mosaic compositions made with diverse materials.

# LE CHEMIN DES DAMES
MICHELIN LOCAL MAP 306: C-6 TO F-6

Chemin des Dames, which means Ladies' Way, follows a ridge separating the Aisne Valley from the Ailette Valley. It derives its name from the daughters of Louis XV, known as "Mesdames", who followed this route to get to the Château de la Bove, home of their friend the Duchess of Narbonne. The site still bears the marks of the bitter fighting which took place during the First World War.

## A Bit of History

### Nivelle Offensive
In 1914, after the Battle of the Marne, the retreating Germans stopped here, having realised that the location was an excellent defensive spot which they fortified by making use of the quarries (*boves* or *creuttes*), hollowed out of the ridge.
**General Nivelle**, commander of the French armies from December 1916, searched for a way of penetrating their defence along Chemin des Dames. In spite of the difficult terrain, riddled with machine gun nests, on 16 April 1917 he sent an army under Mangin to attack the German positions. The French troops occupied the ridges following the first assault but the Germans clung onto the slopes of the Ailette Valley: the terrible French losses that ensued, together with the failure of the venture, caused a crisis of morale which provoked mutinies in parts of the French army.
General Nivelle and General Mangin were dismissed; **Marshal Pétain** (then a general) took over and suppressed the rebellion. There are people today who think the mutineers should have been pardoned because they were only driven to despair by the horrors of war.

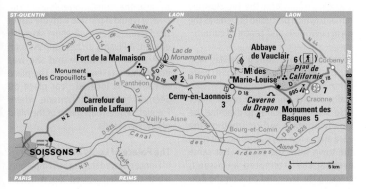

# COMPIÈGNE★★★

**POPULATION 108 234**

**MICHELIN LOCAL MAP 305: H-4 OR MAP 106 FOLD 10**

Compiègne, which was a royal residence long before it hosted the brilliant parties and receptions of the Second Empire, is bordered by one of the most beautiful forests in France. It was there that the armistice of 11 November 1918 was signed; today it is a hiker's paradise, with deer roaming freely.

- **Information:** Pl. de l'Hôtel-de-Ville, 60200 Compiègne. ☎ 03 44 40 01 00. www.mairie.compiegne.fr.
- ▶ **Orient Yourself:** Most of the city occupies the left bank of the Oise River. The Palace dominates Place du General de Gaulle. Three blocks south in the centre of town stands the city hall (hôtel de ville), which houses the tourist office. Nearby, on Place du Change, is a provincial market Les Halles du Grenier à Sel (see Address Book).
- **Parking:** There are parking areas around the Palace, near St-Jacques church and on Cours Guynemer along the river. The train station, on the opposite side of the river, provides parking space.
- **Don't Miss:** The palace, of course, with its two museums. Driving tours no 1 and no 2 are particularly worth a trip, combining viewpoints and history.
- **Organizing Your Time:** Allow at least 2hr for the palace, and more if you want to explore the grounds. The Additional Sights includes two museums, so plan on another 2hr. Hikers and cyclists will want to take their time in the Compiègne Forest. Each of the driving tours requires 1hr to 1hr30min.
- **Especially for Kids:** Though not tailored specifically to children, the Excursion is close to town, and includes a barge hold and a tour of a lock, something kids should find interesting.
- **Also See:** Longueil-Annel; Ourscamps; Pierrefonds.

## A Bit of History

**Origins** – Charles the Bald had a palace built to resemble the one in Aix-la-Chapelle (Aachen) built for Charlemagne and ceded to Charles' brother, Louis, in 843 when the Treaty of Verdun divided up the Carolingian Empire. He also founded an abbey which from the 10C preserved the relics of St Cornelius. The town developed around this royal abbey of St Cornelius (today only the 14C cloisters remain), which preceded St Denis as the royal necropolis and centre of culture.

**Joan of Arc Imprisoned** – In May 1430 the Burgundians and the English were camping beneath Compiègne's town walls, on the north side of the River Oise. Joan of Arc came to examine the enemy position and returned on the 23rd after a few days' absence, entering the town from the south. That same evening she attempted an assault, crossing the river and chasing the Bur-

gundian vanguard from their Margny encampment. However, reinforcements came to the aid of the Burgundians from Clairoix and Coudun, while the English came from Venette, stealing along the Oise to attack from the rear; the French had no choice but to give ground. The 'Maid of Orléans' covered the retreat with a handful of men. She reached the moat just as the commanding officer in Compiègne gave the order to raise the drawbridge, fearing the enemy would slip inside with the last of the French soldiers. A short skirmish ensued. A Picardy archer toppled Joan of Arc from her horse and she was immediately taken prisoner. The place of capture is located near place du 54ème-Régiment-d'Infanterie, where Frémiet's equestrian statue of the Maid of Orléans stands.

**The Palace of Louis XV** – All the kings of France enjoyed staying in Compiègne, which they often visited. Yet, with four main buildings haphazardly arranged around a central courtyard, the château was not an obvious royal residence. Louis XIV said, "At Versailles, I am lodged like a king; at Fontainebleau, like a prince; and at Compiègne, like a peasant." He had new apartments built facing the forest. His 75 visits here were marked by sumptuous feasts and, in particular, great military camps.

When Louis XV ordered the complete reconstruction of the palace in 1738 he was less interested in outdoing his predecessor, who had built so much, than in having a place where he could reside with his court and ministers. The architect Jacques Gabriel and his successor **Jacques-Ange Gabriel** were limited by the town and its ramparts, which obliged them to rebuild on the old foundations. As a further inconvenience, they could not destroy an old building until a new one had been completed, as the King refused to curtail his visits to Compiègne during the rebuilding work. Louis XV's master plan of 1751 was brought to a halt by the Seven Years War. Louis XVI continued the project and achieved a great deal but left it unfinished. In fact, it was not until 1785 that he was finally able to occupy the royal apartments, which would later accommodate Napoleon I. The south wing was finished that same year. Marie-Antoinette had personally overseen its arrangement, decor and furnishing but never actually stayed there herself. A great terrace was built in front of the palace's façade, which looked out onto a park. This terrace was connected to the gardens by a monumental central flight of steps, replacing the moat that had formerly been part of Charles V's fortifications.

After the Revolution the palace served first as a military school, then as an engineering college. In 1806 it became an Imperial residence and Napoleon I had the place entirely restored by the architect Berthaut, the painter Girodet and the decorators Redouté and the Dubois brothers.

**Wedding Palace** – It was in Compiègne Forest that, on 14 May 1770, the future Louis XVI was introduced to Marie-Antoinette of Austria for the first time; the young Dauphin was paralysed with shyness.

On 27 March 1810 the great-niece of Marie-Antoinette, Marie-Louise of Austria, was to arrive in Compiègne. She had married Napoleon I by proxy and this time the groom was impatient. Despite torrential rain, the Emperor ran to meet the princess and threw himself soaking wet into her carriage, smothering the terrified Marie-Louise with demonstrations of affection. The dinner planned in Soissons was cancelled and instead the Emperor and his bride had supper at Compiègne. Some days later the wedding ceremonies were celebrated at St-Cloud, serving only as the consecration

*Palace*

Ph. Gajic/ MICHELIN

of a union imposed at Vienna and willingly accepted at Compiègne.

In 1832, Louis-Philippe, who transformed the real tennis court into a theatre, married his daughter Louise-Marie to the first king of Belgium, Leopold of Saxe-Coburg.

**The Second Empire "Series"** – Compiègne was the favourite residence of Napoleon III and Empress Eugénie. They came every autumn for four to six weeks to enjoy the hunting season. They also received the celebrities of the time, arranged in five "series" of about 80 people, grouped by "affinities". Lodging the guests often posed great difficulties and many distinguished individuals had to content themselves with rooms under the eaves.

The hunts, theatrical evenings, cvharades and balls left the guests with little free time. Romantic and political intrigue mixed freely. One rainy afternoon, to amuse the Imperial couple and their guests, the writer Mérimée composed his famous dictation, comprising the words with the greatest spelling difficulties in the French language. The Empress made the highest number of mistakes, 62; Pauline Sandoz, Metternich's daughter-in-law, had the least with three. The luxuries and endless frivolities intoxicated the courtiers, who delighted in waltzes and long forest outings. The events of 1870 interrupted this joyous life and the work on the new theatre.

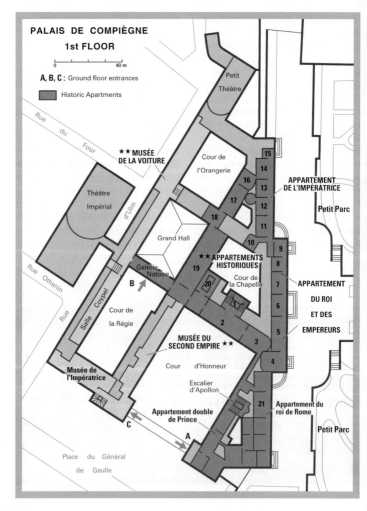

During the Emperor's long periods of residence at Compiègne most of the First Empire furniture was replaced.

**The World Wars** – From 1917 to 1918 the palace was the general headquarters of generals Nivelle and then Pétain. In 1919 a fire damaged most of the royal apartments. The armistices of 11 November 1918 and 22 June 1940 (♿ *see Forêt de COMPIÈGNE: Clairière de l'Armistice*) were signed in the forest. Compiègne suffered heavy bombing during the Second World War. Royallieu, a district south of the town, served from 1941 to 1944 as a centre from which prisoners were sent to various Nazi concentration camps (a memorial stands at the entrance to the military camp as well as in Compiègne railway station).

## Visit

# Palace★★★

Viewed from the square the palace is paradoxically "a Louis XV château built almost entirely from 1751 to 1789". This austerely Classical château covers a vast triangular area (3ha/7.5 acres); indeed, the regularity of its arrangement is even rather monotonous. The decoration inside and the collection of 18C and First Empire tapestries and furnishings is, however, exceptional. Among the many details unifying the various apartments are fine *trompe-l'œil paintings* by Sauvage (1744-1818) over the doors. The new theatre, on which work began in 1867 during the reign of Napoleon III, was never completed because of the Franco-Prussian War in 1870. An association was set up in 1987 to rehabilitate it and organise productions there. As a result, the **Théâtre Impérial**, in which the interior layout is reminiscent of the opera house in Versailles, has become popular as a venue for concerts and operettas.

## Appartements Historiques★★

♿*Open Mar-Oct: ☀☀ guided tours (1hr, last admission 45min before closing) daily except Tue 10am-6pm; Nov-Feb: daily (except Tue) 10am-5.45pm.* ♿*Closed 1 Jan, 1 May, 1 Nov, 25 Dec.* 5€ *(under 18, no charge); no charge 1st Sunday in the month.* ☎ *03 44 38 47 00. www.musee-chateau-compiegne.fr.*

The Historic Apartments of the palace begin with rooms devoted to its history; beyond them rises the Queen's Grand Staircase, or Apollo Staircase, which led directly to the Queen's apartments; farther still is the entrance hall or Gallery of Columns which precedes the Grand Staircase (1). Climb the staircase with its beautiful 18C wrought-iron balustrade to the landing where a great Gallo-Roman sarcophagus lies; it once served as the font in the abbey church of St Cornelius and is a relic of very early Compiègne. The first-floor Guard-room (1785) (2) leads into the antechamber or Ushers' Salon (3), which gave access to both the King's apartment (*left*) and the Queen's (*right*).

### Appartement du Roi et des Empereurs

The **King's and Emperors' apartment** houses exceptional groups of objects, works and memorabilia.

**Salle à manger de l'Empereur** (4) – The decor and furnishings in the dining room are First Empire (early 19C). Pilasters and doors, surmounted by *grisaille* paintings by Sauvage, stand out against the fake rose-pink onyx. One of Sauvage's paintings is an extraordinary trompe-l'œil representing Anacreon. It was here that on 1 May 1814 Louis XVIII entertained Czar Alexander, who was still hesitating about returning the Bourbons to the throne of France. During the Second Empire a private theatre was established here, with those close to the empress taking part in charades and revues.

**Salon des cartes** (5) – First designated as the Nobles' Antechamber under Louis XVI, then as the Senior Officers' Salon under Napoleon I, this room ended up as the Aide-de-Camp Salon or the Card Salon under Napoleon III. The furnishings comprise elements from the First Empire (chairs covered in Beauvais tapestry) and from the Second Empire. Note the games: quoits and a pin table.

**Salon de famille** (6) – This room was once Louis XVI's bedchamber (large mirrors hide the alcove). The **view**★ onto the park extends the length of the avenue to

*Emperor's bedchamber*

Ph. Gajic/ MICHELIN

the Beaux Monts.

The furnishings recall Empress Eugénie's taste for mixing styles: Louis XV armchairs, unusual little seats for two (*confidents*) or for three (*indiscrets*) etc.

**Cabinet du Conseil (7)** – Together with Versailles and Fontainebleau, Compiègne was one of the three châteaux where the king held counsel. Representatives of the Republics of Genoa and of the Kingdom of France signed two successive treaties here (1756 and 1764) which accorded France the right to garrison troops in the maritime citadels of Corsica. An immense tapestry illustrates the *Crossing of the Rhine by Louis XIV*.

**Chambre de l'Empereur (8)** – The Emperor's bedchamber has been restored to its appearance during the First Empire, with Jacob-Desmalter furnishings and friezes representing eagles.

**Bibliothèque (9)** – Formerly the King's Great Cabinet, this room was used as a library during the First Empire. The bookcase and the furnishings are by Jacob-Desmalter; the painted ceiling is the work of Girodet.

## Appartement de l'Impératrice

These rooms comprised the queen's principal apartments, the **Empress' Apartment**, the only ones in which Marie-Antoinette ever stayed. Later, they were particularly favoured by Empresses Marie-Louise and Eugénie.

**Salon du Déjeuner (10)** – The delight-ful breakfast room, with pale blue and yellow silk hangings, was prepared for Marie-Louise in 1809.

**Salon de musique (11)** – This was one of Empress Eugénie's favourite rooms; she furnished it herself. The Louis XVI pieces, from the apartment of Marie-Antoinette at St-Cloud, recall that the last sovereign consort of France kept the memory of the unfortunate queen alive.

**Chambre de l'Impératrice (12)** – The majestic tester bed is enclosed by white silk curtains and gold-embroidered muslin. Paintings by Girodet represent the seasons, and the Morning Star appears in the centre of the ceiling. The round boudoir leading to the bedchamber, also built for Marie-Louise, served as a dressing-room and for taking baths.

The last three of these interconnecting rooms form a decorative First Empire ensemble. Seats are arranged formally around a couch in the **Grand Salon (13)**; the **Salon des Fleurs (14)** owes its name to the eight panels painted with lily-like flowers, after Redoute; the **Salon Bleu (15)** strikingly contrasts blue walls and seats with a red marble fireplace and console tables. These rooms belonged to the imperial prince at the end of the Second Empire.

**Salle à manger de l'Impératrice (16)** – The walls of this modestly sized room are lined with stucco-marble, of a caramel colour more elegantly known as "antique yellow". It was here that the Archduchess Marie-Louise dined with the Emperor for the first time.

**Galerie des chasses de Louis XV** – The room is hung with Gobelins tapestries, which were woven as early as 1735 in accordance with sketches by Oudry. One represents a hunt along the River Oise and includes the silhouettes of Compiègne and the old Royallieu Abbey. The series continues in the **Galerie des Cerfs (17)**, formerly the Queen's Guard-room, then the Empress' Guard-room.

**Galerie du Bal** – The room (39×13m/128×43ft) was constructed within a few months for Marie-Louise's arrival, by gutting two floors of small apartments. The ceiling paintings glorify the Emperor's victories; the mythological scenes at the end of the room are by Girodet.

Throughout the Second Empire the gallery served as a dining room at the time of the "series", the sovereigns presiding from the centre of an immense table set up for the occasion.

**Galerie Natoire and Salle Coypel** – These were built by Napoleon III to lead to the **Grand Théâtre** (never finished). Their decoration illustrates *The Story of Don Quixote*, **tapestry drawings**★ by Natoire (1700-77).

**Chapel** – The First Empire chapel is surprisingly small for such a vast château, as the great chapel planned by Gabriel was never built. It was here on 9 August 1832 that the marriage took place between Princess Louise-Marie, eldest daughter of Louis-Philippe, and Leopold I, King of Belgium. Princess Marie of Orléans, the French king's second daughter, designed the stained-glass window.

**Appartement double de Prince** – Napoleon I had this apartment arranged to receive a foreign sovereign and his or her consort. This excellent group of Empire rooms comprises a dining room, four salons and a great bedchamber (original wallpaper, silk hangings and furniture).

**Appartement du roi de Rome** – The apartment has been restored to its appearance in 1811, when Napoleon I's son (five months old at the time) stayed in it for one month. All the original furnishings adorn the salon-boudoir, bathroom, boudoir, bedchamber and main drawing room. In the middle of the apartment a room (**18**) has been restored to appear as it did at the end of the 18C (Queen Marie-Antoinette's games room).

## Musée du Second Empire★★

The museum is located in a series of small, quiet drawing rooms and presents life at Court and in the outside world, and

the arts, during the Second Empire. Beyond the first room, displaying Daumier's humorous drawings, a space is devoted to the "beauties" of the period. Princess Mathilde (1820-1904), one of the reign's great figures, has pride of place here. She was for a brief time the fiancée of Louis-Napoleon, her close cousin. After her Spanish marriage she devoted herself entirely to her salon in rue de Courcelles, which was much frequented by the important writers and artists of the day, and to her château in St-Gratien.

The museum owns the famous painting *The Empress with her Ladies-in-Waiting* by Winterhalter (1855). Among the many sculptures by Carpeaux in the last rooms, note the bust of Napoleon, aged by the fall of the Empire, and the statue of the Imperial Prince with his dog.

**Musée de l'Impératrice** – This collection was bequeathed by Mr and Mme F Ferrand and includes memorabilia of official life and life in exile, as well as popular objects associated with Empress Eugénie. Among the more moving items are those evoking the Empress and her son, the Imperial Prince, who was massacred by the Zulus.

## Musée de la voiture et du tourisme★★

The museum was created in 1927 on the initiative of the Touring Club of France. None of the authentic royal carriages has been preserved in France. The collection of antique carriages features berlin coaches for travelling or ceremonial use in particular; these carriages were mounted on a base with two shafts, safer than a single shaft, to which the horses were harnessed.

**Grand Hall** – About 50 carriages are on

## The Motorcar's "first steps"

Vehicles of note include the Panhard No 2, the first car equipped with a four-stroke Daimler engine, the 1895 vis-à-vis by Bollée & Son which was one of the entrants in the race from Paris to Marseille-en-Beauvaisis (north of Beauvais), the De Dion-Bouton series, the large 1897 break belonging to the Duchess of Uzès, the first woman driver, the 1899 "Never-satisfied" on Michelin tyres, which was the first car to attain speeds of 100kph/62mph, and the 1900 4-CV Renault, the first saloon car. Steam, combustion and electric motors are also exhibited, showing the various ideas of the researchers and creators of the automobile industry.

display in what was formerly the kitchen courtyard, now covered over: the oldest, a travelling berlin coach, which belonged to the kings of Spain, dating from c 1740; the berlin coach used by the Pope in Bologna, and the one in which Bonaparte made his entrance to the town in 1796. Also on show are 18C and 19C travelling carriages, a mail-coach, charabancs, a Madeleine-Bastille omnibus and Orsay broughams.

De Dion's and Trépardoux's steam car and the 1924 Citroën from the Croisière Noire (the first trans-African car expedition) are among the finest exhibits.

**Kitchens and Outbuildings** – The evolution of the two-wheeler, starting with the heavy ancestors of the bicycle, hobbies (1817) which the rider set in motion by pushing off, can be seen in the former pantries. Pedals appeared with the 1863 Michaux velocipede. The penny-farthing, built out of iron tubing, had an unusually large front wheel to increase its speed. Developments such as the invention of the chain belt, which first appeared on the English tricycle, rendered wheels of disproportionate size unnecessary. The true bicycle became possible in about 1890. The army took advantage of the idea by developing a folding velocipede just before the First World War.

**First Floor** – These rooms are devoted to foreign vehicles and their accessories: Dutch and Italian cabriolets, a Sicilian cart, palanquin, sleighs, coachmen's clothes etc.

## The Gardens

*Main entrance gate is to the left, when facing away from town.* The gardens are known as the **Petit Parc** (the Grand Parc surrounds the gardens and is part of the forest). The Emperor's guiding idea was "to link the château as soon as possible to the forest, which is the true garden and the real beauty of this residence". The enclosing wall which blocked the view of the woods was taken down and replaced by iron railings. Beyond, the openness of avenue des Beaux-Monts creates a magnificent linear perspective (4km/6mi long), which was originally to have been closed with a monumental gateway to remind the

Emperor's young bride of Schönbrunn. Impatient to reach the forest without having to go through the town, Napoleon had a central ramp built for carriages between the terrace and the park; this was unfortunately at the expense of the glorious flight of steps by Gabriel. From then on the Petit Parc was replanted as a formal English garden and lost its importance. The present layout dates from the Second Empire.

## Additional Sights

### Hôtel de ville

This remarkable building was constructed under Louis XII in the late-Gothic style. It was restored during the 19C and the façade statues date from this period. They represent, from left to right around the central equestrian statue of Louis XII: St Denis, St Louis, Charles the Bald, Joan of Arc, Cardinal Pierre d'Ailly who was born in Compiègne, and Charlemagne.

The belfry consists of two floors and a slate-covered spire, flanked by four pinnacled turrets. At the base of the spire, three figures, called picantins and dressed as Swiss foot-soldiers from the period of François I, ring the hours and the quarter-hours.

### Musée de la Figurine historique★

*In the Hôtel de la Cloche, to the right of the Hôtel de Ville.* ♿ ⊙*Mar-Oct: daily, 9am-noon, 2-6pm, Sun and public holidays 2-6pm; Nov-Feb: daily, 9am-noon, 2-5pm, Sun and public holidays 2-5pm.* ⊙*Mon, 1 Jan, 1 May, 14 Jul, 1 Nov, 25 Dec.* ✆*2€ (under 18, no charge); no charge 1st Sun of the month.* ☎ *03 44 20 26 04.*

The museum houses over 100 000 model figures in tin, lead, wood, plastic, paper and cardboard; they are sculpted wholly or partly in the round, or are flat. A visit offers an interesting retrospective of the development of dress, along with an evocation of historical events connected with Compiègne (Joan of Arc, royal hunting parties, Napoleonic wars, the First World War).

### Église St-Jacques

The church features a 15C tower, the

highest in the town, at one of the corners of its west front. This was the parish church of the king and the court, hence funds provided for the chancel to be reworked in marble in the 18C and for the addition of carved-wood panels at the base of the nave's pillars. The harmony of the Gothic style at the time of St Louis is particularly evident in the chancel with its narrow, clerestory lit triforium and the 13C transept. An ambulatory was added in the 16C.

The 13C stone Virgin and Child in the north transept, known as "Our Lady of the Silver Feet" (*Notre-Dame aux pieds d'argent*), is the subject of much veneration.

A chapel in the north aisle houses three 15C painted wooden statues.

▸  *From place St-Jacques, cross rue Magenta to reach rue des Lombards.*

Lovely houses include a timber-framed one dating from the 15C: **Vieille Cassine**, where the masters of the bridge once lived.

### Musée Antoine-Vivenel

⊙*Open Mar-Oct: daily (except Mon) 9am-noon, 2-6pm, Sun 2-6pm; Nov-Feb: daily (except Mon) 9am-noon, 2-5pm, Sun 2-5pm.* ⊙*Closed 1 Jan, 1 May, 14 Jul, 1 Nov, 25 Dec.* ⊚*2€; no charge 1st Sun of month.* ☏ *03 44 20 26 04.*

Compiègne's municipal museum is located in the Hôtel de Songeons; it is a pleasant building dating from the early 19C, the garden of which is now a public park.

**Antiquity**: Greek and Roman marbles and bronzes; Antique ceramics including a remarkable group of **Greek vases**★★ discovered in Etruria and Southern Italy (*Magna Graecia*); successive civilizations, from prehistory to the end of the Gallo-Roman period, are evoked through the tools, weapons and various objects found at excavation sites; note the three bronze helmets dating from c 600 BC. The first-floor rooms have preserved their Directoire wainscoting. The painting collections are displayed here (large altarpiece representing the Passion by Wolgemut, Dürer's teacher), together with ceramics (pitchers in "Flemish stoneware," Italian majolicas), ivories, Limousin enamels).

# Excursions

### Longueil-Annel

*6km/3.7mi northeast along N 32.* This village lies on the banks of the River Oise and of the canal running alongside it. The Cité des Bateliers, which offers visitors a journey on the theme of inland waterways, includes a visit to a former boatmen's café turned into a small museum, a look at a barge hold, a stroll along the banks of the canal and a tour of the Janville lock.

## Forêt de Compiègne★★

The State forest of Compiègne (14 500ha/ 35 800 acres) is a remnant of the immense Cuise Forest which extended from the edge of the Île-de-France to the Ardennes. It embraces delightful beech groves, magnificent avenues, valleys, ponds and villages.

The forest occupies a sort of hollow with the valleys of the River Oise and River Aisne on two sides. A series of hills and promontories sketches a sharply defined crescent to the north, east and south. These peaks rise on average 80m/262ft above the sandy base of the hollow, which is grooved with numerous rivulets. The largest of these, the Ru de Berne, links a series of ponds.

The forest is criss-crossed by 1 500km/ 930mi of roads and footpaths. François I first cut great rides through the trees, with Louis XIV and Louis XV later contri-

*Hôtel de Ville*

A. de Valroger/ MICHELIN

buting to extend this network in order to create an ideal place for hunting. The grounds, once the lands of Frankish kings, are today used by three different hunts.

**Types of Trees** – The most common species in the forest are beech (40%), oak (30%) and yoke-elm (15%). Beech in particular occupies the southern plateau and its slopes, and the area immediately surrounding the town. Oak, which was planted long ago, thrives in the better-drained clay soil, as well as on the Beaux Monts. Since 1830 Norway pine and other conifers have grown in the poor, sandy soil where oaks would find it difficult to thrive.

▶ *A paved cycle path runs between Compiègne (east from carrefour Royal along route Tournante) and Pierrefonds.*

**Fishing regulations** – A board in front of the forest warden's house at Étangs de St-Pierre lists the clubs and organisations that issue permits and licences.

## Driving Tours

### 1 Les Beaux Monts★★

*18km/11mi – about 1hr*

▶ *Leave Compiègne by avenue Royale. At carrefour Royal, turn left onto route Tournante; the road crosses the long perspective of avenue des Beaux-Monts in two bends. At carrefour du Renard turn right onto route Eugénie.*

### Carrefour d'Eugénie

Some of the forest's oldest **oak trees**★ stand around this junction. The most ancient ones date from the time of François I.

▶ *Take the winding road on the left which climbs to Les Beaux Monts.*

### Les Beaux Monts★★

Stop at the summit, near the Beaux Monts viewpoint (*point de vue*); from here the **view**★ stretches along the straight line of the avenue through the

forest all the way to the palace, barely visible 4km/ 2.5mi away.

▶ *Continue to the junction and turn right (viewpoint).*

### Point de vue du Précipice (Precipice Viewpoint)

Here the extensive **view**★ overlooks the woody stretches of the valley of the River Berne and Mont St-Marc.

▶ *Return to the junction and take the road on the right down from Les Beaux Monts.*

The road runs through a magnificent grove of oak and beech to a junction.

▶ *Turn right, cross route Eugénie and take the first road on the right.*

### Chapelle St-Corneille-aux-Bois

The secluded chapel was founded in 1164; it later passed to the abbey of St-Corneille in Compiègne. François I added a hunting lodge but its appearance today dates only from the time of Viollet-le-Duc (19C); the Gothic construction of the 13C chapel, however, has remained intact. The wardens of Compiègne Forest came here before the French Revolution to hear Sunday mass.

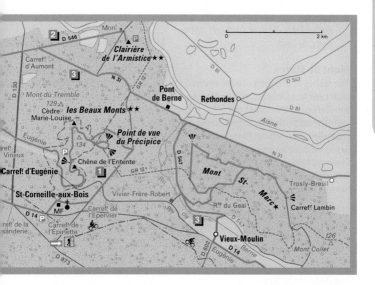

▶ *Continue to D 14; turn right to return to Compiègne (Vieux-Moulin-Compiègne).*

## 2 Clairière de l'Armistice★★

*6km/3.5mi northeast*

▶ *Leave Compiègne by N 31. Go straight across carrefour d'Aumont and carry straight on (D 546) to carrefour du Francport and the car park.*

A site where a network of tracks existed for heavy artillery installations was cleared to make room for the private train of the allied forces' commander-in-chief, Field-Marshal Foch, and for that of the German plenipotentiaries. The tracks were linked to the Compiègne-Soissons line at Rethondes station. Today, rails and flagstones, marking the site of the railway carriages, surround a memorial commemorating the date.

### Wagon du maréchal Foch

🕐*Apr-mid-Oct: daily (except Tue), 9am-12.15pm, 2-6pm; mid-Oct to end Mar: daily (except Tue), 9am-noon, 2-5.30pm.* ⊜*4€ (7-13, 2€).* ☎ *03 44 85 14 18. www.armistice.chez.tiscali.fr.*

The original, historic dining-car, which was converted into an office for Field Marshal Foch, was exhibited in the courtyard of the Invalides in Paris from 1921 to 1927 then returned to the forest clearing and placed in a shelter built for the purpose. Transported to Berlin as a trophy in 1940, it was destroyed in the Thuringia Forest in April 1945. In 1950 it was replaced by another carriage from a similar series. The places occupied by the delegates are indicated and the actual objects they used in 1918, put aside safely at the time, are now back inside the carriage.

The shelter also houses a large room devoted to the two armistices (11 November 1918 and 22 June 1940); the display includes contemporary newspapers, original documents, photographs, dummies in military uniform and remains of the original carriage.

## 3 Le Mont St-Marc★

*26km/16mi – about 1hr 30min*

▶ *Leave Compiègne by N 31.*

### Pont de Berne

It was here that the Dauphin, the future Louis XVI, met Marie-Antoinette for the first time; the future queen had just arrived from Vienna.

▶ *Turn right toward Pierrefonds. At Vivier-Frère-Robert turn left onto route du Geai.*

## Mont St-Marc★

The slopes of this long rise are covered with beeches. On reaching the plateau, turn left onto the forest road that follows the edge; there are good views of the valleys of the River Berne and River Aisne, Rethondes and Laigue Forest.

The road follows the northern promontory of the hill. Some 2.5km/1.5mi farther along, Carrefour Lambin offers a particularly fine view of the Aisne Valley.

▶ *Return by the same road and fork left onto the first road suitable for vehicles. Drive down Route du Geai and continue toward Pierrefonds. Turn right and continue along the main street in Vieux-Moulin.*

## Vieux-Moulin

This former woodcutters' village later became a wealthy community of holiday homes. The little church was rebuilt in 1860 at Napoleon III's expense.

## Address Book

⏧*For coin ranges, see the Legend on the cover flap.*

### WHERE TO STAY

◯ **Auberge de la Vieille Ferme** – *60880 Meux. ☎ 03 44 41 58 54. Closed 28 Jul to 19 Aug, 22 Dec to 7 Jan and Sun evening* – 🄿 *– 14 rms – ⊑ 9.50€ – restaurant* ◯◯. This old farmhouse built of Oise Valley brick offers rooms that are simple but well-kept and practical. The restaurant sports exposed beams, rustic furniture, a tile floor and gleaming copperware. The menu offers traditional and regional cuisine.

◯◯ **Hôtel Les Beaux Arts** – *33 cours Guynemer. ☎ 03 44 92 26 26 – www. lesbeauxarts.com – 35 rms – ⊑ 10€.* Located along the Oise water-front, here's a contemporary hotel whose modern, well-soundproofed rooms have been furnished in teak or laminated wood. Some are larger and have a kitchenette.

### WHERE TO EAT

◯◯ **Le Bistrot des Arts** – *35 cours Guynemer. ☎ 03 44 20 10 10. Closed Sat lunch and Sun.* Located on the ground floor of the Hôtel des Beaux-Arts, an appealing, authentic bistro decorated with various objects and etchings. In the kitchen, the chef concocts appetizing dishes using market-fresh produce.

◯◯ **Auberge du Buissonnet** – *825 r. Vineux, 60750 Choisy-au-Bac – 5km/3mi NE of Compiègne via N 31 and D 66. ☎ 03 44 40 17 41. Closed Sun evening, Tue evening and Mon.* Ask for a table near the bay windows of the dining room or on the terrace, weather permitting, and watch ducks and swans glide peacefully over the pond, then shake themselves off and waddle proudly toward the garden.

◯◯ **Le Palais Gourmand** – *8 r. Dahomey – ☎ 03 44 40 13 13. Closed 1 to 7 Mar, 2 23 Aug, 24-28 Dec, Sun evening and Mon.* This spruce timbered house (1890) has a string of rooms and an attractive verandah where heaters, Moorish pictures and mosaics create an agreeable atmosphere. Traditional cuisine.

◯◯ **Le Nord** – *Pl de la Gare. ☎ 03 44 83 22 30. Closed 25 Jul – 17 Aug, Sat lunch and Sun evening.* This has become quite an institution locally for its seafood dishes. The dining room is modern and bright.

### SHOPPING

**Les Halles du Grenier à Sel** – *place du Change. ☎ 03 44 23 19 55. Tue-Sat, 8am-12.30pm, 3-7pm.* What better way to get close to the French way of doing things than to wander around a provincial market. This mini-market is at the centre of town, close to the beautiful church of St-Jacques (*open Sat 8am-7pm*).

### ON THE TOWN

**Sweet Home Pub** – *49 r. St-Corneille. ☎ 03 44 86 51 00 – Mon 6pm-1am, Tue-Sat 11.30am-1am.* This is, without a doubt, the most enjoyable pub in town. Beyond the handsome wood facade, the owners hold highly entertaining evenings that feature folk and rock concerts, theatre, or literary readings.

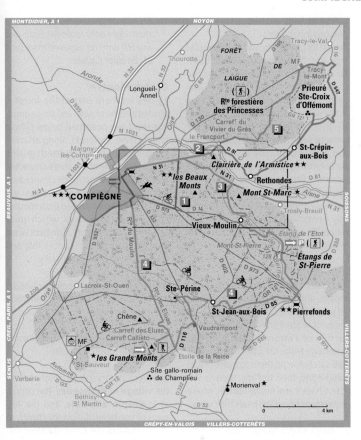

> ▶ *Turn left at the junction with the war memorial and take route Eugénie (on the south bank) to Étang de l'Étot.*

## Étangs de St-Pierre

These ponds were created to stock fish; they were dug by members of the Celestine community from the priory of Mont-St-Pierre, to the west.

Empress Eugénie's former chalet is now a forest warden's house with exhibitions on the forest.

> ▶ *About 1km/0.5mi beyond the last pond, at a fork near the edge of the forest, take the small road left that climbs up to the hilltop districts of Pierrefonds.*

## ④ **Les Grands Monts★**

*27km/17mi – about 1hr 30min*

## Château de Pierrefonds★★

⚐ *See PIERREFONDS*

> ▶ *Leave Pierrefonds by D 85, heading west.*

The road first rises to a wooded plateau, where the beautiful beech groves were largely destroyed during storms in 1984; it then descends into St-Jean-aux-Bois.

## St-Jean-aux-Bois

This charming village was appropriately renamed "Solitude" in 1794. The 12C monastic buildings which were at the heart of the village can be seen along one side of it, marked by a moat filled with water. The Benedictine nuns left their abbey for Royallieu (on the outskirts of Compiègne) in 1634 as the forest was no longer safe; for a while Augustine canons took their place but in 1761 St-Jean was abandoned by its religious inhabitants.

The old fortified gate leads to the esplanade and the last vestiges of the abbey: the church, the chapter-house and the doorway to the "Small Courtyard" (formerly farm buildings). The architectural purity of the 13C **church**★ is remarkable. Inside, the sober harmony of the transept and chancel create an impression of grandeur. The slenderness of the columns separating each transept arm into two bays emphasises the church's height. The arrangement here, that was common later in the 16C, is the only example in the region from that period. The grisailles recall the luminous atmosphere of the nave in the 13C.

### Ste-Périne

The pond surrounded by plane trees and poplars, and the woodland house in an old priory form an attractive sight.

The nuns of Ste-Périne (a linguistic contraction of Pétronille) occupied this hermitage from 1285 to 1626. Fear for their safety forced them to move first to Compiègne, then to Paris, then La Villette, Chaillot and finally Auteuil, where a retirement home still bears their name.

▶ *Turn round; turn right onto the main road to Crépy-en-Valois and at Vaudrampont turn right onto D 116.*

*At Étoile de la Reine roundabout turn sharp right onto route des Éluas and first left onto an unpaved road; park at carrefour Callisto.*

### Grands Monts★

🚶 This southern part of the forest is divided into the plateau and the swamps. The short trip described below (*30min on foot there and back*), along an overhanging path shaded by beech groves, introduces some of the area's characteristics. Walk down route des Princesses; immediately after the barrier turn left onto the well-maintained path marked with yellow indicators which goes around the promontory. Turn back when the path becomes less accessible and reaches the bottom of the gully.

▶ *Turn round; continue along route des Éluas, which runs downhill and round a hairpin bend.*

▶ *Return to Compiègne by following the long route du Moulin.*

Another itinerary (no. 5) might take in the **village of Rethondes**, the church at **St-Crépin-aux-Bois**, and the 16C ruins of the beautiful priory church of the old **Prieuré Ste-Croix-d'Offémont**. The route des Princesses is a popular starting point for rambles.

# CORBIE

POPULATION 6 317
MICHELIN LOCAL MAP 301: I-8

Corbie is a small town situated between the River Somme and the River Ancre. It developed around a Benedictine abbey, where powerful abbots held the title of Count and were allowed to mint coinage.

🛈 **Information:** Pl. de la République, 80800 Corbie, ☎ 03 22 96 95 76. www.bocage3vallees.com.

## A Bit of History

**A Cradle for Saints** – The monastery was founded in 657 by **Ste Bathild**, wife of the Frankish king Clovis II, and in Carolingian times became a centre of Christian civilization under the direc-

tion of **St Adalard**, Charlemagne's cousin. More than 300 monks took part day and night in the constant worship of the Lord; St Paschase Radbert wrote the first theological treatise on the Eucharist; apostolic activity developed. The abbey spread to Corvey in West-

*Somme Valley, Corbie*

phalia, which was to become the main centre of evangelism in northern Europe under the impetus of **St Anschaire** (or Oscar), who was born in Corbie in 801.

In the 11C **St Gerard**, a monk from Corbie, retreated to the area between the Garonne and the Dordogne, founding the monastery known as La Sauve Majeure. **Ste Colette** (1381-1447), the daughter of a local carpenter, lived as a recluse and was favoured with numerous visions. She came out of seclusion to establish several convents of Poor Clares.

# Sights

### Museum

⊙*Daily (except Sun and Tue), mid-Jun to mid-Sep: 2.30-5.30pm.* ⊶*Possibility of guided tours by arrangement with the tourist office.* ☎*03 22 96 43 37. www. perso.orange.fr/musee.corbie.*

This is essentially devoted to the history of the abbey and contains Carolingian pottery, 16C coins, copies of manuscripts from the former library and a relief map of the siege of Corbie in 1636.

From the vast place de la République go through the 18C **monumental gateway** to the abbey; the cloisters and convent buildings were razed during the Revolution.

### Abbatiale St-Pierre

⊶*Guided tours by appointment at the tourist office: 10am-noon, 2.30-6pm (Jul and Aug, 2.30-6pm).* ⊛*(guided tour) 2.50€ (unaccompanied, 0.50€).* ☎*03 22 96 95 76.*

The construction of the former abbey church lasted from the 16C to the 18C but in 1815 the transept and chancel were knocked down, since they were by then in a state of collapse.

The stylistic unity of the remaining buildings is due to the architects' continued use of the Gothic style throughout the Renaissance and Classical periods: this accounts for the ribbed vaults in the three aisles, the rose-window, the twin towers pierced by twin bays, and the west front featuring three doorways with broken arches, all following the style of Gothic cathedrals. Part of the decoration borrows from the Classical repertory, notably the cartouches on the porch coving.

The **interior** is now only about 36m/118ft long, as opposed to 117m/384ft originally (see the model of the church

---

### WHERE TO EAT

⊜⊜ **L'Abbatiale** – Pl. Jean-Catelas – ☎03 22 48 40 48. Closed Sun. This down-to-earth family establishment facing the St-Pierre church welcomes guests with benevolence and simplicity. Two menus await diners: a brasserie-type formula and the traditional restaurant fare; a few rooms are available. Very affordable prices.

---

## Mysterious Blue Springs

In the Corbie area, in particular in Daours, Pont-Noyelles and Fréchencourt, there are mysterious fresh-water springs where water gushing out of the ground has hollowed out craters from which a strange blue light appears to emanate. The phenomenon has given rise to supernatural legends, but it is most likely related to specific characteristics of the surface of the water in such pools, which seems to reflect the wavelength of blue light.

before the Revolution). The Treasury at one time contained 113 reliquaries which were often venerated by the French kings and some of which have been preserved. The works of art include:

- the 15C statue of Our Lady of the Door (*south aisle, last pillar*);
- Ste Bathild, an example of majestic 14C statuary (*end of south aisle, right of altar*);
- a head of St Peter (13C) (*a pillar in the north aisle*);
- the 15C tomb of Abbot Raoul de Roye, the tutor of Ste Colette (*north aisle*).

### Chapelle Ste-Colette

The chapel was built in 1959 on the site of the house in which Ste Colette was born and contains a 16C statue of the saint kneeling.

## Excursions

### Église de La Neuville

*2km/1mi west, on the right bank of the River Ancre.*

Above the doorway of the early-16C church is a large, interesting **high-relief carving**★ showing Christ's entry into Jerusalem on Palm Sunday. The relief is remarkable for its clarity and wealth of detail: spectators perched in the trees, in the background a miller wearing a cotton bonnet at the window of his mill.

### Australian Memorial

*3km/2mi south. Leave Corbie by D 1 (towards Amiens) and in Fouilloy turn left onto D 23 toward Villers-Bretonneux.*

In spring 1918 the hills around **Villers-Bretonneux** were fiercely fought over by the Germans and the Australians, following the German offensive on Picardy; more than 10 000 Australian men lost their lives. A memorial and a cemetery recall their sacrifice. Extended **view** towards the River Somme and Amiens.

# LA CÔTE D'OPALE ★
**MICHELIN LOCAL MAP 301: C-2 TO D-3**

The Opal Coast extends from Baie de Somme to the Belgian borde. Its name derives from the opalescent colour of the waves washing against the coast. A local painter, Édouard Lévêque, first used the name in 1911, but the landscapes had long been an inspiration for painters and writers such as Corot and Victor Hugo. The most spectacular part of the coastline lies between Boulogne and Calais, where the cliffs skirt the Boulonnais hills. Between the sea and the sky, there is only the Opal Coast bluff, characterized by promontories separating the small, dry valleys (**crans**). A strong north-south current wears away the base of the cliffs, sometimes causing large parts to collapse. Research has shown that the cliff is eroding by about 25m/27yd every 100 years. The Côte d'Opale forms the western part of the **Parc naturel régional des Caps et Marais d'Opale.**

- **Information:** Office du tourisme de la Terre des Deux Caps, pl. de la Mairie, 62179 Wissant ☎ 03 21 82 48 00.
- **Orient Yourself:** The Opal coast borders the English Channel and the North Sea from Mers-les-Bains to Bray-Dune. Use the D 940 to explore.
- **Don't Miss:** Enjoy *moules et frites* and other seafood at Mers-les-Bains; they don't come any better than by the sea.
- **Especially for kids:** Make the most of the beach as Wissant.
- **Also See:** Marquenterre nature reserve. Cap Blanc Nez and Cap Gris Nez.

## Driving Tour
*9km/30mi – about 2hr 30min*

### Boulogne-sur-Mer ★
*See BOULOGNE-SUR-MER.*
*Leave Boulogne by D 940.*
D 940 is a winding coastal road that offers glimpses of the sea, the ports and the beaches, leading across hill crests which are intermittently bare or covered with closely cropped meadows.
To the north the road comes to the Escalles cran, resembling a mountain pass but at an altitude of less than 100m/328ft. Car parks flank the road, allowing access to the sea or to walks among the dunes.

### Swimming Beaches
*On a beach with lifeguards in attendance, pay attention to the colour of the flag flying near the lifeguard station:*

- **Green** – *Lifeguards in attendance. Swimming authorised and not considered dangerous.*
- **Orange** – *Lifeguards in attendance. Swimming considered dangerous.*
- **Red** – *Swimming prohibited.*

### Wimereux ☆☆
The opening to the Wimereux Valley (*see Le BOULONNAIS*) is the site of a large and popular seaside resort for families, awarded the "Station Kid" label on account of the activities offered to children. A walk on the promenade built along the sand and pebble beach affords views of the Straits of Dover, the Grande Armée Column and Boulogne. The promenade narrows to a path leading to **Pointe aux Oies**, where on 6 August 1840 the future Napoleon III landed prior to his attempt to win over the garrison stationed at Boulogne.

- *Between Wimereux and Ambleteuse, the road runs beside tall dunes.*

### Ambleteuse
This picturesque village stands above the mouth of the River Slack, where boats can beach. Ambleteuse was formerly a naval base protected by **Fort d'Ambleteuse** (*open Jul-Aug, Sat, Sun 3-7pm; mid-Apr to end Jun and Sep-Oct, Sun 3-7pm (last admission 1hr before closing). ☜3€. ☎ 03 20 54 61 54),* built by Vauban between 1685 and 1690. Napoleon based part of his flotilla here

## Address Book

*⏚For coin ranges, see the Legend on the cover flap.*

### WHERE TO STAY

⊜ **La Grand' Maison Bed and Breakfast** – *Hameau de la Haute-Escal-les, 62179 Escalles – 2km/1.2mi E of Cap-Blanc-Nez via D 243.* ☎ *03 21 85 27 75 – ⊟ – 6 rms.* Here's an appealing 18C flower-filled farm located between the two headlands and facing the British Isles. Fans of hiking, horse riding or windsurfing will heartily appreciate this site between land and sea. The prestige guest rooms, equipped with TVs, are more comfortable. Three self-catering cottages.

⊜⊜ **La Goélette** – *13 digue de Mer, 62930 Wimereux.* ☎ *03 21 32 62 44. 4 rms.* Who could resist this charming villa from the early 1900s, ideally situated on the promenade? The rooms, all renovated, have recovered their original panache (mouldings, maritime pine furnishings). The blue and yellow rooms offer captivating views of the sea.

### WHERE TO EAT

⊜⊜ **La Sirène** – *62179 Audinghen.* ☎ *03 21 32 95 97. Closed 15 Dec to 25 Jan, evenings except Sat from Sep to Easter, Sun evening and Mon.* Situated on the Cap Gris-Nez beach, this restaurant commands a great view of the sea.

Choose a table in one of the two large dining rooms with large bay windows for a meal of grilled lobster (the house speciality) or other seafood dishes.

⊜⊜ **Liégeoise et Atlantic Hôtel** – *digue de Mer, 62930 Wimereux.* ☎ *03 21 32 41 01. Closed Feb, Sun evening and Mon lunch .* For a satisfying seafood meal, choose between the roomy bar on the seafront promenade or the panoramic dining room upstairs. If you plan to stay over, be sure to obtain a room with a view of the ocean.

### LEISURE ACTIVITIES

**Eden 62** – *62930 Wimereux* – ☎ *03 21 32 13 74. Jul to end Aug* ⌁ Guided tours of several natural areas along the Opal Coast: Platier d'Oye, Cap Gris-Nez, Cap Blanc-Nez, estuary and dunes of the Slack, Canche Bay and the Authie dunes.

**Char à Voile Club Wissantais** – *Sea front, 62179 Wissant.* ☎ *03 21 85 86 78.* Sand yachting.

**Station Kid** – *62930 Wimereux.* Located on the Nord de Wimereux dike, the children's beach has a well-equipped play area. The Iodie Beach Club welcomes 3- to 12-year-olds. Dig'enfants offers other activities (workshops, shows): ☎ 03 21 33 90 41.

**Wishbone Center** – *Résidence Bas-Moulin, 62179 Wissant.* ☎ *03 21 85 40 55.* Windsurf and speedsail.

at the time of the Boulogne Camp (⏚ *see BOULOGNE-SUR-MER*). Today it is a beach from which Boulogne's harbour entrance and the white cliffs of the English coast are visible.

The **Musée Historique de la Seconde Guerre Mondiale** (⏚ ⏱ *open Jul-Aug, 9.30am-7pm, Sat, Sun and public holidays, 10am-7pm; Apr-Jun and Sep-mid-Oct, 9.30am-6pm, Sat, Sun and public holidays, 10am-6pm; mid-Oct-Mar, Sat, Sun and public holidays, 10am-6pm. ⊜6€.* ☎ *03 21 87 33 01. www.musee3945.com)* on the outskirts of Ambleteuse retraces the full story of the Second World War, from the conquest of Poland in 1939 to the Liberation. About 100 different uniforms are exhibited, together with equipment worn or used by the armies involved in the war.

▶ *3km/2mi after Audresselles, turn left onto D 191.*

### Cap Gris-Nez★★

This "grey-nose cape" looks out to the English coast less than 30km/19mi away. The gently sloping cliffs rise to 45m/148ft. The lighthouse (28m/92ft tall) with beams visible 45km/28mi away, was rebuilt after the war. It stands at the tip of a bare, windswept peninsula dotted with the remains of ruined German pillboxes. The Gris-Nez branch of CROSS (Centre Régional d'Opération de Secours et de Sauvetage) is located underground; the organisation is responsible for watching over these waters, where maritime traffic is the heaviest in the world, and provides aid of any kind when needed. The crumbling debris

## Flobart from Wissant

These fishing boats, whose origin goes back to the 17C, were used all along the Opal Coast for fishing herring, mackerel, cod and sole. Built of wood in the shape of half a walnut shell, they measured 5m/16ft in length and 2m/6.5ft in width and could land on a beach or any other place where there was no harbour. In addition, owing to their flat bottom and reduced draught, they hardly felt the impact of the waves. In the 1950s, engines replaced the traditional sails and the boats were launched with the help of tractors. Most of them have now been replaced by more efficient vessels; however, a few flobarts are still used as pleasure sailing boats. A flobart festival takes place every year during the last weekend in August.

from the cliffs mingles with the rocky reef known as "the Whales" (*Les Épaulards*) because, seen from a distance, it looks humpbacked and throws up spray. Straight ahead, the **view**★ extends to the English cliffs which appear white next to the blue of the sky. On the French side, the folds of the coastline, including the dry valleys between the cliffs, are visible. Cap Blanc-Nez (*right*) and Boulogne (*left*) may also be seen. The **Musée du Mur de l'Atlantique** (◯open Jun-Sep, 9am-7pm; mid-Feb-May and Oct-mid-Dec 9am-noon, 2-5pm. ◠5.50€. ☎ 03 21 32 97 33) is in the Todt battery, a Second World War pillbox which served as a German missile launching base; missiles 2m/6ft long were fired on England from here. There are collections of arms and uniforms inside the museum. Note, in particular, the naval gun on rails (280 bore, made by Krupp in 1943), which is 35m/115ft long, could fire 15 times per hour and had a range of 62-86km/38.5-53.4mi.

### Wissant ☖

Kids This splendid beach of fine, firm sand is well sheltered from the eastern winds and currents. It forms a vast curve between Cap Gris-Nez and Cap Blanc-Nez. Villas stand among the dunes overlooking the shore. The activities offered to children have earned the resort the "Station Kid" label.

The **Musée du Moulin** (◯open 2-6pm; ◠2.50 €; ☎ 03 21 35 91 87) is housed in a flour mill driven by hydraulic power. It is well preserved and features pine-wood parts, cast-iron waterwheels and a conveyor belt to lift the goods.

### Cap Blanc-Nez★★

The "white-nose cape" is a vertical mass of chalk cliffs rising 134m/440ft above the waves, offering extensive **views**★ of the English cliffs and the French coast from Calais to Cap Gris-Nez.

▶ *Retrace your steps to Mont d'Hubert.*

Cap Gris-Nez

Y. Tierny / MICHELIN

The **Musée National du Transmanche** (☉*open mid-Apr to mid-Dec, daily (except Mon), 2-6pm (last admission 45m before closing)* ⊜*3.80€.* ☎ *03 21 85 57 42)* located on Mont d'Hubert, faces Cap Blanc-Nez; it retraces the turbulent history of the strait, which scientists and scholars have always used to promote their ideas. The story began in 1751 with Nicolas Desmarets, who was the first person to think of linking France to England. Later, Aimé Thomé de Gamond suggested a variety of options: a tunnel constructed of metal tubes, a concrete undersea vault, a pontoon, an artificial isthmus, a mobile bridge and a viaduct-bridge. He even dived to the bottom of the strait several times to collect numerous geological samples. Channel crossings were eventually achieved by balloon (Blanchard), plane (Blériot), steamboat (the first regular line was established in 1816), raft, on skis, etc.

Lower down the hill, near D 940, stands the monument to **Latham** (1883-1912), the pilot who attempted, unsuccessfully, to cross the Channel at the same time as Blériot.

Between **Sangatte** and Blériot-Plage, the chalets are built directly on the sea-washed dunes. It is here that the Channel Tunnel emerges.

### Blériot-Plage

The beautiful beach extends along to Cap Blanc-Nez. At Baraques (*500m/550yd west of the resort*), near D 940, a monument commemorates the first aerial crossing of the Channel, by **Louis Blériot** (1872-1936). On 25 July 1909 he landed his aeroplane in a valley on the Dover cliffs, after a flight of approximately half an hour.

### Calais

♿ *see CALAIS.*

# COUCY-LE-CHÂTEAU-AUFFRIQUE★

POPULATION 995
MICHELIN LOCAL MAP 306: B-5

Coucy extends along a promontory overlooking the Ailette Valley on an impressive defensive **site**★, further sheltered by its medieval walls, which used to incorporate 28 towers. Unfortunately, during the First World War the town suffered greatly from being in the front line of battle, and in 1917 the Germans blew up the castle keep.

- **Information:** Office du tourisme de Coucy-le-Château, 8 r. des Vivants, 02380 ☎ 03 23 52 44 55. www.coucy.com.
- ▶ **Orient Yourself:** 12 miles north of Soissons, and reached by the D 1, D 934 or the D 13.
- **Don't Miss:** The view of the port of Soissons.
- **Organizing Your Time:** you will need two hours to explore the ramparts, and another hour for the museum.
- **Also See:** The forest of Saint Gobain, and Soissons.

## A Bit of History

**The Lord of Coucy** – "I am not a king, nor a prince, a duke or a count either. I am the Lord (Sire) of Coucy," was the proud boast of Enguerrand III (1192-1242), the castle's owner who, after fighting loyally and valiantly at Bouvines, sought to take possession of the French throne during Blanche of Castille's regency.

A "*son et lumière*" show is staged in July.

# Sights

## Château

⊙Open daily May-Aug 10am-1pm, 2-6.30pm, Sat-Sun 10am-12.30pm, 2-7pm (last admission 30min before closing). Sep-Apr 10am-1pm, 2-5.30pm. ⊙Closed 1 Jan, 1 May, 1 and 11 Nov, 25 Dec. ⊜5€ (no charge, first Sun of month, Oct-Apr) ☎ 03 23 52 71 28.

Visitors enter a bailey before the castle proper. To the right of the bailey entrance the Guard-room (Salle des Gardes) contains a model and documents relating to Coucy. The foundations of a Romanesque chapel are visible on the approach to the castle, which stands as an irregular quadrilateral at the end of the promontory. The great round towers built with hoardings that used to surround the castle were over 30m/98ft high and the keep destroyed by the Germans in 1917 reached a height of 54m/177ft.

The dwellings were rebuilt by Enguerrand VII at the end of the 14C, then finished at the end of the 15C by Louis of Orléans, Charles VI's brother, who had bought Coucy from Enguerrand VII's daughter. Remains of two large chambers (Salle des Preuses and Salle des Preux) still exist, with a cellar underneath. From the west tower there is a good view over the valleys of the River Ailette and River Oise.

## Porte de Soissons

This gate, which was built in the 13C, is reinforced by the Coucy tower and now houses the **Musée historique** (⊙open Jun-Sep, 10am-7pm; Mar-May and Oct,

### WHERE TO EAT

⊜ **Le Belle Vue** – Ville haute, 02380 Coucy-le-Château. ☎ 03 23 52 69 70 – hotel.restaurant.belle.vue@wanadoo.fr. Closed 1 wk at Christmas – ℗ – 7 rms – ☐ 5 € – restaurant ⊜. This simple hotel is well situated in the upper town. Ask for a room on the second floor and enjoy an unbeatable view of the château and the plain beyond. The rather old-fashioned dining room serves traditional fare.

2-6pm; Nov-Feb, pre-booked visits only. ⊙closed 1 Jan and 25 Dec. ☎ 03 23 52 44 55 or 03 23 52 22 22). A model of the town and the castle are among the exhibits, together with engravings and old photographs, and figures dressed in period costume. From the platform there is a good view over the Ailette Valley.

## Porte de Laon

This entrance dates from the 13C and played a major defensive role at the base of the promontory; it is the only entrance with easy access and is therefore guarded by two huge round towers, with walls 8m/26ft thick at their base.

## Domaine de la Grangère

This garden belonged to the Governor's House where in 1594 César, Duke of Vendôme, was born, the bastard son of Henri IV and Gabrielle d'Estrées, Duchesse de Beaufort. The lip of the well is made from a keystone from the castle keep.

| | |
|---|---|
| Château R. du | 2 |
| Gouverneur R. du | 3 |
| Hôtel-de-Ville Pl. de | 4 |
| Laon R. de | 5 |
| Longue-Paume R. de la | 6 |
| Marché Pl. du | 7 |
| Pot-d'Étain R. du | 8 |
| Traversière R. | 9 |
| Truande R. | 10 |
| Vivants R. des | 12 |

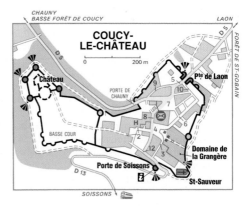

## Driving Tour

▶ *Leave Coucy by Porte de Chauny; at the junction at the foot of the promontory, take D 934 toward Noyon, through Montoir.*

### Bois du Montoir

A 380mm mortar was concealed in this stretch of woodland. On several occasions in 1915, it fired on Compiègne which is 40km/25mi away, causing enormous shell holes.

### Folembray

The kennels of the Rallye-Nomade Hunt are located here. The hounds are used for deer hunting. François I enjoyed staying in the château with his mistress Françoise de Châteaubriand.

# CRÉCY-EN-PONTHIEU

POPULATION 1 611
MICHELIN LOCAL MAP 301: E-6

The name of Crécy conjures up images of the Hundred Years War, particularly the defeat of King Philippe VI of France at the hands of Edward III of England on 26 August 1346. Today Crécy is a peaceful little town facing the plateau on which Crécy Forest stands.

- **Information:** Office du tourisme de Crécy-en-Ponthieu, 32 r. Mar. Leclerc-de-Hauteclocque, 80150. ☎ 03 22 23 93 84. www.crecyenponthieu.com.
- ▶ **Orient Yourself:** On the edge of a farmed basin at the source of the River Maye, the town is accessed from Abbeville by the D 928 and the D 12.
- **Parking:** Limited town centre parking; grab the first place you find and walk in.
- **Don't Miss:** A tour in the nearby forest of Crécy.
- **Organizing Your Time:** Include Crécy in a tour of the Somme valley; stop off here for lunch.
- **Also See:** The Bay of the Somme viewed from St Valery-sur-Somme; the Gardens of Valloire; Saint Riquier.

## A Bit of History

### The Battle of Crécy

Crécy was the site of the bitter defeat inflicted on Philippe VI of France by Edward III of England at the beginning of the Hundred Years War. **Edward III** had landed in Normandy with 3 900 knights, 11 000 longbow men and 5 000 armed Welshmen; they rampaged through Normandy as far as Poissy and took up a defensive position at Crécy. Philip VI advanced with 1 200 knights, 6 000 Genoese archers and 20 000 men-at-arms. An attack was then launched by the French cavalry, in a spirited but ill-planned move. The assault disintegrated under the hail from the English archers, reinforced for the first time in European history by bombardments; in the resulting carnage, 11 princes, 1 542 knights and 10 000 soldiers fell on the battlefield.

## Sights

### "Croix du Bourg"

The cross erected in the lower part of the town around the 12C remains a mystery. The top part is certainly post 1600.

### Moulin Edouard III

*1km/0.5mi north on D 111.*
Beside the road (*right*) stands a hillock on the site of the windmill from where the King of England directed the battle. From the top there is a good view over the undulating plain (*viewing table*).

### "Croix de Bohême"

*On D 56 southeast of Crécy.*
Philip's ally John the Blind, the old king of Bohemia, was killed while being carried to his badly wounded son at the heart of the battle; the spot where he

## The Valois Dynasty

In 1328, the death of Charles IV, last son of Philip IV the Fair, marked the extinction of the direct line of Capetians. The House of Valois followed, through Philip VI of Valois, first cousin of Charles IV, who was chosen by the nobility and the clergy in preference to Edward III of England, Philip the Fair's own grandson through his mother. Edward decided not to accept his eviction and in 1340 he landed in Normandy, thus starting the Hundred Years War. The House of Valois prospered nevertheless and in turn founded the dynasty of the dukes of Burgundy. The grandson of Philip VI, Charles V, was a wise monarch who strengthened the State and recovered the major part of the territories lost to the English thanks to his constable, Du Guesclin. The last representatives of this dynasty which lasted until 1589, Charles VIII, François I, Henri II and III, contributed to the development of Italian, therefore Renaissance, art in France, while giving kingship a new, authoritarian stamp.

fell is marked with the Cross of Bohemia (Croix de Bohême).

## Driving Tour

*29km/18mi round trip – about 1hr*

The Forêt de Crécy, which covers an area of 4 300ha/10 625 acres, has been laid out for tourism with lay-bys and picnic areas, eight signposted footpaths and bridlepaths, and the "Circuit des vieux chênes" or "Old Oak Trail" which can be followed by car or bike. The forest lies on the plateau to the south of the River Maye and is the natural habitat of deer, wild boar and pheasants. It is carpeted with lily-of-the-valley in springtime. Viewing tables have been set out on the edge of the forest in Forêt-Montiers and Forêt-l'Abbaye.

▶ *From Crécy, take the Forêt-l'Abbaye road (D 111) to the crossroads at Le Monument then turn right onto the Forest-Montiers road through the woodland.*

The Forêt-Montiers road runs past some superb beech and oak copses.

▶ *Continue to Le Poteau de Nouvion then turn right onto the forest road called Le Chevreuil, to the crossroads at Les Grands-Hêtres hunting hide.*

### Hutte des Grands-Hêtres

This part of the forest, crossed by a footpath called Sentier des deux Huttes, is absolutely outstanding.

▶ *Return to Poteau de Nouvion and turn right towards N 1 and Forêt-Montiers.*

### Forêt-Montiers

It was here that St Riquier founded a hermitage, later to become a monastery (*moutier* in French). It was also here that François I's son, Charles, died of plague at the age of 23.

▶ *Take N 1 in a northerly direction.*

### Bernay-en-Ponthieu

This village, lying on the south-facing slopes of the Maye Valley, has retained its old **posting house** opposite the church. The street façade of the former **coaching inn** dates from the 15C: the corbelled upper floor rests on a beam carved with garlands and grotesques.

### WHERE TO EAT

**Ferme-auberge La Table de Ferme** – *Hameau d'Estruval, 80150 Ponches-Estruval – 8km/4.8mi N of Crécy via D 12, D 212 and secondary road –* ☎ *03 22 23 54 02. Open Sat evening, Sun lunch and public holidays Mar-Dec; Thu-Sun in Jul-Aug – reserv. required.* Built from cob, white stone and brick, this farm is 250 years old. Geese, ducks and chickens wander merrily in the farmyard, whilst tempting vegetables grow in the kitchen garden. Don't resist the pleasure of enjoying a farm-fresh meal in this relaxing setting.

The River Maye forms a myriad of lakes and ponds in the area around Bernay-en-Ponthieu.

▶ *Turn right onto D 938 and return to Crécy-en-Ponthieu.*

The road overlooks the wide **Maye Valley** with its alternating fields of crops, meadows and thickets. The southern slopes are topped by the Crécy Forest.

# CHÂTEAU DE DAMPIERRE★★

MICHELIN LOCAL MAP 311: H-3, MAP 101 FOLD 31 OR 106 FOLD 29

Dampierre is closely associated with two distinguished families, the Luynes and the Chevreuse. The château still belongs to the latter. From 1675 to 1683 Jules Hardouin-Mansart rebuilt the Château de Dampierre for Colbert's son-in-law the Duke of Chevreuse, a former student at Port-Royal and the mentor of the Duke of Burgundy. The castle and its park, laid out by Le Nôtre, form one of the rare estates close to Paris to have been so well preserved.

- **Information:** ☎ 01 30 52 53 24. www.chateau-de-dampierre.fr.
- ▶ **Orient Yourself:** Situated in the narrow upper part of the Chevreuse Valley, 27 miles southqwest of Paris; accessible by the A 12.
- **Organizing Your Time:** You should allow half a day to get the best out of your visit.

## Visit

### Château★★

*Open Apr to mid-Oct,* ✎ *guided visits (45mn), 11am-6.30pm; Sun and public holidays, 11am-noon, 2-6.30pm; grounds, 11am-6.30pm;* ⊕*9.50 €; grounds only, 6€.* ☎ *01 30 52 53 24.* The main body of the château, surrounded by a moat, opens onto a courtyard flanked by stables and outbuildings. In front of it are two buildings with arcades. The pinkish tones of the brick harmonise with the sober stone string courses and columns, contrasting sharply with the darker hues of the park.

On the ground floor, visitors may admire Cavelier's statue of Penelope (1848) in the hall leading to the drawing rooms embellished with Louis XV wainscoting, the suite occupied by Marie Leszczynska, and an imposing dining room decorated with Louis XIV panelling.

The first floor houses the **Royal Suite**, which accommodated Louis XIV, Louis XV and Louis XVI. The splendid 17C and 18C furnishings are beautifully preserved and reminiscent of the King's suite at Versailles. Note the furniture, portraits, wainscoting, medallions and overdoor panels by old masters.

The most amazing achievement stands at the top of the great staircase. The Salle de la Minerve is a formal reception room dating from the 19C when the castle was restored by Duban. Ingres was commissioned to paint a fresco representing the Golden Age; it was never completed. The Duc Honoré de Luynes, who conceived the whole project, ordered a colourful 3m/10ft statue of Minerva, a miniature replica of the legendary gold and ivory Minerva of the Parthenon executed by Phidias in the 5C BC.

### Park★

A walk round the castle starting from the right will lead you to a large ornamental pond, the favourite spot of many anglers. Water is omnipresent in this vast romantic park: canals, fountains and waterfalls embellish this green open space in the heart of the forest, in the middle of the picturesque Chevreuse Valley. The park and the castle form one of the rare protected estates near the capital.

## Address Book

*For coin ranges, see the Legend on the cover flap.*

### WHERE TO STAY

Abbaye des Vaux de Cernay – 78720 Cernay-la-Ville – 2.5km/1.5mi W of Cernay via D 24. 01 34 85 23 00 – www.abbayedecernay.com – – 57 rms – 16 € – restaurant . To fall asleep in the superb Cistercian abbey and awake to the monastic quietude of its magnificent park: heavenly! The spacious rooms are a successful blend of modern comfort and antique building materials. Restaurant and tearoom.

### WHERE TO EAT

Country Road – 20 Grande-Rue, 78720 Dampierre-en-Yvelines. 01 30 52 52 07. Closed 24 Dec to 5 Jan, Mon-Wed and evening. This delightful house in the heart of the village features a tearoom and an interior decoration shop. The carefully chosen painted wood furniture, tablecloths and tableware create something of a British atmosphere that complements the menu, offering mixed salads, pastries, brunch and daily specials.

# Excursion

### Vaux de Cernay

*4km/2.5mi south by D 91 to Cernay-la-Ville, then right onto D 24 (30min to 2hr walk).*

The road weaves up the wooded narrow valley, past a restaurant and across a brook by a mill, Moulin des Roches.

▸ *Park near the Chalet des Cascades.*

### Étang de Cernay

The pond was created by the monks of the local abbey to stock fish. A memorial to the 19C landscape painter Léon-Germain Pelouse stands at the top of the embankment, near a stately oak tree. The walk may be continued for another 30min or 1hr by following the wide path which veers right and leads straight up to the wooded plateau. From the edge of the plateau turn back, bear right and return along the cliff path that skirts the promontory.

### Abbaye des Vaux-de-Cernay★

Now a hotel, the abbey was founded in the early 12C. It came under Cistercian rule and reached its heyday in the 13C, but in the 14C it suffered from epidemics of plague and successive wars and started to decline. In 1791 it was abandoned by its last 12 monks and sold. The Rothschild family who bought the abbey in 1873 restored and preserved it until the Second World War. On the **grounds**, the ruins of the abbey church may be seen (late-12C façade with rose-window), and the monk's building, now a concert hall.

# DISNEYLAND RESORT PARIS★★★

### MICHELIN LOCAL MAP 312: F-2 OR MAP 106 FOLD 22

Disneyland is a place to relive your childhood dreams. Not far from the hotels, the main entertainment centre called Disney Village re-creates the American way of life with shops, restaurants and entertainment. A short distance from the complex lies Golf Disneyland Paris, with its 27-hole course.

- **Information:** ☎ 0825 306 030. www.disneylandparis.com.
- ▶ **Orient yourself:** This unique development in Europe stands on the Brie plain about 30km/18mi east of Paris.
- **P** **Parking:** On site parking: cars 8€.

## A Bit of History

### A Magician called Walt Disney

Walt Disney's name is linked to innumerable animated cartoons that have entertained children throughout the world. No one can forget the heroes of his creations (Mickey Mouse, Minnie, Donald, Pluto, Pinocchio, Snow White, and others) .

Born Walter Elias Disney in Chicago in 1901, the fourth child of Flora and Elias Disney, Walt soon showed great ability at drawing. After the First World War, in which he served as an ambulance driver in France, he returned to the US where, in Kansas City, he met a young Dutchman called Ub Iwerks, who was also passionate about drawing. In 1923 the pair produced in Hollywood a series of short films called *Alice Comedies*. In 1928 Mickey Mouse, the future international star, was created. There next followed the era of the Oscar-winning, full-length animated cartoon films: *The Three Little Pigs* (1933), *Snow White and the Seven Dwarfs* (1937), and *Dumbo* (1941). Disney also produced films starring real people, such as *Treasure Island* (1950) and *20 000 Leagues Under the Sea* (1954). In 1966 the man who had spent his life trying to bring dreams to life died. Walt Disney Studios continued to make films, remaining faithful to Walt's ideas.

## Disneyland Park★★★

Kids ⏰*Open Jul-Aug 9am-11pm (9pm for Walt Disney studios). Sep to mid-Jan 10am-8pm (weekends and public holidays, 9am-8pm. Rest of year 10am-8pm (Sat, 9am-8pm. ☞1-day pass 51€ (3-11 years, 43€); 3-day pass 113€ (3-11 years 92€). ☞ Guided tours, go to City Hall, on Town Square in the Main Street: 15€ (under 12s, free).*

The large Disneyland Paris site (over 55ha/135 acres) comprises five territories or"lands", each with a different theme. As well as the spectacular shows featuring amazing automatons in particularly detailed settings, each region has shops, ice cream vendors, restaurants and self-service restaurants.

### How old is Mickey?

The famous young mouse has not got a single wrinkle, yet he was born in 1928 thanks to Disney and the cartoonist of Dutch origin, Ub Iwerks. Mickey first appeared in a small film entitled *Plane Crazy*, based on Charles Lindbergh's achievement. However, it was on 18 November of the same year that he made his debut as a star, together with the delightful Minnie, in the first silent cartoon film entitled *Steamboat Willie*. One small detail: age has caused Mickey to lose, not his hair, but his tail!

Every day, the **Disney Parade★★**, a procession of floats carrying all the favourite Disney cartoon characters, takes place. On some evenings and throughout the summer the **Main Street Electrical Parade★★** adds extra illuminations to the fairytale setting.

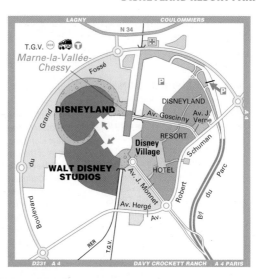

## Main Street USA

The main street of an American town at the turn of the 20C, lined with shops and restaurants with Victorian-style fronts, is brought to life as though by magic. Horse-drawn street cars, limousines, fire engines and Black Marias transport visitors from Town Square to Central Plaza (the hub of the park) while colourful musicians play favourite ragtime, jazz and Dixieland tunes. On each side of the road are **Discovery Arcade** and **Liberty Arcade** (exhibition and diorama on the famous Statue of Liberty at the entrance to New York harbour). From Main Street station a small steam train, the **Disneyland Railroad★**, travels across the park and through the **Grand Canyon Diorama**, stopping at the station in each land.

## Frontierland

The conquest of the West, the gold rush and the Wild West with its legends and folklore are brought together in Thunder Mesa, a typical western town, and Big Thunder Mountain, a strange, arid wall of rock like the mountains of Monument Valley (Arizona, Utah). Big Thunder Mountain rises on an island washed by the Rivers of the Far West. The waters here are plied by two handsome **steam-boats★**, the *Mark Twain* and the *Molly Brown*.

## Big Thunder Mountain★★★

In the mountain, there's an old gold mine. On the banks of the lake, in the buildings belonging to a mining company, are crowds of travellers patiently waiting to board the **Mine Train**. The trip in the hurtling carriages racing down the track at top speed includes explosions and risks of rock falls. A thrilling ride for those who enjoy heart-pounding excitement.

## Phantom Manor★★★

A dilapidated manor house stands high above the Rivers of the Far West. It used to be the home of people who had struck it lucky during the gold rush. Inside, strange things happen. The walls stretch and shrink. The tour through the rooms and basement continues in small black cars that take you to the ghost town of Thunder Mesa. When you leave, take a stroll to the **Boot Hill** cemetery and have a look at the strange tombstones.

## Pirates or corsairs?

Pirates were adventurers without any scruples who roamed the seas, boarding and plundering merchant ships for their own profit. Corsairs, on the other hand, were commissioned by their government to track down merchant ships from enemy countries. The most famous corsairs were Jean Bart, Duguay-Trouin and Surcouf.

## Address Book

For coin ranges, see Legend on the cover flap.

### GENERAL INFORMATION

**Booking a show** – Entertainment programmes and booking facilities are available from City Hall, located in Town Square, just inside Disneyland Park.

**Currency exchange** – Facilities are available at the main entrance to the park.

**Handicapped guests** – A guide detailing special services available can be obtained from City Hall (Disneyland Park) or from the information desk inside Walt Disney Studios Park.

**Storage areas** – Near the main entrance and beneath Main Street Station.

**Animals** – These are not allowed in the theme parks, in Disney Village or in the hotels. The Animal Care Centre is located near the visitors' car park.

**Baby Care Center, Meeting Place for Lost Children, First Aid** – Near the Plaza Gardens Restaurant (Disneyland Park) or in Front Lot (Walt Disney Studios Park).

### MAKING THE MOST OF THE THEME PARKS

To avoid long queues at popular attractions, visit these attractions during the parade, at the end of the day or better still to get a **Fast Pass** issued by distributors outside the most popular attractions in both parks; this ticket bears a time slot of one hour during which time you may have access to the attraction within a few minutes.

**Disneyland Park**: Indiana Jones (Adventureland); Peter Pan's Flight (Fantasyland); Big Thunder Mountain (Frontierland); Space Mountain and Star Tours (Discoveryland).

**Walt Disney Studios Park**: Rock'n Roller Coaster (Backlot); Flying Carpets (Animation Courtyard); Studio Tram Tour (Production Courtyard).

### WHERE TO STAY

For the total Disney experience, you can choose your accommodation among the park's hotels. All managed by Disney, their decor is inspired by different regions of the United States.

**Camping Base de Loisirs de Jablines-Annet** – *77450 Jablines –* *6km/3.6mi N of Disney via N 34 and D 45.* ☎ *01 60 26 09 37. Open 28 Mar to 2 Nov – reserv. advisable – 150 sites.* Offering every sport – or nearly – the Île-de-France's biggest beach is spread before you while Disneyland is right around the corner! The sites, with large, paved alleys along the edges, give onto pretty views of the surrounding landscapes.

**Bellevue Bed and Breakfast** – *77610 Neufmoutiers-en-Brie – 10km/6mi S of Disney. Take A 4, D 231 then D 96.* ☎*01 64 07 11 05 – www.bellevue.fr.st – 7 rms.* Don't turn around when you see the modern buildings, you'd be sorry. Nestled in an attractive garden, this residence is most pleasant: both simple and elegant, close to Paris and Disneyland, it is a charming stopover in the heart of the Brie region.

**Les Hauts de Montguillon** – *22 r. de St-Quentin, in Montguillon, 77860 St-Germain-sur-Morin – 3km/1.8mi NE of Disney.* ☎ *01 60 04 45 53 – http://perso. wanadoo.fr/les-hauts-de-mont-guillon/ – reserv. required – 3 rms - meals .* This recently restored farmhouse located a few minutes from Disneyland is an opportune, comfortable halt. Bedrooms are a successful blend of old and new; bathrooms are stylish and ultra-modern. Quiet garden.

**Hôtel Santa Fé** – *In Disneyland.* ☎ *01 60 45 78 00 – 1000 rms.* Welcome to New Mexico! A larger than life poster of Clint Eastwood, straight out of *The Good, The Bad and The Ugly*, welcomes you on your way to rooms cooled by ceiling fans. The Tex-Mex restaurant is enlivened by mariachi bands.

**Hôtel Cheyenne** – *In Disneyland.* ☎ *01 60 45 62 00 – 1000 rms.* Come play cowboys and Indians with your kids in this reconstructed Far West town! Simple rooms designed for family visits; restaurant with a self-service menu and costumed service staff who put on a Western-style show.

**Hôtel Séquoia Lodge** – *In Disneyland.* ☎ *01 60 45 51 00 – 1001 rms.* The Rocky Mountain wilderness inspired the decoration scheme of this hotel where you'll be greeted by park rangers. Comfortable rooms. Two restaurants with an alpine bent proposing buffet menus. Pool and fitness area.

🍴🍷🍽 **Newport Bay Club** – *In Disneyland*. ☎ *01 60 45 55 00 – 1093 rms.* On the shores of Lake Disney, discover the charm of an early 20C New England coast resort, complete with rocking chairs on the veranda. Two restaurants: the Cape Cod, serving buffet meals, and the Yacht Club, featuring seafood.

## WHERE TO EAT

### INSIDE DISNEYLAND

For a quick snack or a leisurely meal, a multitude of restaurants awaits you. Here's a sampling:

🍷 For a nibble, take a quick trip to Italy via la **Bella Notte**, have a seat on **Colonel Hathi's** terrace, or enjoy the buffet at the **Plaza Gardens**. If you have more time, you might opt for one of the restaurants – you'll enjoy a fine meal in original surroundings. Remember to reserve your table by phone (☎01 64 74 28 82) or at the City Hall, just left of the park entrance.

🍷🍽 **Silver Spur Steakhouse** – *Frontierland. Closed Mon-Tue* . You can leave your horse at the entrance of this Far West saloon. While you probably won't run into cowboys or rich cattle farmers, you will be able to savour grilled meat prepared ranch-style. Impressive lighting fixtures adorned with silver spurs.

🍴🍷🍽 **Blue Lagoon Restaurant** – *Adventureland* . Tropical moonlight and Caribbean ambience among luxurious greenery, where island specialities include seafood, *accras de morue* (cod fritters), West Indian *boudin* (blood pudding) and the Creole *rougail de poisson*. Have a seat along the Pirate of the Caribbean's river and tuck in.

🍷🍽 **Walt's Restaurant** – *Main Street. Closed Wed-Thu*. After having climbed the sweeping staircase of this handsome Victorian mansion on Main Street and admired the photos of Mr. Disney that line the walls, choose a table in one of the cosy salons of this comfortable restaurant. Our favourite dining areas are Discoveryland and the Library.

🍷🍽 **Auberge de Cendrillon** – *Fantasyland*. Once upon a time Cinderella's Inn stood at the foot of a lovely castle. A beautiful girl in glass slippers would come by coach – so the legend says – to savour the tenderly simmered dishes served in front of the big fireplace or on the flowered terrace in summer.

In the **Walt Disney Studios park** – 🍷🍽 **Rendez-vous des Stars Restaurant** – *Production Courtyard*. This buffet restaurant in the Art Deco style is where Hollywood's greatest stars convene. The walls are covered with portraits of the most famous celebrities of the Big Screen – maybe you'll be lucky enough to meet one of them.

### OUTSIDE THE THEME PARKS

🍷 **Annette's Diner** – *Disney Village*. ☎ *01 60 45 70 37*. Interested in experiencing a blast from the past, as seen in the 1950s-era film *American Graffiti*? Come in and order true-to-life hamburgers, hot dogs, milk shakes… Waiters and waitresses leave their posts every now and again and start dancing – they may well invite you to join them!

🍷🍽 **Rainforest Café** – *Disney Village*. ☎ *01 60 43 65 53 – www.rainforestcafe. com*. You'll need to cross a shop, not an ocean, to get to this Amazonian rain forest. Gorillas, elephants and other exotic beasts observe you as you dine on mildly spicy dishes served in a sensational equatorial decor.

🍷🍽 **The Steakhouse** – *Disney Village*. ☎ *01 60 45 70 45. Closed Sat lunch*. Connoisseurs of juicy steaks and fine wines: this place is for you. Before your meal arrives, enjoy the superb decor inspired by prohibition-era Chicago. If you have children along, don't miss Sunday brunch in the company of Disney heroes.

🍷🍽 **L'Ermitage** – *allée Jean-de-la-Fontaine, Ecluse de Chalifert, 77144 Chalifert – 6km/3.6mi N of Disneyland via N 34 and D 45*. ☎ *01 60 43 41 43 – www.notrermitage.com. Closed 29 Jul to 29 Aug – reserv. required*. The oldest guinguette on the banks of the Marne, founded in 1860, is still packed every weekend. Patrons of all ages come here to enjoy the unique festive atmosphere during dinner or a thé-dansant. Disco Fridays, cabaret Saturdays and retro Sundays.

## Famous fairy-tale writers

Charles Perrault (1628-1703): *Sleeping Beauty*; Charles Lutwidge Dodgson, better known as Lewis Carroll (1832-98): *Alice in Wonderland*; the Grimm Brothers: *Snow White and the Seven Dwarfs*; anthology of German fairy tales; Carlo Collodi: *Pinocchio*; Hans Christian Andersen (1805-1875): *The Little Mermaid*; James Matthew Barrie (1860-1937): *Peter Pan*.

### Adventureland

From Central Plaza, go through Adventureland Bazaar, a sort of desert fortress containing several exotically foreign shops. Adventureland conjures up pictures of exotic adventures, travel to far-distant lands, treasure island, and pirates.

### Pirates of the Caribbean★★★

This fortress is easy to spot – the skull and crossbones fly at the top of its walls. Cross the underground passages which reserve a few surprises then board a small boat and watch the attack and ransacking of a Spanish harbour town by pirates. There are several different scenes, all with superb decors and lots of action.

### Indiana Jones et le Temple du Péril… à l'envers★★★

In the jungle lies a ruined temple; courageous archaeologists in wagons enter it in reverse and defy the laws of gravity. This is not for the faint-hearted.

### La Cabane des Robinson★★

The Swiss Family Robinson survived a shipwreck and were able to salvage a few objects and building materials that enabled them to build a tree house in a giant banyan tree (an Indian fig). A staircase leads up to the various rooms with their wonderful furniture.

### Le Château de la Belle au bois dormant★★ (Sleeping Beauty's Castle)

On the upper floor, stained-glass windows and Aubusson tapestries recount episodes from this famous fairy story. Below, in the depths of the castle, a huge scaly dragon appears to be sleeping. From the ramparts, there is a magnificent view of Fantasyland.

### It's a Small World★★

A "cruise" takes visitors past dolls dressed in national costume, singing and dancing in sets that represent their home countries. A hymn in praise of the gentleness and liveliness of children all over the world.

*Space Mountain*

### Alice's Curious Labyrinth★

An episode from *Alice in Wonderland* in which the path to the Queen of Heart's castle is full of surprises.

### Peter Pan's Flight★★

Like the flight of Peter Pan, the boy who never grew up, the trip takes visitors over the rooftops of London and the Never-Never Land, and past episodes from the story of Peter Pan, all in small boats.

### Blanche-Neige et les Sept Nains★ (Snow White and the Seven Dwarfs)

In the mysterious forest crossed by small wagons is the wicked witch who cast a spell on Snow White.

### Space Mountain★★★ – De la Terre à la Lune

This superb attraction, which is unique to Disney, was inspired by Jules Verne's novel *From the Earth to the Moon*. A huge copper and bronze mountain encompassing a gigantic cannon pointing skyward awaits the most audacious visitors. After being catapulted toward the cosmos, you experience a mind-bending, and highly acrobatic, intergalactic trip.

### Star Tours★★★

A breathtaking trip on a spaceship. Based on George Lucas' famous film, *Star Wars*. A stopover at the **Astroport Services Interstellaires** is highly recommended. Use the **Photomorph** to change your looks (peals of laughter guaranteed) and have your photo taken.

### Chérie, j'ai rétréci le public★★★ (Honey I've shrunk the audience)

An extraordinary experience awaits you in the hall of the Imagination Institute: the famous professor Wayne Szalinski is giving a public demonstration of his shrinking machine. Are you volunteering? If so, hang on: the settings may not be spot on!

### Le Visionarium★★

Ever dreamt of travelling back in time? This is your chance, in an amazing machine which offers a "voyage through time". Using the surround-vision process, the audience travels right across Europe and meets a number of famous people.

## Walt Disney Studios Park★★★

Inaugurated on 16 March 2002, this park is entirely dedicated to the wonders of the cinema. It offers its guests a chance to take a trip backstage and discover some of the secrets of filming, of animation techniques and of television. The park is divided into four production areas, each including an amazing variety of shows and attractions.

### Front Lot

The park entrance is overlooked by a 33m/108ft-high water tower, a traditional landmark in film studios. In the centre of the Spanish-style courtyard, planted with palm trees, stands a fountain dedicated to Mickey.

**Disney Studio 1** is the reconstruction of a famous Hollywood film set, Hollywood Boulevard, lined with restaurants and boutiques.

### Animagique★★★

This attraction celebrates Disney's full-length animation films; spectators find themselves at the centre of a 3D cartoon, next to Mickey, Donald Duck, Dumbo's pink elephants, Pinocchio.

## Visionaries

Leonardo da Vinci (1452-1512): as early as the 15C, he had conceived the parachute and the helicopter. Jules Verne (1828-1905) used to state: "Everything a man can imagine other men can realise". His science fiction novels show how right he was. Herbert George Wells (1866-1946): this master of fantasy shook the Americans with his novel entitled *War of the Worlds*, which Orson Welles interpreted on radio in 1938.

## Why Buffalo Bill?

Having taken part in the conquest of the Wild West, the Civil War, the war against the Cheyennes and the Sioux, William Cody became famous for his skill as a marksman and for hunting buffaloes during the building of the Kansas Pacific Railroad. A journalist, who later wrote about his achievements, gave him the nickname of Buffalo Bill. As for our hero, he travelled through the United States and then Europe, staging his adventures in a particularly lively show entitled *Buffalo Bill's Wild West Show*.

### Art of Disney Animation★★

An interactive discovery of the secrets of animation.

### Flying Carpets★★

Guests wait backstage for instructions which direct them to the main film set where Aladdin's Genie guides them onto flying carpets!

### Production Courtyard

Here spectators are allowed to see what happens in the usually out-of-bounds backstage areas of cinema and television studios: how film sets and special effects are created, how costumes are made.

### Cinémagique★★★

When fiction meets reality, spectators literally go through the screen and become the actors and heroes of the film.

### Television Production Tour★★

You are offered a guided tour of Disney Channel France and the possibility to watch the live filming of *Zapping Zone*.

### Studio Tram Tour★★

Sit back and enjoy this guided tour aboard a small tramway through amazing film sets, until you reach **Catastrophe Canyon★★★**!

### Armageddon★★

The Russian space station is threatened by meteorites, a gripping (and particularly loud) experience!

### Rock'n Roller Coaster★★★

A unique "musical" experience awaits you inside a recording studio; be prepared to be propelled at full speed on a breathtaking journey…(not for the faint-hearted!).

### Moteurs… Action!★★★

A hero chasing some villains through a village in the south of France, an occasion to see some superb stunts.

# Disney Village★

The main street of this American town offers continuous entertainment and a convivial atmosphere. On summer evenings, it is particularly lively once the theme parks are closed for the night. Shops, restaurants and bars are crowded. In the street, games of skill take place while tightrope walkers, acrobats on stilts, jugglers and musicians arouse the crowd's enthusiasm. Night-owls can then go on to the discotheque **Hurricanes**. The quality of the shows, the increasing number of cinemas in the **Multiplexe Gaumont**, and the reputation of establishments such as **Planet Hollywood** have insured the success of this "village" which attracts a growing number of visitors from the Île-de-France region.

### Buffalo Bill's Wild West Show★★

The famous adventures of pioneer William Frederick Cody (1846-1917), alias Buffalo Bill, inspired this dinner-show which, complete with horses, bison, cowboys and Indians, evokes the epic days of the Wild West. The Texas-style meal is served on tin plates. There is non-stop action with unexpected turns, special effects and plenty of laughs.

# DOUAI★

**POPULATION 137 607**

**MICHELIN LOCAL MAP 302: G-5**

Standing on both banks of the River Scarpe, the town has preserved the 18C layout and buildings that gave it the aristocratic look Balzac evoked in his *Recherche de l'Absolu*. Douai is proud of its two peals of bells, one in the belfry and the other a peripatetic peal of 50 bells which travels the length and breadth of France. A French bell-ringing school was founded in Douai by Jacques Lannoy, who still runs it today.

**Information:** Office du tourisme de Douai, 70 pl. d'Armes, 59500, Douai. ☎ 0327 88 26 79. www.ville-douai.fr.

## A Bit of History

**Industrial, legal and intellectual centre** – Large industrial firms, comprising metallurgy, chemicals and food, a national printing works and an important river freight trade all contribute to the town's economic prosperity. In addition, Douai is a major legal centre, with a Court of Appeal, a relic of the Flanders Parliament which sat here from 1714 to the Revolution.

The town also enjoys a distinguished reputation for intellectual activity, which began with the elegiac poetess **Marceline Desbordes-Valmore** (1786-1859) who was born here, and is maintained by the many educational institutions which have taken the place of the university, founded in the 16C but transferred to Lille in 1887.

**Gayant's town** – On 16 June 1479, Douai narrowly escaped falling into French hands. A procession was organised to thank the patron saint of the town and when peace with France was signed 60 years later, this annual event became more colourful with each corporation supplying a float decorated with symbolic characters. The wicker-workers' guild provided a *gayant* (giant in Picard dialect); a year later the fruiterers supplied him with a wife… the children soon followed.

**Gayant's misfortunes** – In 1770, the bishop of Arras forbade the procession, which celebrated a French defeat, and replaced it with another one on 6 July, intended to celebrate the arrival of French troops in Douai in 1667. The giants were given another lease of life in 1778, only to be wiped out again by the Revolution. They reappeared in 1801 and were given their present costumes 20 years later. Destroyed in 1918 and 1944, they were rebuilt each time with the same care.

### Jean Bellegambe (1470-1534)

This artist, who seems to have spent his entire life in Douai, was a likeable character with wide-ranging artistic talent.

He mastered the transition from the Gothic tradition (religious subjects treated with realistic detail and harmonious colours) to the Italian influence of the Renaissance (works decorated with columns, pilasters, shells and garlands) which he linked with the objective, intimate realism of the Flemish School and the intellectualism of the French School. The latter is marked by a choice of subjects which are sometimes difficult to understand.

Bellegambe worked a great deal for the abbeys of the Scarpe Valley, and Douai's landscape and buildings can often be recognised in his works: the belfry and town gates, the towers of the abbey church of Anchin, Flines woods and the watery landscapes of the River Scarpe and River Sensée.

## Address Book

*For coin ranges, see the Legend on the cover flap.*

### WHERE TO STAY

**Hôtel de la Terrasse** – *36 terrasse St-Pierre.* ☎ *03 27 88 70 04 – P – 26 rms – ☎ 8.50€.* The perfect starting place for a morning stroll along the nearby banks of the Scarpe. The func-tional, soundproofed rooms are housed in three separate buildings. One of the dining rooms is adorned with pieces from the owner's private art collection.

### WHERE TO EAT

**Le Storez** – *116 r. Storez.* ☎ *03 27 98 88 80. Closed Sat lunch, Sun evening and Mon.* Opposite the Porte d'Arras, a remnant of the city's old ramparts, this brick house has been serving customers since 1896. Today's fare consists of dishes with a maritime accent, served in a retro-style decor.

**Le Chat Botté** – *Château de Bernicourt, 59286 Roost-Warendin – 10km/6mi NE of Douai via D 917 and D 8.* ☎ *03 27 80 24 44. Closed 1-15 Aug, Sun evening and Mon.* To savour a moment of quietude in the middle of a shady park, visit the Château de Bernicourt. The restaurant, set up in the outbuild-ings, has a dining room decorated with coloured rattan chairs and canvases signed by a family artist.

**Au Turbotin** – *9 r. de la Massue.* ☎ *03 27 87 04 16. Closed 7-20 Feb; Aug, Sat lunch, Sun evening and Mon.* This former seed merchant's shop is brightly decorated and popular with people in the legal profession. Seafood menus.

**La Terrasse** – *36 terrasse St-Pierre.* ☎ *03 27 88 70 04.* Comprising three adjacent houses in a narrow street at the centre of town, opposite the church, this popular restaurant serves traditional cuisine in spacious and refined dining rooms decorated with paintings and violins. Excellent wine list of over 800 bottles.

### SHOPPING

**Aux Délices** – *68 r. de la Mairie – Opposite the belfry.* ☎ *03 27 88 69 19. Mon 2-7.30pm, Tue-Sat 9am-12.30pm, 2-7.30pm. Closed Sun.* Caramel lovers come here to buy one of Douai's oldest specialities: Gayantines, milk caramel sweetmeats with a butter caramel centre flavoured with vanilla or chicory. Other tempting treats include Boulets du Ch'ti and Tuiles du Nord.

### ON THE TOWN

**Aux Grès** – *2 pl. St-Amé.* ☎ *03 27 86 83 53. Tue-Thu 6pm-1am, Fri 6pm-2am, Sat 8pm-3am. Closed Sun-Mon, Aug and public holidays.* A tile awning above the bar, sawed-off tree trunks for tables, brick walls and an old fireplace lit at the first signs of chilly weather comprise the decor of this cheery pub. Darts and chess.

### SHOWTIME

**L'Hippodrome** – *Pl. du Barlet, BP 79.* ☎ *03 27 99 66 66 – www.hippodromed-ouai.com – see programme; Mon 1pm-7pm, Tue-Sat 3pm-7pm. Closed school and public holidays and Sun – 7 to 20€.* This state-funded theatre has a 12-sided stage that can be modified according to the needs of the current performance. From classical drama to techno nights, the theatre's audacious programming appeals to a variety of audiences. The annual 'Météores' festival, held in March, draws artists from the four corners of the planet. Art and experimental films are also screened here.

### LEISURE

**Boating along the Scarpe** – *Jul-Aug: Thu-Sun, and public holidays 2pm-7pm; May-June and Sep: Sat, Sun and public holidays 3-7pm. (From the Palais de Justice landing stage). 4.50€ (children: 3€).* Kids This pleasant outing along the river Scarpe (30min), once crowded with barges, takes you past banks lined with venerable old residences.

**Rambles** – *R. de la Plage, 59265 Aubigny-au-Bac.* ☎ *03 27 80 91 40 or 03 27 89 24 24.* There are many marked trails in the area. Ask for a map at the Office de Tourisme.

**Les Brasseurs de Gayant** – *63 fg de Paris.* ☎ *03 27 93 26 22 – www.brasseurs-gayant.com.* Tours of this brewery.

# Walking Tour

Start from **Porte de Valenciennes**, which is Gothic on one side (15C) and Classical on the other (18C) and walk to place d'Armes, a part-pedestrian zone with outdoor cafés and fountains. The **Hôtel du Dauphin** is the only remaining 18C house here; its façade is adorned with trophies. It now houses the tourist office.

▶ *Walk along rue de la Mairie.*

## Town Hall and Belfry★

🕐*Open Jul and Aug:* 🚶 *guided tours (1hr), 10-11am, 2-6pm; rest of year, daily 11am (except Mon), 3pm, 4pm, 5pm.* 🕐*Closed 1 Jan and 25 Dec.* ✎3.50€. ☎ *03 27 88 26 79. www.ville-douai.fr.*
The construction of this Gothic ensemble, over which towers the austere belfry, began in 1380 and was resumed several times between 1471 and 1873. Inside the **town hall** (*Hôtel de Ville*) the Gothic Council Chamber (15C), the old chapel (now the main hall), the White Salon with 18C wood panelling and the state room are open to visitors. The **belfry** is one of the best known in northern France and has been made famous not only by the description given by Victor Hugo who stopped briefly in the town in 1837, but also by Corot's fine painting, now in the Louvre. It is an imposing square Gothic tower, sombre and grim, completed in 1410; it stands 64m/210ft tall (40m/131ft from the ground to the platform).
The current **peal of 62 bells** is on the fourth floor. The bells replaced those destroyed by the Germans in 1917. They play the tune of the Scottish Puritans on the hour; on the half-hour, a boating song; at quarter past and quarter to the hour, a few notes of Gayant's tune. From the top of the tower (192 steps), Douai and its industrial suburb may be seen through the louvre-boarding.

▶ *Follow the vaulted passageway and cross the courtyard of the town hall to rue de l'Université.*

## Rue de la Comédie

To the right stands the **Hôtel d'Aoust**, a beautiful example of Louis XV architecture. Note the Rococo door and the allegorical statues representing the four seasons decorating the façade overlooking the courtyard.

▶ *Continue along rue de la Comédie and turn right onto rue des Foulons.*

## Rue des Foulons

Along the left-hand side of rue des Foulons, literally "Fullers' Street", a reminder of the linen-drapers of the Middle Ages, are a few 18C houses. At no 132, note the **Hôtel de la Tramerie** built in the Louis XIII style.

▶ *Follow rue de la Mairie on the right then rue Gambetta to rue Bellegambe.*

## Rue Bellegambe

The Modern Style boutique in rue Bellegambe (*opposite the church*) features a shop front decorated with sunflowers. Slightly farther on (no 5) is the birthplace of painter Henri-Edmond Cross.

▶ *Walk back along the street and turn left toward the town hall.*

# Sight

## Musée de la Chartreuse★★

🕐*Open daily (except Tue) 10am-noon, 2-6pm.* 🚶 *Guided tours (1hr) possible by arrangement.* 🕐*Closed 1 Jan, 1 May, Ascension, 14 Jul, 15 Aug, 1 and 11 Nov and 25 Dec.* ✎3€, *no charge 1st Sunday in the month.* ☎ *03 27 71 38 80.*
The museum is installed in an interesting group of 16C, 17C and 18C buildings, which were once the old charter house. On the left is the Hôtel d'Abancourt; on the right, beneath a huge square tower, is the building in the Flemish Renaissance style constructed for the Montmorency family. This is where the first Carthusian monks settled in the 17C. They built the small cloisters, the refectory, the chapter-house and the chapel, which was completed in 1722. The great cloisters and the monks' cells were destroyed in the 19C.

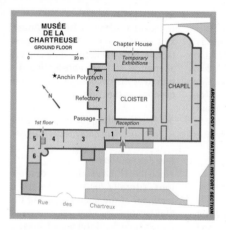

The museum is in two parts: the Fine Arts Section, and the Archaeology and Natural History Section.

## Fine Arts

The collections consist principally of fine early paintings.

**Rooms 1 to 3** – Early Flemish, Dutch (the Master of Manne, the Master of Flemalle) and Italian paintings. Large 16C altarpieces from other abbeys are on display here. Especially noteworthy are **Anchin Polyptych**★ by Bellegambe (*room 2*) portraying the Adoration of the Cross or the Adoration of the Holy Trinity, depending on whether the leaves are open or closed, and the Marchiennes Polyptych by Van Scorel (Utrecht School, 16C), dedicated to St James and St Stephen. Two masterpieces of the Italian Renaissance: Veronese's *Portrait of a Venetian Woman* and Carracci's *Scourging of Christ*, a work of rare intensity, are on display in room 3. The bronze *Venus of Castello* recalls the work of the famous sculptor and architect Giambologna. Although he conducted most of his career in Italy – Rome and particularly Florence – he was born in Douai in 1529 and trained in Flanders.

**Rooms 4 to 6** – Relief map of Douai in 1709. 16C Flemish and Dutch Mannerism is exhibited: works by Roland Savery, the Antwerp artists Jean Matsys, son of Quentin, and Frans Floris, the Dutchmen Van Hemessen, Van Reymerswaele, Goltzius, Cornelis Van Haarlem etc.

▶ *Take the staircase in room 4 to the first floor.*

**Rooms 7 and 8** – Works by Rubens (*Céres and Pan*) and Jordaens (Study of a head); landscapes by Momper and Govaerts; a witchcraft scene by David Teniers. Interesting series of lesser 17C Dutch masters.

**Rooms 11-12** – The French School (17C-19C) is well represented here by portrait painters: Le Brun (*Louis XIV on Horseback*), Vivien, Largillière, Boilly, David (*Mme Tallien*) etc.

Works by Impressionist painters are also on show: Renoir, Sisley and Pissaro and Post-Impressionists.

▶ *Return to the ground floor.*

**Cloisters** – The cloister vaults are pointed despite having been built in 1663, in the middle of the Classical period. The red brickwork contrasts pleasantly with the white stone of the ribs and the framing, carved with Baroque designs.

**Chapter-house** – The chapter-house was built in the same year as the cloisters (1663) and in the same style; it now holds temporary exhibitions.

## Archaeology and Natural History

▶ *Turn left on leaving the Charter house and left again onto rue St-Albin.*

The evolution of man is traced from the Palaeolithic Age to AD 400 through the findings of excavations in the north of France (*first floor*). The collection includes a cast of Biache Man's skull, discovered at Biache-St-Vaast, about 13km/8mi from Douai; the man is thought to have lived about 250 000 years ago.

The Gallo-Roman period is illustrated through material found at Bavay (statuettes) and at Lewarde (busts). There are some interesting models of the Merovingian village of Brebières and the necropolis at Hordain.

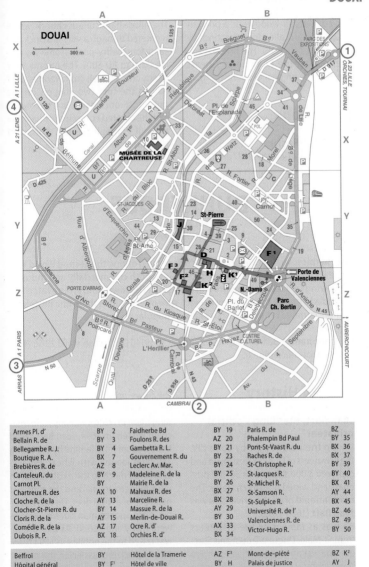

| | | | | | | | |
|---|---|---|---|---|---|---|---|
| Armes Pl. d' | BY | 2 | Faidherbe Bd | BY | 19 | Paris R. de | BZ |
| Bellain R. de | BY | 3 | Foulons R. des | AZ | 20 | Phalempin Bd Paul | BY 35 |
| Bellegambe R. J. | BY | 4 | Gambetta R. L. | BY | 21 | Pont-St-Vaast R. du | BX 36 |
| Boutique R. A. | BX | 7 | Gouvernement R. du | BY | 23 | Raches R. de | BX 37 |
| Brebières R. de | AZ | 8 | Leclerc Av. Mar. | BY | 24 | St-Christophe R. | BY 39 |
| Canteleu R. du | BY | 9 | Madeleine R. de la | BY | 25 | St-Jacques R. | BY 40 |
| Carnot Pl. | BY | | Mairie R. de la | BY | 26 | St-Michel R. | BX 41 |
| Chartreux R. des | AX | 10 | Malvaux R. des | BX | 27 | St-Samson R. | AY 44 |
| Cloche R. de la | AY | 13 | Marceline R. | BX | 28 | St-Sulpice R. | BX 45 |
| Clocher-St-Pierre R. du | BY | 14 | Massue R. de la | AY | 29 | Université R. de l' | BZ 46 |
| Cloris R. de la | AY | 15 | Merlin-de-Douai R. | BY | 30 | Valenciennes R. de | BZ 49 |
| Comédie R. de la | AZ | 17 | Ocre R. d' | AX | 33 | Victor-Hugo R. | BY 50 |
| Dubois R. P. | BX | 18 | Orchies R. d' | BX | 34 | | |

| | | | | | | |
|---|---|---|---|---|---|---|
| Beffroi | BY | | Hôtel de la Tramerie | AZ F³ | Mont-de-piété | BZ K² |
| Hôpital général | BY F¹ | Hôtel de ville | BY H | Palais de justice | AY J |
| Hôtel d'Aoust | ABZ F² | Hôtel du Dauphin | BZ K¹ | Théâtre | BZ T |

# Additional Sights

### Palais de Justice

⏲ *Open Jul-Sep: 2nd and 4th Tue of month and public holidays (Jul-Aug: Sat 3.30pm).* 🚶 *Guided tour into the Parliament Chamber.* 🎫*3.50€.*

The law courts date from the early 16C but were almost entirely rebuilt in the 18C; they were once the refuge of Marchiennes Abbey and then became the seat of the Flanders Parliament. The

main front, rebuilt under Louis XVI by the architect Lillois Lequeux, has a severe-looking central porch.

The old prison, from which a famous 18C French adventurer escaped, has been turned into an **exhibition centre** *(enter from the riverside)*. The items on show illustrate the history of the town and the law courts.

The first-floor courtroom, called the **Grande Salle du Parlement** (1762), is furnished with a vast marble fireplace, carved Louis XV woodwork, a portrait of Louis XIV and allegorical paintings by Nicolas Brenet (1769). The brick façade overlooking the River Scarpe bears traces of the original Gothic arching.

## Excursions

### Flines-les-Raches
*11km/7mi north-east by D 917 and D 938.*

The village has a curious **church**, which is entered through a very old brick and sandstone belfry-porch (some say dating back to AD 800). The narrow nave opens onto chapels from various periods. In the first two chapels on the right, the roof beams are decorated with historiated corbels; they bear the arms of Philippine Torck, Abbess of Flines from 1561 to 1571.

# DUNKERQUE
### POPULATION 191 173
### MICHELIN LOCAL MAP 302: C-1

**The "heroic town" of Dunkirk was 80% destroyed during the Second World War. Since its rebuilding, it has expanded rapidly, both commercially and industrially, owing to the enormous growth of its port. The town centre, renovated and extended through the Neptune project, now offers visitors three fine museums, and the carnival brings in its fair share of popular rejoicing.**

🖪 **Information:** Beffroi, r. de l'Amiral-Ronarc'h, 59140 Dunkerque. ☎ 03 28 66 79 21. www.ot-dunkerque.fr.

## A Bit of History

### Jean Bart, the "king's official privateer"
During the wars fought by Louis XIV, the privateers of Dunkirk destroyed and captured 3 000 ships, took 30 000 prisoners and wiped out Dutch trade. The most intrepid of all the privateers was **Jean Bart** (1650-1702).
He was as famous as the privateers from St-Malo, Duguay-Trouin and Surcouf, and was a virtuoso of the North Sea trade routes. Unlike pirates, who were outlaws attacking any and every passing ship and, in many cases, murdering

the crews, privateers were granted "letters patent" from the sovereign entitling them to hound warships and merchant vessels. In 1694, Jean Bart saved the kingdom from famine by capturing 130 ships loaded with wheat. His success owed much to the existence of an ultra-modern arsenal and the constant presence of a royal fleet. He was a simple, plain-spoken man but his exploits were many and varied. As a result, he was raised to the nobility in 1694 then, three years later, was given the rank of Commodore. It is said that Louis XIV announced the appointment personally. "Jean Bart, I have appointed you to

### Dunkirk Carnival

The carnival began at the end of the 19C. Before leaving town for several months to go fishing for cod in the frozen Icelandic waters, the "*visscherbende*" (groups of fishermen in Flemish) would organise a lively feast at the shipowners' expense. Afterwards they said goodbye and left. Today the Dunkirk Carnival is one of the most popular in the north of France. It means five weeks of mass hysteria: processions of over-excited people, accompanied by fifes and drums, winding through the streets, dancing side by side, and a long succession of popular balls (Bal des Corsaires, Nuit des Acharnés) with plenty to drink of course!

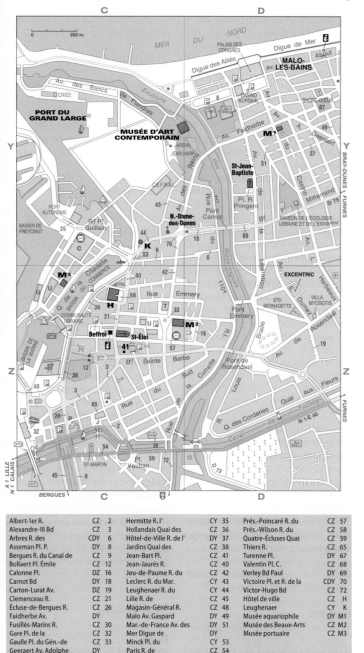

| | | | | | |
|---|---|---|---|---|---|
| Albert-1er R. | CZ 2 | Hermitte R. l' | CY 35 | Prés.-Poincaré R. du | CZ 57 |
| Alexandre-III Bd | CZ 3 | Hollandais Quai des | CZ 36 | Prés.-Wilson R. du | CZ 58 |
| Arbres R. des | CDY 6 | Hôtel-de-Ville R. de l' | DY 37 | Quatre-Écluses Quai | CZ 59 |
| Asseman Pl. P. | DY 8 | Jardins Quai des | CZ 38 | Thiers R. | CZ 65 |
| Bergues R. du Canal de | CZ 9 | Jean-Bart Pl. | CZ 41 | Turenne Pl. | DY 67 |
| Bollaert Pl. Émile | CZ 12 | Jean-Jaurès R. | CZ 40 | Valentin Pl. C. | CZ 68 |
| Calonne Pl. | DZ 16 | Jeu-de-Paume R. du | CZ 42 | Verley Bd Paul | DY 69 |
| Carnot Bd | DY 18 | Leclerc R. du Mar. | CY 43 | Victoire Pl. et R. de la | CDY 70 |
| Carton-Lurat Av. | DZ 19 | Leughenaer R. du | CY 44 | Victor-Hugo Bd | CZ 72 |
| Clemenceau R. | CZ 21 | Lille R. de | CZ 45 | Victor R. du | CZ H |
| Écluse-de-Bergues R. | CZ 26 | Magasin-Général R. | CZ 48 | Leughenaer | CY K |
| Faidherbe Av. | DY | Malo Av. Gaspard | DY 49 | Musée aquariophile | DY M1 |
| Fusillés-Marins R. | CZ 30 | Mar.-de-France Av. des | DY 51 | Musée des Beaux-Arts | CZ M2 |
| Gare Pl. de la | CZ 32 | Mer Digue de | DY | Musée portuaire | CZ M3 |
| Gaulle Pl. du Gén.-de | CZ 33 | Minck Pl. du | CY 53 | | |
| Geeraert Av. Adolphe | DY | Paris R. de | CZ 54 | | |

the rank of Commodore." The brave seafarer is said to have replied, "Sire, you were right to do so." The following year he avoided combat with nine large ships while taking the Prince de Conti to Poland. Once the danger was past,

the prince said to him, "Had we been attacked, we should have been captured". "Never," replied Jean Bart, "We should all have been blown sky high for my son was in the munitions hold and he had orders to set light to a powder keg as soon as I gave the command."

**Church of the Dunes** – Until the 7C the site on which Dunkirk stands was covered by sea. Its name, which means "church of the dunes," did not appear until 1067. Until the end of the 17C, possession of this poorly defended fishermen's town was fought over by Spanish, French, English and Dutch alike. In 1658 it was taken by Turenne after the Battle of the Dunes and fortified shortly after by Vauban.

**Evacuation of Dunkirk (May-June 1940)** – From 25 May to 4 June Dunkirk was the scene of a bloody battle at the time of the evacuation of Allied forces who were cut off from their bases after the German breakthrough at Sedan and the subsequent push toward the coast. The boats in Dunkirk's port and on the beaches from Malo to Bray-Dunes made the journey back and forth between the French coast and England. Despite the limpet mines, torpedoes, bombs and the pounding of heavy German shells, almost 350 000 men were rescued, about two-thirds of them British.

# The Port★★

Dunkirk's harbour traffic is largely dependent on the importance of the town's industrial complex founded on steel, petroleum and petrochemical products. The shipyards closed down in 1987 after turning out more than 300 ships.

Since then, the eastern and western ports have been linked by a **deepwater canal** to the Nord-Pas-de-Calais region of France, Belgium and the Paris Basin. The port installations extend along 15km/9mi of coastline.

### Port-Est

The eastern port is serviced by an outer harbour (80ha/198 acres) and three locks, with the largest, the Charles-de-Gaulle Lock (365×50m/400×55yd), able to accommodate ships up to 115 000 tonnes. The **harbour basin** (6km/4mi long) is divided into six open basins and specialised industrial basins, in addition to storage installations. Well equipped for ship repairs, the port has four dry docks and one floating dock.

① **Walking Tour** – *About 1hr.*

▶ *Start from place du Minck (fish market) between the Bassin du Commerce and the Cale aux Pêcheurs and cross the old citadel district, where the customs forwarding agents are established today. The channel and the marina are on the right. Cross Trystam Lock and turn right toward the lighthouse.*

Built between 1838 and 1843, the **lighthouse** (*guided tours Jul and Aug, Sun, 3-6pm. 2.50 €, 7-12 years 2€, family 6€. ☎ 03 28 63 33 39*) is 63m/207ft tall and its 6 000 watts produce beams which can be seen 48km/30mi away. From the top the **view** extends to the impressive harbour installations, the beach at Malo-les-Bains and the surrounding area.

② **Boat trips**
*Open Jul and Aug: daily (except Mon) 2.30pm and 4.30pm (weekends and public holidays, 3pm and 5pm). Mar-Jun and Sep-Oct call ☎ 03 28 59 11 14 (landing stage) or 03 28 66 79 21 (tourist office). 7.50€ (child, 5.50€, family, 22€).*
Boats leave from the Bassin du Commerce, the largest of the three old basins, and cruise the entire length of the port. The trip takes visitors past the tug basin, the workshops (dry docks), the various locks, the wet docks and storage areas, the sugar terminal (Transterminal Sucrier), the BP refinery and the petroleum wharves, the EDF power station etc.

# The Town

### Belfry
*Open Jul-Aug and public holidays: guided tours (30mn) 10am, 11am, 2pm and 3pm. Apr-Jun and Sep-Oct. 2pm, 3pm, 4pm and 5pm. Rest of year: by arrangement with tourist office. 2.80€ (7-12 years, 2€). ☎ 03 28 66 79 21. www.ot-dunkerque.fr.*

Built in the 13C and heightened in 1440, this served as the bell-tower to **Église St-Éloi** which burnt down in 1558. This high tower (58m/190ft) contains a peal of 48 bells which play "Jean Bart's tune" on the hours and other popular tunes on the quarter hours. The tourist office is housed on the ground floor. A war memorial has been erected under the arch opposite Église St-Éloi.

# Sights

### Musée portuaire★

♿ Kids ⏱Open Jul-Aug 10am-6pm.Rest of year daily (except Tue) 10am-12.45pm, 1.30-6pm. ⏱Closed 1 Jan, eve of Shrove Tuesday, 1 May, 25 Dec. ☞4€ (7-12 years, 3€). ☏ 03 28 63 33 39. www.musee portuaire.fr.
Laid out in a former tobacco warehouse dating from the 19C, this attractive museum gives an insight into the history and operating of the port of Dunkirk, Northern France's huge maritime gateway. Dunkirk used to specialise in fishing and trade but, from the 1960s onward, it also became a major industrial port. The work of the pilots, access to the harbour, ship repairs, product handling, coastal fishing and Icelandic fishing are all described through dioramas, model ships, maps, paintings, engravings and the tools once used by dockers.

In the 17C, Dunkirk became the main privateering harbour, with Jean Bart to defend it. *The Battle of Texel* (a copy of a painting by Isabey kept in the Musée de la Marine in Paris), engravings, and models of privateers' boats illustrate Bart's exploits.

Opposite the museum are several interesting ships including a three-master, the *Duchesse Anne*, once a sailing school ship (1901); a light vessel, the *Sandettie* (1949); and an old barge, the *Guilde* (1929), which houses an exhibition on inland navigation in its hold.

### Musée des Beaux-Arts★ (Fine Arts Museum)

⏱Open daily (except Tue) 10am-noon, 2-6pm. ⏱Closed 1 Jan, carnival Sunday, 1 May, 1 Nov, 25 Dec. 4.50€, no charge 1st Sunday in the month. ☏ 03 28 59 21 65.
This museum (rebuilt in 1973) houses beautiful collections of 16C to 20C paintings and documents tracing Dunkirk's history. One room is dedicated to the privateer Jean Bart. Note the strange 17C money box in the shape of a chained captive from the Église St-Eloi. The money placed in it was used to buy back slaves.

### Musée d'Art Contemporain★

⏱Open daily (except Tue) 10am-12.15pm, 1.45-6pm. ⏱Closed 1 Jan, carnival Sunday, 1 May, 1 Nov, 25 Dec. ☞3.05€, no charge 1st Sunday in the month. ☏ 03 28 59 21 65.
Architect Jean Willerval bore in mind the existing garden when he built his modern concrete building sheathed in white ceramic. In 1994, the museum changed its original purpose and, as a result, its collection of paintings and sculpture was transferred to the Museum of Fine Arts. It is now devoted to contemporary earthenware and glassware. Working with the theme **"Dialogues in ceramics"**, the museum aims to increase public awareness of this art form.

The Museum of Contemporary Art stands in the middle of a **sculpture park**★ designed by landscape gardener Gilbert Samel. The paths climb outcrops and run down slopes, leading past great stone pieces by the sculptor Dodeigne, metal structures by Féraud and compositions by Viseux, Arman and Zvenijorovsky, all against the backdrop of the North Sea.

# CHÂTEAU D'ÉCOUEN★★
## MICHELIN LOCAL MAP 305: F-6, MAP 101 FOLD 6 OR 106 FOLD 19

Nestling in a park (17ha/42 acres) overlooking the plain, Château d'Écouen was originally intended for Constable Anne de Montmorency and his wife, Madeleine of Savoy, who lived here from 1538 to 1555. When Constable Anne's grandson Henri II de Montmorency was beheaded in 1632, the château reverted to the Condé family but was later confiscated during the Revolution. Napoleon I salvaged the estate in 1806 by founding the first school for the daughters of members of the Légion d'Honneur there. In 1962 the château and its grounds were ceded to the Ministry of Culture, who undertook to turn it into a state museum devoted to Renaissance art.

🄸 **Information:** Access is through the forest, on foot.
🄿 **Parking:** Cars must be parked at the entrance to the forest.

## Visit 1hr

### Exterior
The Château d'Écouen reflects the transition of French art from the Early Renaissance period (Château of the Loire) to the High Renaissance during Henri II's reign.
**Courtyard** – The buildings feature pavilions at each corner and are surmounted by elaborate dormer windows with carved pediments. The beautiful east range was destroyed in the 18C and replaced by a low entrance wing.
Porticoes with Classical-style columns decorate the buildings. The most outstanding one is to the left, on the south wing (Anne de Montmorency's residence) built by Jean Bullant to house Michelangelo's famous *Slaves* in the niches on the ground floor. The statues (*the originals are in the Louvre*) were a gift to Anne de Montmorency from King Henri II.

*Painted fireplace in the Château d'Écouen*

R. Mazin/ PHOTONONSTOP

**North Terrace** – Sweeping **view** of the surrounding cereal-growing countryside.

### Musée National de la Renaissance★★
♿ 🕐*Open daily (except Tue) 9.30am-12.45pm, 2-5.15pm (5.45pm in summer).* 🕐*Closed 1 Jan, 1 May and 25 Dec.* ∞*4.50€, no charge 1st Sunday in the month.* ☎ *01 34 38 38 50. www.musee-renaissance.fr.*
Some of the exhibits on display belonged to the Renaissance collections of the Cluny Museum in Paris. Écouen Museum presents a wide range of works dating from the 16C and early 17C, which introduce visitors to the various branches of the decorative arts: furniture, wainscots, tapestries and embroideries, ceramics, enamels etc. Most of the exhibits were made in France, Italy or the Netherlands. They represent a small selection but the ambience they create is in keeping with the life of wealthy nobility during the Renaissance.
The original interior decoration consists mainly of grotesques, painted on the friezes below the ceiling and the embrasures of the windows. But it is for its **painted fireplaces**★ that Écouen is famed. Created during the reign of Henri II, these chimney-pieces are representative of the first Fontainebleau School: the central biblical scene is painted on an oval or rectangular medallion, surrounded by grotesques, garlands of fruit and motifs in leather; the hazy landscapes depicting antique ruins, fortresses and humble cottages are in imitation of Niccolo dell'Abbate.

**Ground Floor** – The monograms A and M (Anne de Montmorency and Madeleine of Savoy) have been included in the decoration of the chapel, built in 1544 and covered with painted vaulting resting on diagonal arches. This heraldic motif reappears in different places (musicians' gallery, panelling in the oratory, and the vaulting in the sacristy). The Passion Altarpiece is adorned with enamelling and a copy of Leonardo da Vinci's *Last Supper*.

Several rooms are devoted to a particular trade or technique and illustrate various aspects of Renaissance life; note a clock of German origin in the shape of a ship known as Charles V's clock, now shown incorporated into a 16C collector's cabinet and, in the reconstruction of a 16C goldsmith's workshop, a goldsmith's work bench set in an inlaid chest. This comes from the Kunstkammer of Augustus I in Dresden. The northwest pavilion was formerly occupied by Catherine de' Medici.

**First Floor** – In the south wing, visitors are shown round the constable's bedroom and Madeleine of Savoy's suite, both interesting on account of the period furniture. The west wing is almost entirely taken up by the **Tapestry of David and Bathsheba**★★★ (1510-20) which runs from the Abigail pavilion to the king's bedchamber, along the Psyche Gallery. The 75m/246ft hanging divided into 10 sections tells of the romance between King David and Bathsheba. The outstanding quality of the tapestry – woven with wool and silk threads, as well as silver braid – is equalled only by that of *The Hunts of Maximilian* in the Louvre, without doubt the two most precious examples of 16C Brussels tapestry work existing in France.

The hanging ends in the King's Apartment, situated in the northwest pavilion.

⚫ *For explanations of the monograms read the paragraph entitled "Henri II's Château" in the chapter on Fontainebleau.*

The king's suite occupied the northern wing. One of the rooms contains the floor tiles made specially for the château in 1542 by the Rouen potter Masseot Abaquesne. The winged victory on the central panel of the monumental fireplace was taken from a similar design in the François I Gallery at Fontainebleau.

The two tapestries are part of the famous *Fructus Belli* made in Brussels to cartoons by Jules Romains.

**Second Floor** – In the northeast pavilion, many pieces of Isnik pottery (mid-16C to early 17C) are exhibited in glass cabinets, illustrating the exotic tastes of 16C collectors. The first room in the north wing presents religious stained glass painted in *grisaille*; admire the Virgin and Child, dated 1544.

The second hall deals entirely with French ceramics (Bernard Palissy, Saint-Parchaira, and Masséat Abaquesne's work, *The Flood*) and there is a reconstruction of another floor designed specially for the château, showing the arms of the Constable, those of his wife, of Henri II and Catherine de' Medici.

The 15 marriage chests (*cassoni*) on show in the northwest pavilion form a remarkable ensemble; these painted panels are taken from wooden chests that were presented to newlyweds in sets of two.

The southwest pavilion concentrates on silverware (cutlery, jewellery), mainly of German origin. There is an extraordinary Daphne by the great Nuremberg goldsmith, Wenzel Jammitzer (1508-85). Above the chapel is the former library of Constable Anne which still has some of the original gilded wainscoting. It is representative of the world of books during the Renaissance period.

## Additional Sight

### Église St-Acceul

*On request at the town hall.*
☎ 01 39 33 09 00.

The chancel by Jean Bullant is the most interesting part of the building. The complex rib patterns of the vaulting (*temporarily concealed by supporting timber*) date it to the 16C.

St Acceul features several Renaissance **stained-glass windows**★; those in the north aisle are dated 1544: Dormition and Assumption of the Virgin, Annunciation and Visitation, Nativity and Adoration of the Magi.

# CHÂTEAU DE FERRIÈRES★

MICHELIN LOCAL MAP 312: F-3, MAP 101 FOLD 30 OR 106 FOLDS 21, 22

The shooting parties on Ferrières estate, the luxurious furnishings of the château and the precious collections gathered by the members of the Rothschild dynasty were the talk of the town for over 100 years. The landscape park, created at the same time as the Bois de Boulogne, is extremely attractive, especially in the vicinity of the lake. The nearby town got its name from iron ore *(fer)* extracted in great quantities during the 16C and 17C.

🗎 **Information:** ☎ 01 64 66 31 25. www.chateauferrieres.com

## A Bit of History

### A Challenge to Tradition

In 1829 James de Rothschild, founder of the French line of the family, acquired 7 500 acres of hunting grounds formerly belonging to Fouché, with a view to building a villa which would accommodate his invaluable collections. The baron did not choose a professional architect; he broke with tradition and hired **Joseph Paxton**, the English glasshouse and garden designer with a penchant for modern materials such as iron and glass. Already famed for the Crystal Palace in London (*destroyed in 1936*), Paxton erected a rectangular building flanked by square towers, with a central hall equipped with zenithal lighting. Construction work was completed in 1859. The decoration, left in the hands of the baroness, was entrusted to the French specialist Eugène Lami.

On 16 December 1862 Napoleon III paid an official visit to the Rothschilds in their new residence. Delighted by the splendid apartments and the 800 head of game for his day's shoot, the Emperor planted a sequoia tree as a commemorative gesture.

Less than 10 years later, Jules Favre – in charge of Foreign Affairs in the new National Defence government – turned up at the gates of the château on 19 September 1870. In his capacity as Minister, Favre came to see Chancellor Bismarck, who was staying at Ferrières with Kaiser Wilhelm I of Prussia, to ask him to agree to an armistice. The chancellor however made this conditional on the surrender of Strasbourg, Toul and Bitche, and further implied that the cession of Alsace and part of Lorraine was inevitable. Jules Favre left the premises the following morning. On 28 January 1871, Paris fell to the hands of the enemy.

*Ferrières*

In 1977 Baron Guy de Rothschild and his wife Marie-Hélène donated their château and part of the estate to the Confederation of Paris Universities.

## Visit 2hr

### Exterior

The castle's architecture reflects the various styles of the Renaissance period, including the odd eccentricity that was acceptable in the 19C. Although balusters, galleries and colonnades reigned supreme, the façades were each different. The most striking and the most typically English is the main front overlooking the lake, with its centrepiece flanked by turrets and its display of superimposed galleries. Step back to take in the tall decorative stone chimneys, reminiscent of the Château de Chambord.

### Interior

A pavilion sporting a large clock is fronted by the main entrance porch which bears the baron's monogram (JR) and the family coat of arms (the five Rothschild arrows).

The main staircase leads to the central hall – 40m/130ft wide and 12m/40ft high under the glass ceiling – now stripped of its paintings and tapestries. Above the main door, a row of telamones and caryatids in bronze and black marble support a musicians' gallery. The use of such statues was a popular decorative feature in the mid-19C. The Salon Bleu, overlooking the park, has busts of the Empress Eugénie and Bettina de Rothschild, the first proprietress of the château. The Louis XVI salon is the most typical example of Eugène Lami's work: it features off-white wainscoting with pinkish hues, a painted ceiling inspired by Boucher and reproduction Louis XVI furniture. Opposite is the Salon Rouge, in which the 1870 negotiations took place. It now presents an exhibition on the history of the estate.

### Musée de l'Imaginaire

🕐Open May-Sep: daily except Mon and Tue, 2-7pm. ☜8€. ☎ 01 64 66 31 25.

**WHERE TO STAY**

☖☖ **St-Rémy** – 77164 Ferrières-en-Brie. ☎ 01 64 76 74 00 – 25 rms – ☲ 8€ – restaurant ☖☖☖. Located right behind the church, this late-19C house has given up most of its original features following a total overhaul. Note the upstairs ballroom, originally decorated by the Rothschild family. Pretty modern furnishings in the restaurant and comfortable bedrooms.

This small museum housed on the second floor showcases a changing collection of paintings and sculptures by an international group of contemporary artists who express their extravagant visions in the style known as Fantastic Realism. The works are shown here before being offered for public sale.

### Park★

🕐Open May-Sep: daily except Mon and Tue, 2-7pm. 🕐1 Jan and 25 Dec. ☜5€. ☎01 64 66 31 25.

The park designed by Paxton boasts a number of superb compositions, mainly consisting of ornamental coniferous trees: cedars of Lebanon, numerous Atlas cedars – including the highly decorative blue form – and sequoias, introduced into France around 1850.

Several individual trees also deserve a mention: a Lebanese cedar with unusually long, spread-eagled branches, swamp cypresses with twigs which turn deep russet and drop off in winter, copper beeches, groves of plane trees and, on the far side of the lake, feathery weeping species, adding an autumnal touch to the tableau.

Outside the park, the allée des Lions presents an imposing driveway of stately sequoias.

### Forêt de Ferrières

In 1973, the Île-de-France region acquired the forest surrounding the castle and covering 2 800ha/ 6 919 acres. The forest now includes parking and picnic areas as well as numerous footpaths and cycle paths accessible all year round. The Étang de la Planchette is an angler's paradise (☜ fishing permits delivered on the spot).

# FONTAINEBLEAU★★★

POPULATION 15 942

MICHELIN LOCAL MAP 312: F-5 OR MAP 106 FOLDS 45, 46

It was not until the 19C that Fontainebleau started to develop, owing to the growing popularity of country residences and the general appreciation of its unspoilt forest. The area owes its name to a spring at the heart of a forest abounding in game, which was known as the "Fontaine de Bliaut" or "Blaut", probably after a former owner. However, Fontainebleau essentially owes its fame to the castle and the park named on UNESCO's World Heritage list. In addition, the town is the ideal starting point for excursions to Vaux-le-Vicomte, Barbizon or Courances.

**Access from Paris:** *SNCF rail link from Gare de Lyon*

- **Information:** Office du tourisme du pays de Fontainebleau-Avon, 4, r. Royale, 77300 Fontainebleau ☎ 01 60 74 99 99 – www.fontainebleau-tourisme.com.
- ▶ **Orient Yourself:** Fontainebleau is 60km from Paris, via the A 6, and then the N 37.
- **Don't Miss:** The Renaissance features of the castle, especially its famous horse-shoe staircase.
- **Organizing Your Time:** You can spend a whole day here, and probably will.

## A Bit of History

The Palais de Fontainebleau owes its origins to royalty's passion for hunting; it owes its development and decoration to the kings' delight in amassing works of art and displaying them in their "family home." This palace has an extremely distinguished past; from the last of the Capetians up to Napoleon III, it was designed for and occupied by French rulers.

### A hunting lodge

A spring – called Bliaut or Blaut fountain in the middle of a forest abounding in game – prompted the kings of France to build a mansion here. The exact date is not known but it was probably before 1137 as a charter exists issued under Louis VII from Fontainebleau, dating from that year. Philip Augustus celebrated the return of the Third Crusade here during the Christmas festivities of 1191 and St Louis founded a Trinitarian convent, whose members were called Mathurins; Philip the Fair was born here in 1268: unfortunately he also died here following a serious riding accident.

### The Renaissance

Under François I almost all the medieval buildings were pulled down and replaced by two main edifices, erected under the supervision of Gilles Le Breton. The oval-shaped east pavilion – built on the former foundations – was linked to the west block by a long gallery. To decorate the palace, François I hired many artists; he dreamed of creating a "New Rome" furnished with replicas of Classical statues.

The actual building consisted of rubble-work as the sandstone taken from the forest was too difficult to work into regular freestones. The harled façades are enlivened by string-courses of brick or massive sandstone blocks.

### Henri II's château

Henri II pursued the efforts undertaken by his father. He gave orders to complete and decorate the ballroom, which remains one of the splendours of Fontainebleau Palace. The monograms – consisting of the royal H and the two intertwined Cs of Catherine de' Medici – were legion. In a form of ambiguity that was generally accepted in its day, the two C's placed immediately beside

*Castle*

Ph. Gajic MICHELIN

the H form a double D, the monogram of the King's mistress Diane de Poitiers.

When Henri II was killed in a tournament, his widow Catherine de' Medici sent her rival to Chaumont-sur-Loire (*see The Green Guide Châteaux of the Loire*) and dismissed the architect in charge of the building work, Philibert Delorme, who was Diane's protégé. He was replaced by the Italian Primaticcio; those working under him, including Niccolo dell'Abbate, favoured light, cheerful colours.

### Henri IV's palace – 17C

Henri IV, who adored Fontainebleau, had the palace enlarged quite significantly. The irregular contours of the Oval Court were corrected and he gave orders to build the Kitchen Court and the Real Tennis Court (*Jeu de Paume*). These he had decorated by a new group of artists

of largely Flemish, and not Italian, inspiration: frescoes were replaced by oil paintings on plaster or canvas. In the same way, the plain wood panelling highlighted with gilding gave way to painted wainscot. This was the Second Fontainebleau School, whose representatives moved in Parisian circles.

### The House of Eternity

Louis XIV, XV and XVI undertook numerous renovations aimed at embellishing their apartments. The Revolution spared the château but emptied it of its precious furniture. Napoleon, who became consul, then emperor, thoroughly enjoyed staying at the palace. He preferred Fontainebleau to Versailles, where he felt haunted by a phantom rival. He called the palace "The House of Eternity" and left his mark by commissioning further refur-

## Military and Equestrian Tradition

Throughout French history, whether under monarchic or republican rule, independent units have been posted to Fontainebleau. Tradition, it seems, favoured the cavalry, present in the 17C with the king's bodyguard. A number of racecourses and riding schools were created under Napoleon III; the Centre National des Sports Équestres perpetuates this tradition ( *see Calendar of Events*), while the forest caters to riding enthusiasts.

The history of the town has been marked by several military organisations, notably the École Spéciale Militaire (1803 to 1808, before St-Cyr), the polygon-shaped École d'Application d'Artillerie et du Génie (1871 to 1914) and the SHAPE (Supreme Headquarters, Allied Powers, Europe) headquarters of NATO, which gave the town a cosmopolitan touch from 1947 to 1967.

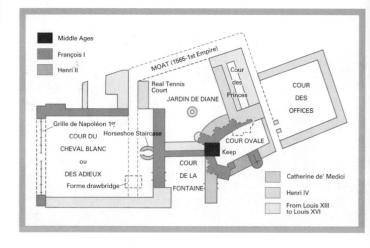

bishments. The last rulers of France also took up residence in this historic palace. It was eventually turned into a museum under the Republic.

## The Palace★★★

### Exterior *1hr*

**Cour du Cheval Blanc or des Adieux★★** – This former bailey was used only by domestics, but its generous size soon earmarked it for official parades and tournaments. It was sometimes called the White Horse Court after the day Charles IX set up a plaster cast of the equestrian statue of Marcus Aurelius in Rome; a small slab in the central alley marks its former location.

The golden eagles seemingly hovering above the pillars of the main gate remind visitors that the Emperor had this made into his main courtyard. He gave orders to raze the Renaissance buildings that lay to the west of the court, but kept the end pavilions. It is clear, walking between the two long wings, that only the one on the left with its brick courses has retained the elegance that characterised the work of Gilles Le Breton, François I's favourite architect. The right wing – which boasted the Ulysses Gallery decorated under the supervision of Primaticcio – was dismantled by Louis XV and rebuilt by Jacques-Ange Gabriel.

At the far end of the court the main block, fronted by a balustrade marking the site of the former moat, was completed in several stages from the reign of François I to that of Louis XV. Nonetheless the façades show a certain unity of style. The large horizontal planes of the blue slating are broken by the white

## The Farewell

On 20 April 1814 Emperor Napoleon Bonaparte appeared at the top of the horseshoe staircase; it was 1pm. The foreign army commissioners in charge of escorting him away were waiting in their carriages at the foot of the steps. Napoleon started to walk down the staircase with great dignity, his hand resting on the stone balustrade, his face white with contained emotion. He stopped for a moment while contemplating his guards standing to attention, then moved forward to the group of officers surrounding the Eagle, led by General Petit. His farewell speech, deeply moving, was both an appeal to the spirit of patriotism and a parting tribute to those who had followed him throughout his career. After embracing the general, Bonaparte kissed the flag, threw himself into one of the carriages and was whisked away amid the tearful shouts of his soldiers.

façades, the trapezoidal roofs and the tall chimneys of the five pavilions. The celebrated horseshoe staircase executed by Jean du Cerceau during the reign of Louis XIII is a harmoniously curved, extravagant composition showing clearly royalty's taste for splendour.

**Cour de la Fontaine★** – The fountain at the edge of the pond (*Étang des Carpes*) used to yield remarkably clear water. This was kept exclusively for the king's use and to that end the spring was guarded by two sentinels night and day.

The present fountain dates back to 1812 and is crowned by a statue of Ulysses. The surrounding buildings feature stone masonry and the whole ensemble forms a pleasant courtyard. At the far end, the Galerie François I is fronted by a terrace; it rests on a row of arches which once opened onto the king's bathroom suite.

The **Aile de la Belle cheminée** on the right was built by Primaticcio around 1565. The name originated from the fireplace that adorned the vast first-floor hall until the 18C. At that point in history Louis XV – who had turned the room into a theatre and rechristened it Aile de l'Ancienne Comédie – dismantled the fireplace, and the low-relief carvings were scattered. The monumental external steps consist of a dog-legged staircase with two straight flights in the Italian style.

On the left the Queen Mothers' and Pope's wing ends in the Grand Pavilion built by Gabriel.

**Étang des Carpes★ (Carp Pond)** – In the centre of the pond – alive with carp – stands a small pavilion built under Henri IV, renovated under Louis XIV and restored by Napoleon. It was used for refreshments and light meals.

**Porte Dorée★** – Dated 1528, this gatehouse is part of an imposing pavilion. It was the official entrance to the palace until Henri IV built the Porte du Baptistère. The paintings by Primaticcio have all been restored and the tympanum sports a stylised salamander, François I's emblem. On the two upper levels are Italian-style loggias. The first floor – its loggia sealed off by large bay windows – used to house Mme de Maintenon's suite.

The ballroom is flanked by an avenue of lime trees. The view from the bay windows is splendid and it is regrettable that the initial plans to build an open-air loggia were changed on account of the climate. The east end of the two-storeyed chapel dedicated to St Saturnin can be seen in the distance.

**Porte du Baptistère★** – The gateway opens onto the Oval Court. The base of the gateway is the rustic entrance with decorative sandstone that once held the drawbridge across the old moat.

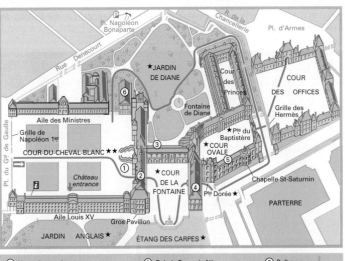

① Horseshoe staircase
② Aile des Reines-Mères et du Pape
③ Galerie François 1er
④ Aile de la Belle Cheminée
⑤ Ballroom
⑥ Real Tennis Court

It opened onto the Cour du Cheval-Blanc and was designed by Primaticcio. It is crowned by a wide arch surmounted by a dome. The gateway is named after the christening of Louis XIII and his two sisters, Élisabeth and Chrétienne, celebrated with great pomp on a dais on 14 September 1606.

**Cour Ovale★** – This is by far the most ancient and the most interesting courtyard of Fontainebleau Palace. The site was the bailey of the original stronghold; of the latter there remains only the keep, named after St Louis, although it was probably built prior to his reign. François I incorporated it into the structure he had erected on the foundations of the old castle, shaped like an oval or rather a polygon with rounded corners. Under Henri IV, the courtyard lost its shape, although not its name; the east side was enlarged, and the wings were aligned and squared by two new pavilions framing the new Porte du Baptistère. The general layout of the palace was preserved.

**Cour des Offices** – The entrance faces the Porte du Baptistère and is guarded by two arresting sandstone heads depicting Hermes, sculpted by Gilles Guérin in 1640. The Cour des Offices was built by Henri IV in 1609; it is a huge oblong, sealed off on three sides by austere buildings alternating with low pavilions. With its imposing porch executed in the style of city gates, it bears a strong resemblance to a square. Walk through the gate and admire its architecture from place d'Armes; the sandstone front presents rusticated work and has a large niche as its centrepiece.

Continue the tour of the palace exterior. The east and north wings of the Cour des Princes are two functional buildings designed or redesigned under Louis XV to provide further accommodation for members of the court.

**Jardin de Diane★** – The queen's formal garden created by Catherine de' Medici was designed by Henri IV and bordered by an orangery on its northern side. In the 19C the orangery was torn down and the park turned into a landscape garden. Diana's fountain, an elegant display of stonework dated 1603, has survived in the middle of the grounds. It has now resumed its original appearance; the four bronze dogs formerly exhibited in the Louvre Museum sit obediently at the feet of their mistress, the hunting goddess.

### Grands Appartements★★★

  *Open Jun-Sep: daily (except Tue) 9.30am-6pm; Oct-May: daily (except Tue) 9.30am-5pm; last admission 45min before closing. Closed 1 Jan, 1 May, 25 Dec. 6.50€ (children under 18: no charge), no charge 1st Sunday in the month.* ☎ *01 60 71 50 60. www.musee-chateau-fontainebleau.fr.*

The main apartments are reached by the stucco staircase (**a**), the Galerie des Fastes (**b**) and the Galerie des Assiettes

*Ballroom*

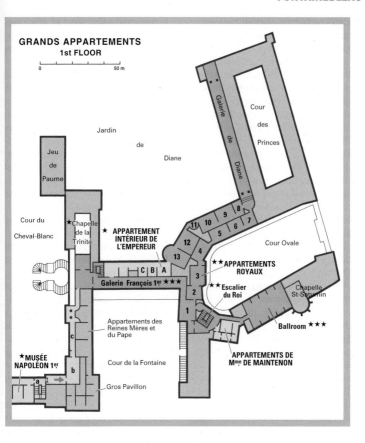

**GRANDS APPARTEMENTS**
1st FLOOR

0      50 m

Jardin de Diane

Jeu de Paume

Cour du Cheval-Blanc

★Chapelle de la Trinité

★ **APPARTEMENT INTÉRIEUR DE L'EMPEREUR**

Galerie de Diane

Cour des Princes

Cour Ovale

★★ **APPARTEMENTS ROYAUX**

★★ **Escalier du Roi**

Chapelle St-Saturnin

C | B | A

**Galerie François 1er** ★★★

Appartements des Reines Mères et du Pape

★**MUSÉE NAPOLÉON 1er**

Cour de la Fontaine

Gros Pavillon

**Ballroom** ★★★

**APPARTEMENTS DE Mᵐᵉ DE MAINTENON**

(c) which features 128 beautifully decorated pieces of Sèvres porcelain.

**Chapelle de la Trinité★** – The chapel takes its name from the Trinitarian church set up on the premises by St Louis. Henri IV had the sanctuary reinforced by vaulting and then decorated. Martin Fréminet (1567-1619), one of the lesser-known followers of Michelangelo, painted the arches with strong, vigorous scenes characterised by perspective and a daring use of foreshortening. The scenes represent the mystery of the Redemption and a number of figures from the Old Testament.

It was in this chapel that Louis XV was wedded to Marie Leszczynska in 1725 and that Louis Napoleon, later to be Napoleon III, was christened in 1810.

**Galerie de François I★★★** – This gallery was built from 1528 to 1530 and was originally open on both sides, resembling a covered passageway.

When Louis XVI enlarged it in 1786, he filled in the windows looking onto Diana's garden. A set of false French windows was fitted for reasons of symmetry. The greater part of the decoration – closely combining fresco and stucco work – was supervised by Rosso, while the wood panelling was entrusted to an Italian master carpenter. François I's monogram and his emblem the salamander were widely represented.

The scenes are difficult to interpret (there are no explanatory documents), though they seem to split into two groups, one on either side of the central bay which is adorned with an oval painting depicting two figures: Danaë by Primaticcio and *The Nymph of Fontainebleau* (1860) after Rosso.

The east side, near a bust of François I, features mostly violent scenes, perhaps referring to the recent misfortunes of the French king (the defeat of Pavia, the king's captivity in Madrid), the inescapable nature of war and death (the battle between the Centaurs and the Lapiths, Youth and Old Age, the Destruction of the Greek fleet). Beneath the vignette depicting Venus and Love at the edge of a pond, note the miniature picture set in a tablet, representing the château around 1540 with both the gallery and the Porte Dorée clearly visible.

On the west side, near the entrance, the decor exemplifies the sacred qualities of the royal function – Sacrifice, the Unity of the State – and the concept of filial piety in the old-fashioned sense of the word (the twins Cleobis and Biton): the king, his mother Louise of Savoy and his sister Marguerite d'Angoulême were devoted to one another.

The most striking scene is the portrait of an elephant whose caparison bears the royal monogram; the pachyderm no doubt symbolises the perennity of the monarchy.

**Escalier du Roi★★** – The staircase was built in 1749, under Louis XV, in what was once the bedchamber of the Duchess of Étampes, François I's favourite. The murals – the history of Alexander the Great – are by Primaticcio (note Alexander taming Bucephalus above the door) and dell'Abbate (Alexander placing Homer's books in a chest, on the far wall). Primaticcio's stucco work is highly original; the upper frieze is punctuated by caryatids with elongated bodies.

**Salle de Bal★★★ (Ballroom)** – This room (30m/100ft long and 10m/33ft wide) was traditionally reserved for banquets and formal receptions. It was begun under François I and completed by Philibert Delorme under Henri II. A thorough restoration programme has revived the dazzling frescoes and paintings by Primaticcio and his pupil dell'Abbate. The marquetry of the parquet floor, completed under Louis-Philippe, echoes the splendid coffered ceiling, richly highlighted with silver and gold. The monumental fireplace features two telamones, cast after Antique statues in the Capitol Museum in Rome.

**Appartements de Mme de Maintenon** – Note the delicate wainscoting in the Grand Salon, most of which was executed in the 17C.

**Appartements royaux★★** – At the time of François I, Fontainebleau featured a single suite of apartments laid out around the Oval Court. Towards 1565, the regent Catherine de' Medici gave orders to double the curved building between the Oval Court and Diana's Garden. Subsequently, the royal bedrooms, closets and private salons overlooked Diana's Garden. The original suite now houses antechambers, guardrooms and reception rooms where the king used to entertain his guests.

**Salle des Gardes (1)** – Late-16C ceiling and frieze.

A wide arch leads from the **Salle du Buffet (2)** to a chamber in the oldest tower of the castle.

**Salle du Donjon (3)** – Until the reign of Henri IV this sombre room was occupied by French kings who used it as a bedroom, hence its other name, the St Louis Bedroom. The equestrian low-relief sculpture (c 1600) portraying Henri IV on the fireplace came from the "Belle Cheminée." It was carved by Mathieu Jacquet.

**Salon Louis XIII (4)** – It was here that Louis XIII was born on 27 September 1601. His birth is evoked by the coffered ceiling which depicts Cupid riding a dolphin (the word dauphin means both dolphin and heir to the throne). The panel with painted wainscoting is crowned by a set of 11 pictures by Ambroise Dubois; the Romance between Theagenes and Chariclea, works dating from c 1610.

**Salon François I (5)** – Of Primaticcio's work there remains only the fireplace.

**Salon des Tapisseries (6)** – This room, having been the queen's chamber, the guard-room and the queen's first antechamber, became the empress's principal drawing room in 1804, the guard-room once more in 1814 and finally the Tapestry Salon in 1837.

The fireplace dates from 1731 and the Renaissance ceiling in pine wood is the work of Poncet (1835). The furniture was made during the Second Empire (mid-19C). The tapestries telling the story of Psyche were manufactured in Paris in the first half of the 17C.

*Throne Room*

**Antichambre de l'Impératrice** (7) – Formerly the queen's guard-room, this chamber was built on the site of the old royal staircase; the ceiling and panelling are both dated 1835. The Gobelins tapestries, executed after cartoons by Le Brun, illustrate the four seasons. The Second Empire furniture features a console, a carved-oak writing desk (Fourdinois, 1865) and a set of armchairs of English inspiration. Note the two Indian-style enamel vases produced by the Sèvres factory.

**Galerie de Diane** – This long gilt passageway (80m/263ft) was decorated during the Restoration and turned into a library under the Second Empire.

**Salon blanc- Petit salon de la Reine** (8) – In 1835 the room was decorated with furnishings from an earlier period: Louis XV wainscoting, Louis XVI fireplace inlaid with bronze etc. The furniture is Empire: chairs in gilt wood by Jacob Frères, settee, armchairs and chairs from St-Cloud, mahogany console and heads of fantastic animals in bronzed, gilt wood (Jacob Desmalter).

**Grand Salon de l'Impératrice** (9) – This drawing room, formerly the queen's gaming room, features a ceiling painted by Berthélemy; the scene is Minerva crowning the Muses.

The furniture dates from the reign of Louis XVI (chests by Stöckel and Beneman, seats upholstered with painted satin, a carpet made by the Savonnerie works) or from the First Empire (seats and chests

by Jacob Desmalter, the so-called "Seasons Table" made of Sèvres porcelain and painted by Georget in 1806-7, and a carpet rewoven to an old design). The two sets of furniture are displayed in turn.

**Chambre de l'Impératrice** (10) – This used to be the queen's bedroom. The greater part of the ceiling was designed for Anne of Austria in 1644; the wood panelling, the fireplace and the top of the alcove were created for Marie Leszczynska in 1747 and the doors with arabesque motifs were installed for Marie-Antoinette in 1787. The brocaded silk was rewoven according to the original pattern in Lyon at the end of Louis XVI's reign. Among the furniture note Marie-Antoinette's bed, designed in 1787 by Hauré, Séné and Laurent, a set of armchairs attributed to Jacob Frères and several commodes by Stöckel and Beneman (1786). The vases are Sèvres porcelain.

**Boudoir de la Reine** (11) – This delightful room was designed by Marie-Antoinette. The wainscoting was painted by Bourgois and Touzé after sketches by the architect Rousseau. The ceiling – representing sunrise – is the work of Berthélemy. The roll-top writing desk and the work table were made by Riesener in 1786.

**Salle du Trône** (12) – This was the king's bedroom from Henri IV to Louis XVI; Napoleon converted it into the throne room. The ornate mural paintings, dating from several periods, were harmonised in the 18C. Above the fireplace is a full-length portrait of Louis XIII, painted in Philippe de Champaigne's studio.

**Salle du Conseil** (13) – This room was given a semicircular extension in 1773. The ceiling and panelling are splendid examples of Louis XV decoration.

Five pictures by Boucher adorn the ceiling, representing the four seasons and Apollo, conqueror of Night. The wainscoting presents an alternation of allegorical figures painted in blue or pink monochrome by Van Loo and Jean-Baptiste Pierre.

**Appartement Intérieur de l'Empereur★** – *Visit included in the tour of the Grands Appartements.* **Napoleon** had his suite installed in the wing built by Louis XVI, on the garden side running parallel with the François I Gallery.

**Chambre de Napoléon** (A) – Most of the decoration – dating from the Louis XVI period – has survived. The furniture is typically Empire.

**Petite chambre à coucher** (B) – A little private study which Bonaparte furnished with a day bed in gilded iron.

**Salon de l'Abdication** (C) – According to tradition, this is the room in which the famous abdication document was signed on 6 April 1814. The Empire furniture in this red drawing room dates back to that momentous time.

The François I Gallery leads to the Vestibule du Fer-à-cheval, at the top of the curved steps of the same name. This was the official entrance to the palace from the late 17C onwards. Both the gallery of the chapel and the Appartements des Reines-Mères give onto this hall.

**Musée chinois★** – ₺ ⒸOpen intermittently, check the information each day. Jun-Sep: daily (except Tue) 9.30am-6pm; Oct-May 9.30am-5pm. ⒸClosed 1 Jan, 1 May, 25 Dec. Admission included in the ticket for the visit to the Grands Appartements. ☎ 01 60 71 50 60.

This small museum, commissioned by Empress Eugénie on the ground floor of the Gros Pavillon, comes as a surprise because of the contrast between the comfortable, heavy furniture and the slender elegance of the objects on show. The collection was originally the booty captured during the Franco-British conflict with China in 1860, especially as a result of the ransacking of the imperial palace. The following year, a delegation of Siamese ambassadors completed the collection with a number of opulent presents, an event which was faithfully recorded in a painting by Gérôme.

The tour begins in the **antechamber** decorated with two luxurious Siamese palanquins. The "**nouveaux salons**" beyond are decorated with crimson wall hangings, padded armchairs, ebony furniture and objects from China and Siam. Most of the collection, however, is to be seen in the **cabinet de laque** decorated with 15 panels from an 18C Chinese fan. Note the four large tapestries on the ceiling and the huge glass-fronted cabinet filled to the brim with objects, including a copy of the Siamese royal crown.

## Musée Napoléon I★

The **museum** ₺ (🕐 1hr15 guided tours on request: daily (except Tue): Jun-Sep: 9.30am-6pm; Oct-May 9.30am-5pm. Ⓒ1 Jan, 1 May and 25 Dec. Telephone in the morning for information. ⊛3 €. ☎ 01 60 71 50 60) is dedicated to the Emperor and his family; it occupies 15 rooms on the ground level and first floor of the Louis XV wing. Exhibits include portraits (paintings and sculptures), silverware, arms, medals, ceramics (Imperial service), clothing (coronation robes, uniforms) and personal memorabilia. Thanks to the numerous works of art and furniture adorning their interior, these apartments have kept their princely character.

The rooms on the first floor evoke the Coronation (paintings by François Gérard), the Emperor's various military campaigns, his daily life (remarkable folding desk by Jacob Desmalter), the Empress Marie-Louise in formal attire or painting the Emperor's portrait (picture by Alexandre Menjaud) and the birth of Napoleon's son, the future King of Rome (cradles).

The ground floor presents the Emperor's close relations. Each of the seven rooms is devoted to a member of the family: Napoleon's mother, his brothers Joseph, Louis and Jérôme and his sisters Elisa, Pauline and Caroline.

## Petits Appartements et Galerie des Cerfs

*Guided tours (1hr15) on request daily (except Tue):* ⏱*Jun-Sep: 9.30am-6pm; Oct-May 9.30am-5pm.* ⏱*1 Jan, 1 May and 25 Dec. Telephone in the morning for information.* ✆*3 €.* ☎ *01 60 71 50 60.*

These rooms are located on the ground floor below the François I Gallery and the Royal Suite overlooking the Jardin de Diane.

**Petits Appartements de Napoléon I** – This suite comprises François I's former bathroom suite (located beneath the gallery and converted into private rooms under Louis XV for the king, Mme de Pompadour and Mme du Barry), and the ground floor of the new Louis XVI wing, situated under the Imperial Suite. The rooms opening onto the garden have been decorated with Louis XV wainscoting and Empire furniture.

**Appartements de l'Impératrice Joséphine★** – This suite of rooms adorned with Louis XV panelling was designed for Joséphine in 1808. It lies beneath the grand royal suite.

The study, with its large rotunda, is located beneath the Council Chamber (*first floor*). The Empire furniture here has a feminine touch: Marie-Louise's tambour frame, her easel etc. The Salon Jaune constitutes one of the palace's most perfect examples of Empire decoration. The gold-coloured wall hangings provide an elegant setting for Jacob Desmalter's choice furniture set off by a large Aubusson carpet with a white background.

**Galerie des Cerfs★** – The gallery is decorated with numerous deer heads (only the antlers are genuine). The mural paintings were renovated under Napoleon III; they show palatial residences at the time of Henri IV, seen in perspective. It was in this gallery that Queen Christina of Sweden had her favourite, Monaldeschi, assassinated in 1657. The original casts used to make Primaticcio's 1540 replicas of Antique statues are on display in the gallery.

# Gardens★

These consist of the Jardin de Diane (⏱ *see above*), the Landscape Garden, the parterre and the park.

▶ *Follow the route indicated on the map below.*

## Grotte du Jardin des Pins★

This rare ornamental composition carved in sandstone reveals the popular taste, copied from the Italians, for ponds,

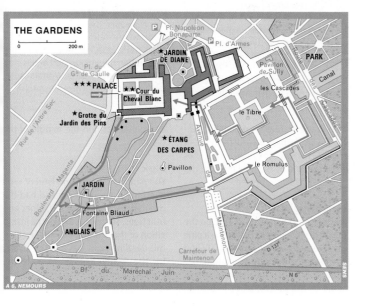

## Address Book

*⏾For coin ranges, see the Legend on the cover flap.*

### WHERE TO STAY

⊖ **Hôtel Victoria** – *112 r. de France.* ☎ *01 60 74 90 00 – resa@hotelvictoria.com* – 🅿 *– 20 rms –* ⊇ *8€.* This 19C building is a pleasant, relaxing place to stay. Most of the rooms on its three floors have been redone in shades of yellow and blue; five of them have a marble fireplace. Breakfast is served on the veranda or the terrace looking toward the garden.

⊖ **Hôtel de la Chancellerie** – *1 r. de la Chancellerie.* ☎ *01 64 22 21 70 – hotel.chancellerie@goformet.com – 25 rms –* ⊇ *5.50€.* This small hotel in the heart of the city is located in the former buildings of the chancellery. The small rooms are bright and practical and the reception is amiable. An appealing address for those on a budget.

### WHERE TO EAT

⊖⊜⊜ **Croquembouche** – *43 r. de France –* ☎ *01 64 22 01 57. Closed Aug, Christmas school holidays, Sun evening, Thu lunch and Wed.* A plain and simple restaurant in centre city frequented by regular patrons who appreciate the warm reception, the inviting dining room decorated in soothing colours, and the traditional food prepared from fresh produce.

⊖⊜ **L'Île aux Truites** – *6 chemin de la Basse-Varenne, 77870 Vulaines-sur-Seine – 7km/4.2mi E of Fontainebleau dir. Samoreau.* ☎ *01 64 23 71 87. Closed 20 Dec to 25 Jan, Thu lunch and Wed – reserv. required.* A pretty thatched-roof country house well-situated on the banks of the Seine. Diners can savour trout and salmon culled from the restaurant's fish tank while enjoying an incomparable view of the river and forest. Summertime, meals are served outdoors.

### ON THE TOWN

**Le Franklin-Roosevelt** – *20 r. Grande.* ☎ *01 64 22 28 73 – Mon-Sat 10am-1am.* This wine bar aims to please. Note the inviting decor featuring mahogany furniture and red leatherette wall seats, the library dedicated to the period between 1890 and 1920, the intimate ambience with jazz in the background and some fine vintages on the wine menu. Heated terrace.

### SHOPPING

**La Ferme des Sablons** – *19 r. des Sablons.* ☎ *01 64 22 67 25 – Tue-Fri 8am-1pm, 3:30pm-7:30pm; Sat 8am-7:30pm; Sun 8am-1pm. Closed Aug.* A third of the 130 varieties of cheese sold by this cheese shop are matured on site, including the house speciality, le Fontainebleau, a soft white cheese with cream. There is also a selection of local products. A pleasant, pastoral setting.

### SPORT

**Jeu de Paume de Fontainebleau** – *Château de Fontainebleau.* ☎ *01 64 22 47 67 – jdp-fontainebleau@wanadoo.fr – daily 11am-7pm.* The jeu de paume, a sport whose descendants include tennis and squash, has been played since 1601 in this indoor court of the Château de Fontainebleau. Visitors can watch a match or try a game themselves.

---

man-made features and bucolic landscapes in vogue toward the end of François I's reign. The rusticated arches are supported by giant telamones. The frescoes have disappeared.

### Jardin anglais★

The garden was created in 1812 on the site of former gardens (featuring a pine grove) redesigned under Louis XIV and abandoned during the Revolution. The Bliaut or Blaut fountain, which gave its name to the palace, plays in a small octagonal basin in the middle of the garden.

### Park

The park was created by Henri IV, who filled the canal (in 1609) and had the grounds planted with elms, pines and fruit trees. Sixty years before the installation of the Grand Canal at Versailles, this dazzling sight was a great novelty for the *Ancien Régime*, as were the aquatic displays.

# FORÊT DE FONTAINEBLEAU ★★★

MICHELIN LOCAL MAP 312: F-5 OR MAP 106 FOLDS 44, 45 AND 46

This lovely (25 000ha/62 000 acres) forest surrounding Fontainebleau is largely State-owned and has always provided magnificent hunting grounds. It is immensely popular with ramblers and climbing enthusiasts. The forest was damaged in several places by the violent storm of December 1999.

- **Information:** Office du tourisme du pays de Fontainebleau-Avon, 4 r. Royale – 77300 Fontainebleau ☎ 01 60 74 99 99 – www.fontainebleau-tourisme.com
- ▶ **Orient Yourself:** Fontainebleau is 60km from Paris, via the A 6, and then the N 37.
- ▣ **Parking:** There are few designated parking areas in the forest, but ample opportunity to pull off the road. Take care, however, not to damage the ecology of the area – and take your litter home with you.
- **Don't Miss:** The chance to take a walk in the woodlands
- ⏱ **Organizing Your Time:** Allow as much time as you want; the area is excellent for walking. So, take a picnic and make a day of it.

## Geology of the Forest

**Geological formation** – The relief of the forested area comprises a series of parallel sandstone ridges thought to be the result of a tropical spell during the Tertiary Era, when strong winds gradually accumulated sand deposits. The sand dunes subsequently solidified into a hard sandstone matrix and then buried beneath deposits of Beauce limestone, resulting in the preservation of the area's rolling landscape.

Where the limestone has eroded revealing the sandstone, the resultant rocky areas are known locally as **platières**.

These **moorlands** covered with heather and other shrubs are often cracked and dotted with ponds. When the sandstone layer has many crevices and holes, water seeps through and starts to wash away the underlying sands. The upper sandstone stratum is no longer supported and crumbles as a result, producing picturesque rocky clusters, the famous Fontainebleau **rochers**. **Vales** or **plains** averaging 40-80m/130-260ft in height are found where the sandstone layer has been eroded away, exposing the sand or the Brie marl and limestone beneath. The planting of conifers fertilises the soil, making it possible to grow beeches. These produce humus and are eventually replaced by oaks, the ideal tree species for a forest.

**Forest layout** – The forest is divided into 747 plots and consists of copses and thickets, moorland and rock. Sessile oak covers 8 000ha/19 768 acres, Norway pines 7 500ha/18 532 acres, and beeches 1 500ha/3 706 acres. The other species (hornbeam, birch, maritime and Corsican pine, larch, chestnut, acacia, and service trees) are reminders of older attempts at acclimatisation or the remains of lightly wooded moorland. Some 416ha/1 433 acres constitute a biological reserve.

**Denecourt-Colinet footpaths** – Footpaths laid out by the "two Sylvains" (Denecourt and Colinet) take you to the most famous spots in the forest. Sylvain Denecourt served with Napoleon's Grande Armée. He removed rocks and boulders from caves, cleared the finest beauty spots, and laid out 150km/93mi of waymarked footpaths. On carefully selected trees (see the guide book entitled *Guide des Amis de la Forêt*) or rocks, discreet blue lines topped by numbers (1 to 16) indicate the main paths. Blue letters (also explained in the guide) and stars are also used as markings on specific sights. Colinet, once a civil servant with the Ponts et Chaussées (Ministry of Public Buildings and Works) continued where his predecessor had left off. The markings were completed, after 1975, by the inclusion of white enamelled signposts bordered in green at all the main junctions.

## Address Book

*For coin ranges, see the Legend on the cover flap.*

### WHERE TO STAY

**Hôtel du Pavillon Royal** – *40 av. Gallieni, 77590 Bois-le-Roi – 10km/6mi N of Fontainebleau. Take N 6, D 116 and D 137 – ☎ 01 64 10 41 00 – ⊡ – 26 rms – ☲ 7 €.* Located next to the Hydraulic Institute, this modern hotel receives many foreign visitors in its well-soundproofed, spacious rooms. You'll enjoy taking strolls in the garden and dips in the pool.

### WHERE TO EAT

**La Marine** – *52 quai Olivier-Metra, at l'Écluse (the lock), 77590 Bois-le-Roi – 10km/6mi N of Fontainebleau. Take N 6, D 116 and D 137. ☎ 01 60 69 61 38. Closed 14-29 Feb, 15 Sep to 1 Oct, Mon-Tue .* On the banks of the Seine, just opposite the lock gate, here's an engaging restaurant whose terrace resembles the prow of a barge. Dining room with exposed beams; traditional cuisine.

**Auberge de la Treille** – *5 r. Grande, 77210 Samoreau – 6km/ 3.6mi E of Fontainebleau via D 210. ☎ 01 64 23 71 22. Closed 7-22 Apr, 18 Aug to 9 Sep, Thu evening and Sun evening .* An ancient grape vine covers the façade of this attractive country inn. The dining room is prolonged by a quiet garden terrace, to be enjoyed without moderation as soon as the sun comes out. Fixed-price menus proposing traditional cuisine.

**Hostellerie du Cheval Noir** – *47 av. J.- Jaurès, 77250 Moret-sur-Loing – 11km/6.6mi SE of Fontainebleau via N6 – ☎ 01 60 70 80 20.* Built opposite one of the city gates, here's an 18C coaching inn-cum-restaurant featuring a luminous dining room-veranda. Decorated with Alfred Sisley prints, it sets the stage for a meal of creative cooking that tends toward the sweet and spicy. A few guest rooms named after famous artists.

### DISCOVERING THE FOREST

**Caution!** The fragile ecosystem of this forest must be respected. Making fires, leaving trash behind, gathering plants, cutting branches off trees and wandering off the trails are all prohibited!

**Rambles** – Over time, an increasing number of paths have been cleared. Their markings sometimes overlap, making orientation difficult.
Grande Randonnée (GR): Red and white.
Petite Randonnée (PR): Yellow.
Tour du Massif de Fontainebleau (TMF): Green and white (vertical lines).
Denecourt and Colinet's original trail markers (blue), much older than the current ones, have been maintained on certain trails.
The *Guide des Sentiers de Promenade dans le Massif Forestier de Fontainebleau* (A Guide to the Fontainebleau Forest's Hiking Trails) is published by the *Association des Amis de la Forêt de Fontainebleau*. It may be purchased in the Office de Tourisme or in bookshops.

**Cycling** – The asphalt roads criss-crossing the forest, many of which are open to bicycles and closed to cars, are much appreciated by cyclists. A map is available at the Office National des Fôrets. Trailbikes are also permitted on certain trails.
For organised outings and cycle hire contact Top Loisirs, 10 passage Ronsin, 77300 Fontainebleau, ☎ 01 60 74 08 50 (by reservation). www.toploisirs.fr

**Centre hippique de la Marlotte** – *25 r. Allongé, 77780 Bourron-Marlotte – ☎ 01 64 45 94 04* (horse riding).

**Centre équestre de Recloses-Fontainebleau** – *R. Clos de la Bonne, 77760 Recloses – ☎ 01 64 24 21 10 – www.centre-equestre77.com* (horse riding).

**Club Alpin français, Île-de-France** – *24 av. Laumière, 75019 Paris – ☎ 01 53 72 88 00* (mountaineering).

**Rock climbing** – *91405 Orsay Cédex – CoSiRoc (Comité Défense Sites Rochers Escalade). Bâtiment 510, Centre Universitaire.*

**Orienteering** – *77300 Fontainebleau – www.toploisirs.fr. Guidance and equipment rentals at Top Loisirs (see above for address).*

**Fitness trail (Parcours de santé)** – *77300 Fontainebleau.* In the Forêt de Fontainebleau at the Faisanderie, near the Carrefour du Coq.

**"Bleau" and "Bleausards"** – By 1910, a few climbing enthusiasts from the Club Alpin Français had already begun to train at Le Cuvier-Châtillon, La Dame-Jeanne, L'Éléphant etc camping overnight near their favourite rock if necessary.

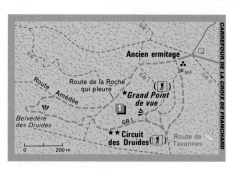

In the inter-war years, the idea of a rock climbing school became commonplace among climbers in France. Fontainebleau was the ideal spot for climbers living in Paris. The compact sandstone in the forest provides a challenge and a few valuable examples of potential difficulties: overhanging ledges, and slabs of rocks which, if there are many in succession, are a good preparation for climbs in the Alps, Himalayas or Andes.

There are more than 100 climbs marked out with arrows on the rocks. Each of them is a succession of climbs, descents and, in some cases, jumps; there are never any walks along paths.

## Driving in the Forest

🚗 Some of the roads running through the forest carry heavy traffic and turning left onto minor forest roads is often forbidden; for this reason, it is advisable, when planning a sightseeing tour of the forest, to avoid N 6, N 7 and route Ronde between the Table-du-Roi and Grand-Veneur crossroads.

## Hiking Tours

### 1 Gorges de Franchard★★

🚶 30min to 2hr on foot round-trip.

From the Croix de Franchard crossroads, drive to the spacious shady esplanade at the Ermitage de Franchard, a very popular spot at weekends. However, do not expect to find waterfalls here – no river, not even a stream runs through this gorge. Among the different species of trees, note cedar trees from the Atlas mountain range (North Africa), pine trees from Vancouver (Canada) and horse-chestnut trees.

**Ancien ermitage de Franchard** – A hermitage developed here in the 12C, and in the 13C a community moved in to look after the pilgrims. By the 19C, the pilgrimage had become a country fête held on the Tuesday after Whitsun. Today only the chapel walls remain, incorporated into the forest warden's house.

**'Grand Point de vue★** – 🚶 30min on foot round-trip. Beyond the warden's garden skirt the sandy track on the left and climb towards the rocks without changing direction. This leads to a very sandy road (route de Tavannes); after 300m/330yd a mushroom-shaped rock will appear ahead. At the plateau turn right and on reaching the rock bear left to a bench overlooking the ravine. The view of the gorge is breathtaking.

▶ To return to the hermitage, walk down three steps and bear left. This path returns to the route de Tavannes.

**Circuit des Druides★★** – 🚶 2hr – Beyond the Grand Point de Vue shown on the map, go down three steps and turn right. Follow the blue markings indicating Denecourt-Colinet path 7 which wends its way through a labyrinth of half-splintered boulders, some of them forming overhangs. At the bottom of the "gorge", cross a sandy road beside an isolated oak tree and climb back up among the rocks (follow the "÷" signs) to the "second belvedere" marked by a star.

Remain on the edge of the plateau. There is a wonderful view of the gorge and across the **Belvédère des Druides** (marked "P"). Go down to the easterly footpath and, at the bottom of the gorge, join the "route Amédée". Turn

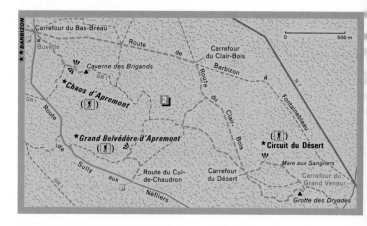

right. At the first crossroads, turn left onto the route de la Roche-qui-Pleure which climbs back up the hill and through a gap in the side of the plateau to the hermitage. (*Do not follow the path with the blue signs; it zigzags its way up through the rocks on the left.*)

### ② Gorges d'Apremont★

*10km/6mi round-trip – about 3hr 30min on foot*

Leave Barbizon by allée aux Vaches, the continuation of Grande Rue, a magnificent tree-lined avenue that was so well known to artists. This road leads to the carrefour du Bas-Bréau, an intersection near a cluster of trees now protected by a preservation order spearheaded by a group of artists.

**Chaos d'Apremont★** – 🚶 *45min on foot round-trip from the crossroads.*
Follow the path marked in blue left of the refreshment chalet (buvette) and continue up amid the rocks; at the top bear right and follow the edge of the plateau. Views are over the wooded slopes of the gorge and the Bière plain. The path veers left: a clump of acacia and pine trees marks the entrance to the **Caverne des Brigands** (*take a torch*).

▶ *Return to the car. Take the Sully road through the woods to the bare plateau high above the distant ravines.*

**Grand Belvédère d'Apremont★** – 🚶 *15min on foot.* About 1 700m/1mi from the crossroads called Le Bas-Bréau, park at the junction with the "road" to

Le Cul-de-Chaudron. Progress along the plateau and turn left onto the path with blue markings. At a crossroads with a Denecourt-Colinet sign, turn right.
The path runs downhill past boulders and rocks. Bear left, remaining above the rocks. Below is the "gorge", its slopes strewn with blocks of stone. To the west is the Plaine de Bière.

254

▶ *Return to the car and to carrefour du Bas-Bréau.*

**Circuit du Désert★★ –** 🚶
*3hr 30min on foot.* This part of the forest is famous for its barren and desert-like appearance that was so well known to artists and, later, to film directors.

Take the old road from Barbizon to Fontainebleau; after 1.6km/1mi turn south onto the road to Le Clair Bois. Take the first lane on the right, route de la Chouette, over a pass and down to the Désert d'Apremont, a valley dotted with oddly shaped boulders. Bear left onto path no 6 marked in blue. On reaching the rock resembling an animal with two snouts (trail marker N), bear right. At the carrefour du Désert take the blue-marked path that lies between route du Clair-Bois and route

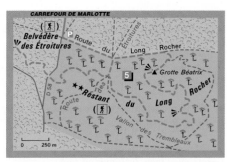

de Milan; it leads to a ravine framed by boulders, then along a rocky ledge. Immediately after the Grotte des Dryades, marked with a star, bear left and

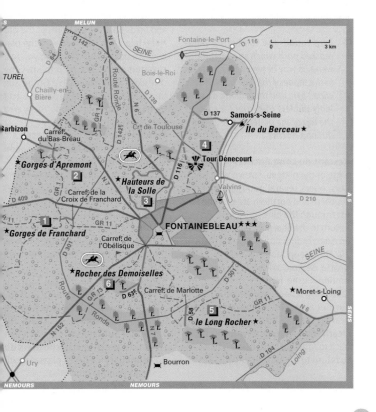

walk down path "6-6" and up the far side of the valley to the raised platform; the pond called Mare aux Sangliers lies to the left. The prominent part of the plateau offers a good **view** of the Désert d'Apremont and the Bière plain.

▶ *Return to the car via carrefour du Désert and route de Clair-Bois.*

## 5 Le Long Rocher
*1.5km/1mi – then 2hr30min on foot round-trip. From route Ronde branch off toward Bourron-Marlotte (D 58).*
Start from carrefour de Marlotte. After 1km/0.6mi, before reaching a steep slope, turn left onto route du Long Rocher, a sandy forest lane (ONF board: "Zone de Silence de la Malmontagne").

▶ *Park at the next crossroads (barrier). Take route des Étroitures (first turning on the right). After 100m/110yd, turn right onto path no 11, marked in blue.*

**Belvédère des Étroitures** – 🚶 *Trail marker U.* Admire the view of Marlotte and the Loing Valley.

▶ *Turn round and follow the blue-marked path which soon begins to wend its way between the boulders in the shade of the pine trees. It then winds here and there along a seemingly aimless route until it reaches the top of the plateau, the "Restant du Long-Rocher".*

**Restant du Long Rocher★★** – 🚶 The edge of the plateau, strewn with boulders, offers several good views of the southern and northern areas of the forest through the pine trees.
Return to the blue path and continue in an easterly direction. Leave the plateau via the steep slope which includes Grotte Béatrix. Walk past a series of boulders used for exercise by mountaineering schools (red arrows).
Further along, the path rises slightly; branch off left and take the steep, clearly marked track down. This leads back to route du Long Rocher; bear left to return to the starting point.

## 7 Les Trois Pignons★
*2.5km/1.5mi – then 3hr on foot round-trip.*

▶ *Leave from the southern end of Arbonne (junction of the Fontainebleau-Milly road). Take the Milly road but immediately turn left onto the Achères-la-Forêt road (D 64). After 1.6km/1mi the road veers toward the motorway; turn right under it. Park the car.*

Les Trois Pignons massif is an unusual extension of Fontainebleau Forest: it is a stony, barren site, unique in Île-de-France, with dry valleys, eroded peaks and other peculiarities which are common to sandstone landscapes.
From the car park go straight ahead and follow the road past two houses on the right. At the corner of the fencing, bear right and walk to the edge of a sandy depression, to the starting point of the Denecourt-Colinet path (no 16).
🚶 On the other side of the depression, directly opposite the plaque, is the first blue mark. The path crosses a flat stretch of land dotted with boulders and leads past the platform of the old Noisy telegraph transmitter to the plateau. An hour's walk will bring you to a chestnut grove. The path follows the recesses of the impressive Gorge aux Chats and continues southeast and then south, crossing a sandy, rocky area cleared of trees.
**Point de vue de la Vallée Close★★** – 🚶 The edge of the plateau offers a good **view★★** of the uplands. In the foreground, a monument crowned by a cross of Lorraine honours the local Resistance network.
The blue path then turns north and descends eastward, avoiding the wide sandy track previously explored to lead through oak coppices and heather back to the starting point.
**Suggestions for Additional Tours:**
● North of Fontainebleau 3 **Hauteurs de la Solle★** along **route Louis-Philippe★** and **route du Gros-Fouteau★** through ancient groves and then to the **Rochers du Mont Ussy★** where a pleasant path leads through pine trees;

- A round trip northeast of the town
  4 taking in **Tour Dénecourt**, a 19C
  tower offering **panoramic views**★,
  and **Samois-sur-Seine**, an attractive and once-important town on
  the banks of the river;

- To the southwest 6, pleasant rambles through the Cirque des Demoi-
  selles and to the **Rocher des De-
  moiselles**★.

# GUÎNES

POPULATION 5 221

MICHELIN LOCAL MAP 301: E-2

Guînes, now a busy cereal market town, was the seat of a powerful count, a
vassal of the English crown for more than 200 years, from 1352 to 1558. Surrounded by forests and marshland, the town is the pleasant starting point for
tours of the Trois Pays area. A "*son et lumière*" show takes place in June.

- **Information:** Office du tourisme de Guines, 14 r. Clemenceau – BP 37 – 62340
  ☎ 03 21 35 73 73 – www.calais-cotedopale.com.
- **Orient Yourself:** Guînes is 8km south of Calais, along the D 231 or the D 127.
- **Don't Miss:** the Fortresse de Mimoyecques
- **Organizing Your Time:** Guînes is a small place, but allow half a day.

## Sight

### Forêt de Guînes

The road from Guînes enters this hilly
area which is densely covered with varied species (oak, beech, hornbeam,
birch) and extends (785ha/1 940 acres)
to the northern edge of the Boulonnais
region.

The road ends at the **Clairière du Bal-
lon**. To the left and slightly set back, the
**Colonne Blanchard** in marble marks
the spot where, on 7 January 1785, the
balloon flown by Jean-Pierre Blanchard
(1753-1809) and the American physician
John Jeffries landed, having achieved
the first aerial crossing of the Channel.

## Excursions

### Fortresse de Mimoyecques

♿ ◐Open Jul and Aug: 10am-7pm; Apr-
Jun and early Sep to mid-Nov: 11am-6pm,
Sun and public holidays 10am-6pm.
6€. ☎ 03 21 87 10 34. 10km/6mi southwest by D 231 and D 249 from Landrethun-
le-Nord.

Because of its position 8km/5mi from
the coast and 150km/93mi from London,
Mimoyecques was chosen as the launch
site for the formidable V3 Howitzer,
invented after the V1 and V2, to bom-
bard London. To fire these shells the
Germans had developed enormous,
130m/426ft-long cannon. Work began
in September 1943 when thousands of
prisoners were forced to dig the 600m/1
968ft rail tunnel under 30m/98ft of
chalk, and the trenches where the cannon were to be installed. The Allied
forces bombed Mimoyecques from
November 1943, and in July 1944 a Tallboy bomb pierced the concrete roof;
this resulted in flooding which put an
end to the works.

The huge scale of the project can still
be seen, including the impressive tunnel where over 40 trains daily brought
materials from Germany.

# COUPOLE
# D'HELFAUT-WIZERNES★★

MICHELIN LOCAL MAP 301: G-3

This gigantic rocket-launching pad, built in 1943, is one of the most imposing relics of the Second World War. The site 🔣 has now been turned into a *Centre d'Histoire de la Guerre et des Fusées* (centre devoted to the history of war and rockets), which serves both as a memorial and an instructive venue.

▶ **Orient Yourself:** Situated in the Pas-de-Calais, 5 km from the town of Saint-Omer.
🕐 **Organizing Your Time:** Allow 2-3 hours for your visit

## A Bit of History

**A project out of all proportion** – Following the destruction in 1943 of the Éperlecques Bunker, Hitler decided to build a new one. The Todt organisation built a protective dome 72m/236ft in diameter and 5m/16ft thick, railway tunnels to convey the rockets, and miles of underground galleries to stock them.

**Tallboy versus V2** – In spite of the heavy bombing which lasted from March to September 1944 and involved 5t Tallboy bombs, the dome was hardly damaged but the thrust forward of Allied forces in July 1944 forced the Germans to abandon the site before the launching pad was completed. V2 rockets were launched subsequently toward London and Antwerp from mobile bases, causing heavy casualties.

**First rockets to reach the stratosphere** – Adjusted in a top secret centre headed by Wernher von Braun in Peenemünde, on an island in the Baltic Sea, V2 rockets were built by the prisoners of the DoraNordhausen concentration camp who were made to work day and night. These formidable 14m/46ft-high weapons comprised 22 000 pieces; they could achieve a speed of 5 800kph/3 604mph and reach a target 300km/186mi away. They marked the beginning of man's venture into space.

**Race to conquer space** – At the end of the war, Von Braun joined the Americans and became one of the initiators of the Apollo space programme. This signalled the start of a race to conquer space between America and the Soviet Union.

## Visit

♿🕐*Open Jul and Aug: 10am-7pm; Sep-Jun: 9am-6pm.* 🕐*over Christmas period.* 💶*9€ (children: 6€).* ☎*03 21 93 27 27. www.lacoupole.com.*

The tour starts in a tunnel through which travelled all trains arriving from Germany and continues along underground galleries intended for the storage of rockets. You then take a lift up a 40m/131ft shaft which brings you beneath the huge dome weighing 55 000t. Two exhibitions, relying heavily on audiovisual techniques (documentaries lasting 7 to 20min including rare archive pictures; laser show) present German secret weapons (V1 flying bombs and V2 rockets) and the life of the local population in northern France from 1940 to 1944.

One of the most moving sequences of the tour is focused on the last letter of a young member of the Resistance which shows up on a reconstruction of the Mur des Fusillés (execution wall) of the Lille citadel. An area is devoted to rockets and the conquest of space from 1945 to 1969 with models of Titan, Soyouz, Saturn, Ariane and a 20min film entitled *From the Earth to the Moon*.

A working model shows the firing site as it should have been; next to it, visitors can see a V1 flying bomb and an authentic V2 rocket, 14m/46ft high weighing 12t.

On the way back, the itinerary takes in the large octagonal hall, which remained unfinished, where rockets were prepared for launching (they were loaded with liquid oxygen and explosives) before being conveyed upright through two tunnels leading to two outside launching pads.

# L'ISLE-ADAM

**POPULATION 11 163**

MICHELIN LOCAL MAP 305: E-6 OR MAP 106 FOLD 6

L'Isle-Adam 🏊 has one of France's largest inland beaches, now a popular water sports centre: it features numerous facilities for yachting, sailing, rowing, canoeing etc. In 1014 a castle built on one of the islands in the River Oise was ceded to Adam de Villiers by Robert II the Pious, Hugh Capet's son. The former erected a priory on the estate.

Honoré de Balzac was a regular visitor to L'Isle-Adam and several of his novels are set in the area. In the 19C Villiers de L'Isle-Adam, the author of *Cruel Tales*, was to become one of the great names of French literature. L'Isle-Adam was also home to Henri Prosper Breuil (1877-1961), the renowned archaeologist.

The old bridges – in particular Cabouillet Bridge, a 16C stone construction with three arches – command a pleasant view of the Oise, which is still frequented by traditional rowing boats *(boat hire office on the beach)*.

🛈 **Information:** 46 Grande-Rue, 95290 L'Isle-Adam, ☎ 01 34 69 41 99, www.ville-isle-adam.fr

▶ **Orient Yourself:** Situated north of Paris along the Oise Valley

🅿 **Parking:** There are plenty of free parking areas

## Sights

### Musée Louis-Senlecq

*46 Grande-Rue (between the post office and the church). Temporarily closed for restoration.*

Housed in a former 17C school, this art and history museum displays the town's collections gathered since 1939. The painting gallery is particularly interesting; it contains the works of important groups of artists (Émile Boggio, Jules-Romain Joyant and Jules Dupré). Note the fine painting by Vlaminck entitled *Houses Under Snow*.

### Centre d'Art Jacques-Henri-Lartigue

*31 Grande-Rue.* ♿ 🕐*Daily (except Tue), 2-6pm.* 🕐*1 Jan, 1 May, 25 Dec.* ⊚*3.50 € (no charge, Wed and under 18 yrs).* ☎ 01 34 08 02 72.

Jacques-Henri Lartigue (1894-1986) was a famous photographer and a prolific painter: his foundation owns no fewer than 300 of his paintings exhibited in rotation. His style changed with time but his vigorous brushstrokes and his very bright colours are easily recognisable. The centre also organises temporary exhibitions featuring contemporary artists.

### Pavillon Chinois de Cassan

*To the northeast, along rue de Beaumont. Enter through the main gateway of the former park.*

This quaint pavilion overlooking a lake was built to adorn the landscaped park of Cassan. The estate used to belong to the financier Bergeret (1715-85), an enthusiastic art lover and patron of Fragonard; the rest of the estate has been turned into a residential area.

The pagoda, brightly decorated in red, green and saffron tones, stands on a stone base resting upon arches that house the spillway for the waters of the park (ponds and canals).

The pagoda-shaped roof is supported by a row of eight wooden pillars (a

**WHERE TO EAT**

⊜⊜ **Le Cabouillet** – *5 quai de l'Oise.* ☎ *01 34 69 00 90. Closed Feb school holidays, Sun evening and Mon – reserv. advisable weekends.* Everyone who's anyone in L'Isle Adam frequents this 200-year-old establishment. The setting, in shades of deep yellow and blue, is as refined as the cuisine. Tables upstairs look onto the River Oise; those on the terrace are very popular in summer.

*The pagoda at Cassan*

"peristyle"). It conceals the elaborate network of overlapping domes that act as a lantern and, inside, crown the room, decorated with paintings. The mast at the top of the pavilion features several tiers of rings adorned with small bronze bells.

### Forêt de L'Isle-Adam

This State-owned forest, which covers an area of 1 500ha/3 800 acres, is separated from the Forêt de Carnelle by the Presles Valley. Oak trees make up two-thirds of the thickets and copses; the remainder of the forest is beech, chestnut, hornbeam, birch and lime.

The forest was very carefully enclosed and maintained for hunting by the Princes de Conti until 1783 (reflecting this initiative, the words portes and grilles, both meaning "gate", are frequently found in local place names). Nowadays, several major roads cut through it including D 64 to Paris and N 184, newly routed to avoid the banks of the River Oise.

The forest varies in altitude from 27m/88ft to 193m/627ft. The forest is in fact a series of copses. The area adjacent to L'Isle-Adam is fairly flat. The area near Maffliers is higher and more hilly. It is crossed by a network of roads fanning out from the remarkable star-shaped crossroads known as **Le Poteau La Tour**.

# ABBAYE DE JOUARRE★

MICHELIN LOCAL MAP 312: H-2 OR MAP 106 FOLD 24

Jouarre stands on a hilltop high above the last loop of the River Petit Morin before it flows into the Marne. The town already had two abbeys in the 7C. The monastery was short-lived, but the convent adopted the Benedictine rule and survived. It soon acquired a prestigious reputation and the great ladies of France, among them Madeleine d'Orléans, François I's half-sister, were flattered to receive the title of abbess. In 1572, during the Wars of Religion, one of the abbesses, *Charlotte de Bourbon* was attracted by the new Calvinist ideas. She fled from Jouarre with several nuns and a handsome sum of money and renounced the Catholic religion. She later married William of Nassau, the founder of the Dutch Republic.

Badly damaged during the Hundred Years War, the abbey was rebuilt several times, particularly in the 18C. When the abbey was seized during the Revolution, it was the residence of a fervent, united religious community, close observers of monastic rules and widely praised by Jacques Bossuet. The monastery resumed its activity c 1837.

- **Information:** ☎ 01 60 22 06 11. http://perso.orange.fr/abbayejouarre
- **Orient Yourself:** Just under 1hr from Paris via the autoroute A4 (leave at the exit for St Jean les deux Jumeaux) -then take the RN3 (direction La Ferté sous Jouarre), and then D 402.
- **Organizing Your Time:** Allow two hours for your visit.

## Visit

⊙ *Daily (except Tue), 9.45am-12.15pm, 2.30-6pm (5.30pm in winter); Sun and public holidays 10.15am-12.15pm and 2.30-6pm.* ⊛ *4.50 €.* ☎ *01 60 22 06 11.*

### Tower

Only the tower remains from the old medieval sanctuary; it once served as bell tower and porch to the 12C Romanesque church. The interior has been carefully restored: three vaulted rooms, furnished by Madeleine d'Orléans in the 16C, house abbey memorabilia (note the armorial bosses) and temporary exhibitions.

### Crypt★

*Guided tours (30min); daily (except Tue): Apr to Sep: 10.15-11.15am, 2.15pm, 3.15pm, 4.15pm, 5.15pm; Nov to end Mar (also closed Mon): 10.15-11.15am, 2.15pm, 3.15pm, and 4.15pm.* ⊙ *Closed 1 Jan, 1 May, 1 and 11 Nov, 25 and 26 Dec.* ⊛ *4.50€.* ☎ *01 60 22 64 54. The crypt*

---

## Address Book

### WHERE TO STAY

⊖ **Plat d'Étain** – *77260 La Ferté-sous-Jouarre – 4.5km/2.7mi N of the abbey via D 402.* ☎ *01 60 22 06 07 – hotel-le-plat-d-etain@wanadoo.fr. Closed 1-12 Oct, 17-31 Dec, Sun evening and Fri –* ℗ *– 18 rms –* ⊇ *6 € – restaurant* ⊖. While this inn, a stone's throw from the abbey was built in 1840, its rooms are up to date. A pewter plate (*plat d'étain*) adorns the wall of the charming, faintly outmoded dining room. Traditional fare.

### WHERE TO EAT

⊖⊖ **Le Bec Fin** – *1 quai des Anglais, 77260 La Ferté-sous-Jouarre.* ☎ *01 60 22 01 27. Closed Sun evening, Tue evening and Mon – reserv. advisable weekends.* This restaurant, ideally located near the River Marne and the Charles-de-Gaulle bridge, is popular with the locals. The delightfully 'retro' decor and excellent reception accompany traditional cuisine with an accent on seafood.

lies behind the parish church, at the end of place St-Paul. The square presents an imposing 13C cross resting on a stone base with the Virgin and Child in the centre of a four-lobed medallion. The crypt consists of two formerly underground chapels which were linked in the 17C.

**Crypte St-Paul**, the mausoleum of the founding family, is considered to be one of the oldest religious monuments in France.

The crypt is divided into three aisles by two rows of

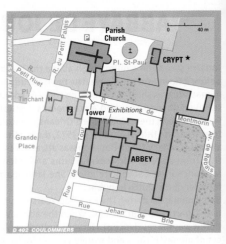

three columns dating from Gallo-Roman times, made of marble, porphyry or limestone. It is believed that the capitals were made of white marble from the Pyrenees. The famous Merovingian wall near the entrance presents a primitive stone mosaic with geometric motifs (oblongs, squares, diamonds etc). The most striking sarcophagus is the Tomb of St Agilbert, Bishop of Dorchester and later of Paris, the brother of Abbess Theodechilde; Christ sits enthroned, surrounded by the Chosen Few with upraised arms. One of the galleries affords a good view of the bas-relief at the head: Christ circled by the four Evangelists' symbols (man, lion, bull, eagle). The tomb of St Osanne – an Irish princess who allegedly died in Jouarre – presents a 13C recumbent figure. The most elaborate decoration is that of the sarcophagus of Theodechilde, the first abbess of Jouarre. A display of large cockleshells adorns a Latin inscription in honour of the wise Virgins.

The **crypte St-Ébrégésile** is a small Romanesque church beyond the first crypt. An archaeological dig carried out in 1989 revealed that it had been built between Merovingian walls. The capitals in the crypt are also Merovingian, as is Bishop Ebrégésile's sarcophagus, which was discovered in 1985 to the left of the altar.

Recent excavations have revealed the nave of the modest St-Ébrégésile Church, along with several Merovingian sarcophagi.

## Musée Briard

◐ *Open Apr-Oct:* 🚶 *guided tours (30min) daily (except Tue) 10am-noon, 2-6pm; Nov-Mar: daily (except Tue) 10am-noon, 2-5pm.* ◐ *Closed 1 Jan, 1 May, 1 and 11 Nov, 25 and 26 Dec.* 🎫*2.50€.* ☏ *01 60 22 64 54.*

Above these two crypts, a former chapel (17C) houses the museum which displays exhibits relating to regional folklore and history: costumes, tools, paintings, etc.

## Église Paroissiale

*Enter by the south transept (see plan) at the end of the cul-de-sac.*

This was rebuilt after the Hundred Years War and completed in the early 16C.

The north arm of the transept features a 16C Entombment (studio of Michel Colombe), a 15C *Pietà* and two reliquaries (12C and 13C) covered in silver-gilt with enamels, cabochons and filigree work. The south aisle contains a 16C statue of Our Lady of Jouarre.

# Excursion

## Doue

*10km/6.2mi southeast of Jouarre.*

Doue hill (181m/594ft) offers a view of the Plateau de la Brie des Morins in the distance. The squat nave of the **Église St-Martin** contrasts with its lofty Gothic chancel and transept. Inside, note the luminosity of the chancel with its openwork design, characteristic of the Early Gothic style (13C).

# JOUY-EN-JOSAS

POPULATION 8 042

MICHELIN LOCAL MAP 311: J-3 OR MAP 106 FOLD 30

This town has retained a noble appearance owing to the neat, tidy houses and the substantial estates, partly preserved after being ceded to various research and academic centres. The village was once a secluded spot favoured by memorable visits from Victor Hugo. In rue Victor-Hugo, a plaque indicates the small house rented by the poet for his mistress Juliette Drouet in 1835. His stay here inspired the writing of *Olympio*.

The former French President Léon Blum and the bacteriologist Professor Albert Calmette, who discovered the vaccine against tuberculosis, are buried in Jouy cemetery.

- 🛈 **Information:** 29 bis av. Jean-Jaurès, 78350 Jouy-en-Josas, ☎ 01 39 56 62 69.
- ▶ **Orient Yourself:** 6km south-east of Versailles.
- 🅿 **Parking:** Limited parking opportunity in town centre (charged)
- 🐾 **Don't miss** The Musée Français de la Photographie
- 🕘 **Organizing Your Time:** Allow an hour or so for each museum, but if you have little time, visit the photographic museum first.

## A Bit of History

### A textile centre

In the 17C, printed cotton was imported from India, thus posing a serious threat to local manufacturers who obtained from Louis XIV a ban on printed material. The ban was lifted in 1759 and a year later, at the age of 22, **Christophe-Philippe Oberkampf** founded his first textile workshop, specialising in a type of printed calico known as *toile de Jouy*. In 1783 the factory became the Royal Works; business thrived. Oberkampf recruited his first skilled workers in Switzerland, and they in turn trained new apprentices. Showing a great interest in scientific advancement and modern machinery, this gifted manufacturer employed up to 1 300 workers, a remarkably high number for the time.

However, the Napoleonic Wars, the foreign invasion and the advent of competition dealt a deathblow to the Royal Works. In 1843 the company was forced to file a petition for bankruptcy and the factory was demolished twenty years later.

## Sights

### Musée de la Toile de Jouy★

♿ *54 rue Charles-de-Gaulle.* 🕘*Open daily (except Mon) 11am-6pm.* 🕘*Closed 1 Jan.* *4.50 €.* ☎ *01 39 56 48 64.*

The museum is housed in the 19C Château de l'Églantine, close to the site of the former manufacture. The rooms on the ground floor contain displays explaining the techniques used and the history of this famous product. Copper plates and cylinders or blocks of wood were used to print the pattern on the fabric. The Salon d'Oberkampf has been reconstructed with waxwork figures, some superb pieces of furniture stamped with the name of the cabinetmaker (Jacob), Jouy hangings and family portraits.

On the first floor are some fine showcases containing dresses, shawls and panels dating from the 18C and 19C. Floral motifs and pastoral scenes were the first to become fashionable, then came antique motifs. Note the various sets of bedclothes. The museum shop sells interesting reproductions of the original patterns.

### Maison de Jeanne et Léon Blum

*4 rue Léon-Blum.* 🕘*Open May, Jun, Sep and Oct: Sun and public holidays 2-5pm.* *4€.* ☎ *01 30 70 68 46.*

*Toile de Jouy*

Musée de la Toile de Jouy

This was the home that the former French president acquired in 1945 and in which he lived until his death in 1950 with his wife Jeanne (whom he had married in 1943 in Buchenwald concentration camp). Several of the rooms contain documents relating to his early days, his literary works (essays, reviews) and his role in both the Socialist movement and French current affairs. The main room houses his writing desk and most of his private collection of books.

## Excursion

### Bièvres

Lying in the valley of the River Bièvre, which flows into the Seine in Paris, Bièvres has retained memories of Victor Hugo who stayed in the area many times.

### Maison littéraire de Victor Hugo

&#9855; *45 rue de Vauboyen.* Guided tours, *Sat, Sun, 2.30-6.30pm.* Closed Dec-Feb. *4€.* 01 69 41 82 84.

The Château des Roches belonged to the director of a newspaper, the *Journal des Débats*, who held a literary salon and was a friend of Victor Hugo. The museum founded in 1991 by a patron of

the arts, Daisaku Ikeda, has been carefully restored in its original romantic style to house mementoes of the poet: letters written by Victor Hugo himself and by some of his contemporaries, hastily scribbled drafts, annotated proofs of *Les Misérables* and *Les Contemplations* and photos. There are regular temporary exhibitions devoted to famous writers.

### Musée Français de la Photographie★

*78 rue de Paris, in the direction of Le Petit Clamart.* Open daily (except Tue) *10am-noon, 2-6pm.* Closed public holidays. *4€.* 01 69 35 16 50.

The museum presents a history of photography from technical and artistic viewpoints. Some 15 000 items, including 300 Kodak cameras, and about a million photographs are on show. Exhibits range from Da Vinci's studies to the very latest equipment, relying on sophisticated technology. The crucial discoveries of Nicéphore Niepce, who took the first photograph on 5 May 1816, are explained, as are Daguerre and his photographic process, the advent of amateur photography in 1888 (George Eastman-registered trademark "Kodak"), the invention of the miniature camera (Leica) in 1925 etc.

The museum highlights the continuous, sometimes naive quest for technical advancement, together with the craftsmanship involved; the large-format cameras are masterpieces of cabinet-making and leatherwork.

The first aerial photograph was taken in 1858 by Félix Tournachon, known as Nadar (1820-1910), from a hot-air balloon hovering over Bièvres. A stele, erected at the intersection of RN 118 and A 86, recalls his achievement, and every year Bièvres hosts an internationally renowned photography fair on the first weekend in June.

# LAON★★

POPULATION 26 265

MICHELIN LOCAL MAP 306: D-5

Laon occupies a superb **site★★**, perched (over 100m/328ft high) like an acropolis on a rock, crowning a tall outcrop of land which overlooks the plain. The Carolingian town is a celebrated tourist destination on the borders of Picardy, the Paris Basin and Champagne, incorporating a famous cathedral, and interesting sights and houses in medieval streets overlooking a wide horizon.

There are two districts in the Ville Haute: the **Cité**, Laon's original heart around the cathedral; and the **Bourg**. An automatic cable railway, the **Poma**, links the old town to the railway station in the modern town at the base of the mount.

The **Le Nain brothers** (17C), born here, evoked the life and people of Laon in their paintings, and **Louis Cotte** (1740-1815), a native of Laon and a member of the Jesuit order, was one of the founders of modern weather forecasting.

- **Information:** Pl. duParvis-Gautier-de-Mortagne, 02000 Laon. ☎03 23 20 28 62. www.tourisme-paysdelaon.com.
- ▶ **Orient Yourself:** Laon is 130km from Paris via the N 2, and just 50km from Reims by the N 44.
- **Parking:** Driving is awkward and parking extremely limited in the Ville Haute. Leave your car in the Ville Basse (*underground parking, Place de la Gare*), and travel to the Ville Haute via cable-drawn mini-metro. ⏺*See Le Poma.*
- **Don't Miss:** A guided tour of the old town.
- **Organizing Your Time:** Half a day will suffice is you just want to explore the town, but allow another half day if you want to take in the museums.

## A Bit Of History

### Carolingian Capital

Ancient Laudunum was the capital of France for a time during the Carolingian period (9C-10C). Berthe au Grand Pied, Charlemagne's mother, was born in Samoussy (northeast of Laon) and Charles the Bald, Charles the Simple, Louis IV d'Outremer, Lothar and Louis V all lived on "Mount Laon" in a palace near the Ardon Gate. The reign of the Carolingians finally came to an end with the arrival of Hugh Capet, who took Laon by treachery; Charlemagne's descendants were driven out and Capet established himself in Paris.

From the Carolingian period on, Laon became a renowned religious and intellectual centre, thanks to Jean Scot Erigène and Martin Scot in the 9C; Anselm and Raoul of Laon in the 11C, under whose auspices the "Laon School" flourished; and Bishop Gautier de Mortagne in the 12C, who had the cathedral built. In the 13C the town was surrounded with new ramparts and from the 16C Laon was a powerful military stronghold which was besieged on several occasions, once by Henri IV in 1594. In 1870 the munitions magazine exploded; over 500 people were killed or injured.

## Tour of the Ville Haute

### Palais épiscopal

The palace, today used by the law courts, is preceded by a courtyard offering a view of the east end of the cathedral. The 13C building on the left rests on a gallery of pointed arches, its capitals decorated with plant motifs. Upstairs, the Grande Salle du Duché (over 30m/98ft long) today serves as the Assize Court.

The building at the far end was built in the 17C; it contained the bishop's apartments which lead directly to the two-storey 12C chapel. The lower chapel was reserved for servants and was used mainly for the Eucharist; the upper chapel, in the form of a Greek cross,

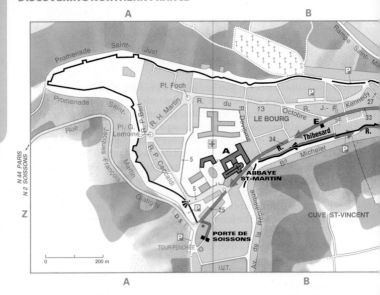

| | | | | | | |
|---|---|---|---|---|---|---|
| 13-Octobre R. du | ABZ | Cordeliers R. des | CZ 18 | Nord Prom. du | CDZ | |
| Ardon Rampe d' | CZ | Couloire Prom. de la | CDZ | Pasteur R. | DZ | |
| Arquebuse R. de l' | CZ 2 | Devisme R. | BZ | Rabin Promenade Yizthak | CZ 30 | |
| Aubry Pl. | CZ 3 | Doumer R. Paul | CZ 19 | République Av. de la | BZ | |
| Bert R. P. | AZ | Ermant R. Georges | CZ 21 | Roosevelt R. Franklin | CZ 31 | |
| Berthelot R. Marcelin | AZ 5 | Gambetta Av. | CDZ | St-Jean R. | BZ 33 | |
| Bourg R. du | BCZ 8 | Glatigny R. | | St-Just Promenade | AZ | |
| Briand Av. A. | CZ | Jacques-François | AZ | St-Marcel Rampe | BY | |
| Ceccaldi R. P. | CZ | Jur Prom. Barthélémy de | CZ 24 | St-Martin Promenade | AZ | |
| Change R. du | CZ 9 | Kennedy R. J.-F. | BZ | St-Martin R. | BZ 34 | |
| Châtelaine R. | CZ 13 | Libération R. de la | ABZ 25 | Scheffer R. | DZ | |
| Chenizelles R. des | BCZ | Marquette R. Père | BZ 27 | Sérurier R. | CZ | |
| Churchill R. Winston | DZ | Martin R. H. | AZ | Signier R. de | CZ 36 | |
| Citadelle Prom. de la | DZ | Martinot Allée Jean | DZ 28 | Thibesard R. | BZ | |
| Cloître R. du | CZ 15 | Michelet Bd | BZ | Timbaud R. P. | DZ | |
| Combattants d'Afrique | | Mortagne Pl. Gautier de | CZ 29 | Valise R. de la | DZ | |
| du Nord Pl. des | DZ 16 | Le Nain R. | CY | Vinchon R. | CZ 40 | |

| | | | | | | |
|---|---|---|---|---|---|---|
| Abbaye St-Martin | BZ | Hôtel du Petit St-Vincent | BZ E | Porte de Soissons | AZ | |
| Bâtiments abbatiaux | ABZ A | Hôtel-Dieu | CZ | Porte des Chenizelles | CZ | |
| Cathédrale Notre-Dame | CZ | Maison des Arts | CZ | Prieuré du Val des | | |
| Chapelle des Templiers | CZ | Musée de Laon | CZ | Écoliers et Refuge de | | |
| Citadelle | DZ | Palais épiscopal | CZ | l'Abbaye du Val-St-Pierre | CZ K | |
| Cloître | CZ B | Porte d'Ardon | CZ | Rempart du Midi | CZ | |

served for religious ceremonies in the bishop's presence.

The **Maison des Arts et loisirs** (⊙open daily (except Sun and Mon, and during events) 1.30-6pm. ⊙closed from mid Jul to end Aug and public holidays. No charge. ☏ 03 23 26 30 30) opposite the palace, opened in 1971. It stands on the site of the third hospital founded in the 13C. The cultural centre comprises an exhibition hall, reading room, theatre, meeting rooms and a function or conference room.

In rue Sérurier no 53 has a 15C entrance and no 33 bis incorporates the 18C door of the old town hall. The 16C-17C Dau-

phin Inn, at no 7-11 rue au Change, still has its beautiful wooden gallery.

### Cathédrale Notre-Dame★★

Laon boasts one of the oldest Gothic cathedrals in France; it was begun in the 12C and completed in about 1230. The cathedral's main features are the traces of Romanesque architecture evident in its structure, in common with the cathedrals of Noyon and Soissons. These traces may be seen in the lantern tower and galleries, in the shape of some of the rounded arches and in the style of many capitals. There were originally seven towers: two on the west

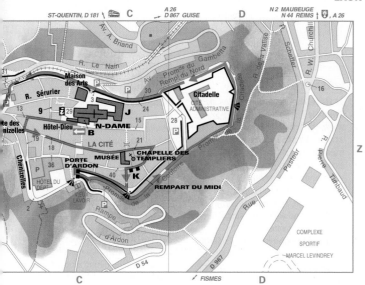

front, one over the transept crossing and four on the transept arms, two of which lost their spire during the Revolution.

The west front is one of the loveliest and most unusual in existence. The beautifully balanced appearance is due to the three deep porches decorated with majestic statuary (reworked in the 19C) and in particular the famous towers (56m/184ft tall).

The towers, imposing yet light in appearance, are pierced by large bays and framed by slender turrets. They bear great oxen on their corners, recalling the legend of the ox which appeared miraculously to help a struggling team of yoked oxen working on repairs to the cathedral. The two towers of the transept arms are built in the same way (60m/196ft and 75m/246ft).

**Interior** – The interior is 110m/360ft long, 30m/98ft wide and 24m/78ft high (Notre-Dame de Paris: 130m/426ft, 45m/147ft, 35m/114ft). The **nave**★★★ roofed with sexpartite vaulting, rises to a magnificent height through four levels: great arches, galleries, a blind triforium and a clerestory. Beyond the nave, the wide chancel terminates in a flat east end, as in Cistercian churches.

The transept crossing offers a good view of the nave, chancel, transept arms and the Norman-style lantern tower (40m/131ft high). Beautiful 13C stained-glass windows grace the apse's lancet bays and rose window, dedicated to the Glorification of the Church; the rose window in the north transept also contains 13C stained glass representing the Liberal Arts. Note the chancel railings and the organ dating from the 17C.

Leave the cathedral by the south transept and follow the outer wall of the cloisters, which are decorated with a frieze of sculpted foliage; on the corner is an Angel with a sundial.

## Hôtel-Dieu

In the past the bays and wide tierce-point arches of the 12C two-storey former hospital opened onto the street; today they are bricked up. The building has retained its great Gothic ward with three aisles that now houses the tourist office, and the room on the ground floor called the Passers-by Room.

▶ *Follow rue Châtelaine, then one of the two lanes on the left leading to rue des Cordeliers. Cross place des Frères-Lenain and continue along rue G.-Ermant.*

## Chapelle des Templiers★

🕐 *Open Tue–Sun Jun–Sep 9am–6pm (Sat, Sun and public holidays, 11am–6pm); Oct–May: 9am-6pm (Sat, Sun and*

## Address Book

*For coin ranges, see the Legend on the cover flap.*

### WHERE TO STAY

**Hôtel du Commerce** – *11 pl. des Droits-de-l'Homme. 03 23 79 57 16 – www.hotel-commerce-laon.com – P – 24 rms – 5€.* Located a stone's throw from the train station, this unpretentious establishment is very convenient for vacationers who travel by train; those who arrive by car will appreciate the hotel garage. The rooms, simply furnished and well maintained, have just been renovated.

**Hôtel Les Chevaliers** – *3 r. Sérurier. 03 23 27 17 50.* Originally built in the Middle Ages, this skilfully restored residence was given a new lease on life when it opened as a hotel. The stones, bricks, beams, cosy décor and hospitable welcome combine to give it the personality and charm of a homely guesthouse.

**Hostellerie Saint Vincent** – *Av. Charles-de-Gaulle b 03 23 23 42 43 – www.stvincent-laon.com. Closed Christmas period – P – 47 rms – 7.50€ – restaurant .* A modern motel at the base of the upper town; spacious rooms, and restaurant serving Alsacienne cuisine.

### WHERE TO EAT

**Bistrot Le Saint-Amour** – *45 bd Brossolette. 03 23 23 31 01 – w.marc. zorn@wanadoo.fr. Closed 23-29 Feb, 21-28 Apr, 4-17 Aug, Sat lunch, Mon evening and Sun except public holidays.* This lovely, simple little bistro is a real pleasure if you don't mind dining elbow-to-elbow. Express formula and bistro-style cuisine in keeping with the ambience.

---

*public holidays, 2-6pm).* Closed 1 Jan, 1 May, 14 Jul, 25 Dec. 03 23 20 19 87. The building recalls the Temple commandery founded here in the 12C which, after the order was suppressed, passed on to the Knights of St John of Jerusalem. A peaceful flower garden has replaced the Knights Templar's cemetery, but the Romanesque chapel has been preserved; it is octagonal with a gabled bell tower and a small chancel with a semicircular apse. The porch and the gallery were added in the 13C and 14C. The interior houses two statue-columns of prophets removed from the west front of the cathedral, and the 14C recumbent effigy of **Guillaume de Harcigny**, Charles VI's doctor and a forerunner of psychoanalysis in France.

▶ *On leaving, turn right onto rue G Ermant and round onto rue Vinchon.*

The street is lined with old houses: no 44 was the 13C Val des Écoliers Priory (15C chapel and 18C portal) and no 40 the Val-St-Pierre Abbey refuge (15C-16C).

### Rempart du Midi and Porte d'Ardon★

The 13C Porte d'Ardon or Porte Royée (belonging to the roi, the king in French), stands at the end of the south ramparts, flanked by watchtowers with pepper-pot roofs; the gate overlooks a picturesque old public wash-house and drinking trough.

The south ramparts end in a **citadel** built for Henri IV by Jean Errard; walk round it along Promenade de la Citadelle which offers views of the plain dotted with other, small Tertiary Age hillocks.

▶ *Continue to the St Rémi rampart, turn left toward place du Général-Leclerc. Walk along rue du Bourg, rue St-Jean and rue St-Martin.*

### Hôtel du Petit St-Vincent

The building was constructed in the first half of the 16C as the town refuge for St Vincent's Abbey, which was outside the ramparts. The main body of the Gothic building by the road is surrounded by turrets and flanked with an entrance vault surmounted by a chapel.

A later wing set at right angles over-looks the courtyard.

## Abbaye St-Martin★

🕭 *Guided tours available Jul-Aug, 2-6pm. ☎ 03 23 20 28 62.*

This 12C-13C former Premonstratensian abbey church, restored after the fire in 1944, is a beautiful example of the Early Gothic style. The square offers a good general view; note the long, Roman-esque-looking nave, the height (35m/114ft) and arrangement of the two towers at the corner of the nave and the transept (Rhenish influence), and the tall south transept with its rose window and arcades.

The west front soars up, pierced by a great bay; its gable is decorated with a high-relief carving of St Martin sharing his cloak with a pauper. The tympana over the side doors depict the Decapitation of John the Baptist (*right*) and the Martyrdom of St Lawrence, who was roasted alive (*left*).

**Interior** – The chancel and the transept chapels have flat east ends, following Cistercian custom. Recumbent figures lie near the entrance: Raoul de Coucy, a Laon Knight (late 12C) and Jeanne de Flandre, his sister-in-law, abbess of Sauvoir-sous-Laon (14C). The wooden panels in the nave are in the Louis XV style and those in the chancel Louis XIII. A 16C Christ of Compassion stands to the right of the Chapelle St-Eloi, separated from the church by a Renaissance stone screen.

**Abbey buildings** – The restored 18C section, visible from the cloisters, houses the library (*bibliothèque*). A fine elliptical stone staircase leads to the first floor.

## Porte de Soissons★

The gate was built in the 13C from quarried stone and reinforced with round towers. It stands in a park containing a monument to Marquette (1637-75), a Jesuit from Laon who discovered the Mississippi River. A curtain wall links the gate to the great **Tour Penchée** or leaning tower, so-named following subsidence.

**Rue Thibesard** follows the sentry path along the ramparts, offering unusual **views**★ of the cathedral; its towers rise above the old slate roofs with their red-brick chimneys.

Continue along the ramparts and **rue des Chenizelles**, an old, cobbled street, to the 13C **Porte de Chenizelles**. The two towers create a narrow passageway through to rue du Bourg.

## Le Poma Funicular Railway

Driving is awkward and parking extremely limited in the Ville Haute. Travel to the upper town via cable-drawn mini-metro, Le Poma. ◐*Open Mon-Sat 7am-8pm (Jul-Aug: Sun 2.30pm-7pm).* ◐*Closed public holidays.* ✺*1€. Information: station (gare).* ☎*03 23 79 07 59. www.tul-laon.net.*

# Additional Sight

## Musée d'Art et d'Archéologie de Laon★

◐*Open daily (except Mon): Jun-Sep: 11am-6pm; Oct-May: 2-6pm.* ◐*Closed 1 Jan, 1 May, 14 Jul, 25 Dec.* ✺*3.40€; no charge Sun (Oct-Mar).* ☎ *03 23 20 19 87. http://perso.orange.fr/musee.laon.*

The archaeological collection is remarkable: Greek art including 1 700 vases, terracotta figurines and sculptures (3C BC Greek head of Alexander the Great). Local finds are also displayed: bronzes and ceramics, Merovingian and Gallo-Roman jewellery.

Several rooms are devoted to painting: works by the Master of the Rohan Hours, the Le Nain brothers, Desportes and Berthélemy (18C).

# LILLE★★

POPULATION 226 800 – METROPOLITAN AREA 1 000 900
MICHELIN LOCAL MAP 302: G-4

Lille, the lively capital of French Flanders, today enjoys a role as a regional and European metropolis owing to its location on major north-south and east-west routes. This lively convivial city has acquired a new lease on life and successfully combines a definite high-tech appeal with its splendid Baroque style.

🛈 **Information:** Palais Rihour, pl. Rihour, 59000 Lille, ☎ 0 891 562 004. www.lilletourism.com.

▶ **Orient Yourself:** 140 miles north of Paris, via the A 1, or 70 miles west via the A 27 from Brussels

🅿 **Parking:** Plenty of car parks in the centre of the city, but these fill up early. Try the parking areas around the TGV station.

☺ **Don't Miss:** A walk in the Bois de Boulogne and around the Citadelle; take time out to explore the Old Town

🕓 **Organizing Your Time:** To get a feel for Lille you will need a few days here, but they will be days well spent. If you have limited time, just explore the Old Town.

**Kids** **Especially for Kids:** The zoo in the Bois de Boulogne

## A Bit of History

### Life in Lille

The typical Lille citizen is reliable and hardworking, but also a *bon vivant* who likes his food and appreciates a beer. Place du Général-de-Gaulle, the pedestrianised place Rihour and nearby streets, particularly rue de Béthune with its numerous cinemas, are always lively.

### Cultural Activity

Lille is now a major cultural centre following the establishment of a philharmonic orchestra, the opening of Opéra du Nord in Lille, the lyric workshop in Tourcoing, the Northern France Ballet Company and the institution of several theatre companies such as the Théâtre du Nord. Several cultural festivals take place here every year; the autumn festival includes concerts, fine arts, and theatre and dance performances.

### Folklore

Folklore still plays an active part in the city, as it does in much of northern France; every district of Lille has its own feast day (*ducasse*). Lille's **giants, Phinaert** and **Lydéric**, are paraded through the streets on holidays. According to legend, in about AD 600 a highwayman

called Phinaert lived in a château where Lille stands today. One day the highwayman attacked the Prince of Dijon and his wife as they were on their way to England; the prince was killed, but his wife was able to escape. Some time later she gave birth to a boy whom she put into hiding, before being caught herself by the highwayman. The baby was taken in by a hermit who baptised him Lydéric and had him suckled by a doe. Once grown to manhood, Lydéric vowed to avenge the death of his parents; he challenged Phinaert to a fight and slew the highwayman. He then married the sister of King Dagobert and was entrusted with protecting the Flemish forests which had belonged to Phinaert.

### The town's new look

Successful efforts over several years to preserve and restore the lovely 17C and 18C buildings and monuments of the old district have turned Lille into an attractive artistic city; at the same time, much modernisation has taken place: the rebuilding of the district known as St-Sauveur and of the Forum; the creation of Villeneuve-d'Ascq and Euralille.

### The "Dallas" of northern France

Owing to its location at the centre of a network of major routes and waterways,

*Lille – Grand'Place*

Lille has always been industrially and commercially important. The town is more than ever the economic centre of northern France. Business facilities (conference centre), traditional industries (textiles, mechanics), computer and technology giants, food production companies and research laboratories all co-exist here, side by side with the universities.

The metropolis of Lille is at the heart of a highly developed network of motorways leading to Paris, Brussels, Dunkirk and Antwerp; further, it has the third largest river port in France and an international airport at Lesquin.

The rail network uses the modernistic Lille-Europe station, built to cater to high-speed trains and the Eurostar service to London and Brussels.

The city boasts the world's most modern metro, the **VAL**, an entirely automatic system. One line links Lille to Roubaix-Tourcoing.

## A Turbulent History

Lille has had a turbulent history having been sometimes Flemish, sometimes French, sometimes under Austrian or Spanish control. The city has faced 11 sieges and destruction many times.

### The Counts of Flanders

The name "l'Isle" (pronounced Lille) first appeared in 1066, in the charter of a donation to the collegiate church (*collégiale St-Pierre*) by Baudoin V, Count of Flanders, who owned a château on one of the islands in the River Deule. The town developed around this château and a port that once existed on the site of the present avenue du Peuple-Belge. Although a French vassal, Flanders was linked, at least economically, with England and the Holy Roman Empire. Faced with Philip Augustus' claims on the northern regions, a coalition was formed which included the counts of Boulogne, Hainaut and Flanders, King John of England and the Holy Roman Emperor Otto IV. The **Battle of Bouvines**, the first great French victory, concluded this war on 27 July 1214. Ferrand was imprisoned in the Louvre, while Jeanne governed Lille.

### The dukes of Burgundy and the Spanish

The marriage of Marguerite of Flanders to Philip the Bold in 1369 made Flanders part of the duchy of Burgundy. The presence of the dukes stimulated trade. **Philip the Good** (1419-67) had Rihour Palace built, where he made the "Pheas-

*Joust on the Deûle*

Médiathèque municiple Jean Lévy

ant Vow" in 1454 promising to leave for the crusades.

The marriage of Marie of Burgundy, daughter of Charles the Bold, to Maximilian of Austria in 1477 brought the duchy of Burgundy, including Flanders, under Hapsburg control; the duchy later became Spanish when Charles V of Spain became emperor.

After the Wars of Religion, gangs of peasants in revolt devastated the countryside and sacked the churches. Lille escaped the assault of the "Howlers" (*Hurlus*) thanks only to the inhabitants' energetic defence, led by the innkeeper **Jeanne Maillotte**.

### Traditional economy

During the Middle Ages Lille became famous for its clothmaking; later the high-warp weavers who had been forced out of Arras by Louis XIV came to establish their tapestry workshops here.

Lille devoted itself to cotton and linen milling in the 18C, whereas nearby Roubaix and Tourcoing specialised in wool. Large-scale industry came to Lille at the end of the 18C, creating an urban proletariat with its accompanying miseries: by 1846 the rate of infant mortality in the slums in St-Sauveur reached 75% and the cellars where workers laboured achieved a notoriety which Victor Hugo evoked in tragic verse.

Another of Lille's specialities was the milling of linseed, rapeseed and poppyseed to produce oil. Last but not least, the town was famous for the production of lace and ceramics.

### Lille becomes French

Following his marriage to Maria-Theresa of Spain in 1663, Louis XIV laid claim to the Low Countries, taking advantage of the rights of his wife to a part of Spain's heritage. In 1667 he personally directed the siege of Lille and triumphantly entered the city after only nine days of resistance, after which Lille became capital of the Northern Provinces. The Sun King hastened to have a citadel built by Vauban and enlarged the town, laying down regulations on the height and style of the houses.

### Lille under Siege

In **September 1792**, 35 000 Austrians laid siege to Lille which was defended by only a small garrison. Cannonballs rained down on the town and many buildings were destroyed; nevertheless, the courageous inhabitants held on and the Austrians eventually raised the siege. It is said that a barber who was shaving clients in the street used the fragment of a shell as a shaving dish.

In early **October 1914**, when six Bavarian regiments tried to breach the fortifications, Lille was very poorly defended. The town was obliged to submit after three days of bloody resistance during which time 900 buildings were destroyed. Prince Ruprecht of Bavaria, receiving the surrender, refused the sword of Captain de Pardieu "in recognition of the heroism of the French troops."

## Sights

### Palais des Beaux-arts★★★

    *Open daily (except Tue) 10am-6pm (Mon 2-6pm, Fri 10am-7pm). Closed 1 Jan, 1 May, 14 Jul, 1st Sat-Sun in Sep, 1 Nov, 25 Dec. 5€. ☎ 03 20 06 78 00.* The art gallery was built between 1885 and 1892 to designs by architects Bérard and Delmas. The majestic building stands on place de la République, opposite the county offices (*préfecture*).

A narrow building 70m/228ft long and 6.5m/19.5ft wide has been built to the rear. It contains the café and restaurant on the ground floor, the drawings section

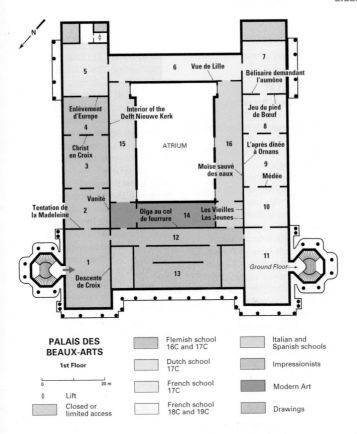

N

**PALAIS DES BEAUX-ARTS**

1st Floor

0 — 20 m

♦ Lift

Closed or limited access

Flemish school 16C and 17C

Dutch school 17C

French school 17C

French school 18C and 19C

Italian and Spanish schools

Impressionists

Modern Art

Drawings

and the gallery's offices.

Between the two buildings is the garden. The middle section has been given a glass surface that lets light into the temporary exhibition halls below.

The vast entrance hall extending the whole length of the façade is lit by two large coloured-glass chandeliers by Gaetano Pesce. There is free access to the atrium where the bookshop, tearoom and café-cum-restaurant are situated (*garden entrance in rue de Valmy*).

### Basement

**Archaeology** – Works from the Mediterranean basin: Egypt, Cyprus, Rome, Greece (three-legged toilet vase known as Exaleiptron, ceramics with black figures).

**Middle Ages and Renaissance** – The chased-bronze Lille incense-burner (12C Mosan art) is displayed in the centre of the first room. Next to it are a few ivory objets d'art from abbeys in north-

ern France such as the *Old Man of the Apocalypse* (12C from St-Omer).

The vaulted galleries contain rare examples of Romanesque sculpture, including

*Musée des Beaux-Arts – Belisarius Begging for aims by David*

Musée des Beaux-Arts, Lille

## Address Book

*For coin ranges, see the Legend on the cover flap.*

### WHERE TO STAY

**B & B (Bed and Breakfast)** – *78 r. Caumartin – ☎ 03 20 13 76 57. http://perso.wanadoo.fr/bedbreakfast-lille. Closed 15 Jul-15 Aug – ⊟ – 3 rms.* "B & B" as in Bed and Breakfast, as well as in Béatrice and Bernard, the current owners of this house built during the reign of Napoléon III. The comfortable rooms – non-smoking only – have been nicely refurbished; two of them have sloping ceilings. Cosy sitting room, breakfast room looking out onto the garden.

**Station Bac St-Maur** – *77 r. de la Gare, Bac St-Maur, 62840 Sailly-sur-la-Lys – 7km/4.2mi SW of Armentières. ☎ 03 21 02 68 20. Closed Nov-Mar – P – 6 rms: – ⊇ 6.50€.* Continue your travels while staying put by taking a room in this old train station converted into a hotel-restaurant. Fans of railway's golden years will enjoy lodging in one of the six compartments of this wagon dating from the 1930s. All aboard!

**Chez Julie** – *8 r. de Radinghem, 59134 Beaucamps-Ligny – 12km/7.2mi W of Lille. Take A 25, exit n° 7, then D 62, Rte du Radinghem. ☎ 03 20 50 33 82 – ⊟ – 3 rms.* One quickly feels at home in this nice red-brick smallholding on the edge of a village near Lille. The pastel-toned bedrooms are well-maintained; a piano, a wood-burning stove and traditional Flemish games round out the breakfast room.

**La Ferme Blanche** – *R. Pasteur, 59840 Lompret – 7km/4.2mi NW of Lille – ☎ 03 20 92 99 12. Closed 15 days in Aug – ⊟ – 3 rms.* A bumpy lane leads to this pretty white farmhouse behind an electric gate (video surveillance). The simple rooms are comfortably installed in the old barn. Small swimming pool in the courtyard.

**Hôtel Flandre Angleterre** – *13 pl. de la Gare, 59000 Armentières. ☎ 03 20 06 04 12 – 44 rms – ⊇ 7€.* Situated opposite the train station and near the pedestrian streets, this family-run hotel presents modern rooms that are comfortable and cosy. Recommended for location and affordability.

**As Hôtel** – *98 r. Louis-Braille, 59790 Ronchin – 3km/1.8mi SE of Lille via the motorway dir. Paris, exit no. 1: Ronchin. ☎ 03 20 53 05 05 – P – 65 rms: – ⊇ 8€ – restaurant.* This cubic hotel offers recently refitted rooms, all with new bedding, and a pleasant dining room in shades of yellow and black. A convenient stopover just off the A1 motorway.

**Hôtel Brueghel** – *5 parvis St-Maurice, 59000 Armentières. ☎ 03 20 06 06 69, www.hotel-brueghel.com – 60 rms – ⊇ 7.50€.* This Flemish-style house is conveniently located in the pedestrian part of town quite near the train station. The rooms have old-fashioned charm and modern bathrooms. The lift, the woodwork and the knick-knacks give the place a nostalgic appeal.

**La Viennale** – *31 r. Jean-Jacques-Rousseau, Centre-Vieux-Lille. ☎ 03 20 51 08 02, http://laviennale.free.fr – 12 rms – ⊇ 5€.* Sculpted woodwork, ceilings with gilded mouldings, period furnishings and Chinese vases. This 18C house has a deliciously kitsch appeal. The spacious rooms, each unique, are named after flowers. Lovely walled garden.

### WHERE TO EAT

**La Taverne de l'Écu** – *9 r. Esquermoise. ☎ 03 20 57 55 66.* Successively a cabaret, a brothel, then a movie theatre, La Taverne has finally found its true calling as a very lively microbrewery. Combine bustling waiters, a gay, noisy atmosphere and mugs overflowing with tasty home-brewed ale and you have one of Lille's favourite watering holes. Traditional fare plus a few regional specialities.

**Flam's** – *8 r. de Pas, 59000 Armentières – ☎ 03 20 54 18 38. Closed 25 Dec and 1 Jan.* Satisfy your flammeküche yen by ordering one in this restaurant specialising in the confection of the inimitable Alsatian tarte. The most popular tables are in the upper dining room, facing the oven. A leisurely meal.

**Domaine de Lintillac** – *43 r. de Gand. ☎ 03 20 06 53 51. Closed 2 wks in Aug, Sun-Mon.* The red facade of the building will lead you directly to this rustic restaurant in old Lille. Wicker baskets hang from the beams and the walls are lined with pots of preserves from southwest France. The plentiful cuisine of the Périgord region is dished up here.

🍺 **Le Bistrot des Brasseurs** – *20 pl. de la Gare.* ☎ *03 20 06 37 27.* The reputation of "The Brewers' Bistro," founded in 1928, is almost as widespread as that of its neighbour, Les 3 Brasseurs, and for good reason! The beer is drawn directly from the brewers' vats of this northern institution. Lively fun of the traditional tavern style; regional fare.

🍺 **Restaurant Le Lapin à Z'os** – *19 pl. de la République, 59830 Cysoing – 15km/9mi SE of Lille via D 955.* ☎ *03 20 79 48 49. Closed Sat lunch, Sun evening, Tue lunch and Mon – reserv. recommended.* This enjoyable restaurant located on the city's main square features an amusing bric-a-brac decor starring none other than Mr. Rabbit himself. The long-eared creature also has the leading role in the kitchen, where he is prepared in a variety of manners. Diners who aren't keen on lapin may prefer the mussels, served in a pot.

🍺 **Le Passe-Porc** – *155 r. de Solférino – 59000 Armentières.* ☎ *03 20 42 83 93. Closed 29 Jul to 19 Aug and Sun – reserv. required.* A bistro after our own hearts. The tiled floor, wall seats and enamelled plaques on the walls act as the backdrop for a remarkable collection of pigs. The hearty ambience and plentiful fare are in perfect harmony with the amusing surroundings.

🍺 **Aux Moules** – *34 r. de Béthune, 59000 Armentières.* ☎ *03 20 57 12 46. Closed Christmas and New Year's.* A multitude of mussels (*moules*) and a few other Flemish specialities await customers in this 1930s style brasserie located in a lively pedestrian street. A must for bona fide shellfish fans and friends.

🍺 **T Rijsel (Estaminet)** – *25 r. de Gand, 59000 Armentières –* ☎ *03 20 15 01 59. Closed first 3 wks of Aug, Sun-Mon.* A sure bet, this *estaminet* is located in a street crowded with restaurants. The appealing Flemish décor features photos, posters and advertisements, while the appetizing regional menu is presented in the form of an old school notebook.

🍺 **Alcide** – *5 r. des Débris-St-Etienne, 59800 Lille.* ☎ *03 20 12 06 95 – bigaradeasynet.fr. Closed mid-Jul to mid-Aug and Sun evenings.* In a picturesque

narrow street near the Grand'Place, this bistro, founded in 1830, although renovated, still retains its original charm. Regional specialities and incomparable mussels (*moules*) and chips.

🍺🍺 **La Robe des Champs** – *10 r. Faidherbe.* ☎ *03 20 55 13 74.* This pretty yellow and blue restaurant in the town centre gives pride of place to the noble potato and its many disguises. Whether your dish was originally concocted in Lille, Paris or rural France, your taste buds will surely be gratified.

🍺🍺 **La Tête de l'Art** – *10 r. de l'Arc, 59000 Armentières.* ☎ *03 20 54 68 89. Closed first 3 wks of Aug, Sun and evenings except Fri-Sat – reserv. essential Sat-Sun.* A charming, lively restaurant is hidden behind the pink facade of this manor built in 1890. Follow the hallway to discover the inviting dining room where denizens of Lille gather for traditional meals. A good selection of wines at reasonable prices.

🍺🍺 **Le Bistrot de Pierrot** – *6 pl. de Béthune, 59000 Armentières –* ☎ *03 20 57 14 09. Closed Sun and public holidays.* Pierrot, the colourful owner of this friendly bistro, is also a local television personality who reveals his culinary secrets on a regional station. A few Flemish specialities figure among the wide variety of dishes offered, with a nice assortment of wines to boot.

🍺🍺 **Restaurant La Cave aux Fioles** – *39 r. de Gand, 59000 Armentières –* ☎ *03 20 55 18 43. www.lacaveauxfioles. com. Closed Sat lunch, Sun and public holidays – reserv. required evenings.* Don't be put off by the gloomy passageway that leads to this restaurant housed in two 17C and 18C residences – the interior is unexpectedly warm and pleasant: brick, wood, beams and paintings by area artists. Convivial ambience; bistro cuisine.

## ON THE TOWN

**L'Échiquier** (*Bar of the Alliance Hotel*), *17 quai de Wault, 59000 Armentières –* ☎ *03 20 30 62 62. Mon-Sat 10am-1am, Sun and public holidays 10.30am-11pm. No musical events Jul-Aug.* This bar, installed in the majestic 17C setting of a former Minim convent, is attached to the Alliance Hotel. A harpist performs Mon-Thu 7.30pm-9.30pm, followed by a pianist Mon-Thu 10pm-11.30pm, Fri and

Sat 7.30pm-11.30pm, Sun 4pm-7pm. Rich selection of champagne and cocktails.

**Les 3 Brasseurs** – *22 pl. de la Gare (Opposite the Lille-Flandres train station), 59000 Armentières.* ☎ *03 20 06 46 29 – daily 11am-12.30am. Closed Aug.* The pungent scent of hops greets visitors to this brasserie, a veritable Lille institution. Sample one or all of the four kinds on beer on draught drawn directly from the tuns behind the counter. Flamme-kueches, sauerkraut and regional fare are on hand for nibblers and the ravenous alike.

**The Tudor Inn After Burn Café** – *12 r. de la Vieille-Comédie (Pl. Rihour), 59000 Armentières.* ☎ *03 20 54 53 35 – Mon-Sat 11am-3am, Sun 3pm-3am. Closed Christmas and New Year's.* An enormous sword dominates the bar of this pub specialised in cocktails, with or without alcohol. Other café highlights include afternoon teas, merry "happy dips" from 6.30pm to 9pm (before-dinner drinks served with appetizers) and "lounge cocktails" later on.

## SHOWTIME

**Useful tip**: The Office de Tourisme publishes a weekly journal, *Sortir*, listing all of the city's current events, concerts and art exhibitions.

**Théâtre Le Grand Bleu** – *36 av. Max-Dormoy.* ☎ *03 20 09 88 44, www.legrandbleu.com – ticket office 9am-noon, 2pm-6pm; performances 8pm, Wed and Sat 3pm, Sun 5pm. Closed Aug – adults: 11€ (children: 8.60€).* This performance hall caters to a young audience. Some of its events appeal to children as young as five years old, others are designed for teens. Dance, circus, theatre, storytelling, hip-hop, etc.

**Les Folies de Paris** – *52 av. du Peuple-Belge, 59000 Armentières.* ☎ *03 20 06 62 64, www.foliesdeparis.com – Tue-Sat dinner: 8pm; show: 10.30pm. Sun 1pm and 3pm. Closed Aug – tickets 39€, 49€, 59€.* This cabaret and dinner show is the area's biggest. It is frequented by a crowd of Lillois and their Belgian neighbours, especially when the work week is over.

**Orchestre National de Lille** – *30 pl. Mendès-France, 59000 Armentières.* ☎ *03 20 12 82 40, www.onlille.com – Mon-Fri 9am-12.45pm, 2pm-6pm. Closed Aug - tickets start at 10 €.* Since 1976,

The Orchestre National de Lille gives an average of 120 concerts per season. Performances are held in the Lille area, the Nord-Pas-de-Calais region and abroad (30 countries altogether). The varied repertoire, featuring performances for young audiences, original pieces, established musicians and fresh talent, exemplifies this orchestra's motto: 'taking music to all who would hear it.'

**Théâtre de Marionnettes du Jardin Vauban** – *R. Léon-Jouhaux, Chalet des Chèvres in the Jardin Vauban, 59000 Armentières.* ☎ *03 20 42 09 95. Open Easter-Oct – tickets 4.20€.* An outdoors puppet show of the Guignol tradition starring characters of local repute, such as Jacques de Lille and Jean-Jean La Plume.

**Théâtre Mariska** – *2 pl. de la Gare, 59830 Cysoing – 15km/9mi SE of Lille via D 955.* ☎ *03 20 79 47 03, www.mariska.fr. 8.30am-noon and 1.30-5.30pm. Closed Aug – tickets 5€.* Created in 1970, this marionette puppet theatre is housed in a typical Flemish residence. The company gives nearly a thousand shows a year, on site and throughout the region, plus workshops for would-be puppeteers. Impressive collection of 120 puppets.

## SPORT & LEISURE

**Prés du Hem** – Kids – *7 av. Marc-Sangnier – 59000 Armentières* – ☎ *03 20 44 04 60 – voile-armentieres@nordnet.fr – closed Jan-Feb – admission 3€.* This outdoors activities centre offers a wide range of activities, including a mini-train, a pleasure steamer, miniature golf, a farm animal zoo and a bird preserve. Water sports, swimming, fishing and pedalos on a 44ha/110 acre lake.

**Ch'ti vélo** – *10 av. Willy-Brandt.* ☎ *03 28 53 07 49. Daily 7.30am-7.30pm (Sat, Sun and public holidays, 9am-7.30pm – 1€/hr, 5€/day, 12€/week. Reservations required. Cycle hire.*

## SHOPPING

**Le Furet du Nord** – *15 pl. du Gén.-De-Gaulle.* ☎ *03 20 78 43 43, contact@furet.com. Mon-Sat 9.30am-7.30pm. Closed 15 Aug.* This bookshop, founded in 1936, spreads over 7,000m² and 9 different levels: a bibliophile's paradise. Stairs, footbridges and a number of passage-ways take you to your chosen destination: books, games, music, videos, comic books, stationery or the ticket agency.

**Leroux SAS** – *86 r. François-Herbo (south-eastern suburb), 59310 Orchies. ☎ 03 20 64 48 00, lamaisondelachicorée@free.fr* – write to make a reser-vation. *Tue-Thu 1pm-5pm. Closed Jul-Aug.* A visit to this factory teaches all about chicory – cultivated locally – and demonstrates how it is transformed into powder, liquid or special, flavoured products.

**Marché de Wazemmes** – *59000 Armentières. ☎ 08 90 39 20 04.* Tues, Thur and especially Sun mornings, the Wazemmes market takes over the Place de la Nouvelle-Aventure and its great covered market built of red brick. Food stands alternate with second-hand bric-a-brac in a merry market for shoppers of all categories.

**Rue Basse** – *59000 Armentières.* This is Lille's main street for antique dealers; you will also find other unusual shops here, such as the Bleu Natier selling furniture, decorative objects, artistic gifts and handcrafted jewellery.

**Rue de Gand** – Paved, animated and highly colourful, La Rue de Gand is well worth a visit. Butcher shops, taverns, bars and especially restaurants serving various types of cuisine line the pavements.

## VISITS AND TOURS

**Lille by bicycle** – *www.lilletourism.com* – *May-Aug: departure from Palais Rihour the 1st and 3rd Wed of the month, 3-5pm;* 7€ *(under 16: 6€).* Cycle hire available. Enquire at the *Office de Tourisme.* A guided ride through Lille's boulevards, streets and alleys.

**Tourist packages** – The Office de Tourisme, ☎ *0 890 392 004* , offers a variety of package deals (discovery, Christmas market, culture, Lille flea market, cabaret) that may include one or several nights in a hotel, a City Tour, museum admission or a show, etc.

**Tour of Lille** – A tour of Lille by mini-bus (1hr) – *May-Oct: dep. hourly from 10am to 6pm (except Sun at 1pm and 6pm, and Mon at 2pm); Nov-Apr: dep. hourly from 10am to 5pm (except Mon, Sun: 1pm).* ♿ *9.50€ (children under 18: 7.50€).* Rendez-vous at Palais Rihour. Headset commentary in eight languages. Schedule sometimes varies: enquire at the Office de Tourisme, ☎ *03 20 21 94 21.*

## TRANSPORTATION

**Lille Métropole City Pass** – This inclusive ticket gives you access to metropolitan Lille's public transportation network (Transpole) plus 25 interesting sites and tourist attractions in Lille, Roubaix, Tourcoing, Villeneuve-d'Ascq and Wattrelos. The passes are valid 1 day (15€), 2 days (25€) or 3 days (30€). Information and sales in the Offices de Tourisme of the cities cited, through the Comité Départemental du Tourisme du Nord and via ☎ *0 820 42 40 40, www.lilletourism.com.*

---

three fragments of a limestone high-relief carving representing the Deposition (c 1170). Note, in the last room, the famous *Wax head of a maiden* resting on a terracotta base (18C).

**Relief maps★** – The large hall contains the plans of 15 towns situated on the northern borders of France at the time of Louis XIV.

## Ground floor

**Ceramics** – A superb collection of 18C faience from Lille, Nevers, Strasbourg, Delft and Rouen, as well as German and Walloon sandstone exhibits and 18C porcelain from China and Japan.

**Sculpture** – The collection gives an overview of 19C French sculpture with Frémiet (*The Knight Errant*), Houdon (bust of *Le Fèvre de Caumartin*), David d'Angers (original terracotta low-relief sculptures from the Gutenberg memorial on place Kléber in Strasbourg), Camille Claudel (*Giganti, Mme de Massary*), and Bourdelle (*Penelope*, c 1909).

## First floor

The art collections are presented by schools around the atrium.

**16C-17C Flemish School** – Hermessan's *Vanity* (the museum's latest important acquisition) represents the 16C. Several characteristic canvases by Jordaens are displayed, ranging in theme from the religious (*The Temptation of Mary Magdalene*) to the mythological (*The Abduction of Europa*) or the rustic (*The Huntsman*); his study of cows was later taken up by Van Gogh.

**17C Dutch School** – Dutch masterpieces by De Witte (*Nieuwe Kerk in Delft*) and Ruysdael (*The Wheat Field*) hang with still-life paintings by Van der Ast and Van Beyeren, Van Goyen's *The Skaters* and Pieter Codde's *Melancholy*.

**17C French School** – Works by Charles de la Fosse (*The Keys to Paradise Are Given to St Peter*), Le Sueur, Chardin, Philippe de Champaigne (*Nativity*), La Hyre (*Pastoral Landscape*) and Largillière (*Jean-Baptiste Forest*).

**18C and 19C French School** – Remarkable works by Boilly (1761-1845), born at La Bassée near Lille, adorn the walls: *Le Jeu du Pied de Bœuf, Marat's Triumph* and numerous portraits. Note the charming paintings by Louis Watteau, who adopted Lille as his permanent home (*View of Lille*) and the work by his son François (*Alexander's Battle*). Other great painters represented include David (*Belisarius Begging for Alms*), Delacroix, Géricault, Courbet and Puvis de Chavannes.

**Italian and Spanish Schools** – Italy is represented by Liss' *Moses Saved from the Waters*, Tintoretto's *Portrait of a Senator* and a sketch of *Heaven* by Veronese.

The few Spanish paintings are of a rare quality: *Time or The Old Women* and *The Letter or The Young People*, two **works**★ by **Goya**, kind and cruel satirist of his period; and El Greco's *St Francis Praying*.

**Impressionists** – The end of the 19C is represented by works from the **Masson Bequest**. The pre-Impressionist paintings include canvases by Boudin (*The Port of Camaret*), Jongkind (*The Skaters*) and Lépine. Impressionism itself is embraced in works by Sisley (*Port Marly, Winter: Snow Effects*), Renoir (*Young Woman in a Black Hat*) and Monet (*The Disaster, The Houses of Parliament*). Paintings by Vuillard, Carrière, Lebourg and several Rodin sculptures complete the collection.

**Modern Artists** – Figurative and abstract works on show are by Léger (*Women With a Blue Vase*), Gromaire (*Landscape of the Coalmining Region*), Poliakoff (*Composition no 2*), Sonia Delaunay (*Colour Rhythm 1076*) and Picasso (*Portrait of Olga, 1923*).

**Drawings** – This is one of the largest collections in France (about 4 000 works) especially talian drawings.

## Old Lille★★

*2hr 30min*

The real renewal of Lille's old district began in 1965, when a few architecture enthusiasts decided to do something to recover the beauty of the 17C and 18C façades, hidden under unsightly roughrendering. The restorations progressed well and whole blocks of buildings changed completely in appearance. Luxury shops, interior decorators and antique dealers settled in the area which is today an attractive place to explore.

### Lille style

The distinctiveness of the Lille style is due to the particular mix of bricks and carved stone. Façades decorated with quarry stones shaped into lozenges (place Louise-de-Bettignies) first appeared in the early 17C; then came the period of the Flemish Renaissance (Vieille Bourse, the Maison de Gilles de la Boé) where the wealth of ornamentation reached its limit. By the end of the 17C the French influence began to be felt in the decoration of the houses and in their arrangement in aligned rows. Ground floors consist of arcades in close-grained sandstone that prevents humidity reaching the upper floors. The brick above alternates with limestone carved into cherubs, cupids, cornucopias, sheaves of wheat etc.

### Place Rihour

The main building on this square is the **Palais Rihour** (○*open 9am-noon, 2-6pm; Sat and Sun 10am-noon, 2-5pm;* ○*closed public holidays, 1 May;* ∞*no charge;* ☎*0891 562 004; www.lilletourism.com*) which now houses the tourist office. This Gothic palace was built between 1454 and 1473 by Philip the Good, Duke of Burgundy. Outside, note the beautiful mullioned windows and the graceful octagonal brick turret. The guard-room, with its tall, pointed arches, still exists on the ground floor. The chapel, known as the Conclave Room, is upstairs; the chapel for the Duke's private worship, reached

Y. Tierny/ MICHELIN
*Façade. Vieille Bourse*

by an elegant stone staircase, has traceried vaults.

## Place du Général-de-Gaulle★

To reach place du Général-de-Gaulle, take a very busy pedestrian precinct lined with outdoor cafés. On the left, note the 17C houses built in a style that is a combination of Flemish and French. This form of architecture became commonplace in Lille after the town was taken over by Louis XIV. The Grand' Place or main square has always been the busy centre of Lille; as early as the Middle Ages it was a market place. The finest building in the square is the Vieille Bourse. *La Voix du Nord*, a daily newspaper, has its offices in the building (1936) with a stepped pediment beside the **Grand' Garde** (1717), which is surmounted with pediments and once housed the king's guard.
The **Colonne de la Déesse** (1845) rises in the middle of the square, a symbol of the city's heroic resistance during the siege of 1792.

## Vieille Bourse★★

The exchange was built in 1653 by Julien Destrée, at the request of the tradesmen of Lille who wanted an exchange to rival those of the great cities in the Low Countries. It consists of 24 mansard-roofed houses around a courtyard that served in the past for commercial deals; today the houses are home to second-hand bookshops.
The profusion of decoration on the façade is due to the fact that Destrée was a wood sculptor. The caryatids and telamones on two storeys, the garlands and masks above the outer windows, and the fruit and flowers carved on the inner court are all reminiscent of a Flemish chest. Bronze busts, and medallions and tablets honouring learned figures and the sciences, can be seen under the arcades.

## Place du Théâtre

The square is dominated by the imposing Nouvelle Bourse which houses the Chamber of Commerce and its neo-Flemish bell tower. Next to it stands the Louis XVI Opera.
Opposite the Nouvelle Bourse stands the "**Rang de Beauregard,**" comprising houses adorned with pilasters surmounted by elegant cartouches. The

### AN OYSTER-LOVER'S PARADISE

**À L'Huîtrière** – *3 rue des Chats-Bossus. ☎ 03 20 55 43 41, www.huitriere.fr. Closed 22 July-25 Aug, Sun evening and public holidays.* A first-rate establishment for fish and seafood lovers which has been duly acknowledged by the profession. The fishmonger's shop with its superb ceramic frescoes adjoins the dining room, decorated with light oak panelling, lamps and wall lights with pendants. The tables are ornamented with different varieties of fish and shellfish.

| | | |
|---|---|---|
| Anatole-France R. | EY | 3 |
| Angleterre R. | EY | |
| Arsenal Pl. de l' | EY | |
| Arts R. des | EY | |
| Auber R. | DZ | |
| Ballon R. du | EY | |
| Barre R. de la | EY | 9 |
| Bart R. Jean | EZ | |
| Basse R. | EY | |
| Bassée R. de la | DZ | |
| Bateliers R. des | EXY | |
| Béthune R. de | EYZ | |
| Bettignies Pl. L. de | EY | 16 |
| Bigo-Danel Bd | DZ | 18 |
| Brandt Av. Willy | FY | |
| Brûle-Maison R. | EZ | |
| Canonniers R. des | EFY | |
| Carnot Bd | EFY | |
| Chats-Bossus R. des | EY | 27 |
| Churchill Av. Winston | EX | |
| Colbert R. | EY | |
| Collégiale R. de la | EY | |
| Concert Pl. du | EY | |
| Le Corbusier Av. | FY | |
| Coubertin Bd Pierre de | FXY | |
| Courtrai R. de | DEY | |
| Danel R. L. | DEY | |
| Debierre R. Ch. | FZ | 43 |
| Delesalle R. E. | EZ | 45 |
| Delory R. G. | EFZ | |
| Déportés R. des | FY | 46 |
| Desmazières R. | DY | 47 |
| Dr-Calmette Bd | FY | 51 |
| Dr-Legay R. du | FX | |
| Doumer R. Paul | FXY | |
| Dubuisson Bd E. | FZ | |
| Esplanade Façade de l' | DY | |
| Esquermoise R. | EY | |
| Faidherbe R. | EY | |
| Faubourg-de-Roubaix R. du | FY | 55 |
| Flandre R. de | DZ | |
| Foch Av. | EY | |
| Fosses R. des | EYZ | 61 |
| Gambetta R. Léon | DEZ | |
| Gand R. de | EY | |
| Gare Pl. de la | EY | 65 |
| Gaulle Pl. Gén.-de | EY | 66 |
| Gaulle R. du Gén.-de | EFX | |
| Gosselet R. | EZ | |
| Grande-Chaussée R. de la | EY | 73 |
| Guérin R. C. | EZ | |
| Halle R. de la | EY | |
| Hoover Bd du Prés. | FZ | |
| Hôpital-Militaire R. | EY | 78 |
| Inkermann R. | EZ | |
| Jacquart Pl. | EZ | |
| Jacquemars-Giélée R. | EZ | 81 |
| Jardins R. des | EY | 83 |
| Javary R. | FZ | |
| Jeanne-d'Arc Pl. | EZ | |
| Jeanne-d'Arc R. | EZ | |
| Jouhaux Av. Léon | DY | |
| Kennedy Av. Prés. | FZ | 86 |
| Lebas Bd J. B. | FZ | 93 |
| Leblanc R. N. | EZ | |
| Leclerc Pl. du Mar. | DZ | |
| Lefèvre R. G. | FZ | 100 |
| Lepelletier R. | EY | 102 |
| Liberté Bd de la | DEYZ | |
| Lion-d'Or Pl. | EY | |
| Lorraine Bd de la | DYZ | |
| Louis-XIV Bd | FZ | |
| Louise Av. | FY | |
| Loyer R. H. | DZ | 103 |
| Magasin R. du | DY | |
| Maillotte R. J. | EZ | 105 |
| Maillotte R. Jeanne | FX | |
| Manuel R. | DZ | 106 |
| Maracci R. | EXY | |
| Masséna R. | DZ | |
| Max Av. A. | DXY | |
| Mendès-France Pl. | EY | 115 |
| Meurein R. | DZ | |
| Molinel R. du | EFYZ | |
| Monnaie R. de la | EY | 120 |
| Nationale R. | DEYZ | |
| Négrier R. | DEY | |

| | | |
|---|---|---|
| Neuve R. | EY | 123 |
| Nouvelle Aventure Pl. de la | DZ | |
| Oignons Pl. aux | DZ | 124 |
| Paris R. de | EYZ | |
| Pasteur Bd L. | FY | 125 |
| Pasteur Carrefour | DY | |
| Petit R. D. | DZ | |
| Peuple Belge Av. du | EY | |
| Philippe-le-Bon Pl. | EZ | |
| Plat R. | EZ | |
| Pont-Neuf R. du | EY | |
| Port R. du | DZ | |
| Postes R. des | EFZ | |
| Prés.-Kennedy Av. du | EFZ | |
| Princesse R. | DEY | |
| Réduit R. du | FZ | 132 |
| République Av. de la | FXY | |
| République Pl. de la | EZ | |
| Richebe Pl. | EZ | |
| Rihour Pl. | EY | 133 |

| | | |
|---|---|---|
| Roisin R. Jean | EY | 135 |
| Roland R. | DZ | |
| Rotterdam Parvis de | FY | 137 |
| Roubaix R. de | EFY | 138 |
| Royale R. | EY | |
| St-André R. | EY | |
| St-Génois R. | EY | 139 |
| St-Jacques R. | EY | |
| St-Sauveur R. | FZ | |
| St-Sébastien R. | EX | |
| St-Venant Av. Ch. | FYZ | 141 |
| Ste-Catherine R. | DY | 142 |
| Sans-Peur R. Jean | EZ | |
| Schuman Bd Robert | DEX | |
| Schuman Pl. Maurice | DZ | |
| Sébastopol Pl. | EZ | |
| Sec-Arembault R. du | EY | 144 |
| Solférino R. de | DEYZ | |
| Stations R. des | DZ | |
| Suisses Pl. des | FY | 146 |

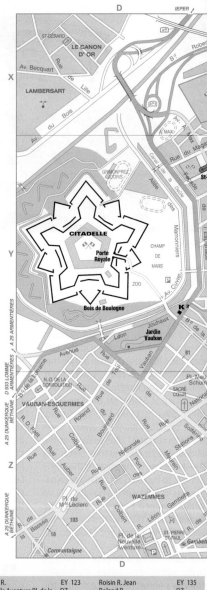

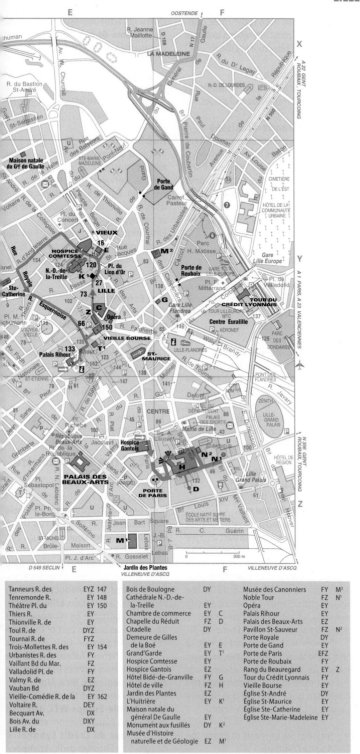

| | | |
|---|---|---|
| Tanneurs R. des | EYZ | 147 |
| Tenremonde R. | EY | 148 |
| Théâtre Pl. du | EY | 150 |
| Thiers R. | EY | |
| Thionville R. de | EY | |
| Toul R. de | DYZ | |
| Tournai R. de | FYZ | |
| Trois-Mollettes R. des | EY | 154 |
| Urbanistes R. des | FY | |
| Vaillant Bd du Mar. | FZ | |
| Valladolid Pl. de | FY | |
| Valmy R. de | EZ | |
| Vauban Bd | DYZ | |
| Vieille-Comédie R. de la | EY | 162 |
| Voltaire R. | DEY | |
| Becquart Av. | DX | |
| Bois Av. du | DXY | |
| Lille R. de | DX | |

| | | |
|---|---|---|
| Bois de Boulogne | DY | |
| Cathédrale N.-D.-de-la-Treille | EY | |
| Chambre de commerce | EY | C |
| Chapelle du Réduit | FZ | D |
| Citadelle | DY | |
| Demeure de Gilles de la Boë | EY | E |
| Grand'Garde | EY | T¹ |
| Hospice Comtesse | EY | |
| Hospice Gantois | EZ | |
| Hôtel Bidé-de-Granville | FY | G |
| Hôtel de ville | FZ | H |
| Jardin des Plantes | EZ | |
| L'Huitrière | EY | K¹ |
| Maison natale du général De Gaulle | EY | |
| Monument aux fusillés | DY | K² |
| Musée d'Histoire naturelle et de Géologie | EZ | M¹ |

| | | |
|---|---|---|
| Musée des Canonniers | FY | M² |
| Noble Tour | FZ | N¹ |
| Opéra | EY | |
| Palais Rihour | EY | |
| Palais des Beaux-Arts | EZ | |
| Pavillon St-Sauveur | FZ | N² |
| Porte Royale | DY | |
| Porte de Gand | EY | |
| Porte de Paris | EFZ | |
| Porte de Roubaix | FY | |
| Rang du Beauregard | EY | Z |
| Tour du Crédit Lyonnais | FY | |
| Vieille Bourse | EY | |
| Église St-André | DY | |
| Église St-Maurice | EY | |
| Église Ste-Catherine | EY | |
| Église Ste-Marie-Madeleine | EY | |

terrace, built in 1687, is the most characteristic and most interesting example of late-17C architecture in Lille.

### Rue de la Bourse
The street is lined with 18C house-fronts decorated with cherubs and masks.

### Rue de la Grande-Chaussée
The old arcaded sandstone houses have been renovated and now contain shops selling luxury goods. Some of the wrought-iron balconies and the upper part of the windows are very intricately worked. Note the first house on the right and nos 9, 23 (ship on the keystone of the window) and 29.

### Rue des Chats-Bossus
The street acquired its curious name ("Street of the Humpback Cats") from an old tanner's sign. **L'Huîtrière,** a famous seafood restaurant, has a typical Art-Deco front dating from 1928.

### Place Louise-de-Bettignies
The square bears the name of a First World War heroine. The **Demeure de Gilles de la Boé**★, at no 29 on a corner, was built in about 1636 and is a superb example of Flemish Baroque. The abundant ornamentation includes cornices and prominent pediments. In the past this building stood on the edge of the Basse-Deûle port, in the days when there was a great deal of river traffic.

### Rue de la Monnaie★
The Mint once stood in this street where the restored houses now attract antique dealers and interior decorators. On the left there is a row of 18C houses (note the apothecary's shop sign of a mortar and distilling equipment at no 3). The houses at nos 5 and 9 are decorated with dolphins, wheat-sheaves, palms etc. At no 10 a statue of Notre-Dame-de-la-Treille adorns the front and at nos 12 and 14 the crow-stepped gable has been rebuilt. Neighbouring houses date from the first third of the 17C and flank the rusticated door (1649) of the Hospice Comtesse (◐ see Additional Sights).

▶ *Take the passageway opposite the Hospice Comtesse.*

On the left is the impressive **Cathédrale Notre-Dame-de-la-Treille**, a neo-Gothic construction that was never completed.

▶ *Return to rue de la Monnaie and walk straight ahead along rue de la Collégiale, then turn left onto rue Négrier and rue Royale.*

### Rue Royale
This was the main route through the elegant district that was built during the 18C between the citadel and the old town. **Église Ste-Catherine**, with its austere 15C tower, stands on the left at the beginning of the street.
Fine French-style mansions line the street: note, at no 68, the former Hôtel de l'Intendance, built in 1787 by Lequeux, a local architect.

### Rue Esquermoise
The street is lined with 17C and 18C houses. At nos 6 and 4 cherubs are shown embracing or turning their backs on each other depending on whether or not they belong to the same house. Opposite is a superb restored house that belonged to a furrier (Gailliaerde).

▶ *Return to place Rihour via the Grand'Place.*

## East of the Town Centre

### Euralille
Covering an area of almost 70ha/173 acres beyond Lille city centre is a whole new urban district designed by Dutch town planner Rem Koolhaas. Since May 1993, Lille's railway station, which was renamed **Lille-Flandres**, has catered to most of the high-speed trains from Paris. Linked by a viaduct with four arches, the new station, **Lille-Europe**, easily recognisable by its huge glass frontage, was built as part of the Paris-London and London-Brussels routes using the Channel Tunnel and for the high-speed train services between Lille and Lyon, Bordeaux, Nice, Montpellier etc. Two towers span the new stations, the **Tour Lille-Europe WTC** designed by architect Claude Vasconi and the L-shaped **Tour du Crédit Lyonnais**★ designed by Christian de Portzampac.

The **Centre Euralille** was designed by the acclaimed French architect Jean Nouvel. Its spacious walkways and two floors contain more than 130 shops, a hypermarket, restaurants and a cultural centre called the Espace Croisé. It also has a theatre, private apartments, and a business school.

## Porte de Roubaix

This massive gate from the 1621 Spanish fortifications is composed of a sandstone base surmounted by a dripstone and a layer in brick. It was opened in 1875 to allow room for tramways and the moats have been turned into gardens. There is a similar gate 600m/656yd to the north, the **Porte de Gand**, reached via rue des Canonniers and rue de Courtrai.

# Quartier St-Sauveur

*Allow 1hr30min*

This former working-class district was known for the misery of its slums which inspired Emile Desrousseaux, author of the famous French lullaby *Le P'tit Quinquin (statue in rue Nationale on the corner of avenue Foch)*. The area has today been completely remodelled into a business centre around the town hall. Relics of the past remain dotted among the modern buildings.

## Porte de Paris★

This gate, built from 1685 to 1692 by Simon Vollant in honour of Louis XIV, is the only example of a town gate which also served as a triumphal arch; it was formerly part of the ramparts. On the outward side, it appears as an arch decorated with the arms of Lille (a lily) and of France (three lilies). Victory stands at the top, honoured by Fames, about to crown Louis XIV represented in a medallion. From the inner side the gate has the appearance of a lodge.

## Hôtel de Ville

The town hall was built from 1924 to 1927 and is overlooked by a tall belfry (104m/341ft). The two Lille giants, Lydéric and Phinaert are sculpted at its base.

## Pavillon St-Sauveur

This is the wing of an 18C cloister, preserved when a hospice was demolished in 1959. The brick and stone arches are surmounted by clerestory windows decorated with flowered medallions.

## Noble Tour

This keep with its truncated appearance is the only relic of the 15C fortifications; it has become a Resistance memorial. There is a beautiful work by the sculptor Bizette-Lindet.

# Additional Sights

## Hospice Comtesse★

*Open daily (except Tue) 10am-12.30pm, 2-6pm (Mon 2-6pm). Closed Jan, 1 May, 14 Jul, 15 Aug, 1st Sat-Sun in Sep, 1 Nov, 25 Dec. 2.30€ (no charge first Sun in the month). 03 28 36 84 00.*

The hospital was built in 1237 by Jeanne de Constantinople, Countess of Flanders, to ask for divine intervention on behalf of her husband Ferrand de Portugal, taken prisoner at Bouvines (*see above*). It was destroyed by fire in 1468 but was rebuilt and enlarged in the 17C and 18C. It became a hospice during the Revolution, then an orphanage. It changed again in 1939 and is today a museum of history and ethnography which also holds concerts and exhibitions.

The monumental 17C main entrance is built from beautiful rusticated sandstone.

**Hospital ward** – A long, sober building, rebuilt after 1470 on the old 13C foundations, flanks the main courtyard. Inside, the immense proportions of the interior and its panelled timber **vault**★★ in the shape of an upturned boat are striking. The ward contains two beautiful tapestries, woven in Lille in 1704. One represents Baudouin of Flanders with his wife and two daughters; the other portrays Jeanne, the hospital's founder, flanked by her first and second husbands. The **chapel**, which extends the length of the interior, was enlarged and isolated by a rood screen after the fire of 1649. The old 15C window and traces of mural paintings have been revealed on the right wall. The vault is decorated with the heraldic arms of the hospital's benefactors.

Château du Vert Bois, Bondues

*16C Bruxelles tapestry*

**Museum** – *In the right wing.* Furniture and artworks evoking the atmosphere of a 17C religious establishment are displayed in the right wing, which was built by the community in the late 15C and heightened in the 17C: the kitchen features blue and white tiles from Holland and Lille; the Baroque overmantel in the dining room frames a 16C Nativity; the sombre Louis XIV panels of the parlour are decorated with a series of 17C votive offerings in the form of portraits of local children. The prayer room is lined with Louis XV wood panelling.

The former dormitory on the first floor has carved ceiling beams. It contains 17C Flemish and Dutch paintings and a superb 16C wooden Crucifixion from Picardy. The cross-bar and main section of the Cross are decorated with medallions depicting the Evangelists. Two rooms flanking the dormitory are filled with exhibits relating to regional history: architectural features, objets d'art, and paintings by Louis and François Watteau representing Lille in the 18C.

## Maison Natale du Général de Gaulle

*9 rue Princesse.* ♿ 🕐*Open Wed-Sun, 10am-1pm and 2-5pm (last admission 1hr before closing).* ⬤5€. ☎ *03 28 38 12 05. www.maison-natale-degaulle.org.*

**Charles de Gaulle** was born on 22 November 1890 in this whitewashed brick house in Lille, where his grandfather had a lace works. The old workshop and the house have been turned into a small museum exhibiting photographs and memorabilia. On display are De Gaulle's christening robe and a replica of the car in

which the General and his wife were travelling on the day of the attempt on their lives in Le Petit-Clamart. The original car was involved in a severe accident in 1971 and was only fit for scrap except the seats, steering wheel and dashboard which were used for the replica.

## Citadelle★ (Citadel)

*The Citadelle is permanently occupied by the military;* ⬤ *guided visits possible by arrangement, call for information.* ☎ *0 891 562 004.*

This citadel is the largest and best preserved in France. It was Louis XIV's first project after the conquest of Lille and is a fine example of Vauban's genius; it is still occupied by the army today. It took three years to build (1667-70) using 2 000 men. The result was this stone-faced brick construction comprising five bastions and five demilune fortifications, which protect the moats formerly fed by the River Deûle. These defences used to enclose a real town.

The **porte Royale**, which bears a Latin inscription praising Louis XIV, gives onto a vast pentagonal parade ground surrounded by buildings by Simon Vollant: the Classical chapel, the officer's quarters and a superb restored arsenal. These stone and brick buildings are representative of the French-Lille style which developed during this period. The citadel could be completely self-sufficient as it had its own wells, bakery, brewery, tailors, cobblers etc.

A **zoo** has been established in the **Bois de Boulogne**, near the Champ de Mars; there is also a tropical house and a playground. The **jardin Vauban** on the

Deûle Canal bank is typical of mid-19C country gardens, with its clumps of trees, winding paths, flower beds and ponds. A statue of the Lille poet Albert Samain (1859-1906) stands within it. During the last two World Wars many French patriots were executed by firing squad in the outer moats. The **Monument aux Fusillés** by Félix Desruelle stands in neighbouring square Daubenton; it dates from 1915 and commemorates the Lille citizens who were shot. Its most striking feature is the nobility of the victims' bearing.

## Musée des Canonniers

🕐 *Open daily (except Sun) 2-5pm.* 🕐 *Closed public holidays, Jan to mid-Feb and the first two weeks in Aug.* ⊜*6€.* ☎ *03 20 55 58 90.*

Housed in the former Hôtel des Canonniers, once a convent. In 1804 the building was given by Napoleon to the corporation of gunners founded in 1483 and known as the Sainte-Barbe Brotherhood. The military museum illustrates the history of the various sieges Lille had to withstand, and Faidherbe and Négrier's feats of arms. Some 3 000 objects are on display: rifles from 1777 to 1945, swords, sabres etc.

## Musée d'Histoire Naturelle et de Géologie

🕐 *Open Jul-Dec daily (except Tue and Sat) 9am-noon, 2-5pm (Sun and public holidays 10am-5pm); Jan-Jun 10am-1pm, 2-6pm.* 🕐 *Closed 1 Jan, 1 May, 15 Aug, 1 Nov, 25 Dec.* ⊜*3€. No charge 1st Sun of the month, except during exhibitions.* ☎*03 28 55 30 80.*

The Natural History and Geology Museum was set up in 1822. Its collections were extended at the beginning of the 20C by two local geologists. Facing visitors as they enter the main hall are two impressive whale skeletons, the remains of creatures washed up on the coast.

The **zoology** collection on the left includes stuffed mammals and birds, reptiles, Batrachia, molluscs, fish, and insects. Dioramas are used to show French fauna in its natural habitat: huge boars, alert deer, beavers etc. The insect houses contain spiders, scorpions and cockroaches. The magnificent ornithological collection boasts more than 5 000 birds, including examples of species that are now extinct such as New Zealand huias or great auks.

The section on the right deals with **geology**. Fossils and rocks illustrate the history of Northern Europe from 600 million years BC to the Gallo-Roman period. Numerous plant fossils found in old mine workings are the remains of the dense forest that covered the region 300 million years ago. The work of miners is illustrated by a reconstruction of a coal seam, with its narrow gallery and heavy cart.

# MAINTENON ★

POPULATION 4 440

MICHELIN LOCAL MAP 311: F-4 OR MAP 106 FOLD 26

This charming town on the banks of the River Eure is renowned for its château, irrevocably linked to the incredible destiny of **Françoise d'Aubigné**. Born in 1635 to a family with Calvinist views, she was orphaned at the age of 12, became the widow of the burlesque poet Paul Scarron at the age of 25, the clandestine governess of Mme de Montespan's children by the age of 34 and, in a secret ceremony, the wife of Louis XIV at the age of 48.

🛈 **Information:** Mairie, pl. Aristide-Briand, 28130 Maintenon, ☎02 37 23 05 04.

▶ **Orient Yourself:** 50 miles from Paris, along the A 10. Access from Paris: SNCF rail link from Gare Montparnasse.

🕐 **Organizing Your Time:** Allow one to two hours to visit the chateau.

# A Bit of History

**The corridors of power** – When her clandestine charge, the Duc de Maine, was legitimised, Françoise Scarron made a public appearance at court. Thereafter Louis XIV, who was extremely fond of his son, used to see her every day. Initially, he found her a trifle pedantic, but soon revised his opinion of "the Scarron widow" and succumbed to her charm, intelligence and strong temperament.

After the Queen's death, Louis XIV secretly married Mme de Maintenon in the winter of 1683-84. The morganatic queen acceded to the rank of peer and marquise in 1688 – a privilege bestowed on her directly by the King – and from then on she became an extremely powerful figure in the country's political life.

**A Herculean task** – Between 1685 and 1688, the area around Maintenon saw one of the century's most ambitious projects: the diverting of the waters of the River Eure to the fountains of Versailles. François Louvois acted as supervisor; he left Sébastien Vauban in charge of the plans and entrusted him with the construction of an 80km/50mi-long aqueduct linking Pontgouin (*Michelin map 311 C 5*) to the Étang de la Tour.

The Maintenon aqueduct was a colossal enterprise, 4 600m/15 000ft in length with three superimposed rows of arches, placed 72m/237ft above the level of the River Eure. In fact, it was only possible to fit in one row of arches.

The operation was carried out like a military campaign; 20 000 soldiers took part in the excavation work, in addition to the 10 000 skilled workers summoned from remote villages and local peasants who helped cart the materials. The River Voise and River Drouette were canalised and used to convey the freestone and sandstone rubble from the Gallardon and Épernon quarries.

In 1689, the wars triggered off by the Augsburg League interrupted the work. The French troops, in poor physical condition, were sent off to the borders to defend their country. The work was never resumed.

# Sights

### Château★

○ *Open Apr-Oct daily (except Tue) 2-5.45pm, Sun and public holidays 10-11.15am and 2-5.45pm; Nov-Mar: Sat-Sun and public holidays 2-5pm.* ○ *Closed end Dec to mid-Jan.* ≈ *6.50€ (children: 3€).* ☎ *02 37 23 00 09.*

The present château occupies the site of a former stronghold circled by the waters of the Eure. The construction work was undertaken by Jean Cottereau, Minister of Finance to Louis XII, François

*Château de Maintenon*

I and Henri II, and completed around 1509 in the Renaissance style.

The estate then came into the hands of the d'Angennes family. In 1674 Louis XIV bought the château from Françoise d'Angennes for 250 000 livres and gave it to the future Marquise de Maintenon. The Marquise left it to her niece, who was married to the Duke of Ayen, son of the first Maréchal de Noailles. The château has remained in this family ever since.

**Exterior** – The archway, flanked by two protruding turrets and bearing Jean Cottereau's arms (three lizards), leads to the inner court which is the starting-point for tours. The square 12C keep, now crowned with an elegant roof, is all that remains of the original stronghold.

The adjoining wing was built by Mme de Maintenon and the narrow door set in the tower still sports the Marquise's emblem, a griffin's head. A door depicting St Michael and bearing the lizard emblem gives onto a staircase leading to Mme de Maintenon's suite. This consists of an antechamber, a bedroom – where Charles X spent the night on 3 August 1830 when he fled Rambouillet – and a small cabinet.

After leaving the central building, visitors are shown round the first floor of the Renaissance wing, redesigned to

accommodate the apartments of Mme de Montespan and her royal charges. The tour ends with the reception rooms furnished by the Noailles family in the 19C. The Grand Salon bears portraits of the two royal rivals, Mme de Montespan and Mme de Maintenon. In the Portrait Gallery, a collection of paintings represents the illustrious members of the family. The mortal remains of the Marquise lie in the chapel of St-Cyr Military Academy.

---

## WHERE TO STAY

🍴🍴 **Les Chandelles (Bed and Breakfast)** – 19 r. des Sablons, in Les Chandelles village, 28130 Villiers-le-Morhier – 8km/4.2mi N of Maintenon via D 116 dir. Coulomb – ☎ 02 37 82 71 59 – 5 rms. A large gate guards the entrance to this pretty farm built in 1840 and surrounded by a garden where horses graze. The bedrooms are decorated in gay, vernal colours, and their bathrooms are very nicely fitted out. Activities proposed include horse riding, fishing and especially golf – the owner, a former golf pro, now teaches the sport and can point you toward the best courses.

---

# MAISONS-LAFFITTE★

POPULATION 21 856

MICHELIN LOCAL MAP 311: I-2, MAP 101 FOLD 13 OR 106 FOLD 18

Maisons-Laffitte, a residential town lying on the banks of the Seine and on the edge of St-Germain Forest, is famous for its castle.

- **Information:** 41 av. de Longueil, 78600 Maisons-Laffitte, ☎ 01 39 62 63 64.
- ▶ **Orient Yourself:** On the westerly outskirts of Paris, in a loop on the River Seine. Access from Paris: SNCF rail link from Gare St-Lazare or RER line A 3/A 5.
- 🕐 **Organizing Your Time:** Allow 1-2 hours to explore the chateau

## A Bit of History

**Président Longueil** – The château was built by the architect **François Mansart** between 1642 and 1651 for René de Longueil, President of the Parlement de Paris, appointed Governor of the royal châteaux at Versailles and St-

Germain. The château was designed to receive royalty as it was one of the official places of residence assigned to French rulers. The palace was inaugurated during a brilliant reception celebrated in honour of Anne of Austria and Louis XIV, then aged 13. The Sun King subsequently took up residence at St-

*Château de Maisons-Laffitte*

Germain and paid frequent visits to Maisons, as did his successors.

From Artois to Lannes – The Comte d'Artois, brother of Louis XVI, acquired the estate in 1777 and gave orders to build the famous racecourse. His extravagant parties were attended by everyone at court.

**Maisons-Laffitte** – In 1818 the famous banker **Jacques Laffitte** (1767-1844) bought the estate, where he entertained the adversaries of the Restoration: General Foy, the Marquis de Lafayette, Casimir Périer, Benjamin Constant etc. Laffitte did much to secure Louis-Philippe d'Orléans' accession to the throne during the Revolution of July 1830 which overthrew Charles X. This shrewd financier was made Prime Minister to the new king in 1830 but proved unable to calm the disturbances that had broken out in the capital; mistrusted by both the Orleanists and the moderates, Laffitte was forced to resign in March 1831. Ruined, in debt to the tune of 50 million francs, he dismantled the imposing stables and used the stone to build houses in the Grand Parc.

The stables had been two long, beautiful buildings designed by Mansart and erected on the avenue du Château (now avenue du Général-Leclerc). They provided a very impressive entrance to the Longueil's estate.

## Château

*2 avenue Carnot. ⏰Open daily (except Tue): Apr to mid-Oct: 10am-12.30pm, 2-6pm (rest of year 5pm, last admission 30min before closing). ⏰Closed 1 Jan, 1 May, 1 and 11 Nov, 25 Dec. ✎6.50€ (no charge 1st Sun in the month Oct-Apr). ☎ 01 39 62 01 49, www.maisonslaffitte.net.* The château dates from the early part of Louis XIV's reign and has always been considered a model of French architecture. From the main driveway, formerly called the King's entrance – royal visitors generally approached from St-Germain Forest, to the west – there is a splendid view of the high-pitched roofs.

The façade facing the Seine is fronted by a dry moat, a terrace and the main staircase. The stone exterior presents Classical ornamentation: Doric on the ground floor, Ionic on the first floor and Corinthian on the attic storey level with the dormer windows. The alternating fluted columns and engaged pilasters form a pleasing, well-balanced composition.

**WHERE TO EAT**

🍽🍽**Rôtisserie Vieille Fontaine** – *8 avenue Grétry, Maisons Laffitte –* ☎ *01 39 62 01 78. Closed 8-14 Aug, Sun evening and Mon .* This stately manor house with three dining rooms specialises in grilled meat dishes prepared before your eyes. The veranda opens onto a small park. Good value for money.

# MARLY-LE-ROI ★

POPULATION 16 759

MICHELIN LOCAL MAP 311: I-2, MAP 101 FOLD 12 OR 106 FOLD 17

Although a number of major property developments have spread across the Grandes Terres plateau since 1950, stretching towards Le Pecq, the name of Louis XIV remains firmly attached to this town. Marly was the Sun King's favourite residence. Unfortunately, its golden age lasted barely 20 years. After the First Empire, only the park remained, an impressive display of greenery bordering the old village, which has welcomed many writers and artists: the two Alexandre Dumas, Alfred Sisley, Camille Pissarro, the sculptor Maillol and the tragedienne Mlle Rachel, to name but a few.

🛈 **Information:** 2 av. des Combattants, 78160 Marly-le-Roi, ☎ 01 30 61 61 35.

▶ **Orient Yourself:** 15 miles west of the centre of Paris, along the A 13

🕐 **Organizing Your Time:** Exploring Marly Park is what will take up your time here.

## A Bit of History

**The early stages** – Marly's construction was due to Louis XIV's desire to retreat from the formal etiquette of Versailles. After the Treaty of Nijmegen in 1678, at the peak of his glory, tired of the continual entertaining at Versailles, the king dreamed of a peaceful country residence, far from the madding crowd. His barony at Marly offered a deep, lush valley which seemed to suit the purpose and he entrusted **Jules Hardouin-Mansart** with the plans.

Mansart came up with an ingenious idea: instead of designing one huge single pavilion, which he knew the king would refuse, he conceived a series of 13 separate units. The royal pavilion would stand on the upper terrace, while the other 12, smaller in size and all identical, would be arranged along a stretch of water. To promote his idea, Mansart explained that the decoration of the king's pavilion could symbolise the sun – Louis XIV's emblem – and that the surrounding buildings could represent the 12 signs of the zodiac. To cut down on costs, it was agreed to replace the carved bas-reliefs by trompe-l'œil frescoes. The King, delighted, gave orders to start building in 1679. It took nine years for the whole project to be completed. After working relentlessly all his life, Mansart died at the château in 1708.

**Further embellishments** – Right until the end of his reign, Louis XIV applied himself to the improvement of his Marly residence and kept a close watch on the various projects under way. He would even show gardeners how to trim the hedges properly.

Behind the royal pavilion rose the steep, wooded slopes of the hillside. The Sun King gave orders to build the River, also called the Grande Cascade, the Wonder of Marly, which was served by the famous "Machine": starting from the top of the hill, an impressive series of falls poured down a flight of 52 steps of pink marble set into the terraced slope. The whole ensemble – adorned with statues, porticoes and rockeries – was completed in 1699.

The same year, the King decided to clear the main perspective and raze the hillock that stood in the way, an enterprise that occupied 1 600 soldiers for a period of four years.

**Life at Marly** – Apart from his close relatives, Louis XIV brought very few guests to Marly; the facilities for accommodation were limited to 24 apartments. It is estimated that 500 lords and 300 ladies altogether were invited to the château over a period of 30 years. The King himself drew up a list of the guests and he personally determined where they should stay; the nearer they were to the royal pavilion, the greater the honour. The "happy few" were not

**WHERE TO EAT**

😊😊😊 **Le Village** – *3 Grande-rue –*
☎ *01 39 16 28 14. Closed Aug, Sat
lunchtime, Sun evening and Mon –
booking essential.* Le Village is located
in the lively pedestrian area of the
old city, where many restaurants are
to be found. You will be delighted
by the warm welcome of the owners
and will relish the succulent,
inventive dishes.

necessarily members of the aristocracy
or high dignitaries, but lively, intelligent
personalities whose wit and charm
would enliven the King's stays.

The formal etiquette of Versailles was
dropped at Marly. The King shared his
meals with his guests, with whom he
conversed in a free, casual manner.
Hunts, forest walks, outdoor games,
card games, games of chance, balls and
concerts were a regular feature of life
here. The standard of comfort at the
place, however, left something to be
desired; in summer the guests caught
fever, in winter they shivered with cold
or choked with smoke because it was
too damp to start a fire. Louis XIV, who
personally undertook to tackle the
heating problem, introduced new systems every year, in vain.

**The end of Marly** – On 9 August 1715,
the King suffered a bout of exhaustion
after following the hunt in his carriage.

*Equestrian statue: the famous Marly Horses*

Ph. Gajic/ MICHELIN

He was taken to Versailles, where he
died on 1 September, aged 77.

Louis XV and Louis XVI stayed in Marly
from time to time. The costly Grande
Cascade was abandoned in favour of
the present "green carpet." The furniture was sold during the Revolution; in
1800, an industrialist bought the estate
and set up a mill there. Having failed in
business, he offered Napoleon the opportunity to buy Marly but he was turned
down. He then proceeded to demolish
the château and sell the building materials. A year later, Napoleon retrieved
the estate which has since been the
property of the French State.

# Marly Park★★

▶ *Enter Marly Park by the Deux Portes.
Take the first right turn through the
woods to the car park near the presidential pavilion.*

A large esplanade flanked by lime trees
in the centre of the park marks the
former site of the royal pavilion. A series
of slabs defines the layout of the building; the large octagonal drawing room
in the centre is surrounded by four corner rooms, separated by vestibules. The
decoration in the King's rooms was red,
the Dauphin's rooms were green (they
were originally intended for the Queen
but she never occupied them); the
apartments for "Monsieur" (Louis XIV's
brother) were blue and those of "Madame," his second wife Elisabeth of Bavaria,
were pale yellow.

This is where the two perspectives of
the park meet: across to the drive leading to the Royal Gates, and along the
route running from St-Germain and the
Seine Valley up to the Grand Mirror fountains and the green "carpet" of lawn.

The present grounds are suggestive of
old Marly, with its terraces, fountains
and hornbeam arbours. Further information can be obtained from the
museum in the new outbuilding near
the Grille Royale.

## Grille Royale

Louis XIV would use this entrance when
he arrived from Versailles. Admire the

perspective of the steep road climbing up the hillside and its continuation on the opposite slope, slicing its way through the trees.

## Musée-Promenade de Marly-le-Roi-Louveciennes

&. ⏰*Open daily (except Mon and Tue) 2-6pm.* ⏰*Closed public holidays.* ⏳*3€ (under 7, no charge).* ☎ *01 39 69 06 26.*
The museum contains precious material on the 13 pavilions and the garden statues which no longer exist; the plans drawn up in 1753 and a miniature model of the whole project give a fair idea of what the king's country residence looked like. Note the interesting 18C approach to ornamental gardening.

The interior decoration of the royal pavilion is represented by Van der Meulen's *Capture of Gray* and by Mme Vigée-Lebrun's *Summer* and *Autumn* which were hung at Marly in 1755. Admire one of Desportes' hunting scenes. The Louis XV period features *Aeneas's Apotheosis* commissioned from Boucher for the King's bedroom, chests of drawers (Mondon, De Loose) originally in the apartments of Madame Elisabeth and the Count of Provence; a number of items including Pajou's statue of *Loyalty* concern Mme du Barry. The collection also contains religious works from St-Vigor Church, in particular a *Lamentation* (1516) and a St-John-the-Baptist from the School of Caravaggio.

Before leaving the museum, visit the small chamber presenting the "Marly Machine"; it contains drawings and plans, together with a model. The mural painting depicts the waterworks of Versailles.

▶ *Return to the car and leave the park by avenue des Combattants. Drive down to the Abreuvoir.*

## Abreuvoir (Horse-pond)

After a steep descent – known as Côte du Cœur-Volant – D 386 leads to the horse-pond, once used as a spillway for the waters of Marly park. From here, the water was conveyed back to the Seine by a system of pipes and drains. The terrace flanked by yew trees above the pond used to display Coysevox' *Winged Horses* and at a later date, Guillaume Coustou's

*Rearing Horses*. Two replicas stand in their place. The original statues once adorned place de la Concorde in Paris and have now been moved to the Louvre.

# Excursions

# Port-Marly

### Château de Monte-Cristo★

⏰*Open Apr-Nov: daily (except Mon) 10am-12.30pm, 2-6pm, Sat-Sun and public holidays 10am-6pm, guided tours Sun (45min) 2-6pm; Nov-Mar: Sun and public holidays 2-5pm.* ⏰*Closed 1 Jan and 25 Dec.* ⏳*5€ Mon-Sat, 6.70 € Sun.* ☎ *01 39 16 49 49.*
Built in 1846 on a hill overlooking the Seine Valley, this extravagant folly expressed the eccentricity of **Alexandre Dumas** through a wonderfully eclectic combination of Gothic, Renaissance and Moorish styles. After holding sumptuous receptions for the fashionable Paris set when his works *The Count of Monte-Cristo* and *The Three Musketeers* were enjoying great success, Dumas ran up enormous debts and was finally forced to sell up. The delightful building, which houses a library and information centre, is decorated with medallions representing the famous writer and the great minds whom he particularly admired, Homer, Aeschylus, Sophocles.

Some of the rooms contain portraits and documents. Visitors can also see the great man's study and the splendid **Moorish drawing room★** in which the exuberance of the carvings and brilliant stained glass is equalled only by the furniture. The restoration of this room in 1985 was sponsored by Hassan II of Morocco, a great admirer of Dumas' works.

A few yards from the château is the little **Château d'If**, a pseudo-Gothic construction designed by Dumas as a place to which he could retire for peace and quiet. Note the titles of his works engraved on the freestone walls.

After being abandoned for many years, the **park** has now been exceptionally well preserved and again provides a charming setting with its grottoes and man-made features. The many natural springs have been skilfully channelled to form tiny waterfalls cascading into the basins and ponds.

## Louveciennes★

This small residential town on the edge of Marly Forest still features several large estates. Many famous people, in particular artists, were attracted by this charming place: the portrait painter: Élisabeth Vigée-Lebrun (1755-1842); the poet André Chénier (1762-94); the sculptor Emmanuel Frémiet (1824-1910), a student of Rude; and above all, several Impressionist painters.

 Two itineraries guide you in the footsteps of the Impressionists, the "Chemin des Impressionnistes" (4km/2.5mi starting from the town hall) and the "Liaison Verte" (6km/3.7mi starting from the Musée-promenade at Marly-le-Roi).

The **church** (12C-13C) on the village square retains a Romanesque look, but the polygonal bell-tower is 19C. The interior boasts an interesting collection of stone piscinae, resting against the east end.

Walk through the public gardens, along rue de l'Étang and down rue du Pont for a pleasant view of the 16C **Château du Pont** (private), the groves of trees and the rippling waters of the moat.

Follow rue du Général-Leclerc to the town hall, opposite which stand three arches of the disused aqueduct that used to convey the waters of the Seine to Versailles thanks to the "Marly Machine."

Return to the church and walk along rue du Professeur-Tuffier, then follow the signposts to reach **Field Marshal Joffre's Tomb**. The Maréchal's estate can be seen on the corner of chemin des Gressets (plaque).

The rotunda-shaped temple seen from the chemin des Gressets was the last resting place of the Victor of the Marne and his wife. Marshal Joffre, who died in 1931, was extremely fond of Louveciennes and insisted on being buried here rather than at Les Invalides in Paris.

## Bougival★ *4km/2.5mi*

In the 19C Bougival was a centre of art, fêtes and bohemian life. Bizet, Corot, Meissonier and Renoir lived here. The "boaters" – fun-loving, young Parisian men and women – who flocked to the dances at La Grenouillère had their carefree lives evoked by Maupassant in his novels and short stories, and captured on canvas by Impressionists (Renoir, Berthe Morisot, Monet).

## Musée Tourgueniev

*16 rue Ivan-Tourgueniev.* ◔*Open Apr to end Oct: Sun 10am-6pm.* ◔*Closed public holidays. 4.60 € (under 12, no charge).* ☏*01 45 77 87 12. Access on foot via a small alleyway off N 13, near the Holiday Inn Hotel.*

Built on the heights, the house where Turgenev lived during his exile was part of the property owned by his friends Louis Viardot and his wife Pauline, a singer like her sister La Malibran.

On the ground floor are some of the writer's documents, photographs of family and friends, engravings, and his piano. His works are evoked through extracts from novels and essays, among them the *Récits d'un Chasseur* published in 1852, in which he predicted the abolition of serfdom in Russia.

On the first floor, the writer's study and the room where he died on 3 September 1883 have been re-created. His body was taken to St Petersburg on 1 October: a photograph captures Ernest Renan giving a speech at the Gare du Nord in Paris (*Adieu Paris*); another shows the funeral procession in St Petersburg.

## The Marly Machine

The Île de la Loge road bridge affords a good view of the 18C buildings (*quai Rennequin-Sualem at Bougival*) that contained the Marly Machine, and the pipes lining the hillside. At the top of the rise stands a white lodge by Ledoux: the **"pavillon de musique" de Madame du Barry** (⚬⚊ *closed to the public*). It was inaugurated on 2 September 1771, during a sumptuous banquet attended by Louis XV.

**A strange machine** – It was decided to divert the waters of the Seine to supply the fountains of Marly and, subsequently, those of Versailles.

Colbert succeeded in finding a Belgian engineer, Arnold Deville, and a master carpenter, Rennequin Sualem, who agreed to take on the daring project of raising the water 150m/493ft above the level of the river. The work started in 1681, took three years and involved a considerable amount of equipment: 13 hydraulic wheels with a diameter of 12m/40ft operated 225 pumps arranged on three levels, by which the water was conveyed from the water tower – 163m/535ft above the Seine – to the Louveciennes reservoirs via an aqueduct with a capacity of 5 000m³/176 575cu ft per day. From there the water was channelled to Marly or Versailles. Since the 19C, several pumping devices have occupied the site; the last disappeared in 1967. *For more information, read the explanations given on the panel located by the River Seine.*

### Forêt de Marly

Once royal hunting grounds, jealously guarded by high walls, The State forest covers a rough but picturesque plateau planted with oaks, beeches and chestnut trees. The total area is estimated at 2 000ha/5 000 acres.

The thicker groves, featuring some beautiful trees, lie west of the road from St-Germain to St-Nom-la-Bretèche, particularly between Étoile des Dames and Étoile de Joyenval.

▶ *Consult Michelin map 101 to see which lanes are closed to traffic (barriers). These may however be recommended as cycling paths.*

# PARC ORNITHOLOGIQUE DU MARQUENTERRE★★

**MICHELIN LOCAL MAP 301: C-6**

The Marquenterre area is an alluvial plain reclaimed from the sea, which lies between the Authie and Somme estuaries. Its name derives from *mer qui entre en terre* (sea which enters the land). The stretches of land are made up of briny marshes, salt-pastures and sand dunes secured to the land by vegetation. Today this reserve is home to 315 species of birds (the continent of Europe has 452 species in all), 350 species of plants, and 40 species of mammals living both on land and in the water, including a large colony of seals; the most inquisitive of them are sometimes spotted at high tide near the quayside at St Valéry-en-Somme and Le Crotoy.

🛈 **Information:** Comité Départemental du Tourisme de La Somme, 21, rue Ernest-Cauvin, 80000 AMIENS. ☎ 03 22 71 22 71. www.somme-tourisme.com.

▶ **Orient Yourself:** The Park lies between the estuaries of the Authie and the Somme, accessible from Abbeville via the D 940, direction Crotoy.

🅿 **Parking:** Large, free parking area.

👁 **Don't Miss:** The aviary, for a close up view of birds

🕐 **Organizing Your Time:** There are three different routes around the reserve from one to three hours duration.

[Kids] **Especially for Kids:** The discovery trails around the park

♿ **Also See:** The bay of the Somme; Le Crotoy, and St Valery-sur-Somme.

## A Bit of History

**Reclaimed from the sea** – The process of reclaiming the land was started in the 12C by monks from St-Riquier and Valloires who erected the first dikes and attempted to canalise the rivers. Many drainage canals were built. Perched on a hill, Rue, the future capital of the Marquenterre area, ceased to be an island in the 18C. During the 19C, dikes and beaches were strengthened, which allowed the development of vegetable and cereal growing. In 1923, the industrialist H Jeanson bought an area of marshland along the coast, which his successors

## Making the Most of the Park

### WHEN TO GO

Each season is interesting and enables visitors to watch different species.

**Spring** is the nesting season for many species such as storks, small waders (avocets, oystercatchers, plovers), grey lag geese, shelduck. The herons' nesting place is particularly spectacular since five species of large waders, including spoonbills, nest at the top of pine trees.

**Summer** is the migrating season for black storks; it is also the time when small waders gather at high tide and when large gatherings of spoonbills, cormorants and egrets can be seen.

**Autumn** sees the mass arrival of many species of ducks coming to spend the winter in the park (up to 6 000 birds, some of them arriving from Russia and Finland, can be observed). The park is the most important wader ringing centre in France, and studies on migration are carried out in cooperation with the Natonal Natural History Museum in Paris.

6km/3.7mi of footpaths lead to different observation points and trained guides are at the disposal of visitors to help them discover the rich environment of the park.

### WHAT TO TAKE WITH YOU

Solid walking shoes, a wind- waterproof coat. A pair of binoculars (also available for rent at the park).

### RIDING TOURS 🏇

Kids *Espace Equestre Henson, 34 chemin des Garennes, 80120 St-Quentin-en-Tourmont – ☎ 03 22 25 03 06, www. henson.fr.* The Henson horse riding centre organises guided riding tours for all levels of ability, including beginners and children.

---

drained and diked using Dutch methods, so that it was eventually possible to grow bulbs. At the same time, trees were planted. But the plans failed, and gave rise to the idea of a bird sanctuary.

**The birth of the bird sanctuary** – The Marquenterre lands have always been an important habitat for migratory and sedentary birds. Alas, it was also a paradise for hunters who brought many species close to extinction.

As a result, the Hunting Commission created a reserve on the maritime land, to ensure the protection of the birds along 5km/3mi of coastline.

The owners of the Marquenterre estate next to the reserve decided to set up a bird sanctuary within it to allow the general public to watch bird life in a natural habitat. Thirteen years later the site became the property of the Conservatoire du Littoral (Office of Coastal Preservation) and was granted in 1994 the status of "protected nature reserve." A riding centre established next to the bird sanctuary organises excursions for beginners and experienced riders (Centre équestre Henson Marquenterre, Domaine du Marquenterre, 80120 St-Quentin-en-Tourmont, ☎ 03 22 25 03 06, www.henson.fr).

### Parc Ornithologique★★ (Bird Sanctuary)

🕐 Open Apr-Sep 10am-7.30pm. Feb-Mar and Oct to mid-Nov 10am-5.30pm. Mid-

---

## The Henson horse breed

This small robust horse is a cross between a French saddle horse and a Norwegian Fjord pony. Its coat varies from light yellow to brown, and its mane is a mixture of black and gold. This breed was developed in 1978 in a small village of the Baie de Somme area, thanks to the determination of Doctor Berquin. Hensons show remarkable endurance; they can remain out in the fields all year round and cover great distances without getting tired. Their docile and affectionate behaviour make them ideal companions for children and long-distance riders. They also fare very well in team competitions and horse shows generally.

*Nov to Jan 10am-5pm. Last admission 2h before closing.* ◯*Closed 1 Jan, 25 Dec.* ∞*9.90€ (children 7.90€).* ☎ *03 22 25 03 06. www.parcdumarquenterre.com. It is advisable to visit on a rising tide when the birds leave the stretches of the Baie de Somme or during the spring and autumn migration periods.*

The Bird Sanctuary covers 250ha/627 acres on the edge of the reserve. Over 300 species of bird have been identified, among them the red-beaked shelldduck, geese, tern, avocet, gulls, herons, sandpipers and spoonbill.

*S. Maire/ MICHELIN*

*Reserve*

**Kids Three different trails are sign posted:**

**Discovery trail** – *Allow 1hr. Explanatory panels.* The tour of the lakes and aviaries at the foot of an old coastal dune offers a close-up view of the birds that live here permanently: ducks, seagulls, geese and herons. Their calls attract wild birds of the same species. A few familiar mammals can be seen on the way: Henson horses, weasels and hares,

as well as amphibians such as toads and elegant insects such as dragonflies.

**Observation trail** – *Allow 2hr.* The 7km/4.3mi walk follows a path through the dunes to various observation hides, a heronry and a large aviary.

**Extended observation trail** – *Allow 3hr.* An additional path (1.5km/1mi) shows the reserve from a completely different angle.

# MEAUX ★

## POPULATION 67 956
### MICHELIN LOCAL MAP 312: G-2 OR MAP 106 FOLDS 22, 23

Nestling inside a deep bend of the River Marne, Meaux lies at the intersection of several main roads, in particular N 3, which runs through the town from east to west. In the summer months, a **son et lumière (sound and light) performance** featuring a cast of more than 2 000 re-enacts Meaux's moments of glory in the charming setting of the Episcopal Precinct (◖*see Calendar of Events*).

- **Information:** 1 pl. Doumer, 77100 Meaux. ☎ 01 64 33 02 26.
- **Orient Yourself:** In Ile de France, 34 miles east of Paris, along the A 4. Access from Paris: SNCF rail link from Gare de l'Est.
- **Parking:** Limited town centre parking; try to find a space near the cathedral.
- **Organizing Your Time:** Allow 1-2 hours to visit the cathedral and episcopal palace.
- **Also See:** Château de Montceaux

## Episcopal Precinct

### Cathédrale St-Étienne★

**Exterior** – The construction of the church continued from the late 12C to the 16C, covering the entire gamut of Gothic architecture. The façade (14C-16C) is pure Flamboyant. The limestone used

for the stonework has crumbled in several places and the exterior decoration is badly damaged. The Wars of Religion brought further destruction.

The south transept façade is an elegant example of Radiant Gothic. In poor condition, the south doorway is dedicated to St Stephen. Only the left tower (68m/

*Cathédrale St-Étienne*

223ft) was completed. The one on the right, a plain bell-tower, is called the Black Tower on account of its dark-coloured shingles.

**Interior** – Last restored in the 18C, the interior of the cathedral contrasts sharply with the badly weathered exterior. The lofty, well-lit nave is an impressive sight. The two bays of the nave next to the transept date from the early 13C. The transepts, in particular the south arm, are superb examples of 14C architecture. Below the huge stained-glass window runs an openwork triforium so fine that it allows a full view of the lancets. The chancel is a pleasing sight with its double aisles and its five apsidal chapels. Note the pretty 15C Maugarni doorway to the left.

A walk round the ambulatory leads to Bossuet's tomb, marked by a slab of black marble in the south part of the chancel.

### Ancien palais épiscopal
○*Open Apr-Sep daily (except Tue) 10am-noon, 2-6pm. Oct-Mar daily (except Mon and Tue) 10am-noon, 2-5pm, Sun 2-5pm.*

---

## Address Book

*For coin ranges, see the Legend on the cover flap.*

### WHERE TO EAT

○○ **Le Cep** – *36 r. du Tan –* ☎ *01 64 34 20 33. Closed Sun evening and Mon – reserv. weekends.* Despite the no-frills decor – walls of mimosa-yellow wood panelling and white tablecloths – connoisseurs file in for perfectly prepared traditional meals. The house specialities, Brie de Meaux pané (breaded and cooked) and salmon in pastry, are simply divine.

### SHOPPING

**Le Bec Fin** – *4 r. St-Rémy – in the vicinity of the cathedral –* ☎ *01 64 33 73 47 – Mon 3pm-7.30pm; Tue-Sat 7am-1pm,* *3pm-7.30pm. Closed 3 wks in Aug.* The shop is sliced in two. On one side, a delicatessen/grocer's shop. On the other, the cheese shop and its cheese maturing cellar starring two specialities: Brie de Meaux and Tancrou, a goat cheese from Seine-et-Marne. All of the products are locally made and nicely presented.

### BOATING

**Marne Loisirs** – *Quai Jacques-Prévert –* ☎ *01 64 34 97 97 – marneloi@aol.com. Open Apr-Oct: daily 9am-noon, 1pm-6pm.* Boat rentals, no special permit required. Boats hold from 2-4 to 10-12 sailors who can discover the charms of the Marne at their leisure.

## The Eagle of Meaux

Having completed his tutorial commitments to the Dauphin, **Jacques Bossuet** was made Bishop of Meaux in 1682 at the age of 55.

The man later known as the "Eagle of Meaux" exercised his ecclesiastic duties with the utmost assiduity; he kept an attentive eye on catechism, was often seen preaching in his own cathedral and assumed full command of the religious communities in his diocese. For instance, despite his great esteem for Jouarre Abbey, he did not hesitate to have the place besieged when the abbess refused to dismiss two nuns whose presence he considered undesirable.

Bossuet enjoyed working in the huge library of the Bishop's Palace, or in his study at the bottom of the garden; it was here that he composed five of his most famous funeral orations including those dedicated to Louis XIV's wife Marie-Thérèse and the Great Condé. He also wrote a number of books defending Gallican orthodoxy.

He died in Paris in 1704, aged 77, at the height of his intellectual powers. As was his wish, he was buried in his cathedral in Meaux.

*Closed 1 Jan, 1 May, 25 Dec. 3€, no charge Wed. 01 64 34 84 45.*

The old palace houses a **museum** largely dedicated to Bossuet. The building was completed in the 12C and altered in the 17C.

The two magnificent **Gothic rooms** facing the park on the ground floor, the lower and the upper chapel are the oldest parts of the palace. The amazing brick ramp leading to the first floor was designed by Bishop Briçonnet in the 16C to enable the mules loaded with grain to reach the attics.

### Musée des Beaux-Arts

The Salle du Synode and the Grands Appartements have been made into a Fine Arts Museum (15C to 19C). The many artists featured include Boullogne, De Troy, Bouchardon, Millet, Courbet, Senelle, Coypel and Van Loo. The Petits Appartements, situated in the west wing, house 19C works by Orientalist painters Gérôme and Decamps and landscape artists Daubigny and Millet.

### Appartement de Bossuet

Located in the east wing, Bossuet's apartment has retained its original layout but the decoration was renewed in the Louis XV style. Admire Mignard's portrait of the bishop and a splendid Cressent commode (early 18C).

### Anciens remparts

*The ramparts are only accessible during the guided tours of the town.*

At the top of the steps stands the humble 17C pavilion which Bossuet used as a study. The bishop would retire here to collect his thoughts or to write in the peaceful hours of the night.

The centre of the terrace affords a good **view**★ of the gardens, the Bishop's Palace and the cathedral.

## Excursion

### Château de Montceaux

*8.5km/5mi east. Leave Meaux by N 3 (east). Beyond Trilport, in Montceaux Forest, turn right onto D 19 (signposted Montceaux-les-Meaux). The lane to the château is on the right.*

Montceaux was known as the Château of the Queens. Catherine de' Medici had it built and Philibert Delorme almost certainly worked on it between 1547 and 1559. On the death of the woman who was "almost Queen," the king gave the château to his bride Marie de Medici who entrusted the works to Salomon de Brosse before he started to build the Luxembourg Palace in Paris. The château then fell into disrepair and after 1650 became uninhabitable. Handsome ruins lurk among the trees, and from the roofless entrance pavilion there is an especially good view of a section of wall with gaping windows.

# MEUDON★
POPULATION 43 663
MICHELIN LOCAL MAP 305: E-8, MAP 101 FOLD 24 OR 106 FOLD 18

The grave of the sculptor **Auguste Rodin** can be seen outside his former residence, now a museum. The remains of Mme de Pompadour's estate, an Observatory, and an art-history museum are some of Meudon's other attractions.

- 🛈 **Information:** Hôtel de Ville, 6 avenue Le Corbeiller, 92195 Meudon. ☏ 01 41 14 80 00. www.ville-meudon.fr.
- ▶ **Orient Yourself:** This residential town is located 2½ miles southwest of central Paris, on the slopes of the plateau covered by the Meudon Forest. Access from Paris: RER line C 5/C 7 or SNCF rail link from Gare Montparnasse.
- 😊 **Don't Miss:** Lunch in the railway setting of Le Brimborion.
- 🕐 **Organizing Your Time:** Allow half a day to explore fully, and then enjoy lunch.

## A Bit of History

In the mid 18C Mme de Pompadour acquired **Bellevue** estate and gave orders to build the château. Louis XV paid frequent visits to the estate and in 1757 he bought Bellevue from his mistress. The last occupants were the two unmarried daughters of Louis XV, the aunts of Louis XVI. They added a botanical garden and a charming hamlet. The estate was pillaged during the Revolution and sold as State property.

All that remains of the former estate is part of the terrace and its balustrade at the junction of rue Marcel-Allégot and avenue du 11-Novembre.

*Observatory*

M.O. Bernard/ MICHELIN

## Château

The stately avenue du Château is lined with four rows of lime trees. Half way down the street, a plaque on the left marks the little house (no 27) where **Richard Wagner** composed the score for the *Flying Dutchman* in 1841.

### Château of the House of Guise
In the 15C, the manor house belonging to the Duchess of Étampes became the property of the Cardinal de Lorraine, who belonged to the House of Guise. For 100 years Meudon remained in the hands of the Guise. The family later sold the estate to Abel Servien in 1654 owing to financial difficulties.

### New owners
The wealthy Abel Servien, Marquis de Sablé and Minister of Finance, commissioned Le Vau to renovate the château at great expense and gave orders to build the terrace, a large-scale project. Servien led a life of luxury and his fortune soon ran out; when he died in 1659, his son sold the estate to Louvois, the lord of Chaville.

The new owner pursued the efforts of his predecessor, renewing the decoration and embellishing the park. He asked Trivaux to create the perspective and entrusted the plans of the gardens to Le Nôtre, then to Mansart. After Louvois' death, his widow agreed to give Louis XIV her domain in exchange for the Château de Choisy, which belonged to the King's son, the Grand Dauphin.

### Royal property

An enthusiastic art lover, "Monseigneur" made considerable changes in the interior decoration and layout of the Old Château.

In 1711 Monseigneur died of smallpox and the following year his son the Duke of Burgundy succumbed to the disease. The château came into the hands of a two-year-old boy, who was to become Louis XV. His great-grandfather Louis XIV administered the estate up to 1715.

## Sights

### Terrace★

The terrace (450m/1480ft long and 136m/447ft wide) is planted with handsome trees and sweeping lawns. It commands an extensive **view**★ of Meudon, the Seine Valley and Paris.

The far end of the esplanade rests on the foundations of the old orangeries of the château. From here, visitors may discover Le Nôtre's beautiful perspective with the modern complex of Meudon-la-Forêt in the far distance.

### Observatoire

⏱Open Visits by arrangement (1 month in advance), 3rd Sat of each month. ⏱Closed school and public holidays. ⊜4.50€. ☎ 01 45 07 75 30.

On the right stands the observatory, housing the astrophysics section of the Paris Observatory. A large revolving dome with a diameter of 18.5m/60ft crowns the central block of the New Château. Founded in 1876 by the astronomer Janssen, this observatory is considered the most important in France. It is also the leading aerospace research centre in France.

### WHERE TO EAT

⊜⊜ **Le Brimborion** – 8 r. de Vélizy – ☎ 01 45 34 12 03. Closed Sat lunch and Sun evening – reserv. required weekends. This restaurant used to be the buffet of the Meudon-Bellevue railway station. Charming decor and delectable menu featuring time-worn recipes updated to suit modern tastes. In fine weather the garden becomes a terrace – a lovely spot where one hardly notices the trains go by.

### Musée d'Art et d'Histoire

11 rue des Pierres, at the foot of the terrace (drive there from the town centre). ⏱Open daily (except Mon and Tue) 2-6pm. ⏱Closed Aug and public holidays. ⊜2€. ☎ 01 46 23 87 13.

The museum, in the house which Molière's wife Armande Béjart bought in 1676, three years after the writer's death, centres on the history of the town, the celebrities who lived there and the châteaux of Bellevue and Meudon (information centre). The formal gardens are dotted with contemporary sculptures by Arp, Bourdelle and Stahly.

### Musée Rodin, Villa des Brillants

19 avenue Auguste-Rodin. ⏱Open Apr-Sep Fri and Sat-Sun 1-6pm (last admission 5pm). ⏱Closed 1 May and 25 Dec. ⊜2€. ☎ 01 41 14 35 00.

An indispensable complement to the Rodin Museum in Paris, the museum stands next to the Villa des Brillants, **Rodin's** residence and studio from 1895. It contains moulds, drawings and rough sketches by the great sculptor, together with a number of original plaster casts (The Gates of Hell, Balzac, The Burghers of Calais). The façade of the museum was taken from the old château at Issy-les-Moulineaux. Rodin died in 1917 and his grave was laid out in front of the museum. Sitting pensively on the tombstone is his famous statue The Thinker.

# MILLY-LA-FORÊT★

POPULATION 4 601

MICHELIN LOCAL MAP 312: D-5 OR MAP 106 FOLD 44

The locality of Milly-la-Forêt developed around the old covered market and it is now an important starting-point for many of the forest lanes crisscrossing the wooded uplands of Les Trois Pignons and Coquibus. Milly has been a long-standing centre for the growing of medicinal plants, including one variety still considered a local speciality: peppermint.

The *Parc Naturel Régional du Gâtinais Français* extends over the north part of the Gâtinais region; 30% of the area is forested and the park was set up to protect and enhance the natural and cultural heritage, promote economic development whilst safeguarding the environment (agricultural activities predominate), improve the quality of life and bring life back to the villages. A few activities intended for visitors are organised (horse-drawn carriages are used to encourage the discovery of the region's traditional heritage) and a guide is available in the park to help and advise tourists.

- **Information:** 60 r. Jean-Cocteau, 91490 Milly-la-Forêt, ☎ 01 64 98 83 17.
- ▶ **Orient Yourself:** Milly-la-Forêt lies 40 miles due south of Paris, via the A6.

## Walking Tour

### Halles

Located on the town square, the market building, made entirely of oak and chestnut wood, dates back to 1479. The imposing roof structure resting on 48 pillars slopes almost down to the ground.

Rue Jean-Cocteau leads to rue du Lau, a no-through road which ends in front of a Romanesque doorway flanked by two turrets; these are in turn linked to the Louis XIII-style former Governor's residence where Jean Cocteau lived from 1947 to his death in 1963 (⚊ *not open to the public*).

## Additional Sights

### Espace culturel Paul-Bédu

*8 bis rue Farnault.* ♿ 🕐*Open daily (except Mon) Jun-Sep 10am-6pm. Rest of the year 10am-5pm Sun and public holidays, 2.30-6pm.* ◉*2€.* ☎ *01 64 98 75 52.* Situated opposite the town hall, this cultural centre stages temporary exhibitions and houses late-19C to early-20C

*Château de Courances, garden façade*

objets d'art and small paintings collected by Paul Bédu, a native of Milly; a collection of lithographs, drawings and ceramics by Cocteau is also on display.

## Conservatoire National des Plantes Médicinales Aromatiques et Industrielles

*Route de Nemours.* ♿ ○*Open mid-Apr to mid-Sep 9am-5.30pm Sat, Sun and public holidays, 2-6pm. Mid-Sep to mid-Oct daily (except Sat, Sun) 9am-5pm.* ◐*4.50€.* ☎ *01 64 98 83 77.*

2ha/5 acres on the edge of the forest have been set aside for the preservation of over 1 200 species of plants: culinary and medicinal herbs (a long-standing tradition in Milly) as well as plants used for dyeing such as woad and madder and a selection of exotic plants. Traditional tools used for growing these plants are on display.

An herb market is held in the market building at the beginning of June.

# Excursions

## Le Cyclop

⬤⬤ *Guided visits only (45mn) May-Oct 2-5pm (Sun 11am-5.45pm).* ⊗*Note: children under 10 are not allowed inside the sculpture.* ◐*7€.* ☎ *01 64 98 95 18 . www.art-public.com/cyclop. Leave Milly on the Étampes road (D 837); follow the signposted road to the parking area.*

This monumental sculpture was donated to the French government in 1987 by artists Jean Tinguely and Niki de Sainte-Phalle. It represents an enormous head 22.5m/73ft high made with 300t of steel. The face sparkles, whereas inside the head there is a strange world of disorder and utopia. On the top of the piece is a vast water-filled basin dedicated to France's most innovative postwar artist Yves Klein (1928-62), noted for his use of a rich ultramarine commonly referred to as Yves Klein blue. Works by other artists are also displayed.

## Address Book

⌖*For coin ranges, see the Legend on the cvoer flap.*

### WHERE TO STAY

◠ **M. Lenoir (Bed and Breakfast)** – *9 r. du Souvenir, 91490 Moigny-sur-École - 3.5 km/2.2mi N of Milly-la-Forêt –* ☎ *01 64 98 47 84 or 06 76 95 56 87. 4 rms – meals* ◠. High protective walls ensure the privacy of this handsome stone house and its heterogeneous garden. The rooms, tastefully decorated, are extremely peaceful. Breakfast room housed in the former chicken coop.

### WHERE TO EAT

◠ **La Truffière** – *14 rte de Boutigny (dir. Ferté-Alais) –* ☎ *01 64 98 70 27. Closed Sun evening.* The warm welcome and attentive service are among the main assets of this restaurant situated in the old Milly railway station. The play area and chicken coop behind the restaurant, just next to the pleasant terrace, are very popular with the youngsters.

### SHOPPING

**L'Herbier de Milly** – *16 pl. du Marché –* ☎ *01 64 98 92 39 – Tue-Sun 9.30am-*

*12.30pm, 2.30pm-7.30pm.* Come discover this herbalist's shop, run by the same family for four generations, where you can sample regional specialities such as Milly peppermint and several kinds of honey. Beginning in May, a visit to the shop's medicinal garden is well worth the detour.

### PARC NATUREL RÉGIONAL DU GÂTINAIS FRANÇAIS

Created in 1999, the Natural Park of the Gâtinais Region extends through the heavily wooded north part of the Gâtinais. Its objective is to protect and develop the natural and cultural heritage of this area, promote economic development while respecting the environment (farming is the local main-stay), generally improve the quality of life, and revitalise the villages. Some tourist activities, such as tours of the region's attractions in horse and wagon, and a tourist brochure covering park territory, are available. *Maison du Parc, pl. de la République, 91490 Milly-la-Forêt,* ☎ *01 64 98 73 93.*

## Château de Courances

⏺ *Open Apr-Oct daily (except Wed) 2-6.30pm.* ☜*7€ (children under 12, no charge).* ☎ *01 40 62 07 71. 4km/2.4mi north.*

Built around 1550 by Gilles le Breton for Cosme Clausse, Secretary of Finance to Henri II, the château acquired its present appearance in the 17C. It is a good example of the Louis XIII style: a brick building with sandstone bonding, pointed roofs and a sparsely decorated exterior. In the 19C the front was embellished with a replica of the horseshoe staircase at Fontainebleau. The château is still surrounded by a moat, and a splendid avenue on the opposite side of the road completes this sweeping perspective.

**Park★★** – The approach to the château is very grand. Walk through the gate and cross the "forecourt," a vast stretch of lawn divided by a central path and flanked by two canals reflecting the plane trees.

The park, designed by Le Nôtre, extends behind the château, and the rear façade overlooks a lush, green lawn. A path leads to the Grand Canal, which receives the waters of the River École. Another path, set at right angles, skirts the small cascades and leads to the flower beds, offering a lovely view of the château mirrored in the crystal-clear water.

**Château** – From the south terrace, there is a view of the park. The tour includes a number of living rooms, low-ceilinged chambers and annexes. Note the corner dining room, tastefully decorated with walnut wainscoting and ornamental plates, and the Monkeys' Gallery, named after three 16C tapestries with scenes of monkeys mimicking man.

## Boigneville

*11km/6.8mi south along D 1 then D 449.* This Gâtinais village boasts one of the largest churches in the whole *département*.

**Notre-Dame-de-l'Assomption** – ⏺*Open first Sun of month, 2-6pm.* ☜*3.80€.* ☎ *01 64 99 40 07.* The crypt of this late-12C to early-13C church contains remarkable frescoes dating from 1677 and depicting the life of the Virgin Mary.

**Écomusée** – Housed in a barn, this museum is devoted to the lifestyle and the natural, historic and cultural background of a rural community from the beginning of the 20C.

# MONTFORT-L'AMAURY★

POPULATION 3 137

MICHELIN LOCAL MAP 311: G-3 OR MAP 106 NORTH OF FOLDS 27, 28

This old town is built on the side of a hill dominated by castle ruins. Before the French Revolution, Montfort 🏰 was an important county town enjoying far more power than nearby Rambouillet. The composer Maurice Ravel and Jean Monnet, one of the founders of the European Union, were among the town's distinguished residents. Today, Montfort-l'Amaury is an elegant holiday resort where antique shops and small "country" restaurants abound.

🛈 **Information:** 6 r. Amaury, 78490 Montfort-l'Amaury, ☎ 01 34 86 87 96. www.ville-montfort-l-amaury.fr

▸ **Orient Yourself:** 30 miles, almost due west of Paris, via the A 12/N 12.

## A Bit of History

The district was founded and fortified in the 11C by the builder Amaury de Montfort. The most famous descendant of this illustrious family was Simon IV, the leader of the Albigensian Crusade against the heretical Cathars of Languedoc.

**A Breton outpost in Île-de-France** – In 1312 the marriage of the Breton Duke Arthur to one of the Montfort daughters made this citadel a part of Brittany. Subsequently, when Anne of Brittany, Comtesse de Montfort married Charles VIII and then Louis XII, Montfort-l'Amaury became a French fief. The duchy became Crown property after the accession of Henri II, the son of François I and Claude de France.

# Sights

## Église St-Pierre★

The rebuilding of the church was commissioned by Anne of Brittany in the late 15C. The decoration work continued through the Renaissance and was completed in the early 17C; the nave was uniformly elevated and the belltower and the façade were both remodelled.

Walk round the church, surrounded by quaint old houses. Observe the striking gargoyles that adorn the walls of the apse and the high flying buttresses supporting the chancel. The pretty doorway on the south front bears medallions portraying the benefactors André de Foix and his wife, whose generosity made it possible to carry out the renovation work in the Renaissance. The interior features a superb set of Renaissance **stained-glass windows**★ in the ambulatory and around the aisles.

## Ancien charnier

This old cemetery is enclosed within an arcaded gallery surmounted by splendid timbered roofing in the shape of an upturned ship. The left gallery is 16C, the other two date from the 17C. In accordance with medieval tradition, these galleries were intended to receive the bones of the dead when there was a lack of space in the graveyard.

## Castle ruins

Take the narrow, twisting road to the top of the hill. Two sections of wall overgrown with ivy are all that remain of the 11C keep. The stone and brick turret belonged to the building commissioned by Anne of Brittany.

The summit offers a good **view**★ of the town, the old-fashioned roofs and the edge of the forest.

## Musée Maurice-Ravel★

*5 rue Maurice-Ravel.* ☚☚ *Tours by request, daily (except Mon and Tue) Apr-Sep 2.30-6pm Sat-Sun at 10am, 11am, 2.30pm, 3.30pm, 4.30pm and 5.30pm;. Oct-Mar: 2.30-5pm, Sat-Sun at 10am, 11am, 2.30pm, 3.30pm and 4.30pm.* ⊙*Closed between Christmas and New Year's Day.* ☚*6.50€.* ☎ *01 34 86 00 89.*

### WHERE TO EAT

☚☚**Hostellerie des Tours** – *Pl. de l'Église –* ☎ *01 34 86 00 43. Closed Tue evening and Wed – reserv. advisable.* There are two storeys to this 19C hostel: on the ground floor, you'll find a pleasant dining room decorated with copper cookware and a 1930s style bar, while in the cellar there's a picturesque vaulted cave. Traditional fare and Provençal specialities.

## Maurice Ravel (1875-1937)

Ravel's relatively late admission to the Paris Conservatory in 1889 makes his precocious output as a composer even more surprising (*Habanera* dates from 1895) unless one is aware of the fact that his father, a music-loving engineer, took great care of his son's musical education. The principal of the Conservatory thought that Ravel made "terrible mistakes in his compositions." However, his composition teacher, Gabriel Fauré, was of another opinion: "a natural musician with new ideas and a disarming sincerity." In 1901, Ravel composed *Jeux d'eau*, and won second prize in the coveted Prix de Rome competition with his cantata *Myrrha*. His name was beginning to be widely known. However, in spite of repeated attempts, he never won the Prix de Rome and the scandal that ensued prompted the principal of the Conservatory to resign and be replaced by Fauré. Ravel then produced some of his major works (*Rhapsodie espagnole*, 1907). In collaboration with Diaghilev's Russian Ballet, he created *Daphnis and Chloé* in 1912. After the war (during which he tried to enlist), his style became balder (*L'Enfant et les Sortilèges*, 1925; libretto by Colette). The *Boléro*, a ballet commissioned by Ida Rubinstein and created in 1928, was one of his major successes in symphonic writing.

## One of the founders of the European Union

Jean Monnet (1888-1979) was an economist, a negotiator and a politician whose career was influenced by his relationship with the Anglo-Saxon world. He was a member of the Allied maritime commission during the First World War. Between the wars he took part in the creation of an investment bank in New York and then played an important role as financial advisor in the co-ordination of the Franco-British war effort in 1939, negotiating the purchase of material in Washington on behalf of the United Kingdom government. He was later sent to the United States by De Gaulle as a member of the French Committee of National Liberation. He once again showed his negotiating skills by obtaining a considerable reduction of the outstanding debt and new funding (Blum-Byrnes agreement). Thanks to his modernisation plan (Plan Monnet 1947) and to the Marshall Plan, France was able to straighten her economy. The Schuman Plan (9 May 1950) laid the foundations of the European Coal and Steel Community, of which he was the first president, thus becoming with Schuman one of the founders of the European Union. He also actively worked for the establishment of the United States of Europe. His memoirs were published in 1976; his ashes were transferred to the Pantheon in Paris on 9 November 1988.

In 1920 the French composer **Ravel** bought a tiny villa in Montfort-l'Amaury. It was in this house – called Le Belvédère – that he wrote most of his music: *L'Enfant et les Sortilèges, Boléro, Daphnis et Chloé* etc. The composer developed a brain tumour but stayed on in Montfort, despite doctor's orders to stop working. He was forced to move back to Paris in 1937, where he died soon afterwards. The rooms are somewhat cramped and Ravel – who was a short man – had several of them made even smaller. The interior decoration has remained intact; much of the painting was done by Ravel himself and featured dark, sombre tones. The museum exhibits include the composer's piano, his gramophone and numerous mementoes reflecting his taste for refinement.

**Jardin zen** – Ravel had spent a fortune on his tiny garden (300m2/359sq yd). It has now been relaid in the Japanese style the composer liked so much: bamboos and azaleas, irises and small trees with gnarled branches; a bonsai specialist takes regular care of it.

## Excursions

### Vicq Musée d'Art naïf de l'Île-de-France

*4km/2.5mi north along D 76.* ♿ ◷*Open daily (except Mon) 10am-6pm.* ◷*Closed 1 Jan, 25 Dec.* ✆5€. ☎ 01 34 86 06 22.

This museum devoted to the world of fantasy contains the Max-Fourny collection – more than 1 500 works displayed in rotation with temporary exhibitions.

### La Queue-les-Yvelines, La Serre aux Papillons

*4.5km/3mi northwest. Leave Montfort by D 155 and drive to La Queue-les-Yvelines.* ♿ ◷*Open end Mar to early Nov 9.30am-12.15pm, 2.30-6pm.* ✆6€. ☎ 01 34 86 42 99. The butterfly house is part of the Jardinerie Poullain. More than 500 butterflies live in it, in tropical conditions.

### Houjarray, Maison Jean-Monnet (Centre d'information sur l'Europe)

*4.5km/3mi east. Leave Montfort by D 13 toward Tremblay-sur-Mauldre. Cross N 191 and turn right to Houjarray before Bazoches-sur-Guyonne. The centre is 1 500 m/1mi farther on in Houjarray.* ◷*Open daily 10am-5pm Sat 1-6pm, Sun and public holidays 9am-6pm.* ◷*Closed 25 Dec.* ☎ 01 34 86 12 43.

Jean Monnet (1888-1979), the political economist and diplomat, bought this country retreat in 1945; it has a thatched roof and a large, gently sloping garden which overlooks the surrounding countryside.

The text of the declaration regarding the Schuman Plan of 1950 (embodied in a treaty that same year) was conceived and written here; it led to the creation of the European Coal and Steel Community (ECSC).

Monnet would return to this haven of peace after his frequent trips around the world and had many famous figures and heads of State to stay. He retired here in 1975, writing his memoirs until his death.

Some of the original furnishings remain, together with various possessions: Monnet's *Memoirs*, letters from Schuman, Roosevelt, Adenauer and de Gaulle, various publications with Monnet on the cover, paintings by his wife Sylvia, a bust of Marianne (1945) by the sculptor Paul Belmondo. Display panels recount the important moments of his career.

# MONTMORENCY★

POPULATION 20 599

MICHELIN LOCAL MAP 305: E, F-7, MAP 101 FOLD 5 OR 106 FOLD 19

This charming town, set on hilly ground, consists of a town centre surrounded by wealthy residences. Its main claim to fame is to have been the home of the celebrated author and social theorist Jean-Jacques Rousseau (1712-78) for a period of his life. From the late 18C to the mid-19C, Montmorency 🚶 and its forest were popular venues for writers, artists, politicians and young Parisian socialites.

- 🛈 **Information:** 1 av. Foch, 95160 Montmorency, ☎ 01 39 64 42 94.
- ▶ **Orient Yourself:** Montmorency is in the Ile de France, a mere 13 miles north of the city centre.
- 👁 **Don't Miss:** Musée Jean-Jacques-Rousseau
- 🕐 **Organizing Your Time:** You could, and should, spend half a day here, plus another half day to explore the forest.

## A Bit of History

### The "First Christian Barons"

The Bouchard family, who held the lordship of Montmorency, had the reputation of being difficult vassals, and it was only after the 12C that they served the French court loyally. Over a period of 500 years, the Montmorency family produced six constables, 12 marshals and four admirals. They had connections with every ruler in Europe and chose to call themselves the "first Christian barons".

The oldest branch of the family died out in 1632 when the constable's grandson Henri II de Montmorency, governor of Languedoc, was beheaded at the age of 37 for having plotted against Cardinal Richelieu.

The duchy passed into the hands of Henri de Bourbon-Condé but the title was given to a member of the Montmorency-Boutteville family by Louis XIV.

### Jean-Jacques Rousseau's Literary Retreat

Rousseau lived in Montmorency from 1756 to 1762. Invited by Mme d'Épinay, a society woman who moved in literary circles, the 44-year-old author took up residence in the Hermitage, a small garden pavilion which has since been taken down. He was living with Thérèse Levasseur, a linen maid whom he later married, but fell passionately in love with his hostess' sister-in-law Mme d'Houdetot, who was nearly 20 years his junior.

His romantic involvements caused him to fall out with Mme d'Épinay in 1757, at which point he moved to Montlouis, a house in the village, where he completed *The New Eloisa* and published *Emilius and Sophia* and *A Treatise on the Social Contract*. These were his three major works.

In 1762 *Emilius and Sophia* was qualified as subversive literature by the Parlement

**WHERE TO EAT**

😊😊 **Au Cœur de la Forêt** – *Av. du Repos de Diane, access via a forest lane* – ☎ *01 39 64 99 19. Closed 5-29 Aug, Thu evening, Sun evening and Mon.* Take the romantic Repos de Diane avenue to this modern restaurant hidden in the forest. In winter, the fireplace warms the dining room, while in summer, the terrace is simply delightful. On your plate, you'll find nicely prepared fresh ingredients and a very agreeable meal!

de Paris and a warrant was issued for Rousseau's arrest. Fortunately, the author was forewarned; he fled Montlouis in the marshal's post-chaise and sought refuge in Switzerland.

## Sights

### Collégiale St-Martin
*Rue de l'Église.*
Started in the 16C by Guillaume de Montmorency and completed by his son Constable Anne, St Martin's is characteristic of the Flamboyant Gothic style. It was originally designed to be the mausoleum of the Montmorency family.

The chapel was specially designed to receive the remains of the Montmorency family and, in the 18C, the tombs of several members of the Condé family. The tombs were destroyed during the Revolution. Some were salvaged and moved to the Louvre, including those of Constable Anne and his wife Madeleine. The others have disappeared save for the funeral slab of Guillaume de Montmorency and his wife Anne Pot, of the famous Burgundian family; it has been placed at the top of the south aisle.

### Stained-glass windows★
The 14 windows that adorn the apse and the five nearest right-hand bays of the chancel provide fine examples of Renaissance decoration, tastefully restored in the 19C. The family connections of the Montmorency are illustrated by the effigies of their ancestors, the brightly coloured coats of arms and the saints they worshipped. The other windows in the nave – executed in the 19C – harmonise well with the earlier Renaissance windows.

### Musée Jean-Jacques-Rousseau
*5 rue Jean-Jacques-Rousseau.* 👁‍🗨 *Guided tours (1hr) daily (except Mon) 2-6pm.* 🕐*Closed between Christmas and New Year's Day and 1 May.* 👁4€. ☎ *01 39 64 80 13. www.ville-montmorency.fr.*
This is the house where the French writer lived from 1757 to 1762 and where he wrote his major works. The museum evokes the daily life of Thérèse and Jean-Jacques. The old part of the house affords a good view of the valley. The arbour planted with lime trees leads through to the small garden pavilion Rousseau used as a study, which he sardonically called his "keep".

The exhibition hall and audio-visual room in the modern part of the museum present particular aspects of Rousseau's life and work. The 18C house on the edge of the grounds contains a library with numerous studies on Rousseau and the town's historic research centre.

## Excursions

### Forêt de Montmorency
Extending over an area of 2 000ha/4 942 acres north of the River Seine, the Montmorency Forest covers the highest hill (195m/640ft) in the Paris region.
The area west of Domont and N 309 is the most interesting section of the forest, with deep wooded vales and patches of moist undergrowth. Oaks and chestnut trees are the dominant species, with the occasional birch.
🚶 The forest boasts several footpaths (GR1, hiking trails), a cycle track which cuts through the forest (**Route du Faîte**), and the Caesar's Camp recreational area.
**Château de la Chasse** – *30min on foot from N 309 (green gate on the left, 2km/1.2mi beyond Montlignon Church).*
🚶 The oddly shaped castle, flanked with truncated towers, stands in a picturesque setting, on the edge of a pond.

# NEW Michelin tourist guides: expand your holiday horizons

- *New cover*
- *New layout*
- *New information*
- *New destinations*

# MONTREUIL★

POPULATION 2 428
MICHELIN LOCAL MAP 301: D-5

Montreuil occupies a picturesque site★ on the edge of the plateau overlooking the Canche Valley. This peaceful town preserves a slightly nostalgic charm in its old streets lined with 17C and 18C houses, its citadel and shaded ramparts commanding vast horizons. Montreuil's proximity to the coast and particularly to Le Touquet attracts numerous tourists in summer.

- **Information:** 21 r. Carnot, 62170 Montreuil, ☎03 21 06 04 27. www.tourisme-montreuillois.com.
- ▶ **Orient Yourself:** Just 11 miles inland from Le Touquet via the N 39, and 30 miles north of Abbeville along the N1.
- 🅿 **Parking:** Limited roadside parking.
- **Don't Miss:** A tour of the ramparts, and the cobbled Rue Clape-en-Bas.
- ⏱ **Organizing Your Time:** You can easily spend a relaxed half day exploring the citadelle and the ramparts.
- **Also see:** The Gardens of Valloires, Le Touquet-Paris-Plage.

## A Bit of History

### Royal patronage

Montreuil developed around two buildings: the monastery founded in the 7C by the Bishop of Amiens, and the fortress built in about 900 by the Count of Ponthieu.

In 1537 Emperor Charles V's troops forcibly seized the town, almost completely destroying it in the process. The ramparts were rebuilt by the engineers of François I, Henri IV and Louis XIII; and Montreuil included up to eight churches. In 1804, at the time of the Boulogne Camp, Napoleon stayed in Montreuil, and in 1916 Douglas Haig, commander of the British troops, made his headquarters here.

## Sights

### Citadelle★

⏱ *Open Mar-Oct daily (except Tue) 10am-noon, 2-6pm.* ⏱ *Closed Dec to Feb.* 2.50€. ☎ 03 21 06 10 83.

Montreuil citadel was built in the second half of the 16C, but contains elements of an 11C and 13C structure. It was completely remodelled in the 17C. On the side facing the town, a demi-lunes protects the entrance. Having crossed this, the tour encompasses:

- the two 13C round towers which flank the royal château;
- Tour Berthe (14C), the tower that served as the entrance to the town until 1594. It is part of a 16C bastion and houses the emblems of the lords killed at Agincourt in 1415.

## A "Storm in the Mind"

Montreuil's setting and surroundings have charmed many writers, among them Laurence Sterne (1713-68), the English writer and author of *A Sentimental Journey through France and Italy*, and also **Victor Hugo**. The latter visited Montreuil in 1837 and used the town as the setting for one of the main episodes in *Les Misérables*. The novel tells how the convict Jean Valjean, reformed by a life of generosity and sacrifice, becomes mayor of Montreuil; when, however, an innocent man is to be tried in his place, Valjean is subjected to a terrible moral dilemma, immortalised by Hugo under the heading "Storm in the Mind".

A "son et lumière" show on the theme of *Les Misérables* takes place in late July – early September.

## Address Book

🎨 *For coin ranges, see the Legend on the cover flap.*

### WHERE TO STAY

🛏 **L'Écu de France** – *5 porte de France –* ☎*03 21 06 01 89. Closed Tue-Wed in winter –8 rms –* 🍽 *5.50€ – restaurant* 🍴🍴. This inviting house with a spotless facade offers modern bedrooms in shades of red and yellow. At mealtime, generous portions of Flemish cooking are served in a medieval decor (stained glass, swords hanging on the walls, and so forth).

🛏 **Manoir Francis** – *1 r. de l'Église, 62170 Marles-sur-Canche – 5.5km/3.3mi SE of Montreuil via D 113 – ☎ 03 21 81 38 80 –* 🍽 *– 3 rms.* Guests must go through an enormous covered porch, then cross the yard abounding in poultry to reach this handsome 17C seigniorial farmhouse. Spacious bedrooms furnished with period pieces and a private sitting room. Magnificent breakfast room.

🍴🍴 **La Commanderie (Bed and Breakfast)** – *Allée des Templiers, 62990 Loison-sur-Créquoise – ☎ 03 21 86 49 87. Closed Feb –* 🍽 *– reserv. recommended in winter – 3 rms.* A long alleyway leads to this splendid 12C residence, formerly belonging to knights of the Templar order. The stylishly decorated rooms have been given girls' names. Beautiful antiques are placed here and there, and there is a pleasant park bordered by a river.

🍴🍴🍴 **Haute Chambre (Bed and Breakfast)** – *124 rte d'Hucqueliers, le Ménage hamlet, 62170 Beussent – 10km/6mi N of Montreuil via N 1 then D 127 – ☎ 03 21 90 91 92. Closed 1-15 Sep and 15 Dec to 15 Jan –* 🍽 *– 5 rms.* If the Canche Valley is a tiara, the Haute Chambre is its brightest jewel. Rather difficult to find, this 1858 manor, marvellously restored by the owners, is sure to please. Whether in the plush bedrooms or the idyllic park, you'll live the aristocratic life at your own rhythm here. The host's sculpture and painting atelier may be visited upon request.

### WHERE TO EAT

🍽 **L'Auberge d'Inxent** – *62170 Inxent – 9km/5.4mi N of Montreuil via D 127 – ☎ 03 21 90 71 19 – auberge.inxent@ wanadoo.fr. Closed 30 Jun to 10 Jul, 22 Dec to 29 Jan, Tue lunch and Mon from 21 Jul to 24 Aug, Tue-Wed from 26 Aug to 5 Jul.* Located in the heart of the village, this pretty blue house dating from 1765 has always been an inn. An agreeable place to stay while visiting the Vallée de la Course, offering comfortable, rather spacious bedrooms. Tasty cuisine of the Artois region. The garden is well worth a visit.

🍽🍽🍽 **Auberge La Grenouillère** – *62170 Madelaine-sous-Montreuil – 2.5km/1.5mi W of Montreuil via D 139 and secondary road – ☎ 03 21 06 07 22. Closed 2-31 Jan, 24-27 Jun, 2-6 Sep, Wed except Jul-Aug and Tue.* In this charming country inn, the guest of honour is unquestionably the frog, whose presence can be seen everywhere: on walls, on paintings dating from 1930, and, for enthusiasts, on the dinner plate. In summer the delectable fare is served outdoors. A few guest rooms.

### SHOPPING

**M. et Mme Leviel** – *Fond des Communes – 62170 Montcravel – ☎ 03 21 06 21 73.* Their speciality: *apérichèvres,* goat cheese hors- d'œuvres.

### SHOWTIME

**Son et lumière** – 'Sound and Light' show – *'Les Misérables',* a show based on Victor Hugo's *chef-d'œuvre.* Late July-early Aug, evenings. *Information at Tourism Office.*

### SPORT

**Club Canoë kayak** – *4 R. des Moulins-des-Orphelins – ☎ 03 21 06 20 16 –* River kayaking centre.

### TOURS

**Visit of in the city** – The Office de Tourisme offers guided tours. Jun-Sep, Sat and Sun. 7€. ☎ *03 21 06 04 27.*

- the sentry walk, which offers attractive **views**★★ over the Canche Valley: the old charter house of Notre-Dame-des-Près and the opening of the Course Valley (*right*), the wetlands of the Canche, the estuary and Le Touquet marked by its lighthouse (*left*).
- the pillboxes built in 1840 and the 18C chapel.

### Remparts★ (Ramparts)

The red-brick and white-stone walls with bastions date largely from the 16C-17C, though some elements of the 13C walls have remained on the west front.

▷ *Leave the citadel by the bridge that crosses the ditch and turn right onto the small path that runs alongside the walls; continue for 300m/330yd towards the gate known as Porte de France.*

From the sentry walk there is a lovely perspective of the curtain walls with their series of 13C towers incorporated into the 16C walls; one side offers a view over the roofs of Montreuil, the other the Canche Valley and the plateau of the Montreuil region.

🚶 For those with time to spare, it is possible to walk right round the ramparts (*1hr*) along a shaded path offering extensive views over the surrounding countryside.

## The Town

### Rue du Clape-en-Bas

This charming cobbled street is lined with low, whitewashed houses with mossy tiled roofs, typical of dwellings in the Canche Valley. Craftsmen work here during the season (weavers, potters etc).

# MORET-SUR-LOING★

POPULATION 4 402

MICHELIN LOCAL MAP 312: F-5 OR MAP 106 FOLD 46

Moret is a charming riverside town at the confluence of the Loing and Seine rivers, close to Fontainebleau Forest.

🛈 **Information:** Pl. de Samois, 77250 Moret-sur-Loing. ☎01 60 70 41 66.
▷ **Orient Yourself:** Near Fontainebleau, 50 miles south of Paris via the A 6/N 6. Access from Paris: SNCF rail link from Gare de Lyon.

## A Bit of History

### A fortified town and a royal residence

Situated near the Champagne border, Moret and its fortified castle defended the king's territory from the reign of Louis VII up to Philip the Fair's marriage to Jeanne of Navarre, the daughter of the Comte de Champagne (1284), which put an end to the feud between the two families. Its keep and curtain wall – the two gates still stand – lost their strategic value, and Fontainebleau became the official place of residence for French rulers. The fortifications remained until the mid-19C and the part of town traversed by the River Loing kept its secluded character.

The history of Moret was marked by a number of famous women, including Jacqueline de Bueil (1588-1651), one of the last loves of Henri IV, who founded the Notre-Dame-des-Anges hospital and convent. Marie Leszczynska was greeted in Moret by Louis XV on 4 September 1725; a commemorative obelisk marks the place where the betrothed met (at the top of the rise along N 5). The following day they were married in Fontainebleau.

## Address Book

♿ *For coin ranges, see the Legend on the cover flap.*

### WHERE TO STAY

⊜ **Auberge de la Terrasse** – *40 r. de la Pêcherie* – ☎ *01 60 70 51 03. Closed mid-Oct to early Nov* – *17 rms* – ⌑ *9.30€.* Enjoy the view of the river from the dining room of this very nicely situated hotel along the Loing. Families will be particularly pleased – the well-fitted, comfortable rooms are free for children under ten, and a children's meal is offered for two adult meals taken.

⊜ **M. Gicquel (Bed and Breakfast)** – *46 r. René-Montgermont, 77690 Montigny-sur-Loing – 7km/4.2mi SW of Moret-sur-Loing via D 104* – ☎ *01 64 45 87 92* – *2 rms.* These august stables and their paved courtyard, nestled in the heart of a tiny village, offer upper-floor bedrooms with sloped ceilings, exposed beams and furniture of yore. The attractive breakfast room gives onto the kitchen.

### WHERE TO EAT

⊜⊜⊜ **Rôtisserie du Bon Abri** – *90 av. de Fontainebleau, 77250 Veneux-les-Sablons - 3,5 km from Moret-sur-Loing* – ☎ *01 60 70 55 40. Closed 26 Jul to 13 Aug, 26 to 30 Dec, 16 to 24 Feb, Tue and Sun evening, and Mon.* The hospitable reception from the Spttieaux family, tastefully designed interior and delect-able traditional cuisine are responsible for the fine reputation of this brasserie-bistro in the town centre.

⊜⊜⊜ **Hôtel La Vanne Rouge** – *77690 Montigny-sur-Loing* – ☎ *01 64 78 52 30 – closed Sun evening, Mon-Tue from Sep to Easter.* Located on the banks of the Loing, this impressive 19C half-timbered house features a rustic dining room furnished with stylish pieces. When the weather is pleasant, ask for a table on the enchanting, linden-shaded terrace.

### SHOPPING

**Sucre d'orge des Religieuses de Moret** – *5 r. du Puits-du-four* – ☎ *01 60 70 35 63 – Apr-Nov: Sun/public holidays 3-7pm; Jun-Sep: Sat, 3-7pm. Closed Feb.* The Nuns of Moret have been making barley sugar since 1638 and this family museum tells their story. A collection of sweets boxes and antique objects complements the video describing the main aspects of small-scale barley sugar manufacturing. One may sample the wares and buy some to take home.

### BOATING

**Bâteaux du Confluent** – *6 quai de Seine, 77670 St-Mammès* – ☎ *01 64 23 25 59 – Oct-Mar: Mon, Wed and Fri afternoons or mornings by appointment; May-Sep daily afternoons (except Sat, Sun, and holidays: all day).* This boat rental company is well situated at the convergence of the Loing and the Seine. Different boats (no special licence necessary) are available depending on the length of your journey, (from one hour to one week). Navigational equipment and souvenirs.

## Walking Tour

### The river banks★

Branch off the road to St-Mammès and proceed toward the Pré de Pin which runs along the east bank of the Loing. Admire the **view** of the lake, the shaded islets, the fishermen, the church and the ancient keep. This view provided inspiration for the Impressionist, Alfred Sisley, who chose Moret and the surrounding area as the theme for some 400 of his paintings.

### Bridge over the Loing

One of the oldest bridges in the Île-de-France, this was probably built around the same time as the town fortifications but was frequently torn down and then widened. On the approach to the Porte de Bourgogne the ramparts and several houses with overhangs – one of which rises out of the Loing waters – come into view.

### Église Notre-Dame

The building is reminiscent of many great churches in the Île-de-France.

*Maison de François I*

The **chancel** is believed to have been consecrated in 1166. The original elevation is visible in the apse and on the south side; the main arches resting on round columns are crowned by a gallery opening onto triple arching, surmounted by clerestory windows. The arches and the bays on the north side were walled up to offer greater support to the structurally unsound bell tower erected in the 15C.

### Ancien hospice

The corner post at rue de Grez bears an effigy of St James. A few steps along rue de Grez a modern cartouche bears the foundation date of the hospital (1638). The place became famous for the Moret barley sugar sweets made by the nuns. This tradition was continued by the town's confectioners.

### Maison de Sisley

**Alfred Sisley** (1839-99), the Impressionist painter of English parentage, spent the latter part of his life in Moret. His studio was at no 19 rue Montmartre (*private*). He turned his back on a life in commerce to paint, and belonged to the Impressionist group but never achieved fame in his lifetime and was continually beset by financial difficulties. A pure landscape painter, Sisley delighted in the scenery of the Île-de-France and showed feeling for portraying water, light and air.

### Rue Grande

At no 24 a commemorative plaque marks the house where Napoleon spent part of the night on his way back from Elba (19 to 20 March 1815).

### Maison François I

*Walk through the town hall porch and into the small courtyard.* Note the extravagant Renaissance decoration of the gallery, and the door crowned by a salamander.

### Porte de Samois

Also known as the Paris Gate. A statue of the Virgin Mary adorns the inner façade. Note the old-fashioned royal milestone that once marked out the highway leading from Lyon to Paris (now N 5).

# MORIENVAL★

POPULATION 1 048

MICHELIN LOCAL MAP 305: I-5 OR MAP 106 FOLD 11

Beautifully set off by the trees and shrubs in the park of the former abbey and the greenery in the surrounding valley, Morienval  is one of the earliest Gothic churches in France.

🛈 **Information:** ☎03 44 88 66 36 or 06 12 22 68 46.
▶ **Orient Yourself:** Located 45 miles northeast of Paris, and south of Compiègne.
🕐 **Organizing Your Time:** Allow one hour to explore the abbey.

## Église Notre-Dame★

🕐*Open 9am-7pm by prior arrangement.*

Notre-Dame church depended on a nunnery said to have been founded by King Dagobert in the 7C. Little has changed since the 12C except for the reconstruction of the clerestory in the chancel. The narrow bays visible today date from the last restoration project (1878-1912).

**Exterior** – The abbey church has a typical silhouette with its three towers, one adjoining the west front and two flanking the chancel; the north tower is marginally shorter and slimmer than the south tower.

Go northward around the church to the apse; note the ambulatory which was squeezed onto the semicircle of the chancel at the beginning of the 12C, to give it extra strength.

**Interior** – The extremely narrow ambulatory is the most unusual part of the church. Its arches, dating from about 1125, are some of the oldest in France. Here for the first time ogee arches have been used in the curved part of a building; however, they are an integral part of the areas of vaulting that they support. The transition from groined vaulting to quadripartite vaulting can be seen.

A large number of memorial stones stand along the wall of the north aisle; one commemorates the great abbess Anne II Foucault (1596-1635). Farther along the same wall, past the northern arm of the transept, is a statue of Our Lady of Morienval (17C).

On the wall of the opposite aisle, 19C engravings show the church as it was before the last restoration. In the southern arm of the transept stands a 16C Crucifixion group once mounted on a rood beam, and a large 17C terracotta St Christopher stands on the same side in the nave near the main doorway.

*Notre-Dame Church*

# GROTTES-REFUGES DE NAOURS★
## NAOURS CAVES
MICHELIN LOCAL MAP 301: G-7 – 13KM/8MI NORTH OF AMIENS

The old village of Naours contains excellent examples of Picardy-style cob houses. Below the surface of the plateau near Naours is the largest number of refuge-caves dug out of limestone; there are many in Picardy and parts of Artois, known as *creuttes*, *boves* **or**, in Naours, *muches*. **During times of trouble the men of the village would hide there.**

Human occupation of the caves of Naours goes back to the 9C and the Norman invasions, although the caves are mentioned in documents only from the 14C. They were much used during the Wars of Religion and the Thirty Years War. In the 18C salt-smugglers used them to avoid the collectors of the hated salt tax. Forgotten for a while, they were rediscovered in 1887 by Abbot Danicourt, the local priest, who explored and cleared them with the help of the villagers. In 1905 treasure was found: 20 gold coins from the 15C, 16C and 17C. In 1942 the caves were occupied by the Germans.

- **Information:** ☎ 03 22 93 71 78. www.grottesdenaours.com.
- **Orient Yourself:** On a limestone plateau, 8miles north of Amiens.
- **Parking:** On site (free)
- **Organizing Your Time:** Tours take about one hour
- **Also See:** Amiens, the chateau of Bertangles.

## Visit

### Caves

**Kids** ⏰*Open Apr-Aug:* ⟶ *guided tours 9.30am-6.30pm; Sep-Mar 9.30am-12.30pm, 2-5.30pm.* ⏰*Closed mid Nov-end Jan.* ⟶*10€ (children: 8€).*

The underground passages form a town which could shelter 3 000 people in its 2km/1.25mi of streets and squares, its 300 rooms, three chapels, cattle sheds and stables, bakery with ovens, storerooms etc. Chimneys link the passages to the surface of the plateau, 30m/98ft above.

During the tour the different layers of the soil are revealed: chalk, clay in fissures and pockets, flint in parallel bands. The small **Musée du folklore** is housed in a few of the chambers; local crafts are presented in enormous dioramas.

It is also possible to climb to the top of the ridge, to the two reconstructed wooden Picardy **post-mills**; there were at one time up to seven windmills in Naours (*bird's-eye view over the town*).

---

### WHERE TO EAT

⊖ **La Chèvrerie de Canaples** –
*172 r. de Fieffes, 80670 Canaples – 6km/3.6mi N of Naours via D 60 and D 933 –* ☎ *03 22 52 93 06. Closed Nov to Mar, Sun and public holidays –* ⟶ *– reserv. required for refreshments.* An original way to round off your tour of the caves. This farm serves mid-afternoon refreshments, farm-style, to groups of at least 10, or lets visitors sample their cheeses (closed lunchtime – noon to 2pm) and discover their goat farm and shop selling regional products.

# COLLINE DE NOTRE-DAME-DE-LORETTE ★

### NOTRE-DAME-DE-LORETTE HILL

MICHELIN LOCAL MAP 301: J-5 – 11KM/7MI SOUTH-WEST OF LENS

In a dramatically bleak setting, under an often grey sky, the hill at Notre-Dame-de-Lorette (166m/544ft high) is the culminating point of the Artois hill range. It overlooks a battlefield and was the target of many attacks during the First World War. **General Pétain** had his command post at La Targette, 7km/4.3mi from Notre-Dame-de-Lorette hill, while the 33rd army corps pierced the German lines.

- **Information:** 100 r. Pasteur, 62153 Souchez ☎ 03 21 72 66 55.
- ▶ **Orient Yourself:** The highest point of the Artois hills; 7 miles southwest of Lens by the D 58E, and from Béthune or Arras by the D 937 then D 58E.

## A Bit of History

Notre-Dame-de-Lorette features in dispatches during the First World War, especially during the first battle of Artois from May to September 1915. Among the many other places mentioned are Carency, Ablain St-Nazaire, Souchez (monument to General Barbot and the 1 500 *"chasseurs alpins"* killed in May 1915), Neuville St-Vaast, Vimy and La Targette (German cemetery).

## Sights

### Tour-lanterne

The main ossuary with its lantern tower (52m/170ft high) and the seven other ossuaries house the remains of 20 000 unknown soldiers. From the top floor, there is a vast **panorama**★ of the mining basin (*north*), the Vimy Memorial (*east*), the ruined church of Ablain St-Nazaire, the towers of Mont-St-Éloi and Arras (*south*).

### Musée vivant 1914-1918

🕘*Open 9am-8pm.* 🕘*Closed 1 Jan and 25 Dec.* ◉4€. ☎ *03 21 45 15 80.*

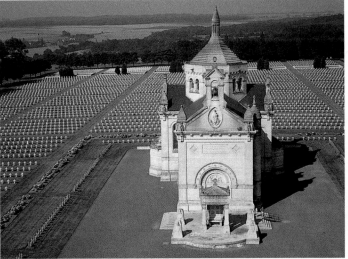

*Notre-Dame-de-Lorette*

T. Demont/ MICHELIN

## WHERE TO EAT

**⊖ Auberge du Cabaret Rouge –**
*1 r. Carnot, 62153 Souchez – 3km/1.8mi
E of N.-D.-de-Lorette via D 58e and D 937
– ☎ 03 21 45 06 10. Open Sat all day
and Sun lunchtime; groups accepted
weekdays – ⌐ – reserv. essential.* This
house near the road has three small
dining rooms decorated with a host
of trinkets. The menu centres on
homegrown vegetables and poultry,
plus other products from neighbouring
farms. Before leaving, ask the owner
to tell the story of the Cabaret Rouge.

Located 100m/109yd from the basilica,
the museum houses many objects
(photographs, uniforms, shells, helmets,
stereoscopic plates), and several reconstructions of underground shelters with
laser effects, which recreate the environment of soldiers. Next to the museum,
the Champ de bataille extends over an
area of 3ha/7.4 acres with its maze of
French and German trenches and its
mementoes of the First World War (guns,
machine-guns, turrets).

### Musée de la Targette

*7km southeast along D 937.* ♿ ⏰*Open
9am-8pm.* ⏰*Closed 1 Jan and 25 Dec.*
⊜*4€.* ☎*03 21 59 17 76.*
The museum contains over 2 000 exhibits,
including ancient weapons, but it is
mainly devoted to the two World Wars
and re-creates fighting in the Artois region
with the help of reconstructed scenes.

# NOYON ★

**POPULATION 14 471**
**MICHELIN LOCAL MAP 305: I, J-3**

Noyon is an ancient religious town with a rich history; its buildings are over-
shadowed by its imposing cathedral. It was the homeland of Calvin (1509-64)
and the sculptor Sarazin (1588-1660). The town lies in the heart of a picturesque
area, known locally as the "Petite Suisse" (small Switzerland), which is today the
main red-fruit producing region in France.

- ⓘ **Information:** 1 pl. Bertrand-Labarre, 60400 Noyon, ☎ 03 44 44 21 88.
www.noyon.com/tourisme.
- ▶ **Orient Yourself:** In a very fruity region, 15 miles northeast of Compiègne
by the N 32.
- ⊛ **Don't Miss:** Musée du Noyonnais
- ⏰ **Organizing Your Time:** A good time to visit is the first weekend of July, for the
fruit festival.

## A Bit of History

From St Médard to Hugh Capet
Originally Gallo-Roman, Noyon was
elevated by St Medard to a bishopric
linked to Tournai in 581. A century later,
St Eligius was one of its bishops. The
town has witnessed the splendour of
two coronations, Charlemagne's in 768
as King of the Franks and Hugh Capet's
in 987 as King of France. Noyon was one
of the first French cities to obtain its
own charter, in 1108.

### Red-fruit festival

The local industrial activity is varied
(smelting, printing works, food products).
Agriculture, favoured by the presence of
canning factories and storage businesses,
is mainly centred on growing red fruit,
90% of the production being destined for
the manufacture of sorbets. In July, when
the red-fruit festival is on (first Sunday),
the square in front of the cathedral is dotted with punnets of mouth-watering
strawberries, red currants, cherries and
black currants. Popular activities include
pastry tasting and competitions of fruit-
stone throwing.

*Chapter library*

# Cathedral★★

🕐*Open daily; times vary.* 🔊 *Possibility of guided visit by arrangement with the Office de Tourisme.*

Four buildings preceded the present cathedral, which was begun with the chancel in 1145 and finished in 1235 with the west front; this remarkable example of the Early Gothic style has a sober, solid Romanesque appearance combined with the breadth and harmony of the great masterpieces of the golden age of cathedral building. It was restored after 1918.

## Place du Parvis

The square is edged with a semicircle of canons' residences, where each entrance is surmounted by a representation of a canon's hat. It has kept its old charm despite the fact that most of these buildings were rebuilt after 1918.

**Exterior** – The sparse front is preceded by an early-13C porch with three bays; it was reinforced in the 14C with two flying buttresses decorated with small gables. The north tower is one of the loveliest types of bell tower built in northern France in the 14C; it is discreetly decorated with fine mouldings and twists of foliage on the gallery arcades, and foliate friezes under the upper shoulders of the buttresses.

To the north stands the old **chapter library** (*private*), a fine 16C timbered building. It is known for housing the precious Gospel Book from Morienval which dates from the 9C. One of the library rooms containing blacklisted works was known as "Hell."

**Interior★★** – The proportions of the nave and chancel are extremely pleasing. The nave has five double bays. The elevation rises through four storeys: great arches, large and elegant galleries with double arcading which are particularly striking viewed from the transept crossing, shallow triforium and clerestory.

The chancel vault is as high as the nave's. The eight ribs of the apse radiate from a central keystone and develop

## WHERE TO STAY AND EAT

⊜⊜ **Hotel Le Cèdre** – *8 r. de l'Évêché, 60400 Crisolles –* ☎*03 44 44 23 24 – www.hotel-lecedre.com –* 🅿 *– 35 rms –* ⊑ *7€.* This hotel built of red brick blends in perfectly with the surrounding cité. The rooms are best described as practical; most give onto the cathedral.

⊜⊜ **Auberge de Crisolles** – *On the D 932 – 60400 Crisolles – 4km/2.4mi NE of Noyon via D 932 dir. Ham –* ☎ *03 44 09 02 32. Closed Sun evening and Mon.* Stylish furnishings, old rose-coloured wallpaper and a nicely composed interior define the restaurant belonging to this pleasant inn on a quiet country road. Traditional cuisine concocted from fresh, top-quality ingredients.

into a cluster of small columns. Nine chapels open onto the ambulatory. Among the furnishings, the Louis XVI high altar shaped liked a temple is of particular interest, as are some largely 18C grilles that enclose the chancel and the chapels in the nave.

Today only a single gallery remains of the **old cloisters** (*north aisle*); the bays with beautiful radiating tracery overlook the garden. The opposite wall is pierced with wide pointed arch windows and a door giving access to the 13C **chapter-house**. The pointed arches rest on a series of columns.

## Additional Sights

### Musée du Noyonnais

*Guided visits by arrangement with the Tourist Office. Apr-Oct daily 10am-noon, 2-6pm. Nov-Mar daily (except Mon) 10am-noon, 2-5pm. Closed 1 Jan, 11 Nov, 25 Dec. 2.50€, no charge first Sunday in the month. ☎ 03 44 09 43 41.*

This brick and stone Renaissance building (a remnant of the old bishop's palace), with a corner turret and a 17C wing which was rebuilt after the First World War, contains collections on local history. Many objects were discovered during excavations in Noyon and the surrounding area (Cuts, Béhéricourt): 12C chess pieces, a cache of Gallo-Roman coins, funeral objects and ceramics. Upstairs, 12C and 13C oak **chests** from the cathedral are exhibited.

### Musée Jean-Calvin

*Guided visits by arrangement with Tourist Office. Apr-Oct 10am-noon, 2-6pm. Nov-Mar daily (except Tue) 10am-noon, 2-5pm. Closed 1 Jan, 11 Nov, 25 Dec. 2.50 €, no charge first Sunday in the month. ☎ 03 44 44 03 59.*

The museum is installed in a house built in 1927 partly on the foundations, and following old plans, of the house where Calvin was born and which was destroyed at the end of the 16C.

An audio-visual display (*10min*) presents Calvin and his time. The great reformer's room has been re-created and contains authentic portraits and engravings, together with a letter written by Calvin. Among other exhibits are 16C French Bibles, including the famous Olivetan Bible and the Lefèvre d'Étaples Bible, models of a 16C printing works and of the round Paradise temple in Lyon (1564) as well as writings by Calvin and his contemporaries. The library holds 1 200 books dating from the 16C to the 20C.

# CHÂTEAU D'OLHAIN★

MICHELIN LOCAL MAP 301: I-5
6KM/3.5MI SOUTH-EAST OF BRUAY-LA-BUISSIÈRE

**Olhain Castle,** set in a romantic lake at the bottom of a vale, is characteristic of fortified castles built in low-lying areas during the Middle Ages. It dates from the 13C-15C and boasts a large bailey that has been transformed for agricultural use.

🔢 **Information:** ☎ 03 21 27 94 76 or 01 39 18 33 14. www.chateau-olhain.com.
▶ **Orient Yourself:** 3.5 miles southeast of Bruay-la-Buissière. From Arras take the D 341, northwest.
**Especially for Kids:** Parc Départemental de Nature et de Loisirs
👓 **Also See:** Béthune, Lens.

## Visit

*Open Jul and Aug, Sat-Sun and public holidays 3pm-6.30pm; Apr-Jun, and Sep-Oct, Sun and public holidays 3-6.30pm. Closed Nov-Mar. 4€.*

The castle has retained its medieval structure. A drawbridge gives access to the bailey and from there to a watchtower (*staircase with 100 steps*), a Gothic room known as the guard-room, cellars with 2-3m/6.5-10ft-thick walls, and a chapel. Pleasant stroll along the edge of the moat.

### Kids Parc Départemental de Nature et de Loisirs
*1km/0.5mi north on D 57E.*
In this nest of greenery in the heart of the mining region, numerous facilities have been established: sports grounds, swimming pool, golf course, tennis courts, playgrounds, picnic areas, footpaths etc.

### Dolmen de Fresnicourt
*3km/2mi on D 57 and a little road to the right (signposted).*
The "Fairies' Table" is situated on the edge of a small, once-sacred oakwood. It is an impressive sight, even though its capstone has slipped.
The crest of the hill on which the megalith stands, separating Flanders from Artois, provides extensive views.

# VALLÉE DE L'OURCQ
## OURCQ VALLEY
MICHELIN LOCAL MAP 312: G-1 TO H-2 OR MAP 106 FOLDS 12, 23, 24

Beyond La Ferté-Milon, the River Ourcq follows a winding course, which skirts the beds of hard coarse limestone in the Brie subsoil. Before the creation of the canal to divert its waters, the Ourcq used to flow into the Marne downstream from Mary-sur-Marne. **Canal cruises** along the Ourcq are available in season. The poet Charles Péguy was one of the many French soldiers killed in the Battle of the Marne (1914).

## Battle of the Marne

The first Battle of the Marne originated with the Battle of the Ourcq, which in fact took place on the heights of the Multien plateau and not in the valley itself. The outcome of this battle did much to secure the success of the general offensive launched between Nanteuil-le-Haudouin, north of Meaux, and Révigny, north-west of Bar-le-Duc.
It is little known that this battle began – on both sides – with the engagement of large reserve units (55th and 56th French Divisions, 4th German Corps). Owing to the hazards of drafting and the movement of retreat, many of the French soldiers were in fact defending their native territory.

## The Battlefield and the Ourcq Valley

### Round-trip starting from Meaux
*96km/58mi – allow 4hr – local map, see next page.*

### Meaux★
*see MEAUX.*

▶ *From Meaux take N 3 (west) toward Paris. After 6.5km/4mi, a memorial paying tribute to Gallieni stands on the left-hand side of the road. Turn right onto D 27, toward Iverny, then right again toward Chauconin-Neufmontiers.*

### Mémorial de Villeroy
This stands on the site of the early operations of 5 September 1914.
The funeral vault houses the remains of 133 officers and soldiers who died in the fields nearby. **Charles Péguy** (1873-1914) was buried with his comrades-in-arms belonging to the 276th Infantry Regiment (reserve). Their collective grave lies to the right of the vault. The cross celebrating the memory of the writer, philosopher and social reformer has been moved to the intersection of D 27 and D 129.
The 19th Company of the 276th Regiment was called in to relieve the Moroccan Brigade who accompanied them and who were dangerously engaged in battle near Penchard. It launched an attack toward Monthyon, under the fire of the enemy, sheltered in the valley around the Rutel brook.

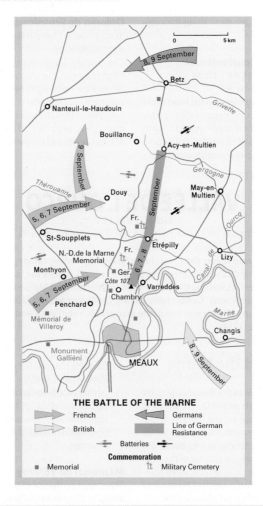

**THE BATTLE OF THE MARNE**

| French | Germans |
| British | Line of German Resistance |

✈ Batteries

**Commemoration**

■ Memorial ‡ Military Cemetery

## Address Book

⏲ *For coin ranges, see the Legend on the cover flap.*

### WHERE TO EAT

🍽🍽 **L'Assiette du Marché** – *1 place du Marché, 77840 Crouy-sur-Ourcq – 5km/3mi east of May-en-Multien by D 94 – ☎ 01 64 35 67 41. Closed 12 Feb-8 Mar, Thur and evenings except Fri and Sat –* 🍴. This city residence on the market square houses a small yet delightful restaurant. The tiny dining room with its neat decoration, reminiscent of a tea shop, offers simple cuisine noted for its original flavours salads, daily specials and meat or fish dishes.

🍽🍽🍽 **Auberge de l'Ourcq** – *Rue Thury, 60890 Mareuil-sur-Ourcq – ☎ 03 44 87 24 14. Closed 22 Jan-12 Feb, 25 July-11 Aug, Mon and evenings except Fri and Sat.* Treat yourself to Sunday lunch at this country-style family inn in the heart of Mareuil village, where the Ourcq Canal commences its course. Warm welcome, traditional French cooking and reasonable prices.

### CANAL CRUISING

Boat trips, with or without lunch on board, are organised along *the Canal de l'Ourcq. Information and bookings,* ☎ *0800 95 21 21 or 01 60 01 13 65.*

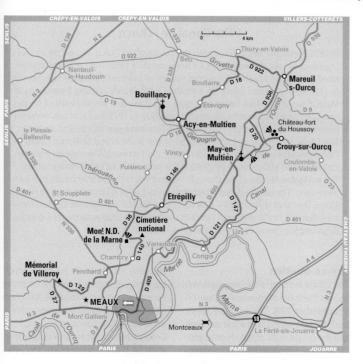

Péguy was the only surviving officer. He told his men to lie down and was inspecting the German positions when he was struck by a bullet.

▶ *At the next crossroads, turn left toward Chauconin-Neufmontiers. Drive through Penchard and follow directions to Chambry. Drive through the village.*

The bell tower of Barcy is visible to the left.

## Cimetière National de Chambry

Most of the soldiers buried here died during the fighting that took place on 6, 7 and 8 September when they were defending the village of Chambry, which was taken, lost and re-taken several times.

Along the road there is a view of the Chambry-Barcy Plateau covered in war graves that seem to mark out the progression of the Allied troops beneath the fire from the lines of German defence.

Located 500m/500yd east of the crossroads, the German military cemetery marks the place where the main German line – which roughly follows the dirt track – crossed the road to Varreddes.

▶ *Turn back, toward Barcy.*

## Monument Notre-Dame-de-la-Marne

This was erected in response to a vow made by Monseigneur Marbeau, Bishop of Meaux, in 1914 and dominates the whole battlefield.

▶ *Turn to the north for a good view of the Multien plateau in the far distance.*

Proceed toward Puisieux. At the crossroads after the old factory, turn right to Étrépilly. In the centre of the village, 200m/220yd before reaching the church, turn left toward Vincy and Acy-en-Multien.

## Étrépilly

The small national cemetery and the memorial evoke the fighting that took place during the night of 7-8 September, reaching a climax near the village graveyard.

## The Canal de l'Ourcq

In 1802 Bonaparte decided to divert the course of the Ourcq by creating a canal-aqueduct to take the waters to La Villette north of Paris. The canal was inaugurated seven years later and permitted navigation between Paris and Claye-Souilly in 1813. By 1821 it had joined up with the canalised river running from Ourcq to Mareuil-sur-Ourcq. Five locks were built and those that already existed on the canalised watercourse were renewed. From 1920 to 1930 the canal was widened between La Villette and Les Pavillons-sous-Bois and a new lock built at Sevran.
The Canal de l'Ourcq supplies the locks of the St-Denis and St-Martin canals in Paris; it also provides water for factories in Paris. Commercial navigation between La Villette and Meaux ceased in 1960: it has been replaced by pleasure boating. The navigable section of the Ourcq is 110km/68mi long and may be divided into three parts. The canalised river (10km/6mi – 4 locks) starts upstream from La Ferté-Milon. The canal (90km/54mi – 6 locks), linking Mareuil-sur-Ourcq to Les Pavillons-sous-Bois, is 1.5m/5ft deep and 11m/37ft wide. Finally, a wide watercourse (no locks) flows into the "Rond-Point des Canaux" in Paris (La Villette).

## Acy-en-Multien

This village nestling in the Gergogne Valley was the scene of intensive warfare on 7 September 1914. The winding alleys, the hillsides planted with small spinneys and the estate walls of the château provided many opportunities for close combat, often ending in tragic death.

▶ *Take the left-hand fork out of Acy toward Nanteuil-le-Haudouin.*

## Église de Bouillancy

Located in the lower part of the village. In the quiet valley – rural life is concentrated in the village on the plateau – lies an Early Gothic church (12C-13C) with harmonious proportions.

▶ *Turn back to Acy and take D 18 up to the plateau.*

Enjoy the view of **Acy** and the elegant village spire. Beyond Étavigny, the road moves away from the battlefield.

▶ *Just before Thury-en-Valois take D 922 to the right.*

The road leads to **Mareuil-sur-Ourcq**, marking the start of the canal.

▶ *Cross Varinfroy to Crouy-sur-Ourcq.*

## Crouy-sur-Ourcq

Just after the level crossing, the road skirts the ruins of the **Château Fort de**

**Houssoy.** In order to see the **keep**, which has remained separate, park the car in the station car park and walk to the courtyard gates. From the top of the tower, there is a fine view of the surrounding area.
**Crouy Church** (*visits by arrangement.* ☎ 01 64 35 63 02) features a Gothic interior with two 16C aisles. Admire the beautifully crafted panelling (1670) in the chancel.

▶ *Turn back, and after the bridge turn left toward May.*

The twisting, hilly road affords extensive **views** of the surrounding landscape.

## May-en-Multien

The village is well situated 100m/330ft above the River Ourcq. It is visible from afar on account of its church tower.

▶ *Drive down to Lizy. Do not cross the canal bridge but go up the hill on the north bank along the road to Congis (D 121).*

**View** of the last loop of the Ourcq, overgrown with greenery.

▶ *Cross Congis and Varreddes and join D 405, south.*

On the left stands the huge **American monument** that pays homage to the Marne combatants. The road dips and leads straight down to Meaux.

# PARIS ★★★

POPULATION 2 152 333 – METROPOLITAIN AREA 9 060 257
MICHELIN PLAN 10 (SINGLE SHEET) OR 11 (ATLAS WITH STREET INDEX)

Paris dominates France's intellectual, artistic, scientific and political life, and has done so since the 12C when the Capetian kings made it their capital. It is today a lively, beautiful city with considerable charm, boasting a wealth of attractions. The map and descriptions on the following pages give an outline of the most important sights in Paris, so that the visitor with just a day or two may become acquainted with the capital's landmarks and treasures. Like any city with a rich and varied history, however, Paris needs a little time to get to know; for longer stays in the French capital, consult Michelin's *Green Guide Paris*.

- **Information:** 25-27 rue des Pyramides, 1er arr., Mo Pyramides, ☎ 0 892 683 000. www.paris-touristoffice.com.
- ▶ **Orient Yourself:** Paris is located 290km (180 miles) from the Channel Port at Calais, and 200km (125 miles) from Le Havre. The city is less than three hours from London by Eurostar rail services. See the "Planning Your Trip" section of the guide for detailed information on getting to Paris.
- **Parking:** It simply doesn't bear thinking about. Driving in the city is a nightmare, ill-advised at best, and finding somewhere to park, other than very early in the morning, is impossible. Use public transportation or a sightseeing bus instead.
- **Don't Miss:** With so much that is wonderful to see, it is impossible to give an adequate overview. But certain sights are unmissable: the Eiffel Tower, of course, but you may have to queue; the Louvre; Arc de Triomphe; Champs Elysées; the artists in Montmartre; a boat trip on the Seine. Lunch in the Musée d'Orsay is quite an experience, too.
- **Organizing Your Time:** Plan carefully; do not try to cram too much into each day or you will be very jaded by Day 3. Start with a walk – from the Arc de Triomphe (*see La Voie Triomphale*), down the Champs Elysées, across the Place de la Concorde, through the Tuileries and up to the Louvre. Take time out to explore the trendy corridors of the Left Bank (Rive Gauche) and sample oysters fresh from the coast.
- **Especially for Kids:** Eiffel Tower; George Pompidou Centre.
- **Also See:** Père Lachaise cemetery; Versailles; Montparnasse; the Bastille.

*Place de la Concorde*

*The Louvre*

# Sightseeing

## Civil Architecture

### The Louvre★★★

The original Louvre was a fortress built in 1190 by Philippe Auguste on the banks of the Seine to protect the weakest point in his new city; it was used as treasure-house, arsenal and archive. In the 14C the fortress ceased its military functions with the erection of a new perimeter and Charles V converted it into a residence, installing his famous library in one of the towers. In 1528 François I took up residence in the Louvre. The keep was razed and defences knocked down but it was not until 1546 that a new royal palace was commissioned, on the site of the old keep, which was to become the residence of the kings of France. It was the architect Pierre Lescot who brought the Italian Renaissance style to the banks of the Seine; Jean Goujon added the sculpture. Over the following centuries, almost all the French monarchs added to and altered the evolving Louvre. The Florentine **Catherine de' Medici**, as Regent for Charles IX, ordered Philibert Delorme to build the Tuileries Palace nearby for her while work continued on the Louvre. Charles IX and Henri III both lived in and added to the Louvre, as did Henri IV and Louis XIII who both added pavilions. In 1662 the young King Louis XIV celebrated the birth of the Dauphin with lavish entertainment here.

The monumental, colonnaded façade facing the city was designed by Perrault, aided by Le Brun and Le Vau. It was begun in 1667 but completed only in 1811. Both Napoleon I and Napoleon III continued with additions, alterations and restorations. In 1871 the Communards set the Tuileries Palace and some of the wings of the Louvre ablaze, most of which were subsequently restored or rebuilt. The Tuileries Palace was finally demolished in 1883.

In 1984 President Mitterrand chose the glazed pyramid designed by the American IM Pei as the contemporary entrance to the Louvre Museum.

The **Louvre**★★★ is one of the largest and most famous museums in the world. It is divided into the following main sections: History of the Louvre and Medieval Louvre; Oriental Antiquities and Arts of Islam; Egyptian Antiquities; Greek, Etruscan and Roman Antiquities; Sculptures; Objets d'art; Paintings; Prints and Drawings. An additional section, Arts of Africa, Asia, Oceania and the Americas, contains a selection of masterpieces from early civilisations, which will later move to a new museum on quai Branly (*recommended access via the Porte des Lions*). Among its innumerable treasures are Mesopotamian statues; the Frieze of the Archers from Darius' Palace; the jewellery of Rameses II; the *Winged Victory of Samothrace* and the *Venus de Milo*; Michelangelo's Slaves; Renaissance master paintings by Giotto, Fra Angelico, Leonardo da Vinci (*Mona Lisa*), through to Veronese, Caravaggio, Van Dyck, Rubens, Rembrandt, Watteau and many more. There are Classical and Romantic works by the great French painters David, Ingres, Delacroix and Géricault.

The objets d'art include the Crown Jewels of France; Brussels and Gobelins tapestries; fine furniture and clocks.

## Hôtel des Invalides★★★

Guns captured at Vienna in 1805 line the Esplanade leading to the huge building (designed in 1671 to 1676 to house old soldiers invalided out of service) with a front (200m/650ft long) featuring dormer windows in the form of trophies. St Louis' Church within the precinct is the resting place of some of France's great soldiers; it also contains flags captured from the enemy. Berlioz' *Requiem* was first performed here in 1837.

The **Église du Dôme**★★★(◑*open Apr-Sep 10am-6pm; Oct-Mar 10am-5pm. ◑Closed first Mon of the month, 1 Jan, 1 May, 1 Nov, 25 Dec. ◉7.50€. ☎01 44 42 37 72, www.invalides.org)* was designed by Jules-Hardouin Mansart and begun in 1677; it is one of the great works in the Louis XIV style. The façade giving onto place Vauban has Doric and Corinthian orders, topped with a pediment carved by Coysevox. The soaring, gilded dome stands on a great columned drum supporting a balcony; an elegant lantern rises above.

The church took on its role as military necropolis when Napoleon had Maréchal de Turenne (d 1685) buried here. There is also a memorial to Vauban, the great military architect, and the tomb of Maréchal Foch. In an impressive crypt of green granite stands the unmarked red porphyry mausoleum, which is **Napoleon's Tomb** ★★★.

## Arc de Triomphe★★★

◑*Open Apr-Sep 10am-11pm (last admission 30min before closing). Oct-Mar: 10am-10.30pm. ◑Closed 1 Jan, 1 and 8 May (morning), 14 Jul, 11 Nov (morning), 25 Dec. ◉8€. ☎ 01 55 37 73 77.*

The great triumphal arch is one of Paris' main focal points; it stands in place Charles-de-Gaulle – known as the Star (L'Étoile) owing to its 12 radiating avenues. The arch was designed in 1806 as one of the landmarks of Napoleon's imperial capital but was finished only in

*Eiffel Tower by night*

A. Eü/MICHELIN

1836, in the reign of Louis Philippe.

In 1921 the arch saw the burial of the Unknown Soldier; two years later the flame of remembrance was kindled for the first time. Sculpture on the arch includes Rude's 1836 masterpiece known as *La Marseillaise*, showing the departure of volunteers to fight the invading Prussians (1792).

## Place de la Concorde★★★

This perfect expression of the Louis XV style was designed by Jacques-Ange Gabriel in 1755 and completed over 20 years. In January 1793 the guillotine was set up here for the execution of Louis XVI and other victims of the Reign of Terror. The square features colonnaded buildings to the north, massive pedestals, magnificent marble sculptures, and the pink granite Luxor Obelisk, 3 300 years old and covered with hieroglyphics, which was brought back from Egypt in 1836.

## Tour Eiffel★★★

*Lift:* ♿ *1st and 2nd floors only.* ⏱*Open mid-Jun to end Aug 9am-12.45am. Rest of year 9.30am-11.45pm. 4.20€ (1st floor), 7.70 € (2nd floor), 11 € (3rd floor). Stairs (1st and 2nd floor only):* ⌖*3.80€.* ☎ *01 44 11 23 23. www.tour-eiffel.fr.*

The Eiffel Tower is Paris' most famous symbol. The first proposal for a tower was made in 1884; construction was completed in 26 months and the tower opened in March 1889.

In spite of its weight (7 000t) and height (320.75m/1 051ft) and the use of 2.5 million rivets, it is a masterpiece of lightness. The tower actually weighs less than the volume of the air surrounding it and the pressure it exerts on the ground is that of a man sitting on a chair.

## Palais de Justice★

This, the main seat of civil and judicial authority, has been the residence of Roman governors, Merovingian kings and the children of Clovis, as well as Dagobert's mint, Duke Eudes' fortress and the royal palace of the rulers of medieval France. The Capetian kings gave it a chapel and a keep and its 1313 Gothic halls were widely admired. Later, Charles V built the Clock Tower (*Tour de l'Horloge*), the first public clock in Paris.

*Eiffel Tower*

The **Conciergerie**★★ (⏱*open Mar-Oct 9.30am-6pm; Nov-Feb 9.30am-5pm. Last admission 30min before closing.* ⏱*Closed 1 Jan, 1 May, 25 Dec.* ⌖*6.10€* ☎*01 53 40 60 80)* served as antechamber to the guillotine during the Reign of Terror; it contains the Prisoners' Gallery, Marie-Antoinette's cell and the Girondins Chapel.

## Palais-Royal★★

In 1632 Richelieu commissioned the huge building which became known as the Cardinal's Palace when it was extended in 1639. On his deathbed Richelieu bequeathed it to Louis XIII who renamed it the Palais-Royal. The formal gardens at the rear and the surrounding arcades were laid out in 1783; the adjoining Théâtre-Français was added four years later. The 260 columns in the outer courtyard were designed in 1986 by Daniel Buren.

## École Militaire★

Though lack of funds curtailed the original design, the military academy designed by Jacques-Ange Gabriel is an outstanding example of 18C French architecture.

It was begun in 1752, partly financed by Mme de Pompadour, and completed in 1772; various wings and buildings were added later. True to its original function, it houses the French Army's Staff College. The main front has a projecting central section with Corinthian columns rising through two storeys, crowned with a quadrangular dome and adorned with allegorical figures and military trophies. The superb **main courtyard**★★ is lined by porticoes with paired columns.

## Panthéon★★

⏱*Open Apr-Sep 10am-6.30pm. Oct-Mar 10am-6.15pm.* ⏱*Closed 1 Jan, 1 May (morning), 14 Jul, 11 Nov (morning), 25 Dec.* ⌖*7.50€.* ☎ *01 44 32 18 00.*

In 1744 Louis XV made a vow in Metz to replace the half-ruined church of St Genevieve's Abbey: in 1758 Soufflot began building on the highest point of the Left Bank. Despite predictions of collapse, the building has stood firm

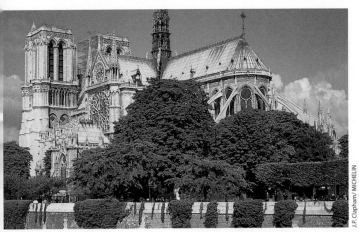

*Cathédrale Notre-Dame*

over the years but has undergone extensive alteration. In 1791 it was closed to worshippers and turned into the last resting place of the "great men of the days of French liberty". The building, in the shape of a Greek Cross, is still crowned by Soufflot's dome; the pediment of the Corinthian portico was carved by David d'Angers in 1831. The crypt houses the tombs of the famous.

### Opéra Garnier★★

⊙Open 10am-5pm (unless matinée or special event taking place). ☞ Guided tours (1h15) of the public foyers and the museum: noon (arrive 15min in advance). ⊚7€. ⊙Closed 1 Jan and 1 May. ☎ 01 40 01 25 40, www.operadeparis.fr.
The National Academy of Music opened in 1875, designed by Charles Garnier. The sumptuous interior is embellished with marble and a ceiling by Chagall.

### Palais de Chaillot★★

These elegant buildings constructed for the 1937 World Fair house the prestigious Théâtre national de Chaillot, the Musée de la Marine (naval museum), Musée de l'Homme (anthropology, ethnography, *closed until further notice*), and Musée des Monuments Français (*closed for refurbishment*). There is a **superb view**★★★ over the Seine, the Eiffel Tower and the Champ-de-Mars.

## Religious Architecture

### Cathédrale Notre-Dame★★★

The metropolitan church of Paris is one of the triumphs of French architecture. People have worshiped here for 2 000 years and in many ways Notre-Dame is the cathedral of the nation. Work was begun by Maurice de Sully in 1163 on what turned out to be the last great galleried church and one of the first with flying buttresses.

The chancel was built during the reign of Louis VII and consecrated in 1182 in the reign of Philip Augustus. The double ambulatory and the tracery reinforcing the wide windows set new trends, and the extended spouts of the flying buttresses formed the first gargoyles. By 1210 the first bays of the nave had been built; within 10 years it was completed and the 28 statues of the Kings' Gallery were in place. By 1245 the bulk of the work was complete; St Louis held a ceremony for the knighting of his son and placed the Crown of Thorns here until the Sainte-Chapelle was ready to receive it. In 1250 the twin towers were finished and the nave given side chapels.

In 1430 the young Henry VI of England was crowned King of France in the cathedral; in 1455 a ceremony was conducted to rehabilitate Joan of Arc; in 1558 Mary Stuart was crowned here on becoming Queen of France by her marriage to François II; and in 1572 the

J.P. Clapham/ MICHELIN

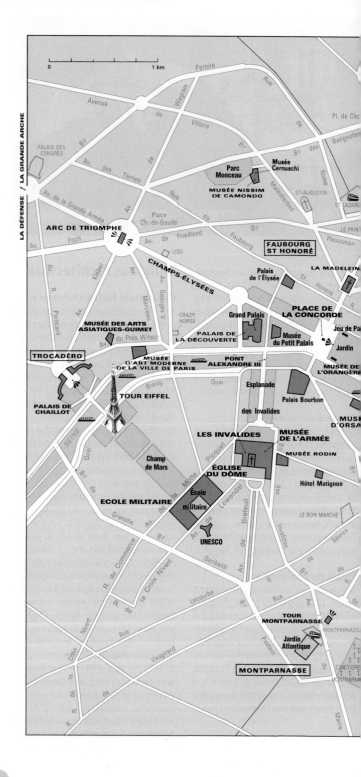

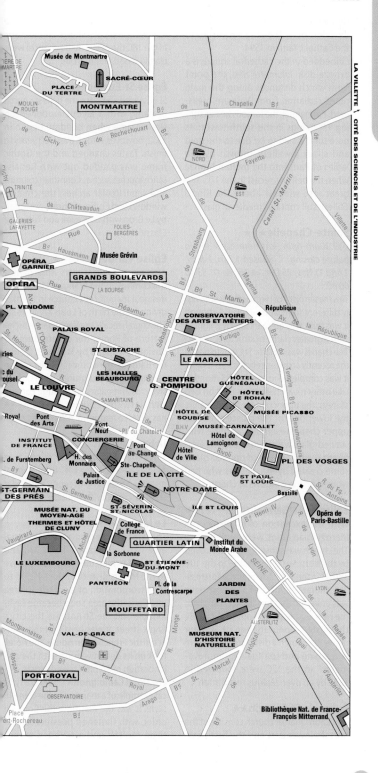

Musée de Montmartre

**SACRÉ-CŒUR**

**PLACE DU TERTRE**

MOULIN ROUGE

**MONTMARTRE**

Bᵈ de la Chapelle

de Clichy

Bᵈ de Rochechouart

de Strasbourg

NORD

EST

Fayette

Canal St. Martin

la Villette

TRINITÉ

R. de Châteaudun

La

de

GALERIES LAFAYETTE

FOLIES-BERGÈRES

Rue

Bᵈ Haussmann

**Musée Grévin**

**OPÉRA GARNIER**

**OPÉRA**

Rue

**GRANDS BOULEVARDS**

LA BOURSE

Bᵈ St Martin

Magenta

République

**PL. VENDÔME**

Av. de l'Opéra

Réaumur

Bᵈ St

Av. de la République

St. Honoré

**PALAIS ROYAL**

Sébastopol

**CONSERVATOIRE DES ARTS ET MÉTIERS**

Turbigo

Bᵈ du Temple

**ST-EUSTACHE**

**LE MARAIS**

ries

: du ousel

**LE LOUVRE**

**LES HALLES BEAUBOURG**

de

**CENTRE G. POMPIDOU**

**HÔTEL GUÉNÉGAUD**

**HÔTEL DE ROHAN**

**MUSÉE PICASSO**

Beaumarchais

SAMARITAINE

Royal

Pont des Arts

Pont Neuf

Bᵈ

**HÔTEL DE SOUBISE**

B.H.V.

**MUSÉE CARNAVALET**

Pl. du Châtelet

Hôtel de Lamoignon

**INSTITUT DE FRANCE**

**CONCIERGERIE**

Pont au Change

**Hôtel de Ville**

Rivoli

. de Furstemberg

H. des Monnaies

Ste-Chapelle

**PL. DES VOSGES**

**ST-GERMAIN DES PRÉS**

Palais de Justice

**ÎLE DE LA CITÉ**

**NOTRE DAME**

**ST PAUL-ST LOUIS**

R du Fᵍ St Antoine

St. Germain

**Bastille**

**MUSÉE NAT. DU MOYEN-AGE THERMES ET HÔTEL DE CLUNY**

**ST-SÉVERIN-ST-NICOLAS**

**ÎLE ST LOUIS**

Bᵈ Henri IV

**Opéra de Paris-Bastille**

Vaugirard

Michel

Collège de France

**QUARTIER LATIN**

**Institut du Monde Arabe**

R. de Lyon

**LE LUXEMBOURG**

St.

la Sorbonne

**ST ÉTIENNE-DU-MONT**

SEINE

Quai

LYON

**PANTHÉON**

Pl. de la Contrescarpe

**JARDIN DES PLANTES**

de la Rapée

Montparnasse

Bᵈ

**VAL-DE-GRÂCE**

Rue Monge

**MOUFFETARD**

AUSTERLITZ

Raspail

**MUSEUM NAT. D'HISTOIRE NATURELLE**

Quai

d'Austerlitz

**PORT-ROYAL**

Bᵈ de Port Royal

St.

Marcel

Quai de l'Hôpital

Place ert-Rochereau

OBSERVATOIRE

Bᵈ

Arago

de

Bᵈ

**Bibliothèque Nat. de France-François Mitterrand**

Huguenot Henri IV married Marguerite de Valois here; the king converted to the Catholic faith in 1594.

Embedded in the cathedral square is a bronze disk, *kilomètre zéro*, the point from which distances along the main roads radiating from Paris are measured. Emmanuel, the famous bell weighing 13t, hangs in the south tower; its pure tone is said to be due to the gold and silver jewellery thrown by the ladies of Paris into the molten bronze when the bell was recast in the 17C. The great rose window above the Kings' Gallery still contains medieval glass.

### Sainte-Chapelle★★★

🕐*9.30am-6pm (last admission 30min before closing).* 🕐*Closed 1 Jan, 1 May, 1 and 11 Nov, 25 Dec.* ✆*7€.* ☎ *01 53 40 60 80.*

This masterpiece of High Gothic is strikingly different from Notre-Dame. Although it was built only 80 years later it is lighter, with a greater clarity of structure.

The chapel was built for St Louis to house the recently acquired relics of the Passion; it was completed in a record 33 months. Like other royal chapels it is built on two storeys, the upper one for the monarch, the lower one for the palace staff. The upper chapel resembles a shrine with stained-glass walls; 720 of the 1 134 different scenes are still of original glass, some created by the masters who had worked on the windows at Chartres.

### Église de St-Germain-des-Prés★★

With the exception of Clovis, all the Merovingian kings were buried here. The church was subsequently destroyed by the Normans but restored in the 10C and 11C; the west tower has a fortress-like character. Around 1160 the nave was enlarged and the chancel rebuilt in the new Gothic style. From 1631 to 1789 the austere congregation of St Maur made the church a distinguished centre of learning and spirituality. "Improvements" in the 17C were followed in 1822 by an over-zealous restoration.

### Église de St-Séverin★★

This Latin Quarter church consists of the portal's lower part and the first three bays of the nave in High Gothic, with the rest largely Flamboyant – note the famous spiral pillar in the ambulatory. In the 18C the pillars in the chancel were clad in wood and marble.

### Église St-Eustache★★

St Eustache was once the richest church in Paris, with a layout modelled on Notre-Dame when building began in 1532; however, it took over 100 years to finish. Tastes changed and the Gothic frame was padded out with Renaissance touches such as Corinthian columns and semicircular arches; the chancel windows and Colbert's tomb, designed by Le Brun with Coysevox and Tuby, are Classical.

### Église Val-de-Grâce★★

After many childless years, Anne of Austria commissioned François Mansart to design a magnificent church in thanksgiving for the birth of Louis XIV in 1638. The church recalls the Renaissance architecture of Rome; the ornate dome is obviously inspired by St Peter's. Inside, the Baroque spirit prevails: polychrome paving, highly sculptured vaults, massive crossing pillars and a huge canopy with six twisted columns. The **dome**★★ has a fresco featuring 200 figures.

### Urban Design

Since the sweeping away of much of medieval Paris in the 19C, three central districts have come to typify particular stages in the city's evolution.

### Le Marais★★★

This smart shopping and residential area has Renaissance, Louis XIII and Louis XIV architecture. Charles V's move to the Marais district in the 14C led to the incorporation of a suburban area into Paris; the area soon became fashionable and rue St-Antoine the city's finest street. It was here that the characteristic French town house, the *hôtel*, took on its definitive form with the collaboration of architects and artists.

The **Hôtel Lamoignon**★ (1584) is a typical example of a mansion in the Henri III style. It was the first time the Colossal order, with flattened pilasters, Corinthian capitals and a sculpted stringcourse, was seen in Paris. The Henri IV

Allison M. Simpson/ MICHELIN

*Arc du Carrousel*

style appeared in the symmetrical **place des Vosges**★★★ (completed 1612). The 36 two-storey houses of alternate brick and stone facings have steeply pitched slate roofs pierced with dormer windows. Louis XIII's reign heralded the Classical style; in 1624 the **Hôtel de Sully** was built, with a gateway flanked by massive pavilions and a main courtyard with triangular and curved pediments and scrolled dormer windows. The early Louis XIV style is seen in Mansart's fine **Hôtel de Guénégaud**★★ (1648) with its simple lines, majestic staircase and small formal garden; in the **Hôtel de Beauvais**★ with its curved balcony on brackets; in the **Hôtel Carnavalet**★★ (now the Museum of Parisian History) built in 1655 by Mansart; and in Cottard's theatrical **Hôtel Amelot de Bisseuil**★ with its cornice and curved pediment decorated with allegorical figures. The Louis XIV style is seen in the **Hôtel de Rohan**★★ with its sculpture of the *Horses of Apollo* and the adjoining **Hôtel de Soubise**★ with its horseshoe-shaped courtyard and double colonnade; both have raised ground floors, massive windows, roof balustrades and sculpture on the projecting central sections.

## La Voie Triomphale★★★ (From the Tuileries to the Arc de Triomphe)

A great road leading from the courtyard of the Louvre to St Germain had been planned by Colbert but today's "Triumphal Way" was laid out under Louis XVI, Napoleon III and during the years of the Third Republic.

### Arc du Carrousel★

This pastiche of a Roman arch is decorated with statues of Napoleonic military men. An impressive perspective runs from the Louvre through the arch to the obelisk in place de la Concorde, then on to the Arc de Triomphe.

### Jardin des Tuileries★

The gardens were first laid out in the 1560s by Catherine de' Medici in the Italian style. A century later they were remodelled by Le Nôtre who created the archetypal formal French garden.

### Champs-Élysées★★★

In 1667 Le Nôtre extended the road from the Tuileries to a new focal point, the Rond-Point. The avenue was a service road at the back of smart houses but when refreshment stalls were set up along it crowds began to cluster. In 1724 the Duke of Antin planted rows of elms to extend the "Elysian Fields" up to the Étoile. In 1729 street lanterns lit the evening scene. Finally, in 1836 the **Arc de Triomphe**★★★ (☾*see above*) was completed. The Champs-Élysées became fashionable during the reign of Louis-Napoleon, when high society flocked to its restaurants.

### La Défense★★

This modern business centre with sky-scrapers and pedestrian terraces descending toward the Seine was planned as an entire project, the individual buildings subordinated to the overall design.

The precincts are overlooked by the enormous cube of the marble-faced **Grande Arche** (1989) ♿ (*Open all year 10am-7pm (last admission 45min before closing). ☞7.50€. ☎ 01 49 07 27 27. www.grandearche.com*) by Danish architect Johan Otto von Spreckelsen, which straddles the view stretching along to the Étoile and the Champs-Élysées. The area is also known for its public sculpture: works by Miró, Calder, Takis, Venet, Kowalski etc make it virtually an open-air museum.

## The Political Capital

### Palais de l'Élysée

This has been the Paris residence of the President of France since 1873. It was built in 1718 and was once the property of the Marquise de Pompadour. During the Revolution it housed a public dance hall, a gaming salon and a picture gallery. In Napoleon's time, Marie-Louise had a boudoir here and the young King of Rome, their son, a set of rooms.

### Palais Bourbon★

This has been the seat of the Lower House of France's Parliament, the Assemblée Nationale, for over 150 years. The Assembly consists of directly elected members; it examines and where necessary amends all draft legislation.

The palace was built in 1722; during the Revolution it was the seat of the Council of Five Hundred. The decorative treatment of the façade (1804) which overlooks place de la Concorde was chosen by Napoleon.

### Palais du Luxembourg★★

This is the seat of the Senate, the French Upper House. Its 283 members are elected for a period of 9 years but a staggered system ensures that a third of them face reselection every three years.

After the death of her husband the king, the regent Marie de Medici decided to move from the Louvre; in 1615 she commissioned a palace, something to remind her of the Pitti Palace in Florence, from Salomon de Brosse. The result has an exterior with ringed columns and rusticated stonework; a courtyard with columns, semicircular windows, curved pediments, balconies and roof balustrades; a south front with a quadrangular dome, a massive pediment and garden terraces.

### Hôtel de Ville★

Central Paris is governed from city hall. Municipal government was introduced in the 13C under the direction of leading members of the powerful watermen's guild appointed by Louis IX. The place has long been the hub of uprising and revolt: during the Revolution it was held by the Commune; in 1848 it was the seat of the Provisional Government. The Republic was proclaimed from here in 1870 and, in March 1871, the Communards burnt it down. It was rebuilt from 1874.

## The Intellectual and Artistic Capital

### Intellectual Life

The city as a whole functions as the capital of the country's intellectual life, though there is a particular concentration on the Left Bank, in the Fifth and Sixth *arrondissements*. The capital's most venerable institutions stand in the area around Mont Ste-Geneviève, in the **Latin Quarter** (so-called because Latin was the language of instruction right up to the French Revolution).

### Institut de France★★

The institute originated as the College of Four Nations founded by Mazarin for scholars from the provinces incorporated into France during his ministry (Piedmont, Alsace, Artois and Roussillon). Its building, which dates from 1662, was designed by Le Vau and stands over the river from the Louvre; it is famous for its dome, its semicircular flanking buildings and the tomb of Mazarin in the vestibule. The Institute is made up of five academies:

*Pont des Arts and Institut de France*

A. Éli/ MICHELIN

The **Académie Française**, the most prestigious of all, was founded in 1635 by Richelieu; its membership is limited to 40. The members, "Immortals," devote themselves to upholding the quality of the French language and enshrining it in the *Dictionnaire de la langue française*, the country's standard dictionary.

The **Académie des Beaux-Arts** dates from 1816. It has 50 members who cover painting, sculpture, architecture, engraving and music.

The **Académie des Inscriptions et Belles Lettres** was founded by Colbert in 1663. It deals with literary history and maintains an archive of original documents.

The **Académie des Sciences**, founded by Colbert in 1666, has 66 members working in astronomy, mathematics, medicine and natural sciences.

The **Académie des Sciences morales et politiques**, the last one to be founded (1832), is dedicated to philosophy, ethics, law, geography and history.

### Collège de France

The college was founded in 1529 by François I under the name of the College of Three Languages (Latin, Greek, Hebrew) in order to combat the narrow scholasticism of the Sorbonne. The present buildings date from the time of Louis XIII, who renamed it the Royal College of France;

it underwent major reconstruction in 1778. It was here, in 1948, that Frédéric Joliot-Curie formulated the laws controlling the process of nuclear fission and built a cyclotron to test his theories.

### Sorbonne

This is the country's most illustrious university, the successor to the theological college founded in 1253 by Robert de Sorbon for 16 poor scholars. In 1469 France's first printing press was installed here by Louis XI. For many years, the university court constituted the highest ecclesiastical authority beneath the Pope.

The **Sorbonne Church**★, built by Lemercier from 1635, is a fine example of Jesuit architecture. **Richelieu's tomb**★ (1694) by Girardon lies inside.

## Entertainment and Culture

Paris remains a thriving cultural centre, with a large number of different shows, exhibitions and events on at any one time.

**Entertainment** – There are **about 60 theatres** and over **400 cinemas** in the capital. **Music hall, variety shows** and **reviews** take place at the Crazy Horse, the Folies Bergères, the Moulin Rouge. There are numerous **concert halls**, some with resident orchestras, as well as the Opera and the Comic Opera. There are also nightclubs, jazz clubs, cabarets, café-theatres, circuses, concerts, recitals in churches etc. *The Green Guide Paris lists a selection of places to go for entertainment, as well as hotels and restaurants.*

**Exhibitions** – Paris boasts about 100 museums and 120 art galleries, plus about another 30 places for temporary shows. Museums include the world-famous Louvre, the **Musée d'Orsay**★★★ (1848-1914 art) ⬥ *(Ⓛopen daily (except Mon) 9.30am-9.45pm. ☎ 01 40 49 48 14. www.musee-orsay.fr)* the Centre Pompidou, the **Musée de Cluny**★★ (Museum of the Middle Ages) *(Ⓛopen daily (except Tue) 9.15am-5.45pm (last admission 30min before closing). Ⓛclosed 1 Jan, 1 May and 25 Dec. ⬥6.50€, no charge first Sunday in the month. ☎ 01 53 73 78 16),* the **Musée Rodin**★★ *(Ⓛopen daily (except Mon) Apr-Sep 9.30am-5.45pm (last admission 30min before closing); Oct-Mar daily (except Mon) 9.30am-4.45pm. Ⓛclosed 1 Jan, 1 May and 25 Dec. ⬥7€, no charge first Sunday in the month. ☎ 01 44 18 61 24),* the Military Museum at the Invalides and the fascinating **Cité des Sciences et de l'Industrie**★★★ *(☎ 01 40 05 80 00. www.cite-sciences.fr)* at La Villette.

**Tourist Paris** – Certain parts of the city have come to be identified in the visitor's mind with the very essence of Paris itself.

### Montmartre★★★

The "Martyrs' Mound" became the haunt of artists and Bohemians in the late 19C; its steep and narrow lanes and precipitous stairways still evoke the atmospheric village it once was. The mound rises abruptly above the city's roofs and at its centre is **place du Tertre**★★ with its "art market."

The exotic outline of the **Sacré-Cœur Basilica**★★, a place of perpetual pilgrimage, rises nearby. The basilica offers an incomparable **panorama**★★★ over the whole city.

### Centre Georges-Pompidou★★★

⬥ *Pompidou centre: Ⓛopen 11am-10pm (last admission 1hr before closing); museum and exhibitions: 11am-9pm, Thu 11am-11pm. Ⓛclosed Tue and 1 May. ⬥10€, no charge for the museum first Sunday in the month. ☎ 01 44 78 12 33. www.centrepompidou.fr.*

The old Beaubourg district has been transformed by the construction of this cultural centre with its library, exhibitions and **Musée National d'art Moderne** *( guided tours of the National Museum of Modern Art and temporary exhibitions: call for information on 01 44 78 12 33).*

# PÉRONNE

POPULATION 9 000

MICHELIN LOCAL MAP 301: K-8

At the confluence of the River Cologne and the Somme stands the old fortified town of Péronne, stretching between fish-filled lakes and **"hardines"**, marshland vegetable gardens similar to the **"hortillonages"** of Amiens. This is an eel centre, which is reflected in the local gastronomy; specialties include eel pâté and smoked eels. Colvert is the local beer.

🛈 **Information:** 1 r. Louis-XI, 80200 Péronne ☎ 03 22 84 42 38. www.ot-peronne.fr.

▶ **Orient Yourself:** At the confluence of the Cologne and the Somme, between Amiens and Saint Quentin. Accessed by the N 29, then the N 17 or the D 44.

🅿 **Parking:** Large car park near the Historial, but also ample on-street parking.

🕐 **Organizing Your Time:** You will need two hours to get full value from the Historial, but the town deserves another couple of hours, and maybe a stop for lunch.

# A Bit of History

### The Meeting in Péronne

In 1468, a meeting was attended by **Charles the Bold** and **Louis XI**, who both wanted Picardy as part of their territory. Louis was a sly, wily man who had supported the uprising of the town of Liège against Charles; as a result he had been shut away in Péronne by his rival. Before he could recover his freedom, the King of France was forced to sign a humiliating treaty that went against the grain and his interests since it obliged him to take up arms against the people of Liège. He was to remember the insult in future years and tradition has it that his bitterness was kept alive by a parrot which kept repeating, "Péronne! Péronne!"

### Miseries of War

In 1870 Péronne was besieged by the Prussians who bombarded the town for 13 days. During the Battle of the Somme in 1916 Péronne was occupied by the Germans. That year and the next saw the destruction of virtually the entire town.

# Sights

### Historial de la Grande Guerre★★

&. ◔*Open daily 10am-6pm.* ◔*Closed mid-Dec to mid-Jan.* ⊛*7€.* ☎ *03 22 83 14 18. www.historial.org.*
The unusual and innovative Museum of the Great War is housed in a modern building standing on piles behind the 13C castle, on the banks of the Étang du Cam. Access to the museum is through an opening carved into the wall of the **castle**. Louis XI was held prisoner by Charles the Bold in one of the towers here.
The museum presents an insight into European society on the eve of the *daily (except Mon)* First World War and throughout the hostilities.
Maps, some of them illuminated, illustrate at regular intervals the develop-

*Miniature aeroplane made from shrapnel and bullets*

ment of various fronts. A large collection of objects, works of art, documents, letters and postcards reveal the thoughts and the pattern of daily life for those caught up in the conflict.
In shallow white-marble excavations representing the trenches are uniforms, arms and personal effects.

### Hôtel de Ville

*Place du Cdt-Daudré.*
The town hall has a Renaissance façade flanked by turrets looking toward the square, and a Louis XVI front looking toward rue St-Sauveur. Inside, the **Musée Danicourt** (◔*open daily (except Sun and Mon) 2-5.30pm, Sat 9am-noon, 2-4.30pm;* ◔*closed public holidays, 3 weeks in May, and Christmas to New Year;* ☎ *03 22 73 31 10; www.ville-peronne.fr)* contains a collection of ancient coins and Greco-Roman and Merovingian jewellery.

### Porte de Bretagne

*Off rue St-Sauveur.*
This gateway dates from 1602 and was one of two entrances giving access through the town walls, which were destroyed before the First World War. It is now a free-standing brick pavilion with a slate roof, and is adorned with the emblem of Péronne. The wooden gates have been retained.
Beyond the moat, walk through the gate of the demilune and follow the old brick **ramparts** with stone courses (16C-17C) for an attractive view over the lakes and the "hardines".

# CHÂTEAU DE PIERREFONDS★★
MICHELIN LOCAL MAP 305: I- 4 – ALSO SEE MAP UNDER FORÊT DE COMPIÈGNE

This famous castle, rising above a pretty town, which in its heyday was a fashionable spa resort, has since 1924, been the setting of many films. A small lake adds to the romantic image.

- **Information:** Pl. de l'Hôtel-de-Ville, 60350 Pierrefonds ☎ 03 44 42 81 44
- ▶ **Orient Yourself:** Almost exactly due south-east of Compiègne, reached by the D 973.
- ⏱ **Organizing Your Time:** Allow two hr for a tour of the chateau.
- **Also See:** The town of Compiègne, the forest and the Armistice Clearing.

## A Bit of History

### Louis of Orléans' Castle
A castle has stood on this site since the 12C. The Valois earldom – which was elevated to a duchy when Charles VI gave it to his brother, Louis of Orléans – consisted of the castellany of Pierrefonds 🚶 together with Béthisy, Crépy and La Ferté-Milon.

Louis of Orléans assumed the regency during the king's madness but was assassinated in 1407 by his cousin John the Fearless, Duke of Burgundy. Before his death he constructed a chain of fortresses on his Valois lands, of which Pierrefonds was the linchpin.

The medieval castle was rebuilt by the King's architect, and Pierrefonds triumphantly withstood sieges by the English, the Burgundians and the royal troops. In the 16C the castle passed to Antoine d'Estrées, Marquess of Cœuvres and father of the beautiful Gabrielle. On the death of Henri IV the Marquess took sides with the Prince of Condé against the young Louis XIII; besieged once again by the royal forces, the castle was finally seized and dismantled.

### Viollet-le-Duc's Castle
In 1813 Napoleon I bought the castle ruins for a little under 3 000 francs. Napoleon III, an enthusiastic archaeologist, and since his days in the army passionate about the art of siege warfare, entrusted its restoration in 1857 to **Viollet-le-Duc**. It was only a matter of returning parts of it (the keep and annexes) to a habitable condition, leaving the curtain walls and towers as "picturesque ruins". At the end of 1861, however, the programme of works took on an altogether different, larger dimension; Pierrefonds was to be transformed into an Imperial residence. Work lasted until 1884.

*Château de Pierrefonds*

Fascinated by medieval life and Gothic architecture in particular, Viollet-le-Duc set about a complete reconstruction of the castle, following the basic shapes that were already outlined by the numerous walls and fragments remaining at the time.

## Visit

*Leave the car in place de l'Hôtel-de-Ville and approach the main entrance to the castle at the foot of the Arthus Tower. Walk round the castle along the route Charretière.* ⏱*Open May to Sep: 9.30am-6pm. Rest of year daily (except Mon) 9.30am-12.30pm, 2-5.30pm. Last admission 45min before closing.* ⏱*Closed 1 Jan, 1 May, 1 and 11 Nov, 25 Dec.* ⊜*6.50€.* ☎*03 44 42 72 72. www. monum.fr.*

**Exterior** – The quadrangular castle (103m/337ft long, 88m/288ft wide) has a large defensive tower at each corner and in the middle of the walls. On three sides it overlooks the village, almost

vertically; to the south a deep moat separates the castle from the plateau. The walls have two sentry walks, one above the other: the covered lower one is dressed with machicolations. The towers (38m/124ft high with 5-6m/16-20ft thick walls) are crowned with two storeys of defences; from the cart track (*route charretière*) they are a formidable sight. Eight statues of named military heroes adorn them, indicating the building's political significance.

Having walked along the esplanade, cross the first moat to the forecourt known as Les Grandes Lices. A double drawbridge (1) – one lane for pedestrians, the other for vehicles – leads to the castle doorway which opens into the **main courtyard**.

**Interior** – A permanent exhibition in the barracks celebrates Viollet-le-Duc and his work (engravings, paintings, photographs of the ruins, history of the castle etc). Another exhibition, devoted to the **Monduit workshops**, displays a collection of works of art in lead, including the lion weathervane of the Arras

---

## Address Book

ℹ*For coin ranges, see the Legend on the cover flap.*

### WHERE TO STAY

⊜⊜ **Domaine du Bois d'Aucourt** – *1.1km/0.7mi W of Pierrefonds via D 85, dir. St-Jean-aux-Bois –* ☎*03 44 42 80 34 –* ⊡ *– 11 rms –* ⊡ *8 €.* No two rooms are alike in this quiet 19C manor house in the heart of the Compiègne forest. Depending on your fancy you may rest in surroundings reminiscent of Scotland, Seville, Tuscany, a Zen meditation chamber or a tropical island.

⊜ **Camping La Croix du Vieux Pont** – *02290 Berny-Rivière – 19km/11.5mi NE of Pierrefonds. Take D 335, D 81 and D 91 –* ☎*03 23 55 50 02 –* ⊅ *– reserv. recommended – 370 sites: Food service.* Featuring both a lake and a river, this is an angler's paradise! The well-designed campsite also offers activities such as pony rides for kids, pedalo outings and swimming in the pools, one of which is covered.

### WHERE TO EAT

⊜ **Aux Blés d'Or** – *8 r. Jules-Michelet –* ☎*03 44 42 85 91. Closed 3 to 16 Jan, 19-27 Feb, 29 Nov-12 Dec, Tue and Wed.* This inn is a pleasant, family-friendly stopover with recently fitted-out rooms that are simple, comfortable and well maintained. The impressive silhouette of the medieval château can be admired from the restaurant's terrace. Good choice of fixed-price menus with an accent on traditional fare.

### LEISURE

**Petit train touristique** – *tourist train station – from town centre parking – Apr to mid-Nov: 1st trip at 2.30pm. 5€ (under 10, 2.50 €).* ☎ *03 23 55 26 85 or 06 08 40 68 76.* A sightseeing loop round the city (1/2hr).

**Boat ride on the Lac de Pierrefonds** – *Apr to Oct: 9am-8pm (10pm Fri-Sat).* Embark and discover the thermal springs developed under Napoléon III and the local aquatic fauna.

belfry, the Cupid of Amiens Cathedral and some of the gargoyles decorating Notre-Dame Cathedral in Paris. The exhibits are authentic since they were made in the Monduit workshops at the same time as the commissioned items. They were used to illustrate the workshops' skills on the occasion of world exhibitions.

The **main front** appears with its basket-handled arcading forming a covered shelter, surmounted by a gallery. Neither of these existed in the original castle, but were created by Viollet-le-Duc, freely inspired by the courtyard at the Château de Blois. The equestrian statue of Louis of Orléans (2) by Frémiet (1868) stands before the monumental stairway. The inside of the **chapel**, heightened by Viollet-le-Duc, presents a bold elevation with a vaulted gallery above the apse, which was another of the architect's inventions. The doorway pier incorporates a figure of St James the Great with Viollet-le-Duc's features.

The **keep**, where the lord had his living quarters, stands between the chapel and the entrance. Viollet-le-Duc accentuated its residential function by giving it an elegant open stairway. It is flanked by three towers. The two on the outside are round whereas the one on the inside is square.

The **provisions courtyard** between the keep and the chapel communicates with the main courtyard by means of a postern gate and with the outside world by another postern, 10m/30ft above the foot of the castle walls. To introduce food and other supplies into the fortress, a steeply inclined wooden ramp was lowered; provisions were then dragged up.

### Keep (Logis au donjon)

Reaching the first floor of the keep, the tour leads through the Imperial couple's rooms: the **salle des Blasons** or Grande Salle (3) with woodwork and a few, rare pieces of furniture designed by Viollet-le-Duc. Among the symbolic decorative motifs, notice the Napoleonic eagle, the thistle (Empress Eugénie's emblem) and on the chimney-piece the heraldic arms of Louis of Orléans (the "broken" arms of France) and another family emblem, a knotted staff. Beyond the Chambre de l'Empereur (4) – which enjoys a view down over the fortified entrance – the tour leads to the Salle des Preuses, leaving the keep.

### Salle des "Preuses"

This timber-ceilinged hall (52×9m/170×29ft) was created by Viollet-le-Duc. The roof is shaped like an upturned ship. The mantelpiece of the double fireplace (5) is decorated with statues of nine women, heroines from tales of chivalry. The central figure of Semiramis, Queen of Assyria and legendarily of captivating beauty, has the features of the Empress whereas the others are portraits of ladies of the court.

### Tour d'Alexandre et Chemin de Ronde Nord (Sentry walk)

The original walls on this side of the ruins still stand 22m/72ft high; note the different colour of the stones. Along the sentry walk Viollet-le-Duc highlighted the last step forward in defence

CHÂTEAU DE PIERREFONDS
1st FLOOR

systems before the arrival of the cannon: level walkways without steps or narrow doorways, which allowed the defenders (housed in nearby barracks) to muster quickly at critical points without blundering into obstacles. The view extends over Pierrefonds Valley.

### Salle des Gardes ou des Mercenaires

A double spiral staircase (6) leads down to this guard-room which now houses beautiful lapidary fragments: remains of the original 15C statues of the heroic figures on each tower. The tour ends at the model of the castle.

# POISSY

POPULATION 36 101

MICHELIN LOCAL MAP 311: I-2, MAP 101 FOLD 12 OR 106 FOLD 17

The town of Poissy, situated on the banks of the Seine, was a royal residence as early as the 5C. St Louis was christened here in 1214; the king's private correspondence was even signed Louis de Poissy. The castle used to stand on place Meissonnier but it was demolished by Charles V.

Up to the middle of the last century, Poissy was the main Paris cattle market. Today, it is the site of a large automobile plant (Peugeot).

- **Information:** 132 r. du Gén.-de-Gaulle, 78300 Poissy, ☎ 01 30 74 60 65
- **Orient Yourself:** A little over 20 miles from the centre of Paris, on the Seine. Access from Paris: RER line A 5 or SNCF rail link from Gare St-Lazare
- **Organizing Your Time:** You should allow half a day to explore here; if you have children, head for the toy museum. The Peugeot factory is an interesting visit, but has very limited opening times.
- **Especially for Kids:** Musée du Jouet.

## Sights

### Collégiale Notre-Dame★

*Guided tours Sun 3-6pm.*
☎ 01 39 65 08 03.

The greater part of the collegiate church is Romanesque, dating from the 11C and 12C. The front tower, built in the Romanesque style, once served as a belfry-porch. The square base of the tower develops to an octagonal section

*16C Entombment, Collégiale Notre-Dame*

J.-L. Bohin/ EXPLORER

on the highest level, ending in a stone spire. The central tower is eight-sided through two floors, and ends in a timberwork spire.

**Interior** – The nave is a rare example of transitional style. The capitals of the south columns in the first two bays were recarved in the 17C. The other capitals feature interlacing monsters and foliage motifs. Some of them are thought to be older than this building and were probably taken from another church. The nave is very well lit owing to the installation of a triforium by Viollet-le-Duc in the three bays nearest to the chancel, which is circled by an ambulatory with groined vaulting. The side chapels – added in the 15C – pay homage to the various trade guilds: butchers, fishermen etc.

The first chapel to the right of the doorway contains fragments of the font used for St Louis' christening. For many centuries, the faithful would scrape the stone sides of the font, dissolve the dust in a glass of water and drink the potion as a remedy for high fever. This explains why the font is in such bad condition.

The most impressive furnishings are in the first chapel on the right: majestic 15C statues of John the Baptist and St Barbara, and a superb 16C Entombment (see below) portraying Mary, John, Mary Magdalene, the Holy Women, Nicodemus and Joseph of Arimathea.

### Musée d'Art et d'Histoire

*12 rue St-Louis.* ⌖ *Temporarily closed for refurbishing.*

The history of Poissy from Merovingian times (sarcophagi) up to the late 1940s (automobile industry) is presented in a simple, pleasing manner. One of the glass cabinets displays numerous seals, some of which date back to the 12C. Other exhibits include a painting by Meissonnier depicting summer bathing in the Seine, a splendid 16C painted wooden statue taken from the Church of Our Lady etc.

### Musée du Jouet

*1 enclos de l'Abbaye.* ◷*Open daily (except Mon) 9.30am-noon, 2-5.30pm.* ◷*Closed public holidays.* ⌒*3.50€* ☎ *01 39 65 06 06.*

[Kids] The toy museum is housed in the building flanked by two towers that used to mark the fortified entrance to the abbey. The toys and games exhibited in the museum cover the period from 1850 to 1960. There are a large number of dolls showing the changes in fashion over a century. On the first floor, there is a display case full of clockwork toys, another filled with teddy bears and yet another with lead and paper soldiers dating from the 19C. On the top floor are collections of cars and trains, some clockwork, others powered by steam. An electric train track dating from the 1930s operates automatically as visitors approach.

### Villa Savoye★

*82 rue de Villiers.* ◷*Open daily (except Mon): May-Aug: 10am-6pm; Mar-Apr and Sep-Oct: 10am-5pm; Nov-Feb: 10am-1pm, 2-5pm.* ◷*Closed 1 Jan, 1 May, 1 and 11 Nov, 25 Dec.* ⌒*7€. No charge first Sun of month (Oct-May).* ☎ *01 39 65 01 06.*

This masterpiece of modern architecture was designed in 1929 by **Le Corbusier** and **Pierre Jeanneret** for the industrialist Savoye. The use of cylindrical piles made it possible to do away with load-bearing walls and introduce huge glass surfaces. The main rooms

---

### The Poissy Symposium

An Augustinian convent founded in the 11C was given to the Dominican order by Philip the Fair. From 9 September to 13 October 1561 the abbey refectory hosted the Poissy Symposium; Catholics and Protestants were invited to discuss their differences at the instigation of Chancellor Michel de l'Hôpital. The debate was attended by the papal legate, 16 cardinals, 40 bishops and the general of the Jesuit order on the one side, and by an important group of theologians led by Theodore Beza on the other. The symposium lasted 17 days, but these high-level talks proved to be in vain for the divide between the two parties was even greater after the conference.

## Address Book

*For coin ranges, see the Legend on the cover flap.*

### WHERE TO STAY

**Les Romanciers** – *Quai de Seine, 78670 Médan – 6km/3.6mi W of Poissy via D 153 and D 164 –* ☎ *01 39 75 82 22. Closed end Dec to mid-Jan and Sun evening –* P *– 10 rms –* ☐ *8€ – restaurant 25/30€.* Situated opposite the Médan-Villennes beach and near Emile Zola's house, here's a pleasant stopping place betwixt land and sea. The large, well-appointed rooms all overlook the Seine; meals are served at the water's edge in high season.

### WHERE TO EAT

**Le Bon Vivant** – *30 av. Émile-Zola –* ☎ *01 39 65 02 14. Closed 23 Feb-1 Mar, Aug, Sun evening and Mon.* This Belle Epoque guinguette on the banks of a branch of the Seine is perfect for a weekend getaway. Two agreeable dining rooms – one of which is adorned with hunting trophies – and a terrace are the setting for traditional cuisine.

### SHOPPING

**Noyau de Poissy** – *105 r. du Gén.-de-Gaulle –* ☎ *01 39 65 20 59 – www.noyaudepoissy.com – Tue-Sat 9:30am-12:30pm, 3pm-7pm; Sun 9:30am-12:30pm. Closed 1 May.* Come visit this hundred year-old distillery to learn how the famous Noyau de Poissy liqueurs are made. Enjoy the guided tour and then stop in the attached shop, a most practical place for stocking up on delicacies to take home.

---

are located on the first floor, at a height of 3.5m/12ft. They are arranged around a large terrace which opens onto the countryside, as does the solarium occupying the top level of the house. The Villa Savoye features a ramp leading to the upper levels and a spiral staircase with vertical lines deliberately brought in to counter the horizontal configuration of the villa.

## Centre de Production Peugeot

*Guided tours (3hr) first Wed in the month at 2pm, by appointment 1 month in advance. Closed end Jul to end Aug and end Dec to early Jan, Easter Mon, 1 May, Ascension, 14 Jul, 1 Nov.*
*PSA Peugeot Citroën, site de Poissy, Visites d'usine, 45 r. J.-P.-Timbaud, 78307 Poissy Cedex.* ☎ *01 30 19 91 28.*

The Talbot trademark has a long-standing, partly British tradition since it evolved from the association of the French industrialist Adolphe Clément with Lord Talbot, Earl of Shrewsbury. The French concern within the group was bought back in 1934; SIMCA was founded the same year. After the war, small car manufacturers were taken over by larger ones and, although Talbot-Lago won the 24-hour competition at Le Mans in 1950, it was taken over by the second-largest French manufacturer in 1958. In 1960, SIMCA was split into two concerns controlled by Chrysler and Fiat. In 1978, Peugeot bought Chrysler's European subsidiaries, including Talbot. Just like the Renault factory in Flins, the Peugeot-Talbot factory in Poissy has contributed to shape the Seine Valley. Today, this ultra-modern car plant has a large number of industrial robots. It produces more than 1 200 cars every day.

# ABBAYE DE PORT-ROYAL-DES-CHAMPS★

MICHELIN LOCAL MAP 311: I-3, MAP 101 FOLD 22 OR 106 FOLD 29

Little remains of this famous abbey, which was the scene of a serious religious dispute for more than 100 years of French history.

**Information:** ☎ 01 30 43 74 93.

## A Bit of History

### An abbess aged eleven

In 1204 a Cistercian convent was founded in Porrois, a town later known as Port-Royal ⬛. Although this order was supposed to be strict, the rules grew extremely lax over a period of five centuries and by the turn of the 17C, the ten nuns and six novices who resided at the abbey were leading a most unsaintly life; the cloisters had become a promenade, fasting was a bygone practice and the vows of poverty were hardly compatible with the entertaining carried out at the abbey, including Carnival celebrations. In 1602 **Angélique Arnauld**, the 11-year-old daughter of an influential family of lawyers was passed off as 17 and appointed Abbess of Port-Royal.

### A reformer without mercy

Recovering from a bout of ill health, Mother Angélique began a series of reforms at the convent, reinstating the enclosure and imposing Cistercian rule, meditation and manual labour. After moving to Paris in 1625 as growth of the abbey soon led to cramped conditions, Arnauld returned in 1648 as the community now split its time between Port-Royal-des-Champs and Paris.

### Theological battles

Over the course of the 17C, Port-Royal-des-Champs became a hotbed of theological controversy as the "Petites Ecoles" at the abbey produced some of the greatest minds of the day, promoting **Jansenism** to the great indignation of the Jesuits.

After numerous interventions by State and religious organizations into the theological battle, the monastery buildings were razed to the ground in 1710. In 2000 a plot of land was planted with vines as a reminder of the vineyard that once covered the south-facing slopes. Renovations have also taken place, restoring much of the buildings and renewing orchards and meadows.

## Ruins and Museums

The tour of Port-Royal estate comprises two parts. The pilgrimage to the abbey ruins is enhanced by a visit to the park (Porte de Longueville, canal, view of the ruins). The Little Schools building is situated on a plateau, surrounded by pleasant, shaded grounds. It now houses a national museum, containing a wide range of documents on the former teaching colleges.

*Angélique Arnauld by Philippe de Champaigne (Musée de Versailles)*

## Racine at Port-Royal

Jean Racine lived at Port-Royal between the ages of 16 and 19, with a break at college in Paris. He was taught Greek and Latin and French versification, and was lectured on diction and rhetoric. The French poet learned much from his tutors and he soon became an outstanding reader. Louis XIV was spellbound by his beautiful voice and Racine's advice was sought by many an actor. The good Dr Hamon, of whom he was very fond, often used to take Racine with him when he went to treat poor patients, knitting clothes for them as he trotted along on an old donkey.

## Ruins and Abbey Museum

Open daily (except Tue) 2-6pm, Sat-Sun and public holidays 11am-noon, 2-6pm. Closed 1 Jan, 25 Dec. 3€. 01 30 43 74 93.

The tour begins in a square area defined by avenues of lime trees, which was the site of the former cloisters. The grave-yard where the Cistercian nuns were buried after 1204 has been planted with grass. The church adjoined the cloisters. Because the Solitaires had raised the floor level in an attempt to ward off the dampness, the building was razed down to the paving. When the original level was restored, the work uncovered the base of the pillars and the walls of the first building.

Next to the dovecote, a 17C barn houses a collection of paintings, engravings and memorabilia which illustrate and enliven the tour of the estate.

Les Granges, where the Solitaires lodged, lies above the valley on the north side screened by trees. Ascending and descending the steep slope daily to attend Mass in the abbey must have required great effort; it is said that the Hundred Steps were designed by the Messieurs themselves. The Hundred Steps are no longer open to the public.

## Musée National des Granges de Port-Royal

Open mid-Mar to end Oct: daily (except Tue) 10.30am-6.30pm; early Nov to mid-Mar: 10am-noon, 2-5pm (Sat-Sun 10.30am-6.30pm) last admission 1hr before closing. Closed between Dec. 25 and 1 Jan. 3€. 01 39 30 72 72.

The building was specially designed for the Little Schools (established by the Messieurs at the Abbey to provide religious education) in 1651-52 and presents a suitably austere front. In the 19C a Louis XIII-style wing was added. Most of the rooms have been restored to their former condition and contain books, engravings and drawings on the history of the abbey and the Jansenist movement, the Solitaires and the Little Schools. Other exhibits include a series of portraits by Philippe de Champaigne depicting the principal Jansenist leaders.

Although the Jansenists were sceptical about the Arts, they accepted paintings inspired by authentic religious feeling. The exhibition hall dedicated to Philippe de Champaigne reminds visitors of the strong ties that linked this painter to the abbey: every day the nuns could admire his two works *Ecce Homo* and *Mater Dolorosa*.

The museum building overlooking the farmyard once accommodated Blaise Pascal who came here on a retreat and wrote his *Mystery of Jesus* here in 1655. Tradition has it that his knowledge of mathematics came in useful during his stay at the abbey when he produced calculations for a new winch for the well: this enabled the nuns to draw a huge bucket as big as nine ordinary buckets from a depth of 60m/197ft with no extra effort.

## In Racine's footsteps

A 7km/4.3mi footpath dedicated to **Jean Racine** (1639-99) starts from the Granges de Port-Royal. Poems written by Racine in his youth to celebrate the beauty of the site are inscribed on panels dotted along the way. The path crosses D 91, runs through the hamlet of La Lorioterie, past the Fauveau mill, then across the Roi de Rome and Madeleine crossroads and ends at the church in Chevreuse.

# PROVINS★★

POPULATION 12 091
MICHELIN LOCAL MAP 312: I-4

Whether approaching Provins 🔝 from the Brie plateau to the west or from Champagne and the Voulzie Valley, this medieval town presents the eye-catching and distinctive outlines of the Tour César and of the dome of St-Quiriace Church. The splendid ramparts contribute to the town's medieval atmosphere and the rose gardens add to its visual appeal. The lower town, a lively shopping centre, sits at the foot of the promontory and extends along the River Voulzie and the River Durteint. The town, which boasts 58 historic monuments, is now a UNESCO World Heritage Site.

- ℹ️ **Information:** Chemin de Villecran, 77160 Provins. ☎ 01 64 60 26 26. www.provins.net.
- ▶ **Orient Yourself:** In the Ile de France, 54 miles southeast of Paris via the A 4 and then D 231. Access from Paris: SNCF rail link from Gare de l'Est.
- 🅿️ **Parking:** While you are trying to figure out the one-way traffic system, you will encounter a number of car parks, mostly charged. Try in the Place Honore de Balzac, the rue Vieille Notre-Dame or the rue de Temple. Or park near Porte St-Jean, near the tourist office.
- 👁 **Don't Miss:** A tour of the ramparts and the upper town. If you are staying for a few days, consider buying a Provins Pass (*Office du Tourisme*); it can save you money.
- 🕐 **Organizing Your Time:** The town is surprisingly compact, but you should still allow at least half a day, or more, to get the most from your visit.
- 🧒 **Especially for Kids:** The falconry display at Les Aigles des Remparts. Medieval knights jousting and fighting at La Légende des Chevaliers.
- ♿ **Also See:** Troyes, Reims.

## A Bit of History

### The Provins fairs

In the 10C Provins became one of the economic capitals of the Champagne region, thanks to its two annual fairs which, with those of Troyes, were among the largest in the region. Traders from the north and from the Mediterranean came here to do business.

Linens, silks, spices from the Orient and wine were traded, attracting people from many walks of life: money agents and merchants among whom mingled the hard-working bourgeoisie of the region. These fairs were prosperous until the early 14C, when the political and economic weight shifted to Paris, eclipsing the Champagne region.

### Roses

According to tradition it was **Thibaud IV** the Troubadour who brought roses back from Syria and grew them successfully here in Provins. Edmund Lancaster (1245-96), brother of the King of England, married Blanche of Artois and was for a while suzerain of Provins, at which time he introduced the red rose into his coat of arms.

*Common Rose of Provins*

BN, Paris

## Address Book

*For coin ranges, see the Legend on the cover flap.*

### WHERE TO STAY

**Ferme du Chatel (Bed and Breakfast)** – *5 r. de la Chapelle-St-Jean –* ☎ *01 64 00 10 73 – 5 rms.* This farm, built between the 12C-18C, boasts a splendid situation in the heart of the medieval town. The rooms, with exposed timberwork, are quiet and impeccably maintained. A vast garden planted with fruit trees.

**Christine and Jean-Claude Dormion (Bed and Breakfast)** – *2 r. des Glycines, 77650 Lizines – 15km/9 mi SW of Provins via N 19 and D 209 –* ☎ *01 60 67 32 56 – 5 rms.* Agriculture is still the mainstay of this 300 year-old farm offering perfectly maintained, rustic bedrooms, each equipped with a kitchenette corner. The breakfast room, brightened by a large bay window, is most pleasant, and the garden and orchard are enticing indeed.

**La Ferme de Toussacq** – *In the Toussacq hamlet, along the Seine – 77480 Grisy-sur-Seine – 20km/12mi S of Provins. Take N 19, rte de Nogent-sur-Seine via D 78 and D 411 –* ☎ *01 64 01 82 90 – www.hameau-de-toussacq.com/ferme. html – 5 rms.* Amidst a bucolic setting on the banks of the Seine, come discover this group of 17-19C edifices offering simple bedrooms in the château's out-buildings. Meals, featuring long-simmered dishes made from farm produce, occasionally include vegetarian fare.

### WHERE TO EAT

**La Patache** – *6 pl. H.- de- Balzac –* ☎ *01 64 00 01 19. Closed Sun evening and Mon.* The pleasant welcome and traditional dishes with a Provençal slant keep customers coming back to this restaurant decorated in tones of blue, yellow and white. The terrace, set on a quiet square, is quite popular in summer.

**Le Petit Écu** – *9 pl. du Châtel (upper town) –* ☎ *01 64 08 95 00.* Located on the charming Place du Châtel in the heart of old Provins, this fine half-timbered house offers a weekend special in season that includes a country buffet.

**Auberge de la Grange** – *3 r. St-Jean, (upper town) –* ☎ *01 64 08 96 77. Closed Feb and Nov school holidays, Sun evening*

*in winter, Tue evening and Wed.* Located in the upper town, opposite the grange aux dîmes (tithes barn), this half-timbered house purportedly dates from the 11C. Depending on the season, you may dine in the decidedly rustic décor of the dining room or on the terrace set up in a pretty, flower-filled courtyard.

### ON THE TOWN

**Chez Denis "Auberge du Chatel"** – *2 r. Couverte, 77160 Provins –* ☎ *01 64 08 97 34 – chez-denis@provins.org. Daily 9am-1am – 13/16 €.* The eclectic decoration scheme of this bar-brasserie gives it something of a retro feel. Displayed paintings and statuettes may be purchased. Terrace in a shaded courtyard in the centre of town.

### SHOWTIME

**À l'Assaut des Remparts – War Machines** [Kids] – ☎ *01 64 60 26 26 – www.provins.net – Apr-Jul. Tickets and schedule at the Office de tourisme – 6.10€ (children: 4.50€).* Near the Porte Saint-Jean towards the back of the moat, you'll be transported into the Middle Ages thanks to a faultlessly realistic performance demonstrating the use of long-gone military equipment and defensive weapons.

**Les Aigles des Remparts (Eagles of the Ramparts)** [Kids] – ☎ *01 60 58 80 32 – www.provins.net – end Mar to early Nov: daily. Tickets and timetable at the Office de Tourisme – 8.50€ (children: 5.50€).* One of the nobility's favourite pastimes during the Middle Ages was watching birds of prey swoop through the skies. After the show, the falconers will invite you to visit the aviary.

**La Légende des chevaliers** [Kids] – ☎ *01 64 60 26 26 – www.provins.net – mid-Jun to late Aug. Tickets and schedule at the Office de tourisme – 10.50€ (children: 7.50€).* From within the rampart ditches, witness a jousting match featuring knights on horseback, battling with lances and swords, and on foot, fighting with studded flails and battleaxes.

### SHOPPING

**Gaufillier** – *2 av. Victor-Garnier –* ☎ *01 64 00 03 71 – Tue-Sat 8am-12.30pm, 2.30pm-7.15pm; Sun 8am-12.30pm.*

For over ten years, this chocolatier-confectioner-pastry chef has been pampering customers with rose-flavoured treats: jam, ice cream, sweets, fruit pastes, nougat, tea, lemonade, syrup, and, more recently, caramels. Yummy!
**La Ronde des Abeilles** – *3 rue des Beaux-Arts, Ville-Haute* – ☎ *01 60 67 65 97.*

*Daily (except Tue) 2pm-7pm.* The speciality of this pretty confectioner's shop is Provins rose honey. They also sell many other products of the hive (royal jelly, pollen, beeswax) as well as other delicacies including cooked and honey-preserved fruits and vegetables, gingerbread and hydromel (a light alcohol made from honey).

## Upper Town★★

*It is advisable to park in the car park near Porte St-Jean. This is the location of the tourist office and the departure point for the small tourist train.*

### Porte St-Jean

St John's Gateway was built in the 13C. This stocky construction is flanked by two projecting towers which are partially hidden by the buttresses that were added in the 14C to support the drawbridge.

▸ *Follow allée des Remparts which overlooks the old moat.*

### Remparts★★

The town walls were built in the 12C and 13C along an existing line of defence, then altered on several occasions. They constitute a very fine example of medieval military architecture. A house straddling the curtain wall was the home of the Provins executioners. The last one to live here was Charles-Henri Sanson who executed Louis XVI. The most interesting part of the ramparts runs between Porte St-Jean and Porte de Jouy. The Tour aux Engins, on the corner, links the two curtain walls; it derives its name from a barn nearby in which engines of war were housed. In summer, on a space behind this

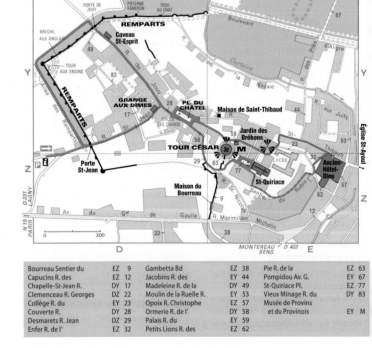

| | | | | | | |
|---|---|---|---|---|---|---|
| Bourreau Sentier du | EZ 9 | Gambetta Bd | EZ 38 | Pie R. de la | EZ 63 |
| Capucins R. des | EZ 12 | Jacobins R. des | EY 44 | Pompidou Av. G. | EY 67 |
| Chapelle-St-Jean R. | DY 17 | Madeleine R. de la | EY 49 | St-Quiriace Pl. | EZ 77 |
| Clemenceau R. Georges | DZ 22 | Moulin de la Ruelle R. | EY 53 | Vieux Minage R. du | DY 83 |
| Collège R. du | EY 23 | Opoix R. Christophe | EZ 57 | Musée de Provins | |
| Couverte R. | DY 28 | Ormerie R. de l' | DY 58 | et du Provinois | EY M |
| Desmarets R. Jean | DZ 29 | Palais R. du | EY 59 | | |
| Enfer R. de l' | EZ 32 | Petits Lions R. des | EZ 62 | | |

tower, within the ramparts, the falconers of the "Aigles de Provins" company put on a show of birds of prey; other birds of prey are displayed in shelters. Beyond the 12C Porte de Jouy take rue de Jouy, which is lined by picturesque low houses with long tiled roofs or an overhanging upper storey.

## Place du Châtel

This vast, peaceful square, rectangular in shape, is bordered by attractive old houses: the 15C Maison des Quatre Pignons (southwest corner), the 13C Maison des Petits-Plaids (northwest corner), and the Hôtel de la Coquille to the north. The remains of Église St-Thibault (12C) stand on the northeast corner.

Walk past the **Musée de Provins et du Provinois** (ℰ see Additional sights), housed in one of the town's oldest buildings, the "Maison Romane" (Romanesque house).

## Tour César (Caesar's Tower)★★

ⓘOpen Apr-Oct: 10am-6pm; Nov-Mar: 2-5pm. ⓘClosed 25 Dec. ⓈⒶ3.40€. ☎ 01 64 60 26 26.

This superb 12C keep, 44m/144ft high and flanked by four turrets, is the emblem of the town. It was once part of the walls of the upper town. The pyramidal roof was built in the 16C.

The guard-room on the first floor is octagonal and 11m/36ft high; it is topped by vaulting formed of four arcades of pointed arches ending in a dome and pierced by an orifice through which the soldiers on the floor above were passed supplies. The gallery encircling the keep at turret-level was originally roofed over. The view★ extends over the town and the surrounding countryside.

▸ Return to Porte St-Jean via place du Châtel, then rue St-Jean on the left.

🐾 **Guided tour of the city** 2 hrs
Provins, an official City of Art and History, offers two-hour discovery tours led by guides certified by the Ministry of Culture and Communication. ⓘFrom early June to late August: weekends and holidays at 3pm. ⒶⒶ6.10€. For information, contact the Office du Tourisme ☎ 01 64 60 26 26 or visit www.provins.net.

Tour César

## Additional Sights

### Grange aux Dîmes★

Rue St-Jean. ⓘOpen Apr-Aug Sat, Sun and public holidays 10am-6pm; Sep and Oct 2-6pm (Sat-Sun 10am-6pm. ⓘClosed Nov-Mar. ⒶⒶ3.40€. ☎ 01 64 60 26 26, www.provins.net.

This massive 13C building belonged to the canons of St-Quiriace, who hired out the space to merchants during the major fairs. When the fairs went into decline the barn became a store for the tithes (dîmes) levied on the harvests of the peasants.

The vast hall on the ground floor houses a permanent exhibition (audio-guided tour) re-creating the atmosphere of the town's famous fairs: scenes and dummies evoke craftsmen and shopkeepers of bygone days.

### Musée de Provins et du Provinois

ⓘOpen daily: Apr-mid Jun noon-5.30pm. Mid Jun-mid Sep 11am-6.30pm. Mid Sep-Oct noon-5.30pm. ⓘClosed 27 Aug, 25 Dec-1 Jan. ⒶⒶ3€. ☎ 01 64 01 40 19. www.provins.net.

On the ground floor are displayed **the sculpture and ceramic collections**★, valuable works of local medieval and Renaissance art.

Exploiting the underground clay quarries enabled potters to produce pieces now noted for their remarkable variety and timelessness.

### Souterrains à graffiti

*Entrance in rue St-Thibault, left of the doorway to the Ancien Hôtel-Dieu.* ⏰ 🔦 *guided tours (45min): Apr-Jul and Sep-Nov Mon-Fri at 3pm and 4pm Sat-Sun and public holidays 10.30am-6pm. Jul-Sep 1.45-6pm. Nov-Mar: Sat-Sun, public and school holidays at 2pm, 3pm and 4pm.* ⏰ *Closed 25 Dec.* 🎫 *3.70€.* ☎ *01 64 60 26 26. www.provins.net.*

There is a substantial network of underground passages around Provins, some marked with ancient graffiti. The section that is open to the public runs through a layer of tufa that lies parallel to the base of the spur on which the Upper Town stands. The entrance is through a low-roofed chamber with ribbed vaulting in the old hospice.

# LE QUESNOY★

POPULATION 4 917

MICHELIN LOCAL MAP 302: J-6

This quiet town of low, whitewashed houses lies in a lush, lake-filled setting close to Mormal Forest and is a fine example of French military architecture.

- 🛈 **Information:** 1 r. du Mar.-Joffre, 59530 Le Quesnoy, ☎ 03 27 20 54 70.
- ▶ **Orient Yourself:** In a strategic position between the Oise and the Cambrésis, accessed from Valenciennes or Bavay by the N 49 then the D 934, and from Cambrai by the D 942.
- 🅿 **Parking:** Limited parking within the fortifications (fee); it is better to park near the Étang du Pont Rouge.
- 👁 **Don't Miss:** Take a tour of the ramparts, or a gentle stroll in the Mormal Forest.
- ⏰ **Organizing Your Time:** Two hours should be allowed to tour the fortifications; do this in the morning, then take a picnic in the forest.
- 👁 **Also See:** Valenciennes, Bavay.

## Fortifications★

The perfectly preserved fortifications still show clearly the unique qualities of the old stronghold. Built of coarse stone, flint and lime mortar covered with bricks, they form a polygon of defensive curtain walls with projecting bastions. Despite apparently being in the style of Vauban these defences, particularly the bastions with projecting towers, in fact date in part from the time of Emperor Charles V (16C). Various all-season paths offer pleasant walks, enabling enthusiasts of military architecture to study the layout of the defences (information panels).

▶ *Leave from place du Général-Leclerc and head for the postern gate by avenue d'Honneur des Néo-Zélandais.*

The gateway gives access to the moat, to the spot where the men of the New Zealand Rifle Brigade scaled the walls in November 1918. The Monument des Néo-Zélandais commemorates their exploits.

▶ *Follow the moat around the south front of the ramparts.*

From **Étang du Pont Rouge** continue to **Lac Vauban** which lies at the foot of

### WHERE TO EAT

🍽 **Au Canard Gourmand** – *80 rte de Valenciennes* – ☎ *03 27 49 12 95. Closed Mon – reserv. required.* This recently opened establishment was a sensation in no time. It undoubtedly owes its success to the inviting dining room framed in red-brick walls, the delicious dishes featuring the cuisine of southwest France, and the very reasonable prices. A shop sells homemade delicacies fresh from the farm.

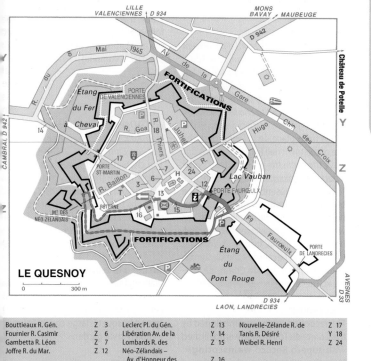

| | | | | | | |
|---|---|---|---|---|---|---|
| Boutrieaux R. Gén. | Z | 3 | Leclerc Pl. du Gén. | Z | 13 | Nouvelle-Zélande R. de | Z | 17 |
| Fournier R. Casimir | Z | 6 | Libération Av. de la | Y | 14 | Tanis R. Désiré | Y | 18 |
| Gambetta R. Léon | Z | 7 | Lombards R. des | Z | 15 | Weibel R. Henri | Z | 24 |
| Joffre R. du Mar. | Z | 12 | Néo-Zélandais – | | | | | |
| | | | Av. d'Honneur des | Z | 16 | | | |

the ramparts to each side of the Porte Fauroeulx.

The bridge provides a lovely view of the red-brick curtain walls and bastions and their reflection in the calm waters.

**Étang du Fer à Cheval**

Lying northwest of the town, the lake was dug to a design by Vauban during Louis XIV's reign. The calm and verdant setting is extremely peaceful.

# RAMBOUILLET★

### POPULATION 24 758
### MICHELIN LOCAL MAP 311: G-4 OR MAP 106 FOLD 28

**The combination of an attractive château, park and forest makes Rambouillet one of the main sights in the Île-de-France. Since 1883 it has been the official summer residence of the President of the French Republic. Distinguished guests include Hosni Mubarak (Egypt, August 1998), Nelson Mandela (South Africa, July 1996), Boris Yeltsin (Russia, October 1995), George Bush (United States, July 1991) and Mikhail Gorbachev (USSR, October 1990).**

- **Information:** Hôtel de Ville, pl. de la Libération, 78120 Rambouillet, ☎ 01 34 83 21 21.
- ▶ **Orient Yourself:** 33 miles southwest of the centre of Paris, Rambouillet is reached via the A 13 and A 12. Access from Paris: SNCF rail link from Gare Montparnasse.
- **P Parking:** You can park near the chateau or on the place Jeanne d'Arc (charge).
- **Don't Miss:** Visit the deer observation hides in the Forêt des Cerfs, but be very quiet.
- **Organizing Your Time:** The chateau itself will not take more than an hour or so, but you can spend all day exploring the forest.
- **Especially for Kids:** Espace Rambouillet, a massive wildlife park with aviaries and free flight shows. The toy train collection (Musée Rambolitrain).

## Château

🎧 *Guided tours (30min) daily (except Tue).* ⏰*Open 10-11.45am, 2-4.30pm (Apr-Sep: 5.30pm).* ⏰*Closed 1 Jan, 1 May, 1 and 11 Nov, 25 Dec and during presidential visits.* ⊚*7€, no charge first Sun in the month from Oct to end May.* ☎ *01 34 83 00 25.*

Leave from place de la Libération, the site of the town hall (*if the car park is full, leave the car in the park Château's park – parking is tolerated in certain spots*).

The château presents a triangular shape owing to the fact that Napoleon dismantled the left wing. The large round tower, where François I is believed to have died, belonged to the 14C fortress. It is difficult to distinguish because of the numerous additions made by the Comte de Toulouse. The façades are essentially 19C.

### Mezzanine

The reception rooms commissioned by the Comte de Toulouse are embellished with superb Rococo **wainscoting**★. Note the charming boudoir designed for the Comte's wife.

The corridor adjoining the François I tower leads through to the Imperial bathroom suite, adorned with Pompeian frescoes. This opens onto the Emperor's Bed-chamber, where he spent the night of 29 June 1815, and the study. It was in the dining room – the former ballroom – that Charles X signed the abdication document. The view of the park is stunning.

## Park★

&. ⏰*Open daily: May-Sep 8am-7pm (Jun-Aug: 7.30pm). Feb-Apr 8am-6pm. Nov-Jan: 8am-5pm.* ☎ *01 34 94 28 79.*

The château is set in a pleasant park, renowned for the variety of its gardens remodelled throughout the 17C and 18C, which reflect the evolution of taste during that period, from the formal parterres to the winding alleyways lined with exotic trees.

### Jardin à la française

Walking back toward the château, one goes through the "petit bosquet" (small copse), the "miroir" (mirror) and the "grand bosquet" (large copse) forming a French-style garden.

### Quinconce

This quincunx, situated to the east of the château and created in 1710, comprises a group of lime trees from Holland planted according to a chequered pattern known as a "quinconce". In its centre stands *La Barque* solaire, a bronze sculpture by Karel, inaugurated in 1993.

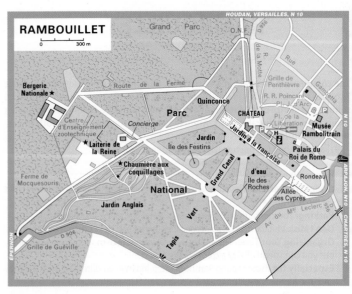

## International meetings in Rambouillet

Let to various persons after the abdication of Charles X, Rambouillet Château came back into State ownership on the fall of the Second Empire. In 1897, it became one of the official country residences of the presidents of the Republic. De Gaulle organised hunting parties on the estate. On the initiative of Valéry Giscard d'Estaing, the château was the venue of the first summit meeting of industrialised countries, which began as an informal get-together of six western heads of state. More recently, the Rambouillet conference of March 1999 attempted to find a solution to the Kosovo problem, unfortunately without success.

## Jardin à l'anglaise

In 1779, Hubert Robert designed an English-style garden beyond the green carpet of lawn. It is essentially planted with exotic species. The **Grotte des Amants** (Lovers' grotto) was named after a couple of lovers who took refuge inside during a thunderstorm. Canals crisscross the park, forming small islands: Île des Festins, Îles des Roches etc. 18C follies are scattered among the greenery.

## Chaumière des Coquillages★

Guided tours only (45min). Open daily (except Tue) 10am-noon, 2-5.30pm (Oct-Mar: 4.30pm). Closed 1 Jan, 1 May, 1 and 11 Nov, 25 Dec. 3.50€. 01 34 94 28 79.

The **landscape garden** in the park features a charming cottage built for the Princesse de Lamballe. The walls of the rooms are encrusted with a variety of sea shells, chips of marble and mother-of-pearl. A small boudoir with painted panelling adjoins the main room.

## Laiterie de la Reine★

Guided tours only (45min). Open daily (except Tue) 10am-noon, 2-5.30pm (Oct-Mar: 4.30pm). Closed 1 Jan, 1 May, 1 and 11 Nov, 25 Dec. 3.50€. 01 34 94 28 79.

Louis XVI had the Dairy built in 1785 to amuse his wife Marie-Antoinette. The small sandstone pavilion resembling a neo-Classical temple consists of two rooms. The first – which houses the actual dairy – features marble paving and a marble table dating from the First Empire. The Sèvres porcelain bowls and jugs used for tasting have disappeared.

The room at the back was designed as an artificial grotto adorned with luxuriant vegetation. It includes a marble

composition by Pierre Julien depicting a nymph and the she-goat Amalthea (1787).

# Additional Sights

## Palais du Roi de Rome

Open only during exhibitions: Daily (except Mon and Tue), 2-6pm. 01 30 88 77 77. www.ot-rambouillet.fr.

This mansion was built in 1813 at the request of Napoleon who intended to give it to his son the king of Rome. Two wings framed the central building which has now disappeared. However, it was only very briefly used by the king of Rome before he left for Austria with his mother, Maria-Louise. The right-hand wing stages themed exhibitions.

## Musée du Jeu de l'Oie

Open daily (except Mon), 2-6pm. 2.50€ (4.50 € combined ticket including the musée Rambolitrain). 01 30 88 73 73.

The left-hand wing houses Pierre Dietsch's collection including 80 games of snakes and ladders dating from the 17C to the 20C.

## Jardin

Open daily Apr-Sep, 2-8pm. Oct-Mar, 2-5pm.

Laid out according to its original plan, this romantic garden covering 5 000m²/ 5 980sq yd contains a stele erected in memory of the "young king of Rome".

## Musée Rambolitrain

4 place Jeanne-d'Arc. Open daily (except Mon and Tue) 10am-noon, 2-5.30pm. Closed 1 Jan and 25 Dec. 3.50€. 01 34 83 15 93.

An astounding collection of more than 4 000 toy trains and models explains the history of the railway from its early beginnings to the present day. A large O-shaped circuit occupies the whole of the second floor.

### Bergerie Nationale★

  Open Mar-Oct: Sat and Sun, 2-6pm; Nov-Feb: daily (except Mon and Tue), 2 5.30pm. Possibility of guided visits on Sat and Sun. Closed from 24 Dec to mid-Jan. 4€. 01 61 08 68 00. Inside the park, 1.5km/1mi from the main gate: follow the signposts.

In 1785, Louis XVI decided to add to his experimental farm the production of fine wool and so he purchased a flock of merino sheep from Spain, Angora goats from Turkey and cows from Switzerland. The sheep farm buildings were completed during the Second Empire.

# FORÊT DE RAMBOUILLET★

MICHELIN LOCAL MAP 312: A-4 TO B-4 OR MAP 106 FOLD 28

This vast forest has some delightful footpaths for those who enjoy walking, as well as 60km/40mi of cycle tracks. Some 20 or more lakes with picturesque banks, including the Étangs de Hollande, and a number of villages with old houses that are now holiday homes give it a very special charm.

- **Information:** Hôtel de Ville, pl. de la Libération, 78120 Rambouillet, ☎01 34 83 21 21.
- **Orient Yourself:** 33 miles southwest of the centre of Paris, Rambouillet is reached via the A 13 and A 12. Access from Paris: SNCF rail link from Gare Montparnasse.
- **Organizing Your Time:** You can easily spend an entire day in the forest, walking, cycling and picnicking.
- **Especially for Kids:** Espace Rambouillet (see below).

## A Bit of History

Rambouillet is part of the ancient Yveline Forest, which in Gallo-Roman times stretched as far as the outskirts of Nogent-le-Roi, Houdan, Cernay-la-Ville and Etampes. A large part of it is now included in the Parc Naturel Régional de la Haute Vallée de Chevreuse.

Of the total 20 000ha/50 000 acres, 14 000ha/35 000 acres are State owned. They cover a clay plateau with an altitude of between 110m/358ft and 180m/585ft, crisscrossed by sandy valleys. In the Middle Ages, wide-scale deforestation took place and the vast clearances now divide it into three main areas of woodland: St-Léger and Rambouillet itself, the most popular areas with tourists situated north of Rambouillet, and Yvelines to the south, which is rather more divided up into private estates.

### Flora and fauna

The forest around Rambouillet is damper and has more rivers, lakes and ponds than the one at Fontainebleau. From time immemorial it has been particularly well stocked with game such as deer, roe-deer and wild boar – and it remains so today.

## Visit

### Espace Rambouillet

Open Apr and Jul-Oct, daily 10am-6pm (Sat, Sun and public holidays 6.30pm). Feb, Mar and Nov daily (except Mon) 10am-5pm. May-Jun daily 9.30am-6pm (Sat, Sun and public holidays 6.30pm). Closed Dec-Jan. 8.80€ (children: 6.60 €), but there are seasonal price variations; check website for details. ☎ 01 34 83 05 00. www.onf.fr/espacer-amb. Car park and visitors centre 500m/540yd to the southwest of the Rambouillet-Clairefontaine road (D 27).

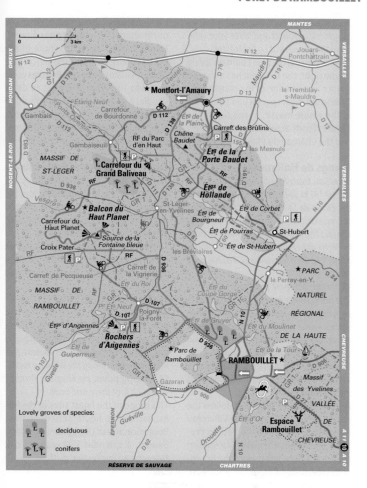

This 250ha/625-acre wildlife park has been divided into various areas (binoculars are recommended):

**Forêt des Cerfs**, where observation hides provide a view of deer, stags, and wild oxen.

**Forêt Sauvage**, a 180ha/450-acre site in which the animals roam free.

**Forêt des Aigles**, with more than 100 birds of prey in aviaries. Free flight shows.

**Coin des Fourmis**, where young children can get acquainted with these industrious insects (ants).

## Hikes and Tours

The **GR 1** trail runs through the forest from north to south between Montfort-l'Amaury and Rambouillet. The **GR 22** trail runs in a northwest/southwest direction from Gambaiseuil to St-Léger-en-Yvelines.

### Rochers d'Angennes

*8.5km/5.3mi from Rambouillet via D 936 then D 107. Leave from the parking area of the "Zone de Silence des Rabières." Walk 100m/110yd through the village up the steeper slope of the valley to find the right path leading to the summit.*

🔼 Go past an arena-shaped shelf circled by boulders to reach the crest: **view** of the Guesle Valley and Angennes Lake, bordered by bulrushes, reeds and other aquatic plants.

### Balcon du Haut Planet★

*12km from Rambouillet along D 936 to Carrefour du Haut-Planet, then turn right* onto the unsurfaced road which crosses rough, hilly ground and leave your vehicle in the car park at La Croix Pater.

After passing the Blue Fountain spring on the right, the lane reaches a shaded terrace on the edge of the plateau, unfolding the most spectacular panorama of the whole massif: to the north, the **view** extends across the Vesgre Valley and the Château du Planet.

### Étangs de Hollande

*8km/5mi from Rambouillet along N 10 then D 191 to St-Hubert; leave the car near the Étang de St-Hubert. For information on regulations for fishing in the ponds, contact the Fédération des Yvelines pour la Pêche et la Protection du Milieu Aquatique, 19 r. du Docteur-Roux, 78520 Limay ☎ 01 34 77 58 90.*

*4hr on foot there and back.*

The ponds were part of one of Vauban's projects to create reservoirs for Versailles' water requirements. A series of six ponds separated by paths was laid out near the **Étangs de Hollande**. Only the two end basins are filled with water. In summer, the ponds offer **swimming** and **fishing** facilities.

Head west out of St-Hubert, follow the Corbet forest track, cross the Villarceau alleyway, and walk to the Petites-Yvelines crossroads then the Malmaison crossroads. Turn left toward the Bourgneuf crossroads and, to the southeast, the Route des Étangs which skirts the north shore of the **Bourgneuf** pond. Follow D 60 to the south shore of the **Corbet** pond. Walk past the sluice-gate which separates it from the **Pourras** pond and skirt the Pourras woods to Croix Vaudin. A path on the left runs through the woods to the Pont Napoléon; on the right lies the **St-Hubert** pond. This leads back to the Corbet forest track.

### Carrefour du Grand Baliveau

*8km/5mi from Montfort-l'Amaury via D 138. At the crossroads, follow the path to the right of the panel marked "route forestière du Parc-d'en-Haut." 30min on foot there and back.*

The path offers a charming walk through a lovely green glade. One of the clearings affords a good **view**★ of a secluded valley.

### Étang de la Porte Baudet ou des Maurus

*4km/2.5mi from Montfort by D 112 and D 13: go past the turning to Gambais (right) and turn left onto rue du Vert-Galant. Follow the plateau along the winding road.*
*Starting point: parking des Brûlins; 45min on foot there and back.*

This is one of the finest sites in the forest; farther on, Route Belsédène then Route Goron lead (1km/0.6mi) to Chêne Baudet, a splendid 550-year-old oak tree with an impressive girth.

# CHÂTEAU-FORT DE RAMBURES★

MICHELIN LOCAL MAP 301: D-8 – 6KM/4MI NORTH-EAST OF BLANGY-SUR-BRESLE

Surrounded by an English-style park and an arboretum, **Rambures Castle** is an interesting example of 15C military architecture; during the Hundred Years War it played an important role as a French enclave in the middle of the English-occupied territories, and it came to be called "the key to the Vimeu." The castle has remained in the same family since the 15C. Henri IV stayed in the castle.

- **Information:** www.chateaufort-rambures.com.
- **Orient Yourself:** From Abbeville (15 miles) take the D 928, and then the D 180.
- **Don't Miss:** The rosary in the park.
- **Organizing Your Time:** Allow 2 hr to wander around this delightful place.

# Visit

🐾 *Guided visits (1h)* 🕐*Mar-Oct: 10am-noon, 2-6pm. Nov-Feb Mon-Sat by arrangement, Sun 2.30-6pm (last admission 1hr before closing).* 🕐*Closed 1 Jan, 25 Dec.* ⊗*6€.* ☎ *03 22 25 10 93.*

**Exterior** – The castle retains the look of a powerful fortress, with its enormous machicolated round towers and its rounded curtain walls (so that there were no level surfaces for the enemy to fire against), its deep moat and its tall watchtower. It was designed to resist the artillery of the time and its brick walls are 3-7m/10-23ft thick. In the 18C the castle was converted into a country residence and the courtyard façade was pierced with huge windows.

The English-style park is planted with ancient trees.

**Interior** – For many of the rooms the only source of daylight is still through loopholes, though the alterations begun in the 18C did provide reception rooms decorated with woodwork and marble chimney-pieces (*first floor*).

After a glance over the 15C watch-path, the tour continues on the second floor, to the library-billiards room hung with a collection of portraits.

The kitchen is located in the old guard-room above the dungeons; the cellars were used to shelter the villagers during invasions.

# LA ROCHE-GUYON★

POPULATION 550

MICHELIN LOCAL MAP 305: A-6 OR MAP 106 FOLD 2

This village developed at the foot of an old stronghold; its crumbling keep still dominates the steep, rocky ledge. Life at La Roche-Guyon 🔝 has resumed its peaceful character since the bombings of July 1944 and the Battle of Normandy, when Marshal Rommel established his headquarters in the castle. The village has retained some of its cave dwellings and fine old houses .

🔢 **Information:** 8 rue du Général Leclerc, 95780 La Roche-Guyon. ☎ 01 34 79 70 55. www.larocheguyon.fr.

▶ **Orient Yourself:** Between the Seine and the Vexin plateau, 50 miles west of Paris, via the A 13.

🅿 **Parking:** Large free car park at west side of the village.

☺ **Don't Miss:** A visit to see the troglodyte caves along the Route des Crêtes.

🕐 **Organizing Your Time:** This tranquil village will consume more than the 1-2 hr needed to see the chateau.

## A Bit of History

### The La Rochefoucauld estate

In the 13C, a residential château was erected at the foot of the cliff not far from the fortress; it was linked to the keep by a flight of steps carved in the rock. François I and his numerous retinue took up residence here in 1546. La Roche-Guyon was made a duchy peerage in 1621. In 1659, the title came into the hands of **François de La Rochefoucauld**, who wrote many of his famous *Maximes* at the château.

## Sights

### The banks of the Seine★

The quayside promenade commands a good **view**★ of the sleepy countryside and the meandering river. Behind, the two castles stand side by side. The abutment pier of the former suspension bridge (dismantled in the 19C) provides a good observation point.

### Château★

🕐*Open mid-Mar to mid-Nov (last admission 1hr before closing) 10am-6pm, Sat-Sun and public holidays 10am-7pm. Mid-*

## The Duke and the young Romantic writers

In 1816 Louis-François Auguste, **Duc de Rohan-Chabot**, acquired the estate. He lost his wife in 1819 and took holy orders at the age of 31. Then he continued to entertain at the château, combining acts of charity with the fashionable manners of pre-Revolutionary France. Among the guests were fellow students at St-Sulpice Seminary and the young Romantic authors Victor Hugo, Alphonse de Lamartine, Hugues Lamennais, Henri Lacordaire and Father Dupanloup.

They delighted in the grand services celebrated in the underground chapel to the strains of a superb Italian organ. In 1829 the duke was appointed Archbishop of Besançon, and then Cardinal, and sold the château and its grounds to François de la Rochefoucauld-Liancourt. La Roche-Guyon has remained in this family ever since.

*Nov to mid-Mar: 10am-4pm, Sat-Sun and public holidays 10am-5pm.* ◷*Closed during Christmas school holidays.* ⬯*7.50€.* ☎ *01 34 79 74 42.*

The superb wrought-iron gates bearing the La Rochefoucauld crest open onto the courtyard and 18C stables which now house the reception desk and temporary exhibitions. The house still has some 13C features such as the towers flanking the main apartments. Built in the 16C, they stand on a terrace supported by arcaded foundations. The rooms are empty of furniture. The parapet walkway and "south-east" tower provide some wonderful panoramic views of the Seine Valley. A newly restored corridor leads to the three chapels. The main one is dedicated to Our Lady of the Snows. During the German occupation, numerous pillboxes were built into the cliffs. They now house a retrospective look at Rommel's stay at the château. The remainder of the buildings in the cliffs, including the

orangery, are now used as the backdrop for a sound and light show on regional art, entitled **"Parcours de lumière en Vallée de Seine".**

# Excursions

### Route des Crêtes★
*Round-trip of 4km/2.5mi.*

Take the road to Gasny which passes the entrance to the famous troglodyte caves or stables called **boves**, carved in the chalk. On reaching the pass, turn right onto D 100, also known as "Route des Crêtes". When the estates no longer conceal the view of the river, park the car on a belvedere near a spinney of pine trees. There is a **view**★★ of the meander of the Seine carpeted with the trees of the Forêt de Moisson and, further along the promontory, of the spurs of the Haute-Isle cliffs. Note, in the foreground, down below, the truncated **keep** of the Château de La Roche-Guyon.

Continue along D 100. At the first junction, turn right onto Charrière des Bois, which leads back to the starting point. The road follows a steep downward slope and passes under the 18C aqueduct that supplies water to the village and the château.

### Arboretum de La Roche
*On D 37 towards Amenucourt.*

The arboretum, which spreads over 12ha/29 acres, has been planted to reproduce the geography of the Île-de-France area. Each *département* is distinguished by a different species: oak for Seine-et-Marne, maple for Essonne, hornbeam for Val-de-Marne, ash for Val-d'Oise, cherry for Seine-Saint-Denis, lime for

*La Roche-Guyon – The castle and the keep*

A. de valroger/MICHELIN

Les Hauts-de-Seine, and beech for Yvelines. The plane-trees in the middle represent Paris. They are all young trees, apart from the 20-year-old Lebanese cedar at the central roundabout. Among the plantations, snaking stretches of lawn evoke the valleys.

## Vétheuil

*6km/3.7mi east along D 913.*
This former wine-growing village has a lovely riverside setting: it lies on the steep banks of one of the Seine's meanders. The village houses – built with a fine pale-yellow stone – are characteristic of the French Vexin region. The small town was made famous by the Impressionists, in particular Claude Monet who lived here for three years and whose wife Camille died in Vétheuil in 1879.

## Domaine de Villarceaux

*10km/6.2mi northeast. From Chaussy, follow D 71 toward Magny-en-Vexin. Drive past the Louis XV-style castle and take the first road to the right (signposted "La Comté"). A little farther on the right, a new access road leads to a vast parking area.* ⏱*Open mid-Jun to mid-Sep: guided tours (2hr) daily except Mon 2-6pm (last admission 1hr before closing); mid-Sep to mid-Jun: Wed, Sat-Sun 2-6pm.* ⏱*Closed end Oct to end Apr.* ☎*01 53 85 72 10 or 01 34 67 74 33.*
Villarceaux estate is graced by a magnificent setting and two châteaux: a 15C-16C manor house which belonged to the celebrated beauty Ninon de Lenclos, and a Louis XV château.
Approaching the estate from the south, the road from Villers-en-Arthies offers a glimpse of a third edifice, the Château du Couvent surrounded by a golf course.

### WHERE TO STAY

🛏🛏 **Prieuré Maïalen** – *4 allée du Jamburee, 78840 Moisson – 2km/1.2mi E of La Roche-Guyon via D 124 –* ☎ *01 34 79 37 20 – blevi@free.fr –* 🍴 *– 3 rms – meal, 21 €.* In the heart of a village dear to Monet, here's an old 16C priory, entirely refurbished, where each bedroom has been decorated according to a given theme: Provence, Scheherezade and The Boat.

### WHERE TO EAT

🍽 **Les Bords de Seine** – *21 r. du Dr-Duval, 95780 La Roche-Guyon –* ☎ *01 30 98 32 52 – reserv. advisable .* This big house with blue shutters is very nicely situated along the Seine. The sparkling new bedrooms, the restaurant's maritime décor and the delightful terraces add up to a lovely sojourn.

Prolonged by vast outbuildings forming a courtyard, the Manoir de Ninon replaced in the 16C a former fortified house now reduced to the Tour St-Nicolas. Ninon's pavilion ends with Ninon's tower which houses a charming Italian closet and an intriguing hideout dimly lit by a loophole.
**Gardens★** – These illustrate the evolution of gardens through the centuries. The former Renaissance terraces on the left of the entrance are overlooked by the unusual St-Nicolas Tower, known as the "tower of the condemned" because witches were hanged there. The tour of the large pond leads past Ninon's pool, supplied by an Italian waterfall, and reveals a **view★** of the south front of the Louis XV castle. The other façade of the 18C castle overlooks the open Vexin countryside.

### Ninon de Lenclos

When Ninon (1616-1706) died at the age of 90, she had witnessed Louis XIII's reign and the absolute monarchy of Louis XIV. She was acquainted with all the leading personalities of her time and became a legendary figure of the 17C because of her charm and her wisdom; few of her contemporaries could claim to possess such an impressive collection of memories. It was at Villarceaux that she received the young Françoise d'Aubigné, the future Mme Scarron and Mme de Maintenon, who 32 years later was to marry Louis XIV. It was also here that she had a love affair with Louis de Mornay, the Marquis de Villarceaux. The youthful Voltaire was officially presented to her shortly before her death.

# ABBAYE DE ROYAUMONT★★

MICHELIN LOCAL MAP 305: F-6 OR MAP 106 FOLD 7

Royaumont Abbey is an impressive symbol of the wealth that often accrued to the great French abbeys of the Middle Ages. A tour of this sanctuary is strongly recommended, particularly when a concert is scheduled.

The abbey, founded in 1228 and completed in 1235, was occupied by members of the Cistercian order. It was richly endowed by the king and his successors, which explains the size and beauty of the buildings. Six of St Louis' relatives – three children, a brother and two grandsons – were buried in the abbey. Their remains have since been moved to St-Denis.

In 1793 Royaumont was sold as State property and the church dismantled. Since 1923 the abbot's palace and the grounds forming the estate have been separated from the abbey itself.

In 1964 the last owners Isabel and Henri Gouïn (1900-77) created the Royaumont Foundation for the Advancement of Human Science, to which they donated the estate.

- **Information:** ☎ 01 30 35 59 91. www.royaumont.com.
- ▶ **Orient Yourself:** Located 22 miles north of Paris, 17 miles from Paris CDG Airport and the Roissy TGV train station, the Abbey is easy to reach by the A1 and A16 autoroutes.
- ⏱ **Organizing Your Time:** Allow yourself 1 hr to tour the abbey.

## Visit

 ♿ ⏱*Open daily, all year, 10am-6pm (Nov-Feb 10am-5.30pm). 👣 Guided tours (without extra charge) Sat, 2.30pm, 3.30pm and 4.30pm; Sun and public holidays: 11.45am, 2.30pm, 3.45pm and 5pm (Nov-Feb 11.45am, 2.30pm, 3.30pm and 4.30pm). 👛5.50€ (children: 4 €).*

### Church ruins

*See plan.* Royaumont Church, consecrated in 1235, is, unlike traditional Cistercian churches, an unusually large edifice (101m/330ft long) in keeping with its royal origins.

The chancel and its radiating chapels break with Cistercian tradition in that they do not feature a flat east end (e.g. Fontenay in Burgundy). A corner turret (1) belonging to the former north transept gives a fair idea of its elevation (the keystone was 28m/91ft above ground).

### Cloisters

These surround a delightful garden. The west gallery (*opposite the entrance*) is paralleled, at the back, by a narrow, un-

*Abbaye de Royaumont*

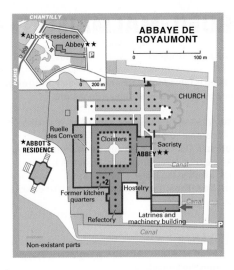

covered passageway known as the "ruelle des Convers." It was built for the lay brothers in order that they might have access to their wing and to the church without passing through the cloisters, habitually reserved for the monks.

## Refectory

This spacious dining hall – which consists of two aisles – is a masterpiece of Gothic architecture. It could accommodate 60 monks without difficulty (note the monolithic shafts of the columns). St Louis would take his turn at serving the monks at table while they sat in silence listening to the reader who stood erect in a pulpit carved out of the thick stone wall.

## Former kitchen quarters

The kitchens house a statue of the Virgin of Royaumont (2), carved in the 14C. The strange building resting on 31 semicircular arches astride the canal is the **latrines and machinery building**. In former times, the water reached a higher level and activated the machinery in the workshops. One of the water wheels has remained intact.

## Abbot's Residence (Palais Abbatial)

Built on the eve of the Revolution for the last commendatory abbot of Royaumont, this white cubic construction is reminiscent of an Italian villa. In neo-Classical style, it is the work of Louis Le Masson. The façade facing the road to Chantilly is reflected in the waters of a charming pond.

### A cultural mission

In 1978 the abbey was assigned a new cultural mission. The Centre Culturel de Rencontre set up on its premises ensures the preservation of the abbey; it also organises concerts, lectures, training seminars and exhibitions in its regional vocal arts centre, literary centre and ethnology centre.

# RUEIL-MALMAISON★★

POPULATION 73 469

MICHELIN LOCAL MAP 311: J-2, MAP 101 FOLDS 13, 14 OR 106 FOLD 18

**The town of Rueil is famed for Malmaison, the delightful estate that remains firmly attached to the name of Napoleon Bonaparte.**

- **Information:** 160 av. Paul-Doumer, 92500 Rueil-Malmaison, ☎ 01 47 32 35 75. www.rueil-tourisme.com
- **Orient Yourself:** On the edge of Paris, 9 miles from the centre, in a loop in the Seine. Take the N 13. Access from Paris: RER line A 1.
- **Don't Miss:** a walk in the forest.
- **Organizing Your Time:** If you want to get round all the museums you will need most of a day.

## A Bit of History

### Malmaison during the Consulate

Marie-Joseph-Rose Tascher de la Pagerie, born in Martinique in 1763, the widow of Général de Beauharnais, married General **Bonaparte** in 1796. Three years later, while Napoleon was away on campaign, she bought Malmaison and the 260ha/640 acres surrounding the château.

When Napoleon was First Consul he lived at the Tuileries, which he found "grand and boring." He decided to spend the end of each 10-day "week" at Malmaison. These were the happiest moments of his married life. Elegant, lively **Josephine** – she had 600 dresses and would change five or six times a day – was the spirit of the party at Malmaison. Life was carefree and formal protocol was dropped.

F. Jalain/EXPLORER

*The dining room at Malmaison*

### Malmaison in Imperial times

Crowned Emperor in 1804, **Napoleon** had no alternative but to stay at St-Cloud, Fontainebleau and the Tuileries, which were the official places of residence. Visits to Malmaison were too rare for the Empress' liking; she began to miss her splendid botanical and rose gardens, unparalleled in France. Josephine was a generous person with expensive tastes who spent money unstintingly. When she ran into debt, her husband would complain bitterly but invariably gave in.

### Malmaison after the divorce

Josephine returned here after her divorce in 1809. Napoleon had given her Malmaison, the Élysée and a château near Évreux. She fled the estate in 1814, but the Allied powers persuaded her to return. She behaved a little rashly by entertaining the Russian Tsar and the King of Prussia at Malmaison. She caught cold while staying with her daughter Hortense at the Château de St Leu and died on 29 May 1814, at the age of 51. The debts she left behind were estimated at 3 million francs.

### The farewell to Malmaison

Ten months after Josephine's death, Napoleon escaped from Elba and revisited Malmaison.

At the end of the Hundred Days he return-ed to the estate and stayed with

Hortense, who had married Napoleon's brother, Louis, and was to give birth to Napoleon III. On 29 June 1815 the Emperor paid a last visit to the château and his family before leaving for Rochefort and St Helena.

### A succession of owners

After Josephine's death, the Château de Malmaison and its 726ha/1 800 acres of land passed to her son Prince Eugène, who died in 1824. The château was sold in 1828 and changed hands several times until it was bought by Napoleon III for the sum of one million francs. The Emperor undertook to restore the architecture and interior decoration to its former glory.

By 1877 the château was in a sorry state and the grounds reduced to a mere 60ha/148 acres. Malmaison was sold as State property and saw yet another succession of owners. The last proprietor, a Mr Osiris, acquired the estate – by now reduced to 6ha/15 acres – in 1896, restored the château and gave it to the State in 1904.

The site of the Mausoleum of the Imperial Prince was bequeathed to Malmaison by Prince Victor-Napoleon. Mr and Mrs Edward Tuck, an American couple who owned Bois-Préau Château, also gave their residence and its 19ha/47 acre park, formerly part of Josephine's private gardens.

## Sights

### Museum

⏱*Open daily (except Tue) (last admission 45min before closing): Apr-Sep: 10am-5.45pm (Sat and Sun 10am-6.15pm); Oct-Mar: 10am-12.30pm, 1.30-5.30pm.* ⏣*4.50€, no charge first Sun in the month.* ☎ *01 41 29 05 55.*

When Josephine bought it in 1799, the **château**, built around 1622, featured the central block and two jutting pavilions dating from the 18C.

The museum was founded in 1906. It houses many exhibits which were purchased, donated or taken from either Malmaison, St-Cloud and the Tuileries, or from other national palaces connected with the Imperial family.

### Pavilions

The **Pavillon Osiris** contains all the collections that have been donated over the years: the works of art and Antique pieces belonging to Mr Osiris, a remarkable selection of snuff boxes, glass objects and caskets relating to the Napoleonic legend. The central area is dominated by Gérard's full-length portrait of Tsar Alexander I. The **Pavillon des Voitures** displays several Imperial carriages, including the landau that Blücher captured at Waterloo in June 1815.

### Musée d'Histoire locale

*6 avenue Paul-Vaillant-Couturier, inside the former town hall.* ⏱*Open daily (except Sun) 2.30-6pm.*⏱*Closed Aug and public holidays.* ☎ *01 47 32 66 50.*

This museum, housed in the old town hall, offers an interesting overview of Rueil's history (Cardinal Richelieu, barracks, Swiss guards etc) and of the town's main economic activities in the past: wine-growing, laundering (note the cast-iron oven used to heat irons). One room on the first floor is devoted to the Consulate and Empire periods (impressive collection of tin soldiers representing Napoleon's Grande Armée led by the Emperor himself). Another room illustrates the importance of Rueil at the beginning of the 20C (postcard-printing).

### Musée des Gardes suisses

*5 place du Mar.-Leclerc.* ⏱*Open Thu 2.30-6pm; by request on other days.* ⏱*Closed Jul and Aug.* ⏣*2€.* ☎ *01 47 32 66 50.*

Documents, weapons, personal objects and uniforms illustrate the lifestyle of the Swiss guards stationed in the Rueil barracks over a period of 200 years.

---

### CHINESE CUISINE

⏥⏥⏥**Le Bonheur de Chine** – *6 allée A.-Maillol* – ☎ *01 47 49 88 88. Closed Mon.*The sculpted wooden façade and decorative fixtures shipped back from the Far East confirm that you are in China! Everything here is extravagant, ranging from the marble reception area and its giant fish-tank to the dining halls and even the menu.

# ST-AMAND-LES-EAUX

POPULATION 17 175

MICHELIN LOCAL MAP 302: I-5

The town is set on the west bank of the River Scarpe; its name derives partly from St Amand, who, in the 7C, founded a Benedictine monastery here which became one of the most important abbeys in the north of France, and partly from its hot springs, used for the treatment of rheumatism and respiratory disorders. The four mineral springs produce water bottled by the Société des Eaux Minérales de St-Amand, the fifth largest producer in France. Culinary specialities include acorn tarts, hazelnut-flavoured flat cake and the local beer, known as "abbey beer".

- **Information:** Grand'Place, 59230 St-Amand-Les-Eaux, ☎ 03 27 22 24 47. www.saint-amand-les-eaux.fr
- **Orient Yourself:** Close to the border with Belgium, 18 miles southeast of Lille via the D 955.
- **Organizing Your Time:** Allow a full day and make the most of your time in the forest.

## Sights

### Abbey

The last reconstruction of these monastic buildings was undertaken c 1625 by Abbot Nicolas du Bois, with their solemn inauguration in 1673. After the Revolution, only the impressive abbey tower and the magistrates' buildings remained.

### Abbey Tower – Museum★

*Open daily (except Tue) Apr-Sep 2-5pm (Sat-Sun 10am-12.30pm, 3-6pm); Oct-Mar: 2-5pm (Sat-Sun 10am-12.30pm, 2-5pm). Closed 1 Jan, 1 May, 14 Jul, 1 Nov, 25 Dec. 2€. ☎ 03 27 22 24 55.*
This colossal building (82m/269ft high) in a traditional Baroque style was the narthex of a church with a nave (non-extant) that occupied much of what is now the public garden.

### Établissement thermal

*4km/2.5mi east by D 954 and D 151.*
Fontaine-Bouillon was known to the Romans for the curative powers of the spring water and was also a place of worship. When the exploitation of the waters began again in the 17C, under Vauban's direction, several ex-voto wooden statues left by those who had taken the waters in the past were found at the bottom of the basin.
The waters and mud, bubbling up at a temperature of 26°C/82°F, are among the most radioactive in France; they are used mainly for the treatment of rheumatism and for respiratory ailments.

The **établissement thermal**, which was rebuilt after the Second World War, also houses a hotel and a casino; its park (8ha/20 acres) extends into the forest along Drève du Prince, which was marked out on the orders of Louis Bonaparte, who took the waters here in 1805.

### Forêt de Raismes-St-Amand-Wallers★

This forest (4 600ha/11 370 acres), an important section of a larger Regional Nature Park (**Parc naturel régional Scarpe-Escaut**), is however only a sliver of the great mantle that covered the Hainault region in the Middle Ages. The flat sand and clay soil, combined with the quarries of former mining works, has resulted in marshes and small lakes throughout the forest, which is made up of oak, beech, birch and poplar groves.

### Maison de la Forêt

*(Étoile de la Princesse)* ♿ *(open Apr-Oct Wed 2-6pm (Sun and public holidays, 3-6.30pm). During school holidays daily except Sat 2-6pm (Sun and public holidays 3-8.30pm). Closed Nov-Mar. 2€ (children: 1€). ☎ 03 27 36 72 72)* provides a wealth of information on the

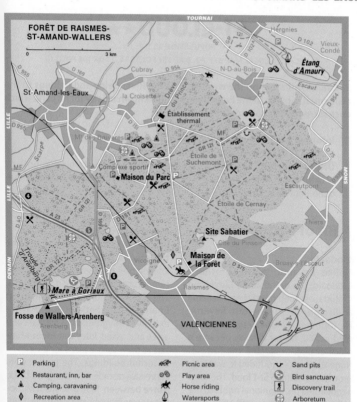

FORÊT DE RAISMES-ST-AMAND-WALLERS

| | Parking | | Picnic area | | Sand pits |
|---|---|---|---|---|---|
| | Restaurant, inn, bar | | Play area | | Bird sanctuary |
| | Camping, caravaning | | Horse riding | | Discovery trail |
| | Recreation area | | Watersports | | Arboretum |

history of the forest, its fauna and flora and on the former mining activities.

Amenities include trails, bridleways, picnic areas, a recreation area (*base de loisirs*), a water sports centre at the 100ha/247-acre **Amaury Lake** (*étang d'Amaury*) and the **Goriaux Pool** (*Mare à Goriaux*) bird sanctuary (*réserve ornithologique*) where numerous bird species such as the crested grebe, the common coot and the little ringed plover live.

# ST-CLOUD ★★

POPULATION 28 157

MICHELIN LOCAL MAP 311: J-2, MAP 101 FOLDS 14, 24 OR 106 FOLD 18

St-Cloud is situated on the west bank of the River Seine and belongs to the residential suburbs of the French capital. It is known mostly for its park, which once surrounded a splendid château.

- **Information:** Hotel de ville - 13, place Charles de Gaulle, 92210. ☎01 47 71 53 00. www.ville-st-cloud.fr.
- ▶ **Orient Yourself:** St-Cloud is located on the very western edge of Paris (9.6km/6mi from the city center), accessible by Metro Line 10 (station: Boulogne-Pont de St-Cloud).

## A Bit of History

### Clodoald

Unlike his unfortunate brothers, Clodoald, the grandson of Clovis and Clotilda, escaped murder and became a disciple of the hermit Severin. He founded a monastery, where he died in 560; his tomb soon became a place of pilgrimage and the town of Nogent, which surrounded it, was subsequently renamed St-Cloud. The saint bequeathed his seigniorial rights to the bishops of Paris who, until 1839, held the title of dukes of St-Cloud and peers of France.

### The assassination of Henri III

In 1589 Henri III laid seige to Paris, which had fallen into the hands of the **Catholic League**: this religious alliance between members of the French nobility (led by the Guise and Montmorency families) and Spain had been formed in order to gain military and political power during a time of weak monarchy in France.

Following the King's alliance with his cousin, the Protestant Henri of Navarre, a vengeful young Jacobin friar called Jacques Clément gained admission to the King's presence and stabbed him in the abdomen. Henri III died two days later.

### Monsieur's Castle

In 1658 the episcopal building became the property of Louis XIV's brother, known to all as "Monsieur." His first wife Henrietta of England died there in 1670. The Sun King's brother later married Charlotte-Elisabeth of Bavaria. He extended the grounds to 590ha/1 460 acres and asked Jules Hardouin-Mansart to draw up the plans for a series of beautiful buildings. The park and its impressive cascade were designed by **Le Nôtre** between 1690 and 1695. Marie-Antoinette bought the estate in 1785 but it became State property during the Revolution.

### The 18 Brumaire

When General Bonaparte returned from his campaign in Egypt, the army troops and the French people saw him as the leader who would restore peace and order. On 18 Brumaire of the year VIII the new French calendar (9 November 1799), the seat of the Consulate was moved to St-Cloud.

The following day, the Five Hundred held a meeting at the orangery, presided over by Napoleon's brother Lucien Bonaparte. The General was greatly disconcerted by the hostile reception he got and was saved only by the swift intervention of

### St-Cloud porcelain

Founded by Pierre Chicaneau in 1677, the porcelain manufacture functioned for almost a century. The delicate, translucent porcelain objects are characterised by blue-monochrome lambrequin motifs enhanced by gold decorations. Some items are adorned with oriental motifs. The trademark is a blue sun.

## Pont de St-Cloud

In the 8C a bridge was built across the River Seine. According to tradition, no king was to set foot on it, or he would die a sudden death. Until the middle of the 16C, French rulers would cross the river in a boat.

However when François I died in Rambouillet, it was decided that the funeral procession would cross the famous bridge; no ill omens were feared as the King was already deceased. This put an end to the long-standing tradition. François' son Henri II replaced the old wooden bridge with a magnificent stone construction featuring 14 arches. The local people were astonished by such a massive display of stonework, which they claimed was the Devil's work, and the bridge had to be exorcised.

his brother who had the assembly room cleared by Murat. The Directoire was abolished.

### St-Cloud during the Empire

In 1802 Bonaparte was appointed consul for life and St-Cloud became his favourite official residence. He celebrated his civil wedding with Marie-Louise on the estate and followed it with a religious ceremony in the Square Salon of the Louvre (1810).

Later, in 1814, the Prussian Marshal Gebhard Blücher took up residence at the château. In an act of vengeance, he cut the silk hangings to ribbons, and wrecked both the bedroom and the library.

It was at St-Cloud that Charles X signed the Ordinances of July 1830, which abolished the charter and precipitated his downfall. It was also from St-Cloud that he went into exile.

On 1 December 1852 the Prince-President Louis-Napoleon was made Emperor. A meeting was held at the Château de St-Cloud on 15 July 1870, during which it was decided to declare war on Prussia. The building was badly damaged in a fire three months later; it was finally razed to the ground in 1891.

## Park★★

ⓘ *Open May-Aug 7.30am-10pm. Mar-Apr and Sep-Oct: 7.30am-9pm. Nov-Feb: 30am-8pm. ⌕3.50€ per car, 2.50€ motorbikes, mopeds, etc., no charge for pedestrians. ☎01 41 12 02 90. www.monum.fr.*

The 450ha/1 110-acre park which spreads from the slopes of the Seine Valley to the Garches plateau has retained most of the original layout designed by Le

Nôtre. In the former stables, a **Musée Historique** (ⓘ*open daily (except Mon and Tue) 10am-1pm and 2-6pm. ⌕2.50€. ☎ 01 41 12 02 90)* tells the story of the estate and its château.

### Grande Cascade★

Designed in the 17C by Lepautre, these impressive falls were later enlarged by Jules Hardouin-Mansart. Dominated by allegorical statues of the River Seine and River Marne, the waters of the cascade flow into a series of basins and troughs before reaching the lower falls, from where they are channelled down to the edge of the park. The whole works are about 90m/296ft long. The **Grandes Eaux★★** fountain display, staged every Sunday in June, is quite remarkable.

### Grand Jet

Nestling in greenery near the Great Cascade, this is the most powerful fountain in the park and rises to a height of 42m/138ft.

### Terrace

A cluster of yew trees and a marble layout mark the former site of the château, which was also the start of the Grande

### HORSE RACES

**Hippodrome de Saint-Cloud** – *1 r. du Camp Canadien* – ☎ *01 47 71 69 26.* The Saint-Cloud racetrack is well known among enthusiasts. Situated at the foot of Mont Valérien, it spreads over 75 hectares and has a rather unexpected golf course in the middle. Several renowned events take place here, including the Grand Prix de Saint-Cloud and La Journée de l'Élégance.

Perspective, a succession of parterres, lawns and ponds and their continuation, the allée de Marnes, stretching over a distance of 2km/1.2mi. The private gardens used to spread on either side. The terrace offers a superb **panorama**★★ of Paris, stretching from the Bois de Boulogne to the woods at Clamart and Meudon.

### Terrasse de l'Orangerie

Some 50 orange trees and oleanders spend the summer months here from May to October. In winter they take shelter inside the orangery in Meudon.

### Jardin du Trocadéro★

These gardens were laid out on the site of the former château; they date from the Restoration period. This beautiful landscaped garden features a charming pond and an aviary.

The far end of the terrace commands a view of Paris. In the foreground, note the Pavillon d'Artois, part of which was built in the 17C.

### Tapis vert

Running from the Grande Gerbe to Rond-Point des 24 Jets, these lawns command a lovely view of the flower beds and the city of Paris.

### Rond-Point de la Balustrade

On this site Napoleon erected a monument surmounted by a lantern which was lit when the Emperor was staying at the château. It was based on a model from ancient Greece, which is why the Parisians called it Demosthene's lantern. It was blown up by the Prussians in 1870.

### Pavillon de Breteuil

This 18C pavilion – St-Cloud's former Trianon – houses the Bureau International des Poids et Mesures (World Centre for Scientific Measurement). The Bureau still has the old standard metre.

### Institut Pasteur★
### Musée des Applications de la Recherche

*3 avenue Pasteur and 3 boulevard Raymond-Poincaré.*

In 1884 when **Louis Pasteur**, who had already done considerable research work, lacked space in Paris to pursue his studies on rabies, a decree ruled that he could move to the now State-owned Villeneuve-l'Étang estate; in 1885 he successfully invented the first vaccine for human use, crowning a lifelong career. The museum is housed in the Hundred Guards' Pavilion, occupied by Napoleon III's soldiers in the 19C. The room where Pasteur died in 1895 remains intact and features the family measuring rod bearing inscriptions made by Mme Pasteur.

## Town

Overlooked by the spire of the Église St-Clodoald (1865), the steep, narrow streets of the old town wind their way up the hillsides of the Seine Valley.

### Église Stella-Matutina★

*Place Henri-Chrétien along avenue du Maréchal-Foch.* ○*Open Mon-Fri 9am-noon, 2-6pm, Sat 10am-noon.* ☎ *01 41 12 80 80.*

The church was consecrated in 1965; it is shaped like a huge circular tent made of wood, metal and glass. It is fixed to a concrete base by nine pivots and fronted by a porch roof in the shape of a helm. The converging lines of the copper roofing and the pine timbering create an impression of loftiness and soaring height, which is further emphasised by the concentric rows of pews round the altar.

# ST-DENIS★★

POPULATION 85 832

MICHELIN LOCAL MAP 305: F-7, MAP 101 FOLD 16 OR 106 FOLDS 19, 20

St-Denis is an industrial and cultural town dating far back in history. For centuries, its destiny was directly linked to that of the abbey, then of the cathedral, which contains a unique collection of tombs and recumbent effigies dating from the 12C to the 16C. The style of the basilica offers a striking contrast to the futuristic architecture of the **Stade de France**, inaugurated for the 1998 World Football Cup.

- 🔲 **Information:** 1 r. de la République, 93200 St-Denis, ☎01 55 87 08 70. www. saint-denis-tourisme.com - Stade de France, r. Jules-Rimet (Porte G), 93200 St-Denis. www.ville-saint-denis.fr.
- ▶ **Orient Yourself:** Just 6 miles to the north of Paris. Access from Paris: Metro line 13 (station: St-Denis-Basilique). By RER, line B (station: La Plaine-Stade-de-France) or line D (stations: Saint-Denis and Stade-de-France).
- 🅿 **Parking:** Parking in St Denis can be difficult, but there are a number of charged car parks both near the basilica and the information office in r. de la République.
- 🔯 **Don't Miss:** Fête des Loges, which takes place every year in the St-Germain Forest and last for seven weeks from the end of June (🔖 see panel below).
- 🕐 **Organizing Your Time:** Allow half a day to take in St Denis. Visit on Tue, Fri or Sat to experience the Marché du Monde.
- 🔯 **Also See:** Rueil-Malmaison. Auvers-sur-Oise.

## A Bit of History

### "Monsieur St-Denis"

St Denis was a preacher, and the first Bishop of Lutetia. Legend has it that, after being beheaded in Montmartre, he picked up his head and walked away. He finally died in the country and was buried by a pious woman. An abbey was built over the grave of the man popularly known as "Monsieur (or Monsignor) St-Denis" and soon attracted large crowds of pilgrims. That, at least, is the legend. In fact, a Roman town stood on the site of St-Denis. It was called Catolacus and it had stood since the 1C AD, as it was possible to keep watch over the Paris-Beauvais road and the river from this spot. In AD 475, the first large church was built. Dagobert I had it rebuilt in AD 630 and set up a Benedictine community there with orders to take charge of the pilgrimage. The building we see today dates mainly from the 12C and 13C.

### Abbot Suger

Suger is the outstanding figure in the history of St-Denis. He came from a poor family and was "given" to the abbey at the age of 10. His exceptional gifts gave him immense power over his fellow pupil, the son of Louis VI the Fat, who became a close friend of the young monk, summoned him to the royal court and consulted him on every possible subject. Suger was elected Abbot of St-Denis in 1122 and drew the plans of the present minster himself.

### Annual event

The Fête des Loges, which goes back to St Louis, takes place every year in the St-Germain Forest on a site known as "Les Loges". This convivial funfair lasts for seven weeks from the end of June to the Sunday following 15 August. The numerous attractions and stands appeal to around 3 million visitors who also enjoy the roast chickens, sauerkraut and beer on offer…

## Address Book

### THEATRE

**Théâtre Gérard-Philipe** – *59 bd Jules-Guesde – M Saint-Denis-Basilique – ☎ 01 48 13 70 00 – shows at 8.30pm – see programme. Closed Jul-Aug and 1 May.* The young director Stanislas Nordey and his team have been running the Théâtre Gérard Philippe since 1998. TGP has a vocation as a "people's theatre", catering to middle and lower-class neighbourhoods and their denizens. It produces young troupes and offers new creations and the works of contemporary authors (Pasolini), in addition to classics and children's plays. Low ticket prices encourage theatre-goers to stop in regularly.

### SHOPPING

**Le Marché du Monde** – St-Denis has remained faithful to its fairground reputation with the Marché du Monde (World Market), one of the Île-de-France's largest. It overflows from the Halle Garnier, built in 1893, with 300-odd tradespeople and a variety of booths selling Middle Eastern doughnuts, spices, fabrics, clothes and inexpensive tableware, etc. *Tue, Fri and Sat from 8am to noon.*

# Basilica★★★

## The burial ground of kings

For 1200 years from Dagobert to Louis XVIII, almost all the kings of France were buried here. In 1793, Barrère asked the Convention for permission to destroy the tombs. The bodies were thrown into communal graves. Alexandre Lenoir saved the most precious tombs by taking them to Paris, storing them in the Petits-Augustins which was to become the Musée des Monuments Français. In 1816, Louis XVIII returned the tombs to the basilica.

*Window in the Basilica*

Ph. Gajic/ MICHELIN

## Construction

The structure is of prime importance in the history of architecture. It had the first large chancel and was a prototype, providing inspiration for the architects of countless late-12C cathedrals such as the ones in Chartres, Senlis and Meaux.

**Decline and Fall** – In later years, the basilica was poorly maintained and the French Revolution brought with it further damage. Napoleon had the most urgent repairs carried out and returned the basilica to the Church in 1806.

**Restoration** – The architect Debret took charge of the church in 1813 but he knew little or nothing about medieval architecture and his work raised public indignation. He began to work on the magnificent spire, but used materials that were too heavy and the delicate balance was destroyed. In 1846, the spire threatened collapse and had to be removed.

**Viollet-le-Duc** – Replacing Debret in 1847, Viollet-le-Duc gathered up documents that enabled him to restore the building to its original condition. From 1858 until his death in 1879, he undertook a considerable amount of work and the church we see today is due to his efforts.

Today the basilica is surrounded by gardens laid out on the site of medieval buildings which have disappeared.

# Visit 1hr

## Exterior

The absence of the north tower mars the harmony of the west front. In the Middle Ages the building was fortified and some crenellations are still visible at the base of the towers. The tympanum on the central doorway represents the Last Judgment, that on the right doorway (it has been re-carved) depicts the Last Communion of St Denis and on the left the Death of St Denis and his companions Rusticus and Eleutherus (also re-carved). The door jambs feature the Wise and Foolish Virgins (*centre*), the labours of the months (*right*) and the signs of the Zodiac (*left*).

The basilica is floodlit every night; the lighting by Yann Kersalé which illuminates the west front re-creates the warm colours of stained glass.

## Interior

⊙*Open Apr-Sep 10am-6.15pm (Sun and public holidays, noon-6.15pm). Oct-Mar 10am-5.15pm (Sun and public holidays, noon-5.15pm). Last admission 30min before closing.* ⊷*Guided visits possible.* ⊙*Closed 1 Jan, 1 May, 25 Dec.* ⊜*6.50€, no charge first Sun in the month, Oct-Mar.* ☎ *01 48 09 83 54.*

The cathedral is 108m/354ft long, 39m/128ft wide in the transept and 29m/95ft high, making it slightly smaller than Notre-Dame in Paris.

The elegant nave is attributed to Pierre de Montreuil. The bays in the triforium open onto the exterior (one of the first examples of such arrangements). The stained-glass windows in the nave are modern.

## Tombs and recumbent effigies★★★

St-Denis houses the tombs of 46 kings, 32 queens and 63 royal children, as well as those of leading personalities who served the French court, such as Bertrand du Guesclin (1). The tombs have been empty since the Revolution.

After the 14C it was the custom to remove the heart and viscera from the bodies of kings before embalming them. The inner organs, the heart and the body were all buried in different places; the bodies in St-Denis.

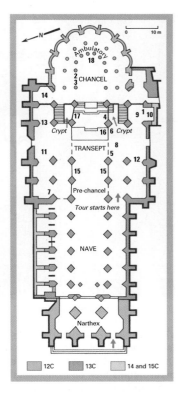

Up to the Renaissance, the only sculpture adorning tombs were **recumbent figures**. Note the tombs of Clovis (2) and Fredegunde (3), featuring a copper cloisonné mosaic made in the 12C for St-Germain-des-Prés Church.

Around 1260 St Louis commissioned a series of effigies of all the rulers who had preceded him since the 7C. The figures were purely symbolic but they provide a telling example of how royalty was portrayed toward the mid-13C. They include the imposing tomb of Dagobert (4), with its lively, spirited scenes, the recumbent effigies of Charles Martel (5) and Pepin the Short (6) and a female effigy carved in Tournai marble (7).

The tomb of Isabelle of Aragon and of Philippe III the Bold (8), who died in 1285, shows an early concern for accurate portraiture.

Toward the middle of the 14C well-known people had their tomb built when they were still alive. The effigies of Charles V by Beauneveu (9), Charles

*Effigies of Marie-Antionette and Louis XVI*

VI and Isabella of Bavaria (**10**) are therefore extremely lifelike.

During the Renaissance, these **mausoleums** took on monumental proportions and were lavishly decorated. The upper level featured the king and his queen, kneeling in full regalia. On the lower level, the deceased were pictured lying down as naked cadavers. Admire the twin monuments built for Louis XII and Anne of Brittany (**11**), and that of François I and Claude de France (**12**), sculpted by Philibert Delorme and Pierre Bontemps.

**Catherine de' Medici**, who survived her husband Henri II by 30 years, gave orders to build the royal tomb. When she saw how she had been portrayed according to tradition, she fainted in horror and ordered a new effigy which substituted sleep for death. Both works are on display in the cathedral. Their making was supervised by Primaticcio (**13**), and Germain Pilon (**14**), respectively.

### Chancel

The beautiful pre-Renaissance stalls (**15**) in the forward part of the chancel and the carved wooden door inside the basilica, leading to the south-side necropolis, were taken from the Nor-

man Castle in Gaillon. On the right stands a splendid 12C Romanesque **Virgin Mary**★ in painted wood (**16**), brought from St-Martin-des-Champs. The bishop's throne opposite (**17**) is a replica of Dagobert's royal throne (*the original is in the Medals and Antiquities Gallery at the Bibliothèque Nationale in Paris*).

At the end, the modern reliquary of the saints Denis, Rusticus and Eleutherius (**18**) flanks Suger's **ambulatory**★, characterised by wide arches and slender columns.

### Crypt★★

The lower ambulatory was built in the Romanesque style by Suger (12C) and restored by Viollet-le-Duc (capitals with plant motifs). In the centre stands a vaulted chapel known as Hilduin's Chapel (after the abbot who had it built in the 9C).

Beneath the pavement lies the burial vault of the Bourbon family, which houses the remains of Louis XVI, Marie-Antoinette and Louis XVIII. The communal grave in the north transept contains the bones of kings and queens, royal highnesses, princes of the blood, Merovingians, Capetians and members of the Orléans and Valois dynasties.

# Additional Sights

## Musée d'Art et d'Histoire

*22 bis rue Gabriel-Péri.* ○*Open daily (except Tue) 10am-5.30pm, Thu 10am-8pm, Sat-Sun 2-6.30pm.* ○*Closed public holidays.* ◎*4€, no charge first Sun of month.* ☎ *01 42 43 05 10.*

The museum is set up in the former Carmelite convent, part of which has been restored. The refectory and the kitchen contain archaeological exhibits discovered in St-Denis (fragments of medieval pottery). Many of the items on display come from the old hospital, including a superb reconstruction of an apothecary's shop that is of particular interest to ceramics enthusiasts (17C and 18C jars), and an apothecary's collection of ceramic phials and jars (17C and 18C).

The cells on the first floor contain many works of art, mementoes and paintings, including several by Guillot, evoking the daily life of the Carmelite nuns. Mystical adages have been inscribed on the walls.

On the second floor, once reserved for the king when he visited his daughter, there are numerous drawings, paintings and documents relating to the Paris Commune of 1871.

The former Louis XV pavilion, now renovated, houses an exhibition of the works of Paul Éluard, with a collection of personal memorabilia.

## Musée Bouilhet-Christofle

*112 rue Ambroise-Croizat.* ○*Open daily (except Sat-Sun) 9.30am-1pm and 2-5.30pm.* ○*Closed public holidays.* ◎*5€.* ☎*01 49 22 40 40.*

The famous gold and silverware manufacturing company (founded by Charles Christofle in 1830) – the first to apply the principle of electroplating – set up premises here in 1874. They became the official supplier to Napoleon III and their silver pieces still adorn the tables of many heads of State and rulers throughout the world. The museum presents more than 2 000 rare exhibits and some beautiful reproductions crafted in the St-Denis workshops in the late 19C. Note, in particular, sets of tableware created for 19C luxury hotels or for the Normandie liner.

## Stade de France

☎*01 55 93 00 00. www.stadefrance.com.* The 1998 World Football Cup was the force that generated the stadium, and now it is the biggest multifunction Olympic-sized stadium in the world. The elliptic structure is 270m/295yd long, 230m/ 240yd wide, 35m/115ft high and covers an area of 17ha/42 acres. Thanks to its variable capacity, it can host all kinds of sporting and entertainment events. The circle of stands (25 000 seats) nearest the track can be reconfigured to accommodate athletics competitions. The middle stand has a capacity of 30 000 and the upper stand 25 000. When the field is used for concerts, the total capacity reaches 100 000.

## Parc de la Courneuve

*2.5km/1.5mi east along rue de Strasbourg and N 301 (on the right).*

This 350ha/865-acre stretch of greenery features a cycling track, bridlepath, a ski jump, a little train, sports facilities, and playgrounds for children. Rowing boats and pedaloes may be hired to explore the 12ha/30-acre lake (◎*bathing prohibited*).

# ST-GERMAIN-EN-LAYE★★

### POPULATION 40 162
### MICHELIN LOCAL MAP 311: I-2, MAP 101 FOLD 12 OR 106 FOLDS 17, 18

St-Germain is both a residential district and a popular resort, with many tourists attracted by its château, its huge terrace and its forest. The town owes its name to St Germain, a Paris bishop, and *laye* which probably means "forest path."

- **Information:** Maison Claude Debussy, 38 r. au Pain, 78100 St Germain-en-Laye. ☎ 01 34 51 05 12.
- ▶ **Orient Yourself:** Not far from the Sine, 14 miles west of the centre of Paris, via the N 13 and A 14. Access from Paris: RER line A 1.
- **Don't Miss:** Lovers of classical music should take time to visit the Maison Debussy.
- **Organizing Your Time:** There is a goodly amount to see, so allow half a day.
- **Also See:** St Cloud. Rueil-Malmaison. Versailles.

## A Bit Of History

### The old castle

In the 12C Louis VI, the Fat, eager to exploit the strategic position of the St-Germain hillside, built a fortified stronghold on the site of the present château. The fortress was destroyed during the Hundred Years War and restored by Charles V around 1368.

In 1514 Louis XII married his daughter Claude de France to the Duc d'Angoulême, who became François I the following year. The young ruler was acquainted with Italian culture and the ancient citadel was hardly suited to his taste for palatial comfort and luxury. In 1539 he had the whole building razed with the exception of Charles V's keep and the chapel built by St Louis.

### New Château

Even the new building presented itself as a fortified structure equipped with machicolations and de-fended by a garrison numbering 3 000. Henri II, who wanted a real country house, commissioned Philibert Delorme to draw up plans for a new château on the edge of the plateau. The château became famous on account of its fantastic location and the terraces built along the slopes overlooking the River Seine.

The area beneath the foundation arches has been arranged into artificial grottoes where hydraulically propelled automatons re-enact mythological scenes: Orpheus playing the viola and attracting animals who come to listen, Neptune's chariot in full motion etc.

### Chronology of court events

The court occupied both the new château and the old castle, which were used as a palatial residence, or a safe retreat when riots broke out in Paris.

Henri II, Charles IX and Louis XIV were all born at St-Germain. Louis XIII died here. Mary Queen of Scots lived here between the ages of 6 and 16. In 1558 she married the Dauphin François, aged only 15, and was crowned Queen of France the following year.

### Mansart's improvements

Louis XIV – who was born, christened and brought up at St-Germain – grew fond of the château. As king, he paid frequent visits to the estate.

The apartments of the old castle had become too cramped for Louis' liking and he commissioned **Jules Hardouin-Mansart** to build five large pavilions as a replacement for the five corner turrets adjoining the outer walls. Le Nôtre drew up the plans for the park, the terrace and the forest; in 1665 the grounds were replanted with five and a half million trees. In 1682 the court moved from St-Germain to Versailles. In 1689 the deposed King of England James II came to stay at the old castle, where he died in great financial straits in 1701, a well-

*Château de St-Germain-en-Laye*

loved figure (funeral monument in St-Germain Church, facing the château).

### Final developments

In 1776 the badly dilapidated new château was ceded to the Comte d'Artois by his brother Louis XVI. The future king Charles X had the building demolished, except for the Henri IV pavilion on the terrace and the Sully Pavilion, in Le Pecq. The remains, together with the park, were sold during the Revolution. The old castle was stripped of its furniture. Under Napoleon I it was the seat of a cavalry college; under Louis-Philippe it housed a military penitentiary but Napoleon III ordered its closure in 1855. It was then entirely restored under the guidance of the architect Millet, succeeded by Daumet.

In 1862 Napoleon III inaugurated the National Museum of French Antiquities which he had set up on the premises. The signing of the 1919 peace treaty with Austria took place in the château at St-Germain.

## The Château And Its Neighbourhood

The most striking approach to the château is from the north, along the road from Les Loges. The tour starts from the square beside the château, place Charles-de-Gaulle.

### Château★

The château is the shape of an imperfect pentagon. The feudal foundations are distinguishable together with the covered watch-path and a series of machicolations restored by Daumet. The roof, laid out as a terrace edged with vases and a balustrade and dominated by tall chimneys, was an innovative idea.

The royal suites were on the first floor; the king and the dauphin lived in the wing facing the parterres, the queen's suite looked toward Paris and the children's rooms were in the wing which now faces rue Thiers. Under Henri IV 12 of the 14 royal infants, born to five different mothers, romped noisily in these quarters.

### Ste-Chapelle★

Built by St Louis from 1230 to 1238, this chapel precedes the Ste-Chapelle in Paris by some 10 years. It was probably designed by the same architect, Pierre de Montreuil, but its tall windows do not have the stained glass that gives such dazzling splendour to its counterpart in Paris.

Within the thickness of the keystones are carvings of figures thought to represent St Louis, his mother Blanche de Castille, his wife, and other people close to him. If this is true, it would make these precious images the oldest pictures of royal families in existence.

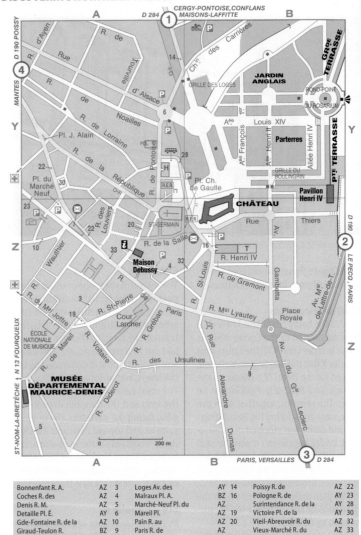

| | | | | | | |
|---|---|---|---|---|---|---|
| Bonnenfant R. A. | AZ | 3 | Loges Av. des | AY | 14 | Poissy R. de | AZ | 22 |
| Coches R. des | AZ | 4 | Malraux Pl. A. | BZ | 16 | Pologne R. de | AY | 23 |
| Denis R. M. | AZ | 5 | Marché-Neuf Pl. du | AZ | | Surintendance R. de la | AY | 28 |
| Detaille Pl. É. | AY | 6 | Mareil Pl. | AZ | 19 | Victoire Pl. de la | AY | 30 |
| Gde-Fontaine R. de la | AZ | 10 | Pain R. au | AZ | 20 | Vieil-Abreuvoir R. du | AZ | 32 |
| Giraud-Teulon R. | BZ | 9 | Paris R. de | AZ | | Vieux-Marché R. du | AZ | 33 |

## Musée des Antiquités Nationales★★

&. ⓒOpen daily (except Tue): May-Sep: 9am-5.15pm (Sat and Sun, 10am-6.15pm); Oct-Apr: 9am-5.15pm. ⓒClosed 1 Jan and 25 Dec. ⊚4€. ☎ 01 39 10 13 00, www.musee-antiquitesnationales.fr.
The museum contains many rare archaeological exhibits relating to France's early history, ranging from prehistory to Charlemagne's reign.

## Prehistory and protohistory (Mezzanine)

The Palaeolithic or early Stone Age goes back one million years before our era. The glass cabinets on the right provide general information on materials such as stone (flint), quartz, bone and antlers, and display toolmaking techniques of that period. Note the traces of man's existence in prehistoric times: photographs of the handprints at Gargas, mould of the footprints found in a cave at Aldène. The left-hand cabinets displaying the results of the excavations are in chronological order. The major works of art dating from the Palaeolithic Age are surprisingly small: the **Lady of Brassempouy** (3.6cm/1.44in high), the oldest human face found to date (c 20000 BC), a bison licking itself (Magdalenian – c 16000 BC), the Bruniquel baton in the shape of a jumping horse (c 13000 BC), the Mas-d'Azil head of a neighing horse (c 10000 BC) etc. During the Neolithic Age, man developed farming and cattle rearing, community life in huts and the use of ceramics. He produced arms and tools by polishing very hard stones (jadeite). The discovery of an alloy combining copper and tin led to the early stages of metallurgy (Bronze Age). Gold too was widely used and the museum displays several objects and pieces of jewellery made of solid gold or gold leaf. Note

## Address Book

*For coin ranges, see the Legend on the cover flap.*

### TOURISM INFORMATION

*Maison Claude Debussy, 38 r. au Pain, 78100 St-Germain-en-Laye, ☎ 01 34 51 05 12*

### WHERE TO STAY

**Havre Hôtel** – *92 r. Léon-Desoyer – ☎01 34 51 41 05. Closed 3 wks in Aug – 10 rms:– 6.50€.* Outside of the historical heart of the city, this small, colourful hotel has simple, pleasant rooms. The three overlooking the cemetery are the quietest. A good, dependable address in town.

### WHERE TO EAT

**Bistrot du Boucher** – *8 bis av. Carnot – take N. 12 – ☎ 01 39 73 07 29. Closed 3 wks in Aug, Sun evening and Mon.* Open the door of this bistro with its 1930's décor to discover top-quality fare and the friendly atmosphere that prevails day and night. Emblematic slate menu, waiters in black aprons and dishes evoking treasured family recipes.

**Top Model** – *24 r. St-Pierre – ☎ 01 34 51 77 78. Closed 3-10 Jan, 3-23 Aug, Sun evening and Mon – reservations essential.* A very appealing address in the heart of St-Germain-en-Laye where the attractive, modern dining room is entirely done in white. Traditional cuisine is the mainstay, and there's an Iranian caviar menu for aficionados.

### ON THE TOWN

**Forum Café** – *18 r. de Poissy – ☎ 01 30 61 04 84 – www.osullivanspubs.com – Mon-Tue 10am-midnight, Wed-Thu 10am-1am, Fri-Sat 10am-2am.* For the past 30 years, this long, wood-bedecked establishment has been bridging the generation gap by making everyone – from high school students to their grandparents – welcome. The giant screen, good choice of beer (seven on tap), music and theme evenings (paella, Beaujolais, etc ...) make this one of the liveliest spots in town.

**Couleur Café** – *18 r. de la Salle – ☎ 01 39 10 07 70. Daily 8am-8pm.* A novel little café à l'Italienne clad in chrome and blue wood. Since the café itself can't seat more than 20, the terrace on the pedestrian street is heated. St. Germain natives in the know come here for a cup of coffee (eight blends to choose from), tea or cocoa while nibbling on a blueberry muffin or a cookie and reading a newspaper. Light meals.

### SHOWTIME

**La Clef** – *46 r. de Mareil – ☎ 01 39 21 54 90 – www.rockinfo.fr/laclef – see programme.* Advance ticket purchase at La Clef and the FNAC. Zebda, Miossec, Louise Attaque and even Compay Segundo, the famous Cuban musician, have played this concert hall. Varied, often quite talented, performances.

### SHOPPING

**Ferme expérimentale du Domaine de Grignon** – *78850 Thiverval-Grignon – ☎01 30 54 37 34 – www.inapg.inra.fr – shop open Wed-Sun 2pm-7pm, except Sat 10am-noon, 2pm-7pm; visitors welcome.* Visit this experimental farm and its dairy division for a fun learning experience. Follow the signposts to take the free tour, then visit the shop and discover products collected from agricultural lycées (schools) all over the country.

the numerous weapons (daggers, axes with curved blades) and the metal necklaces and other decorative objects (open bracelets) which give these particular collections the sparkle that characterised some of the so-called "primitive" civilizations of the modern world.

**Gallo-Roman and Merovingian Antiquities (First floor)** – The lengthy period of Roman peace (*Pax Romana*), the indulgence of the victors and the deeply rooted religious feeling for indigenous gods gave rise to a flourishing industry of mythological and funeral sculpture (until then the Celts had shown little interest in statuary art).

Ceramic pieces played an important role in domestic life; one of the cabinets offers a fairly comprehensive presentation of "sigillate" ceramics, decorated with stamped motifs, made in workshops at Lezoux, La Graufesenque, Banassac etc (1C-4C AD).

Little is known about the following period (3C-8C AD), though its heritage consists mostly of Merovingian burial places rich in arms – swords with damascene blades – and items of finery: heavy flat buckles for belts, S-shaped clasps etc.

The large ballroom in the château – also called the Salle de Mars – is dedicated to comparative archaeology; a superb selection of objects from all five continents makes it possible to draw parallels between techniques and lifestyles belonging to geographically distant civilizations, from very different historical periods.

### Exterior

**Parterres** – Enter the gardens through the gate on place Charles-de-Gaulle and skirt the château. Built into the façade is the loggia opening onto the inner main staircase. The moat contains restored megalithic monuments and replicas of Roman statues.

The east esplanade – now the site of a pillbox – was the scene of the last judicial duel during which the will of God was invoked. The duel between Jarnac and La Châtaigneraie was attended by Henri II, accompanied by his retinue of courtiers. La Châtaigneraie, one of the finest swordsmen in Europe, was confident about the outcome of the battle. Jarnac, however, had learnt a new tactic: he severed the left hamstring of his adversary, who collapsed and slowly died.

**Pavillon Henri-IV** – The brick pavilion was built on the very edge of the escarpment; it is crowned by a dome, and, together with the **Sully Pavilion** set lower down on the hillside at Le Pecq, is all that remains of the new château. It contains the Louis XIII oratory where Louis XIV was baptised on 5 September 1638, the day he was born.

The hotel which opened in this historic building in 1836 became an important meeting place for 19C writers, artists and politicians. Alexandre Dumas wrote *The Three Musketeers* and *The Count of Monte Cristo* while he was staying here, Offenbach composed *The Drum Major's Daughter* and Léo Delibes produced the ballet *Sylvia*. The statesman and president Thiers died here in 1877.

**Terrace★★** – The Small Terrace starts beside the hotel and extends to the Rosarium roundabout. There, a worn Touring Club of France viewing table is a reminder of past views toward the western suburbs of Paris.

The Grand Terrace extends beyond the roundabout. It is one of Le Nôtre's finest accomplishments and was completed in 1673 after four years of large-scale construction work. Lined with stately lime trees, it is 2 400m/8 000ft long and is one of the most famous promenades around Paris.

The **vista**★ from the terrace being the same all the way along, visitors pressed for time may return to their car through the lovely **English-style garden**★.

## Additional Sights

### Maison Debussy

*38 rue au Pain.* ○*Open daily (except Sun and Mon) Mar-Oct 2-6pm, Sat 10am-12.30pm, 2-6pm (Nov-Feb 5pm).* ○*Closed public holidays.* ☎ 01 34 51 05 12.

This house was the birthplace of the composer Claude Debussy on 22 August 1862. The restored building contains the tourist office and mementoes of the composer.

## Musée Départemental Maurice-Denis★

🕐Open daily (except Mon) 10am-5.30pm, Sat-Sun 10am-6.30pm (last admission 1hr before closing). 🕐Closed 1 Jan, 1 May, 25 Dec. ⊛4€. ☎ 01 39 73 77 87. www.musee-mauricedenis.fr.

The Priory was founded in 1678 by Mme de Montespan and was originally designed as a royal hospital. In 1915 it became the property of the painter **Maurice Denis** (1870-1943), who moved here with his large family and freely entertained his friends of the Nabis movement.

The museum explains the origins of the **Nabis** group – founded by Paul Sérusier in 1888 – and illustrates their passion for various forms of pictorial and decorative expression: painting, posters, stained glass etc. The works assembled in the priory testify to the considerable influence the symbolic movement – the "search for the invisible" – had on the art world at large: literature, decorative arts, sculpture, painting and music. Rejecting Realism and Naturalism, this movement claimed the necessity to put feeling at the centre of every work of art.

The first floor displays *Eternal Spring*, a set of ten panels by Maurice Denis, depicting women bathing, near a fountain or in a garden, gathered together for the sake of music or conversation.

**Chapelle** – The chapel was entirely decorated by Maurice Denis between 1915 and 1928: stained glass, frescoes, liturgical furnishings.

**Atelier** – Maurice Denis had this studio built by his friend Auguste Perret in 1912 when he was working on the decoration for the ceiling of the Théâtre des Champs-Élysées. Vast profane and religious projects are on display.

**Park** – A series of terraced flower beds are pleasantly dotted with statues by Antoine Bourdelle. The park offers a charming vista of the priory façade and its elegant severity.

# FORÊT DE ST-GOBAIN★★

ST-GOBAIN FOREST
MICHELIN LOCAL MAP 306: C-5

This beautiful forest ⚡ (6 000ha/14 000 acres) between the River Oise and River Ailette covers a plateau pitted with quarries and furrowed with vales that are dotted with lakes.

The region is rich in deer and used to be the home of wolves and wild boar. Deer-hunting, a tradition here since the time of Louis XV, still continues today. Signposted trails lead through the forest; in season, the area provides a rich crop of mushrooms and lily of the valley.

🛈 **Information:** Syndicat d'initiative de Chauny, pl. du Marché-Couvert, 02300. ☎ 03 23 52 20 79.

▶ **Orient Yourself:** Use the D 7 to reach the forest from Laon, and the N 44 then D 13 from Saint Quentin. The D 13 also links via the D 1 with Soissons.

😊 **Don't Miss:** Take a Sunday afternoon break at the Auberge de Bernagousse.

🕐 **Organizing Your Time:** Allow 3 hr to take the 14-mile round tour of the forest.

👣 **Also See:** Laon, Coucy-le-Château-Auffrique.

## Forêt de St-Gobain

### St-Gobain

The town was established as a consequence of pilgrims visiting the Irish hermit Gobain, who settled in the forest and lived there for 20 years until he was beheaded by the Vandals. St-Gobain lies on the edge of a limestone ridge that reaches a height of 200m/656ft in parts. St-Gobain is best-known for its **Mirror Factory** (*manufacture de glaces*) founded by Louis XIV at Colbert's request, and established in 1692 in the ruins of the castle that had belonged to the lords of Coucy. It was the first to use a method

**WHERE TO EAT**

🍽 **Auberge de Bernagousse** –
*02700 Barisis-aux-Bois – 5km/3mi SW
of St-Gobain via D 534 – ☎ 03 23 39 56
05. Closed 19-26 Feb, 3-10 Sep, Sun
evening and Mon – reserv. requested
weekends.* Treat yourself to a relaxing
break in this rather basic inn hidden
in the bosom of the forest. The
Sunday after-noon 'tea' has a faithful
following – the pies and cider served
therein give ramblers the strength
they need to continue their journey.

of casting which allowed the production
of very large mirrors. This manufacture
preceded the St-Gobain Company, now
part of the St-Gobain-Pont-à-Mousson
group, one of the top producers of
glazes in the world.

▶ *Take D 7 (Laon road) east for 3km/
2mi; at the crossroads (La Croix-des-
Tables) turn left onto D 730.*

🚶 The **Roches de l'Ermitage** (*15min on
foot there and back*) are very picturesque.
There are three hiking trails: the pond
(2hr, blue markings), the abbeys (4hr,
red markings) and the rocks (20min,
white markings).

▶ *D 730 joins D 55. Turn right onto D 55
and first left onto D 556.*

### Le Tortoir★

The walls of Le Tortoir, a 14C fortified
priory and once a daughter-house of
the abbey of St-Nicolas-aux-Bois, appear
in a clearing surrounded by lakes where
teal and moorhen are to be found.

▶ *Return to D 55 and continue south.*

Soon after the village of St-Nicolas-aux-
Bois, the ruins of the abbey become
visible (*right*).

### Abbaye St-Nicolas-aux-Bois★

The Benedictine abbey, the remains of
which have been incorporated into a
private property, occupied a delightful
setting here on the floor of a valley. The
road first skirts the moat which protected the abbey walls and then two
ponds encircled by greenery, beyond
which the 15C abbey buildings appear.

### Croix Seizine

*400m/440yd from D 55.* This expiatory
monument was erected by Enguerrand IV,
Lord of Coucy, who was condemned in
1256 by St Louis for having executed
four students from St-Nicolas-aux-Bois
who were caught hunting on his land.

▶ *Continue along D 55. At the picturesque
village of Suzy turn right onto D 552.*

### Abbaye de Prémontré★

*Apr-Oct: 9am-7pm; Nov-Mar: 9am-5pm.
No charge.*

*Former Priory Le Tortoir*

This former abbey nestling in a wooded valley was founded by **St Norbert**, who was born at the end of the 11C near the Rhine in the Duchy of Cleves. He lived a worldly life until, one stormy day, he was thrown from his horse like St Paul and a voice reproached him for his dissolute living. Touched by grace, Norbert sold all his possessions and retreated to Prémontré where he founded the abbey and the order which took its name. The abbey was rebuilt in the 18C, convert-ed to a glass-works in 1802 and is now a psychiatric hospital. The main body has a round outer porch with an unusual curved triangular pediment, with a cardinal's shield above. The wings are simpler; their porches are topped with a shell framed by monumental urns.

▶ *Follow D 14 to Septvaux.*

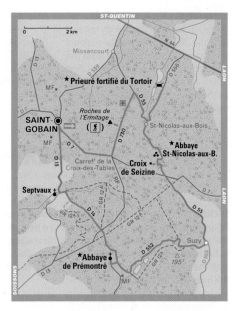

### Septvaux

The Romanesque church with its two belfries stands on a rise overlooking the lovely 12C wash-house (*on the road to Coucy*).

▶ *D 13 returns to St-Gobain.*

# ST-LEU-D'ESSERENT ★

POPULATION 4 867

MICHELIN LOCAL MAP 305: F-5 OR MAP 106 FOLDS 7, 8

NORTHWEST OF CHANTILLY

The Archbishop of Sens, St Leu, who died in 623, gave his name to several French localities. St-Leu-d'Esserent, located on the banks of the River Oise, boasts a magnificent church which the philosopher and historian Ernest Renan once compared to a Greek temple on account of its pure, harmonious lines.

🗊 **Information:** R. de l'Église, 60430 St-Leu-d'Esserent, ☎ 03 44 56 38 10.

▶ **Orient Yourself:** Mid-way between Paris (34 miles), via the N 16, and Compiègne (28 miles) by the D 200/D 201.

🕐 **Organizing Your Time:** Allow half an hour.

## Church ★

The bridge over the Oise affords the best **general view** of the church from a distance. Nearby quarries produced the lovely stone that was used for the construction of many other churches and cathedrals, as well as the palace at Versailles.

The Germans converted these quarries into workshops for their V1 missiles. As a result, the town was repeatedly bombed and the church wrecked in 1944.

### Exterior

The façade has been significantly restored since the 19C – in particular the sculpted decoration – and is separate from the nave. It forms a Romanesque block (first half of the 12C) presenting a porch and, on the upper level, a gallery, each consisting of three bays.

### Interior★

The nave is filled with a golden light filtering through modern stained glass (1960). The chancel and the first two bays of the nave are Romanesque (12C) whereas the rest of the nave is 13C.

# ST-OMER★★

POPULATION 15 747

MICHELIN LOCAL MAP 301: G-3

St-Omer is an aristocratic, wealthy and religious town which has largely retained its ancient appearance. It is characterised by quiet streets lined with 17C and 18C pilastered mansions and houses with sculpted bays. The cathedral is said to have some of the finest furniture in France. This refined atmosphere contrasts with the simpler nature of the northern suburbs, where low Flemish houses line the quays of the River Aa.

- **Information:** *4 r. du Lion d'Or, 62500 St-Omer.* ☎ *03 21 98 08 51. www.tourisme-saint-omer.com.*
- ▶ **Orient Yourself:** Close to the channel port of Calais (30 miles via A 26), and 160 miles north of Paris, via the A 26/A 1.
- **Parking:** There is limited town centre parking, but you may find a place (charged) near the cathedral, or the tourist information centre.
- **Don't Miss:** A trip on the flat-bottomed boats, known as *bacôves*, that take visitors round the Marais Audomarois, which specialises in market gardening.
- **Organizing Your Time:** If the cathedral is your objective you should allow at least 2hr. With a wider viewpoint, you might spend 2 or 3 days in the area to discover the region known as Audomarois.
- **Kids Especially for Kids:** The Fontinettes Barge Lift at Arques is fascinating.

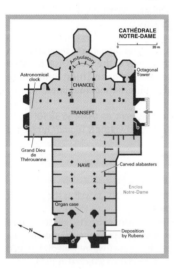

## Cathedral District★★

### Cathédrale Notre-Dame★★

The cathedral is the most beautiful religious building in the region and is surprisingly large and majestic. It stands in the heart of a peaceful area which was formerly the canons' "Notre-Dame cloister". The **chancel** dates from 1200, the transept from the 13C, and the nave from the 14C and 15C. The powerful west front tower (50m/164ft) with its network of vertical, English-style blind arcades is crowned by 15C watch-turrets. The pier of the large south door is ornamented with a 14C Virgin Mary and the tympanum bears a Last Judgment in which the chosen are very few. In a corner of the chancel stands an octagonal Romanesque tower.

## Address Book

*For coin ranges, see the Legend on the cover flap.*

### WHERE TO STAY

**Le Vivier** – *22 r. Louis-Martel* – ☎ *03 21 95 76 00. Closed early Jan and Sun evening – 7 rms – ☐ 6€ – restaurant*. The perfect location for those who choose to stay in town. The rooms, with blonde wood furnishings, are quiet and well fitted out. The restaurant, decorated in shades of beige, pink and magenta, serves dishes with an accent on seafood.

**Hôtel Les Frangins** – *5 r. Carnot* – ☎ *03 21 38 12 47 – 26 rms: – ☐ 7.50€ – restaurant 8/20€*. Located in the historical centre of St-Omer, near shops and museums, 'Les frangins' – slang for 'the brothers' – offers renovated rooms that are practical and quiet.

### WHERE TO EAT

**Le Cygne** – *8 r. Caventou* – ☎ *03 21 98 20 52. Closed 10-30 Aug, Sun evening and Mon except public holidays.* Close by the cathedral, this restaurant has, rightly so, become the principal eatery in town serving traditional French cuisine, using the local produce.

**Hostellerie St-Hubert** – *62570 Hallines – 6km/3.6mi SW of St-Omer via D 928 and D 211* – ☎ *03 21 39 77 77. Closed Sun evening, Tue lunch and Mon.* Screened by the huge trees planted in its park, this bourgeois 19C residence has retained the sumptuous trappings of its era. The dining room ceilings and walls are decorated with fine wood carvings. A few spacious bedrooms.

### ON THE TOWN

**Le Queen Victoria** – *15 pl. Foch* – ☎ *03 21 88 51 17 – Sun-Thu 9am-1am, Fri-Sat 9am-2am.* Here's a warm, intimate pub featuring an old parquet floor and brick walls. The bar has chairs you can lean back on and the small dining room in the rear has a delightful chimney for chilly winter evenings. There's also a large terrace on the square.

### SHOPPING

**Les Chocolats de Beussent** – *30 r. des clouteries* – ☎ *03 21 12 66 82* –

www.choco-france.com. *Tue-Sat 10am-12.30pm, 2-7pm.* Do you wonder what that sausage is doing hanging in the window of this tiny chocolate shop in a pedestrian street? It is in fact chocolate impersonating pork, and its name is Choconaille, a take-off on the French *cochonaille* – delicatessen. It is but one of a number of cocoa-rich house specialities.

**Le Terroir** – *31 r. des clouteries* – ☎ *03 21 38 26 51. Mon 2-7.30pm, Tue-Sat 8.30am-12.30pm, 2-7.30pm. Closed public holidays.* Hédiard teas, Méo coffee, fruits and vegetables, bottles of whisky, cognac and armagnac, fine delicatessen and foie gras preserves – the only problem is deciding which to choose! Ideally situated in a pedestrian street near the Hôtel de Ville, a boutique that puts the accent on regional specialities and produce from small farms.

### LEISURE

**Distillerie Genièvrerie** – *Mme Persyn* – *D 207 between Moulle and Eperlecques* – *62910 Houlle* – ☎ *03 21 93 01 71* – www.genievredehoulle.com – *by appointment at 9am. Closed public holidays.* A 1h30min guided tour of one of the last three gin-making enterprises in France. The alcohol is made in traditional stills.

**Isnor Clairmarais** – *3 r. du Marais, 62500 Clairmarais* – ☎ *03 21 39 15 15* – www.isnor.fr – *Apr, May, June, Sep: open Sat-Sun and public holidays; Jul-Aug, 10am-6pm. Closed 15 Dec to 15 Jan – 6.20€ (children: 5.30€).* Dinghies, canoes, rowboats and motorboats (electric or heat engines) are available for outings in the wetlands, alone or with a guide.

**Mme Lalart** – *Pont de la Guillotine, Rivage de Tilques, 62500 Tilques* – ☎ *03 21 95 10 19 – 10am-8pm – 6€ (children: 4.90€).* Boat trips aboard a *bâcove*, a flat-bottomed boat typical of the St-Omar wetlands.

**Arques Plaisance** – *Base nautique, r. d'Alsace, 62510 Arques,* ☎ *03 21 98 35 97.* Boat hire – by the day, weekend or week.

**Bal Parc** – *207 r. du Vieux-Château, 62890 Tournehem* – ☎ *03 21 35 61 00* – *Jun-Aug – 7€.* Amusement park.

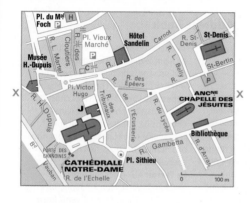

mechanism dating from 1588 (*north transept*) and the Flamboyant rose window above.

▶ *Take rue des Tribunaux.*

The street runs behind the east end of Notre-Dame and in front of the **palais épiscopal**, which dates from the 17C and now houses the law courts, leading to place Victor-Hugo. The square is the busy centre of St-Omer and features a fountain placed there to celebrate the birth of the Count of Artois, the future Charles X.

### Works of Art★★

Among the numerous interesting pieces, note in particular:

- the 13C cenotaph (1) of St-Omer (*left of the nave*);
- the 16C mausoleum (2) of Eustache de Croy, Provost of the St-Omer Chapter and Bishop of Arras. This striking work by the Mons artist Jacques Du Broeucq presents the deceased kneeling in his episcopal robes and also lying naked in the Antique manner (*right of the nave*);
- the 13C statue of Notre-Dame-des-Miracles (3), a highly venerated object of pilgrimage (*south transept*);
- a 13C low-relief Nativity (4); the 8C tomb of St Erkembode (5), Abbot of St Bertin's (*ambulatory*);
- the Astronomical Clock with a

### Hôtel Sandelin and museum★

 &#9855; &#128337;*Open 10am-noon, 2-6pm.* &#128337;*Closed Mon, Tue and public holidays.* &#9096;*4.50€.* ☎ 03 21 38 00 94.

The house was built in 1777 for the Viscountess of Fruges. It is set between a courtyard and a garden, with access through a monumental portal with an elegant Louis XV gate.

**Ground Floor** – The drawing rooms overlooking the gardens form a charmingly old-fashioned suite of rooms with light-coloured, finely carved wainscoting and 18C fireplaces that form a beautiful setting for the Louis XV furniture and the paintings from the bequest of Mme du Teil-Chaix d'Est-Ange. Among the paintings are Lépicié's *Rising of Fanchon* in the style of Chardin, the portrait of *Mme de Pompadour as Diana the Huntress* by Nattier and four lively works by Boilly (*The Visit, The Improvised Concert, The Quenching of the Flame of Love, The Jealous Lover*).

The woodcarving room (religious sculptures and medieval tapestries) and the Salle Henri Dupuis containing ebony cabinets made in Antwerp lead to the **Salle du Trésor** where exhibits include the famous gilt and enamelled **base of the St Bertin Cross★** (12C), a masterpiece of Mosan art. It is decorated with the Evangelists and enamelled scenes from the Old Testament and comes

*Bacôve in the Audomarois*

Y. Tierny/MICHELIN

from the abbey of St Bertin, as does the beautiful ivory representing one of the old men of the Apocalypse. Note, too, the **cross reliquary** with its double crossbar (1210-20) from the abbey in Claimarais. The rear has fine filigree work and is encrusted with gemstones.

The small wall cabinets in the chapel corridor (so-called because of the impressive altar made of ebony, tortoiseshell and gilded bronze) contain various pieces of gold and silverware and ivories.

**First and Second Floors ★**– Collection of ceramics including some produced in St-Omer. Also an outstanding series of **Delftware** (750 items).

## Musée Henri-Dupuis

Open daily (except Mon, Tue and public holidays): 10am-noon, 2-6pm. 3€. ☎ 03 21 38 24 13.

The museum is housed in an 18C mansion with a beautiful period Flemish kitchen. The ground floor houses a large collection of **birds** in their natural habitat, covering an area from the Arctic to Indonesia (dioramas, information panels). On the first floor, an impressive collection of **shells★** is on display, reminding visitors of an 18C natural history room.

# Town Walk

## Jardin public★

This vast park (20ha/48 acres) is located on part of the old 17C ramparts. The moat has been turned into a formal French garden; on the slope is an English garden with winding paths shaded by beautiful trees. There are lovely views of the bastion, the roofs and the cathedral tower. The large moat south of the garden now contains a swimming pool.

## Place du Maréchal-Foch

The town hall was built between 1834 and 1841 using stone from the former abbey church dedicated to St Bertin. A theatre was set in the centre of the building. At 42 bis, the **Hôtel du Bail-lage** (now the Caisse d'Épargne or savings bank) was originally the royal courthouse which challenged the authority of the town's aldermen.

▶ *Follow rue L.-Martel, walk across place Victor-Hugo and take rue des Epeers and rue St-Bertin.*

## Ruines de St-Bertin and Faubourg Nord

All that remains of the abbey are a few arches and the lower part of the tower (1460). Rue St Bertin provides a lovely view of the ruins surrounded by great trees. Via place du Vanquai, one can stroll through the Faubourg Nord (north suburb), along quai des Salines and quai du Commerce lined with low Flemish houses reflected in the still waters of the canalised River Aa.

▶ *At the end of quai des Salines, turn left on rue de Dunkerque then right on rue St-Sépulcre.*

## Église St-Sépulchre

This hall-church (the three aisles are of the same width and height) was consecrated in 1387 and used to be the seat of the largest parish in the town. The name of the church is uncommon; there are only seven churches named after the Holy Sepulchre in France. It comes from the involvement of three local lords in the Crusades.

▶ *Rue de Dunkerque leads back to place du Maréchal-Foch.*

# L'Audomarois

This region gets its name from the Latin word Audomarus meaning "Omer" and it covers the area around St-Omer. It also forms one of the sectors in the regional country park. The area known as the Marais Audomarois, or Omer Marshes, is one of the most unusual parts of the park. www.audomarois-online.com.

## Grange-Nature

Open mid-Apr-Sep: daily (except Mon): 2-6pm. Closed May. ☎ 03 21 38 52 95.
This is the visitor centre for the Audomarois section of the **Parc Naturel Régional des Caps et Marais d'Opale**. The centre is also the starting point for footpaths, some within the Romelaëre Nature Reserve (observation and study trails).

## Marais audomarois

The marshes sit in a vast depression (3 400ha/8 401 acres) stretching from Watten in the north to Arques just south of St-Omer, and from Clairmarais Forest (northeast) to the Tilques watercress beds (northwest).

Today the marshes encompass a series of small plots of land linked by **waterways** (*watergangs*), which are used by large flat-bottomed boats known as *bacôves*. For a proper **tour of the marshes**, hire a boat or join one of the tours in a *bâcove* or other vessel.

# Excursions

## Forêt de Rihoult-Clairmarais

*4.5km/ 2.5mi east.*

🚶 When he stayed at St-Omer, Charlemagne hunted here in the oak groves; in the 12C the forest was the property of Cistercian monks.

The forest (1 167ha/2 884 acres) is now managed with tourists in mind (*picnic tables*), especially around **étang d'Harchelles**, the last of seven ponds dug by the Cistercians for peat and fish.

## Arques

*4km/2.5mi southeast. Leave St-Omer by N 42.*

Arques, which is an industrial town known chiefly for its crystal glassware, is also an important port at the junction of the canalised Aa and the Neuffossé Canal, linking the River Aa to the River Lys.

## Arc International★

♿ 🎧 *Guided tours (1hr30min) by request daily (except Sun and public holidays) by prior arrangement 9am–12.30pm and 1.30-5.30pm. ◎5.50€ (children 3.50€) Minimum age: 8 years. ☎ 03 21 12 74 74.*

Founded in 1825, the Verrerie-cristallerie d'Arques is now, under its new name, a world leader in fine tableware production. Every day, six million items are manufactured in glass, opal and crystal. A tour of the premises provides a close look at the materials used to make cooking utensils and decorative items. Glass is made from a mixture of sand, soda, lime and cullet (ground glass).

## Maison du Parc Naturel Régional des Caps et Marais d'Opale

🕐 *Open daily (except Sat and Sun), 8.30am–noon and 1.30-6pm.* 🕐 *Closed public and Christmas holidays.* ☎ *03 21 87 90 90.*

Le Grand Vannage houses the Maison du Parc, a white-stone and pink-brick building spanning the Aa. The sluice gate room where the river level is regulated can be visited.

▶ *In Arques, take N 42 east toward Hazebrouck; about 1km/0.5mi beyond the bridge over the Aa, turn right onto a small road marked "Ascenseur des Fontinettes" which ends near a factory.*

## Ascenseur à Bateaux des Fontinettes★ (Fontinettes Barge Lift, Arques)

🧒 🕐 *Open Apr-Sep: 10am–noon, 2-6pm, Sat, Sun 2-6pm (last admission 45mn before closing). ◎3€. ☎ 03 21 12 90 23.*

The barge lift, which was in use from 1888 to 1967 was built on the Neuffossé Canal to replace the five locks needed to negotiate the 13.13m/ 43ft drop in the canal. The principle was simple: the barges took their place in one of two water-filled basins, attached to two enormous pistons which served as a kind of hydraulic balance; one went up while the other simultaneously went down. Displays in the engine room and a working model explain how it functioned.

## Esquerdes

*8km/5mi southwest along D 211.*

This village lies in the Aa Valley and has been famous for papermaking since 1473. It still has several paper mills.

## Maison du papier

🕐 *Open mid-Apr-May and Jun-Sep: daily (except Mon) 2-6pm.* 🕐 *Closed 8 May. ◎4€. ☎03 21 95 45 25.*

Exhibitions here explain papermaking techniques from the earliest used in China to the most modern. Visitors can try making their own sheet of paper in the workshop, an unusual souvenir to take home.

# ST-QUENTIN

**POPULATION 103 781**
**MICHELIN LOCAL MAP 306: B-3**

St-Quentin is perched on a limestone hill riddled with caves and underground passages, and overlooks the canalised River Somme which flows across the Isle marshlands. St-Quentin's waterways and railways link it to the north European capitals and the Ruhr, making it a transportation centre between Paris, the English Channel, the countries north of France and the Champagne region.

- **Information:** 27 r. Victor-Basch, 02100 St-Quentin ☎03 23 67 05 00. www.tourisme-saintquentin.fr.
- ▶ **Orient Yourself:** High on a limestone hill overlooking the Somme. 100 miles north of Paris, and mid-way between Cambrai and Laon.
- **Parking:** There is a limited number of car parks in the town centre, as well as on-street parking. Park at the first opportunity as you near the town centre, and walk in.
- **Don't Miss:** The art deco façades, which date from the time when the town was rebuilt after the first World War.
- **Organizing Your Time:** Allow 2 hr to explore the town, plus another hour in the basilica. Take a break in the Parc des Champs-Élysées.
- **Especially for Kids:** Check out the hundreds of butterflies in the Musée des Papillons.
- **Also See:** The Forêt de Saint-Gobain. Laon. Péronne.

## Town Walk

### The Art Deco Trail

St-Quentin suffered extensive damage during the First World War and was partially rebuilt during the 1920s to designs by the architect Guindez. A walk through the town's streets reveals numerous house fronts decorated with bow windows, projecting balconies, floral or geometric motifs, coloured mosaics, wrought-iron work etc.

Among the most outstanding buildings are the post office (*rue de Lyon*), the council chamber in the Hôtel de Ville (town hall), the Carillon cinema (*rue des Toiles*), the music school (*47 rue d'Isle*), the buffet in the railway station and, next to it, the bridge flanked by lantern towers.

▶ *Walk from place de l'Hôtel-de-Ville to rue des Canonniers.*

### Rue des Canonniers

The 18C **Hôtel Joly de Bammeville** has a staircase with wrought-iron banisters. It houses the town library. The entrance

---

## St-Quentin Canal

Before the Canal du Nord was built, this was the busiest canal in France. It links the basins of the River Somme and River Oise to the River Escaut (Scheldt), flowing for about 100km/62mi between Chauny and Cambrai. Napoleon considered it one of the period's greatest achievements.

It is made up of two sections: the Crozat Canal, running between the River Oise and River Somme, which was named after the financier who had it constructed, and the St-Quentin Canal proper, which crosses the plateau between the River Somme and River Escaut partly through tunnels at Tronquoy (1km/0.5mi long) and Riqueval. It is the St-Quentin Canal which is used for regular shipments of sand, gravel and especially grain to the Paris region. The enlargement of the canal, which is part of a long-term project, will improve the town's links with Dunkirk.

to the old **Hôtel des Canonniers** (*no 21*) has military trophies carved in low relief.

▶ *Return to place de l'Hôtel-de-Ville and follow rue des Toiles. Walk round the basilica, cross rue du Gouvernement near the east end of the basilica. Rue E.-Ovres leads to the Champs-Élysées gardens.*

## Champs-Élysées

The site of the original fortification was turned into a pleasant park during the Restoration (10ha/24 acres): playgrounds, sports field, flower garden.

▶ *The Marais de l'Isle is accessible via boulevard Gambetta and place du 8-Octobre leading to the quai Gayant bridge; turn left after crossing the bridge.*

## Marais d'Isle

  ♿ ⏱*Open Apr-Sep: 8am-8pm. Oct-Mar: 9am-5pm.* ☎ *03 23 05 06 50.*
This zone covering over 100ha/247 acres has been provided with fishing and water sports facilities, and it also includes a **nature reserve** which lies along the route taken by migratory birds from Northern and Eastern Europe.
The flora of the wetlands is very varied and includes rare species like water hemlock (also known as dropwort or cowbane) or strange ones like bladderwort, a carnivorous plant. Among the numerous birds here there are nest-building species (crested grebes) and overwintering species (ducks).
The **Maison de la Nature** (♿ ⏱*Open 8am-noon, 2-5.30pm, Sat, Sun and public holidays, 10-noon, 2-5.30pm.* ☎ *03 23 05 06 50*), a small visitor centre in Rouvray presents an audio-visual show and documents relating to the ecosystem of the lake.

# Sights

## Hôtel de Ville★

💬 *Guided visits by prior arrangement with the tourist office.* ☎ *03 23 67 05 00.*
This is a gem of Late Gothic architecture (early 16C). The vigorous design of the façade includes ogival arches topped with pinnacles, mullioned windows and a traceried gallery beneath three gables. It is decorated with picturesque carvings in the Flamboyant Gothic style. The campanile was rebuilt in the 18C. It houses a peal of 37 bells.
Every summer, the town hall square is turned into a beach.

## Espace St-Jacques

*14 rue de la Sellerie.*
**Musée des Papillons** – Kids ⏱*Open daily (except Tue) 2-6pm, Sun and public holidays 3-6pm.* ⏱*Closed 1 Jan, 1 May, Whitsun, 14 Jul, 1 Nov, 25 Dec.* 💶*2.50€ (under 16 free on Wed)* ☎ *03 23 06 93 93.*
This collection of butterflies and other insects is the largest in Europe. It includes about 600 000 specimens, of which about a fifth are exhibited at any given time.

## Basilica★

⏱*Open Tue – Sat 9am-5pm, Mon noon-5pm, Sun 1.30-5.30pm.*
The basilica of St-Quentin is a mainly Gothic building that could rival many of the great cathedrals. It began as a collegiate church dedicated to St Quentin, who worked as a missionary in the region and was martyred at the end of the 3C; it became a basilica in 1876.
**Exterior** – The west front incorporates a massive belfry-porch; its lower part dates from the late 12C whereas the upper storeys were rebuilt in the 17C and the top after 1918. The spire dates from 1976 and reaches the height of the original one (82m/269ft).
**Interior** – The impressively large 13C **chancel** consists of a double transept, double aisles, an ambulatory and radiating chapels. The vaulting of the chapels right of the ambulatory rests on two

columns, following the elegant arrangement of the Champagne region.

The 15C nave (34m/111ft high) has a long maze (260m/284yd) traced on its floor, which the faithful followed on their knees. The sculpted Tree of Jesse, at the start of the south aisle, dates from the early 16C; the second chapel bears 16C mural paintings.

### Musée Antoine-Lécuyer

🕐 *Open daily (except Tue) Jul and Aug: 10am-noon, 2-6pm, Sun 2-6pm. Rest of year 10am-noon, 2-5pm, Sat, 10am-noon, 2-6pm, Sun, 2-6pm.* 🕐 *Closed 1 Jan, 1 May,* *Whitsun, 14 Jul, 1 Nov, 25 Dec.* ⊗*2.50€.* ☎ *03 23 06 93 98.*

The pride of the museum is the splendid portrait **collection**★★ by the pastel artist **Quentin de La Tour** (1704-88), who was born and died in St-Quentin. La Tour, who painted all the important 18C society figures, is representative of an age marked by the importance of individuality. His works, both sensitive and honest, are "incomparable illustrations of moral anatomy": each smile has its own personality, whether spontaneous, ironic, mischievous, benevolent, embittered etc.

# ST-RIQUIER★

**POPULATION 1 186**

**MICHELIN LOCAL MAP 301: E-7**

This ancient fortified town boasts an imposing Gothic church to rival many cathedrals and a picturesque turreted belfry with look-out posts. St-Riquier 🚶 grew around an ancient Benedictine abbey which is the setting, in July, of a renowned classical music festival. Visitors arriving from Abbeville are greeted by the Maison Petit, a house built for a soldier in Napoleon's Grande Armée with an oddly shaped gable recalling the Emperor's famous hat.

🛈 **Information:** Le Beffroi, 80135 St-Riquier ☎ 03 22 28 91 72.

▶ **Orient Yourself:** From Abbeville, 6 miles to the southwest, take the D 925. If using the A 16, leave at Junction 22 (Abbeville) and use the Ni to reach the D 9265.

🅿 **Parking:** There is a parking area in the centre of town.

🖑 **Also See:** Abbeville; the valley of the Somme.

## A Bit of History

### A hermit and a son-in-law

The town was called Centule when, in 645, the hermit **Riquier** died in Crécy Forest, near what is now the village of Forest-Moutiers. This monk who came from a noble family had previously evangelised the Ponthieu region; after his death his body was transported to Centule where it inspired many pilgrimages.

A Benedictine monastery was founded as a result and prospered so much that in 790 Charlemagne gave it to his son-in-law, the poet **Angilbert**, the "Homer of the Palatine Academy". Angilbert, to whom the Emperor paid several visits, gave a new lease of life to the abbey and had the buildings rebuilt in the most precious materials: Italian porphyry, marble and jasper.

## Sights

### Church★

🖑 🕐*Open daily except Mon Apr-Sep 10am-noon, 2-5pm (Sun, 2-5pm).* 🕐*Closed Oct-Mar.* ☎ *03 22 28 20 20.* 👣 *Guided visits (1 hr) in the Treasury.* ⊗*3€.*

Despite having been destroyed and rebuilt several times, the present, largely Flamboyant (15C-16C) church has nevertheless retained some 13C architectural elements (lower parts of the transept and chancel).

## A NIGHT IN ST-RIQUIER

🍽🍽🍽🍽 **Hôtel Jean de Bruges** – ☎ 03 22 28 30 30 – www.hotel-jean-de-bruges.com. Closed Jan – 11 rms – 🛏 14 €. Built in the 17C of white stone, this handsome residence opposite the church is an inviting halt in the bosom of the medieval city. Transformed into a hotel by a Belgian barrister, the combination of modern and antique furniture results in elegantly understated guest rooms. Pretty terrace-patio.

### Exterior

The west front is essentially made up of a large square tower (50m/ 164ft high) flanked by stair towers and covered in abundant, finely carved ornamentation. Above the central doorway, the gable bears a Holy Trinity surround-ed by two abbots and the Apostles.

### Interior★★

The beauty, size and simplicity of the architecture are worth admiring. The two storeys of the large central nave (13m/42ft wide, 24m/78ft high, 96m/314ft long) are separated by a frieze and a balustrade. The chancel still has its 17C decoration and furniture: wrought-iron **grilles**★, lectern and monks' stalls, marble screen surmounted by a large wooden Crucifix by Girardon.

The south transept is unusual: its end is cut off by the sacristy and the treasury above it which occupy three bays of the cloister gallery. The wall of the treasury is decorated with fine sculptures and statues.

The Lady Chapel contains stellar vaulting with ribs running down to historiated corbels (Life of the Virgin Mary); at the entrance, *The Apparition of the Virgin to St Philomena* (1847) is by Ducornet, an artist who painted with his feet as he had no arms. In St Angilbert's Chapel the five polychrome statues of saints are typical of 16C Picardy sculpture: they show (*left to right*) Veronica, Helen, Benedict, Vigor and Riquier.

### Treasury

This was the abbot's private chapel. The walls of the beautiful early-16C vaulted chamber are decorated with murals from the same period; the best of them depicts the Meeting of the Three Dead and the Three Living, which symbolises the brevity of life.

The treasury contains a 12C Byzantine Crucifix, 13C reliquaries, a 15C alabaster altarpiece and a curious 16C handwarmer.

### Abbey buildings

Rebuilt in the 17C during the d'Aligre abbacy, they now house the **Centre culturel départemental de l'abbaye de St-Riquier** (🕒 open Jul and Aug 10am-6pm. May, Jun and Sep 10am-noon, 2-6pm. Mid Mar, Apr and Oct to mid Nov 2-6pm (Sat-Sun and public holidays 10am-noon, 2-6pm); ☎03 22 28 20 20) that includes a **museum** of rural life and crafts and a **conference centre** with seminar rooms and accommodation.

# ST-VALERY-SUR-SOMME★

POPULATION 2 686

MICHELIN LOCAL MAP 301: C-6

St-Valery (pronounced Val'ry), the capital of the Vimeu region, occupies a lush setting overlooking the peaceful countryside of the Somme Bay. It consists of a walled upper town with half-timbered houses and a lower town beside the port used by coasters, yachts and fishing boats known as *sauterelliers* (a *sauterelle* is a grey shrimp). Every year the coast around St Valery becomes the playground of an important colony of seals. Salt-meadow lamb is a local speciality.

St-Valery began as an abbey founded by a monk called Walrick from Luxeuil in Lorraine. In 1066 William the Conqueror rested here before invading England; a medieval pageant celebrates his departure on the second weekend in June. Joan of Arc passed through the town in 1430 as prisoner of the English, on the way from Le Crotoy. The town prospered in the 18C through the import of salt from the Vendée region.

- **Information:** 2 pl. Guillaume-le-Conquérant, 80230 St-Valery-Sur-Somme ☎ 03 22 60 93 50. www.saint-valery-sur-somme.fr.
- **Orient Yourself:** On the banks of the Somme, 13 miles northwest from Abbeville by the D 3 and D 40. From A 16, leave at Junction 23.
- **Parking:** There is plenty of paid parking along the harbour and overlooking the bay.
- **Don't Miss:** The tranquility of the Herbarium des Remparts, or *moules et frites* across the bay in Le Crotoy.
- **Organizing Your Time:** St Valéry has a happy knack of consuming a lot of your time. Ideally, you should spend a night or two here, and use it as a very agreeable base to explore around the bay.
- **Especially for Kids:** Écomusée Picarvie
- **Also See:** Le Crotoy. Abbeville. Fort-Mahon-Plage (if you want a family fun beach). The Parc ornithologique du Marquenterre.

## Ville Basse

The lower town extends for almost 2km/1.25mi, to the mouth of the River Somme where the port is located.

### Digue-promenade★

The promenade, which is shaded in summer by plane and lime trees, leads to a sheltered beach and offers lovely **views** over the Somme Bay to Le Crotoy and the headland at Le Hourdel. Pleasant villas set in gardens stand inland; beyond the Relais de Normandie are the ramparts of the upper town, overlooked by St Martin's church.

### Écomusée Picarvie★

*Open May-Sep Wed-Sun 10am-12.30pm, 1.30-6pm.* ☜*5.25€(children: 4.20€)* ☎ *03 22 26 94 90.*

This appealing little museum faithfully recreates regional life before the industrial age. Reconstructions of workshops and stalls show the work of basket weavers, cobblers, locksmiths, coopers, blacksmiths, joiners etc and there is

*Ecomusée Picarvie*

S. Sauvignier/ MICHELIN

## Address Book

*For coin ranges, see the Legend on the cover flap.*

### TOURISM INFORMATION

⬚ *2 pl. Guillaume-le-Conquérant, 80230 St-Valery-Sur-Somme, ☎ 03 22 60 93 50. www.saint-valery-sur-somme.fr.*

### WHERE TO STAY

😐 **Mme Servant (Bed and Breakfast)** – *117 r. Au-Feurre – ☎ 03 22 60 97 56. Closed Christmas week – ⌂ – 4 rms.* This characteristic house and its well-tended garden are located right near the gracious Porte Guillaume. Each bedroom has a different decoration scheme: marine (blue and white), cinema (old movie posters on the walls) and garden (green hues, wrought-iron furniture).

### WHERE TO EAT

😐😐 **La Colonne de Bronze** – *43 quai Romerel – ☎ 03 22 60 80 07 – la-colonne-de-bronze@wanadoo.fr. Closed 25 Dec to 5 Feb, Tue lunch off-season and Mon except evenings in Jul-Aug.* The bronze column that stood here in Napoleon Bonaparte's time is long gone, but this wood-bedecked restau-rant is still well worth a visit. Follow in the footsteps of the Prince of Wales (who dined here in 1917) and have a meal in this restaurant serving tasty fare made of select ingredients.

### SPORT

**Association Quesnoy** – *Quai Jeanne-d'Arc, Baie des Phoques – ☎ 03 22 60 08 44 or 06 08 46 53 34 (M. Petitleon) – www.baiedesphoques.org. Closed Nov-Mar – starting at 14 €.* Discovery outings in sea kayaks or Polynesian dugouts in the Baie de Somme!

also a village with a school, café and barber's shop. An entire period farm has been recreated on the first floor, with the bedroom, kitchen, cowshed, stable, cider-press and the barn where flax, grown in the surrounding villages, was beaten to make linen.

## Ville Haute

### Porte de Nevers

The name of this 14C gate, which was heightened in the 16C, harks back to the dukes of Nevers who owned St-Valery in the 17C.

### Porte Guillaume

The 12C gate stands between two majestic towers and offers an extensive view over the Somme Bay.

### Herbarium des Remparts

*36 rue Brandt.* ⏱*Open daily May-Oct 10am-5.30pm (weekends and public holidays 10am-12.30pm and 3-6pm (7pm May-Aug).* ⏱*Closed during hot weather.* ⬚*5€. ☎ 03 22 26 90 72.*

A garden that once belonged to the nuns in charge of the hospital is being preserved by an association of local residents as an unspoilt natural area, overgrown with wild flowers. A remarkably tranquil spot.

### Chapelle St-Valery or Chapelle des Marins

Take rue de l'Abbaye beyond the Porte Guillaume: **St Valery's Abbey** used to lie in the vale to the left. The abbey's brick and stone château survives, with a carved 18C pediment.

🚶 *From place de l'Ermitage take the path up to the chapel (30min there and back).*

The chequered sandstone and flint chapel houses the tomb of St Valery. Overlooking the Somme Bay, the chapel offers an extensive **view**★ of the salt meadows and the estuary as far as the Marquenterre reserve in the distance.

# SCEAUX★★

POPULATION 19 494

MICHELIN LOCAL MAP 312: C-3, MAP 101 FOLD 25 OR 106 FOLD 31

The town of Sceaux, a suburb of Paris, boasts one of the finest parks for which the Île-de-France region is famous.

🏛 **Information:** 70 r. Houdan, 92330 Sceaux, ☎ 01 46 61 19 03. www.sceaux.fr.

▶ **Orient Yourself:** A southern suburb of Paris, 7 miles from the city centre, and within the outer *péréphérique*. Access from Paris: RER line B 2 (town centre), B 4 (park)

🅿 **Parking:** Within the park and chateau grounds.

## A Bit of History

### Colbert's Sceaux

In 1670 Louis XIV's superintendent of buildings **Jean-Baptiste Colbert** commissioned Claude Perrault, Le Brun, Girardon and Coysevox to build a superb residence in Sceaux. The two groups of sculptures flanking the entrance pavilion were created by Coysevox: the dog and the unicorn, representing loyalty and honesty, were Colbert's emblems. The canal, basins and fountains were supplied by the waters diverted from the hillsides of Le Plessis-Robinson. The château was inaugurated in 1677 at a lavish reception attended by the Sun King in person; one of the many attractions that night was the performance of Jean Racine's famous tragedy *Phaedra*.

### Sceaux in the hands of the Duc du Maine

In 1700 the estate became the property of the Duc du Maine, the legitimised son of Louis XIV and Mme de Montespan. The King often came to stay with his favourite son.

The Duchesse du Maine, the Great Condé's granddaughter, surrounded herself with a large court of brilliant personalities. She entertained on a grand scale, providing opera, ballet, comedy and tragedy for her many guests. The dazzling "Nights of Sceaux", enhanced by superb displays of fireworks and twinkling lights, were the talk of all Paris and Versailles.

On the eve of the Revolution, the estate of Sceaux belonged to the Duc de Penthièvre, the Duc du Maine's nephew, for whom the fabulist Florian acted as librarian. The domain was confiscated

*The rose garden at L'Haÿ-les-Roses*

M.O. Bernard/MICHELIN

*The Grandes Cascades at Sceaux*

M.O. Bernard/ MICHELIN

and subsequently sold to a tradesman who had the château razed to the ground and the park turned into arable land.

**Sceaux today** – In 1856 the Duc de Trévise, who inherited the estate through his wife's family, built the château that stands today. The grounds gradually slipped into a state of neglect; Alain-Fournier found inspiration there for his novel *Le Grand Meaulnes*. In 1923 the château was bought by the Seine *département*, which undertook to restore both the building and its park. The Île-de-France Museum was installed in 1936. The estate now belongs to the Hauts-de-Seine dé-partement.

The famous physicists **Pierre** (1859-1906) and **Marie** (1867-1934) **Curie** and their daughter **Irène Joliot-Curie** (1897-1956) lived in Sceaux. Their remains were transferred to the Panthéon in Paris in 1995.

# Château and Park★★

## Main Entrance

&. ◷*Open May-Jul: 7am-9pm. Apr and Aug 7am-8.30pm. Sep: 7.30am-8pm. Jan and Nov 8am-5pm. Feb 8am-6pm. Mar 7.30am-7pm. Oct 8am-7pm.* ☎ *01 41 87 28 60.*

Designed for Colbert, the two entrance pavilions with sculpted pediments are flanked by two small lodges surmounted by Coysevox's groups of statues.

## Orangerie

This conservatory (60m/196ft long) was designed by Jules Hardouin-Mansart in 1685. It is decorated with a series of carved pediments. In summer it was used as the ballroom – note the interior decoration – and in winter it sheltered the 300 orange trees of Sceaux Park.

Today the orangery is a venue for conferences, exhibitions and concerts (*For the programme, write to the "Saison Musicale d'été de Sceaux", BP 52, 92333 Sceaux Cedex,* ☎ *01 46 60 07 79*).

## Musée de l'Île-de-France★

&. ◷*Open daily (except Tue) 10am-6pm (Oct-Mar 5pm).* ◷*Closed 1 Jan, 1 May, 14 Jul, 15 Aug, 1 Nov, 25 Dec.* ⊚*3.30€, no charge first Sunday in the month.* ☎*01 41 87 29 50.*

The museum is housed in the château that once belonged to the Duc de Trévise. It was refurbished in 1994 and is laid out on the basis of four themes: Sceaux, the estate and its owners; ceramics from the Paris Basin; royal and princely residences; and scenery in the Paris Basin from the 18C to the 20C.

The oval room is given over to Sceaux faience and boasts the largest existing collection of this local production. The "Japanese-style faience" (&. *see Introduction, Faience and porcelain*) by J Chapelle makes renewed use of the Rococo style. Two other rooms are part of this section of the museum. The library has 18C porcelain (Vincennes, Sèvres, St-Cloud etc) and the Millet room on the first floor includes fine 19C faience recognisable for its unusual background colouring and decoration (rope-work for Montereau, flowers for Creil).

The luxurious residences built in the vicinity, some of which have since been demolished, are illustrated at length. There are etchings by Rigaud, oils including the *Château de St-Cloud* by C Troyon, furniture such as the elegant bureau made by Riesenburg (Château de St-Hubert) and Caroline Murat's bed produced by the Jacob brothers (Château de Neuilly).

The variety of landscapes in the Paris Basin has provided much inspiration for artists such as A-H Dunoy, G Michel, Lebourg, Utrillo, Luce etc. The museum has a large collection of works by Paul Huet, André Dunoyer de Ségonzac and Jean Fautrier.

Painted wainscoting from the folly built by the famous 18C dancer "La Guimard" in Pantin decorates a small drawing room.

### Grandes Cascades★

🕐 *Open Wed, Sat-Sun and public holidays: 11am-6pm. No charge.* ☎ *01 41 87 28 60.*
The waters are approached from allée de la Duchesse; they spring out of carved masks by Rodin and tumble down a series of 10 terraces before flowing into the Octagonal Basin. The sight of these various fountains and cascades is particularly spectacular when all the fountains are playing during the **Grandes Eaux**★. This perspective is continued by a green lawn.

### Grand Canal★

This is as long as the Petit Canal at Versailles (1 030m/3 380ft) and flanked by a double row of Lombardy poplars.

### Pavillon de l'Aurore

🕐 *Open Apr-Sep: Sat-Sun and public holidays 10am-6pm; Oct-Mar: Sat-Sun and public holidays, 10am-5pm.* 🕐 *Closed 1 Jan, 1 May, 14 Jul, 25 Dec.* 👓 *3.30€, no charge first Sun in month.* ☎ *01 41 87 29 50.*
This charming pavilion crowned by a dome is attributed to Claude Perrault. It is approached by a series of steps featuring dainty, neatly arranged balusters. The interior decoration forms a harmonious ensemble: wainscot, flooring, ceilings and a superb dome by Le Brun, reproducing the delicate tints of sunrise.

It was here that Colbert received the French Academy in 1677. For this momentous occasion the poet Quinault composed a poem of 900 lines on the subject of Le Brun's fresco. He read it out to the members of that prestigious assembly, who spent most of the evening craning their necks toward the ceiling to follow Quinault's detailed explanations.

# SENLIS★★

POPULATION 16 327

MICHELIN LOCAL MAP 305: G-5 OR MAP 106 FOLDS 8, 9

Senlis derives its romantic charm from its picturesque old streets, its connections with Frankish rulers, enterprising bishops and abbots, the rich cornfields of Valois and the wooded horizons.

- **Information:** Pl. du Parvis-Notre-Dame, 60300 Senlis, ☎ 03 44 53 06 40. www.ville-senlis.fr.
- **Orient Yourself:** Accessed via the A 1 from Paris (32 miles), leave at Junction 8 for Senlis. Access from Paris: SNCF rail link from Gare du Nord to Chantilly; bus link to Senlis.
- **Parking:** The car park near the cathedral fills early in the day; try those off the r. de la République.
- **Don't Miss:** Take a horse drawn tour of the town in a *calèche* (in French).
- **Organizing Your Time:** There is a lot to see and do in Senlis; allow at least a full day, or stop over for a couple of nights.
- **Also See:** Château de Chantilly.

## A Bit of History

### The election of Hugh Capet

The conquerors of Senlis built a massive stronghold over the first Gallo-Roman ramparts of the town. The kings of the first two Frankish dynasties would often take up residence here, lured by the game in the nearby forests. The Carolingian line died out when Louis V suffered a fatal hunting accident. In 987 the Archbishop of Reims called a meeting at

Senlis Castle in which he and the local lords decided that Hugh Capet – the Duc de France – would be the next king. Senlis went out of fashion as a royal place of residence and was gradually replaced by Compiègne and Fontainebleau.

# Cathédrale Notre-Dame★★

Construction of the cathedral was started in 1153 – 16 years after St-Denis and 10 years before Notre-Dame in Paris – but progressed at a slow pace due to insufficient funds, and was not consecrated until 1191. It was only toward the mid-13C that the right tower was crowned with the magnificent **spire**★★ which was to have such a strong influence over religious architecture in the Valois area (⊙ see below). The **main doorway**★★ – is strongly reminiscent of the doorways at Chartres, Notre-Dame in Paris, Amiens and Reims.

### South front

Constructed by Pierre Chambiges in the 16C, the **south front**★★ contrasts sharply with the west front. It is interesting to follow the evolution of Gothic architecture from the austere 12C to the 16C,

when Late Flamboyant already showed signs of Renaissance influence, introduced after the Italian wars. The clerestory and its huge Flamboyant windows were also completed in the 16C. The lower part (12C) of the east end and the radiating chapels are intact. The galleries – dating from Romanesque times – support the nave and chancel with the help of Gothic flying buttresses.

### Interior

The church interior is 70m/230ft long, 19.2m/63ft wide and measures 24m/79ft to the keystone. Above the organ, the 12C vaulting which escaped the ravages of a fire in 1504 marks the original height of the church. The nave and the chancel, comparatively narrow in spite of their height, are graced with an airy lightness. The first chapel to the right of the south doorway features superb vaulting with pendant keystones, a 14C stone Virgin Mary and a lovely set of stained-glass windows. These are the only original panes to have remained intact. A statue of St Louis from the 14C is placed in the south aisle of the ambulatory. The north transept chapel houses a 16C Christ made of larch. The left-hand aisle features an elegant statue of St Barbara dating back to the late 16C-early 17C.

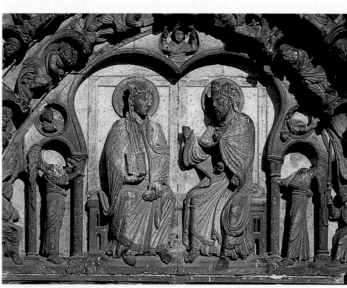

*Main door of Notre-Dame cathedral*

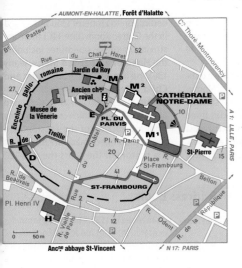

### SENLIS
#### Quartier Ancien

| | |
|---|---|
| Apport-au-Pain R. de l' | 2 |
| Aulas-de-la-Bruyère Pl. | 4 |
| Flageards R. aux | 10 |
| Halle Pl. de la | 12 |
| Leclerc Av. Gén. | 15 |
| Petit-Chaâlis R. du | 20 |
| Puits-Tiphaine R. du | 27 |
| Tonnellerie R. de la | 41 |
| Villevert R. de | 52 |
| Hôtel de la Chancellerie | D |
| Hôtel de ville | H |
| Hôtel des Trois-Pots | E |
| Musée d'Art et d'Archéologie | M¹ |
| Musée de l'hôtel de Vermandois | M² |
| Musée des Spahis | M³ |

## North side

The cathedral's setting on this side is much less solemn; it features several patches of greenery and is extremely picturesque. Skirt the little garden that follows the east façade of what was once the bishop's palace. The building rests on the ruins of the old Gallo-Roman ramparts; the base of one tower remains. Lovely view of the cathedral's east end.

## Old Town  *1hr*

### Jardin du Roy

These gardens occupy the former moat of the Gallo-Roman ramparts which, at their widest point, measured 312m/ 1 024ft across and at their narrowest 242m/794ft. Twenty-eight towers (7m/ 23ft high and 4m/14ft thick) defended the city walls; 16 remain today, some still intact, others badly damaged.

### Ancien Château royal

Before entering the castle courtyard, start to walk up rue du Châtel to see the original fortified entrance to the stronghold, now walled up. Adjoining the old doorway, the 16C Hôtel des Trois Pots proudly sports its old-fashioned sign. The fortified site was occupied at least as early as the reign of the Emperor Claudius (AD 41-54). Throughout its history, up to the time of Henri II, it featured a charming collection of ruins.

Although apparently dating from the Middle Ages, the castle's history is not entirely clear. It now houses the Musée de la Vénerie (& *see SIGHTS below*).

### Old Streets★

Rue du Châtel used to be the main street through Senlis for those travelling from Paris to Flanders. In 1753 it was succeeded by rue Neuve de Paris, now called rue de la République. Its southern continuation, named "rue Vieille de Paris", thus refers to the ancient thoroughfare.

Take the charming **rue de la Treille** and walk to the "Fausse Porte", which was the postern of the former Gallo-Roman ramparts. On the left stands the Chancellerie, flanked by two towers.

The **town hall** (Hôtel de Ville) on place Henri-IV was rebuilt in 1495. The front bears a bust of Henri IV and an inscription conveying his affection for the town of Senlis. These date back to a visit by Charles X on his return from his coronation in Reims Cathedral (1825).

## Sights

### Musée d'Art et d'Archéologie★

*Place Notre-Dame.* ◯*Open Feb-Oct daily (except Tue) 10am-noon, 2-6pm (Wed 2-6pm; Sat, Sun and public holidays 11am-1pm, 2-6pm). Nov-Jan 10am-noon, 2-5pm (Wed 2-5pm; Sat, Sun and public*

holidays 11am-1pm, 2-5pm). ⊙Closed 1 Jan, 1 May, 25 Dec. ≤4.20€ – combined ticket for four museums. ☎ 03 44 32 00 83. www.ville-senlis.fr.
The Gallo-Roman collections are exhibited on the ground floor: glass, Merovingian jewellery, small bronze statues, strange votive offerings carved in stone from a small sanctuary in Halatte Forest (& see below), and a **bronze base**★ dating from AD 48 and engraved with a

dedication to Emperor Claudius.
In the Gothic Room (late 14C) there are striking medieval sculptures including the **Head of a Bearded Man**★ (early 13C) and a majestic marble **Virgin and Child** (late 14C). Note also the entertaining series of small figures of painted and gilded wood which came originally from a depiction of the Passion on a late-15C altarpiece made in Antwerp. At the bottom of the stairs the mid-12C

## Address Book

&For coin ranges, see the Legend on the cover flap.

### WHERE TO STAY

⊖⊖ **Mme Passemier (Bed and Breakfast)** – 2 r. Mortefontaine, 60520 Thiers-sur-Thève – 9km/5.4mi S of Senlis dir. Paris, then secondary road – ☎ 03 44 54 98 43 – 4 rms. A 19C hunting lodge opening its doors onto a large, impeccably manicured garden. The smart bedrooms successfully blend different styles and periods. Living room with a fireplace that invites you to curl up with your book .

⊖⊖ **Hostellerie de la Porte Bellon** – 51 r. Bellon – ☎ 03 44 53 03 05 – www.portebellon.com. Closed 21 Dec to 6 Jan – 18 rm – ⊑ – restaurant ⊖⊖. At a few paces from the city centre, this handsome manor – a former coaching inn – welcomes guests to pleasant, well fitted-out bedrooms. The splendid paved and shaded courtyard leads to the garden where breakfast may be taken when the weather allows. Pretty vaulted cellar.

### WHERE TO EAT

⊖ **Les Jardins de Séraphine** – 18 r. de Beauvais – ☎ 03 44 60 04 00. Closed 15 days in Aug, Sun evening and Mon – reserv. required weekends. Crêpes, salads and one daily special: voilà the simple fare served in this crêperie in the heart of Senlis. True, the décor is nothing special, but the reception is warm and the prices reasonable. Terrace.

⊖⊖ **La Vieille Auberge** – 8 r. Long-Filet – ☎ 03 44 60 95 50. Closed 11-20 Jul, 25 Dec, 1 Jan, Sun evening and Wed. The Old Inn's name is particularly apt – construction

commenced in 1588! The dining room, decorated in warm tones and English style furniture, serves contemporary cuisine. And for fine weather there's an agreeable terrace set up at the back.

⊖⊖ **Auberge des Trois Canards** – 3 pl. de l'Église – 60810 Ognon – 6km/3.6mi NE of Senlis via D 932A – ☎ 03 44 54 41 21. Closed 15 Feb to early Mar, 15 Aug to early Sep, Sun evening, Mon and Wed – reserv. advisable weekends. Decorated in shades of yellow and carmine, this venerable old inn has retained its country flavour. At the end of the terrace there's an enclosed garden with children's games.

### SHOPPING

**Les Sorbets du Valois** – 7 rue de la Tannerie – 8km/6.4mi NE of Senlis via D 582 and D 134 – 60810 Rully – ☎ 03 44 54 71 80 – May-Jul: Tue-Sat 10am- noon, 3pm-7pm; Sun 10am-noon. This Valois farm, specialised in fruit production – especially strawberries – sees its harvest transformed into sor-bets. The secrets of sorbet making are passed along during a short tour of the establishment, and each visitor is given a container of sorbet or ice cream of their choice, well protected in a freezer bag, upon leaving.

### CARRIAGE RIDE

**Senlis en Calèche** – Pl. de la Cathédrale – ☎ 03 44 53 10 26 – www.senlis-en-caleche.com – Apr-Dec 10.30am-noon, 2.30-5.30pm. Closed Jan-Mar. 1-3 persons. 38€ (children: 10 €). Enjoy a horse-drawn tour of the streets of Senlis. Recorded commentary in French.

stained-glass windows recount the creation of Eve and the Temptation of Adam and Eve.

Paintings dating from the 17C to the 20C are on display in the four rooms on the first floor: Philippe de Champaigne, Luca Giordano, Francesco Solimena, Corot, Boudin, Sérusier, and Thomas Couture (1815-79) who was born in Senlis. Centring on works by Séraphine Louis, nicknamed Séraphine de Senlis, is a collection of works by 20C naive artists.

## Musée des Spahis

*By the entrance to the old Royal Castle.*
◔*Same opening hours and admission prices as for the Musée d'Art et d'Archéologie.*

This museum retraces 150 years of history of the North African cavalry, which held a special place in the French Army from 1780 to 1814 and from 1830 to 1964. It largely concentrates on the old Spahis (native Algerian horsemen), Goumiers (indigenous horsemen and foot soldiers), Meharists (dromedary riders) and Saharans (cameleers).

## Musée de la Vénerie (Hunting Museum)

◔ *Guided visits (1 hr) Feb-Oct Mon, Thu and Fri 10am-noon, 2-6pm; Wed 2-6pm; weekends and public holidays 11am, 1pm, 2-5pm. Nov-Jan Mon, Thu and Fri 10am-noon, 2-5pm; Wed 2-5pm; weekends and public holidays 11am-1pm, 2-5pm.* ◔*Closed 1 Jan, 1 May, 25 Dec.* ◉*4€– combined ticket for four museums.* ☏ *03 44 32 00 81.*

In the 13C St Louis founded St-Maurice priory next to the Royal Castle. The relics of St Maurice of Agaune were kept here by the monks until the Revolution.

The works presented here were chosen from among the many illustrations of stag hunts which have enriched French culture. The walls are hung with numerous trophies and stags' heads.

The display of historical hunting gear renders the exhibition particularly interesting. The hunting costume of the Condé – fawn and amaranth-purple – can be seen on a figure representing a Chantilly forest warden, and in the painting depicting the young Duc d'Enghien (1787).

*Senlis*

## Musée de l'Hôtel de Vermandois

◔*Same opening hours and admission prices as for the Musée d'Art et d'Archéologie.*

This small museum installed in a 12C mansion illustrates the history of the town and its cathedral through an audio-visual presentation. Sculpture plays a large part: a 12C head of an angel from one of the doorways of Notre-Dame; carved capitals and consoles from the cathedral and from the priory chapel. The original spire of the cathedral has been placed in one of the two rooms.

## Chapelle Royale St-Frambourg

◔*Open May-Oct Sat, Sun and public holidays 3-6pm; Nov-Apr Sun 3-5pm.* ◉*4.50€.* ☏ *03 44 53 39 99.*

Hugh Capet's wife, the pious Queen Adelaide, founded this chapel before 990 to house the relics of a recluse from the Bas-Maine, known as St Frambourg or St Fraimbault.

The chapel was restored as the Franz Liszt Auditorium in 1977, through the efforts of the pianist Georges Cziffra. The Cziffra Foundation (*www.fondation-cziffra.org*) organises concerts and exhibitions for lovers of classical music.

*Castle wall, Raray*

# Excursions

### Forêt d'Halatte★

This large forest north of Senlis includes beech groves, cherished by the Capetians, and oaks, hornbeams, pine trees etc to the south.

### Pont-Ste-Maxence

*11km/7mi north by N 17.*
Because of its old bridge spanning the River Oise, the town has always been an important staging post. It owes the second part of its name to an Irish saint who was martyred here in the 5C. East of the town stands **Abbaye du Moncel**★ *(○ ⌖ Guided tours (1hr) daily (except Wed) 10am-noon, 2-5pm. ○closed between 25 Dec and 1 Jan. ⌖5€. ☎ 03 44 72 33 98)* which Philip

the Fair had built next to a royal castle, two towers of which still remain. The main façade still looks medieval and offers two imposing chimneys. The **courtyard**★ is surrounded by three wings crowned with tall roofs of brown tiles (restored). Other elements of note include one of the galleries from the 16C cloisters and the amazing 14C **timberwork**★ above the nuns' dorter, made with oak from Halatte Forest.

### Château de Raray

*13km/8mi northeast by D 932A. At Villeneuve-sous-Verberie, turn right.*
Standing on the edge of a charming hamlet, the château (now part of a golf club) is famous for the striking decoration of its main courtyard, used in Jean Cocteau's film *Beauty and the Beast.*

### St-Vaast-de-Longmont

*16km/10mi northeast by D 932A.*
Seen from the village cemetery, the Romanesque bell tower and its stone spire appear to be extremely ornate: cornices with billet moulding, arcades resting on small columns ornately decorated.
At **Rhuis** nearby *(west on D 123)*, the 11C Romanesque church has an elegant bell tower with a double row of twinned windows. The tower is believed to be one of the oldest in Île-de-France. The interior features four bays and an apsidal chapel with no vaulting.

### WHERE TO EAT

⊖⊜ **Auberge du Vieux Logis** –
*105 r. du Gén.-de-Gaulle, 60700 Fleurines – 5km/3mi N of Senlis via N 17 –* ☎ *03 44 54 10 13 – aubergeduvieuxlogis@wanadoo.fr – reserv. required.*
It's easy to forget the national road that goes by this country inn thanks to the flavoursome cuisine served in a rustic décor of exposed beams and stones. In summer, there's a terrace in the garden where an old tile kiln has been preserved.

# SÈVRES ★★

POPULATION 22 534

MICHELIN LOCAL MAP 305: E-8, MAP 101 FOLD 24 OR106 FOLD 18

The Manufacture Nationale de Porcelaine (National Porcelain Factory) established here in the 18C has made the town of Sèvres 🔟 famous throughout the world. Situated between the Parc de St-Cloud and Meudon Forest, Sèvres is now a suburb of Paris.

🔲 **Information:** Hôtel de Ville, 54, Grande Rue, 92311 Sèvres. ☎ 01 41 14 10 10. www.ville-sevres.fr.

▶ **Orient Yourself:** A suburb of Paris 14km (8 miles) southwest of the centre of Paris, close by the Seine. Access from Paris: Metro line 9 (station: Pont de Sèvres).

🕐 **Organizing Your Time:** Allow a couple of hours to visit the museum.

👶 **Also See:** St Cloud. Rueil-Malmaison. Versailles.

## Musée National de la Céramique ★★

♿ 🕐 Open daily (except Tue) 10am-5pm. 🕐 Closed public holidays. ☜ 4€, no charge, first Sun in the month. ☎ 01 41 14 04 20.

Founded in 1824 by Brongniart, the museum has an outstanding collection of pottery, faience, and porcelain classified by origin and by historical period. On the **ground floor** are the collections of Islamic ceramics, some very old and very rare pottery (8C-18C) and a superb collection of Renaissance faience. Opposite is an exhibition and sale room presenting a range of pieces made in the factory, some of them traditional models and others contemporary creations.

The collections on the **first floor** show changes in clay and decorative techniques in Sèvres, Europe and worldwide. In the central room, note the Chinese porcelain (*famille verte and famille rose*) and the decoration on the pieces of Meissen from Saxony (Kakiemon and Imari styles).

The rooms on the right focus on softpaste porcelain (18C-20C). French works are well represented through Chantilly, St-Cloud, Vincennes and Sèvres. In the raised display cabinets, note the various background colours (green, purple, blue). The 19C collection includes the industrial arts service painted by Devely from 1823 onwards. It is representative of the Sèvres porcelain which, unlike others, must include gold.

RMN

*Sèvres pot-pouri vases (18C)*

## A HILLTOP RESTAURANT

⊜⊜**Auberge Garden** – *24 route du Pavé des Gardes* – ☎ *01 46 26 50 50. Closed 7-29 Aug, 24 Dec-2 Jan, Sat lunchtime and Sun evening and Mon.* This former inn perched on the heights of Sèvres is gradually being refurbished by its current owners. The menu is highly attractive and made with delicious produce. Traditional dining room with movable partitions and a piano. Terrace for the sunny days.

The rooms on the left have some splendid pieces of high-fired ceramics from French and European works. The decoration can be in a range of blues, like the porcelain from Rouen or Marseille (late 17C), but much of the high-fired porcelain has multicoloured decoration. This is shown in the magnificent pieces of regional porcelain dating from the 18C. The last rooms are given over to Nevers and Delft.

## Additional Sight

### Maison des Jardies

*14 avenue Gambetta.* 🕐━ *Guided tours (45min) Thu, Fri and Sat-Sun 2.30pm-6pm.* 🕐*Closed 1 Jan, 1 May, 25 Dec.* ⊜*4€, no charge first Sun-day in the month (Oct-May).* ☎ *01 45 34 61 22.*
This modest gardener's lodge was once part of the Jardies estate, where Honoré de Balzac settled in 1838 and attempted to cultivate pineapples, unsuccessfully. Corot stayed here and Gambetta died here on 31 December 1882. Several of the politician's mementoes have been kept and are on show to the public.

# SOISSONS ★

POPULATION 29 453
MICHELIN LOCAL MAP 306: B-6

Soissons rises in the midst of rich agricultural land which is overlooked by the tall spires of the town's abbey visible from afar. Although the town was largely rebuilt after the First World War, it retains its Gothic cathedral and an ancient abbey, one of the most flourishing monasteries of the medieval period.

- **Information:** 16 pl. Fernand-Marquigny, 02200 Soissons. ☎ 03 23 53 17 37. www.ville-soissons.fr.
- ▶ **Orient Yourself:** 100km (62 miles) from Paris and accessed from Saint Quentin and Coucy-le-Château-Auffrique by the D 1, and from Rouen, Beauvais or Reims by the N 13/E 46. From Paris or Laon use the N 2.
- 🕐 **Organizing Your Time:** Allow one hour to explore the cathedral, and about the same for the museum.
- **Kids Especially for Kids:** Try an evening at the dog races (👆 *Address Book*).
- 👆 **Also See:** Laon. The Saint Gobain forest. Coucy-le-Château-Auffrique.

## A Bit of History

### The Frankish capital

The town played an important role at the time of the Frankish monarchy; it was at this town's gates that Clovis defeated the Romans, ruining them for his own benefit. The famous story of the **Soissons Vase** took place after this battle: Clovis demanded that his booty include a vase which had been stolen from a church in Reims. A soldier angrily opposed him, broke the vase and cried "You will have nothing, O King, but that which Destiny gives you!" The following year, while Clovis was reviewing his troops he stopped before the same soldier, raised his sword and split the soldier's skull saying, "Thus you did with the Soissons vase".

# Sights

## Ancienne Abbaye de St-Jean-des-Vignes★★

⏰*Open daily Apr-Sep 9am-noon, 2-6pm, weekends and public holidays 9am-noon, 2-7pm. Oct-Mar 9am-noon, 2-5pm, weekends 9am-noon, 2-6pm.* ⏰*Closed 1 Jan and 25 Dec.* ☎ 03 23 53 58 80.

The old Abbey of St John of the Vines, which was founded in 1076, was one of the richest monasteries of the Middle Ages. The generosity of the kings of France, bishops, great lords and burghers allowed the monks to build a great abbey church in the 13C and 14C. In 1805, however, an imperial decree approved by the Bishop of Soissons ordered its demolition, so that its materials could be used to repair the cathedral; the resulting outcry led to the preservation of the west front.

### West front

The cusped portals are delicately cut and surmounted with late-13C gables; the rest of the front dates from the 14C except for the bell towers which were built in the 15C. An elegant openwork gallery separates the central portal from the great rose window, which has lost its tracery. Statues of the Virgin Mary and the saints are placed in pairs beside the piers on the towers.

The two Flamboyant bell towers are extremely graceful. The **north tower** is the larger, taller and more ornate: the platform of the buttresses is finely worked; the spires of the openwork turrets bear prominent groins and crockets; on the western side, against the mullion of the upper window, a Christ on the Cross stands with statues of the Virgin Mary and St John at his feet.

### Réfectoire★

The **refectory** was built into the extension of the west front, at the back of the great cloisters. The 13C construction has two naves with pointed vaulting. The transverse arches and ribs rest on seven slender columns with foliate capitals. Eight great lobed rose windows pierce the east and south walls. The reader's pulpit still exists.

---

## Address Book

🪙*For coin ranges, see the Legend on the cover flap.*

### WHERE TO STAY

🍽 **Ferme de la Montagne (Bed and Breakfast)** – *02290 Ressons-le-Long – 8km/4.8mi W of Soissons via N 31 and D 1160 –* ☎ *03 23 74 23 71. www.lafermedelamontagne.free.fr. Closed Jan-Feb –* 🍴 *– 5 rms.* This farm belonging to the abbey of Notre-Dame de Soissons is situated on a plateau where it lords over the Vallée de l'Aisne. The splendid landscape may be admired from the drawing room. Each guest room has its own entranceway – a thoughtful touch indeed.

### WHERE TO EAT

🍽🍽 **Hostellerie du Lion d'Or** – *1 pl. du Gén.-de-Gaulle, 02290 Vic-sur-Aisne – 12km/7.2mi W of Soissons via N 31 and D 2 –* ☎ *03 23 55 50 20. Closed 15-31 Jul, 1 wk in Aug, Sun evening, Tue evening and Mon – reserv. requested weekends.* A good address for enjoying a hearty meal in a hospitable setting. Since 1580, diners have been gathering round this restaurant's hearth for delectable, generous meals cooked from market-fresh ingredients. Before leaving, ask to see the 'historic album'.

🍽 **Le Grenadin** – *19 rte de Fère-en-Tardenois, 02200 Belleu –* ☎ *03 23 73 20 57. Closed Sun evening and Mon.* A warm reception and attentive service staff await you in the two bright dining rooms of this soft yellow establishment. When the weather is favourable, tables are set out in the pleasant garden.

### DOG RACES

**Le Cynodrome** – *10 bd Branly – every other Sun at 2pm. Closed Oct-Apr.* Greyhounds come from all over Europe to race on this 450m track. Dancing and entertainment are organised on Grand Prix days – the ambience is friendly and festive. A rare treat, not to be missed. The public may watch training sessions.

*St-Jean-des-Vignes*

## Cloîtres

All that remains of the **great cloisters**★ are two 14C galleries. The pointed arches separated by elaborate buttresses had a graceful blind arcade, remains of which can be seen in the south bays.

## Cathédrale St-Gervais-et-St-Protais★★

🕐 *Open daily May-Sep 9.30am-noon, 2-6.30pm. Rest of year 9.30am-noon, 2-5.30pm.*

Construction of the cathedral began in the 12C with the south transept; the chancel, nave and side aisles rose during the 13C; the north transept and the upper part of the façade were not completed until the early 14C. The Hundred Years War brought work to a halt before the north bell tower was built; it was never to be finished.

## Additional Sights

### Musée Municipal de l'Ancienne Abbaye de St-Léger

*Guided tours daily (except Wed): Apr-Sep 9am-noon, 2-6pm (weekends and public holidays 2-7pm). Oct-Mar 9am-noon, 2 5pm (weekends and public holidays 2 6pm).* 🕐 *Closed 1 Jan, 1 May and 25 Dec.* ☎ *03 23 93 30 50. www.musee-soissons.org.*

St Leger's Abbey was founded in 1139 but devastated in 1567 by Protestants who also demolished the nave of the church.

**Museum** – The museum's various collections are housed in the old monastery buildings.

The first floor is devoted to 16C-19C painting: Northern School (note in particular the anonymous Flemish painting entitled *Allegory of Winter* c 1630-50, representing a bearded old man), Italian School and French School (Largillière, Courbet, Boudin and Daumier). The other room has maps, documents, paintings and models tracing the history of the town.

# LA BAIE DE SOMME★★

SOMME BAY

MICHELIN LOCAL MAP 301: C-6

The Baie de Somme 🚶 is a wonderful area for visitors who wish to relax while watching seals sprawled on the sand and migratory wild ducks, or riding on the tourist train which merrily whistles across the countryside. The bay offers open spaces, luminous landscapes and, at low tide, its endless stretches of sand and grass where you may spot students earning a few euros by gathering samphire.

🛈 **Information:** Office du tourisme du Crotoy, 1 r. Carnot, 80550 ☎ 03 22 27 05 25.

▶ **Orient Yourself:** Accessible from Abbeville by the D 940.

🕐 **Organizing Your Time:** To really get a feel for the environs of the Bay you need a morning in Le Crotoy, followed by lunch, and then an afternoon in St Valéry-sur-Somme. You can easily spend a whole day at the Parc Ornithologique du Marquenterre.

**Especially for Kids:** Parc Ornithologique du Marquenterre. Chemin de fer de la Baie de Somme. Maison de l'Oiseau.

**Also See:** St Valéry-sur-Somme. Fort-Mahon-Plage.

## A Bit of History

### Slow silting-up process

Like all bays, the Somme experiences the flow of water and silt which settles and tends to widen the sandbanks; these become covered with grass, creating the **mollières** or salt-pastures where lambs now graze.

The silting-up combined with a gradual increase in the size of boats in general has considerably affected the formerly active traffic here; the development of the Somme canal from 1786 to 1835 and the creation of a sheltered port at Le Hourdel merely slowed its decline. It is worth noting, however, that during the First World War the bay served as a British base: in 1919, traffic reached an exceptional 125 000t.

### Hunting and fishing

The bay's three fishing ports (St-Valery, Le Crotoy and Le Hourdel) specialise in shellfish and squid fishing.

When the tide is out fish are also caught in the channels, pools and ruts on the shore: cockles, mullet, eels and flatfish, either speared or just picked up by hand. Wildfowl hunters lie in wait in special boats or in hides formed in grassy mounds pierced with firing holes, using domestic or artificial ducks as decoys.

## Around the Bay

### Chemin de fer de la Baie de Somme

*Steam train departing Le Crotoy and St-Valéry-sur-Somme:* 🕐*Jul and Aug*

### Chinese cemetery in Noyelles

This is the largest Chinese cemetery in France. Situated along the road from Sailly-Flibeaucourt to the hamlet of Nolette, the cemetery includes more than 800 white tombstones engraved with Chinese characters. Following an agreement signed in 1916, thousands of Chinese nationals, most of them farmers from the north of China, undertook to serve in the British army in exchange for a salary. The first contingent landed in April 1917; between 1917 and 1919, the camp welcomed 12 000 workers who worked in difficult conditions, were kept apart from the local population and could not come and go as they pleased. Some were killed in the fighting but most succumbed to the epidemic of Spanish influenza which hit the area in the autumn of 1918. At the end of 1919, most of the workers went back home, although a few chose to remain in France.

## Address Book

🔔 *For coin ranges, see the Legend on the cover flap.*

### WHERE TO EAT

🍽 **Le Parc aux Huîtres** – *Le Hourdel, 80410 Cayeux-sur-Mer* – ☎ *03 22 26 61 20. Closed 2 wks in winter and 2 days/wk.* The perfect place for a memorable fish and seafood meal. All of the tables have a view of the Hourdel fishing harbour and the water ballet performed by the fishing boats therein.

🍽 **La Clé des Champs** – *80120 Favières – 5km/3mi NW of Crotoy via D 940 and D 140* – ☎ *03 22 27 88 00. Closed 3-14 Jan, 6-20 Feb, 23-31 Aug, Mon-Tue except public holidays.* An epicurean address in the heart of a tiny village. Amidst a decor of copper plates and cooking ware, relax at one of the round tables set in this simple country inn and savour the fare proposed in the chef's carefully composed menus.

🍽 **Mado** – *6 quai Léonard, 80550 Le Crotoy* – ☎ *03 22 27 81 22.* A local institution housing three dining rooms. Those on the ground floor are pleasant enough, with their etchings of birds and the sea, but if you fancy dining while enjoying a peerless view of the Baie de Somme, you'll need to book a table upstairs.

🍽🍽 **La Marinière** – *27 r. de la Porte du Pont, 80550 Le Crotoy* – ☎ *03 22 27 05 36. Closed 10 Jan to early Feb – reserv. recommended.* A pleasant restaurant located in one of Le Crotoy's shopping streets. Marie-Ange welcomes you into the inviting dining room with a frank smile, while Patrice dons the chef's hat and concocts tasty seafood and other dishes with a local flavour.

### SPORT & LEISURE

**Plan d'eau de St-Firmin A.N.C.R**. – *104 r. Principale – 80550 Le Crotoy –* ☎ *03 22 27 04 39. May-Sep: Mon-Fri 1.30pm-5.30pm, weekends and public holidays 1pm-7pm, school holidays 10am-7pm. Closed Nov-Mar.* Sailing classes, sailboard rentals, catamarans, dinghies and optimists.

**Centre équestre le Val de Selle** – *1832 r. de l'Authie, 80120 Fort-Mahon-Plage –* ☎*03 22 27 45 58.* Horseback rides along the beach (1-3 hr) and day trips (with a guide).

---

daily, spring holidays, 2nd fortnight in June and first fortnight in Sep, Wed, weekends and public holidays. Oct Sun and public holidays. Diesel train departing Cayeux mid-Jul to end Aug: daily (except Mon and Fri). Bicycles carried free. For timetable and charges ring ☎ 03 22 26 96 96 or visit the Office de Tourisme. www.chemin-fer-baie-somme.asso.fr. A train comprising old carriages with viewing platforms pulled by steam or diesel engines runs between Le Crotoy, Noyelles, St Valery and Cayeux-sur-Mer providing a journey (16km/10mi) of discovery through this lush area bordered by the River Somme's grassy sandbanks.

### Parc Ornithologique du Marquenterre★★

Kids 🔔 *See Parc Ornithologique du Marquenterre.*

### Le Crotoy ⚓

The resort is reached by a scenic route (D 940) which runs alongside grass-covered sandbanks (*mollières*). The town was once a fortress, with a castle in which Joan of Arc was imprisoned in 1430 before being taken to St-Valery and then to Rouen. Today it is an attractive and popular seaside resort overlooking the Somme Bay. The port, close to place Jeanne d'Arc, the resort's lively centre, is used by small coastal fishing trawlers (that catch shrimps, flatfish and herrings); casting on the Somme's bed brings in plaice and eel.

**Beach sports** such as speedsailing, kite-flying and landsailing (as far as Fort-Mahon-Plage) are very popular. In addition, the **St-Firmin sailing centre** offers sailing enthusiasts a wide choice of crafts (sailboards, sailing dinghies, catamarans etc).

## Maison de l'Oiseau★

Kids ⅋ ⏰*Open Apr-Sep 10am-6pm (last entry 1hr before closing). Oct-Mar 10am-5pm.* ⏰*Closed 1 Jan and 25 Dec.* ⊜*6.30€–9.90€ (children, 4.60€–7€).* ☎*03 22 26 93 93. www.maisondeloiseau.com.*

A superb collection of stuffed birds assembled by an inhabitant of Cayeux was the basis for the Bird House, which is fittingly located in the ornithologically rich Somme Bay area. A building round a courtyard was especially constructed, following the layout of traditional farms.

Inside, displays highlight local birds in their natural habitat: cliffs, sand and mudflats, dunes and gravel pits. In a room dedicated to ducks, a reconstructed hide looks out over a pond behind the house where wild ducks, geese, waders and other fowl live. Films, exhibitions and information for fledgling birdwatchers complete the presentation.

A **bird-of-prey show** takes place from April to August: *call for times of displays.*

## Le Hourdel

The typical Picardy houses of this small fishing harbour and yachting marina stand at the tip of an offshore bar which begins at Onival. The bar consists of pebbles which are crushed to make emery powders and filtering materials. Views over the bay.

With a good pair of binoculars, it may be possible to observe a colony of some 20 seals sprawled on the sand lining the estuary, ready to flee at the first sign of danger. A surveillance system has been set up by Picardie Nature to reduce human interference so that females can give birth without being disturbed.

## Cayeux-sur-Mer

This resort is bordered by a promenade and a 2km/over 1mi-long wooden path lined with more than 400 cabins. The long beach of hard sand extends from the Hâble d'Ault to the Pointe de Hourdel; footpaths crisscross the woods of Brighton-les-Pins.

# VALLÉE DE LA SOMME★

SOMME VALLEY

MICHELIN LOCAL MAP 301: D-7 TO K-8

The slow-moving waters of the River Somme 🔝, "which made Picardy as the Nile made Egypt" (Mabille de Poncheville), often burst their banks to spill into silvery ponds or dark peat bogs, and have formed a wide, lush valley in Picardy's chalky plateau.

As the Somme is a natural barrier and has long been a regional frontier, it has been the site of numerous encounters and has given its name to two battles, one in 1916, the other in 1940.

🔢 **Information:** Comité Départemental du Tourisme de La Somme, 21, rue Ernest-Cauvin, 80000 Amiens. ☎ 03 22 71 22 71. www.somme-tourisme.com.

⊘ **Don't Miss:** A ride on the flat-bottomed boats in the Hortillonnages in Amiens.

⏰ **Organizing Your Time:** The whole region of the Somme is a place you can spend a whole week. If you have limited time visit Amiens and then head out to the coast.

Kids **Especially for Kids:** Parc Samara.

⅋ **Also See:** Amiens, Péronne, Albert.

# A Bit of History

## Meandering river

The source of the river is upstream of St-Quentin, at an altitude of 97m/318ft; from there it flows 245km/152mi west-ward. The gentleness of this descent, together with the absorbent quality of the peat through which the river meanders, largely explains the lazy pace of the waters.

During their journey, the waters wind

*Parc Samara – Reconstructed Prehistoric dwellings*

past peat bogs hidden under tall grasses, and meadows where laundry used to be spread out to bleach in the sun; past farmed fields and slopes pitted with quarries; past woods revealing shaded springs. In places, the bogs have been drained and turned into vegetable plots (*hortillonnages*).

### Navigation

Navigation on the river has always been limited owing to the fords and the shallowness of the water, but the River Somme nevertheless once carried **grib-annes** between Amiens and St-Valery. These heavy skiffs transported wheat from Santerre and wool from Ponthieu downstream; salt and wine were brought upstream.

The **Somme Canal**, finally completed in the 19C, links St-Quentin and St-Valery. Sometimes it follows the course of the river, at other times it runs alongside it or takes shortcuts across the meanders. The canal has hardly been used, however, as there has never been a true maritime port at the end.

### Hunting and Fishing

Hunting chiefly consists of lying in wait for wildfowl, in either a boat or the shelter of a hide (♿ *see ST-VALERY*). A great quantity of duck and snipe provide the game here; hunting wild swans, however, has not been allowed since the early 18C.

# Péronne to Amiens

▶ *63km/38mi – about 1hr 30min. Leave Péronne on D 938 (northwest).*

The road crosses the Canal du Nord, passing the Étangs de la Haute-Somme near Cléry, then crosses the motorway. As you drive along the plateau, you can see the valley below.

▶ *At the entrance to the town of Maricourt, turn left on D 197, then left again on the chemin de Vaux.*

### Belvédère de Vaux★

This spot is a good place to enjoy the **panorama**★ over the meanders of the River Curlu and the red rooftops of the hamlet of Vaux. Péronne is in the distance, visible on a clear day. The road goes down to Vaux and crosses the River Somme.

▶ *Take the road to Cappy, which runs along the canal.*

### Cappy

This former river port is now an attractive marina. The 12C Romanesque Église St-Nicolas, remodelled in the 16C, has a massive square tower surmounted by a turreted steeple.

▶ *In Cappy, cross the river and follow D 1 to Bray.*

## Bray-sur-Somme

This old port town has a lovely **church** with a big square bell tower and a Romanesque chancel. ⏱*Open daily (except Wed) 9.30am-5.30pm.* ☎ *03 22 76 11 38.*

## Froissy

This town on the canal has a little **train museum** in the old covered market; in the summer months visitors can ride in an old train, the **P'tit train de la Haute Somme**, which was used to supply the trenches during the First World War. ⏱*Open May to end-Sep Sun and public holidays 2.15pm, 3.15pm, 4.15pm, 5.15pm (mid-Jul to end Aug: daily (except Sun and Mon), 2.30pm and 6pm).* 👛*8€ (children: 5€).*

▸ *Return to Bray and take D 1F.*

The drive takes you through the middle of two landscapes: lakes and ponds, sometimes hidden in the fronds of forest ferns, on one side, and steep cliffs on the other. You can see the towers of **Corbie** on the horizon at certain bends in the road.

## Corbie and La Neuville

♿ *See CORBIE*

After La Neuville, the road passes through an area where watercress is grown and rises up a hill. Drive through Daours, continue along D 1; about 11km/7mi beyond the town, you may have your first glimpses of Amiens and its cathedral.

# Amiens to Abbeville

*58km/36mi – about 3hr*

▸ *Leave Amiens on N 235 (west) toward Picquigny; follow the road parallel to the Paris-Calais railway line.*

## Ailly-sur-Somme

The market town is overlooked by the sober lines of the modern church: its unusual design comprises a great slanting roof like the sail of a boat, which on one side rests on a stone wall and on the other, the ground.

▸ *Cross to the north bank of the Somme and turn left toward La Chaussée Tirancourt.*

## Parc Samara★

Kids ⏱*Open Mar-Sep 9.30am-5.30pm (weekends 6pm) (Jul-Aug 10am-6.30pm).* 👛*9€ (children: 7€).* ☎ *03 22 51 82 83.* *www.samara.fr.*

This park (25ha/62 acres) lies at the foot of a Celtic settlement overlooking the River Somme (known as the Samara in the days of the Gauls). Footpaths lead to an **arboretum** (110 species), a botanical garden with some 600 flowering plants, some of them rare, the marshes at the bottom of the valley and reconstructions of dwellings from the Neolithic, Bronze and Iron Ages. The working of flint, wood and pottery is brought to life by demonstrations of prehistoric techniques. Various ecosystems are cultivated and explained in this educational park, including the peat bog, where peat is extracted using techniques that were once common and have almost completely gone out of use.

Daily life in Picardy from the Palaeolithic era to the Gallo-Roman period is evoked in the **exhibition pavilion**: a reindeer hunter's house, a bronzesmith's and an Iron Age ironsmith's workshops, a Gallic village street, Gallo-Roman kitchen etc.

▸ *Take D 3 (north-west) out of Picquigny.*

## Hangest-sur-Somme

👄 *Guided tours daily (except Sat-Sun) by request at the town hall.* ☎ *03 22 51 12 37.*

The village specialises in growing watercress. The 12C-16C church contains 18C furniture from the Abbaye du Gard. In 1940 the German 7th Tank Division commanded by **Rommel** crossed the River Somme between Hangest and **Condé-Folie** using the only railway bridge that had not been blown up. There is a large French military cemetery at Condé-Folie.

## Longpré-les-Corps-Saints

The town derives its name from the relics which the church founder, Aléaume de Fontaine, sent from Constantinople during the Crusades.

▸ *1km/0.5mi beyond Longpré, turn right at Le Catelet onto D 32 toward Long.*

The road crosses the floor of the valley, dotted here with ponds, offering a lovely view of the Château de Long.

## Long

The great **church** in this pretty hillside village was rebuilt in the 19C, in the Gothic style, but retained its 16C spire; Cavaillé-Coll organ.

The elegant Louis XV **château** has a slate mansard roof and red brick and white stone. Note the unusual, rounded wings and the graceful openings surmounted by keystones carved with masks and other ornamentation (○━ *not open to the public*).

▶ *Cross the Somme again and follow D 3.*

## Église de Liercourt

The charming Flamboyant **church** with its gable tower stands just before the village. The fine basket-handled door-

way is surmounted by the arms of France and a recess containing a statue of St Riquier.

▶ *Turn right onto D 901, crossing the Paris-Calais railway line.*

## Château de Pont-Remy

This château was built on an island near Pont-Remy in the 15C but was rebuilt in 1837 in the "Gothic Troubadour" style. Fine landscaped park.

▶ *Return to D 3.*

The road runs along the bottom of the hillside, skirting ponds and meadows, and approaches the Monts de Caubert.

▶ *Turn right to Abbeville.*

## Abbeville
♿ *See ABBEVILLE*

# LA THIÉRACHE★

MICHELIN LOCAL MAP 306: D-3 TO G-4

The Thiérache region forms a green patch in the bare, chalky plains of Picardy and Champagne. The high altitude (250m/820ft in the east) provides greater rainfall which, combined with the terrain's lack of porousness, creates a well-watered area, devoted to forestry and especially grazing. The main lines of communication follow the deep valleys of the River Oise and River Serre and their tributaries. The area between Guise and Hirson is ideal country for hikers and the whole region, abounding in brick-and-stone fortified churches, is the paradise of history buffs.

The woodland is interspersed with meadows, cider-apple orchards and a scattering of farms. Basket-making is a speciality around **Origny**, which is not surprising, in light of the many graceful willows growing there.

▪ **Information:** Office du tourisme de Vervins et du Vervinois, pl. de l'Hôtel de Ville, 02240. ☎03 23 98 11 98. www.ot-vervins.com.
▪ **Don't Miss:** The fortified churches for which the region is renowned.
▪ **Organizing Your Time:** This is a fascinating area to explore, and needs at least 2, even 3, days, although the two circuits given below can be completed in a day.

## Fortified Churches★

Until the reign of Louis XIV the Thiérache region was a frontier and so repeatedly invaded – by 14C mercenaries led by Du Guesclin, by German foot soldiers and by vagabonds – particularly during the Hundred Years War, the Wars of

Religion and the conflicts between France and Spain under Louis XIII and Louis XIV. From the late 16C and during the 17C, local inhabitants, lacking fortresses and ramparts, fortified their churches. This accounts for the watch-turrets, round towers and square keeps pierced with arrow slits found on most

## Address Book

**WHERE TO STAY AND EAT**

☞ **Mme Piette (Bed and Breakfast)** –
*7 pl. des Marronniers, 02120 Chigny –
15km/9mi east of Guiset via N 29 and
D 26 – ☎ 03 23 60 22 04 – ⌺ – 6 rms.*
Here's a home that exudes the quaint
charm of old manor houses. In a décor
where time seems to stand still, Mme
Piette is very attentive to her guests'
needs. Three of the bedrooms do not
have private bathrooms.

☞ **Le Cheval Noir** – *Opposite the church
– 02140 Vervins – ☎ 03 23 98 04 16 –
🅿 – 11 rms – ⌹ 6€ – restaurant ☞.*
This former coaching inn built on
the Vervins ramparts offers spacious,
tastefully refurbished guest rooms,
two inviting dining rooms and a
bar decorated with a good deal of
imagination. Regional cookery and
tempting beer list.

of the 12C and 13C buildings, resulting
in an uncomfortable architectural mix
of brick and stone. Other fortress-churches,
such as that at Plomion, date entirely
from the turn of the 17C.

# 1 Round Trip starting from Vervins

*79km/49mi – about 3hr*

## Vervins

The charm of the town, which is the
region's capital, lies in its ramparts, its
cobbled and winding streets and its
squares bordered by houses with steeply
pitched slate roofs and brick chimneys.
The **church** features a 13C chancel, 16C
nave and imposing brick tower (34m/
111ft tall) with stone string courses (note
the double buttresses on the corners).
Inside, 16C mural paintings adorn the
piers and a huge, brightly coloured composition by Jouvenet (1699) portrays
*Supper in the House of Simon.* Also on
view are an 18C organ case and pulpit.

▶ *Leave Vervins by D 372 (southeast);
at Harcigny take D 37 east.*

## Plomion

The 16C church features a fine west front
flanked by two towers; note the square
keep with its great hall leading up to
the garret.
A large covered market in front of the
church testifies to Plomion's commercial activities.

▶ *Take D 747 east toward Bancigny
and Jeantes.*

## Jeantes

The façade of the **church** is flanked by
two towers. Expressionist frescoes on
the walls of the interior, representing
scenes from the Life of Christ, are the
work of painter Charles Van Eyck (1962).
Note the 12C font.

## Dagny

This old village has preserved its cob
houses and half-timbered houses with
brick courses.

## Morgny-en-Thiérache

The chancel and nave of the church
date from the 13C. Fortification mainly
affected the chancel, which was raised
by a storey to create an extra room for
those seeking a safe refuge.

## Dohis

There are many half-timbered and cob
houses here. The church (12C nave) is
particularly interesting because of its
porch-keep, added in the 17C.

▶ *Turn around from the church and
take the first road on the left (south);
fork left to Parfondeval.*

## Parfondeval

This lovely village stands perched on a
hill, its warm-toned brick houses clus-
tering around a broad green. The 16C
**church** rises at the end of the square,
an indisputable fortress behind a fortification of neighbouring houses. The
white stone portal is in the Renaissance
style. On the walls, glazed bricks form a
crisscross design.

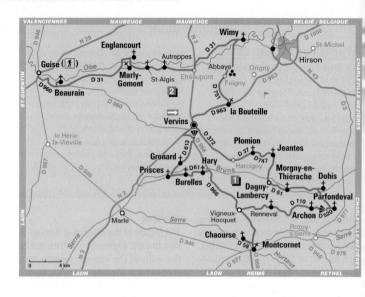

▶ *Back at the entrance to the village take D 520 (west) to Archon.*

The road offers a good view over Archon and the undulating countryside dotted with copses.

## Archon

Cob-walled and brick houses encircle the church, which is guarded by two great towers; a footbridge between the towers also served as a look-out point.

▶ *Follow D 110 west through* **Renneval** *(stone church with fortified chancel) to Vigneux.Head for Montcornet along D 966.*

## Montcornet

The Gothic Église St-Martin, believed to have been built by the Knights Templars in the 13C, boasts a chancel ending in a flat east end, which is almost as long as the nave. 16C additions include a Renaissance porch and eight bartizans with defensive loopholes.

▶ *Continue along D 966 toward Vigneux then turn left onto D 58.*

## Chaourse

This village used to be the main centre of activity in the area but it gradually declined and was overtaken by Mont-cornet. The 13C **church** (nave and tower) was fortified in the 16C. Interesting view of the Serre Valley.

▶ *Turn back to rejoin D 966 and drive on to Hary.*

## Hary

A 16C brick keep rises above the chancel and nave of this 12C Romanesque church.

▶ *D 61 follows the Brune Valley.*

## Burelles

The 16C and 17C village **church** has a number of defences: arrow slits, a reinforced keep with watch-turret, barbicans and watch-turrets above the north transept, the chancel flanked by a turret. The upper floor of the transept has been turned into a vast fortified room.

## Prisces

*Restoration work in progress.*
The 12C chancel and nave of the **church** were given an enormous, square brick keep (25m/82ft tall) with two turrets on diagonally opposing corners. The four floors inside allowed about 100 soldiers to take shelter with their arms and provisions.

▶ *Cross the River Brune and follow D 613 to Gronard.*

## Gronard

The façade of the **church** is almost hidden behind lime trees. The keep is flanked by two round towers.

▶ *Return to Vervins along D 613 and D 966.*

The route offers a picturesque view of Vervins and its surrounding area.

## 2 From Vervins to Guise

*51km/32mi – about 2hr*

This tour largely follows the Oise Valley which also features many fortified churches.

## Vervins
◔ *See above.*

▶ *From Vervins take D 963 to La Bouteille.*

## La Bouteille

The church has thick walls (over 1m/3ft) and is flanked by four turrets. It was built by Cistercians from the nearby **Abbaye de Foigny**, now in ruins.

▶ *D 751 and VC 10 lead to Foigny. Cross D 38 and take the little road which runs beside the abbey ruins, to Wimy.*

## Wimy

The enormous keep of the fortified church is flanked by two large, cylindrical towers. Two fireplaces, a well and a bread oven were added inside. The first floor has a vast room for those seeking refuge.

D 31 crosses Etréaupont and continues through **Autreppes**, a village of brick buildings. The road runs in front of the fortified church and continues past the village of **St Algis** which is overlooked by its church keep.

## Marly

The 13C and 14C sandstone church has a beautiful, pointed arch portal to which two great watch-turrets were added. The large arrow slits near the base allowed crossbows to be used.

▶ *Take D 774 north to Englancourt.*

## Englancourt

The fortified **church**, in a pretty location overlooking the River Oise, has a west front flanked by watch-turrets, a square keep in brick and a chancel with a flat east end reinforced by two round towers.

▶ *Return to D 31 via D 26.*

## Beaurain

The **church** stands isolated on a hill that rises from lush surroundings. The beautiful fortress dates entirely from the same period. The great square keep is flanked by towers, as is the chancel. A Romanesque font stands by the entrance.

## Guise
◔ *See Guise.*

# CHÂTEAU ET PARC DE THOIRY★

**POPULATION 969**

**MICHELIN LOCAL MAP 311: G-2 OR MAP 106 FOLDS 15, 16**

Thoiry 🚶 is a vast estate comprising a large Renaissance château and 250ha/ 625 acres of gardens and park. The family who has owned it for the past 400 years or more has undertaken a considerable amount of work to turn it into a magical spot where history and nature merge.

ℹ️ **Information:** www.thoiry.net

▶ **Orient Yourself:** 53km (33 miles) west of Paris. By car, take A 13 then A 12 to St-Quentin-en-Yvelines. Leave the motorway at the Bois d'Arcy exit toward Dreux and follow N 12 to Pontchartrain, then turn onto D 11 to Thoiry.

🕐 **Organizing Your Time:** Make a day of it.

🧒 **Especially for Kids:** All of it, but especially the African wildlife park.

## Sights

### Château

♿ 🕐*Opening hours vary considerably. See website for details.* 🎫*Combined tickets for château, gardens, labyrinthe, wildlife park, etc 22.90€ (children: 15.90€).* ☎ 01 34 87 53 76. www.thoiry.net.

Raoul Moreau, Treasurer to Henri II, was passionately interested in alchemy and esoterics. It was he who had this "solar house" built on a magnetic fault, to designs using the Golden Section. This outstanding position on a hilltop enables the château to act as a solar instrument, with spectacular sights such as the sunrise or sunset in line with the façade at the solstices.

The house is also a "time machine" which has come down to us through the centuries and now gives an insight into an eventful history. The ancestors conversing from their picture frames in the portrait gallery (no, you are not dreaming!) and the spicy tales uncovered in the 50 trunks full of family archives are all rather unconventional means of taking a look at history.

### Zoological and botanical park

🧒 ♿ 🕐*Opening hours vary considerably. See website for details.* 🎫*Combined tickets for château, gardens, labyrinth, wildlife park, etc 22.90€ (children: 15.90€).* ☎ 01 34 87 53 76. www.thoiry.net.

The area of park adjacent to the château has been laid out as a zoo, with numerous special events. The most impressive section is the tiger enclosure which visitors cross on a concrete footbridge among the trees. It is also possible to see the animals from the glass tunnel in which only the armoured glass separates visitors from the claws and teeth of these wild beasts. Various trails pass the elegant but fearsome black panthers, the emus and cassowaries, the mandrill island, and a tribe of lemurs running free. There are demonstrations of birds of prey in flight. The trees, too, speak to visitors about the natural environment. Do not miss the impressive Asian dragons (5m/16ft long) and become familiar with the ecosystem of European rivers (otters).

### African wildlife park

🧒 ♿ 🕐*Opening hours vary considerably. See website for details.* 🎫*Combined tickets for château, gardens, labyrinthe, wildlife park, etc 22.90€ (children: 15.90€).* ☎ 01 34 87 53 76. www.thoiry.net.

The park is visited by car only (all windows closed) as the animals roam free. For your own safety, please comply with the rules.

The park is so huge that many species of African wildlife are able to live together quite happily. The road covers a distance of 10km/6mi and you will see antelopes, bison, giraffes, zebras, elephants, rhinos, hippos, and much more. A drive through two high-security enclosures provides a close-up view of lions and bears.

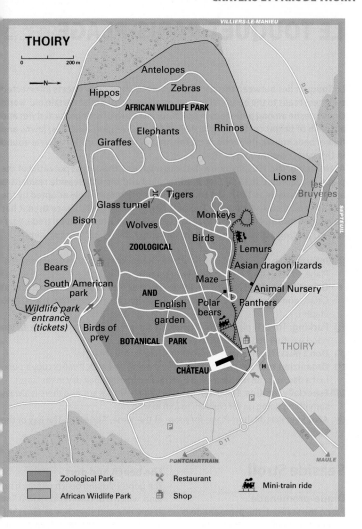

**THOIRY**

0 — 200 m

—N—▶

VILLIERS-LE-MAHIEU

Antelopes

Hippos

Zebras

**AFRICAN WILDLIFE PARK**

Elephants

Rhinos

Giraffes

Lions

les Bruyères

Tigers

Glass tunnel

Monkeys

Bison

Wolves

Birds

Lemurs

**ZOOLOGICAL**

Asian dragon lizards

Bears

Maze

Animal Nursery

South American park

**AND**

Polar bears

Panthers

*Wildlife park entrance (tickets)*

English garden

Birds of prey

**BOTANICAL   PARK**

**CHÂTEAU**

THOIRY

H

P

P

PONTCHARTRAIN

D 11

MAULE

SEPTEUIL

D 11

D 45

| | Zoological Park | ✗ | Restaurant | 🚂 | Mini-train ride |
|---|---|---|---|---|---|
| | African Wildlife Park | 🏪 | Shop | | |

# LE TOUQUET-PARIS-PLAGE ≈≈≈

POPULATION 5 299

MICHELIN LOCAL MAP 301: C-4

Le Touquet lies between the sea and the forest, its parallel streets intersected by access roads to the beach. Villas and establishments with a certain old-world charm nestle among pine trees in a picturesque clash of architectural styles and a splash of bright colours: white walls with blue edging, red tiles, lawns and flower beds impeccably hedged in. The holiday spirit is in the air all-year-round in this vast "seaside garden."

At the end of the 19C, an English businessman saw the tourist potential of the place and founded the Touquet Syndicate Ltd and the first seaside residences appeared as early as 1882. The resort was almost immediately adopted by the English and took the name Le Touquet Paris-Plage in 1912. Since then it has developed into an all-year European resort with a substantial hotel trade, year-round sporting activities and a thalassotherapy (sea-water therapy) centre.

- 🔲 **Information:** Palais de l'Europe, Pl. de l'Hermitage, 62520 Le Touquet-Paris-Plage. ☎ 03 21 06 72 00. www.letouquet.com.
- ▶ **Orient Yourself:** On the coast, 68km (43 miles) south of the Channel port at Calais, and accessible by the A 16 (leave at Junction 26 and take the N 39 to Étaples.
- 🅿 **Parking:** There is plenty of paid parking along the Digue-promenade, but in good weather you will need to be there early.
- 🔄 **Don't Miss:** The maritime forest of the 'Jardins de la Manche'.
- 🕐 **Organizing Your Time:** If you take the recommended walk, it will occupy around half a day. You can then hire a bike and spend another half day in the forest.
- 🚸 **Especially for Kids:** The beach has the 'Station Kid' award, and there is always something going on for children to join in with.
- 👐 **Also See:** Fort-Mahon-Plage for more of the same, Abbeville, The Bay of the Somme.

## Seaside Stroll

### Digue-promenade

Along the seafront, the **promenade** is edged by numerous gardens and car parks. The south end leads to a sand-yachting club and a thalassotherapy centre.

*Having fun on the beach*

S. Sauvignier/MICHELIN

### The beach and port

The gently sloping beach of fine, hard sand, which is uncovered for 1km/0.5mi at low tide and stretches as far as the mouth of the River Authie (12km/7.5mi), attracts many sand yachts. The **coast road** follows the line of the dunes and leads to the marina and the water sports club, well sheltered by the headland known as Pointe du Touquet.

### Sports and leisure activities

Near the attractive shopping galleries of the Hermitage district are the **Sports Centre**, the select **Casino du Palais** and the **Palais de l'Europe** where conferences and cultural exchanges take place.

The **Museum** (🕐*Open Jun-Sep daily (except Tue) 10am-1pm, 2-6pm (Sun 10am-1pm, 3-6pm). Oct-May daily (except Tue) 2-6pm (Sun 3-6pm).* 🔒*Closed public* *holidays.* ⚅*3.80€.* ☎ *03 21 05 62 62)* displays works by the Étaples School (1880-1914). It also includes paintings by Le Sidaner and a section devoted to modern art.

## "Jardins de la Manche"

The forest (800ha/1 900 acres) was planted in 1855; its maritime pine, birch, alder, poplar and acacia trees protect about 2 000 luxury villas – either Anglo-Norman in style or resolutely modern –

from the wind. Some 45km/28mi of bridlepaths and 50km/31mi of forest tracks reserved for hikers run across the woods and the residential districts with their neat gardens.

🚶 **Four walks** start from place de l'Hermitage: **La Pomme de Pin** for "amateurs", **Le Daphné** for serious hikers, **La Feuille de chêne** for keen "explorers" and **L'Argousier** for really "experienced" hikers (*leaflets available from the tourist office*).

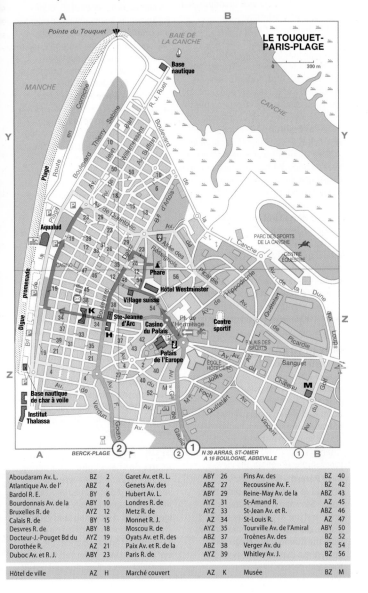

| | | | | | | | | |
|---|---|---|---|---|---|---|---|---|
| Aboudaram Av. L. | BZ | 2 | Garet Av. et R. L. | ABY | 26 | Pins Av. des | BZ | 40 |
| Atlantique Av. de l' | ABZ | 4 | Genets Av. des | ABZ | 27 | Recoussine Av. F. | BZ | 42 |
| Bardol R. E. | BY | 6 | Hubert Av. L. | ABY | 29 | Reine-May Av. de la | ABZ | 43 |
| Bourdonnais Av. de la | ABY | 10 | Londres R. de | AYZ | 31 | St-Amand R. | AZ | 45 |
| Bruxelles R. de | AYZ | 12 | Metz R. de | AYZ | 33 | St-Jean Av. et R. | ABZ | 46 |
| Calais R. de | BY | 15 | Monnet R. J. | AZ | 34 | St-Louis R. | AZ | 47 |
| Desvres R. de | ABZ | 18 | Moscou R. de | AYZ | 35 | Tourville Av. de l'Amiral | ABY | 50 |
| Docteur-J.-Pouget Bd du | AYZ | 19 | Oyats Av. et R. des | ABZ | 37 | Troènes Av. des | BZ | 52 |
| Dorothée R. | AZ | 21 | Paix Av. et R. de la | ABZ | 38 | Verger Av. du | BZ | 54 |
| Duboc Av. et R. J. | ABY | 23 | Paris R. de | AYZ | 39 | Whitley Av. J. | BZ | 56 |
| | | | | | | | | |
| Hôtel de ville | AZ | H | Marché couvert | AZ | K | Musée | BZ | M |

## Address Book

*For coin ranges, see the Legend on the cover flap.*

### WHERE TO STAY

**Hôtel de la Forêt** – *73 r. de Moscou –* ☎ *03 21 05 09 88. Closed 15 Dec to 15 Jan – 10 rms – 6.50€.* This small family hotel in the centre of town is just 0.5km/0.3mi from the shore. The small, simple bedrooms are being renovated one by one. They are well soundproofed and absolutely shipshape.

**Le Chalet** – *15 r. de la Paix –* ☎ *03 21 05 87 65 – 15 rms – 8€.* Although only 50m/55yds from the beach, this hotel looks like it migrated here from the Alps. Spruce bedrooms decorated along a seaside or mountain theme; breakfast room featuring old wooden skis and clogs. Charming!

**Les Embruns** – *89 r. de Paris –* ☎ *03 21 05 87 61. Closed 15 Dec to 14 Jan – 19 rms – 6€.* Located near the water, here's a house with an appealing façade boasting rooms that have mostly been renovated. Those giving on to the back are quieter. Small sitting room and library.

**Hôtel Le Manoir** – *by the golf course – 2.5km/1.5mi S of Touquet –* ☎ *03 21 06 28 28 – P – 41 rms – restaurant*. A pretty, ivy-covered manor situated on the edge of the golf course where you will enjoy the cosy, intimate quietude of the sitting room and bar. Very popular with the golf crowd. Ground-level guest rooms in bungalows outside.

### WHERE TO EAT

**Restaurant Côté Sud** – *187 bd Jules-Pouget –* ☎ *03 21 05 41 24. Closed Mon morning, Sun evening and Wed out of season*. A gorgeous restaurant decorated in the colours of the south of France. The sun-drenched food is also of southern inspiration: rabbit in rosemary sauce, and spicy red mullet, for example. Gorgeous sea views!

**Pérard** – *67 r. de Metz –* ☎ *03 21 05 13 33.* Connoisseurs take note – fish soup is this restaurant's pride and joy! As with other seafood dishes, the ingredients come directly from the fishmonger's shop next door, given that both are owned by the same person.

**Le Nemo** – *Bd de la Mer, Aqualud –* ☎ *03 21 90 07 08. www.lenemo.com. Closed Dec-Jan.* Enter this restaurant inspired by Jules Verne and dive 20 000 leagues under the sea! Nothing is missing – you'll find deep-sea diving suits, mariners' charts, woodwork, pewter pieces, marine curios. Pleasant terrace on the ocean side.

**La Brasserie du Marché** – *In the covered market –* ☎ *03 21 05 30 30*. An agreeable bistro ambience reigns in this bright dining room lined with mirrors. The welcome is friendly and the pretty terrace is very popular in summer. The varied menu includes several tasty regional dishes.

**Le Village Suisse** – *52 av. St-Jean –* ☎ *03 21 05 69 93. Closed 3 wks in Jan, early Dec, Sun evening from Oct to Easter, Tue lunch except Jul-Aug, and Mon*. Situated directly over the "village" shops, here's an elegant restaurant resembling a Swiss chalet. Its strong points? A comfortable, inviting dining room, courteous staff and delicious food that evolves with the seasons.

### ON THE TOWN

**Le Philæ Café** – *28 r. St-Jean –* ☎ *03 21 05 16 99 – daily 6pm-4am.* This luxurious café's decoration scheme faithfully reproduces the Egyptian frescoes and colourful columns adorning the temple of Philæ. The coffee tables are engraved with hieroglyphs and some of the walls sport bas-reliefs. Jazz and rock concerts habitually accompany tropical cocktails; Friday evenings are earmarked for karaoke relayed on a giant screen – things start heating up after 10pm. Until then, you can take out your hieroglyph phrasebook and decipher the symbols!

### SPORT & LEISURE

**Centre de Char à Voile** – *Base nautique Sud –* ☎ *03 21 05 33 51 – reception: 10am-noon, 2-5pm. Closed mid-Dec to mid-Jan.* Touquet's lovely beach is the ideal spot for discovering sand yachting. This novel sport is practised on over 15km/9mi of fine sand under the expert eye and guidance of Bertrand Lambert, quintuple world champion and fastest yachtsman (151.55km/94.12mph) to date.

**Centre Équestre Régional du Touquet** – *Av. de la Dune-aux-Loups –* ☎ *03 21 05 15 25 – daily: 9am-noon, 2pm-6pm.* This centre, which occupies over 50ha/125acres in the forest, boards over 150 magnificent steeds, most of which belong to private owners. The club's 40 horses and ponies are available for outings of different lengths, depending on the rider's ability and experience.

**Golf** – *Av. du Golf – A 16, exit 26 –* ☎ *03 21 06 28 28. www.opengolfclub. com.* A handsome course (two 18-hole and one 9-hole) running through a pine forest and wild dunes.

**Centre de Soins Marins** – *4 bd de la Canche – Mercure Grand Hôtel –* ☎ *03 21 06 88 84 – www. accorthalassa. com – 8.30am-7pm, Sun 8.30am-6pm. Closed Christmas and New Year's Day.*

**Institut Thalassa** – *On the beach –* ☎*03 21 09 86 00.* Thalassotherapy and fitness.

**Parc d'Attractions Aqualud** – *Bd de la Mer –* ☎ *03 21 90 07 07 – www.aqualud.com. Daily 10.15am-5.45pm (Jul-Aug 10.15am-6.45pm, summer late-nights 8pm-midnight). Closed Nov-Jan.* A 4000m² water sports amusement park with a covered section where the air is 27°C/81°F and the water 29°C/84°F year-round. Giant slides, river with inner tubes and surprises, wave pool, jacuzzi, Black Hole, Twister… and lifeguards for parents' peace of mind. Cafeteria.

**Boobaloo** – *38 r. Saint-Louis* ☎ *03 21 05 66 47. Open weekends, public and school holidays 9am-7pm. Closed Jan.* Cycle hire.

## SHOPPING

**Magasin Atem** – *110 r. de Metz –* ☎ *03 21 05 61 58 – www.letouquet.net/ atem – 9.30am-noon, 3.30pm-7pm. Closed Jan, Tue afternoon and Wed except during holidays.* This is where you can buy a good kite and learn to fly it properly.

---

**Three golf courses** extend south of the forest. Along the River Canche are the **racecourse**, the **equestrian centre**, the **shooting range** (*archery*) and the **airport**.

# Balade 1900

▶ *From place de l'Hermitage, take avenue du Verger.*

This is Le Touquet's most fashionable avenue, lined on the right with flower beds and white-painted boutiques (1927) recalling the Art Deco style. Further on the **Hôtel Westminster** is one of the resort's most prestigious establishments with its red-brick façade and protruding windows.

▶ *Bear left and walk along rue St-Jean.*

The **Village Suisse** (1905) on the left is in mock medieval style with turrets and crenels. The shopping arcades have terraces upstairs.

▶ *Return to the hotel and follow avenue des Phares.*

Situated on the right, behind the hotel, the red-brick **lighthouse** was rebuilt by Quételart in 1949. Its hexagonal column, resembling a Doric column, is crowned with two white balconies.

▶ *Cross avenue des Phares and follow rue J.-Duboc leading to boulevard Daloz.*

**Villa Cendrillon** (1923) on the corner of the boulevard boasts a lovely loggia and an unusual overlapping roof. At no 44 along the same boulevard, **Villa La Wallonne** stands at the beginning of the lively shopping centre. Note the façade of **Villa des Mutins** (1925) at no 78 with its two gables overlooking rue de Lens; it was the home of Louis Quételart. **Villa Le Roy d'Ys** at no 45 looks like a traditional house from Normandy with its timber-framed stone walls.

The **Hôtel de Ville** was built from local stone in 1931 in Anglo-Norman style with cemented timber-framing; it is flanked by a belfry (38m/125ft tall).

▶ *Follow rue Jean-Monnet toward the beach.*

## Jean-Baptiste Carpeaux

Jean-Baptiste Carpeaux (Valenciennes 1827-Courbevoie 1875) was a sculptor, painter and draughtsman. He won the Grand Prix de Rome in 1854.

Having become an official sculptor, he produced a large number of elegant busts of celebrities during the Second Empire and was also involved in the decoration of public buildings:

◆ *Triumph of Flora,* a low relief for the pediment of the Louvre's Flora pavilion in Paris;
◆ *Dance,* a group sculpture for the front of the Paris Opera House, now in the Musée d'Orsay;
◆ *The Four Quarters of the Globe,* for the fountain at the Observatoire in Paris;
◆ A statue of Watteau in Valenciennes.

A commemorative statue by Félix Desruelles was erected in memory of the great man in avenue du Sénateur-Girard in Valenciennes. Other works, plaster casts or earthenware models can be seen in the Musée d'Orsay and the Musée du Petit Palais in Paris, the Musée Roybet-Fould in Courbevoie and the Musée des Beaux-Arts in Valenciennes.

**Villa Le Castel** (1904) at no 50 combines the neo-Gothic and Art Nouveau styles. Rue Jean-Monnet continues through the arch of the **covered market** (1927-32), a half-moon-shaped ensemble, and leads to boulevard Pouget on the seafront lined with other holiday houses.

▶ *Take avenue du Verger which leads back to place de l'Hermitage.*

## Excursions

### Stella-Plage
*8km/5mi. leave Le Touquet along avenue F.-Godin and after 5km/3mi, turn right onto D 144.*

Behind the dunes that extend along the beach are villas dotted across the woods forming a continuation of the woods in Le Touquet.

### St-Josse
*10km/6mi southeast on N 39, D 143 and D 144 (views of Étaples).*

St-Josse, which stands on a hill, was once the home of an abbey founded by Charlemagne in memory of St Josse, a 7C pilgrim and hermit whose reliquary is venerated in the church's early-16C chancel.

About 500m/550yd east, in the middle of a wooded close, stand St Josse's Chapel, which is a place of pilgrimage, and St Josse's fountain.

# VALENCIENNES
POPULATION 357 395
MICHELIN LOCAL MAP 302: J-5

This busy commercial town, located on the River Escaut (Scheldt), is surrounded by boulevards which replaced the former ramparts. Only the 15C Tour de la Dedenne has survived.

Valenciennes was once the capital of the steel industry and metallurgy in the north, while the coal basin nearby was fully active. Today these industries have decreased markedly but have been replaced by others: rolling stock, car manufacturing, paints, pharmaceutical laboratories, mechanical engineering, electronics etc.

The presence of a science faculty has contributed to the development of the town, which is today an important cultural centre with fine collections of paintings by Watteau and sculpture by Carpeaux.

Among the culinary specialities of Valenciennes is *langue Lucullus*, smoked ox tongue cut into slices and covered in foie gras.

- **Information:** Maison du tourisme de Valenciennes, 1 r. Askievre, 59300 Valenciennes ☎ 03 27 46 22 99. www.ville-valenciennes.fr.
- ▶ **Orient Yourself:** Close to the Belgian border, southwest of Lille (56km/ 35 miles) and linked by the A 23.
- **Parking:** Valenciennes is a nightmare of one-way streets, but there are plenty of small-ish car parks. The problem is finding out how to get back to the one you spotted.
- **Organizing Your Time:** The Musée des Beaux-Arts is well worth a couple of hours.
- **Especially for Kids:** The Parc d'attractions Le Fleury.

## A Bit of History

### Athens of the North
Valenciennes earned this nickname because of the town's long-standing interest in the arts and the many artists who were born here.

Native sculptors include André Beauneveu (14C) – the "image-maker" of Charles V – who was also a painter, Antoine Pater (1670-1747); Saly (1717-76) who went to work for the court of Denmark, and in particular **Carpeaux** (1827-75), who brought new life to French sculpture.

Famous local painters are also numerous: in the 18C, the great **Antoine Watteau** (1684-1721) and Jean-Baptiste Pater (1695-1736) who both specialised in genre painting in the *fête galante* style; Louis and François Watteau, grand-nephew and great-nephew of Antoine; and in the 19C, the landscape painter Henri Harpignies (1819-1916).

## Sights

### Maison espagnole
This 16C half-timbered, corbelled house was built during the Spanish occupation. It has been restored and is today the home of the tourist office.

### Musée des Beaux-Arts★
♿ ⏲ *Open daily (except Tue) 10am-6pm (Thu 10am-8pm).* ⏲ *Closed 1 Jan, 1 May, Mon following the 2nd Sun in Sep, 25 Dec.* ⊜ *4.80€, no charge first Sun in the month.* ☎ *03 27 22 57 20.*

This vast museum, which was built at the beginning of the last century, has a particularly large collection of works from the 15C-17C Flemish School (Rubens), 18C French works and 19C sculptures (Carpeaux). It has been renovated throughout and now has a bookshop and gift shop, café, lecture hall etc.

## Address Book

🖎 *For coin ranges, see the Legend on the cover flap.*

### WHERE TO STAY

◯◯ **Château d'En Haut (Bed and Breakfast)** – *Château d'en Haut, 59144 Jenlain – 6km/3.6mi SE of Valenciennes via D 934 and D 59 – ☎ 03 27 49 71 80 – ⊲ – 6 rms.* This particularly well-run 18C château is remarkable for its décor – including marquetry, antiques and period paintings – and the charming welcome. The rooms feature canopy beds and windows facing the garden. Guests have access to the library and chapel.

### WHERE TO EAT

◯ **Au Vieux St-Nicolas** – *72 r. de Paris – ☎ 03 27 30 14 93. Closed 1 wk at Easter, 14 Jul to 15 Aug.* This restaurant in a house dating from 1735 is well-situated near the St-Géry church. The traditional cuisine is served under the kindly eye of Old Saint Nick – in the form of a 16C statue presiding over the back of the room.

### LEISURE

**Parc d'attractions Le Fleury** – 🛝 – *5 r. de Bouchain, 59111 Wavrechain-sous-Faulx – ☎ 03 27 35 71 16 – www.lefleury.fr – Jul-Aug 9am-7pm; mid-Apr to Jun: phone for open hours (usually 10am-6pm). Closed Oct-Apr. 9.50€.* Spreading over 23ha/57 acres, this amusement park offers several different aquatic attractions. One may also visit the Animal Garden or go for a workout in the sports area.

## Excursions

### St-Saulve

*2km/1.25mi northeast. Leave Valenciennes by avenue de Liège, N 30.*

**Chapelle du Carmel** – *1 rue Barbusse.* 🕐*open 9-11.30am, 1-5pm ☎ 03 27 46 24 98.* This Carmelite chapel, which was completed in 1966, was inspired by a model created by the sculptor Szekely and then built to plans prepared by the architect Guislain who favoured effects of mass and the use of simple materials. The chapel stands back from the road and is flanked by an asymmetrical bell tower. The interior is bathed in a gentle light which filters in above the altar through stained-glass windows featuring geometric designs.

### Sebourg

*9km/5.5mi east. Leave Valenciennes by D 934 toward Maubeuge, turn left at Saultain on D 59; beyond Estreux turn right onto D 350.*

This little market town attracts people from Valenciennes owing to its rural appearance and stretches over the verdant slopes of the Aunelle Valley.

The 12C-16C **church** (👣 *guided visits 9am-noon, 2-6.30pm, by arrangement. ☎ 03 27 26 52 78)* is the destination for pilgrimages to St Druon; the 12C shepherd-hermit is invoked to cure hernias. In the south aisle lie 14C recumbent effigies of Henri of Hainault, Lord of Sebourg, and his wife.

### Denain

*10km/6mi southwest by N 30.*

After the discovery of coal in 1828, this rural village became a major industrial centre. The town had up to 15 mine shafts at one time (the last one, the Puits du Renard, was closed in 1948 but its slag heap still dominates the town). It was in this town and in the countryside nearby that Zola came to seek inspiration for his work *Germinal*. Traces of the town's heyday are still visible. One large building (1852) remains of the mining community in avenue Villars; it is now the Academy of Music. It was here that the poet-miner Jules Mousseron (1868-1943) lived.

The **Cité Ernestine** (*park your car and take the alleyway between 138 and 140 rue Ludovic-Trarieux*) has retained its working-class atmosphere. It consists of 20 or more semi-detached miners' houses (known as *corons*). The **Cité Bellevue** to the north consists of a fine group of foremen's houses, some of them built to each side of the bread oven.

# ABBAYE ET JARDINS DE VALLOIRES ★★

MICHELIN LOCAL MAP 301: D-5

The old Cistercian abbey is located on a remote site in the Authie Valley, surrounded by woods and orchards; it is a rare and beautiful example of 18C architecture. The Jardin des "Îles" forms an ocean of greenery dotted with colourful islands and the rose garden offers thousands of sweet-smelling roses.

- **Information:** See entries for the abbey and the gardens below.
- ▶ **Orient Yourself:** Argoules is in the north of the department of the Somme 35km (22 miles) north of Abbevile, from where it is reached via the A 16 (leave at Junction 24).
- **Parking:** On site
- **Organizing Your Time:** Allow half a day to visit the whole site.
- **Especially for Kids:** The Garden of the Five Senses.
- **Also See:** Crécy-en-Ponthieu. Montreuil-sur-Mer. Fort-Mahon-Plage.

## A Bit of History

The abbey was founded in the 12C by a count of Ponthieu and became a burial place for his family. In 1346 the bodies of knights killed at Crécy were transported here.

In the 17C the abbey was ravaged by several fires, but the monks were wealthy and in 1730 the abbot ordered that huge amounts of wood be cut in order to begin rebuilding. Reconstruction, following plans by Coignard, took place from 1741 to 1756. The decoration is the work of Baron **Pfaff de Pfaffenhoffen** (1715-84) from Vienna, who was forced to leave his city after a duel.

## Abbey ★

🐾 Guided visits (1hr): Jun-Aug daily 10.30am-5.30pm (Sun, view the abbey's organ 5.30pm). Apr-May and Sep daily 11.30am-4.30pm. Oct-mid-Nov daily 11.30am-5.30pm (4.30pm at weekends and public holidays). ☜6.50€. ☎ 03 22 29 62 33. www.abbaye-valloires.com.

A 16C dovecote stands in front of the long building which is extended to the left and rear by the east front of the **abbey lodgings**; these in turn are surrounded by smaller buildings.

The simple cloister gallery has groined vaulting. The refectory is located on the ground floor of the east wing; the abbot's rooms and the monk's cells are upstairs. The vestry is decorated with wood panels by Pfaffenhoffen and paintings by Parrocel.

## Church ★

Inside, the **organ** (1) is supported by a gallery carved by Pfaffenhoffen with musical instruments; the statues at each side symbolise religion. The balustrade and small organ case are decorated with *putti* and cherub musicians. The beautiful **grilles** ★ (2) are of a graceful and light design: the central part is surmounted by the Valloires arms and Moses' brazen serpent (prefiguration of the Crucifixion), framed by baskets of flowers.

Two angels in gilded lead by Pfaffenhoffen are located around the high altar (3), dominated by a curious abbot's crook. The south transept houses recumbent effigies of a count and countess of Ponthieu (4). In the north transept is the window through which sick monks could follow services.

Carved religious emblems adorn the stalls (5); those reserved for the abbot and the prior stand on either side of the entrance to the apsidal chapel, which is decorated with wood panels by Pfaffenhoffen.

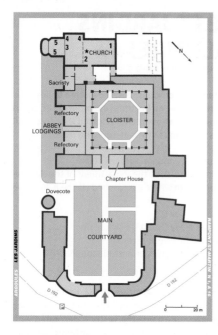

## Gardens★★

🕐*Open daily mid-Mar to mid-Nov 10am-6pm.* 🎫*7.50€* ☎ *03 22 23 53 55. www.jardinsdevalloires.com.*

This 7ha/17-acre park, landscaped in 1987 by Gilles Clément, contains 5 000 species of plants and trees, most of them from the northern hemisphere.

### Jardin à la française

Part of this is laid out in the formal French style reminiscent of Cistercian rigour. The plant cloister is surrounded by yew trees evoking the pillars of the abbey church. The white garden is matched by the yellow garden.

### Jardin des îles

The English-style park is laid out on high ground and includes an Island Garden whose colours change with the seasons. The **winter** island displays the subtle hues of maple and birch trees; the **gold** island is home to elder and hazelnut bushes; the **shadow** island contains plants which dislike sunlight such as weeping mulberry trees; the **cherry-tree** grove, near the **lilac** island, contains several flowering varieties of prunus; the **silver** island is located next to the **viburnum** island and its display of velvety white flowers. Other areas with evocative names include the **crimson-foliage** island, the **autumn** grove, the **butterfly** island and the island of **decorative fruit**, temptingly beautiful but sometimes poisonous, as well as the "**bizarretum**" where oddly shaped plants are gathered.

### Éspace Lamarck

This garden is dedicated to the evolution of species. It is named after the botanist **Jean-Baptiste Lamarck** (1744-1829) who was the first person to outline a theory of the evolution of living beings linked to the variations of their natural environment.

## Address Book

### WHERE TO STAY

⌂ **Hostellerie de l'Abbaye de Valloires** – *In the abbey* – *80120 Valloires* – ☎ *03 22 29 62 33. Closed 11 Nov to 1 Apr* – *18 rms* – 🍽 *6€.* This hostel, located in the very bosom of the Cistercian abbey, is an exceptionally fine setting for a contemplative retreat. Offering varying degrees of comfort, the rooms give onto the splendid gardens or the cloister (the latter offer private showers but the WCs are shared).

### SHOPPING

**Cité des artisans** – *80120 Valloires* – ☎ *03 21 81 83 94* – *Jul-Aug: 10am-noon, 2.30-7pm; Apr-Jun, Sep, Dec 2.30-7pm; Oct-Nov: Sat-Sun 2.30-7pm.* A big hall with booths selling all kinds of crafts: pottery, wooden toys, jewellery, etc. Regional products for sale include honey, preserves and sweets.

### Jardin des 5 sens

Kids The Garden of the Five Senses contains a selection of plants and trees connected with the different senses: strawberries and apples (taste), thorny plants (touch), aspens with leaves that rustle with the slightest breeze (hearing), colourful petunias (sight), jasmine, lily and mint (smell).

### Roseraie

The magnificent rose garden contains 2 000 plants of 100 different varieties, including the Valloires rose created in 1992 and the Delarle Cistercians' rose created in 1998 for the 900th anniversary of the Cistercian order. The roses grow among aromatic plants and medicinal herbs, such as would have been found in the monks' garden.

### Jardin de marais

Lower down lies the wilder Marsh Garden with its artificial canal reminiscent of the arm of the River Authie which used to flow across the estate.

# CHÂTEAU DE VAUX-LE-VICOMTE★★★

MICHELIN LOCAL MAP 312: F-4 OR MAP 106 FOLDS 45, 46

This château built by Fouquet, foreshadowed the splendour of Versailles and remains one of the greatest masterpieces of the 17C. A walk through the gardens laid out by Le Nôtre offers an unforgettable experience as does a tour of the château by candlelight.

- **Information:** ☎ 01 64 14 41 90. www.vaux-le-vicomte.com
- ▶ **Orient Yourself:** 6km (4 miles) northeast of Melun, and 57km (36 miles) south of Paris via the D 51 and then A 5.
- P **Parking:** On site.
- ◷ **Organizing Your Time:** Allow half a day.

## A Bit of History

### The rise of Nicolas Fouquet

Born to a family of magistrates, Fouquet became a member of the Parlement of Paris by the age of 20. He was made Procureur Général of this respectable assembly and was appointed Superintendent of Finances under Mazarin. Intoxicated with success, Fouquet chose a squirrel as his emblem – in Anjou patois *fouquet* means a squirrel – and decreed his motto would be *Quo non ascendam* (How high shall I not climb?).

In 1656 Fouquet decided to grace his own seignory of Vaux with a château worthy of his social standing. He showed excellent taste when it came to choosing his future "collaborators": the architect **Louis Le Vau**, the decorator **Charles Le Brun** and the landscape gardener **André Le Nôtre**. He was equally discerning in other matters; the famous chef Vatel was hired as his major-domo and La Fontaine as close adviser.

The builders were given carte blanche. A total of 18 000 workers took part in the project, which involved the demolition of three villages.

Le Brun created a tapestry works at Maincy to fulfil his commission. After Fouquet's fall it was moved to Paris, where it became the Manufacture Royale des Gobelins. The whole operation took five years to complete and the result was a masterpiece that Louis XIV wished to surpass with the construction of Versailles.

### An invitation to royal vexation

On 17 August 1661 Fouquet organised a fête for the King and his court, who were staying at Fontainebleau. The reception was one of dazzling splendour. The King's table featured a service

## WHERE TO STAY AND EAT

**Labordière (Bed and Breakfast)** –
*16 r. Grande, La Borde hamlet –
77820 Châtillon-la-Borde – 12km/7.2mi
SE of Vaux-le-Vicomte. Take D 215
and D 47 (via Blandy) then D 47E –
☎ 01 60 66 60 54. Closed Nov – 2 rms.*
This smallholding dating from 1850
adjoins the Borde town hall. Enjoy
the serenity of the large, leafy garden
and discover regional produce fresh
from the farms during your table d'hôte
meal. The bedrooms are somewhat
old-fashioned; the largest has
a sloping roof.

**La Ferme du Couvent** –
*77720 Bréau – 14.5/8.8mi east of Vaux-
le-Vicomte. Take D 408 Rte de Provins,
then left on D 227 – ☎ 01 64 38 75 15 –
9 rms.* A relaxing sojourn is guaranteed
in this 18C Briard farm set in a verdant
7ha/17 acre park. The rooms, with
sloping roofs, are all decorated with
creamy colours and modern furniture.

in solid gold; this detail annoyed him
intensely as his own tableware had
been sent back to the smelting works to
meet the expenses incurred by the
Thirty Years War.

After a banquet at which Vatel surpassed
himself, the guests feasted their eyes
on the garden entertainments, enhanced
by 1 200 fountains and cascades. The programme included country ballets, concerts, aquatic tournaments and lottery
games in which all the tickets won
prizes. It also included the première of
*Les Fâcheux,* a comedy ballet by Molière,
performed by the author and his
troupe against a delightful backdrop
of greenery.

The King was vexed by such an extravagant display of pomp and luxury, unparalleled at his own royal court. His first
impulse was to have Fouquet arrested
immediately but Anne of Austria managed to dissuade him.

### The fall of Nicolas Fouquet

Nineteen days later, the Superintendent
of Finances was sent to jail and all his
belongings sequestrated. The artists
who had designed and built Vaux
entered the King's service and were
later to produce the Palace of Versailles.
At the end of a three-year trial, Fouquet
was banished from court but this sen-
tence was altered by the King to perpetual imprisonment.

On account of her dowry, Fouquet's wife
was entitled to recover the ownership of
the château. After the death of her son,
the estate was bought by the Maréchal
de Villars in 1705, when it was made a
duchy peerage. It was sold in 1764 to one
of Louis XV's ministers, the Duc de Choi-
seul-Praslin, and survived the Revolution
without suffering too much damage.

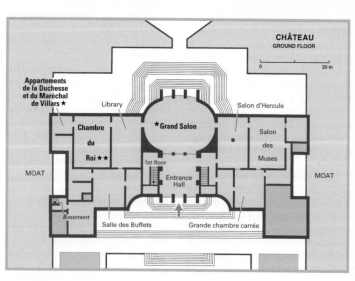

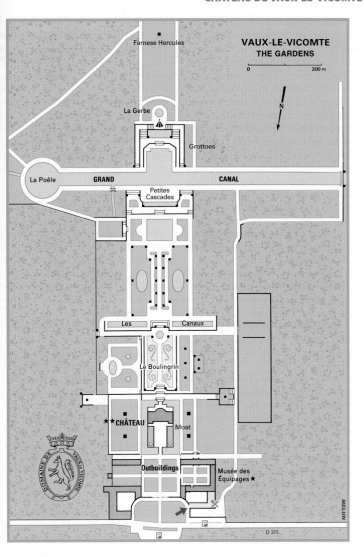

**VAUX-LE-VICOMTE**
THE GARDENS

0        200 m

Farnese Hercules

La Gerbe

Grottoes

La Poêle    **GRAND        CANAL**

Petites
Cascades

Les        Canaux

Le Boulingrin

**★★CHÂTEAU**    Moat

**Outbuildings**    Musée des
Équipages ★

MELUN

D 215

In 1875 Vaux was bought by a wealthy industrialist Mr Sommier, who applied himself to restoring and refurnishing the château, as well as refurbishing its grounds.

## Visit

*Available to visitors: L'Écureuil Restaurant, a boutique, 4-seater electric cars and "nautils" (animal-shaped boats to glide along the canal).*

### Château★★

*Open mid-Mar to mid-Nov 10am-6pm. May to mid-Oct candlelight visit Sat 8pm-midnight (Jul and Aug Fri and Sat). 12€; (candlelight visit 15€). 01 64 14 41 90. www.vaux-le-vicomte.com.*

The château stands on a terrace surrounded by a moat. The impressive approach leads toward the château's imposing northern front, with its tall windows indicating the *piano nobile* on a raised ground floor.

The first floor is occupied by the **suites of Mr and Mme Fouquet**.

You are shown the superintendent's antechamber (large ebony desk inlaid with gilt copper), his study and his bedroom (superb ceiling attributed to Jean Cotelle), followed by Mme Fouquet's boudoir, the Louis XV study and bedroom embellished with contemporary furniture and the Praslin bedchamber.

It is possible to climb another 80 steps to see the timberwork of the roof and the lantern of the dome which offers a super panoramic **view**★★ of the park.

Back on the ground floor, the **Grande Chambre carrée**, has the only Louis XIII interior in the château, with a French-style ceiling.

Six reception rooms looking onto the gardens are laid out on either side of the Grand Salon.

**Grand Salon**★ – This room, crowned by the central dome, was left unfinished after Fouquet's arrest and lacks decoration. The only remains of the original furnishings are two marble tables, as well as six statues and six paintings discovered by Mr Sommier when he moved in.

**Chambre du Roi**★★ – The King's bedchamber communicates with the former antechamber (now a library beautifully furnished in the Regency style). Its decoration is characteristic of the Louis XIV style that was to leave its mark on the State Apartments at Versailles.

**Appartements de la Duchesse et du Maréchal de Villars**★ – The Duchesse de Villars' boudoir formed part of the king's apartments; note the allegorical portrait of the duchess by Coypel and *Queen Marie Leszczynska's Visit to Vaux* in 1728. After the Maréchal's study, which houses archives of his campaigns, comes his bedroom with a splendid **baldaquined bed**★★, decorated with embroidered draperies.

**Salle à manger**★ – The Salle des Buffets probably served as a dining room in Fouquet's time. It gives onto a wood-panelled passageway hung with paintings, where a long row of dressers would receive the bowls of fruit and other dishes brought from the distant kitchens.

A tour of the basement shows a number of rooms (Salle des Plans, Salle des Archives) and the kitchen quarters, which were used up to 1956. Note the servant's dining hall, complete with a fully laid table.

**Outbuildings** – The **Musée des Équipages**★ *(as for the château)* lies in the western outbuildings, next to the visitors' entrance. It presents harnessing and saddlery, an old-fashioned smithy and fully equipped carriages.

## Gardens★★★

*Same opening hours as for the château.*

Mr Sommier carefully restored Le Nôtre's masterpiece, of which the most striking feature is its sweeping perspective. The grounds offer several "optical illusions," including the discovery of basins which are not visible from the château.

Walk to the far end of the upper terrace to get a good view of the southern façade. The central dome and its surmounting lantern turret, the corner pavilions, heavier than on the north side, and the decoration of the forepart, crowned by statues, form an impressive, if somewhat heavy, composition.

The three main water perspectives – the moat, the two rectangular canals and the **Grand Canal** – suddenly come into view in a most impressive manner.

The Grand Canal – known as the *"poêle"* (frying pan) on account of its rounded extremity – is approached by a steep flight of steps level with the Petites Cascades located opposite the grottoes. The niches at each end house two statues of river gods, some of the most important examples of 17C sculpture at Vaux; these Mlle de Scudéry fondly imagined to be the Tiber and the Anqueuil (local name given to the Almont stream).

Skirt the Grand Canal and walk up to the foot of the Farnese *Hercules* which hides the great perspective. The very last basin aptly called the spray – La Gerbe – affords an extensive **view**★ of the château and its stately grounds.

# CHÂTEAU DE VERSAILLES★★★

MICHELIN LOCAL MAP 311: I-3, MAP 101 FOLDS 22, 23 OR 106 FOLDS 17, 18

Versailles epitomises the golden age of French royalty and, except under the Regency, it remained the seat of government and the political centre of France from 1682 to 1789. The outstanding royal residence consists of the palace, its grounds and the Trianons. When night falls, the château glitters as some 500 lighting devices enhance the elegance of the palace gates and of the avenue leading to the château, highlighting the chapel and the Marble court. The prestigious domain is now protected as one of UNESCO's World Heritage sites.

▶ **Orient Yourself:** 18km (11 miles) west of Paris. Access from Paris: By car: A 13 motorway toward Rouen, exit Versailles, Vaucresson. By RER: Line C to Versailles-Rive-Gauche. By train: from St-Lazare Station to Versailles-Rive-droite; from Montparnasse Station to Versailles-Chantiers. The various tours start from different entrances. (👣 see the "Visiting Tips" box for a list of entrances). Use the small site plan for an overview of the complex. The larger plan of the château can help guide you through the various rooms on all three floors.

🅿 **Parking:** There is an entrance fee for cars of 4.50€ (5.50€ on weekends and public holidays)

👓 **Don't Miss:** The Garden Façade; the Chapel, the Salon d'Hercule, the Grand Appartement, the Louis XiV and Louis XV suites, and of course, the Hall of Mirrors. For an unforgettable experience, make a point of visiting Versailles when the fountains are in operation throughout the gardens (👣 see Parc du château VERSAILLES).

🕐 **Organizing Your Time:** Plan to spend an entire day at Versailles. Guided tours of individual sections of the château (such as the King's Quarters) generally average one hour each. Even a quick tour of the gardens requires three hours. The grounds are open from sunrise to sunset, so arrive early. They can be explored before and after the buildings close. Factor in time for the outdoor evening festivities as well (👣 see Address Book in Parc du château VERSAILLES).

Kids **Especially for Kids:** Children will enjoy a boat ride, or the mini-train around the grounds (👣 see Address Book in Parc du château VERSAILLES).

Palace gates, Versailles

Ph. Gajic/MICHELIN

# A Bit of History

### Louis XIII's hunting lodge
In the 17C the locality of Versailles was the seat of a medieval castle perched on a hillock. At the foot lay the village, surrounded by marshes and woodland abounding in game. Louis XIII used to come hunting here often, and in 1624 he bought the lordship of Versailles from the Gondi family and commissioned a small château built of brick, stone and slate.

### The glorious task of taming nature
The year 1661 marked Louis XIV's accession to power. The King hired the various artists, builders, designers and landscape architects who had produced Vaux-le-Vicomte and entrusted them with an even more challenging task. Louis was wary of settling in Paris following the Fronde uprisings and so searched for a site on the outskirts of the capital. He chose Versailles as he had spent many happy days there as a boy and, moreover, he was fond of hunting. It was by no means an ideal site; the mound was too narrow to allow Louis XIII's château to be enlarged.

### An ambitious project
In the early stages, **Louis Le Vau** built a stone construction around the small château in 1668; it was reminiscent of Italian architecture and was aptly named the "Enveloppe". André Le Nôtre designed the new gardens and created his celebrated perspectives. Up to 36 000 men worked on the site. The first receptions were held at the new château in 1664.

In 1678 **Jules Hardouin-Mansart**, aged only 31, was appointed head architect. From 1661 to 1683 **Charles Le Brun** supervised a team of accomplished painters, sculptors, carvers and interior decorators. **Le Nôtre** applied himself to the embellishment of the grounds. When designing the waterworks, he joined forces with the Francines, a family of Italian engineers. It was necessary to build a hill to accommodate the entire length of the château (680m/2 230ft). Whole forests were transplanted and the King's gardeners produced 150 000 new flowering plants every year.

The problem of water supply was of great concern. The waters of Clagny Pond – located near the present Rive Droite railway station – proved insufficient and the builders were forced to divert the course of the Bièvre and drain the Saclay plateau. The Marly Machine conveyed the waters pumped from the River Seine, but the diversion of the Eure ( *see Maintenon*) was a fiasco.

It took 50 years to complete the structural work on the palace at Versailles.

### Life at Court
When the King and his entourage moved to Versailles, the palace and the adjacent outbuildings were required to lodge at least 3 000 people.

## Louis XIV's artistic taste

Louis XIV, whose education was neglected owing to the rebellion known as the "Fronde", inherited from his mother, Anne of Austria, an inclination for politeness and refinement and acquired from Mazarin a collector's passion. The festivities organised at Vaux-le-Vicomte showed him how splendid garden entertainment and fountains could be. The King, who spoke Italian and Spanish fluently, made his court the melting pot of his own aesthetic values reflected by festivities, balls, games and fashion. Until 1671, the King performed on stage (dressed as the Sun in the *Ballet de la Nuit* in 1653), playing the roles of gods or mythological heroes, Roman emperors, even Alexander the Great. He particularly liked music and had a good ear. He often played the guitar, "better than a master" according to Palatine, and learned to play the harpsichord which he appreciated at the end of his life thanks to Couperin; he kept himself informed of Delalande's compositions and Lully's operas, attended rehearsals and sang arias. Evolved from a hunting lodge, Versailles was thus designed for music with the chapel as its temple.

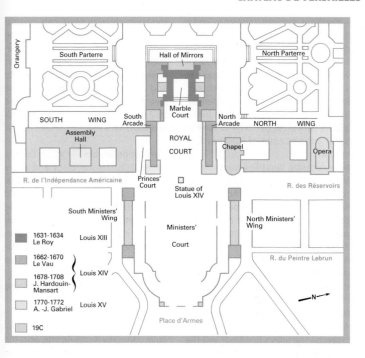

The Fronde movement had been a humiliating experience for the King, who had witnessed many intrigues involving men in high places. Consequently, his main concern was to keep the aristocracy with him at court, in an attempt to stifle opposition that might threaten the stability of the throne. The lavish entertainments suited his extravagant tastes and served to keep the nobility under his thumb. For the first time in French history, the royal suites in the palace were given fixed, permanent furnishings. Thanks to Colbert's efforts to encourage the production of luxury goods (tapestries, furniture, lace etc) on a national scale, the palace – which remained open to the public – offered a standing exhibition of arts and crafts in France.

Strict etiquette governed the visits that the French people would pay to Versailles. The famous chronicler Saint-Simon described a day at court as a "clockwork ceremony" consisting of a series of banquets, audiences and entertainments.

## Versailles in the 18C

When Louis XIV died in 1715 his successor was still a young boy. The Regent Philippe d'Orléans ad-ministered the King's affairs from the Palais-Royal in Paris. During this time, the court left Versailles and moved to the Tuileries.

In 1722 **Louis XV**, aged 12, decided to settle at Versailles. In order that royal etiquette might not interfere with his private life, he gave orders to convert several of the private apartments. He dreamed of having the front of the palace remodelled, a task he entrusted to Jacques-Anges **Gabriel**. Unfortunately, no major alterations could be carried out owing to insufficient funds, but the Petit Trianon was built.

**Louis XVI** commissioned no major works. However, he gave Marie-Antoinette the Petit Trianon completed by Gabriel in 1768 and had the hamlet designed for her in 1774. On 6 October 1789, the national insurrection forced the royal family to return to Paris. After that date, Versailles ceased to be a place of residence for the kings of France.

## To the glory of France

After the storming of the Tuileries and the fall of the monarchy on 10 August 1792, most of the furniture was removed and auctioned. The major works of art

– paintings, carpets, tapestries and a few items of furniture – were kept for the art museum which opened in the Louvre in August 1793. After the renovation work undertaken by Napoleon and Louis XVIII, Versailles was threatened once more; it was spared demolition by Louis-Philippe, who contributed a large part of his personal fortune to turn it into a museum of French history in 1837.

More recently, Versailles was restored following the First World War, thanks to the generosity of the Academy of Fine Arts and the handsome contributions made by a number of wealthy patrons, including the American JD Rockefeller.

A major **restoration** campaign was launched in the early 1950s, permitting the renovation of the Royal Opera, the installation of central heating and electric lighting, and the completion of various refurnishing and maintenance projects. The King's Bedroom and the Hall of Mirrors, in particular, were both restored to their 18C splendour. More restoration work undertaken in 1995 is scheduled to be completed in 2015.

# The Château And Its Surroundings

*The courtyards of the château and of the Trianon as well as the grounds can be visited freely every day from sunrise to sunset. Entrance fee for cars: ⊜4.50€ (5.50€ on Sat-Sun and public holidays). An entrance fee is also charged for visits to the château gardens during the Musical Fountains events and from Apr to end Oct: ⊜3€ (Musical Fountains: 6€). ☎ 01 30 83 78 98.*

## Courtyards★★

The wrought-iron railings date from the reign of Louis XVIII. Beyond them stretches a series of three courtyards.

The forecourt or **Cour des Ministres** is flanked by two long wings linking the four pavilions in which the King's ministers were accommodated.

An equestrian statue of Louis XIV, commissioned by Louis-Philippe, stands in the middle of the drive. The **Cour royale** was separated from the outer courtyard

by railings through which only persons of high rank (peers, princes of the blood, noblemen etc) might pass in carriages. The two wings lining this court were originally separate from the palace and used as outbuildings. They were joined to the main building and fronted by a set of colonnades under Louis XV and Louis XVIII.

The **Cour de Marbre**★★ (Marble Court) – paved with slabs of black and white marble – has been raised to its original level. It is surrounded by Louis XIII's old château, the façades of which were altered and greatly improved by Louis Le Vau and Jules Hardouin-Mansart: balustrades, busts, statues, vases etc. On the first floor of the central pavilion, the three arched windows belonging to the king's bedroom are fronted by a gilded balcony resting upon eight marble columns.

## Garden Façade★★★

*Walk under the North Arcade, skirt the main part of the palace and step back to get a good view.*

The huge building occupies a total length of 680m/2 230ft and yet its general appearance is not monotonous; the central body stands proud from the wings, and the length of the façade is articulated with intermittent rows of sculpted columns and pillars to break the rigidity of the horizontal lines. The flat roof, built in the Italian style, is concealed by a balustrade bearing ornamental trophies and vases. The statues of Apollo and Diana, surrounded by the Months of the Year, surmount the central body which housed the Royal Suite. Certain members of the royal family, including several of the King's children, stayed in the South Wing.

The terrace extending in front of the château commands an extensive view of the park and its many perspectives. It bears two **giant vases**★, one at each end; the one to the north was executed by Coysevox and symbolises War, while the south vase, attributed to Tuby, is a representation of Peace. They are appropriately placed outside the bay windows of the Salon de la Guerre and the Salon de la Paix respectively.

At the foot of the main building lies a row

of four sculptures, the very first to be cast by the Keller brothers who drew inspiration from a classical model: Bacchus, Apollo, Antinoüs and Silenus.

The terrace offers a general **view**★ of the grounds and their distinctive features (*description below*): in the foreground the Water Gardens (*Parterres d'Eau*), with a sweeping perspective as far as the Grand Canal: on the left the South Parterre (*Parterre du Midi*); on the right the North Parterre (*Parterre du Nord*) and groves (*Bosquets du Nord*), cut across by another canal leading to the Neptune Basin. *Return to the Cour de Marbre through the South Arcade in the south wing.*

## Music

Concerts of works by 17C and 18C French composers are given by the Baroque Music Centre (October to December) in various venues: the Opéra royal, the Chapelle royale, the Salon d'Hercule, the Galerie basse…Information and reservations ☎ 01 39 20 78 10.

The success which the château enjoys leads to overcrowding, which can be unpleasant. This problem already existed during the reign of the Sun King: courtiers in sedan chairs, tradesmen, footmen, musicians and workers cluttered the corridors of the château and a great number of Swiss guards were required to keep this colourful crowd under control.

# Tour of the Grands Appartements

🕓 *Open daily (except Mon) Apr-Oct: 9am-6.30pm. Nov-Mar 5.30pm.* ☜ *7.50€. Last admission 30min before closing time.* 🕓 *Closed 1 Jan, 1 May, 25 Dec.* ☎ 01 30 83 76 20.

The visitors' entrance (Entrance **A**) leads through to a vestibule which houses the ticket office. From there, go to the Salles des Croisades.

## Salles des Croisades★

The five rooms, decorated in a neo-Gothic style, illustrate events that took place during the crusades and contain a collection of paintings commissioned by Louis-Philippe. The emblems of the families who took part in the crusades

decorate the pillars, coffered ceilings and part of the walls.

## 17C Galleries

These small rooms – occupying the greater part of the north wing – feature a charming selection of paintings and portraits, also busts and console tables. *Visitors will eventually be able to see all these rooms without joining a guided tour.*

**Ground Floor** – *Group visits only*. The vestibule by the chapel leads to this suite of 11 rooms. The first six were once occupied by the Duc de Maine, the son of Louis XIV and Mme de Montespan, while the last four housed the apartments of the Princes of Bourbon-Conti.

The series of portraits includes Henri IV, who enjoyed visiting the site of Versailles, and Louis XIII, the founder of the original château.

**First Floor** – Portraits of the royal family, Mme de Maintenon, Louis XIV's legitimised children and the celebrated figures of the King's reign, painted by Le Brun, Mignard Van der Meulen, Coypel, Rigaud Largillière etc, bring these rooms to life.

Note the set of portraits of famous men (Colbert, Racine, Molière, La Fontaine, Le Nôtre and Couperin) and the vast battle scenes by Van der Meulen, characterised by attention to detail and a true love of nature.

▸ *You reach the level of the chapel gallery.*

## Chapel★★★

☜ *Guided tours combined with a visit of the Appartement du Roi.*

Only in 1710 was the chapel finished, by which time Louis XIV was 72.

Dedicated to St Louis (Louis IX), the chapel at Versailles is an elegant display of stonework decorated in white and gold tones. This masterpiece is the work of Mansart and was completed by his brother-in-law Robert de Cotte in 1710. The pillars and arches bear exquisite bas-reliefs by, among others, Van Clève, Le Lorrain, Coustou.

As the usual place for an organ is occupied by the royal gallery it stands instead at the east end in the gallery, a splendid

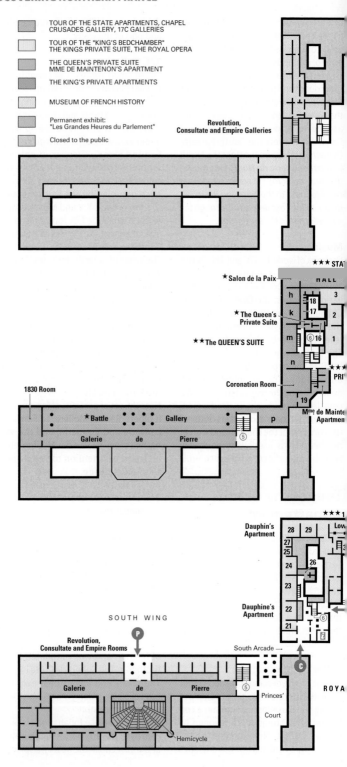

TOUR OF THE STATE APARTMENTS, CHAPEL
CRUSADES GALLERY, 17C GALLERIES

TOUR OF THE "KING'S BEDCHAMBER"
THE KINGS PRIVATE SUITE, THE ROYAL OPERA

THE QUEEN'S PRIVATE SUITE
MME DE MAINTENON'S APARTMENT

THE KING'S PRIVATE APARTMENTS

MUSEUM OF FRENCH HISTORY

Permanent exhibit:
"Les Grandes Heures du Parlement"

Closed to the public

Revolution,
Consultate and Empire Galleries

★★★ STAT

HALL

★ Salon de la Paix

★ The Queen's
Private Suite

★★ The QUEEN'S SUITE

h    18    3
k    17    2
m    6 16   1
n           ★★★
            PRI

Coronation Room

1830 Room    19
             Mme de Mainte
             Apartmen

★ Battle    Gallery    p

Galerie    de    Pierre    5

★★★ 1

Dauphin's
Apartment    28    29    Low

27
25
24    26
23

Dauphine's    22
Apartment    21    6

SOUTH WING

P

Revolution,
Consultate and Empire Rooms

South Arcade

C

Galerie    de    Pierre    5
                          Princes'

Court

ROYA

Hemicycle

# CHÂTEAU DE VERSAILLES

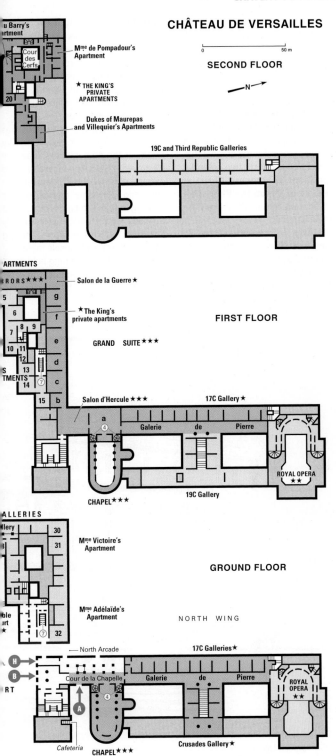

0         50 m

## SECOND FLOOR

—N—→

u Barry's
artment

Cour
des
Cerfs

Mme de Pompadour's
Apartment

20

★ THE KING'S
PRIVATE
APARTMENTS

Dukes of Maurepas
and Villequier's Apartments

19C and Third Republic Galleries

ARTMENTS

RORS ★★★

Salon de la Guerre ★

5

6

g

f

★ The King's
private apartments

## FIRST FLOOR

7

8  9

e

GRAND   SUITE ★★★

10  11

12

d

S

13

TMENTS

⑦

c

14

15

b

Salon d'Hercule ★★★

17C Gallery ★

a
④

Galerie

de

Pierre

CHAPEL ★★★

19C Gallery

ROYAL OPERA
★★

ALLERIES

lery

30

31

Mme Victoire's
Apartment

## GROUND FLOOR

Mme Adélaïde's
Apartment

NORTH   WING

ble
rt
★

⑦

32

North Arcade

17C Galleries ★

H

B

Cour de la Chapelle

Galerie

de

Pierre

RT

A

ROYAL
OPERA
★★

Cafeteria

CHAPEL ★★★

Crusades Gallery ★

piece of craftsmanship by Clicquot, enhanced by fine carvings based on studies by Robert de Cotte.

While the members of the royal family were seated in the gallery, the courtiers stood in the nave.

### Salon d'Hercule★★★

This drawing room stands on the site formerly occupied by the fourth and penultimate chapel of the original château. The room boasts two splendid compositions by Veronese. **Christ at the House of Simon the Pharisee**★ was a present to Louis XIV from the Venetian Republic.

**The ceiling** – representing Hercules entering the Kingdom of the Gods – was painted by François Lemoyne. His work met with widespread acclaim, but the following year the artist suffered a nervous breakdown and committed suicide (1737).

### Grand Appartement★★★

The Grand Appartement consists of six salons, built by Le Vau in 1668 and decorated by Le Brun, running from the Salon d'Hercule, dedicated to a man endowed with divine powers, to the Salon d'Apollon, built in honour of the son of Jupiter and Latona.

In former times, the apartment was approached from the Royal Court by means of the Ambassadors' Staircase (destroyed in 1752). It provides a splendid example of early Louis XIV decoration.

The Grand Appartement symbolised the solar myth to which Louis XIV claimed to belong. Most of the time, it was sparsely furnished with a few stools, folding chairs, pedestal and console tables.

Three times a week, the King held court in the Grand Appartement. The ceremony was enhanced by dancing and gaming.

*Versailles – garden façade*

## 😊 Visiting Tips 😊

### ENTRANCES

The various tours of the château start from different entrances:

Entrance **A**: State apartments (except groups)

Entrance **B**: State apartments (groups)

Entrance **C**: The King' and Dauphin's apartments (audo-guided tours, except groups)

Entrance **D**: Guided tours (same-day bookings, except groups)

Entrance **H**: Access reserved for disabled visitors

Entrance **P**: The milestones of the French Parliament history

**Salon de l'Abondance** (**b**) – At the time of Louis XIV, on the days when the King held court, this reception room contained three buffets: one for hot drinks, and two for cold drinks such as wine, eaux-de-vie, sorbets and fruit juice. The walls are hung with the winter furnishings, made of embossed velvet in deep emerald tones.

**Salon de Vénus** (**c**) – The ceiling of this salon and those of the following rooms were painted by Houasse. It features decorated panels framed by heavy gilt stucco.

**Salon de Diane** (**d**) – This used to be the billiard room under Louis XIV. Observe the **bust of Louis XIV** by Bernini (1665), a remarkable piece of Baroque workmanship. The room displays several paintings by De Lafosse and Blanchard.

**Salon de Mars** (**e**) – The lavish decoration (wall hangings) is a reminder that

D. Hée/ MICHELIN

## Grands Appartements (State Apartments)

These consist of the various reception rooms – the Salon d'Hercule and a suite of six rooms known as the Grands Appartements – together with the famous Hall of Mirrors (*Galerie des Glaces*) and the living quarters where the king and queen would appear in public.

While visiting the palace, it is helpful to remember a few facts concerning the layout of great châteaux of Classical and Baroque inspiration.

Generally speaking, French rulers would spend their day between the ornate reception rooms of the State Apartments – their official, semi-public quarters – and the private apartments which afforded a certain amount of privacy. In the 18C, Louis XV and later Louis XVI enjoyed a greater degree of intimacy in the Petits Appartements.

**A standard example of State Apartments** – The two suites belonging to the king and the queen are placed symmetrically on either side of the central pavilion. Each suite consisted of at least one guard-room, several antechambers, the bedroom, the grand cabinet and a number of private drawing rooms (it was through these that the two royal suites communicated).

At Versailles, this symmetrical disposition was applied only between 1673 and 1682. When Marie-Thérèse died in 1683, there was no question of Mme de Maintenon occupying the apartments of the former queen. Louis XIV moved into new quarters overlooking the Marble Court. His former suite was transformed, at great cost, into a series of reception rooms.

**Summer and winter furnishings** – In the living quarters of the palace, the hangings were changed twice a year, at the beginning of summer and before the onset of winter. Thus the summer furnishings (silk) alternated with the winter furnishings (velvet).

The fabric-dressed walls were then hung with paintings inspired by religious themes, by artists of the Italian School: Poussin, Veronese, Titian etc.

---

this room once belonged to the royal suite (guard-room). Louis XIV subsequently used it for dances, games and concerts. The two galleries which housed the musicians were placed on either side of the fireplace. They were dismantled in 1750. One of the Sun King's favourite paintings hangs above the fireplace: Domenichino's *King David*, in which he is portrayed playing the harp.

**Salon de Mercure** (f) – A fire was lit in this former antechamber on the evenings when the King held court. It was here that Louis XIV lay in state for one week after his death in 1715.

**Salon d'Apollon (Throne Room)** (g) – The former Throne Room. The throne was placed on a central platform covered by a large canopy. The three hooks to which the canopy was attached still remain.

The King received ambassadors in this chamber. When he held court, it was used for dances and concerts. The ceiling sports a fresco by De Lafosse: *Apollo in a Sun Chariot*.

This room marks the end of the Grand Appartement. Set at a perpendicular angle, the Hall of Mirrors and the adjacent rooms dedicated to war and peace occupy the entire length of the main front giving onto the palace gardens.

### Salon de la Guerre★ (War Salon)

This is a corner room joining the Hall of Mirrors and the Grands Appartements; it features a huge oval low-relief sculpture by Coysevox, representing the king defeating his enemies.

### Galerie des Glaces★★★ (Hall of Mirrors)

The Hall of Mirrors was completed by Mansart in 1686. It covered a short-lived terrace (1668-78) that Le Vau had built along the side overlooking the gardens. Together with the Salon de la Guerre and Salon de la Paix, it is the most brilliant achievement by Le Brun and his team of artists. The 17 large windows are echoed by 17 mirrors on the wall opposite. These are made up of 578 pieces of the largest size possible at the time. This hall was designed to catch the golden rays of sunset. The ceiling fresco pays tribute to the early reign of Louis XIV (from 1661 to 1678, up to the Treaty of Nijmegen).

The Hall of Mirrors was used for court receptions, formal ceremonies and diplomatic encounters. On these occasions, the throne was placed under the arch leading into the Salon de la Paix. It is easier to picture the hall during court festivities, when it was thronged with elegant visitors in formal attire, brightly lit by the thousands of flickering candles reflected in the mirrors. The tubs bearing the orange trees, as well as the chandeliers and other furnishings, were made of solid silver in Louis XIV's time.

In 1980 the Hall of Mirrors was restored to its former glory. With its crystal chandeliers and new set of candelabra – cast after the six surviving originals – it presents the same dazzling appearance as in 1770 when Marie-Antoinette was married to the Dauphin, the future King Louis XVI.

It was here that the German Empire was proclaimed on 18 January 1871, and that the Treaty of Versailles was signed on 28 June 1919.

The central windows offer a splendid **view**★★★ of the Grand Perspective.

## Salon de la Paix★ (Peace Salon)

Placed at the southern end of the Hall of Mirrors, this chamber counterbalances the Salon de la Guerre. Originally designed as an extension of the great gallery, it was made into an annex of the Queen's Suite toward the end of Louis XIV's reign; it communicated with the Hall of Mirrors by means of a movable partition.

Above the mantelpiece hangs *Louis XV Bringing Peace to Europe*, a painting by François Lemoyne.

## Appartement de la Reine★★ (Queen's Suite)

This suite was created for Louis XIV's wife Marie-Thérèse, who died here in 1683.

**Chambre de la reine** (h) – In 1975, after a restoration programme lasting 30 years, this room regained its summer furnishings of 1787. Originally designed for Marie-Thérèse, the bedchamber was later occupied by the wife of the Grand Dauphin, Louis XIV's son; by the Duchesse de Bourgogne, wife of the Sun King's grandson, who gave birth to Louis XV here; by Marie Leszczynska, wife of Louis XV (for 43 years); and by Louis XVI's wife Marie-Antoinette. Nineteen children belonging to French royalty – among them Louis XV and Philippe V of Spain – were born in this bedroom.

A long-standing tradition ruled that the delivery of royal infants should be made in public. Even the proud Marie-Antoinette had to comply with this custom, surrounded by curious onlookers.

Note the magnificent silk hangings and furnishings decorated with flowers, ribbons and peacock tails, which were rewoven to the original pattern in Lyon.

**Salon des Nobles de la Reine** (k) – The official presentations to the Queen took place in this former antechamber. It was also here that the queens and dauphins of France used to lie in state prior to the burial ceremony. The original fresco on the ceiling, attributed to Michel Corneille, has been preserved. The rest of the decoration was considered staid and old-fashioned by Marie-Antoinette, who had it entirely refurbished by the architect Richard Mique (1785). Furnished with commodes and corner cupboards by Riesener and embellished with magnificent green silk hangings, the salon looks very much as it would have done on the eve of the French Revolution in 1789.

**Antichambre du Grand Couvert** (m) – This chamber was used as a guardroom under Marie-Thérèse. It was here that Louis XV and Marie Leszczynska – and later Louis XVI and Marie-Antoinette – would dine in full view of the public. A family portrait of Marie-Antoinette and her children (1787) by Mme Vigée-Lebrun hangs here.

Salle des gardes de la Reine (n) – The decoration was the work of Le Brun and N Coypel. It was moved from its original setting – the Salon de Jupiter – when the Hall of Mirrors was completed in 1687; the Salon de Jupiter was subsequently renamed the Salon de la Guerre. On 6 October 1789, several of the queen's guards were stabbed to death by a group of dedicated revolutionaries.

### Salle du sacre (Coronation Room)

This room was initially used as a chapel between 1676 and 1682. The Parlement of Paris used to hold its sessions in this former guard-room. It was altered by Louis-Philippe in order to accommodate several huge paintings depicting the Emperor's coronation. David's second *Coronation of Napoleon* – painted between 1808 and 1822 – lies to the left of the entrance. The original is exhibited in the Louvre Museum (Salle Mollien). On the opposite wall hang David's *Distribution of Eagles on the Champ de Mars* and a painting by Gros representing *Murat at the Battle of Aboukir* (1806). Salle de 1792 (p) – This large, unfurnished room lies at the junction of the south wing and the main central pavilion. The walls are hung with portraits of soldiers, paintings of famous battles and war scenes. Cogniet's work *The Paris National Guard* shows Louis-Philippe proudly sporting his Lieutenant-General's uniform.

### Galerie des batailles★

Created in 1837 on the site of the princes' suite in the south wing, the Galerie des Batailles caused quite a stir because of its huge dimensions (120m/394ft by 13m/43ft).

It was designed to house the 33 paintings of France's major victories under the Ancien Régime, the Empire and the Re-public, from Tolbiac (*first on the left when entering*) to Wagram (*first on the right*) by Horace Vernet, Louis-Philippe's favourite painter (who also painted Iéna, Fontenoy, Bouvines and Friedland), and including works by Eugène Delacroix (Taillebourg) and Baron Gérard (Austerlitz).

### Salle de 1830

Commissioned by Louis-Philippe, this room is devoted to the last king of France, who was known as the "Citizen-king."

▶ *Take the Princes' Staircase V down to the Cour des Princes.*

# Chambre du Roi★★★

*Audio-guided tour. Entrance C. ⌁ Guided tours (1hr) daily (except Mon) 9am-4pm (Apr-Oct 5pm). ⌁4.50€, extra cost to be added to the basic entrance fee. ☎ 01 30 83 77 88.*

### Appartement du Roi★★★ (Louis XIV's Suite)

The king's quarters are arranged around the Cour de Marbre. They were designed by Jules Hardouin-Mansart and set up in Louis XIII's château between 1682 and 1701. The style shows a marked change in the Louis XIV period. The ceilings are no longer coffered but painted white, the marble tiling has been replaced by white and gold panelling, and large mirrors adorn the stately fireplaces.

**Escalier de la Reine** – Toward the end of the Ancien Régime, the Queen's Staircase was the official entrance to the royal apartments. The decoration of the staircase is extremely ornate; from the top landing, admire the elegant display of multicoloured marble designed by Le Brun. The huge *trompe-l'œil* painting is jointly attributed to Meusnier, Poerson and Belin de Fontenay.

The guard-room (1) and a first antechamber (2) lead to the Salon de l'Œil-de-Bœuf.

**Salon de l'Œil-de-Bœuf** (second antechamber) (3) – The Bulls'-Eye Chamber was originally two rooms: the king's bedchamber between 1684 and 1701 – the part nearest to the two windows looking onto the Cour de Marbre – and a small study. The two were united under the supervision of Mansart and Robert de Cotte. Lightness and elegance are the principal characteristics of this charming drawing room, which contrasts sharply with the earlier achievements of Louis' reign. Level with the famous bull's-eye – echoed by a mirror on the opposite wall – runs a frieze depicting children at play. Note Coysevox' bust of Louis XIV.

It was in this antechamber that the courtiers assembled before witnessing the rising and retiring ceremonies of the king.

**Chambre du Roi** (4) – This became Louis XIV's state bedroom in 1701. At the centre of the palace, this bedroom, which looks onto the Cour de Marbre, faces in the direction of the rising sun. Louis XIV, suffering from a gangrenous knee, died here on 1 September 1715. The ritual rising and retiring ceremonies took place in this room from 1701 to 1789. Daytime visitors were requested to make a small bow when passing in front of the bed, which symbolised the divine right of the monarchy.

The King's bedroom is hung with its summer furnishings of 1722 – Louis XV's second year at the palace. Beyond the beautifully restored gilded balustrade is a raised four-poster bed, complete with canopy and curtains.

**Salle du Conseil** (5) – Like the Salon de l'Œil-de-Bœuf, this originally consisted of two rooms: the Cabinet des Termes and the Cabinet du Conseil. The decoration of the present room – created under Louis XV – was entrusted to Gabriel. The mirrors dating from Louis XIV's reign were replaced with wainscoting by Rousseau, who produced a splendid Rococo interior.

Over a period of 100 years, many grave decisions affecting the destiny of France were taken in this council chamber, including that of France's involvement in the American War of Independence in 1775.

## Appartement du Dauphin

*From the Salon de l'Œil-de-Bœuf, go down a small staircase leading to the Dauphin's apartments.*

These rooms have partially retained or regained their 18C ornamentation and have been redecorated and sometimes refurnished. All this contributes to combine artistic appeal and historic interest. Access is through the first antechamber displaying portraits of the main "dauphins" (heirs to the throne).

The entrance was through the **Salle des Gardes** (*on the right*), which is now decorated with splendid Gobelins tapestries. The second antechamber completes the first by exhibiting portraits of Louis XV's daughters by Nattier.

**Chambre du Dauphin** (29) – Occupied from 1684, first of all by Louis XIV's son and then by subsequent heirs to the throne until 1789 (the last occupant was Louis XVI's son), this has retained its original 1747 décor: wardrobe with lacquered panels (Bernard Van Rysenburgh – BVRB), commode by Boudin and an 18C embroidered canopied bed.

**Grand Cabinet du Dauphin** (28) – This room houses portraits of Mesdames Adélaïde, Louise, Sophie and Victoire by Nattier, as well as some beautiful pieces of furniture by Jacob, taken from Louis XVI's gaming room at St-Cloud. The amazing globe was commissioned by Louis XVI for his son's education.

**Bibliothèque** (27) – The library boasts magnificent wooden panelling in deep amber tones, enhanced by turquoise relief work. Admire Vernet's delicate seascapes above the doors. This room leads

---

### Daily life at Versailles

The court included some 4 000 to 5 000 people altogether, and up to 10 000 on crowded days according to Madame de Sévigné. The *Grand Maître de la Maison du Roi* (Grand Master of the King's Household), a post held since 1641 by the Prince de Condé, was in charge of food supplies. Suppliers were keen financiers who advanced the necessary funds and paid themselves back through advantages bestowed by the king. The remains of royal feasts were sold by all those who ordered, prepared and served the dishes. This was a very lucrative business. Meat and fish were sold to the town's shopkeepers through the château's Swiss guards; drinks, coffee, chocolate were sold from kiosks made of plaster or wood, located near the access ramps or the gates. Courtiers had no kitchens and had to be content with warming up dishes bought in this way. Improvised kitchens, dish-warmers and coal shops caused the upper and lower galleries to stink. If you add to this the continuous flow of visitors and lawyers who, provided they were properly dressed (men could hire swords at the castle entrance), mingled with the courtiers hoping to catch a glimpse of the king on his way to the chapel through the Grands Appartements, you can well imagine the crowds.

*Marie-Antoinette and her children by Vigée-Lebrun*

several corner cupboards by Bernard Van Rysenburgh (BVRB). If one compares the Savonnerie tapestry with that of the next room, one notices that the fleur-de-lis motifs have been replaced by stars (Revolution).

**Deuxième antichambre (22)** – The fireplace, adorned with a bust of the Regent, was taken from the Queen's Bedroom at the time of Marie Leszczynska. Savonnerie tapestry.

**Première antichambre (21)** – This houses a number of pictures representing the rulers who succeeded the Sun King: portrait of the five-year-old Louis XV by Alexis Belle (1723), *Cavalcade of the King (Louis XV) after His Coronation on 22 October 1722* by Pierre-Denis Martin.

to the Dauphine's apartments which are visited in reverse order.

### Appartement de la Dauphine

**Cabinet Intérieur de la Dauphine (25)** – This room features Vernis Martin wainscoting as in the Dauphin's library. Note Gaudreaux' commode and a writing desk by Bernard Van Rysenburgh (BVRB). The back rooms were refurbished under Louis XVIII for the Duchesse d'Angoulême, the daughter of Louis XVI: couch formerly belonging to the Comtesse de Provence, antechamber, study-library and servant's quarters.

**Chambre de la Dauphine (24)** – The bedroom contains a Polish-style bed and a magnificent set of six armchairs by Heurtaut. Note Nattier's two portraits of Mme Henriette and Mme Adélaïde, portrayed respectively as Flora and Diana.

**Grand Cabinet de la Dauphine (23)** – This room evokes the marriage of Marie Leszczynska to Louis XV. It also presents Lemaire's sculpted barometer, offered on the occasion of Marie-Antoinette's marriage to the Dauphin, and

## Appartement Privé du Roi★★★

### Appartement intérieur du Roi

This suite of rooms, with its superb wainscoting by Gabriel, provides a delightful feast for the eyes. The fine Rococo carvings are the work of Verberckt.

**Chambre à coucher (6)** – The absence of furniture makes it difficult to picture this room in its original state. Owing to the constraints of court etiquette, Louis XV (after 1738) and then Louis XVI (up to the end of the Ancien Régime) daily had to leave this room and slip away to the State bedroom, where they "performed" the rising and retiring ceremonies. It was here that Louis XV died of smallpox on 10 May 1774.

**Cabinet de la Pendule (7)** – This was a games room until 1769. Passemant and Dauthiau's **astronomical clock★★★** was installed here in 1754. A copper line running across the floor indicates the Versailles meridian.

In the centre of the room stands the equestrian statue of Louis XV by Vassé.

### The rising ceremony

The king was woken up at 7am by his first valet. The first visit he received was that of his doctor. Next came the "grandes entrées" (important guests including members of his family and those who held an office), then the *"secondes entrées"* (less important guests) and finally the nobility. Breakfast was followed by the dressing ceremony, then the king left his apartments to hear Mass in the chapel.

It is a replica of Bouchardon's sculpture which initially adorned place Louis XV – now called place de la Concorde – in Paris and which was destroyed in 1792.

**Antichambre des Chiens (8)** – A charming passageway off the king's private staircase (known as *degré du Roi*). The decoration features Louis XIV panelling, in sharp contrast to the adjoining rooms.

**Salle à manger dite des Retours de chasse (9)** – Between 1750 and 1769 hunts were organised every other day in the forests surrounding Versailles. Louis XV and a few privileged fellow hunters would come here to sup after their exertions.

**Cabinet intérieur du Roi (10)** – This masterpiece of 18C French ornamental art was commissioned by Louis XV. Gabriel and the accomplished cabinet-maker Verberckt were responsible for the stunning Rococo décor.

The celebrated **roll-top desk★★★** by Oeben and Riesener (1769) was among the few prestigious works of art to be spared in 1792.

The **medal cabinet** attributed to the cabinetmaker Gaudreaux (1738) is heavily decorated with gilded bronze: it bears the 1783 candelabra commemorating the role played by France in the American War of Independence, flanked by two Sèvres vases (bronzes by Thomire). Two corner cupboards made by Joubert in 1755 to house Louis XV's ever-increasing collections were added subsequently, as was a set of chairs

attributed to Foliot (1774).

In 1785 the room was the scene of a formal encounter attended by Marie-Antoinette, at which the King informed Cardinal de Rohan that he would shortly be arrested for his involvement in the Diamond Necklace Affair.

The Corner Room leads through to the study where Louis XV and Louis XVI kept all confidential documents relating to State affairs, and where they granted private audiences.

**Cabinet de Madame Adélaïde (12)** – This was one of the first "new rooms" laid out at the instigation of Louis XV. It overlooks the Royal Court and was designed by Louis XV for his favourite daughter Madame Adélaïde (1752). The ornate decoration features delightful Rococo wainscoting and gilded panelling embellished with musical instruments, as well as fishing and floral motifs: the room was used as a music room by the king's daughter. It is believed that the young Mozart performed on the harpsichord before the royal family in this very room, during the winter of 1763-64. Louis XVI later made the room his "jewel cabinet."

**Bibliothèque de Louis XVI (13)** – Designed by the ageing Gabriel and executed by the wood carver Antoine Rousseau, this extremely refined library is a perfect example of the Louis XVI style (1774). The austere appearance of the bookcases, in which the door panels are concealed by a set of false deco-

*Louis XIV's bedroom*

rative backs, is countered by the gay Chinese motifs on the upholstery and the curtains. Next to Riesener's flat-top desk stands the vast mahogany table where the King spent many enjoyable hours correcting geographical maps.

**Salon des Porcelaines (14)** – This room was used as the Hunters' Dining Hall under Louis XV, and from 1769 to 1789 under Louis XVI. It houses numerous exhibits of Sèvres porcelain, painted after drawings by Oudry.

**Salon des Jeux de Louis XVI (15)** – From the doorway admire the full effect of this perfect vignette of 18C furniture and ornamental art: corner cupboards by Riesener (1774), set of chairs by Boulard, curtains and upholstery in rich crimson and gold brocade.

▶ *Walk down the Louis-Philippe staircase X and leave by the North Arcade (a public passageway leading through to the park).*

The room on the ground floor houses a miniature replica of the Ambassador's Staircase (Escalier des Ambassadeurs) under the Louis-Philippe staircase.

### Opéra Royal★★

Gabriel started work on the opera house in 1768 and completed it in time for the wedding ceremony of Marie-Antoinette and the future King Louis XVI in 1770. It was the first oval-shaped opera house in France. Pajou's work, inspired by the classical models of Antiquity, remains surprisingly modern looking. The court engineer Arnoult designed the sophisticated machinery required for the new opera house. For banquets and formal receptions, the floor of the stalls and of the circle could be raised level with the stage. This auditorium – its interior decoration made entirely of wood – enjoys excellent acoustics and can seat 700.

Although initially reserved for members of the court, the opera house at Versailles was later used for lavish receptions organised on the occasion of official visits. A number of foreign rulers were received at the palace, including the King of Sweden (1784), Marie-Antoinette's brother the Emperor Joseph II (1777 and 1781) and Queen

Victoria (1855). The sessions of the National Assembly were held in the Royal Opera between 1871 and 1875. It was here that the Wallon Amendment was voted on 30 January 1875, laying the foundation stone of the Third Republic. The latest restoration ended in 1957 and was marked by an official reception in honour of Queen Elizabeth II and Prince Philip.

## Les Grandes Heures du Parlement★

*Audio-guided tour, Entrance P from the Jardins du Parterre du Midi.* ♿ ⓞ*Open daily (except Mon and Sun) 9am-6.30pm (Nov-Mar 5.30pm). Last admission 1hr before closing.* ⓞ*Closed 1 Jan, 1 May, 25 Dec.* 3€. ☏ 01 39 25 70 70. Versailles is a magnificent reminder of life during the days of the monarchy; it has also been the cradle of French democracy since 1789. Even now, the semicircular chamber in the south wing accommodates members of Parliament when changes are made to the Constitution.

## Cabinets Intérieurs de la Reine★

### (Queen's Private Suite)

These somewhat cramped apartments looking onto two inner courtyards were used as a daytime retreat by the queens of France. Unlike the king, the queen was not allowed to live anywhere but in her State Apartments.

**Cabinet doré (16)** – The panelling by the Rousseau brothers marks the revival of Antique motifs: frieze with rosettes, sphinx, trivets, small censers. A lovely chandelier features among the magnificent bronze works. The commode was made by Riesener. Naderman's harp reminds visitors that the Queen was an enthusiastic musician in her spare time; she would often play with Grétry, Gluck or even his rival Piccinni.

**Bibliothèque (17)** – Note the drawer handles in the shape of a two-headed eagle, the emblem of the House of Hapsburg.

*The King's desk*

**Méridienne** (18) – This little octagonal boudoir was used for resting by Marie-Antoinette. It was designed in 1781 by the Queen's architect Mique in honour of the birth of the first dauphin. The decoration evokes romance and the period leading up to the dauphin's birth: lilies, hearts pierced with arrows and the famous dolphin. The second floor houses Marie-Antoinette's Apartment (*open by prior arrangement*).

## Appartement de Madame de Maintenon

This suite was located away from the throngs of courtiers but next to the King's apartments, reflecting a situation enforced by the King during the last 32 years of his reign, with a view to establishing an atmosphere of tact and mutual respect.

The **Grand Cabinet** (19) was a private drawing room decorated with red hangings where Mme de Maintenon entertained members of the royal family – her favourite was the Duchess of Burgundy – and where Racine recited his famous plays *Esther* and *Athalie*.

## Petits Cabinets du Roi★

### (King's Private Apartments)

*A tour of these apartments is recommended to visitors already acquainted with Versailles and who have a particular interest in 18C decorative art.*

Louis XV did not share the taste for publicity that had been such a dominant trait of the Sun King's personality. Consequently he created a suite of private apartments to which he could retire and receive his mistresses, close friends and relatives.

**Appartement de Madame de Pompadour** – This was the first suite occupied by Louis XV's mistress between

### The king's valets

The Sun King had 28 valets who served and assisted him according to a very precise timetable. What were their privileges? They were close to him daily and could, if the need arose, request a favour from him. In addition, their office automatically made them members of the aristocracy, exempted them from paying the *taille*, a royal tax and provided them with a substantial income. The best known of the king's valets was undoubtedly Marie Du Bois (a man, despite his name), who left a diary, but the most renowned was Alexandre Bontemps, an important member of the court for nearly 60 years, whom Louis XIV trusted implicitly.

*Salle des Hocquetons*

1745 and 1750. The Grand Cabinet features splendid carved woodwork by Verberckt.

**Appartement de Madame du Barry** – The wooden panelling has been meticulously restored to its original colours. The suite looks out onto the Cour des Cerfs and the Cour au Marbre. It consists of a bathroom, a bedroom, a library and a corner **drawing room (20)** which was one of Louis XV's favourite haunts; he would enjoy sitting here and gazing out at the town of Versailles nestling among wooded slopes.

**Appartements des ducs de Maurepas et Villequier** – These apartments were occupied by two ministers of Louis XVI. Most of the furniture was donated by the Duke and Duchess of Windsor.

## MUSEUM★★

The museum houses several thousand paintings and sculptures which present French history from the 17C to the 19C.
**17C Galleries** – *See the Tour of the Grands Appartements.*

## 18C Galleries★★★

**Appartements du Dauphin et de la Dauphine** – *See the Tour of the "Chambre du Roi".*

**Galerie basse** – Divided into apartments under Louis XVI and partly restored under Louis-Philippe, the gallery now stands as it did under Louis XIV. From 1782 to 1789 the rooms in this gallery were used by Marie-Antoinette and her children.

**Appartement de Madame Victoire** – The Sun King's former bathroom and its two marble piscinae underwent several alterations before being used as the antechamber to this suite, occupied by the fourth daughter of Louis XV.

The **Grand Cabinet (30)** is an exquisite corner room with a delightful carved cornice and panelling by Verberckt. It has retained its original fireplace.

Mme Victoire's former **bedroom (31)** has been furnished with some outstanding pieces, set off by the newly restored summer hangings.

**Appartement de Madame Adélaïde** – These rooms housed the second suite of Mme de Pompadour, who died here in 1764. Five years later, Mme Adélaïde moved into the suite.

The **Salle des Hocquetons (32)** was an annex adjoining the former Ambassadors' Staircase, destroyed in 1752. The stately proportions of this room give an idea of how magnificent the flight of stairs once looked. Note the huge **clock★** by Passement and Roque with bronze ornamentation by Germain; it dates from 1754 and illustrates the creation of the world.

The ground-floor suite of Marie-Antoinette, which she occupied during her last days at Versailles, has been partly re-created but as for the furniture in the bedroom and the bathroom **(33)** only the console table and the recently re-embroidered bedspread date from her period.

# PARC DU CHÂTEAU DE VERSAILLES★★★

MICHELIN LOCAL MAP 311: I-3, MAP 101 FOLDS 22, 23 OR 106 FOLDS 17, 18

The park 🔥, forever linked to the name of André Le Nôtre (1613-1700), is the result of Louis XIV's determination to transform the marshland surrounding Versailles into a work of beauty: a variety of gardens, fountains, ponds, a profusion of statues and grottoes, striking rock formations and water everywhere. The park, which can be visited on foot of course, but also in a *barouche* or even in a rowing boat along the Grand Canal, is best seen when the Grandes Eaux (fountains) are in operation (weekends and holidays in summer).

🔹 **Information**: www.chateauversailles.fr.

▶ **Orient Yourself**: The Parc lies northwest both of the town of Versailles and the chateau. (& *See Château de Versailles for access from Paris by road and rail.*)

## A Bit of History

### André Le Nôtre's masterpiece

The palace was built on top of a small hillock consolidated by vast loads of earth. The terrace rises above the Latona Basin by a height of 10.5m/35ft, the Apollo Basin by 30m/100ft, the Grand Canal by 32m/105ft and the Orangery by 17m/56ft.

Before the Revolution, the park was surrounded by a 43km/27mi-long wall punctuated by 22 royal gates. Beyond the actual gardens of the Château (93ha/230 acres), the Versailles estate used to incorporate the **Petit Parc**, which included the Grand Canal and the Trianon, and the **Grand Parc**, a vast hunting reserve dotted with villages. Under the Second Empire the area of the park shrank to around 815ha/2 014 acres and the distance between the palace and its perimeter is about 950m/1 040yd.

## Gardens★★★

🕐 *Quick tour: allow 3hr: Apr-Oct daily 8.30am-7pm. Nov-Mar daily 8.30am-6pm. ☞7€ (no charge Nov-Mar). ☎ 01 30 83 77 88.*

The terrace and parterres provide a perfect balance to the monumental front of the palace which screens the town of Versailles. Lower down, the lawns and the Grand Canal cut across the middle of the grounds, creating a sweeping **perspective**★★★ that extends into the far distance.

Numerous groves and straight paths are laid out on either side of this central axis. The 300 sculptures which adorn the park make it one of the biggest open-air museums of classical sculpture.

In order to return to Le Nôtre's original layout, the team of gardeners has brought down the chestnut trees lining the Allée royale and replanted this stretch framed by six groves so as to re-create the decor which Louis XIV was so fond of: clipped box trees, high hornbeam hedges and a generous use of trellis work.

### The park in figures

🌿 43km/27mi of alleyways

🌿 18 000 trees

🌿 16 000m²/19 136sq yd of box trees

🌿 17km/11mi of hornbeam plantations

🌿 385 topiaries (yew trees clipped into 58 different ornamental shapes)

🌿 180 000 plants needed every year for 9 750m²/11 661sq yd of flower beds

🌿 During the reign of Louis XIV, the plants would be renewed up to 15 times a year

## "Ten thousand trees for Versailles"

Unfortunately the park was severely damaged by the storms which hit the Île-de-France region in December 1999, when thousands of trees, particularly tall ones, were brought down. However, the devastating action of the storm had one positive result: the renovation programme launched in 1990 was moved forward with the invaluable help of numerous patrons, among them Americans, Koreans, Canadians and a village in Switzerland.

# Axe du Soleil

### Parterre d'eau★★

The two huge basins that front the stately palace constitute a sort of aquatic esplanade where the three main perspectives meet: the central view and the line along the North and South Parterres.

### Degré de Latone (Latona Staircase)

An imposing flight of steps and a double ramp flanked with yew trees and replicas of antique statues lead from the Parterres d'Eau down to the Bassin de Latone. From the top of the steps admire the wonderful **view**★★★ of the gardens and the Grande Perspective.

### The two fountains

These were originally called the *Cabinets d'animaux* on account of the bronze works depicting dogs fighting wild beasts. They were named after the most striking statue of the three standing on the edge of the basins.

**The Point du Jour** (1) – Dawn – whose head is crowned by a star – is the work of Gaspard Marsy. The other two figures are Water and Spring.

**Diane chasseresse★** (2) – Le Hongre's statue, Air, is the one looking in the direction of Dawn. At its side stands the hunting goddess Diana, by Desjardins. The third statue was carved by Marsy and represents Venus, the goddess of love. These sculptures are among the finest works in the gardens.

### Bassin de Latone★ (Latona Basin)

This vast composition by Marsy was the very first marble sculpture in the gardens of Versailles (1670). It tells the story of Latona (the statue is a mould of the original), the mother of Apollo and

Diana, who was showered with insults by the peasants of Lycea and prevented from quenching her thirst. She appealed to Jupiter, the father of her children, who promptly avenged the offence by turning the culprits into aquatic animals. Originally the statue of Latona looked toward the palace, a clear indication of how the King viewed the public or private insults concerning his love life.

At the foot of the steps, to the right, lies the charming **Nymph with a Shell** (3), a modern replica of Coysevox' statue. The original work – inspired by the statues of Antiquity – has been moved to the Louvre.

### Allée royale

The "Green Carpet" has been entirely replanted according to Le Nôtre's plans. From the foot of the Esplanade de Latone, admire the Axe du Soleil leading up to the palace and extending beyond the Tapis Vert, toward the Grand Canal.

This long stretch of lawn is lined with a superb collection of ornamental vases and statues. A stroll along the Allée du Midi leads to the **Richelieu Venus** (4), sculpted by Le Gros after an Antique bust that featured among the Cardinal's private collections.

# Bosquets du Midi (South Groves)

### Bosquet de la Salle de Bal★ (5)

This elegant grove, also known as Bosquet des Rocailles, was part of Le Nôtre's original plans and his last creation. Shaped as a circular stage, it is surrounded by gentle slopes, grassy banks and tiered rockeries where small cascades tumble down. This outdoor theatre was used for performances given by members of the court or for dancing.

## Address Book

♨ *For coin ranges, see the Legend on the cover flap.*

### WHERE TO EAT

♨♨ **La Flotille** – *Parc du Château, Grand Canal, 78000 Versailles –* ☎ 01 39 51 41 58 – www.laflotille.fr. *Closed evenings except during nocturnal festivities – reserv. required Sun .*
On the edge of the Grand Canal, in the château's park, here's a small late-19C house brightened by a glass roof. This guinguette-like establishment offers three options: restaurant, brasserie and tearoom. The food is nothing to write home about, but the summer terrace is utterly delightful!

### EVENING FESTIVITIES

The *fêtes de nuit*, or evening festivities, are held seven times each summer at the Bassin de Neptune, with fireworks at the end.

**Les Grandes Eaux musicales** – *During the Grandes Eaux (lit: The Great Waters), the garden must be entered via one of the following: La Cour d'Honneur or Le Passage des Princes; La Grille (The Gate) des Matelots or La Petite Venise near the Grand Canal; or La Grille du Dragon (at the end of the Rue de la Paroisse) from 8:30am to 4:50pm. From midday on, one may also enter via La Grille des Deuxième Cent-marches and La Grille de Neptune.* The Grandes Eaux Musicales, or Musical Fountain Displays, take the spectator back to the magical fountains and groves of 17C Versailles. A brochure describing the itinerary is given out. Spectators await the beginning of the displays above the Bassin de Latone. As soon as the Bassin de Latone fountain begins gushing, follow the plan without dawdling, and make sure not to miss the bosquets (groves) that are only open for these events, especially La Salle de Bal and the Bosquet d'Apollon (invisible from the alleys). The end – and climax – of the show (at 5:20pm, lasting 10mn) takes place in the Bassin de Neptune and the Bassin du Dragon: 99 jets, with one of the latter's reaching 28m/92ft high.

### DISCOVERING THE GARDENS OF VERSAILLES

**Gardens of the Trianon and Hamlet of Versailles** – *78000 Versailles – end Mar to early Oct. Trianon, icehouses and manufactory: weekends at 3pm, tickets at the Grand Trianon ticket booth; hamlet: Sun at 3.30pm, tickets at the Petit Trianon ticket booth.*

**To see Versailles from another angle**
**By bicycle** – *78000 Versailles –* ☎ 01 39 66 97 66. *Daily (except rainy weather) 10am-6.30pm; at the Grille de la Reine and La Porte St-Antoine: Wed 1-6.30pm, weekends and public holidays 10.30am-6.30pm (Jul-Aug: daily 1-6.30pm, weekends and public holidays 10am-6.30pm). From Feb to end Nov there are three cycle hire points in the château's park near the Grand Canal.*
**By boat** – *78000 Versailles –* ☎ 01 39 66 97 66 – *end Mar to end Oct 10am-6pm. 12€ (1hr, 4-person boats).* Departure near La Flotille restaurant.
**By carriage** – *78000 Versailles –* ☎ *Info 01 30 97 04 41 – Jul-Aug: 10am-7pm; May, Jun and Sep: daily (except Mon): 10am-6pm; Oct-Apr: daily (except Mon): 11am-6pm.* A selection of horse-drawn carriages and coaches offer their services.
**By mini-train** – *78000 Versailles –* ☎ 01 39 54 22 00 – *Mar 10.30am-5.30pm; Apr-Sep 10am-6.15pm; Oct 10.30am-6pm; Nov 11am-5pm; Dec-Feb. Call for info.* Sightseeing tour (35mn): stops at the Trianon and the Grand Canal. Departure from the château's Parterre Nord.
**The Château-Trianon shuttle** – *78000 Versailles – 6€ (children: 4.50€). www.train-versailles.com.* From the château's Parterre Nord to the Petit Trianon and the Grand Trianon.
**Promenade du Petit Parc** – *78000 Versailles – 30mn itinerary, rental of horse-drawn vehicles seating 6-7 passengers: 80€ (20mn tours, Apr-Sep 45€).* From the château's Parterre Nord to the Bassin d'Apollon.
**Promenade du Petit Parc, la Petite Venise, Petit Trianon and Grand Trianon** – *78000 Versailles – duration: 50-70mn. Rental of horse-drawn vehicles seating 4-7 passengers – 120€.*

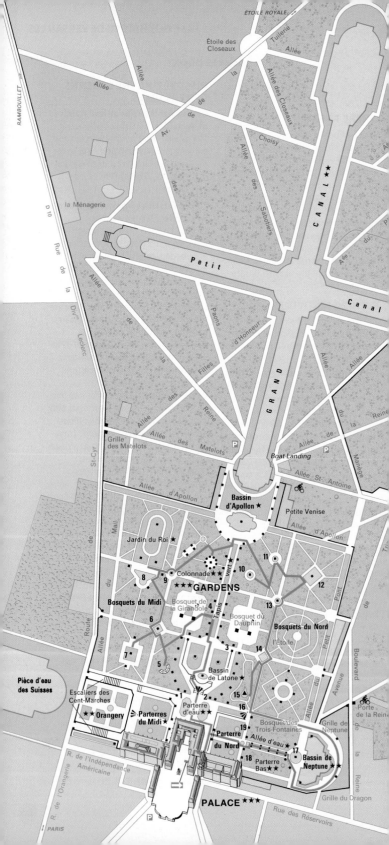

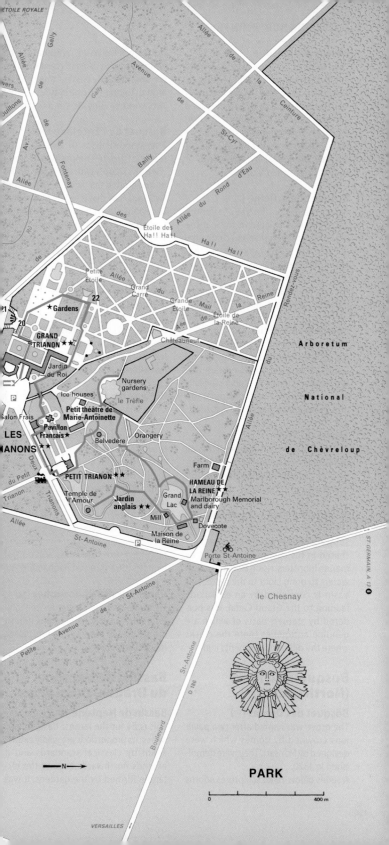

ÉTOILE ROYALE

Allée de Gally

Avenue de

St-Cyr

Allée de la Ceinture

Allée du Rond d'Eau

Étoile des Ha!! Ha!!

Ha!! Ha!!

des

Petite Étoile

Allée

Grand Carré

du

Grande Étoile

Mail

de la Reine

Étoile de la Reine

Rendez-vous

★ Gardens

22

**GRAND TRIANON** ★★

21

20

Jardin du Roi

Ice-houses

Nursery gardens

le Trèfle

Châteauneuf

Salon Frais

Petit théâtre de Marie-Antoinette

**LES TRIANONS**

Pavillon Français ★

Belvedere

Orangery

Jardin du Roi

du Petit Trianon

PETIT TRIANON ★★

Temple de l'Amour

**Jardin anglais** ★★

Grand Lac

Mill

Maison de la Reine

Farm

**HAMEAU DE LA REINE** ★★

Marlborough Memorial and dairy

Dovecote

Porte St-Antoine

Allée St-Antoine

Avenue de Petite

St-Antoine

le Chesnay

**Arboretum**

**National**

**de Chèvreloup**

ST-GERMAIN A 13

Boulevard D 186

**PARK**

0        400 m

N →

VERSAILLES

### Bassin des Saisons

The basins of the Four Seasons are laid out to plans by Le Brun along paths parallel to the Tapis Vert. These groups of lead figures have recently been re-gilded and decorated in "natural tones": Bassin de *Bacchus or Autumn* (6) designed by Marsy, *Saturn or Winter* (9) by Girardon, *Flora or Spring* (13) by Tuby, *Ceres or Summer* (14) by Regnaudin.

### Bosquet de la Reine (7)

This grove lies on the site of a former maze and was created in 1775, at the time of the great replanting campaign. In its centre stand a number of busts and bronze statues cast after Antique models: Aphrodite, a Fighting Gladiator, etc. The maple groves are a magnificent sight in autumn.

### Bassin du Miroir (8)

Of the two basins circling the Royal Isle, the larger one began to silt up and Louis XVIII replaced it by a landscape garden, known as the Royal Garden. The only one to survive is the Bassin du Miroir d'Eau, handsomely adorned with statues.

### Jardin du Roi★

A dazzling sight in summer, when all the flowers are in full bloom, this garden is a welcome change from the formal groves of Versailles.

### Bassin d'Apollon★ (Apollo Basin)

The whole composition was made by Tuby. Apollo the Sun God is portrayed seated in his chariot, surrounded by marine monsters, rising from the ocean waters to bring Light to the Earth. This basin is continued by an esplanade leading to the Grand Canal. It is bordered by statues, parts of which are genuine antiquities (note the cracks where the different fragments join).

## Bosquets du Nord (North Groves)

### Bosquet des Dômes (10)

The grove was named after two pavilions crowned by domes which were designed by Mansart. They were demolished in 1820.

A series of low-relief sculptures adorns the edge of the basin, representing the weapons used in different countries. It has the unmistakably elegant touch of Girardon. Among the fine statues feature two works by Tuby, Acis and Galatea.

### Bosquet de l'Encelade★★ (11)

The stark realism of this recently restored Baroque composition by Marsy contrasts sharply with the other groups dotted around the gardens. A head and two arms is all that is visible of the Titan Enceladus, slowly being dragged down toward the bowels of the earth by the very rocks of Mount Olympus by which the Titan had hoped to reach the sky (a clear warning to Fouquet).

### Bassin de l'Obélisque (12)

Designed by Mansart, this raised basin is surrounded by a flight of stone steps and several lawns. When the fountains are in operation, the central sculpture lets out a gigantic spray of water which resembles a liquid obelisk.

### Bosquet des Bains d'Apollon★★ (15)

*Open only during the fountain display (Grandes Eaux).*

Designed by Hubert Robert in 1776, this grove heralded the Anglo-Chinese style which Marie-Antoinette later adopted for the Trianon park.

On the edge of a small lake, a charming artificial grotto houses the **Apollo Group**★. Its lush, verdant setting is a far cry from the austere 17C Versailles. The Sun God, tired by the day's exertions, is portrayed resting, waited upon by a group of nymphs (Girardon and Regnaudin).

### Carrefour des Philosophes (16)

Flanked by impressive statues, the "philosophers" crossroad offers an interesting sideways **view**★★ of the palace (north-west corner).

## Bassins de Neptune, du Dragon, Allée d'Eau

### Bassin de Neptune★★

This is by far the largest basin in Versailles. Its proportions are wildly extravagant by classical standards and it extends northwards beyond the rectangle formed by the gardens. It was designed by Le Nôtre but acquired its present appearance in 1741, during the reign of Louis XV.

## Bassin du Dragon (17)

This allegorical sculpture evoking the victory over deep-sea monsters is a direct allusion to the crushing of the Fronde Revolt, symbolised by a wounded dragon. Though the dragon's body is the original, the remaining pieces were recast in 1889.

## Allée d'Eau or des Marmousets★

A double row of 22 small white-marble basins bears delightful bronze groups of three children, each holding pink marble vessels.

# The Parterres and Orangery

## Parterre du Nord (North Parterre)

The very first royal suite looked out onto this "terrace of greenery," created in 1668.

## Bassin des Nymphes de Diane (18)

The pond is surrounded by fine low-relief carvings by Girardon which inspired 18C and 19C painters such as Renoir.

## Parterre Bas★★

Close to the groves, the terrace is flanked along its northern and western boundaries by bronze statues representing the four Continents, four Poems, four Seasons and four Temperaments. The lead **Pyramid Fountain**★ (19), made by Girardon from a study by Le Brun, combines grace with originality: dolphins, crayfish and tritons.

At the top of the steps leading to the Parterres d'Eau note the **Knife-grinder**, a bronze replica of a Classical statue. Coysevox' **Venus on a Tortoise** – called *Venus as a Paragon of Modesty* under Louis XIV – is a bronze cast, also inspired by Antique sculpture.

## Parterres du Midi★ (South Parterres)

These flower beds were laid out in front of the queen's apartments. With their vivid blossoms and their pretty boxwood patterns, they are a hymn to Nature. The terrace running along the Orangery

offers a good **view**★ of the 700m/ 2 275ft-long **Pièce d'Eau des Suisses** and, in the far distance, the wooded heights of Satory.

## Orangery★★

One of Mansart's creations (1684), the south-facing Orangery has retained its original double glazing. It extends south by means of two corner pavilions set at right angles which support the colossal **Escalier des Cent-Marches**, a flight of 100 steps. At the time of Louis XIV, the Orangery housed 3 000 rare trees in tubs; 2 000 of these were orange trees. The Orangery looks splendid during the summer season, when the orange trees and palm trees are brought outside and arranged around the flower beds restored in 2001.

## Le Grand Canal★★

The Grand Canal, which was completed in 1670, is shaped like a large cross: the long canal is 1 670m/5 480ft long by 62m/204ft wide; the shorter one measures 1 070m/3 500ft long by 80m/263ft wide. A few years ago, the 1 872 trees lining the Grand Canal were clipped back to a height of 15m/49ft in order to return to the initial perspective.

# Trianons

🕐*Open Apr-Oct noon-6.30pm. (Last admission 30min before closing.) Nov-Mar noon-5.30pm. ⊛5€. ☎ 01 30 83 76 20.*

## Grand Trianon★★ *1hr*

A pavilion known as the Trianon de Porcelaine, faced with blue- and white-Delft tiling, used to be a quiet, secluded meeting place for Louis XIV and his favourite Mme de Montespan. It stood for 18 years, from 1670 to 1687. When Mme de Montespan fell from favour, the pavilion deteriorated and was eventually taken down. In just six months, Jules Hardouin-Mansart completed the Trianon de Marbre, a retreat built by Louis XIV exclusively for the royal family.

## Château★★

Walk past the low railings and enter the semicircular courtyard to discover two buildings with a flat terrace roof, joined by an elegant peristyle.

## Apartments

The austere interior decoration has changed very little since the days of Louis XIV. The apartments were occupied by Napoleon and Louis-Philippe and their respective families. The furniture is either Empire, Restoration or Louis-Philippe and the paintings are by 17C French artists.

The **Salon des Glaces** in the left pavilion was used as a council chamber. Admire the splendid Empire furniture and the lavish silk hangings, rewoven according to the original pattern ordered by Marie-Antoinette (the four Continents of the World).

The **bedroom** contains the bed Napoleon commissioned for his apartments at the Tuileries: it was later altered for Louis-Philippe's use. The wall put in by Bonaparte level with the columns has been dismantled and the room has been restored to its original size.

The **reception rooms** in the right wing were remodelled by Louis-Philippe, who gave them a more personal touch. These salons are enhanced by a collection of paintings by famous 17C French artists, dedicated to mythological subjects.

The **Salon des Malachites** owes its name to the various objects encrusted with malachite given to Napoleon by Tsar Alexander I following their talks in Tilsit (1807): basins, candelabra, bookcase etc.

The **north-facing drawing room** houses four paintings representing the early days of Versailles, following the plans drawn up by Mansart (display of documents showing the palace and the grounds). The two filing cabinets (1810) and the console table (1806) were made by Jacob Desmalter from a drawing by Charles Percier.

The **Salon des Sources** – where Napoleon kept his various maps and plans – leads to the Imperial Suite (*open on request*). Placed at a right angle, the **Gallery**★ houses an extremely precious collection of 21 paintings by Cotelle. They conjure up a vivid picture of the palace and its stately grounds at the time of Louis XIV. The lovely Empire chandeliers were manufactured in the Montcenis glassworks in the Burgundian town of Le Creusot. At the end of the Gallery, the luminous **Salon des Jardins** features a fine set of chairs from the Château de Meudon.

## Gardens★

These derive their simple charm from the impressive displays of flower beds and the absence of allegorical meanings. Some of the flowers in fashion during the 17C and 18C, such as mayweeds, have now been reintroduced.

The terrace of the Lower Gardens (*Jardins Bas*) (**20**) commands a good view of the Lower Basin (Bassin Bas) (**21**), which is reached via a horseshoe staircase, and of the Grand Canal beyond, seen from the side.

Beyond the parterres lies a charming wood featuring fine avenues, rows of stately trees and several small ponds. The only sculpture with a mythological theme is Mansart's Buffet d'Eau (**22**), completed in 1703.

Skirt Trianon-sous-Bois and walk through what was once the king's private garden. It is flanked by two square pavilions that housed the apartments of Mme de Maintenon and Louis XIV toward the end of the Sun King's reign.

## Petit Trianon★★ *30min*

It was Louis XV's love of gardening and farming that prompted the construction of the Petit Trianon. The King gave orders to build a *menagerie* (experimental farm) and commissioned his "botanical expert" Claude Richard to design the greenhouses and botanical gardens. A College of Botanical Science was founded and entrusted to the famous botanist Bernard de Jussieu.

Gabriel finished the Petit Trianon in 1768, shortly before Louis XV's reign ended. Mme de Pompadour, the woman behind the initial project, never saw the château. Louis XVI gave the Petit Trianon to his wife Marie-Antoinette in 1774. The Queen would often come here with her children and her sister-in-law Mme Elisabeth, relieved to get away from court intrigues and the formal etiquette that was expected from a woman of her rank.

*Le Petit Trianon*

D. Hée/MICHELIN

## Pavillon français★

This pavilion was built by Gabriel for Louis XV and Mme de Pompadour in 1750. It is surrounded by an enchanting formal garden. The cornice features a sculpted frieze representing the farm animals that were raised on the estate. Visitors can get a glimpse of the highly refined interior decoration through the large French windows.

## Château★★

The façade facing the courtyard is austere in the extreme. It overlooks the formal gardens and is a perfect example of Gabriel's talent as well as a masterpiece of the Louis XVI style; the four regularly spaced columns are crowned by a balustrade and two fine flights of steps lead down to the gardens.

**First Floor Apartments** – Guibert's craftsmanship is evident in the superb **panelling**★★ in the dining room and the drawing room. The decoration of the dining room presents fruit, flower and foliage motifs, set off against a pale green background, a welcome change from the "Trianon grey" prevalent throughout the 19C. The drawing room – partly refurnished by Empress Eugénie in the 19C (chairs, 1790 pianoforte) – houses one of Riesener's greatest achievements, the famous astronomical writing desk (1771).

## Petit theâtre de Marie-Antoinette

As the queen loved acting, a theatre was designed for her by Mique in 1780; it was linked to the château by a path lined with painted trellis work. The auditorium can accommodate 160 spectators; the stage is lined with blue velvet and satin.

## Le Hameau de la Reine★★
## (the Queen's Hamlet)

The grounds around the lake (Grand Lac) are dotted with a dozen pretty cottages featuring cob walls and thatched or tiled roofs. **Kids** Farm animals (ducks, black pigs, goats) roaming around in the vicinity of the Hameau de la Reine, are a great attraction for children.

## Bosquet des États-Unis

The tulip tree from Virginia was the first tree to be replanted in Versailles Park in 2000 following the devastating storm of the previous winter. After the September 11 terrorist attack on the World Trade Center, 50 trees from the United States were planted in the same grove, including a sequoia from California and a sugar maple from Wisconsin.

# VILLE DE VERSAILLES★★

POPULATION 85 726

MICHELIN LOCAL MAP 311: I-3, MAP 101 FOLD 23 OR 106 FOLDS 17, 18

The town was built as an annex with a view to housing the numerous titled and untitled people who served the French court: dukes, ministers, craftsmen, civil servants etc. Owing to its former duties, the town has retained a certain austere charm with its three avenues converging on the Château, its private mansions, imposing churches and attractive collections which amply justify its title of Royal City.

- 🛈 **Information:** 2bis av. de Paris, 78000 Versailles. ☎ 01 39 24 88 88. www.versailles-tourisme.com.
- ▸ **Orient Yourself:** The town of Versailles lie a little closer to the centre of Paris than the Parc and the Château. Access from Paris: RER C from Invalides station to Versailles at Rive-Gauche; SNCF rail link from Gare Montparnasse to Versailles-Chantiers and from Gare St-Lazare to Versailles Rive-Droite.
- 🕓 **Organizing Your Time:** With the imperial and the verdant so close by, it is easy to overlook the town itself. Take the Town Walk below, and allow half a day to do so.

## A Bit of History

Famous natives of Versailles include **Lazare Hoche** (1768-97), a general in France's revolutionary army, who was sent to Vendée to pacify the region, and **Ferdinand de Lesseps** (1805-94), a diplomat who was responsible for the opening of the Suez Canal, inaugurated in 1869.

### Royal city

In 1671 Louis XIV decided that plots of land would be granted to those citizens who put in a request, in exchange for a levy of five sous for each arpent (3 194m2/3 833sq yd). The new buildings had to conform to the rules laid down by the Service des Bâtiments du Roi, a building commission answerable to the court. The purpose of these measures was to achieve architectural unity. Moreover, in order that the palace might continue to dominate the area, the roofs of the village houses were not to exceed the height of the Cour de Marbre. Today very little remains of these 17C buildings. Most of the old town was completed in the 18C, enlarged and renovated in the 19C.

### Parliamentary town

France's defeat in the 1870-71 Franco-Prussian War enabled Versailles to regain its political role as the seat of the French government. The population rose from 40 000 to 150 000 in a matter of days. Senators and members of the National Assembly, who were unable to find lodgings in town, camped with government ministers at the château which also housed the Banque de France and other official institutions. The president and head of the government found room in the préfecture. This situation lasted until 1879, when Parliament returned to the capital. An amphitheatre was built to house it in the middle of the south wing. During the Third and Fourth Republics, presidential elections were held here. Today the amphitheatre is only used for revising the constitution when both houses are required to sit together.

### Versailles today

More than 200 years after the end of absolute monarchy in France, there are very few 17C houses left in Versailles: most of the old town dates from the 18C with 19C alterations. Having long suffered from being too close to Paris, Versailles has nevertheless managed to develop its own cultural programme and to enhance its exceptional site by restoring its beautiful façades in Quartier St-Louis, for instance. The pedestrianised rue Satory, in the heart of the old town, has become as lively as Quartier Notre-Dame where antique dealers and outdoor cafés abound.

## Transportation

The most practical way to get around is by bus. The main bus stops are at the Rive-Droite station, on Avenue de l'Europe and opposite the Rive-Gauche station.

# Town Walk

## Château surroundings

### Place d'Armes★★

This huge square was the junction of the three wide avenues leading to Paris, St-Cloud and Sceaux, separated by the **Écuries royales**★, the stables built by Jules Hardouin-Mansart in 1683. Identical in size, the Grande and Petite Écuries were so named for reasons of convenience. These imposing buildings housed some 600 horses, as well as riders, grooms, musicians and page boys.

### Grande Écurie

*To the right of the square as you look toward the Château.*
Formerly used for saddle horses, this now houses the **Musée des Carosses** (⏱ *open Apr-Oct Sat and Sun 9am-6.30pm.* ☜2€. ☎ *01 30 83 77 88)* where various sedan chairs and carriages can be seen (carriages used for Napoleon's wedding, Charles X's coronation, presidential elections under the 3rd Republic etc).

### Petite Écurie

*To the left of the square as you look toward the Château.*
This was used for carriages and carriage-horses. Today it houses a school of architecture and workshops specialising in restoration work.

### Rue de l'Indépendance-Américaine

In the 18C this street housed many buildings occupied by ministries and public services, in particular the Grand Commun – built by Mansart in 1684 – which lodged a total of 1 500 officials, cooks etc.

At no 5 stands the former **Ministry of the Navy and Foreign Affairs**, fronted by a magnificent gate crowned by statues of Peace and War. It was here that an alliance was signed (1762) between France and the American "insurrection-aries", acting as a prelude to the 1783 treaties granting the independence of the United States. The mansion has been made into a public library (**bibliothèque municipale**).

### Pièce d'eau des Suisses

*Route de St-Cyr (D 10).*
Separated from the park by the road, this expanse of water extends the Orangery vista to the foot of the wooded Satory heights. At the end stands the statue of Marcus Curtius. The shaded site offers a magnificent view of the Château.

### Quartier St-Louis★

Rue du Vieux-Versailles, lined with carftsmen's workshops, leads to rue Satory: General Hoche's birthplace is at no 18, near the Petite Écurie where his father took care of the horses; note the fine wrought-iron work (*not open to the public*). The St-Louis district boasts a wealth of historic mansions built during the reign of Louis XV and the **Jeu de Paume** where the National Assembly took their famous oath on 20 June 1789; the **Potager du Roi** stretches its chequered layout at the foot of the Château (☝ *see Additional Sights*).

### Cathédrale St-Louis★

St Louis' Cathedral was built in 1754 to serve the "old Versailles" and the Parc aux Cerfs, and lies close to the King's Vegetable Garden (*Potager du Roi*). The west front with its two towers, and the dome above the transept crossing are reminiscent of the great Classical churches.

### Carrés St-Louis

Louis XV gave orders to create a "shopping area" near St Louis' Church, along the streets presently named rue Royale and rue d'Anjou (1755). The market dating

## Address Book

*♨For coin ranges, see the Legend on the cover.*

### WHERE TO STAY

◎◎ **Hôtel Versailles** – *7 r. Ste-Anne, Petite Place* – ☎ *01 39 50 64 65* – *www.hotel-le-versailles.fr* – ℗ – *46 rms* – ⌕ *10€.* This renovated hotel is situated in a quiet side street not far from the château. The Art Deco style rooms are spacious, bright and elegant. Cosy bar-lounge and terrace where breakfast is served in summer.

◎ **Résidence du Berry** – *14 r. d'Anjou* – ☎ *01 39 49 07 07* – *www.hotel-berry.com* – *39 rms* – ⌕ *10€.* Located in the Saint-Louis quarter, this 18C edifice has been entirely restored by Les Bâtiments de France. Comfort and top-quality materials await you in rooms with time-worn beams overhead.
In summer breakfast is taken on a veranda that opens onto the patio.

### WHERE TO EAT

◎ **La Brasserie du Théâtre** – *15 r. des Réservoirs* – ☎ *01 39 50 03 21* – *reserv. advisable evenings.* The walls of this 1895 brasserie situated next to the theatre, as its name would suggest, are covered with photos of artists who have frequented it over the years. 1930s style décor, covered terrace and traditional cuisine.

◎ **Le Bœuf à la Mode** – *4 r. au Pain, (Pl. du Marché Notre-Dame)* – ☎ *01 39 50 31 99. Closed Christmas weekend.* A typical 1930s bistro with a convivial, relaxed atmosphere. The decor – red wall-seats, knick-knacks, posters, mirrors – is a hit and the regional specialities are delicious. Very busy on market days.

◎◎ **La Bodega** – *4 bis r. de la Paroisse* – ☎ *01 30 21 01 73. Closed 25 Dec to 1 Jan, Mon lunch and Sun – reserv. requested weekends.* Come have a royal time at the gates of the château! Tapas, caracoles and other dishes with an Hispanic flavour will satisfy epicureans in quest of the exotic. And to round out the bodega experience, weekend evenings continue late into the night at the Bagheera piano bar.

◎◎ **Le Baladin** – *2 r. de l'Occident (quartier St-Louis)* – ☎ *01 39 50 06 57.*

*Closed Sun evening and Mon lunch in summer – reserv. advisable.* This genial establishment is nestled in the old St. Louis neighbourhood. The dining room, decorated in tones of grey and yellow, is pleasant and the terrace under the horse chestnuts is very popular in fine weather. Delightful, savoury fare.

◎◎ **Au Chapeau Gris** – *7 r. Hoche* – ☎ *01 39 50 10 81. Closed 22 Jul to 22 Aug, Tue evening and Wed – reserv. required.* This restaurant, said to date back to the 18C, is a veritable institution hereabouts. Quintessential Versailles ambience and décor are the setting for appetizing, traditional cuisine. Nothing too wild, just a reliable, very much sought-after establishment.

◎◎ **Valmont** – *20 r. au Pain* – ☎ *01 39 51 39 00. Closed Sun evening and Mon.* This nicely restored old house on the Place des Halles is bound to catch your eye. Venture inside and appreciate the first-rate reception, charming decoration, modern colours, elegant tables and succulent cookery. A meal to look forward to!

### ON THE TOWN

**Cinéma Le Cyrano** – *7 r. Rameau* – ☎ *08 36 68 70 25* – *1-10:30pm.* 8 screens, for up to 1 650 viewers.

**Cinéma Le Roxane** – *6 r. St-Simon* – ☎ *01 30 21 31 50. Daily 1pm-midnight.* Cinema, cine-club, lectures, chamber music concerts.

**Théâtre Montansier** – *13 r. des Réservoirs* – ☎ *01 39 24 05 06* – *tickets: Tue-Sat noon-7pm. Closed mid-Jul to end Aug.* Classical, modern and comic theatre productions, plus dance and children's shows. An eclectic, wide-ranging programme.

**Fenêtres sur cour** – *Passage de la Geôle, Quartier des Antiquaires* – ☎ *01 39 51 97 77* – *Mon-Wed 9:30am-4pm, Thu-Sun 9:30am-11pm. Closed 3 wks Aug.* A restaurant-salon de thé under a glass roof. The bric-a-brac décor – tile floor, carpets, lamps, chandeliers, plaster statues and paintings – is in perfect harmony with the neighbourhood antique shops. Appetizing wine menu. In summer, tables are set outdoors on the Place de la Geôle.

back to Louis XV's reign has been beautifully restored. The shops – featuring mansard roofs – were arranged around four small squares known as *carrés*: Carré au Puits, Carré à l'Avoine, Carré à la Fontaine, Carré à la Terre.

## Quartier Notre-Dame★

The Notre-Dame district features the oldest church in Versailles and a few houses built under Louis XIV, situated near the Notre-Dame marketplace.

### Église Notre-Dame

*35 rue de la Paroisse.*
The church built in rue Dauphine – renamed rue Hoche – by Jules Hardouin-Mansart in 1686 was the parish church to the king and his court. The king would attend Solemn Masses such as Corpus Christi here. The requirements of the *Service des Bâtiments du Roi* explain why the church presents a flattened front flanked by truncated towers.

A large openwork dome graces the church interior, characterised by Doric embellishments. The nave (*explanatory notices*) is surrounded by 12 carved medallions representing Apostles and figures from the New Testament; these were the works presented by the new entrants to the Académie Royale de Sculpture et de Peinture between 1657 and 1689. The 19C axial chapel – the chapel of the Blessed Sacrament – houses the *Assumption*, a 16C painting by Michel Corneille.

▶ *Walk along rue de la Paroisse and turn left onto rue Rameau then onto rue du Baillage.*

### Hôtel du Baillage

*On the corner of rue de la Pourvoierie.*
Built by Gabriel in 1724, this mansion served as the bailiff's tribunal and municipal prison until it was restored and turned into a residence in 1844. The ground floor houses antique dealers. Follow rue de la Paroisse to the **Marché Notre-Dame**, a group of four covered market halls surrounded by picturesque streets such as **rue des Deux-Portes** lined with shops and restaurants.

You could end this stroll by walking along rue Rameau, then turning right onto boulevard de la Reine toward the **Musée Lambinet** (⏾ *see Additional Sights*).

## Additional Sights

### Salle du Jeu de paume

*Call for information.* ☎ 01 30 83 77 88.
This is one of the only remaining Real Tennis Courts or Jeux de Paume. Built for the Court in 1686, it became famous on 20 June 1789 when the Members of the Tiers État (representing the people) and of the lower clergy gathered here after having been excluded from the Hôtel des Menus-Plaisirs where the States General were being held. They then swore that their assembly would not be dissolved until they had given a constitution to the French people.

### Potager du Roi★

*10 rue du Mar.-Joffre.* ♿ ⏾*Open Apr-Oct: 10am-6pm (last admission 30min before closing).* ⏾*4.50€ (6.50€ Sat, Sun and public holidays).* ☎ 01 39 24 62 62. *www. potager-du-roi.fr.*
This "kitchen garden" was commissioned by Louis XIV from **JB La Quintinie** (1624-88) to supply the king's table with a variety of fruit and vegetables many of which are now quite rare. The kitchen garden, which now houses the École nationale du paysage, has survived and its produce is sold in a shop on the grounds. It is divided into sixteen vegetable plots where some 50 different species grow. These plots are surrounded by a dozen orchards planted with 5 000 fruit trees lovingly cared for (there are 130 varieties of apple and pear!).

### Musée Lambinet★

*54 boulevard de la Reine.* ♿ ⏾*Open daily (except Mon 1-15 Aug) 2-6pm (Wed 1-6pm, Fri 2-5pm).* ⏾*Closed public holidays.* ⏾*5.30€.* ☎ 01 39 50 30 32. *www. tourisme.fr/musee-lambinet.*
This museum is housed in the wood-panelled drawing rooms of the charming Hôtel Lambinet built in 1750 for Joseph-Barnabé Porchon, building contractor to the king, whose initials can be seen in the wrought ironwork on the balcony in the middle of the pleasing façade. The atmosphere of an 18C town house

is re-created by the period furniture, paintings and sculptures (Pajou, Houdon). At the same time, the museum illustrates the history of Versailles through numerous pieces of furniture and objects including a collection of French ceramics, watches, miniatures, snuff-boxes, silverware, engraved copper plates used to print the calico known as *toile de Jouy,* and works by local artists, such as the busts of Rousseau and Voltaire by Houdon, the bust of Louis XVI by Pajou or the *Maréchal de Saxe* by Jean-Baptiste Lemoyne.

The first floor houses an extensive collection of items related to Revolutionary events and figures: **Marat's** murder; **Charlotte de Corday's** arrest; events in Versailles during 1789 with, in particular, the Declaration of Human Rights; Général Hoche, one of Versailles' most famous sons. One room is devoted to the **Manufacture d'armes de Versailles**, created in 1793. The factory enjoyed an excellent reputation during the days of the Empire for the quality of the workmanship. This is evident in the collection of ceremonial arms (sabres, rifles) and the very fine boxed pistols with accessories said to have belonged to Général Scherer. The museum displays works by 19C landscape painters (Corot, Eugène Isabey, Charles-Émile Lambinet) as well as genre painting by Louis-Léopold Boilly. The Orientalist painter André Suréda, the Nabis painter Jean Lacombe and the landscape painter Henri Le Sidaner are also among the artists represented.

### Orangerie de Madame Élisabeth

*Impasse Champ-Lagarde.*

The Orangery formed part of the estate offered to Madame Élisabeth in 1783 by her brother, Louis XVI. The building designed by La Brière, Louis XVI's architect, consists of a vast rectangular south-facing room. The house was later turned into a residence which implied the addition of many windows. In 1997, it was bought by the Conseil général des Yvelines and refurbished to house temporary exhibitions of contemporary art. The garden which was also remodelled, has retained the original atmosphere of the place.

## Excursions

### Arboretum National de Chèvreloup

*30 route de Versailles. Via boulevard Saint-Antoine NW on the town plan opposite the Parly II shopping centre.* ○*Open early Apr to mid-Nov Sat-Mon 10am-6pm (last ad-mission 5pm).* ⊸*2.50€.* ☎ *01 39 55 53 80.*

In 1924 a plot of land formerly belonging to the Grand Parc (& *see Parc du château de Versailles*) was offered to the Natural History Museum of Paris so that the Botanical Gardens (*Jardin des Plantes*) could enrich their collection of tree species. The first steps were to set up a Tree Centre. The arboretum houses 2 700 species and varieties from temperate or cold regions (from China to the Caucasus and the United States). An alleyway lined with blue cedar trees from the Atlas mountain range separates conifers from broadleaved trees.

The **Maison de l'arbre** provides valuable information about the arboretum and the development of trees: temporary exhibitions, films.

### Haras de Jardy

*2km/1.2mi northeast along N 182. Leave Versailles by avenue de St-Cloud toward Paris.*

This huge stud farm, a horse-lover's paradise, forms part of an important complex of leisure activities (tennis, golf, riding, show jumping). The vast park offers fine walks and is the site of numerous show jumping competitions.

# VILLENEUVE-D'ASCQ★

POPULATION 65 042

MICHELIN LOCAL MAP 302: G-4 – 8KM/5MI EAST OF LILLE

In 1970 the *communes* of **Annappes, Flers and Ascq** were grouped together to form Villeneuve-d'Ascq, one of nine new towns in France. The three centres of the old towns have remained hubs of activity. The town's name, Ascq, is a reminder of the tragic massacre of 86 patriots on 2 April 1944, which is commemorated by a monument and the **Musée du Souvenir.**

A stroll through the town reveals new concepts in urban living: overhead pedestrian walkways straddle the main roads; residential areas merge into commercial centres; and there are numerous large civic amenities: a 35 000-seat stadium, a cultural centre, museums etc.

The town is linked to the remainder of the Lille metropolitan area by a network of motorways and an automatic *métro* system: the Val.

- **Information:** Office du tourisme de Villebeuve-d'Ascq, Château de Flers, Chemin du Chat-Botté, 59652 ☎ 03 20 43 55 75. www.villeneuvedascq-tourisme.eu.
- **Orient Yourself:** The town lies 8km (5 miles) to the east of Lille, close to the border with Belgium.
- **Parking:** Because the town is a composite of three former towns it is not possible to give parking information that would serve all three, but see map for location of parking in the centre of the new town.
- **Don't Miss:** The windmill museum.
- **Organizing Your Time:** Visit in the morning, and stay for lunch.
- **Especially for Kids:** Forum des Sciences.
- **Also See:** Lille, Tourcoing.

## Rural Heritage

### Musée des Moulins

*Guided tours (1-2hrs) daily (except weekends and public holidays)* ⊙*Open 10am-noon, 2-5pm.* ⊙*Closed Aug, mid-Dec to mid-Jan.* ⊸*From 2.50€ to 6€.* ☎*03 20 05 49 34. www.aram-nord.asso.fr.* In the 19C, the Lille region boasted some 200 mills. After 1976, three of them were reintroduced in Villeneuve-d'Ascq: the **Moulin des Olieux** (an oil mill dating from 1743) which was used for processing linseed, a traditional **flour mill** (1776) and a water mill. After visiting the mills, it is interesting to tour the museum managed by a regionally based association, Les Amis des Moulins. Exhibits describe

## Address Book

*For coin ranges, see the Legend on the cover flap.*

### WHERE TO STAY

⊜⊜ **Ascotel** – *Av. Paul-Langevin, Cité Scientifique* – ☎ *03 20 67 34 34* – ⊞ – *83 rms – restaurant* ⊜⊜. Located in the very heart of the scientific city, close to major roads, Ascotel is a cubic establishment built of red brick. The pale yellow rooms are spacious and well fitted out. Modern-style restaurant.

### TOURS AND VISITS

**Guided walking tours** – *Rendez-vous at 2.30pm at the Château de Flers.* Walks are organized the 2nd Sunday of each month (no charge). Enquire at the Office de Tourisme.

**Passeport Journée** – The Day Passport includes access to museums and meals in a restaurant or a night in one of the hotels participating in the offer. From 19.80€ to 22.90€ (children: 13.70€ to 16.80€). Available at the Office de Tourisme.

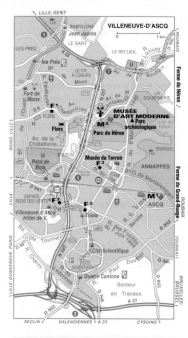

| Ferme D'En-Haut | F¹ |
| Ferme Dupire | F² |
| Ferme Lebrun | F³ |
| Forum des Sciences-Centre F.-Mitterrand | F⁷ |
| Musée des Moulins | M² |
| Musée du Souvenir | M¹ |

the various mechanisms used in the mills, and include the tools used by carpenters, millers, woodcutters etc in the 18C and 19C. There are countless millstones, ranging from a hand-operated prehistoric stone to stones worked by an electric motor.

### Parc du Héron

*The park is accessible from the castle by following the meander of the lake.*

The Chemin du Grand Marais, a pleasant stroll beside the lake, leads to the sailing centre on the edge of Lac Héron. The path runs along the shore, past the bird sanctuary (73ha/180 acres) where herons, mallards, moorhens and partridges find refuge.

### Musée du Terroir

*12 carrière Delporte. Access via rue du 8-Mai. Open Mar-Nov daily (except Sat) 2.30-6pm (Sun 3.30-6pm ( guided visit at 4pm). Closed Dec-Feb. 3€. ☎ 03 20 91 87 57. www.shvam. asso.fr.*

**Delporte Farm** in the old centre of Annappes is built of Lezennes stone and brick; it now houses the folk museum. In the courtyard and buildings a collection of agricultural tools is displayed, along with traditional workshops: foundry, locksmith's, joinery, saddler's, dairy etc.

### Fermes d'antan

There are more than 70 farms in Villeneuve-d'Ascq; the oldest date from the 17C and are built of brick, stone and flint. The **Ferme Lebrun** (1610) is now the home of race horses (*rue de la Liberté*). The **Ferme du Grand-Ruage** (19C) is still a working concern (*rue Colbert*). On the other hand many of these farms have been turned to other uses: a theatre (**Ferme Dupire**, *80 rue Yves-Decugis*), artists' studios (**Ferme d'En-Haut**, *rue Champollion*), **nature centre** (**Ferme du Héron**, 1816, *east of the lake*), the ideal starting point for guided nature walks.

## Sights

### Musée d'Art moderne★★

♿ ☛ *Closed until the spring of 2008. Call for information on opening times and charges. ☎ 03 20 19 68 68.*

Lying by a lawn above Lac du Héron, the huge building (1983) by architect Rolland Simounet suggests a set of brick and glass cubes. The sculpture park displays contemporary works: a mobile and a stabile by **Alexander Calder**, *Southern Cross* (1969) and *Guillotine for Eight People* (1936). Note in particular the *Woman with Open Arms* (1962) by **Picasso**, an idol made of shingles and cement, which looks both colossal and fragile and seems to be as flexible as a sheet of paper. The foyer leads to the permanent and temporary exhibitions (*right*), and to the reception and other services (*left*): library, cafeteria, classrooms used for courses in the plastic arts.

**The collection** – Roger Dutilleul's collection, which contains over 230 works mainly from the first half of the 20C, was presented to the museum by Geneviève and Jean Masurel, Dutilleul's nephew. Dutilleul made his first acquisitions in 1907 and from the beginning recognised the talent of artists who were not then understood: one of the first paintings he bought was Braque's *Houses and Tree* which had just been refused entry at the Salon d'Automne.

The collection contains many Fauvist, Cubist, primitive and abstract works. The Fauvists include Rouault, Derain and Van Dongen (*Pouting Woman* – 1909). Cubism is represented in paintings by **Braque** (*The Factories of Rio Tinto*) and **Picasso** (*Seated Nude, Head of a Woman*); this section also contains collages: Picasso's *Head of a Man* and Braque's *The Little Scout*. Several works by **Fernand Léger** follow his development from a 1914 landscape to his sketch for a mural (1938), encompassing works such as *Woman with a Bunch of Flowers* and *Still-Life with Fruit Dish*. One room is devoted to **Modigliani** paintings, drawings and the unique, white marble *Head of a Woman* (1913); this unfinished work denotes the influence of Khmer and African Art.

Works of abstract art featured are by Kandinsky, Klee and **De Staël**. De Staël knew Roger Dutilleul through the painter **Lanskoy**, who was the collector's protégé, and many examples of the latter's work are also on show. Other artists from the Paris School include **Charchoune**, **Buffet, Chapoval** and **Utrillo**.

## Parc archéologique Asnapio

*Rue Carpeaux.* ◷Open Jul-Aug Tue-Fri 2-5pm. Apr-Jun and Sep-Oct Wed 2-5pm, Sun 2-7pm. ◷Closed public holidays (except Sun). ◉3€. ☎ 03 20 47 21 99.
This 6ha/15 acre park contains reconstructions of regional dwellings from the Neolithic Era to the end of the Middle Ages: houses, barns, workshops.

## Château de Flers

*Visits depending on the open days organised by the tourist office.* ☎ 03 20 43 55 75.
This Flemish castle built in 1661 is surrounded by a moat once spanned by a drawbridge. The brick buildings with stone clamping, surmounted by stepped gables, house the tourist office and an **archaeological museum** (temporary exhibitions).

## Musée du Souvenir

*77 rue Mangin in Ascq.* ◷For hours of opening and charges call ☎ 03 20 91 87 57.
This museum is dedicated to the memory of 86 inhabitants of Ascq (the youngest was only 15) killed in 1944 and recalls the trial of the Germans accused of their massacre.

Eighty-six stones have been laid along the railway line to commemorate this tragic event.

## Forum des Sciences-Centre F.-Mitterrand

*1 place de l'Hôtel-de-Ville.* &. ◷Open daily (except Mon) 10am-5.30pm (weekends and public holidays 2.30-6.30pm). ◷Closed first 3 wks of Sep, 1 Jan, 1 May, 25 Dec. ◉5€ to 7€ depending on the activities. No charge first Sun of month. ☎ 03 20 19 36 36. www.forum-des-sciences.tm.fr.

Kids The Forum is intended to provide an introduction to new technologies through temporary exhibitions. The children's workshop includes an area reserved for three-to six-year-olds and an information centre. The planetarium (its hemisphere has a 14m/46ft diameter) offers an introduction to basic astronomy: observing the sky, the comets, the planets.

# VILLERS-COTTERÊTS

POPULATION 9 839

MICHELIN LOCAL MAP 306: A-7

Villers-Cotterêts is a peaceful little town, almost entirely surrounded by Retz Forest; it was the homeland of the Orléans family until the Revolution and developed owing to the royal passion for hunting. It was the birthplace of Alexandre Dumas senior in 1802.

- **Information:** Office de tourisme de Villers-Cotterêts, 6 pl. A.-Brian (opposite the château), 02600 ☎ 03 23 96 55 10.
- ▶ **Orient Yourself:** 22km (14 miles) from Soissons, and 75km (47 miles) from Paris, to the south of the Aisne.
- ◷ **Organizing Your Time:** Being entirely surrounded by forest, you can make this a place for woodland exploration and picnics. Otherwise, allow half a day to visit the museum and the château.
- ℀ **Also See:** Soissons. The Château de Pierrefonds.

## A Bit of History

**Origins of the national birth registry**
In 1535 François I replaced the first 12C royal castle with a Renaissance building and added to the outbuildings involved in the management of the royal hunts. It was here that the King announced the famous Statute of Villers-Cotterêts in 1539 prescribing the substitution of French for Latin in public registers and legal documents. Among its 192 articles it stated that parish priests should keep registers of the parishioners' dates of birth and death; here then, are the foundations of the modern registry system. Previously, except in noble families where records were kept, ordinary people had to rely on the memory of witnesses to prove identity. It was another 250 years (1792) before the keeping of State registers was entrusted to the local authorities.

**A Child of the Islands**
The first of the three generations – grandfather, father and son – of the famous Dumas family was the son of a Dominican settler, Marquess Davy de la Pailleterie, and Marie-Cessette Dumas, a coloured girl. Thomas-Alexandre assumed his mother's surname and pursued a career in the army where he later rose to become General, but his Republican opinions led to his being disgraced by Napoleon Bonaparte. He retired to Villers-Cotterêts which was his wife's homeland and lived a quiet life until his death, four years after the birth of his son Alexandre, the future novelist.

**Alexandre Dumas' Youth**
Many hard years passed for the widow and her son; Alexandre entered the study of one of the town's notaries and copied deeds there until he was 20. One day his mother told him that only 253 francs remained; Dumas took 53 francs as his share, left the rest for his mother and headed for Paris. He played billiards, gambling the cost of his fare to the capital, and won – which allowed him to arrive in the capital with his nest

### TOURISM INFORMATION

▤ 8 pl. A.-Briand (face au château), 02600 Villers-Cotterêts, ☎ 03 23 96 55 10.

### WHERE TO STAY

◷ **Hôtel Régent** – 26 r. du Gén.-Mangin – ☎ 03 23 96 01 46 – hotel.le.regent@gofornet.com. Closed Sun from Nov to Mar (except public holidays) – ℙ – 25 rms – ⌶ 8€. In memory of the stagecoaches that used to stop here, this 18C post house has preserved its decor of yesteryear. Come in via the porch and admire the paved courtyard and drinking trough. The spacious rooms giving onto the facade feature period furnishings.

egg intact. His beautiful handwriting landed him a job in the secretary's office of the Duc d'Orléans, the future King Louis-Philippe. His prodigious literary career was about to begin.

### Dumas fils (Dumas junior)

Dumas senior married his neighbour who gave birth to a son in 1824. The child was named Alexandre after his father and, like his father, he became a famous writer. His novel, *La Dame aux camélias*, inspired Verdi's opera *Traviata*.

## Visit

### In the footsteps of the three Dumas

Place du Docteur-Mouflier, formerly place de la Fontaine, is mentioned in Dumas senior's memoirs. His grandfather's hotel stood on the square as did the lawyer's office where he was employed and Madame Dumas' tobacconist's shop. The writer's **birthplace**, indicated by a plaque, is at 46 rue A.-Dumas. The titles of his most famous works are written on either side of the garage door. Rue A.-Dumas leads to the square of the same name where a statue of the writer by Rodin used to stand; it was unfortunately melted down by the Germans during the First World War. Only his quill pen was saved and is now in the care of the museum. Rue de Bapaume leads from this square to the cemetery where the Dumas' family grave is located. The other statue of Dumas by Bourret stands in the small public garden on rue L.-Lagrange.

The town boasts three lovely fountains: Clapotis, a crouching young maiden by Ferenc Naguy, on place de la Madelon; Fontaine de Diane, a copy of the Louvre Museum's *Artemis Agrotera (Diana the Huntress)*, on rue L'éveillé; and Fontaine de la Coquille on rue Pelet-Otto.

### Musée Alexandre-Dumas

&. ⏲Open daily (except Tue, last Sun in the month and public holidays) 2-5pm (last admission 45min before closing) ⊚3.10€. ☎ 03 23 96 23 30.

Three small rooms are dedicated to the famous "Three Dumas": letters, novels, paintings, satirical cartoons, busts and objects including the uniform Dumas junior wore as a member of the French Academy.

He was a friend of George Sand and defended the feminist cause. He was elected to the French Academy in 1875.

## Additional Sight

### Château François I

⏲Open May-Oct ➤ Guided tours (1hr) daily (except Mon) 11am and 3pm. Nov-Apr daily (except Sun and public holidays) 11am and 3pm. ⏲Closed 1 May. ⊚4€. ☎ 03 23 96 55 10 (tourist office). In 1806 Napoleon turned the empty château into a workhouse for the *département* of Seine; today it is a retirement home. Within the courtyard, the east and west sides are bordered by buildings which retain Renaissance features: high attic windows in brick flanked by pillars crowned with urns. At the end stands the main front, with a shallow recessed loggia on the first floor, surmounted by a portrait of King François I.

The **main staircase**★ alone is worth a visit; it is a Renaissance masterpiece (1535), a double flight of stairs dating from the period of François I. The carvings on the coffered ceiling – crowned Fs, salamanders, fleurs-de-lis – are from the school of Jean Goujon. The same motifs are used in greater abundance in the State room, which was originally the chapel. The vaulting is concealed by a false ceiling. The stonework of the Renaissance altarpiece remains. At the end of the gallery *(display on local history)* the **King's staircase**, contemporary with the main staircase, has its original decoration of carved mythological scenes from *The Dream of Polyphyle*.

### Parc

All that remains of Le Nôtre's work are the outlines of the parterre and the perspective of the Allée Royale. In the middle of this splendid green expanse, one can still see the base of the circular pond. The white gate at the end of the Allée Royale and the Grandes Allées on the right side of the lawn all lead to the forest (footpaths).

In this index, forests and châteaux are subindexed under "**Forêt**" and "**Château**" respectively.

# A

Abbaye de Jouarre . . . . . . . . . . . . . . . . . .261
Abbaye de Port-Royal-des-Champs . 342
Abbaye de Prémontré . . . . . . . . . . . . . 378
Abbaye de Royaumont . . . . . . . . . . . . 358
Abbaye et Jardins de Valloires. . . . . . .421
Abbaye St-Martin . . . . . . . . . . . . . . . . 269
Abbaye St-Nicolas-aux-Bois. . . . . . . . 378
Abbeville . . . . . . . . . . . . . . . . . . . . . . . . 106
Abbeys . . . . . . . . . . . . . . . . . . . . . . . . . .87
Acy-en-Multien . . . . . . . . . . . . . . . . . . 322
Adam, L'Isle- . . . . . . . . . . . . . . . . . . . . 259
Ailly-sur-Somme . . . . . . . . . . . . . . . . . 407
Aisne . . . . . . . . . . . . . . . . . . . . . . . . . . .59
Albert . . . . . . . . . . . . . . . . . . . . . . . . . .107
Ambleteuse. . . . . . . . . . . . . . . . . . . . . .211
Amiens . . . . . . . . . . . . . . . . . . . 109, 407
Ancienne Abbaye de
    St-Jean-des-Vignes . . . . . . . . . . . . 401
Ancienne Abbaye St-Vaast . . . . . . . . . .126
André, Nélie. . . . . . . . . . . . . . . . . . . . .176
Animals. . . . . . . . . . . . . . . . . . . . . . . . .66
Appartement de Madame de
    Maintenon, Versailles . . . . . . . . . . . 443
Appartement Privé du Roi,
    Versailles. . . . . . . . . . . . . . . . . . . . . 440
Arboretum de La Roche . . . . . . . . . . . 356
Arboretum National de Chèvreloup . 458
Archery. . . . . . . . . . . . . . . . . . . . . . . . .99
Architecture . . . . . . . . . . . . . . . . . . . . .72
Archon . . . . . . . . . . . . . . . . . . . . . . . . .410
Arc International . . . . . . . . . . . . . . . . . 384
Arnauld, Angélique. . . . . . . . . . . . . . . 342
Arques. . . . . . . . . . . . . . . . . . . . . . . . . 384
Arras . . . . . . . . . . . . . . . . . . . . . . . . . . 120
Arras, Treaty of . . . . . . . . . . . . . . . . . . .69
Art . . . . . . . . . . . . . . . . . . . . . . . . 72, 91
Artois Region . . . . . . . . . . . . . . . . . 13, 60
Auberge du Père Ganne . . . . . . . . . . . 140
Auberge Ravoux . . . . . . . . . . . . . . . . . .130
Australian Memorial. . . . . . . . . . . . . . .210
Auvers-sur-Oise . . . . . . . . . . . . . . . . . .130
Avesnes-sur-Helpe . . . . . . . . . . . . . . . 132
Avesnois Region. . . . . . . . . . . . 13, 61, 132

# B

Bailleul . . . . . . . . . . . . . . . . . . . . . . . . .137
Balcon du Haut Planet . . . . . . . . . . . . . 353
Barbizon. . . . . . . . . . . . . . . . . . . . . . . . 140
Barbizon School, The . . . . . . . . . . . 95, 140
Baroque architecture . . . . . . . . . . . . . . .86

Bart, Jean . . . . . . . . . . . . . . . . . . . . . . . 23
Basic Information . . . . . . . . . . . . . . . . . .5
Battle of the Marne . . . . . . . . . . . . . . .31
Bavay. . . . . . . . . . . . . . . . . . . . . . . . . . .14
Beaurain . . . . . . . . . . . . . . . . . . . . . . . .41
Beauvais. . . . . . . . . . . . . . . . . . . . . . . . .14
Beaux Monts, Les. . . . . . . . . . . . . . . . . 20
Beer . . . . . . . . . . . . . . . . . . . . . . . . . . 10
Beguine convents . . . . . . . . . . . . . . . . .17
Bellegambe, Jean . . . . . . . . . . . . . . . 22
Bergues. . . . . . . . . . . . . . . . . . . . . . . . .14
Bernay-en-Ponthieu. . . . . . . . . . . . . . .21
Bêtises de Cambrai . . . . . . . . . . . . . . . 16
Bièvres . . . . . . . . . . . . . . . . . . . . . . . . 26
Billons . . . . . . . . . . . . . . . . . . . . . . . . . .9
Blériot-Plage . . . . . . . . . . . . . . . . . . . .21
Blue-stone oratories. . . . . . . . . . . . . . .13
Boeschepe. . . . . . . . . . . . . . . . . . . . . . .13
Boigneville. . . . . . . . . . . . . . . . . . . . . 30
Bois du Montoir . . . . . . . . . . . . . . . . . .21
Bonaparte, Napoleon. . . . . . . . . . . . . .24
Books and Films. . . . . . . . . . . . . . . . . . .4
Bosquet de la Salle de Bal. . . . . . . . . . 44
Bossuet, Jacques . . . . . . . . . . . . . . . . 29
Bouchon. . . . . . . . . . . . . . . . . . . . . . . .9
Boudin, Eugène . . . . . . . . . . . . . . . . . .9
Bougival . . . . . . . . . . . . . . . . . . . . . . . 29
Bouillancy . . . . . . . . . . . . . . . . . . . . . 32
Boulogne, Forêt de . . . . . . . . . . . . . . .15
Boulogne-sur-Mer. . . . . . . . . . . . 151, 21
Boulonnais, Le . . . . . . . . . . . . . . . . 60, 15
Bouteille, La. . . . . . . . . . . . . . . . . . . . .41
Bouvines, Battle of . . . . . . . . . . . . . . . 27
Bray, Le Pays de . . . . . . . . . . . . . . . . . 14
Bray-sur-Somme . . . . . . . . . . . . . . . . 40
Breteuil, Château de . . . . . . . . . . . . . . 16
Brie. . . . . . . . . . . . . . . . . . . . . . . . . 63, 10
Burelles. . . . . . . . . . . . . . . . . . . . . . . . .41

# C

"Chunnel", The . . . . . . . . . . . . . . . . . . 16
Cabinets Intérieurs de
    la Reine, Versailles . . . . . . . . . . . . . 44
Cabotans . . . . . . . . . . . . . . . . . . . . . . .11
Calais. . . . . . . . . . . . . . . . . . . . . . . . . . 16
Calendar of events . . . . . . . . . . . . . . . .3
Calvin, Jean . . . . . . . . . . . . . . . . . . . . .318
Cambrai . . . . . . . . . . . . . . . . . . . . . . . 16
Cambrésis . . . . . . . . . . . . . . . . . . . . . 6
Canal de l'Ourcq, The . . . . . . . . . . . . . . 32
Canoeing . . . . . . . . . . . . . . . . . . . . . . .3

# INDEX

Cantilius . . . . . . . . . . . . . . . . . . . . . . . . . . . .177
Cap Blanc-Nez. . . . . . . . . . . . . . . . . . . . .213
Capet, Hugh . . . . . . . . . . . . . . . . . . 68, 393
Cap Gris-Nez . . . . . . . . . . . . . . . . . . . . . .212
Cappy . . . . . . . . . . . . . . . . . . . . . . . . . . . 406
Carnival, Dunkirk . . . . . . . . . . . . . . . . . 232
Carnivals. . . . . . . . . . . . . . . . . . . . . . . . . . .97
Carolingians . . . . . . . . . . . . . . . . . . . . . . .68
Carpeaux, Jean-Baptiste . . . . . . . . . . . .418
Carrefour d'Eugénie . . . . . . . . . . . . . . . 204
Car rental . . . . . . . . . . . . . . . . . . . . . . . . .24
Cartignies. . . . . . . . . . . . . . . . . . . . . . . .132
Cassel . . . . . . . . . . . . . . . . . . . . . . . . . . .172
Casteel-Meulen . . . . . . . . . . . . . . . . . . .173
Castles. . . . . . . . . . . . . . . . . . . . . . . . . . . .79
Cathédrale Notre-Dame, Amiens . . . . .112
Cathédrale St-Gervais-et-St-Protais . 402
Cathédrale St-Pierre . . . . . . . . . . . . . . .145
Catsberg. . . . . . . . . . . . . . . . . . . . . . . . .139
Cayeux-sur-Mer . . . . . . . . . . . . . . . . . . 405
Centre d'accueil C. Grimminck . . . . . . .139
Centre de Production Peugeot . . . . . . 341
Cézanne, Paul . . . . . . . . . . . . . . . . . . . . . .96
Chaalis, Abbaye de . . . . . . . . . . . . . . . .174
Chambre du Roi, Versailles. . . . . . . . . . 438
Channel Tunnel, The. . . . . . . . . . . . . . . 164
Chaourse . . . . . . . . . . . . . . . . . . . . . . . . .410
Chapelle des Templiers . . . . . . . . . . . . . 267
Chapelle Royale St-Frambourg . . . . . . 397
Charlemagne . . . . . . . . . . . . . . . . . . . . . .68
Chartres . . . . . . . . . . . . . . . . . . . . 12, 185
**Château**
    d'Auvers . . . . . . . . . . . . . . . . . . . . . . . . . . . 131
    d'Écouen . . . . . . . . . . . . . . . . . . . . . . . . . . .236
    d'If . . . . . . . . . . . . . . . . . . . . . . . . . . . . . . . . . 291
    d'Olhain . . . . . . . . . . . . . . . . . . . . . . . . . . . . . 318
    de Bagatelle . . . . . . . . . . . . . . . . . . . . . . . . . 107
    de Chantilly . . . . . . . . . . . . . . . . . . . . . . . . . . 177
    de Dampierre . . . . . . . . . . . . . . . . . . . . . . . . 218
    de Ferrières . . . . . . . . . . . . . . . . . . . . . . . . . . 238
    de Flers . . . . . . . . . . . . . . . . . . . . . . . . . . . . . . 461
    Fort de Rambures . . . . . . . . . . . . . . . . . . . . . 354
    de la Reine Blanche . . . . . . . . . . . . . . . . . . . 184
    de Montceaux. . . . . . . . . . . . . . . . . . . . . . . . . 297
    de Monte-Cristo . . . . . . . . . . . . . . . . . . . . . . 291
    de Pierrefonds . . . . . . . . . . . . . . . . . . . . . . . . 336
    de Pont-Remy. . . . . . . . . . . . . . . . . . . . . . . . . 408
    de Raray . . . . . . . . . . . . . . . . . . . . . . . . . . . . . 398
    de Vaux-le-Vicomte . . . . . . . . . . . . . . . . . . . 423
    de Versailles . . . . . . . . . . . . . . . . . . . . . . . . . . 427
    et Parc de Thoiry . . . . . . . . . . . . . . . . . . . . . 412
    François I . . . . . . . . . . . . . . . . . . . . . . . . . . . . . 463
Chemin des Dames, Le. . . . . . . . . . . . . .195
Children, Activities for . . . . . . . . . . . . . . .34

Chimes . . . . . . . . . . . . . . . . . . . . . . . . . . .99
Cimetière National de Chambry . . . . .321
Circuit des Druides . . . . . . . . . . . . . . . . 253
Circuit du Désert . . . . . . . . . . . . . . . . . . 255
Cité des Sciences et de l'Industrie . . . 334
Clairière de l'Armistice . . . . . . . . . . . . . 205
Classical architecture . . . . . . . . . . . . . . . .86
Coal Fields . . . . . . . . . . . . . . . . . . . . . . . .101
Colbert, Jean-Baptiste . . . . . . . . . . . . . 391
Colline de Notre-Dame-de-Lorette . . .315
Colonne de la Grande Armée. . . . . . . . .156
Compiègne . . . . . . . . . . . . . . . . . . . . . . 196
Confrérie du Puy Notre-Dame. . . . . . . .114
Conservatoire Botanique National
    de Bailleul. . . . . . . . . . . . . . . . . . . . . . .138
Conservatoire National des
    Plantes Médicinales
    Aromatiques et Industrielles . . . . . 301
Conversion Tables . . . . . . . . . . . . . . . . . . .55
Corbie . . . . . . . . . . . . . . . . . . . . . . . . . . . 208
Corot, Camille . . . . . . . . . . . . . . . . . . . . . .94
Côte d'Opale, La . . . . . . . . . . . . . . 13, 211
Coucy-le-Château-Auffrique . . . . . . . . .214
Coupole d'Helfaut-Wizernes . . . . . . . . 258
Cour de Marbre . . . . . . . . . . . . . . . . . . . 430
Crécy, The Battle of. . . . . . . . . . . . . . . . .216
Crécy-en-Ponthieu . . . . . . . . . . . . . . . . .216
Crossbow . . . . . . . . . . . . . . . . . . . . . . . . . .99
Crotoy, Le . . . . . . . . . . . . . . . . . . . . . . . . 404
Crouy-sur-Ourcq . . . . . . . . . . . . . . . . . . 322
Cruises. . . . . . . . . . . . . . . . . . . . . . . . . . . .44
Cuisine . . . . . . . . . . . . . . . . . . . . . . . . . . .102
Culture . . . . . . . . . . . . . . . . . . . . . . . . . . .72
Currency. . . . . . . . . . . . . . . . . . . . . . . . . . .53
Customs Regulations . . . . . . . . . . . . . . . .20
Cycling . . . . . . . . . . . . . . . . . . . . . . . . . . .32

**D**

Dagny . . . . . . . . . . . . . . . . . . . . . . . . . . . 409
Dampierre, Château de . . . . . . . . . . . . .218
Daubigny, Charles-François . . . . . . . . . .131
Debussy, Claude. . . . . . . . . . . . . . . . . . . .376
Demeure de Gilles de la Boé . . . . . . . 282
Denain. . . . . . . . . . . . . . . . . . . . . . . . . . . 420
Denis, Maurice . . . . . . . . . . . . . . . . . . . . . .96
Discounts . . . . . . . . . . . . . . . . . . . . . . . . . .54
Discovering Northern France. . . . . . . . 105
Disney, Walt. . . . . . . . . . . . . . . . . . . . . . . 220
Disneyland Resort Paris. . . . . . . . . . . . . 220
Dohis . . . . . . . . . . . . . . . . . . . . . . . . . . . . 409
Dolmen de Fresnicourt . . . . . . . . . . . . .319
Domaine de Villarceaux. . . . . . . . . . . . . 357
Douai. . . . . . . . . . . . . . . . . . . . . . . . . . . . 227
Doue . . . . . . . . . . . . . . . . . . . . . . . . . . . . 262

Drievemeulen........................174
Driving in France ....................23
Driving licence ......................23
Ducasse ............................97
Dumas, Alexandre............... 291, 462
Dunkerque......................... 232
Dunkirk........................... 232

# E

Écomusée Picarvie ................ 389
Economy........................... 100
Écouen, Château d' ................ 236
Edward III..........................216
Église de La Neuville................210
Église de Liercourt................. 408
Église Stella-Matutina ............. 366
Electricity...........................52
Emergency services .................52
Englancourt........................411
Eppe-Sauvage .....................135
Ermenonville.......................176
Errard, Jean ........................90
Espace culturel Paul-Bédu .......... 300
Esquerdes ........................ 384
Étrépilly...........................321
Euralille........................... 282

# F

Faïence ............................91
Felleries ..........................133
Ferrières, Château de .............. 238
Ferrières, Forêt de ................ 239
Ferries ............................21
Festivals and Fairs ..................36
First World War......................71
Fishing ............................31
Flanders ....................... 13, 61
Flines-les-Raches.................. 232
Flobart ............................213
Flying buttresses....................83
Folembray .........................216
Folklore............................97
Fontainebleau ..................... 240
Fontainettes, Les .................. 148
Food and Drink.....................102
Forestry ...........................63
**Forêt**
d'Halatte ...................... 398
de Boulogne.................... 158
de Chantilly.................... 184
de Compiègne ................. 203
de Ferrières ................... 239
de Fontainebleau .............. 251
de Guînes...................... 257

de l'Isle-Adam ................. 260
de Marly ...................... 293
Montiers....................... 217
de Montmorency ............... 306
de Raismes-St-Amand-Wallers......... 362
de Rambouillet ................ 352
de Rihoult-Clairmarais.......... 384
de St-Gobain................... 377
Fortresse de Mimoyecques ........ 257
Forum des Sciences-Centre
    F.-Mitterrand ................ 461
Fouquet, Nicolas .................. 423
Fourmies ........................ 257
Franco-Prussian War................70
François I ..........................79
Froissy........................... 407

# G

Galerie des Cerfs ................. 249
Gardens...................... 66, 357
Gardens, Versailles ............... 445
Gâtinais............................63
Gayant........................... 227
General Pétain ....................315
Getting Around ....................22
Getting There .....................21
Giants ............................97
Glassware......................... 100
Go-Karting.........................34
Golf ..............................33
Gorges d'Apremont ............... 254
Gorges de Franchard ............. 253
Gothic architecture.................82
Grandes Eaux ...............365, 393
Grand Point de vue ............... 253
Grands Appartements, Versailles.....431
Grange aux Dîmes................ 347
Grotte du Jardin des Pins ......... 249
Grottes-Refuges de Naours .........314
Guînes........................... 257

# H

Hachette, Jeanne..................143
Hainault...........................60
Hangest-sur-Somme ............. 407
Haras de Jardy ................... 458
Hardelot-Plage....................158
Hardouin-Mansart, Jules........ 289, 372
Hary..............................410
Henri IV...........................79
Henson horse breed, The .......... 294
Hestrud..........................134
Hiking ............................31
Historial de la Grande Guerre ....... 335

# INDEX

History................................68
Holidays .............................53
Horseback riding.....................32
Horse Races........................ 365
Horse Racing.........................35
Hortillonnages.......................115
Hospice Comtesse................. 283
Hot-air ballooning....................43
Hôtel Bouctot-Vagniez...............119
Hôtel de Ville....................... 386
Hôtel Flandre Angleterre ............274
Hôtel Sandelin and museum........ 382
Houjarray........................... 304
How to Use This Guide.................6
Hugo, Victor ....................... 308
Hundred Years War....................68
Hurepoix.............................62
Hydrequent........................ 160

## I
Ile-de-France .............6, 12, 62, 102
Impressionism ......................95
Institut Pasteur – Musée des
    Applications de la Recherche..... 366
Introduction to Northern France ......57

## J
Jacquemart, Nélie ...................176
Jardin archéologique de St-Acheul ...119
Javelin..............................99
Jeantes ........................... 409
Joan of Arc..........................69
Jouy-en-Josas...................... 263

## K
Kayaking............................31
Kermesse ...........................97
Kite flying..........................33
Know Before You Go................. 17

## L
L'Audomarois ...................... 383
L'Isle-Adam ....................... 259
L'Isle-Adam, Forêt de .............. 260
La Baie de Somme.................. 403
La Bouteille ........................411
Lachapelle-aux-Pots............... 148
La Côte d'Opale ....................211
Laffitte, Jacques................... 288
Landsailing ........................33
Landscape painting .................94
La Neuville........................ 407
Laon............................... 265
La Queue-les-Yvelines ............. 304

La Roche-Guyon ................... 355
Lartigue, Jacques-Henri ........... 259
La Thiérache ...................... 408
Lebon, Joseph .....................122
Le Boulonnais......................158
Le Chemin des Dames ..............195
Le COMPA: Conservatoire du
    Machinisme et
    des Pratiques Agricoles ......... 194
Le Crotoy ......................... 404
Le Cyclop ......................... 301
Le Hourdel ........................ 405
Le Long Rocher .................... 256
Le Mont St-Marc and the ponds ..... 205
Lenclos, Ninon de ................. 357
Le Pays de Bray.................... 148
Le Poma Funicular Railway......... 269
Le Portel ..........................157
Le Quesnoy ....................... 348
Les Beaux Monts .................. 204
Les Fontainettes .................. 148
Les Grandes Heures du
    Parlement, Versailles............ 442
Les Grands Monts ................. 207
Les nieulles ........................38
Les Trois Pignons ................. 256
Le Tortoir ......................... 378
Le Touquet-Paris-Plage .............414
Lez-Fontaine.......................134
Licques ...........................159
Liessies ...........................134
Lille.............................. 270
Long.............................. 408
Longpré-les-Corps-Saints.......... 407
Longueil, René de ................. 287
Longueil-Annel ................... 203
Louis of Orléans .................. 336
Louis XIII...........................79
Louis XIV......................... 79, 428
Louis XV ...........................79
Louveciennes ..................... 292

## M
Mail ...............................53
Maillotte, Jeanne ................. 272
Maintenon........................ 285
Maison-atelier de
    Jean-François Millet .............141
Maison Debussy....................376
Maison de Jeanne et Léon Blum..... 263
Maison de l'Oiseau ................ 405
Maison de la Beurière...............156
Maison de la Dentelle...............138

Maison du Parc Naturel Régional
   des Caps et Marais d'Opale . . . . . . . 384
Maison Jean-Monnet . . . . . . . . . . . . . . 304
Maison littéraire de Victor Hugo . . . . 264
Maison Natale du Général de Gaulle . 284
Maison Picassiette . . . . . . . . . . . . . . . . .195
Maisons-Laffitte . . . . . . . . . . . . . . . . . . 287
Manet, Édouard . . . . . . . . . . . . . . . . . . . .96
Mansart, François . . . . . . . . . . . . . . . . . 287
Mantois . . . . . . . . . . . . . . . . . . . . . . . . . . .62
Marly . . . . . . . . . . . . . . . . . . . . . . . . . . . .411
Marly, Forêt de . . . . . . . . . . . . . . . . . . . 293
Marly-le-Roi . . . . . . . . . . . . . . . . . . . . . 289
Marly Park . . . . . . . . . . . . . . . . . . . . . . . 290
Marne, Battle of the . . . . . . . . . . . . . . . .319
Maroilles . . . . . . . . . . . . . . . . . . . . . . . . .132
Marquenterre . . . . . . . . . . . . . . . . . . . . . .59
May-en-Multien . . . . . . . . . . . . . . . . . . 322
Meaux . . . . . . . . . . . . . . . . . . . 295, 319
Medici, Catherine de' . . . . . . . . . . . . . . .324
Mélantois . . . . . . . . . . . . . . . . . . . . . . . . .61
Mémorial de Longueval . . . . . . . . . . 108
Mémorial de Pozières . . . . . . . . . . . . . . 108
Mémorial de Thiepval . . . . . . . . . . . . . . 108
Mémorial de Villeroy . . . . . . . . . . . . . . .319
Mer de Sable . . . . . . . . . . . . . . . . . . . . . .176
Merovingians . . . . . . . . . . . . . . . . . . . . . .68
Metallurgy . . . . . . . . . . . . . . . . . . . . . . . 100
Metro, Paris . . . . . . . . . . . . . . . . . . . . . . .22
Meudon . . . . . . . . . . . . . . . . . . . . . . . . . 298
Michelin Driving Tours . . . . . . . . . . . . . . .12
Michelin Guide France . . . . . . . . . . . . . . .25
Mickey Mouse . . . . . . . . . . . . . . . . . . . . 220
Military architecture . . . . . . . . . . . . . . . . .90
Millet, Jean-François . . . . . . . . . . . . 95, 140
Milly-la-Forêt . . . . . . . . . . . . . . . . . . . . 300
Mimoyecques, Fortresse de . . . . . . . . 257
Monasteries . . . . . . . . . . . . . . . . . . . . . . .86
Monastic buildings . . . . . . . . . . . . . . . . .89
Monastic rules . . . . . . . . . . . . . . . . . . . . .87
Monet, Claude . . . . . . . . . . . . . . . . . . . . .96
Monnet, Jean . . . . . . . . . . . . . . . . . . . . 304
Montcornet . . . . . . . . . . . . . . . . . . . . . . .410
Mont des Cats . . . . . . . . . . . . . . . . . . . . .139
Montfort-l'Amaury . . . . . . . . . . . . . . . . 302
Mont Lambert . . . . . . . . . . . . . . . . . . . . .158
Montmorency . . . . . . . . . . . . . . . . . . . . . 305
Montmorency, Anne de . . . . . . . . . . . . .177
Montmorency, Forêt de . . . . . . . . . . . . . 306
Mont Noir . . . . . . . . . . . . . . . . . . . . . . . . .138
Montreuil . . . . . . . . . . . . . . . . . . . . . . . . 308
Monts de Caubert . . . . . . . . . . . . . . . . . .107
Mont St-Marc . . . . . . . . . . . . . . . . . . . . . 206

Monument de la légion d'honneur . . .15?
Monument de Rousseau et Millet . . . .14?
Monument des Bourgeois de Calais . 16?
Moret-sur-Loing . . . . . . . . . . . . . . . . . . .31?
Morgny-en-Thiérache . . . . . . . . . . . . . . 40?
Morienval . . . . . . . . . . . . . . . . . . . . . . . . .31?
Motorhome Rental . . . . . . . . . . . . . . . . . .2?
Moulin, Jean . . . . . . . . . . . . . . . . . . . . . . 19?
Moulin Edouard III . . . . . . . . . . . . . . . . . .21?
Moustier-en-Fagne . . . . . . . . . . . . . . . . .13?
Multien . . . . . . . . . . . . . . . . . . . . . . . . . . . .6?
Musée Antoine-Lécuyer . . . . . . . . . . . . 38?
Musée Antoine-Vivenel . . . . . . . . . . . . 20?
Musée Benoît-Depuydt . . . . . . . . . . . . .13?
Musée Boucher-de-Perthes . . . . . . . . 10?
Musée Bouilhet-Christofle . . . . . . . . . . 37?
Musée d'Art et d'Archéologie . . . . . . . 39?
Musée d'Art naïf de l'Île-de-France . . 30?
Musée d'Histoire Naturelle
   et de Géologie, Lille . . . . . . . . . . . . . . 28?
Musée Daubigny . . . . . . . . . . . . . . . . . . .13?
Musée de l'Absinthe . . . . . . . . . . . . . . . .13?
Musée de l'hôtel de Berny . . . . . . . . . . .11?
Musée de l'Île-de-France . . . . . . . . . . . 39?
Musée de la Chartreuse . . . . . . . . . . . . 22?
Musée de Laon . . . . . . . . . . . . . . . . . . . . 26?
Musée de la Targette . . . . . . . . . . . . . . . .31?
Musée de la toile de Jouy . . . . . . . . . . . 26?
Musée de la voiture et du tourisme . . 20?
Musée Départemental de l'Oise . . . . .14?
Musée départemental
   Maurice-Denis . . . . . . . . . . . . . . . . . . . 37?
Musée de Picardie . . . . . . . . . . . . . . . . . .11?
Musée des Abris 'Somme 1916' . . . . . 10?
Musée des Antiquités nationales . . . .37?
Musée des Beaux-Arts, Amiens . . . . . .12?
Musée des Canonniers . . . . . . . . . . . . . 28?
Musée du Noyonnais . . . . . . . . . . . . . . .31?
Musée du Second Empire . . . . . . . . . . . 20?
Musée Français de la Photographie . . 26?
Musée Henri-Dupuis . . . . . . . . . . . . . . . 38?
Musée Louis-Senlecq . . . . . . . . . . . . . . . 25?
Musée Municipal de l'Ancienne
   Abbaye de St-Léger . . . . . . . . . . . . . . 40?
Musée Napoléon-I . . . . . . . . . . . . . . . . . 24?
Musée National de la Céramique . . . 39?
Musée National de la Renaissance . . . 23?
Musée National du Transmanche . . . . .21?
Musée Rodin, Villa des Brillants . . . . . 29?
Musée Tourgueniev . . . . . . . . . . . . . . . . 29?
Musée vivant 1914-1918 . . . . . . . . . . . . .31?
Musée Vivant du Cheval
   et du Poney . . . . . . . . . . . . . . . . . . . . . 18?

# INDEX

## N

Nature . . . . . . . . . . . . . . . . . . . . . . . . . . . . . .58
Nature parks . . . . . . . . . . . . . . . . . . . . . . . .45
Nausicaä . . . . . . . . . . . . . . . . . . . . . . . . . . .152
Nieulles, Les . . . . . . . . . . . . . . . . . . . . . . . . .38
Nivelle Offensive . . . . . . . . . . . . . . . . . . . .195
Nord-Pas-de-Calais . . . . . . . . . . . . . . 60, 100
Nôtre, André Le . . . . . . . . . . . . . . . . . . . . 445
Notre-Dame-de-Lorette Hill . . . . . . . . .315
Noyelles . . . . . . . . . . . . . . . . . . . . . . . . . . . 403
Noyon . . . . . . . . . . . . . . . . . . . . . . . . . . . . .316

## O

Oberkampf, Christophe-Philippe . . . . 263
Oise . . . . . . . . . . . . . . . . . . . . . . . . . . . 59, 94
Opal Coast, The . . . . . . . . . . . . . . . . . 13, 211
Orangery, Versailles . . . . . . . . . . . . . . . . .451
Ourcq Valley, The . . . . . . . . . . . . . . . . . . .319

## P

Palais des Beaux-Arts, Lille . . . . . . . . . . 272
Parc-mémorial de Beaumont-Hamel . . 108
Parc archéologique Asnapio . . . . . . . . 461
Parc Astérix . . . . . . . . . . . . . . . . . . . . . . . .128
Parc de la Courneuve . . . . . . . . . . . . . . . 371
Parc Départemental du Val-Joly . . . . .135
Parc du château de Versailles . . . . . . . 445
Parc Naturel Régional des
     Caps et Marais d'Opale . . . . . . . . . . .158
Parc ornithologique du
     Marquenterre . . . . . . . . . . . . . . . . . . . 293
Parc Samara . . . . . . . . . . . . . . . . . . . . . . . 407
Parc zoologique d'Amiens . . . . . . . . . . .119
Parfondeval . . . . . . . . . . . . . . . . . . . . . . . 409
**Paris . . . . . . . . . . . . . . . . . . . . . . . . . . . . .323**
   Arc de Triomphe . . . . . . . . . . . . . . . .325, 331
   Arc du Carrousel . . . . . . . . . . . . . . . . . 331
   Cathédrale Notre-Dame . . . . . . . . . . . 327
   Centre Georges-Pompidou . . . . . . . . . . . 334
   Champs-Élysées . . . . . . . . . . . . . . . . . . 331
   Collège de France . . . . . . . . . . . . . . . . . 333
   Défense, La . . . . . . . . . . . . . . . . . . . . . 332
   École Militaire . . . . . . . . . . . . . . . . . . . 326
   Église de St-Germain-des-Prés . . . . . . . . 330
   Église de St-Séverin . . . . . . . . . . . . . . . 330
   Église du Dôme . . . . . . . . . . . . . . . . . . 325
   Église St-Eustache . . . . . . . . . . . . . . . . 330
   Église Val-de-Grâce . . . . . . . . . . . . . . . 330
   Eiffel Tower . . . . . . . . . . . . . . . . . . . . . 326
   Hôtel des Invalides . . . . . . . . . . . . . . . . 325
   Hôtel de Ville . . . . . . . . . . . . . . . . . . . . 332
   Institut de France . . . . . . . . . . . . . . . . . 332
   Jardin des Tuileries . . . . . . . . . . . . . . . . 331
   La Défense . . . . . . . . . . . . . . . . . . . . . . 332

   La Voie Triomphale . . . . . . . . . . . . . . .323, 331
   Le Marais . . . . . . . . . . . . . . . . . . . . . . . 330
   Louvre . . . . . . . . . . . . . . . . . . . . . . . . . 324
   Marais, Le . . . . . . . . . . . . . . . . . . . . . . . 330
   Metro . . . . . . . . . . . . . . . . . . . . . . . . . . . 22
   Montmartre . . . . . . . . . . . . . . . . . . . . . 334
   Musée d'Orsay . . . . . . . . . . . . . . . . . . . 334
   Musée de Cluny . . . . . . . . . . . . . . . . . . 334
   Musée National d'art Moderne . . . . . . . . 334
   Musée Rodin . . . . . . . . . . . . . . . . . . . . . 334
   Napoleon's Tomb . . . . . . . . . . . . . . . . . 325
   Opéra Garnier . . . . . . . . . . . . . . . . . . . . 327
   Palais-Royal . . . . . . . . . . . . . . . . . . . . . 326
   Palais Bourbon . . . . . . . . . . . . . . . . . . . 332
   Palais de Chaillot . . . . . . . . . . . . . . . . . 327
   Palais de Justice . . . . . . . . . . . . . . . . . . 326
   Palais de l'Élysée . . . . . . . . . . . . . . . . . 332
   Palais du Luxembourg . . . . . . . . . . . . . 332
   Panthéon . . . . . . . . . . . . . . . . . . . . . . . 326
   Place de la Concorde . . . . . . . . . . . . . . 325
   Sainte-Chapelle . . . . . . . . . . . . . . . . . . 330
   Sorbonne . . . . . . . . . . . . . . . . . . . . . . . 333
   St-Eustache, Église . . . . . . . . . . . . . . . . 330
   St-Germain-des-Prés, Église de . . . . . . . . 330
   St-Séverin, Église de . . . . . . . . . . . . . . . 330
   Tour Eiffel . . . . . . . . . . . . . . . . . . . . . . . 326
   Tuileries, Jardin des . . . . . . . . . . . . . . . 331
   Val-de-Grâce, Église . . . . . . . . . . . . . . . 330
Parisis . . . . . . . . . . . . . . . . . . . . . . . . . . . . .62
Passport . . . . . . . . . . . . . . . . . . . . . . . . . . .20
Pasteur, Louis . . . . . . . . . . . . . . . . . . . . . 366
Paxton, Joseph . . . . . . . . . . . . . . . . . . . . 238
Pays de Bray . . . . . . . . . . . . . . . . . . . . . . . .59
Péguy, Charles . . . . . . . . . . . . . . . . . . . . .319
Péronne . . . . . . . . . . . . . . . . . . . . . . . .334, 406
Pétain, Marshal . . . . . . . . . . . . . . . . . . . .195
Petits Cabinets du Roi, Versailles . . . . 443
Peugeot, Centre de Production . . . . . 341
Pévèle . . . . . . . . . . . . . . . . . . . . . . . . . . . . .61
Philip the Good . . . . . . . . . . . . . . . . . . . 271
Picardie, Musée de . . . . . . . . . . . . . . . . .118
Picardy . . . . . . . . . . . . . . . . . . . . 12, 59, 101
Pierrefonds, Château de . . . . . . . . . . . 207
Pigeon-breeding . . . . . . . . . . . . . . . . . . . .99
Pignons, Les Trois . . . . . . . . . . . . . . . . . 256
Pissarro, Camille . . . . . . . . . . . . . . . . . . . .94
Place du Général-de-Gaulle . . . . . . . . 279
Place Rihour . . . . . . . . . . . . . . . . . . . . . . 278
Plankton . . . . . . . . . . . . . . . . . . . . . . . . . . 154
Planning Your Trip . . . . . . . . . . . . . . . . . .11
Plants . . . . . . . . . . . . . . . . . . . . . . . . . . . . .66
Plomion . . . . . . . . . . . . . . . . . . . . . . . . . . 409
Poissy . . . . . . . . . . . . . . . . . . . . . . . . . . . . 339
Poissy Symposium, The . . . . . . . . . . . . . 340

Pont-de-Sains . . . . . . . . . . . . . . . . . . . . . . . .132
Pont-Ste-Maxence. . . . . . . . . . . . . . . . . 398
Poperinge . . . . . . . . . . . . . . . . . . . . . . . . .139
Porcelain. . . . . . . . . . . . . . . . . . . . . . . . . . .91
Port, Dunkirk. . . . . . . . . . . . . . . . . . . . . . 234
Port-Marly . . . . . . . . . . . . . . . . . . . . . . . . 291
Port-Royal-des-Champs . . . . . . . . . . . 342
Porte d'Ardon . . . . . . . . . . . . . . . . . . . . . 268
Porte de Bretagne. . . . . . . . . . . . . . . . . 335
Porte de Paris . . . . . . . . . . . . . . . . . . . . . 283
Porte de Roubaix. . . . . . . . . . . . . . . . . . 283
Porte de Soissons . . . . . . . . . . . . . . . . . 269
Portel, Le . . . . . . . . . . . . . . . . . . . . . . . . . 157
Post . . . . . . . . . . . . . . . . . . . . . . . . . . . . . . .53
Post mills . . . . . . . . . . . . . . . . . . . . . . . . .90
Prisces. . . . . . . . . . . . . . . . . . . . . . . . . . . .410
Provins . . . . . . . . . . . . . . . . . . . . . . . . . . 344
Public Transportation. . . . . . . . . . . . . . .22
Puppets . . . . . . . . . . . . . . . . . . . . . 35, 114

## Q
Quartier St-Leu. . . . . . . . . . . . . . . . . . . . .115
Quartier St-Sauveur, Lille . . . . . . . . . . 283
Quentin de La Tour . . . . . . . . . . . . . . . 387
Quesnoy, Le. . . . . . . . . . . . . . . . . . . . . . 348

## R
Racine, Jean. . . . . . . . . . . . . . . . . . . . . . . 343
Raismes-St-Amand-Wallers,
  Forêt de. . . . . . . . . . . . . . . . . . . . . . . 362
Rambouillet. . . . . . . . . . . . . . . . . . . . . . . 349
Rambouillet Forest . . . . . . . . . . . . . . . . .12
Rambures, Château-Fort de. . . . . . . . . 354
Ramousies . . . . . . . . . . . . . . . . . . . . . . . .133
Rancourt. . . . . . . . . . . . . . . . . . . . . . . . . 108
Ravel, Maurice . . . . . . . . . . . . . . . . . . . . 303
Region Today, The. . . . . . . . . . . . . . . . . 100
Relief maps . . . . . . . . . . . . . . . . . . . . . . 277
Religious Orders. . . . . . . . . . . . . . . . . . . .87
Renoir . . . . . . . . . . . . . . . . . . . . . . . . . . . .96
Rety . . . . . . . . . . . . . . . . . . . . . . . . . . . . . 160
Rhuis . . . . . . . . . . . . . . . . . . . . . . . . . . . . 398
Robespierre, Maximilien de . . . . . . . . .122
Roche-Guyon, La . . . . . . . . . . . . . . . . . . 355
Rochefoucauld, François de La . . . . . . 355
Rocher, Le Long . . . . . . . . . . . . . . . . . . . 256
Rochers d'Angennes. . . . . . . . . . . . . . . 353
Rock climbing. . . . . . . . . . . . . . . . . . . . . .34
Rodin, Auguste. . . . . . . . . . . . . . . 165, 298
Rohan-Chabot, Duc de . . . . . . . . . . . . . 356
Romanesque architecture . . . . . . . . . . .82
Rothschild, James de . . . . . . . . . . . . . . 238
Rousseau, Jean-Jacques . . . . . . . . 176, 305

Rousseau, Théodore. . . . . . . . . . . . . 95, 14
Route des Crêtes . . . . . . . . . . . . . . . . . . 35
Rueil-Malmaison . . . . . . . . . . . . . . . . . . 36

## S
Sailing . . . . . . . . . . . . . . . . . . . . . . . . . . . .3
Sains-du-Nord . . . . . . . . . . . . . . . . . . . .13
Saint-Jans-Cappel . . . . . . . . . . . . . . . . . .13
Saint-Pierre, Eustache de . . . . . . . . . . 16
Santuario . . . . . . . . . . . . . . . . . . . . . . . . 18
Sars-Poteries. . . . . . . . . . . . . . . . . . . . . .13
Savignies . . . . . . . . . . . . . . . . . . . . . . . . 14
Sceaux. . . . . . . . . . . . . . . . . . . . . . . . . . . 39
Sculpture . . . . . . . . . . . . . . . . . . . . . . . . .8
Seasons. . . . . . . . . . . . . . . . . . . . . . . . . . .1
Sebourg . . . . . . . . . . . . . . . . . . . . . . . . . 42
Second World War. . . . . . . . . . . . . . . . . .7
Senlis. . . . . . . . . . . . . . . . . . . . . . . . . . . . 39
Senlisis . . . . . . . . . . . . . . . . . . . . . . . . . . .6
Seurat, Georges . . . . . . . . . . . . . . . . . . .9
Sèvres . . . . . . . . . . . . . . . . . . . . . . . . . . . 39
Shopping . . . . . . . . . . . . . . . . . . . . . . . . .4
Sightseeing . . . . . . . . . . . . . . . . . . . . . . .4
Singing Finch Competitions. . . . . . . . . 10
Sisley, Alfred . . . . . . . . . . . . . . . . . . . . . .31
Skiing. . . . . . . . . . . . . . . . . . . . . . . . . . . . .3
Soissons . . . . . . . . . . . . . . . . . . . . . . . . . 400
Solre-le-Château . . . . . . . . . . . . . . . . . .13
Somme . . . . . . . . . . . . . . . . . . . . . . . . . . .5
Somme Valley, The . . . . . . . . . . . . . . . . 40
Son et Lumière . . . . . . . . . . . . . . . . . . . .3
Souverain-Moulin . . . . . . . . . . . . . . . . .158
Spas . . . . . . . . . . . . . . . . . . . . . . . . . . . . . .3
St-Amand-les-Eaux . . . . . . . . . . . . . . . . 362
St-Cloud . . . . . . . . . . . . . . . . . . . . . . . . . 364
St-Denis . . . . . . . . . . . . . . . . . . . . . . . . . 367
St-Étienne-au-Mont . . . . . . . . . . . . . . . .157
St-Germain-en-Laye . . . . . . . . . . . . . . . 372
St-Germer-de-Fly. . . . . . . . . . . . . . . . . . 148
St-Gobain Forest . . . . . . . . . . . . . . . . . . 377
St-Jean-aux-Bois . . . . . . . . . . . . . . . . . . 207
St-Josse . . . . . . . . . . . . . . . . . . . . . . . . . .418
St-Leu-d'Esserent . . . . . . . . . . . . . . . . . 379
St-Omer . . . . . . . . . . . . . . . . . . . . . . . . . 380
St-Quentin. . . . . . . . . . . . . . . . . . . . . . . 385
St-Riquier . . . . . . . . . . . . . . . . . . . . . . . . 387
St-Saulve. . . . . . . . . . . . . . . . . . . . . . . . . 420
St-Vaast, Ancienne Abbaye . . . . . . . . .126
St-Vaast-de-Longmont . . . . . . . . . . . . . 398
St-Valery-sur-Somme . . . . . . . . . . . . . . 389
Stade de France . . . . . . . . . . . . . . . . . . . 371
Stained Glass. . . . . . . . . . . . . . . . . . . . . .92
State Apartments, Versailles . . . . . . . . 436

# INDEX

Ste-Chapelle . . . . . . . . . . . . . . . . . . . . . . . 373
Ste-Périne . . . . . . . . . . . . . . . . . . . . . . . . 208
Steenvoorde . . . . . . . . . . . . . . . . . . . . . .174
Sterne, Laurence . . . . . . . . . . . . . . . . . 308
Suger, Abbot . . . . . . . . . . . . . . . . . . . . . 367
Symbols, Explanation of . . . . . . . . . . . . .7

## T

Telephones . . . . . . . . . . . . . . . . . . . . . . . .52
Ternois . . . . . . . . . . . . . . . . . . . . . . . . . . . .60
Textiles . . . . . . . . . . . . . . . . . . . . . . . . . 100
Thibaud IV . . . . . . . . . . . . . . . . . . . . . . . 344
Thiérache . . . . . . . . . . . . . . . . . . . . . . . . .61
Time . . . . . . . . . . . . . . . . . . . . . . . . . . . . . .54
Timeline . . . . . . . . . . . . . . . . . . . . . . . . . .68
Tipping . . . . . . . . . . . . . . . . . . . . . . . . . . .54
Tortoir, Le . . . . . . . . . . . . . . . . . . . . . . . . 378
Touquet-Paris-Plage, Le . . . . . . . . . . . .414
Tourist Flights . . . . . . . . . . . . . . . . . . . . .42
Tourist Offices . . . . . . . . . . . . . . . . . . . . .17
Tourist Passes . . . . . . . . . . . . . . . . . . . . .43
Tourist trains . . . . . . . . . . . . . . . . . . . . . .42
Traditional Games . . . . . . . . . . . . . . . . . .99
Traditions . . . . . . . . . . . . . . . . . . . . . . . . .97
**Travel**
    By Coach / Bus . . . . . . . . . . . . . . . . . . . . . . . 22
    By Plane . . . . . . . . . . . . . . . . . . . . . . . . . . . 21
    By Ship . . . . . . . . . . . . . . . . . . . . . . . . . . . . 21
    By Train . . . . . . . . . . . . . . . . . . . . . . . . . . . 22
Trélon . . . . . . . . . . . . . . . . . . . . . . . . . . .136
Trianons, Versailles . . . . . . . . . . . . . . . . .451

## U

Useful Words & Phrases . . . . . . . . . . . . . .49

## V

Valenciennes . . . . . . . . . . . . . . . . . . . . . .419
Vallée de l'Ourcq . . . . . . . . . . . . . . . . . . .319
Vallée de la Somme . . . . . . . . . . . . . . . 405
Valloires, Abbaye et Jardins de . . . . . . .421
Valois . . . . . . . . . . . . . . . . . . . . . . . . . . . . .62
Valois Dynasty, The . . . . . . . . . . . . . . . . .217

Value Added Tax (VAT) . . . . . . . . . . . . . .41
Van Gogh, Vincent . . . . . . . . . . . . . 97, 130
Vauban, Sébastien le Prestre de . . . . . . .90
Vaux . . . . . . . . . . . . . . . . . . . . . . . . . . . 406
Vaux-le-Vicomte, Château de . . . . . . . 423
Vaux de Cernay . . . . . . . . . . . . . . . . . . . . .219
Verne, Jules . . . . . . . . . . . . . . . . . . . . . . . .118
Versailles, Château de . . . . . . . . . . 12, 427
Versailles, Parc du château de . . . . . . 445
Versailles, Treaty of . . . . . . . . . . . . . . . . .71
Versailles, Ville de . . . . . . . . . . . . . . . . 454
Vervins . . . . . . . . . . . . . . . . . . . . . . . . . 409
Vétheuil . . . . . . . . . . . . . . . . . . . . . . . . 357
Vicq . . . . . . . . . . . . . . . . . . . . . . . . . . . . 304
Vieille Bourse . . . . . . . . . . . . . . . . . . . . 279
Villa Savoye . . . . . . . . . . . . . . . . . . . . . 340
Ville de Versailles . . . . . . . . . . . . . . . . . . 454
Villeneuve-d'Ascq . . . . . . . . . . . . . . . . 459
Villers-Cotterêts . . . . . . . . . . . . . . . . . . 462
Vimeu . . . . . . . . . . . . . . . . . . . . . . . . . . . .59
Vimeu Region . . . . . . . . . . . . . . . . . . . . .107
Visa . . . . . . . . . . . . . . . . . . . . . . . . . . . . . .20

## W

Wagner, Richard . . . . . . . . . . . . . . . . . . 298
Wallers-Trélon . . . . . . . . . . . . . . . . . . . .136
Walt Disney Studios Park . . . . . . . . . . . 225
Watou . . . . . . . . . . . . . . . . . . . . . . . . . . .139
Weather . . . . . . . . . . . . . . . . . . . . . . . . . .16
Websites . . . . . . . . . . . . . . . . . . . . . . . . . .17
What to See and Do . . . . . . . . . . . . . . . . .30
When and Where to Go . . . . . . . . . . . . . .14
Where to Stay and Eat . . . . . . . . . . . . . . .25
Wildlife Reserves . . . . . . . . . . . . . . . . . . .46
Wimereux . . . . . . . . . . . . . . . . . . . . . . . .211
Wimereux Valley . . . . . . . . . . . . . . . . . .158
Wimille . . . . . . . . . . . . . . . . . . . . . . . . . 160
Wimy . . . . . . . . . . . . . . . . . . . . . . . . . . .411
Windmills . . . . . . . . . . . . . . . . . . . . . 15, 90
Windsurfing . . . . . . . . . . . . . . . . . . . . . . .30
Wissant . . . . . . . . . . . . . . . . . . . . . . . . . .213
Wormhout . . . . . . . . . . . . . . . . . . . . . . . .174

# WHERE TO STAY

**Abbaye de Jouarre**
Plat d'Étain .......................... 261

**Abbaye et Jardins de Valloires**
Hostellerie de l'Abbaye de Valloires ... 422

**Amiens**
Hôtel Alsace-Lorraine ................ 110
Hôtel Carlton ....................... 110
Le Petit Chateau (Bed and Breakfast).. 110
Mme Lemaitre (Bed and Breakfast).... 110

**Arras**
Château de Saulty
(Bed and Breakfast) ................ 121
Hôtel Diamant ....................... 121
Hotel Le Manoir de Gavrelle .......... 121
Le Clos Grincourt (Bed and Breakfast) . 121

**Avesnes-sur-Helpe**
La Villa Mariani (Bed and Breakfast) ... 135
Les Prés de la Fagne
(Bed and Breakfast) ................ 135

**Bailleul**
Auberge du Vert Mont................ 138

**Barbizon**
La Ferme des Vosves
(Bed and Breakfast)................ 141

**Beauvais**
Hôtel du Cygne ..................... 144
La Ferme du Colombier
(Bed and Breakfast) ................ 144

**Bergues**
Au Tonnelier ....................... 149

**Boulogne-sur-Mer**
Hôtel de la Ferme du Vert............. 153
Hôtel Faidherbe...................... 153
Hôtel Métropole ..................... 153
Le Clos d'Esch (Bed and Breakfast) .... 153

**Calais**
Hôtel Victoria ....................... 166
Le Manoir du Meldick
(Bed and Breakfast) ................ 166

**Cambrai**
Delcambre (Bed and Breakfast) ....... 170

**Chartres**
Hôtel Le Grand Monarque ........... 191
La Ferme du Château
(Bed and Breakfast) ................ 191

**Château de Chantilly**
Château de la Tour ................... 181
Pavillon St-Hubert ................... 181

**Château de Dampierre**
Abbaye des Vaux de Cernay ......... 219

**Château de Ferrières**
St-Rémy ............................. 239

**Château de Pierrefonds**
Camping La Croix du Vieux Pont ...... 337
Domaine du Bois d'Aucourt........... 337

**Château de Vaux-le-Vicomte**
Labordière (Bed and Breakfast) ....... 424
La Ferme du Couvent................. 424

**Compiègne**
Auberge de la Vieille Ferme.......... 206
Hôtel Les Beaux Arts ................ 206

**Disneyland Resort Paris**
Bellevue Bed and Breakfast.......... 222
Camping Base de Loisirs de
Jablines-Annet..................... 222
Hôtel Cheyenne...................... 222
Hôtel Santa Fé ...................... 222
Hôtel Séquoia Lodge ................ 222
Les Hauts de Montguillon ........... 222
Newport Bay Club................... 223

**Douai**
Hôtel de la Terrasse ................. 228

**Fontainebleau**
Hôtel de la Chancellerie ............. 250
Hôtel Victoria ....................... 250

**Forêt de Fontainebleau**
Hôtel du Pavillon Royal.............. 252

**Hardelot**
Hôtel du Parc ....................... 157

**La Côte d'Opale**
La Goélette ......................... 212
La Grand' Maison Bed and Breakfast .. 212

**Laon**
Hostellerie Saint Vincent ............. 268
Hôtel du Commerce.................. 268
Hôtel Les Chevaliers................. 268

**La Roche-Guyon**
Prieuré Maïalen ..................... 357

**La Thiérache**
Le Cheval Noir ...................... 409
Mme Piette (Bed and Breakfast) ...... 409

**Le Touquet-Paris-Plage**
Hôtel de la Forêt .................... 416
Hôtel Le Manoir...................... 416
Le Chalet ........................... 416
Les Embruns ........................ 416

**Lille**
As Hôtel ............................ 274
B & B (Bed and Breakfast)............. 274
Chez Julie........................... 274
Hôtel Brueghel...................... 274
La Ferme Blanche ................... 274
La Viennale ......................... 274
Station Bac St-Maur ................. 274

# INDEX

**Maintenon**
Les Chandelles (Bed and Breakfast) . . . 287
**Milly-la-Forêt**
M. Lenoir (Bed and Breakfast). . . . . . . . 301
**Montreuil**
Haute Chambre (Bed and Breakfast) . . 309
L'Écu de France. . . . . . . . . . . . . . . . . . . . . 309
La Commanderie (Bed and Breakfast) . 309
Manoir Francis . . . . . . . . . . . . . . . . . . . . . 309
**Moret-sur-Loing**
Auberge de la Terrasse . . . . . . . . . . . . . . 311
M. Gicquel (Bed and Breakfast) . . . . . . . 311
**Noyon**
Hotel Le Cèdre . . . . . . . . . . . . . . . . . . . . . 317
**Parc Astérix**
Hôtel des Trois Hiboux . . . . . . . . . . . . . . 128
**Poissy**
Les Romanciers . . . . . . . . . . . . . . . . . . . . . 341
**Provins**
Christine and Jean-Claude Dormion
(Bed and Breakfast) . . . . . . . . . . . . . . . 345
Ferme du Chatel (Bed and Breakfast). . 345
La Ferme de Toussacq . . . . . . . . . . . . . . . 345
**Senlis**
Hostellerie de la Porte Bellon . . . . . . . . 396
Mme Passemier (Bed and Breakfast) . . 396

**Soissons**
Ferme de la Montagne
(Bed and Breakfast) . . . . . . . . . . . . . . . 401
**St-Germain-en-Laye**
Havre Hôtel . . . . . . . . . . . . . . . . . . . . . . . . 375
**St-Omer**
Hôtel Les Frangins . . . . . . . . . . . . . . . . . . 381
Le Vivier . . . . . . . . . . . . . . . . . . . . . . . . . . . 381
**St-Riquier**
Hôtel Jean de Bruges. . . . . . . . . . . . . . . . 388
**St-Valery-sur-Somme**
Mme Servant (Bed and Breakfast). . . . . 390
**Valenciennes**
Au Vieux St-Nicolas. . . . . . . . . . . . . . . . . . 420
Château d'En Haut
(Bed and Breakfast) . . . . . . . . . . . . . . . 420
**Versailles**
Hôtel Versailles . . . . . . . . . . . . . . . . . . . . . 456
Résidence du Berry. . . . . . . . . . . . . . . . . . 456
**Villeneuve-d'Ascq**
Ascotel . . . . . . . . . . . . . . . . . . . . . . . . . . . . 459
**Villers-Cotterêts**
Hôtel Régent. . . . . . . . . . . . . . . . . . . . . . . 462

## WHERE TO EAT

**Abbaye de Jouarre**
Le Bec Fin. . . . . . . . . . . . . . . . . . . . . . . . . . 261
**Amiens**
Ale factory (Les Artisans Brasseurs) . . . 110
L'Os à Mœlle . . . . . . . . . . . . . . . . . . . . . . . 110
Le Bouchon . . . . . . . . . . . . . . . . . . . . . . . . 110
Le Petit Poucet . . . . . . . . . . . . . . . . . . . . . 110
Les Marissons . . . . . . . . . . . . . . . . . . . . . . 110
Le T'chiot Zinc . . . . . . . . . . . . . . . . . . . . . 110
**Arras**
La Table du Troubadour . . . . . . . . . . . . . 121
La Taverne de l'Écu. . . . . . . . . . . . . . . . . . 121
Les Grandes Arcades . . . . . . . . . . . . . . . . 121
**Auvers-sur-Oise**
Auberge Ravoux . . . . . . . . . . . . . . . . . . . . 131
**Avesnes-sur-Helpe**
Auberge de Châtelet . . . . . . . . . . . . . . . . 135
L'Estaminet . . . . . . . . . . . . . . . . . . . . . . . . 135
Marquais . . . . . . . . . . . . . . . . . . . . . . . . . . 135
**Bailleul**
Estaminet "De Vierpot". . . . . . . . . . . . . . 138
**Barbizon**
L'Angelus . . . . . . . . . . . . . . . . . . . . . . . . . . 141
Le Relais de Barbizon. . . . . . . . . . . . . . . . 141

**Beauvais**
La Baie d'Halong . . . . . . . . . . . . . . . . . . . 144
Les Canards de la Landelle. . . . . . . . . . . 144
**Bergues**
Le Cornet d'Or . . . . . . . . . . . . . . . . . . . . . 149
Taverne le Bruegel . . . . . . . . . . . . . . . . . 149
**Boulogne-sur-Mer**
La Raterie . . . . . . . . . . . . . . . . . . . . . . . . . 153
Le Doyen . . . . . . . . . . . . . . . . . . . . . . . . . . 153
Restaurant de Nausicaä . . . . . . . . . . . . . 153
**Calais**
Au Côte d'Argent. . . . . . . . . . . . . . . . . . . 166
La Boudinière. . . . . . . . . . . . . . . . . . . . . . . 166
La Sole Meunière. . . . . . . . . . . . . . . . . . . . 166
Le Channel. . . . . . . . . . . . . . . . . . . . . . . . . 166
**Cambrai**
'Chez Dan' Brasserie Boulonnaise . . . . . 170
La Taverne de Lutèce . . . . . . . . . . . . . . . . 170
Le Bouchon. . . . . . . . . . . . . . . . . . . . . . . . 170
**Cassel**
'T Kasteelhof. . . . . . . . . . . . . . . . . . . . . . . 173
Au Roi du Potje Vleesch . . . . . . . . . . . . . 173
Het Blauwershof . . . . . . . . . . . . . . . . . . . 173
La Taverne Flamande. . . . . . . . . . . . . . . . 173

**Chartres**
Le Café Serpente . . . . . . . . . . . . . . . . . . . . . 191
Le Pichet. . . . . . . . . . . . . . . . . . . . . . . . . . . . 191
Le Tripot . . . . . . . . . . . . . . . . . . . . . . . . . . . . 191
**Château de Chantilly**
Auberge le Vertugadin . . . . . . . . . . . . . . 181
La Belle Bio . . . . . . . . . . . . . . . . . . . . . . . . . 181
La Capitainerie 'Les Cuisines de Vatel'. 181
**Château de Dampierre**
Country Road . . . . . . . . . . . . . . . . . . . . . . . 219
**Château de Pierrefonds**
Aux Blés d'Or . . . . . . . . . . . . . . . . . . . . . . . 337
**Colline de Notre-Dame-de-Lorette**
Auberge du Cabaret Rouge. . . . . . . . . . . 316
**Compiègne**
Auberge du Buissonnet . . . . . . . . . . . . . 206
Le Bistrot des Arts. . . . . . . . . . . . . . . . . . . 206
Le Nord. . . . . . . . . . . . . . . . . . . . . . . . . . . . . 206
Le Palais Gourmand . . . . . . . . . . . . . . . . . 206
**Corbie**
L'Abbatiale. . . . . . . . . . . . . . . . . . . . . . . . . . 209
**Coucy-le-Château-Auffrique**
Le Belle Vue. . . . . . . . . . . . . . . . . . . . . . . . . 215
**Crécy-en-Ponthieu**
Ferme-auberge La Table de Ferme. . . . 217
**Disneyland Resort Paris**
Annette's Diner . . . . . . . . . . . . . . . . . . . . . 223
Auberge de Cendrillon . . . . . . . . . . . . . . 223
Blue Lagoon Restaurant . . . . . . . . . . . . . 223
L'Ermitage . . . . . . . . . . . . . . . . . . . . . . . . . . 223
Rainforest Café. . . . . . . . . . . . . . . . . . . . . . 223
Rendez-vous des Stars Restaurant . . . . 223
Silver Spur Steakhouse . . . . . . . . . . . . . . 223
The Steakhouse . . . . . . . . . . . . . . . . . . . . . 223
Walt's Restaurant . . . . . . . . . . . . . . . . . . . 223
**Douai**
Au Turbotin . . . . . . . . . . . . . . . . . . . . . . . . 228
La Terrasse. . . . . . . . . . . . . . . . . . . . . . . . . . 228
Le Chat Botté . . . . . . . . . . . . . . . . . . . . . . . 228
Le Storez. . . . . . . . . . . . . . . . . . . . . . . . . . . . 228
**Fontainebleau**
Croquembouche . . . . . . . . . . . . . . . . . . . . 250
L'Île aux Truites. . . . . . . . . . . . . . . . . . . . . . 250
**Fôret de Fontainebleau**
Auberge de la Treille . . . . . . . . . . . . . . . 252
Hostellerie du Cheval Noir . . . . . . . . . . . 252
La Marine. . . . . . . . . . . . . . . . . . . . . . . . . . . 252
**Grottes-Refuges de Naours**
La Chèvrerie de Canaples. . . . . . . . . . . . . 314
**Hardelot**
Brasserie l'Océan. . . . . . . . . . . . . . . . . . . . 157

**L'Isle-Adam**
Le Cabouillet. . . . . . . . . . . . . . . . . . . . . . . . 259
**La Baie de Somme**
La Clé des Champs . . . . . . . . . . . . . . . . . . 404
La Marinière . . . . . . . . . . . . . . . . . . . . . . . . 404
Le Parc aux Huîtres . . . . . . . . . . . . . . . . . . 404
Mado. . . . . . . . . . . . . . . . . . . . . . . . . . . . . . . 404
**La Côte d'Opale**
La Sirène. . . . . . . . . . . . . . . . . . . . . . . . . . . . 212
Liégeoise et Atlantic Hôtel. . . . . . . . . . . 212
**Laon**
Bistrot Le Saint-Amour . . . . . . . . . . . . . . 268
**La Roche-Guyon**
Les Bords de Seine . . . . . . . . . . . . . . . . . . 357
**Le Quesnoy**
Au Canard Gourmand . . . . . . . . . . . . . . . 348
**Le Touquet-Paris-Plage**
La Brasserie du Marché . . . . . . . . . . . . . 416
Le Nemo . . . . . . . . . . . . . . . . . . . . . . . . . . . 416
Le Village Suisse . . . . . . . . . . . . . . . . . . . . 416
Pérard . . . . . . . . . . . . . . . . . . . . . . . . . . . . . 416
Restaurant Côté Sud. . . . . . . . . . . . . . . . . 416
**Lille**
À l'Huîtrière. . . . . . . . . . . . . . . . . . . . . . . . . 279
Alcide . . . . . . . . . . . . . . . . . . . . . . . . . . . . . . 275
Aux Moules . . . . . . . . . . . . . . . . . . . . . . . . . 275
Domaine de Lintillac . . . . . . . . . . . . . . . . 274
Flam's . . . . . . . . . . . . . . . . . . . . . . . . . . . . . . 274
La Robe des Champs . . . . . . . . . . . . . . . . 275
La Taverne de l'Écu . . . . . . . . . . . . . . . . . . 274
La Tête de l'Art . . . . . . . . . . . . . . . . . . . . . . 275
Le Bistrot de Pierrot . . . . . . . . . . . . . . . . . 275
Le Bistrot des Brasseurs . . . . . . . . . . . . . 275
Le Passe-Porc . . . . . . . . . . . . . . . . . . . . . . . 275
Restaurant La Cave aux Fioles. . . . . . . . 275
Restaurant Le Lapin à Z'os . . . . . . . . . . . 275
T Rijsel (Estaminet) . . . . . . . . . . . . . . . . . . 275
**Maisons-Laffitte**
Rôtisserie Vieille Fontaine . . . . . . . . . . . 288
**Marly-le-Roi**
Le Village . . . . . . . . . . . . . . . . . . . . . . . . . . . 290
**Meaux**
Le Cep . . . . . . . . . . . . . . . . . . . . . . . . . . . . . . 296
**Meudon**
Le Brimborion . . . . . . . . . . . . . . . . . . . . . . 299
**Milly-la-Forêt**
La Truffière . . . . . . . . . . . . . . . . . . . . . . . . . 301
**Montfort-l'Amaury**
Hostellerie des Tours . . . . . . . . . . . . . . . . 303
**Montmorency**
Au Cœur de la Forêt . . . . . . . . . . . . . . . . . 306